LYTTON STRACHEY

A Critical Biography

Volume I

THE UNKNOWN YEARS (1880–1910)

LYTTON STRACHEY

A Critical Biography

by

MICHAEL HOLROYD

Volume 1
THE UNKNOWN YEARS
(1880–1910)

HOLT, RINEHART AND WINSTON
NEW YORK   CHICAGO   SAN FRANCISCO

To the memory of
HESKETH PEARSON
and to
JOYCE PEARSON

Contents

Illustrations

Frontispiece: *Lytton Strachey, 1904, by Simon Bussy*
(reproduced by courtesy of the late James Strachey)

Preface

Lytton Strachey's reputation has been likened to a meteor, hurrying across the skies to its extinction, and leaving behind it only a whiff of incandescent sulphur. When his posthumous collection of papers, *Characters and Commentaries*, was published, a reviewer in *The Granta*, S. Gorley Putt, made it the occasion for a cautionary lesson, advising future critical scriveners to conserve sufficient energy for a deathbed destruction of miscellaneous essays, lest the piety of less squeamish survivors should later assemble them into a book. This fierce reaction of attitude against Strachey, which had started at his own university, Cambridge, some years before, quickly gathered momentum after his death, spreading to London where it impressed itself strongly upon the metropolitan centre of English culture, and then across the Atlantic to America where in 1936 Douglas Southall Freeman described the author of *Eminent Victorians* and *Queen Victoria* as 'one of the most pernicious influences in modern biography'.

His biographies, however, continued to sell, in Britain, and especially in America, though his literary stock in both countries has remained for the last quarter of a century at a relatively low ebb. Only recently has it looked like making a recovery. Readability was his forte, a readability which delighted the public and dismayed the pundits who saw in it only a reflection of the author's shallowness as a thinker and interpreter of human actions. In an age that has eulogized needless and often clumsy obscurantism, narrative power has been perversely misrepresented as a literary vice, whereas, if not an absolute virtue, it is at least a condition of virtue, a by-product of creative literature which does not render a bad book good but enhances the value of an otherwise fine literary achievement. Famous throughout the world as the most readable of biographers, Strachey was fundamentally an essayist; but his critical essays – so compact and self-contained, yet always elegant and beautifully shaped – are unread by the public and out of fashion with many of the critics. And so it has come about that his rightful place on the literary stage has been usurped by other writers without a tithe of his technical skill, his wit or his genius for narrative.

Unlike a number of his contemporaries, Strachey has received scant attention from biographers, and this omission has tended to encourage some critical misunderstanding. Naturally not all that has been held against him is untrue. But thirty-five years of posthumous literary criticism, unsupported by any significant amount of biographical information, have produced a popular impression considerably distorted and removed from actuality. For most people now the name of Lytton Strachey probably conjures up an image of that stale old gingerbread figure, the sardonic and cynical *dix-huitième-siècle* debunker. Mistakes like that made by Mr Ivor Brown who, in support of his view that the sedentary and enfeebled Strachey underestimated the physical energies of Queen Victoria, presumed that he had never beheld her beloved Cairngorms – which rose, in point of fact, almost out of his back garden in Rothiemurchus – are perhaps slight in themselves. Yet cumulatively they have served to manufacture the myth of a flippant, clever, wholly superficial character, without deep emotions in himself and without an understanding of them in other people, with a restricted appreciation for what is 'polished, pregnant and concise' in the field of art, and with no appreciation whatever of the important facts of real life.

The facts of Strachey's life tell another story. At the age of twenty-five he already seems to have had some premonition of what posterity might be tempted to say of him. He saw himself as a romantic. Do not, he warns his future biographer, write that

> 'He lives outside the world.' Or 'This remark,
> Did I not know his goodness very well,
> Would make me guess that some red imp of Hell
> Had served him with a quill to burn and sting,
> Twisted from out a fallen seraph's wing.'
> No! Neither give your pity; . . . .
> . . . . But strive thus to think of me. –
> 'He has drunk far too deeply of love's wine
> Ever to fear or ever to repine.
> His spirit, calmed with that fierce opiate,
> Sees, and despises, and submits to Fate.
> He knows how wise he is, and by that rule
> He knows without pretence that he's a fool.'

I do not see Lytton Strachey exactly as he saw himself at that early age. But that he was a highly emotional man, with catholic sympathies, is undeniable. For psychological reasons, and owing in part to immediate practical considerations, he was unable adequately to communicate his most passionate feelings in his writings, and this deficiency has misled critics of his prose style to deduce that he was passionless and cold. That he is not among the few very greatest figures in English literature must, for this same reason, be admitted, though he has all the sheer ability of the most consummate artist. The purpose of this book, besides drawing attention to his various literary accomplishments, for long so unfashionable, is to furnish readers with an authentic and hitherto quite unknown portrait of the man so that they may turn back to his works and re-interpret them in a fresh and more personal light.

A minority of critics, often personal friends, have continued loyally to uphold Strachey's literary reputation through these lean times, but they have been singularly unsuccessful in recruiting disciples. The most thorough and scholarly of these, Professor C. R. Sanders, too anxious, it may be, to silence the loud chorus of denigration, has lavished on his subject a volume of generous and unstinted praise which, unfortunately, has done little to restore Strachey's position. It seems unlikely, in any case, that Lytton Strachey himself would have welcomed a hagiographer. 'Discretion', he once wrote, 'is not the better part of biography.' And, by the same token, sentimentality – the deplorable result of suppressed knowledge – is not the better part of literary criticism. But before now a definitive examination of his life and work has not been practical. 'About Strachey's life there is little to say,' reported André Maurois in 1936. 'The biography of the biographer has not yet been written.' A quarter of a century later, when I started on this present volume, it had still not been written. Clive Bell, in an essay on Strachey, has indicated some of the problems which rendered such a biography impossible. 'Lytton could love, and perhaps he could hate,' he explained. 'To anyone who knew him well it is obvious that love and lust and that mysterious mixture of the two which is the heart's desire played in his life parts of which a biographer who fails to take account will make himself ridiculous. But I am not a biographer; nor can, nor should, a biography of Lytton Strachey be attempted for many years to come. It cannot be attempted till his letters have been published or at any rate made accessible, and his letters should not be published till those he cared for and those who thought he cared for them are dead. Most of his papers luckily are in safe and scholarly hands.'

Now, over thirty years after Lytton Strachey's death, his friends and family have combined to put those papers at my disposal without any form of embargo as to how they should be used. The reasons for this necessary delay – an unusually long one in modern times – have been more specifically dealt with by Lytton's younger brother and literary executor James Strachey in the course of an interesting letter to Professor Martin Kallich (2 October 1956). 'As is generally known,' he wrote, 'my brother was to a very large extent homosexual. Traces of his views on that subject are to be found in his published works; but in those days nothing more open would have been permissible. His attitude was strongly in favour of open discussion. But he was never inclined to undue solemnity. There is a large amount of unpublished material – including a very great deal of delightful correspondence – which I hope will become accessible with the gradual advance of civilized opinion. For this advance we owe a good deal, I believe, to Lytton's own influence (though this is not generally known) on his contemporaries, and, of course, more than anything to that of Freud.'

It may seem ironic that, after all this time, the life and work of Lytton Strachey should finally be commemorated by two fat volumes – that standard treatment of the illustrious dead that he was so effective in stamping out. Yet the irony is more apparent than real – no more incongruously relevant, say, than the fact that Lytton Strachey himself should have been jointly responsible for *The Greville Memoirs* – a work in eight fat volumes. He did not, moreover, censure *all* two-volume biographies – admiring, for example, Sir Edward Cook's excellent *Life of Florence Nightingale* – but derided only those which were slipshod and ill-digested, written without detachment or humour, and drenched in a tone of tedious panegyric.

Besides which, there is little proper comparison between Strachey's biographies and the present volumes. Strachey wrote the lives of men and women of action; in dealing with a writer I have attempted also a critical revaluation of his work, since the two are, in a sense, indivisible – Strachey's writings being of a kind that may be re-illumined by the biography of their author serving as commentary. His life, too, was very intimately bound up with his Bloomsbury friends, so that I have been obliged also to offer some re-examination of the Bloomsbury world in the light of Lytton's and their own private correspondence. To divide artificially his life from his books, and both of these from the friends who influenced him and with whom he had dealings, would have been to destroy the polychromatic design and meaning of his life. For this reason, the following pages present more than a biography of one man: they unfold a panorama of the social and intellectual environment of an entire generation.

Strachey, of course, worked almost entirely from published sources which he re-fashioned aesthetically and re-interpreted. I have worked almost entirely from unpublished sources which pose quite a different problem – inspecting over thirty thousand letters from, to, and about my subject, in addition to trunks full of miscellaneous papers, diaries, essays, speeches, autobiographical pieces, poems and so on. In putting together my narrative, I have drawn particularly freely from the letters, since it seems unlikely that any comprehensive selection of these – scattered pretty widely over England and America – will be a practical publishing proposition in the foreseeable future. Lytton was not a ready or eloquent conversationalist, and seems to have been allergic to the telephone. On the other hand he was a copious and very good correspondent, whose letters communicate uniquely his subtle and peculiar personality. 'No good letter was ever written to convey information, or to please the recipient,' he wrote in an essay on Horace Walpole's letters: 'it may achieve both these results incidentally; but its fundamental purpose is to express the personality of the writer.' Where his own letters merely convey information I have paraphrased and blended them in with other sources of information; where the pleasure of the recipient has been the main purpose I have either omitted them altogether or offered some elucidation of this purpose; where I have judged his personality to be best expressed, I have quoted.

Acknowledgements

My book has been made possible by the kindness and co-operation of the late James Strachey, who, besides making accessible a formidable mass of unpublished material, answered the many questions which I put to him during the course of my work and also checked all the biographical facts of my typescript, though he is not to be held responsible for any of the opinions that I have expressed. Among others who have helped me in one way or another and to whom I would like to acknowledge my gratitude and indebtedness are: The Dowager Lady Aberconway, the late J. R. Ackerley, Mr Harold Acton, Lord Annan, Baroness Asquith of Yarnbury, Mrs Barbara Bagenal, Mr Thomas Balston, Bishop Lumsden Barkway, Mr and Mrs J. L. Behrend, the late Clive Bell, Professor Quentin Bell, Mr Gerald Brenan, the Hon. Dorothy Brett, Mr Richard Carline, Mr Noel Carrington, Lord David Cecil, Lady Diana Cooper, Lord Cottesloe, Dr Lissant Cox, the late John Davenport, Mr James Dicker, Professor Bonamy Dobrée, Mr and Mrs Guy Elwes, Mr E. M. Forster, Mr Roderick W. B. Fraser, Mr Roger Fulford, Mr David Garnett, Mrs Angelica Garnett, the Hon. Robert Gathorne-Hardy, Mr William Gerhardie, Mrs Marjorie Gertler, Mrs Julia Gowing (née Strachey), Mr Duncan Grant, Mrs Karin Hall, Sir Roy Harrod, the late Christopher Hassall, Mr R. A. Hodgkin, Mr Basil Holroyd, Mr and Mrs Kenneth Holroyd, Mr Richard Hughes, Mrs Mary Hutchinson, the late Aldous Huxley, Miss Elizabeth Jenkins, Sir Caspar John, Mrs Dorelia John, the late C. H. B. Kitchin, Lady Pansy Lamb, Mr John Lehmann, Miss Rosamond Lehmann, Mr Robert Lescher, the late E. B. C. Lucas, the late F. L. Lucas, Mr André Maurois, the late Professor H. O. Meredith, Mr Gabriel Merle, Mrs Dorothy Moore, Mr Raymond Mortimer, Lady Mosley, Lord Moyne, Dr A. N. L. Munby, Mrs U. Nares, Sir Harold Nicolson, Miss Lucy Norton, Mrs Frances Partridge, the late Hesketh Pearson, Professor Lionel Penrose, Mr Alfred H. Perrin, the Hon. Wogan Philipps (Lord Milford), Mr William Plomer, Mr Peter Quennell, Mrs Nancy Rodd, Sir John

Rothenstein, Sir Steven Runciman, Lord Russell, Mr George Rylands, the late Lord Sackville, Miss Daphne Sanger, Mr Siegfried Sassoon, Mr Alan Searle, Mr Roger Senhouse, Sir John Sheppard, Mr Mauritz Sillem, the Reverend F. A. Simpson, Professor George Kuppler Simson, Professor W. J. H. Sprott, Mrs Alix Strachey, the late Evelyn John St Loe Strachey, M.P., Mr John Strachey, Miss Philippa Strachey, Mr and Mrs Richard Strachey, Sir Charles Tennyson, Dame Sybil Thorndike, Miss Marjorie H. Thurston, Miss Iris Tree, Mrs Igor Vinogradoff, Mr Boris von Anrep, the late Arthur Waley, Sir William Walton, Mrs Ursula Wentzel, Mrs Amabel Williams-Ellis (*née* Strachey), Professor John Dover Wilson, Mr Leonard Woolf, Mr Wayland Young (Lord Kennet).

I should also like to record my thanks to the following: Chatto & Windus Ltd, the Chelsea Public and Reference Library, King's College Library, Cambridge, the National Book League, the Royal Society of Literature, the Society of Authors, and the Slade School of Fine Art.

I must also express my indebtedness to Mr David Machin for his unfailing patience and support over three long years; to Mr Roger Smith for his meticulous checking and preparing of my typescript for the printers; and to Miss Jennifer Holden who helped to correct each page of my work and gave me many valuable suggestions.

The writing of this book was largely made possible by the award, in 1963, of the Eugene F. Saxton Memorial Fellowship for the composition of the first volume; and, in 1965, for the second volume, of a Bollingen Foundation Fellowship.

I am grateful to the following for kindly granting me permission to quote from copyright sources: Lord Annan for *Leslie Stephen* (MacGibbon & Kee); Bishop Barkway for unpublished writings; Rupert Crew Ltd for *The Wandering Years* by Cecil Beaton (Weidenfeld & Nicolson); Professor Sir J. D. Beazley for unpublished writings; the Administratrix of the Estate of Sir Max Beerbohm for letters and *Mainly on the Air* (Heinemann and Alfred A. Knopf, Inc.); Professor Quentin Bell, Chatto and Windus Ltd and Harcourt, Brace & World, Inc. for *Old Friends* by Clive Bell, also Professor Bell for unpublished writings; A. P. Watt & Son for *Queen Victoria* by E. F. Benson (Longmans); A. M. Heath & Co. Ltd for *My Restless Years* by Hector Bolitho (Max Parrish); George Weidenfeld & Nicolson Ltd for *Memories* by C. M. Bowra; Hamish Hamilton Ltd for *South from Granada* by Gerald Brenan, also the author for unpublished writings; William Collins Sons & Co Ltd for Ivor Brown's Introduction to *Queen Victoria* by Lytton Strachey (Collins Classics edition); Mrs

Frances Partridge for unpublished writings by herself, the late Ralph Partridge and Carrington; Lord David Cecil, C.H., for an article in the *Dictionary of National Biography*; Mr John Stewart Collis for *An Artist of Life* (Cassell); Routledge & Kegan Paul Ltd and The Macmillan Company for *Enemies of Promise* by Cyril Connolly (copyright 1948 by Cyril Connolly); William Collins Sons & Co. Ltd for *Two Flamboyant Fathers* by Nicolette Devas; the Society of Authors for unpublished letters by Norman Douglas; Mrs T. S. Eliot for a review and unpublished letters by the late T. S. Eliot; Curtis Brown Ltd for *General Gordon* by Lord Elton (Collins); Mr E. M. Forster, C.H., for unpublished writings; Sigmund Freud Copyrights Ltd for an unpublished letter by Sigmund Freud; Mr Roger Fulford for unpublished writings; Mr David Garnett for *The Flowers of the Forest* and *The Familiar Faces* (Chatto and Windus); Mr William Gerhardie for *Resurrection* (Cassell) and unpublished writings; Mrs Marjorie Gertler for *Selected Letters* by Mark Gertler (Hart-Davis) and for unpublished letters by Mark Gertler; Mr Duncan Grant for an extract from an article and for unpublished writings; Professor G. B. Harrison for unpublished writings; Sir Roy Harrod for *The Life of John Maynard Keynes* (Macmillan); Mrs Dorelia John for *Chiaroscuro* by Augustus John (Cape); Martin Secker & Warburg Ltd and Farrar, Straus & Giroux, Inc. for *The Bloomsbury Group* by J. K. Johnstone (copyright © 1954 by Noonday Press); Sir Geoffrey Keynes for letters by J. M. Keynes; Associated Book Publishers Ltd for *Progress of a Biographer* (Methuen) and *The Return of William Shakespeare* (Eyre and Spottiswoode) by Hugh Kingsmill; the late C. H. B. Kitchin for unpublished writings; Laurence Pollinger Ltd (acting for the Estate of the late Mrs Frieda Lawrence) and The Viking Press, Inc. for letters by D. H. Lawrence (copyright 1932 by the Estate of D. H. Lawrence, 1960 by Angelo Ravagli and C. Montague Weekley) and Laurence Pollinger Ltd and Alfred A. Knopf, Inc. for 'None of That' by D. H. Lawrence; David Higham Associates Ltd for *The Whispering Gallery* by John Lehmann (Longmans); Mr Michael MacCarthy for *Memories* by Desmond MacCarthy (MacGibbon & Kee); Hamish Hamilton Ltd and Alfred A. Knopf, Inc. for *Forty Years with Berenson* by Nicky Mariano; Doubleday & Co. Inc. for *archy's life of mehitabel* by don marquis (copyright 1933 by Doubleday & Company Inc.); Mr Kingsley Martin for *Father Figures* (Hutchinson); the late Professor H. O. Meredith for an unpublished letter; Mrs Igor Vinogradoff for *Ottoline: The Early Memoirs of Lady Ottoline Morrell* (Faber & Faber); Mr Raymond Mortimer for *Channel Packet* (Hogarth Press) and *Duncan Grant* (Penguin); Mr Beverley Nichols for unpublished writings; Sir Harold Nicolson for *The Development of English Biography* (Hogarth Press); Mrs Hesketh Pearson for *Beerbohm Tree* (Methuen) and *Modern Men and Mummers* (Allen & Unwin) by Hesketh Pearson; Mr William Plomer for *At Home* (Cape) and a letter; William Collins Sons & Co. Ltd for *The Sign of the Fish* by Peter Quennell; Mr Kerrison Preston for *Letters from Graham Robertson* (Hamish Hamilton); Hamish Hamilton Ltd for *Summer's Lease* by John Rothenstein; Mr S. de R. Raleigh for letters by Sir Walter Raleigh; Dr A. L. Rowse for a review; Bertrand Russell (Earl Russell, O.M.) for *Portraits from Memory* and *The Autobiography of Bertrand Russell* (Allen & Unwin and Little, Brown) and for unpublished letters; Mr Alan Searle for unpublished writings; Mr Roger Senhouse for unpublished writings; the Reverend F. A. Simpson for unpublished writings and *Louis Napoleon and the Fall of France* (Longmans); David Higham Associates Ltd for *Laughter in the Next Room* by Osbert Sitwell (Macmillan); David Higham Associates Ltd for *The Autobiography of Alice B. Toklas* by Gertrude Stein (The Bodley Head); Mr Frank Swinnerton for *The Georgian Literary Scene* (Dent); Professor Robert H. Tener for a letter; Dame Sybil Thorndike for unpublished writings; Sir Stanley Unwin for *The Truth About a Publisher* (Allen & Unwin); Longmans, Green & Co. Ltd for *Our Partnership* by Beatrice Webb and the Trustees of the Passfield Trust for Beatrice Webb's *Diary*; Mr Edmund Wilson for 'Lytton Strachey' from *The Shores of Light* (Farrar, Straus & Giroux and W. H. Allen); Professor John Dover Wilson, C.H., for an article and an unpublished letter; Mr Leonard Woolf for his own published and unpublished writings and those of Virginia Woolf.

Author's Note

Except in the case of his very early letters, I have tried silently to correct all Lytton's slips of spelling. Where he prefers one variant of a word and I another – as with Tchekhoff or Chekhov, for example – I have, of course, faithfully reproduced his version in the quotations, while keeping my own in other passages. But because Carrington's individual forms of grammar, punctuation and spelling seemed to me to convey her personality so very directly – and that to standardize them would have been to emasculate this strong impression – I have, so far as has been possible throughout Volume II, preserved her original text.

The correspondence of Lytton Strachey with Vanessa Bell, with B. W. Swithinbank, and also some letters he wrote to Lady Keynes, John Hayward and Gertrude Kingston are to be found in the library at King's College, Cambridge. Otherwise, almost all holographs or records of Strachey's papers are either in the possession of Mrs Alix Strachey or the recipients (or their families) of his correspondence. The manuscript of *Elizabeth and Essex* is in the library of Duke University, North Carolina; that of *Queen Victoria* at the University of Texas. The Warren Hastings dissertation was purchased in 1964 by a private American collector. *Eminent Victorians* is in the possession of Mrs Alix Strachey.

The identities and descriptions of certain individuals who appear in this biography have been disguised. The names they are given have been arbitrarily chosen and bear no relation to the originals they replace.

PART I

'We begin life in a very odd manner – like ship-
wrecked sailors. The world is our desert Island.'

Lytton Strachey to Leonard Woolf (July 1904)

CHAPTER I

Lancaster Gate

'To reconstruct, however dimly, that grim machine, would be to realize with some real distinctness the essential substance of my biography.'

Lytton Strachey –
'Lancaster Gate' (1922)

I

THE ANCESTRAL TREADMILL

'Strachey – an old family, small in numbers, but of a marked and persistent type. Among its characteristics are an active interest in public matters, and an administrative aptitude.' So wrote the geneticist Francis Galton defining the essential disposition of the Strachey family. With the majority of writers a survey and assessment of their antecedents is unnecessary. In the special case of Lytton Strachey some knowledge of his family and its inherited culture is fundamental to the understanding of his development and the individual nature of his contribution to critical and biographical literature.

Ever since the late sixteenth century, a large proportion of the family had displayed a taste for letters combined with an unusual degree of competence in the running of public affairs. The first Strachey of note was William, the original secretary of the Virginia Company, who in 1609 had embarked as one of five hundred passengers bound from England for the colony of Virginia. On 2 June, the nine ships in which they were sailing ran into a violent storm, and three of them, including the *Sea Venture* in which Strachey was travelling, becoming separated from the others, were grounded off the coast of Bermuda. The survivors had then set about building two pinnaces on which they voyaged back to England, arriving during September of the following year. Two accounts of their adventures were soon published. But a third, that of William Strachey, did not appear until some fifteen years later, owing to the too-realistic picture it presented of the conditions in Virginia. Scholars are now generally agreed that Shakespeare must have seen the manuscript of this account and made use of it in writing *The Tempest*, either through having known Strachey personally, or through his friendship with the Earl of Southampton, who was treasurer of the Virginia Company, or else indirectly through his acquaintance with Thomas Russell, whose stepson, Sir Dudley Digges, was a member of the Virginia Council.

The next Strachey of some historical interest is John, the grandson of William, who was born in the third decade of the seventeenth century. The English *Zeitgeist* during these years was slowly moving away from what may be described as scientific humanism. The prosaic view of the universe originally formulated by Bacon reached its apotheosis with Locke's *Essay Concerning Human Understanding*. One of Locke's friends was John Strachey, a barrister-at-law and a member of Gray's Inn. His only son, also christened John, was born in 1671 and inherited Sutton Court in Somerset, which was to become the established family residence.

The second John Strachey was of a rather dry disposition, and a notable representative of the new age of materialistic philosophy which Locke had helped to evolve. In him the prosaic fulfilment of the seventeenth-century movement, which was a logical result of the academic endeavour to reduce eternity to explicitness in terms of time, found a most respected embodiment. A cautious scholar and author of learned works on geological and antiquarian subjects, he was elected in December 1719 a Fellow of the Royal Society. In marked contrast to the prudence of his scholasticism was the vigorous activity of his private life. He married twice and became the father of nineteen children, whose education and upkeep was responsible for amassing a debt of twelve thousand pounds against the family estate.

The heir to this debt was Henry Strachey. Brought up during a comparatively lucid interval of English history and in a station of life set at some comfortable distance from the shocks and perils of the rough-and-tumble world, he passed a reasonably unadventurous and contented existence through the first sixty years of the eighteenth century.

The sharp dissimilarity between the first and last halves of this century is strikingly reflected in the unequal personalities of Henry Strachey and his eldest surviving son, who was named after him. Born in 1736, Sir Henry Strachey was a prototype within the family of that breed of aristocratic intelligentsia belonging to the upper-middle classes which, while the British Empire was expanding and consolidating its position, developed into a most powerful section of the ruling caste in Britain.

Unlike both his father and grandfather, products of quieter, less dramatic epochs, Sir Henry was essentially a man of action, a diplomat, politician and 'servant of the British Empire' of a type growing increasingly numerous in this era of colonial aggrandizement. His principal fields of activity concerned America and India, and for his services in both countries he was created a baronet. The first of three succeeding generations of public servants, his most important work was carried out in India where, with the recommendation of George Greville, he had been appointed secretary to Lord Clive during his last visit to India. That his association with Clive was close and cordial is borne out by several incidents. Once, when Strachey discovered that Sutton Court, unable to recover from the mortgage borrowed on it by his grandfather, was being threatened with foreclosure, Clive at once advanced him the whole amount against his future salary. After returning from India, he continued to be retained by Clive as his secretary. Shortly afterwards he married Jane Kelsall, Lady Clive's first cousin, and four years later entered Parliament as the member for Bishop's Castle, one of Clive's boroughs. His loyalty to Clive was extended to one of his celebrated successors, Warren Hastings, and in resolutely refusing Burke's attempts to enlist his support in the impeachment of Hastings he founded a family tradition to which Lytton Strachey was to contribute his full share. Clive's various references to Sir Henry Strachey show him to have been, like his son Edward, a man whose talent was less for dramatic speech-making than for painstaking executive work. Like his son, too, he was fond of letters and produced an historical work which bore the copious title *Narrative of the Mutiny of the Officers of the Army in Bengal in 1766.*

Through succeeding generations, the family had perfected that 'marked and persistent type' which Sir Francis Galton had so clearly observed. The Edward Stracheys present admirable examples of this type. In Edward Strachey himself the twin streams of literary inclination and administrative ability were evenly matched. In addition, he was – as almost all the Stracheys had been – essentially a man of his own time, possessing varied gifts but little true creative originality. His wife Julia exhibited qualities of charm, practical competence in raising a large family, and a keen intelligence unenriched by any exceptional insight – a combination of gifts which characterized several of the Strachey wives, notably Lytton's mother.

Some interesting impressions and comments on the Edward Stracheys have been left by Carlyle, who was first introduced to them in June 1824 at No 4 Myddleton Terrace, the home of his Scottish friends, the Irvings. In the following weeks and months he had been invited to the Stracheys' London house in Fitzroy Square and to their country residence, Goodenough House, at Shooter's Hill near Woolwich – 'a modestly excellent house', as he described it. Here, too, he had met their 'pretty children' (one of them Lytton's father), discovered his first favourable impressions of them confirmed and even excelled, and come to learn something of their history.

Edward Strachey, then fifty years of age, had been educated at Westminster and St Andrews where he evinced an erratic talent for languages, soon learning 'to talk French like English' – an ambiguous though perhaps not inappropriate description of his singular proficiency. During his youth he had travelled through India first as a free-lance writer, then as secretary to his future father-in-law, Colonel William Kirkpatrick, the Resident at Poona, and finally as a judge at Midnapore, Agra, Calcutta and elsewhere. In this faculty he is said to have mastered the Persian language with his usual dexterity, some years later baffling a professor of Persian who completed their mutual confusion by replying in perfect French. On returning from India in 1811, he was appointed one of the three assistants at the Examiner's Office of India House, the other two being Thomas Love Peacock and James Mill, father of the philosopher John Stuart Mill.

Carlyle's desire for a life of action, for ever thwarted, was often to seek vicarious satisfaction in the exploits of others, and it seems probable that Edward Strachey attracted him initially by virtue of his active and unusual career. Closer acquaintance soon showed that he possessed many other attributes more worthy of curiosity and admiration. For, although a profound sceptic, by nature taciturn and abrupt, a man whose rationalistic opinions inevitably clashed with Carlyle's inherited Calvinism, he seldom troubled to force his views upon others, remaining for the most part quite inarticulate on religious and controversial topics. There was about him, too, an ingenuous and downright objection to humbug, which made him a particularly congenial companion to the young writer. Beneath the reserved and unpromising exterior there lay a bizarre compound of personal characteristics. Despite much that was extrovert in his way of life, Edward Strachey cherished a discriminating taste for literature, being fond of Spenser, Shakespeare, Milton and especially Chaucer, whom he read constantly. Besides this literary sensibility, he also retained a wide and rather unlikely knowledge of people and subjects. One of his greatest friends was Mountstuart Elphinstone, the historian, soldier and Indian administrator. Attended by one hundred and fifty servants, eleven camels, ten bullocks, eight elephants and four horses, the two of them had once travelled from Calcutta to Poona, taking more than a year over their journey and discussing as they went an extraordinary variety of writers, a vast library of whose books, ranging from Herodotus to Thomas Jefferson, was carried by their retinue. Strachey achieved, too, the archetype of laborious erudition by publishing in a quarto volume the English translation of a thesis on algebra which, originally in Sanskrit, had been successfully adapted for Hindu readers, re-translated into Persian and thence transposed into the English of 1813. His eccentricities, which greatly amused Carlyle – involving what was best and most poetic in his nature – were by no means all so scholastic. At St Andrews, for instance, his enthusiasm for golf had taken such a hold upon him that he tailored his academic gown into a striking red golfing jacket, while his other recreations apart from golf included the playing of the flute. Yet in spite of these and other pronounced idiosyncrasies, Strachey held in reserve a good store of common sense, and notwithstanding his alternating moods of stubborn silence and irritating logic-chopping, generally impressed the percipient Carlyle as being 'a man of real worth'.

The affection which Carlyle felt for Julia Strachey was naturally more spontaneous and intimate. The member of another distinguished Anglo-Indian family, Julia Woodburn Kirkpatrick had first gone out to India with her elder sister Mrs Buller in the summer of 1807, and had married Edward Strachey within a year of her arrival there. Whereas he was almost twice Carlyle's age, she, at thirty-three, was barely five years his senior. With their complementary natures they got on well from the start. Carlyle's writing, his letters, *Reminiscences* and *Life of Stirling*, all contain graceful references to this 'singular pearl of a woman'. Bright but at the same time serious, her admiration of him was sufficiently intelligent to flatter his self-esteem. All her life she set great store by friendship, in particular the friendship of men whose minds struck her as being original. Well-read without being priggish, still attractive though not frivolous, sincere but not devoid of quiet humour, she would have made an admirable partner for many a man of letters.

That Julia Strachey liked Carlyle is certain; and that she expressed her liking in a peculiarly feminine way, that of making herself respons-ible for finding him a good wife, seems probable. Undoubtedly, to her mind, the most felicitous choice was conveniently close at hand. Her young cousin 'Kitty' Kirkpatrick was the daughter of the Resident of Hyderabad, who had been cunningly seduced by the fourteen-year-old niece of the Nizam. The highly exotic tale of this seduction, contrived by the lovesick girl under the experienced tuition of her mother and grandmother, ended in the conventional rites of Mohammedan and Christian marriage, a practice much frowned on by the authorities. In this case Lord Wellesley himself had felt compelled to investigate the affair, at first resolving to remove Kirkpatrick from his post, but finally deciding instead to recommend him for a baronetcy.

To bring the couple together Julia had invited both Kitty and Carlyle to a small sea-party at Dover. The guests were divided into two groups. Carlyle stayed with his friends the Irvings in a dim, paltry house near the sea, while Kitty and the Stracheys occupied rather brighter apartments near by in Liverpool Terrace. Unfortunately the party got off to a bad start. Perhaps Julia Strachey had expected too much; certainly her husband was not one to make the best of a mediocre situation. Or it may have been that Carlyle, having parted from his physician, was once more suffering from the pains of dyspepsia, aggravated by the extravagantly sceptical Irving. Whatever the cause, it was out of her immediate feelings of disappointment that Julia Strachey suddenly evolved another, more ambitious plan. Carlyle and Kitty, chaperoned by her husband, should go off to France, she suggested, while she herself would remain with the Irvings at Dover. Kitty and the restless Edward Strachey agreed at once, and Carlyle, though he must well have appreciated the dismay that would be excited within his family at the news of such an expedition into what they still (1824–5) regarded as enemy territory, was persuaded without difficulty.

Carlyle's feelings towards Kitty and the prospect of a trip to 'Vanity-fair' were interesting and also, it would appear, quite unsuspected by Julia Strachey. Shy, happy, unassuming and ingenuous as a child, with black eyes and auburn hair, Kitty commanded a striking appearance and personality. And in addition to this, she was the sole mistress of some fifty thousand pounds. No wonder that Carlyle was strongly attracted towards her. In his allusions to her femininity there is a lyrical quality which transcends ordinary affection. But there existed a permanent gulf between his sincere and spontaneous emotions and the bleak inherited Calvinism of his parents. He acknowledged the feelings which he entertained for Kitty – but he did not altogether approve of her. Though she herself believed him for a time to be in love with her, and though his romantic exclamations and dreams of her gave rise to some malicious anxiety from Jane Welsh, languishing in the cold wastes of Scotland, there was little chance that the affair would be translated from the realms of Byronic illusion to those of practical fulfilment.

The three of them travelled together in Kitty's carriage to Montreuil, Nouilles, Abbeville and Beauvais. None of them spoke French well, and Strachey's, which was the worst of all, grew so comic that he soon refused to speak it altogether, falling back on pidgin-English reinforced with an array of extravagant gestures and looks. 'Où est les chevaux?' he used to cry irritably each day. The culmination of this linguistic and mannerly deterioration occurred in Paris. At the end of their tour, the excellent postilion came to the coach window before taking his leave. 'Quelque chose à boire, Monsieur!' he said, respectfully asking for the customary tip. Edward Strachey's answer was short and specific: 'Nong, vous avez drivé devilish slow!'

This glimpse into the lives of Lytton Strachey's grandparents is relevant both on general and particular grounds. In his miniature pen-portrait of Carlyle, Lytton refers briefly and amusingly to his grandfather's riposte to the postilion and, drawing breath, launches upon his criticism of it in a fresh paragraph:

'The reckless insularity of this remark,' he wrote, 'illustrates well enough the extraordinary change which had come over the English governing classes since the eighteenth century. . . . The Napoleonic Wars, the industrial revolution, the romantic revival, the Victorian spirit, had brought about a relapse from the cosmopolitan suavity of eighteenth-century culture; the centrifugal forces, always latent in English life, had triumphed, and men's minds had shot off into the grooves of eccentricity and provincialism.'

These reflections embody the characteristic hostility which Lytton Strachey always manifested towards all forms of John Bullishness. Professor Charles Richard Sanders, the American biographer of Lytton's mind and art, and painstaking chronicler of the whole Strachey family, makes reference to this essay on Carlyle in paradoxical support of his assertion that Lytton 'assimilated the cultural traditions of his family and found life in them'. Lytton Strachey, he states, 'wrote with pride' about his paternal grandfather's association with Carlyle; and to substantiate this claim he quotes one sentence from the initial paragraph where Lytton describes his grandfather as 'an Anglo-Indian of cultivation and intelligence'. But in attempting to reconcile Lytton's writings with his own inexhaustible reverence for an old and illustrious English family, Professor Sanders has given an oversimplified and to some degree false picture of Lytton's attitude towards his forebears. His choice of words represents no straightforward expression of ancestral pride, but constitutes a deliberate literary device used to heighten the contrast, the 'extraordinary change', to quote his own words, between the eighteenth century and the early Victorian era, of which his grandfather was such a typical example. In a more subtle manner the reader is also misdirected by the tone of Professor Sanders's statement, which implies a like sense of cultural inferiority. Lytton's half-amused hostility was indeed a form of inverted respect, but denoted an extension of his self-dislike – a way of purging his romanticism by means of his acute

classical intelligence. He was the culminating product of a long tradition kept alive from the previous generation by artificial stimulants.
Something of the range and limitations of the influence exerted by his
family heritage was suggested by John Russell when, apropos of
Eminent Victorians, he wrote: 'Strachey presents the facts of belief with
the skill bred into a family of gifted administrators; but his minute is
always a hostile one.' Raymond Mortimer struck the same note when,
probably with *Queen Victoria* chiefly in mind, he pointed out that 'the
mastery of a mass of detail, the solid and admirably proportioned
architecture of Mr Strachey's books are an inheritance from generations
of civil servants'. But, as Raymond Mortimer has also written, Strachey
was deeply unconventional, a revolutionary using the very weapons on
the Victorians that had been forged in Victorian homes. Turning his
attention to the cultural inheritance not only of the Stracheys but also
the Stephens, he finds that Lytton Strachey and Virginia Woolf (*née*
Stephen) – 'related to half the most scholarly families in England' – had
in common a certain distinctive characteristic. 'It has some relation to a
voice that is never too loud, a scepticism that remains polite, a learning
that is never paraded and a disregard, that never becomes insulting, for
the public taste. It is a quality of inherited culture. Genius and taste can
only come to terms by something approaching a miracle. In these two
writers this miracle is accomplished.'

Although Lytton remained too much of a genuine original to follow
faithfully the genealogical pattern of the Stracheys, he was at the same
time of too inaudacious a temperament to break completely away from
its potent influence. The family had never been the originators of any
new movement in thought or action, and, for all their wealth of talent,
had never achieved anything creative in the sphere of art. To literary
historians they are interesting chiefly by virtue of their associations with
Shakespeare, Locke, Carlyle and many other celebrated men of letters.
In the case of Lytton Strachey the converse of this is true. Instinctively
he felt the need to become independent of the established traditions of
the past, which had already begun to lose their momentum at his birth
and which threatened to stifle his artistic potential. By the time he went
up to Cambridge at the turn of the century, the superannuated Victorian
family of which he was a very junior member must have appeared to
him like some faded, splendidly old-fashioned illustration from a
schoolroom history book, depicting a social phenomenon already
extinct. The new literary idols of the undergraduate, Ibsen and Shaw,
Samuel Butler and H. G. Wells, were flying in the face of Victorianism and much that the last three generations of Stracheys had
upheld.

The tendency of all mass movements of the human mind is to re-produce the faults of the movement from which they are reacting. The reckless insularity, melodrama and eccentricity which Lytton Strachey uncovered in the Victorians recur, under slightly different guises, in some of his own writing, and are symptomatic of his failure to shake himself loose from the cocoon of family influence which enveloped his early years. What is finest in his achievement is unique. His exquisite craftsmanship, it is true, was derived from generations of civil servants, but it was moulded into a shape peculiar to himself. The weakest elements in his writing – the inverted sentimentality, the rhetoric, the too acutely angled point of view, and the succession of homely plati-tudes which he dipped in phosphorus and turned loose into the night to abash the simple-minded – are the natural symptoms of his maladjust-ment to the past.

'Strachey was a romantic by temperament,' wrote K. R. Srinivasa Iyengar, 'a classicist by training, and often, in his own literary practice, both.' His cast of mind inclined naturally towards critical analysis, but it is in this approach that he was often most shallow and erratic. All too frequently when confronted by some intricate and baffling personality he indulged in one of his brilliant displays of verbal pyrotechnics, elaborating gracefully upon his subject's more colourful traits and smothering his own curiosity by sheer technical dexterity. The method of biography which he instigated, no less than his beautifully shaped critical essays, demanded some profound and enduring analysis of human character if they were to escape the charge of triviality. But, in line with the long practice of his family, he chose his subjects mostly from among men and women of action, concentrating less upon the impulse behind their lives than upon the dramatic effect they produced on those around them. 'To escape the bondage of tradition,' wrote George Carver, 'he created an imaginary past.' His *Queen Victoria* and *Elizabeth and Essex* are, in consequence, most elegant tapestries depict-ing scenes of historical pageantry, and seldom do they pierce far enough below the surface to present an imaginative reconstruction of reality. It is a measure of Lytton's partially attained independence that his bio-graphical technique should be more celebrated for originality than his interpretation of human character.

The overall effects of conformity and revolt on literature and literary criticism are interesting. Towards one end of the scale stands a writer such as Desmond MacCarthy, who believed that a critic – as opposed to an essayist – should propound no opinions of his own. Fascinated by the effect released by any action or piece of writing, he persevered almost exclusively at conveying the sense of enjoyment to be experienced by the average sensitive and intelligent reader, whom he scrupulously kept in mind while composing his essay-reviews. At the opposite end of the scale stands the isolated and disregarded figure of Hugh Kingsmill, who related a book not with its reader but with the original author, with whom he partially identified himself. The one was primarily concerned with reaction to writing, and his essays are spun out with all the careless grace and elegance of fine lace; but, as Strachey himself wrote of Horace Walpole, it is the embroidery which counts more than the material. The other focused upon the personal impulse behind a creative work, and, impatient with the paraphernalia of pure aesthetics, oblivious to his audience, found with dismay that the uncompromising austerity and fine compression of his essays attracted few readers.

Between these two extremes of impressionistic and analytical criticism fluctuates Strachey. He was not a member of the establishment, but of the established opposition. Now impelled by reaction against a coarseness and complacency with which he felt himself hereditarily associated but by which he was temperamentally repelled, his sharp intelligence pricks the inflated reputation of a Victorian hero; now swept headlong by a sentimental nostalgia for Elizabethan drama instilled into him by a vigorously attentive mother, he courses into pure melodrama. First he essays to destroy a legend, then he seasons one with the spice of his own wit garnished with overtones of giggling naughtiness. His immature emotions and wonderfully quick comprehensive mind were seldom harnessed satisfactorily together, so that only spasmodically did he realize his full potential, his powers crystallize into a deep and imaginative penetration.

Indifference rather than passionate indignation against an old establishment is the hallmark of the truly independent and self-sufficient writer, the man who belongs exclusively to no one generation, but is for all time. Strachey stood with one foot in the twentieth century, and one in the past. He was never completely at home in an age of trains and telephones, of squalid industrial suburbs and herded shop-girls; and he stared back ruefully and rather romantically at the more fastidious social refinements of seventeenth- and eighteenth-century France. At least the degradation of those past centuries had been more picturesque, less humdrum and second-rate.

As a true pioneer in the delicate and humane art of biography his place in literature is secure. But his reputation has been damaged by those who initially claimed too much on his behalf. He was not a profound and original psychological thinker; his political and sociological enlightenment was only intermittent; above all it is essential to dispose of the myth that he was the fugleman of inflexible anti-Victorianism, by placing his work in its true chronological context within the stream of literary history. The first and most intense protest against Victorianism had been made in the 'sixties of the previous century, when Swinburne invoked Dolores to 'come down and redeem us from virtue'. The early novels of Ouida echoed this protest in terms more intelligible to the ordinary reader. Samuel Butler, a few years later, inverted Victorian morality in *Erewhon*. The aesthetes, socialists, and imperialists launched their separate attacks on Victorianism in the last decades of the nineteenth century and the first decade of the twentieth, and by 1914 the prestige of the Victorians had sunk to its lowest level. The four most influential writers just before the war were Bernard Shaw, H. G. Wells, Arnold Bennett and G. K. Chesterton. Shaw detested Macaulay, Tennyson and Thackeray, and praised Dickens chiefly as a social reformer. Wells and Bennett detested Thackeray, despised Tennyson, ignored Macaulay and did not relish Dickens. The only Victorians approved by Shaw, Wells and Bennett were those opposing the morals, economics or religion of their age – Carlyle, for example, and Ruskin, Huxley and Samuel Butler. Chesterton, some years younger than the other three, was the first of the Edwardians to stem this anti-Victorian current, erecting Dickens into a bulwark against both socialism and aestheticism, and finding even in the more orthodox Victorians, Thackeray, Browning and Tennyson, much more to praise than to condemn. The war was favourable to the Victorians, who, seen across that gulf, became the objects of a more disinterested appreciation than was possible to men whose earlier years were spent in close quarters with Victorian morality and religion. The only reproach that can be brought against Lytton Strachey, as the earliest post-war critic of the Victorians, is that he desiccated the corpses after the tempest had blown them from their gibbets. *Eminent Victorians* marked, in fact, the initial stage in a more benign treatment of the Victorian age, its acidity being an Edwardian ingredient with which he dispensed almost completely in his next biography, *Queen Victoria*. His disapproval of Victorianism in some respects emphasizes his ties with the past. He was schooled in radical conformity; graduated as a rebel; but ended up largely as a creature of quiet romantic tradition, with a filial affection for the British Raj. He was never able to outgrow this attachment; for, to the end, he could not contend with the complexities of extricating himself from a vast ancestral treadmill which had been revolving in its grooves for generations.

2

PAPA AND MAMA

'The Stracheys are most strongly the children of their fathers, not of their mothers,' Mrs St Loe Strachey wrote in 1930. '"It does not matter whom they marry," said one of St Loe's aunts to me when I was quite young, "the type continues and has been the same for three hundred years."' In the case of Lytton, St Loe's cousin, this dictum no longer holds true. 'You'd never think he was a general's son,' the head porter at the Great Gate of Trinity once remarked to Clive Bell, as the lanky, drooping silhouette of Strachey moved across the quadrangle. And even though the figure of Lieutenant-General Sir Richard Strachey, so stocky and dynamic, might not have fitted a head porter's impression of the typical British general, there was certainly little physical resemblance between him and his fifth son.

Richard Strachey, the third of six sons, had been born at Sutton Court on 24 July 1817. After leaving his public school at Totteridge, he entered Addiscombe, the military seminary of the East India Company, graduating from it two years later at the head of his class and receiving a commission in the Bombay Engineers. He served at Poona and Kandeish, and when war broke out on the Sikh frontier, he was hurried out there to take part in the Sutlej campaign, in which he fought with great gallantry, being awarded a medal with a clasp, and on one occasion having his horse shot from under him.

As the result of successive bouts of fever, he was compelled in 1847 to go to Nan Tal in the Kumaon Himalayas. During his convalescence there he studied botany and geology, and the following year, in company with a gentleman named Winterbottom, he explored the Himalayan provinces, pushing into Tibet as far as the Rakas-Tal and Manasarowar lakes, which his brother, Colonel Henry Strachey, had visited only a few months previously. Together the two explorers carried back a 'significant mass' of scientific data, having collected no less than two thousand botanical specimens. Some thirty-two of their new-found species were named after Strachey, though regrettably, owing to an excess of personal modesty, botanical nomenclature has not been enriched by the introduction of Latin derivatives from the surname of his companion.

In 1849 Richard Strachey made a further expedition, this time with his brother Henry, after which he returned to England to arrange the 'Strachey and Winterbottom Herbarium' and publish his observations

on biological, geographical, geological and meteorological subjects.[1]
After their publication he was elected a fellow of the Royal Society,
and in the same year, 1854, married his first wife, Caroline Anne
Bowles, who died some twelve months later. He then returned to India
where he became associated with the department of public works under
Sir Henry Yule and his future father-in-law, Sir John Peter Grant,
whose secretary he was appointed while in Calcutta during the Mutiny.
His work over the following years showed the immense versatility and
energy of his temperament. Few men have done so much, often in
ways unknown to the outside world, for the improvement of Indian
administration. It was to him that India owed the initiation of her policy
of the systematic extension of railways and canals which increased, to
an incalculable extent, the wealth of the country and profoundly
altered its condition. To him was due the conception of those measures
of financial and administrative decentralization pronounced by Sir
Henry Maine to be by far the greatest and most successful reforms
carried out in India in his time. He established the first adequate forest
service in the country; he completely reorganized the public works
department of which, in 1862, he became the head; he was the first to
advise the amendment of the currency, the delay of which involved the
country in considerable loss; and in his spare time he developed a very
pretty talent for painting. His career in India extended altogether over
thirty years and helped to fashion a stable form of government. By the
time he eventually left in 1871, he commanded a position of very great
power and importance. In public matters he had impressed those with
whom he came into contact as being a man of strong mind, determined
will. On the few occasions when he was indisputably in the wrong – as,
for example, over the vexed topic of railway gauges – he could be
obstinate and inflexible. But despite his outstanding success in public
administration, his real leaning was towards science, and he liked to
think that his more lasting achievements lay in this field. Of all his
scientific investigations, the most zealous were in meteorology; and for
his labours in laying the foundations of the scientific study of Indian
meteorology he was awarded the coveted Symons Medal by the Royal
Meteorological Society. He was also a fine geographical scholar, and was
twice made President of the Royal Geographical Society.

Amid a society of prepotent personages Richard Strachey had more
than held his own. He was not merely a soldier: he was also a scientist,

[1] See for example *Catalogue of the Plants of Kumaon and of the Adjacent Portions of
Garhwal and Tibet*, based on the collections made by Strachey and Winterbottom during
the years 1846–9, and originally prepared in 1852 by Lieutenant-General Sir Richard
Strachey.

civil administrator, explorer, engineer, mathematician and accomplished Victorian gentleman with a large family and a marked knack for water-colours. Yet, though his restless energy overflowed into so many, various channels, his imagination remained exclusively matter-of-fact, and his whole conception of life was of a perfectly humdrum and un-exceptional kind. And in this he was not only carrying out a tradition of high public service, he was also following in the direct footsteps of Edward Strachey and the first Sir Henry Strachey. 'It seems as if the human mind was incapable of changing its focus,' wrote Lytton Strachey in a paper on the Chinese diplomat Li Hung-Chang; and, in words which aptly apply to so many of his own forebears, he continued: 'it must either apprehend what is near to it or what is far off; it cannot combine the two. Of all the great realists of history, the master spirits in the matter-of-fact business of managing mankind, it is difficult to think of more than one or two who, in addition, were moved by philosophical ideals towards noble aims.'

Richard Strachey's second marriage took place on 4 January 1859. Jane Maria Grant was the daughter of Sir John Peter Grant and Henrietta Chichele, daughter of Sir Trevor Chichele Plowden, a prominent member of a rather more aristocratic Anglo-Indian family. She had been born on 13 March 1840, on board the East India Com-pany's strong ship, *The Earl of Hardwicke*, in the middle of a violent storm off the Cape of Good Hope. Eighteen years later, in a sedate Indian withdrawing-room, she had met Richard Strachey for the first time, a black-haired man seated on a yellow sofa, and displaying 'the exact colours of a wasp'.

Physically they were not a well-matched pair. Whereas he, like most Stracheys, was rather short, highly methodical at work but of an abrupt and explosive social temperament, she, by contrast, was tall and stately in appearance, and of a more artistic bent.[1] They had in common, though, an abounding vitality, and since Richard Strachey's energies were directed mainly towards public and scientific matters, it was his wife's less diversified vigour which was experienced more keenly in the home. Certainly his paternal influence with the children seems to have declined sharply with time, while Lady Strachey became increasingly the principal and dominating figure within the family, and most especially, of course, over her younger sons and daughters.

Lytton Strachey was born at Stowey House, Clapham Common, on 1 March 1880, the eleventh of thirteen children, three of whom died in

---

[1] James Strachey recalled that his father was actually as tall as his mother – that is, about five feet eight inches. But he held himself badly and therefore seemed smaller. Photo-graphs of them together make him appear distinctly the shorter figure.

infancy. He was christened Giles Lytton after a sixteenth-century ancestor, Giles Strachey, and his godfather, the first Earl of Lytton, Viceroy of India, who as 'Owen Meredith' achieved some distinction as a poet. For the first three years of his life, however, he appears to have been spiritually nameless, since his christening ceremony, which was combined with that of his younger sister Marjorie, was not performed until the second week of April 1883. As a young child he was high-spirited and loquacious – for the only time in his life. 'Giles is the most ridiculous boy I ever saw,' Lady Strachey wrote to her daughter Dorothy shortly after his third birthday: 'he said to me, "Yesterday in the streets I saw a cow eating the birds!" He then enacted a drama of which the punishment of the unnatural cow was the motive; as a policeman he flung himself on one knee and upraised his arms at the cow with a most fine dramatic gesture of Command; a terrific combat then ensued in which he wielded the peacock broom with might, and finally cried sternly, "Go to be dead!" and laid his broom on the floor saying, "Now the cow is dead." He never ceases talking for a single minute.'

As an infant Lytton was noticeably eccentric. He loved to march up and down Stowey House chanting what was apparently an epic poem full of high-sounding phrases, which always began the same way but varied unpredictably in its later stages. 'It is interspersed with morsels in rhyme called "Dickey Songs",' Lady Strachey noted in her diary on 25 March 1884, 'and sung by the "Bugyler" – the chief hero "Bry-norma", the drummer boy is "Shiptenor", there is "Tellysin" and a "Calorum" and a "Sunsence"; as far as we can ascertain these names are entirely of his own construction. It looks rather as if he were one of the "many children" who could have written Ossian!'

Lytton's father was by this time nearing seventy, though Lady Strachey was still only forty-three. This wide discrepancy of age partly accounts for the differing roles which each played in the household and in the lives of their younger children. Terminating his short, rather impersonal letters in which the formality is relieved only by drawings of obscure botanical specimens to be seen at Kew, and which accompany mathematical booklets and packets of foreign stamps dispatched to Lytton, Richard Strachey invariably signed himself 'Your affnt father, Rd. Strachey'; while his mother, being much closer to him, wrote far longer and more frequent letters and remained, even when Lytton had fully grown up, 'ever darling, your loving Mama'. But while his father's remoteness only served to enhance, as time went on, Lytton's sense of wonder and admiration for him, the strong pressure of emotion laid upon him by his mother made him sometimes feel indifferent towards

her, and in the long run anxious to set himself up independently, free
from her protection and complete in himself.

Although during former days out in India Richard Strachey had
gained the reputation for being forceful and of a peppery temper, now
in England he had grown rather mild in spirit, a little vague and
detached from all that was going on even in the closest proximity.
Lytton's earliest memories of him recalled little but the sheaves of
papers, the voluminous sheets covered with elaborate calculations,
which, to the last, encumbered his desk. During the day he would sit
working at railway or atmospheric matters before this enormous desk
in his study; and Lytton was often sent up from the dining-room to try
and persuade him to descend for lunch. As Lytton grew, so his father
seemed to shrink into 'a little man with a very beautiful head', as
Leonard Woolf later described him, 'sitting all day long, summer and
winter, in a great armchair in front of a blazing fire, reading a novel'.[1]
Over the last few years of his life Sir Richard was seldom seen without
a novel in his hand. Six a week were selected and brought to him on a
silver tray,[2] and these would apparently absorb him all evening until,
shortly after ten o'clock at night, Ellen, the maid, appeared with a shawl
to take him up to bed. Meanwhile Lady Strachey, as she sat playing
patience on the opposite side of the elaborately tiled fireplace, kept an
agonized eye on her husband to see if he was going to be good or not.
Occasionally, very occasionally, he *was* good, soon closed his book,
rose with a smile and shuffled off to bed on Ellen's arm. More often than
not, however, he was naughty and resolved to finish the chapter before
becoming aware that Ellen was in the room. Sometimes Ellen, after
waiting patiently for several minutes, would bend forward and gently
whisper to him that it was late. No notice whatever would be taken of
this announcement. Silent looks of sympathy were then exchanged
between Ellen and Lady Strachey, who shook her head in hopeless
disapproval. But never did she interfere or address any remark to Sir
Richard, and if the proceedings became unusually protracted, one of
her daughters would put her book down, firmly advance and say
'Papa, it's bedtime!' Realizing that the game was up, Sir Richard would

[1] James Strachey, who disputed some details in Leonard Woolf's description, told
the author that the whole change in his father's life to semi-invalidism only took place
after 1897, when he was eighty. 'In that year, which was when he was knighted, he made
the journey by himself from our then country house near Manningtree in Essex, I fancy,
to Osborne for the investiture. He also took Pippa to the Naval Review at Spithead that
year. What happened was that he got an attack of dysentery after a visit to Belgium, and
nearly died. Though he recovered and went on working, he was never so active again.'

[2] This description is based on an account written by Duncan Grant. James Strachey,
however, remembered that half a dozen novels were delivered by van from the library each
week and placed on Sir Richard Strachey's table.

raise his spectacles over his forehead and with an engaging smile pretend that this was the first time he had heard of it. During the day he seemed at all times unaware of the terrific din which constantly surrounded him and which was unfailingly provided by his sons and daughters, sitting through it completely unmoved, Leonard Woolf recalls, and only 'occasionally smiling affectionately at it and them, when it obtruded itself unavoidably upon his notice, for instance, if in some deafening argument one side or the other appealed to him for a decision. He was usually a silent man, who listened with interest and amusement to the verbal hurricane around him; he was extraordinarily friendly and charming to an awkward youth such as I was, and he was fascinating when now and again he was induced to enter the discussion or recall something from his past.'

Part of this benevolent remoteness was occasioned by the increasing deafness which afflicted his later years and which forced him to relinquish several of the official appointments which he still held. Up to the age of ninety, he continued to go to the City and to the Meteorological Office. But he was a dangerous pedestrian, and on several occasions collided with hansom cabs – impacts which, though sometimes bringing on attacks of gout and causing the family the most acute anxiety, always left him in the highest spirits.

Even when Lytton was a young child his father took little active part in the everyday management of family affairs, for in this, as in most other respects, the household was staunchly Victorian. The Strachey tradition was seldom overtly stressed, but an assumption of its sufficiency saturated the atmosphere at Stowey House. The innermost feelings and ideas of the children were seldom contemplated and never discussed – a malpractice which tended in later years to produce in them a reserved manner and an instinctive recoil from all kinds of emotional exhibitionism. Early in his life Richard Strachey had professed to be an atheist, though later he admitted to being an agnostic. The change was not of great significance, for in an age where materialism had assumed the disguise of Christian orthodoxy, atheists and agnostics appeared to share a fundamental quality: they were both conventionally religious. Although no tinge of scepticism or conscious hypocrisy found a place in Richard Strachey's make-up, he attached himself without question to the fashionable ideals and communal virtues of his day. An infinitely painstaking and exhaustive worker, he passed the last active period of his life in the invention and perfection of his instruments for measuring the most minute movements of the highest, least visible clouds, and in giving graphic expression to one or two laws of meteorology. The old man laboured with unmitigated, almost heroic endurance at these pursuits; but that the rules of ethics, the laws and customs of social morality, the psychological complexities of his own children could be subjected to a similarly minute scrutiny was a notion which would have struck him as perverse and fantastic, a lapse from the recognized code of behaviour at once unwarranted and dangerous.

Placed beside her husband, Jane Maria Strachey appears at first sight to have been an unconventional figure. The quality which struck so many of her eminent contemporaries – among them Lord Lytton, Sir Henry Maine and Fitzjames Stephen – was that indefinable one of 'character'. Only a most remarkable woman would have been invited by Lord Bowen to sit beside him in the Court of Appeal, or asked by George Eliot to enter upon a sustained correspondence. Though she had no taste in the plastic arts, and was no intellectual, her personality was striking and agreeable. She was a figure in her own right – and not unaware of the fact. When on 22 June 1897, the date of Queen Victoria's Diamond Jubilee, she opened *The Times* and saw that her husband had been made Knight Grand Commander of the Star of India, she bitterly complained that this had been done without his first being asked. Previously he had declined other honours. And now she would be known as plain Lady Strachey – one of several – instead of *the* Mrs Richard Strachey.

From her earliest years she was addicted to literature and drama, and read especially French literature and Elizabethan drama with untiring relish. Her own publications consisted mostly of verse for children,[1] though she also edited her aunt's celebrated *Memoirs of a Highland Lady*, and in old age wrote 'Some Recollections of a Long Life', extracts from which were printed in the *Nation and Athenaeum*.[2] Some of her other tastes and activities suggest unorthodoxy and enlightenment. A friend of Mrs Henry Fawcett, she worked to promote the Woman's Progressive Movement; she loved classical music, sitting Lytton on her knee while she played songs on the piano; and she inspired him also with her passion for parlour games, amateur

---

[1] Lady Strachey's *Nursery Lyrics*, originally published in 1893 with illustrations by G. P. Jacomb Hood, was reprinted with additions in 1922 as *Nursery Lyrics and other Verses for Children* and illustrated by Philip Hagreen. *Poets on Poets* appeared in 1894. In 1887, she had brought out her children's anthology, *Lay Texts for the Young, in Both English and French*. A copy of this book was presented to Lytton when he was about fourteen. There are no religious authors included in the volume, and, presumably because he was too well known, no Shakespeare. Several of the quotations appear to contradict one another, but the chief qualities held up to be emulated are five in number: truth, reason, balance, virtue and aspiration.

[2] *Nation and Athenaeum* XXXIV (5 Jan., 24 Feb., 1924), pp. 514–15, 730–1; XXXV (12 July, 30 Aug. 1924), pp. 473–4, 664–5. See also XXXIV, p. 514.

theatricals, puzzles, and with something of her zest for billiards, at which she was an expert player. For a number of the social conventions of her time she entertained scant respect, and long before women were generally permitted such habits she smoked, not just ordinary cigarettes, but those of the ultra-modern *American* variety. Even in her seventies she enjoyed particularly the company of young people, throwing herself into their amusements with the unquenchable vivacity of a girl of twenty. Indeed, she was much more 'advanced' in her old age than she had been in her youth – for which progress Lytton was largely responsible. She had been brought up an ordinary, passive Christian, but after reading John Stuart Mill's work *On Liberty* at the age of nineteen she became his fervent disciple. He was the guiding star of her youth, giving her a coherent scheme of thought and an intellectual basis for conduct newly permeated and vitalized by a fresh emotional enthusiasm, when all she had been brought up to believe was shattered to dust and ashes. From this faith she was eventually disabused by Lytton himself, who, reacting to the contrary influence of the philosopher G. E. Moore, came to regard the Utilitarian Mill, so far from being a champion of liberty, as totalitarian, intolerant and inquisitorial. In her anxiety to retain and promote the affection of her son, Lady Strachey endeavoured to alter the course of her mind into more speculative channels. She tried when in her sixties to master the Greek language, and also to match the rather aggressive paganism which Lytton began to adopt as he grew up. 'I should not be surprised,' she wrote hopefully to him on one occasion, 'if the decay of Christianity led to some really interesting appreciations of the New Testament that might stimulate perceptions which, like mine, have been blunted by ceaseless iteration and vitiated by the theological standpoint.' Her attempts to be modern were stamped more by pathos than happiness or success. Lytton, appreciating the personal impulse which lay behind such affirmations of her desire to learn, treated what she said with kindness and respect. But to Maynard Keynes he wrote: 'Oh how dreadful to be a mother. How terrible to love so much and know so little! Will it always be like this to the end of the world?'

Just as the bold spirit of Jane Carlyle had succumbed to the influences that surrounded it, so too, it seemed to Lytton, was his mother a mid-Victorian at heart, whatever new intellectual concepts she might struggle to embrace. The apparent independence of her mind was merely superficial, the eruption of a superabundant and essentially unreflective vitality. In public and political life she campaigned actively for the rights of women as citizens; but at home she instinctively put her husband before herself in every way, and preferred the scientists of her acquaintance – Galton, Huxley, Lubbock, Tyndall and others – to the artists and men of letters. Although she met many eminent writers, including Carlyle, Browning, Ruskin, Tennyson and George Eliot, her recorded observations and comments upon them reveal little genuine perception. She never, for example, noticed anything to suggest that the Carlyles were not on the very best of terms; and when Tennyson declared that *Troilus and Cressida* was probably Shakespeare's finest play, she merely registered shock. On the other hand some of the phrases she used in her letters to Lytton are quite vivid and arresting, and suggest a modest if undeveloped literary talent, swamped by the excessive conformity of an age in which women were still far from attaining reasonable emancipation. Her trivial irregularities from the strictest, most petty conventions of the time were in themselves quite conventional idiosyncrasies, showing how a strain of real originality, if stifled, may become squandered in the form of harmless social eccentricity.

The discrepancy which existed between her potential artistic capability and the actual self-development she attained gave rise to various startling inconsistencies in her behaviour and in the education which she arranged for Lytton. One side of her nature had been furthered by experience at the total expense of the other, and from this ill-proportion seems to have arisen a curious lack of co-ordination. She was invariably dressed in long sweeping clothes of black satin, and, though rather statuesque in appearance, her movements were ungainly; though, too, her energy was unusually concentrated, in demeanour she was often vague and dream-like, and she would frequently enter some room, forget why she had come in and, after gazing round it in distraction for several minutes, be obliged to walk out empty-handed. She suffered also, this majestic-looking lady, from attacks of vertigo, which Lytton inherited, and after one such attack near Marble Arch was arrested by the police on suspicion of drunkenness. Her moods, too, were correspondingly unpredictable. Absent-minded and, like her husband, apparently unaware of what was going on around her for much of the time, she would all at once awake from her reverie and join in a discussion which the family had been carrying on in her presence for the previous hour, arguing her point of view with the most urgent and extreme passion, as if to make up for lost time.

Neither bohemian nor fashion-conscious, something of Lady Strachey's individual temperament was stamped on Stowey House and on the subsequent houses which the family were to occupy. For the children this lack of smartness was altogether refreshing and delightful. They saw the overall dowdiness and confusion as a redeeming element –

something human in the impersonal Victorian atmosphere – and took a ruthless joy in pointing out all the most blatant irregularities both to guests and to their mother. 'Our conventionality,' wrote Lytton, 'slightly mitigated by culture and intelligence, was impinged upon much more seriously by my mother's constitutional vagueness and immateriality, and by a vein in her of oddity and caprice. Her feeling for what was right and proper was unsupported by the slightest touch of snobbery; and while it was very strong and quite unhesitating, it was surprisingly peculiar to herself. That her daughters should go into mourning for the German Emperor, for instance, appeared to her essential; but her own dresses were most extraordinary, designed by herself, quite regardless of fashion. She had all her children christened, but she never went to Church – except in the country when she went with the utmost regularity. She was religious in the payment of calls; but the arrangements of her household, from the point of view of social life, were far below the standard.' From the point of view of domestic administration, her arrangements were more laborious than efficient, and amid the hubbub, the incessant and inevitable *va-et-vient* of her large family, she would sit at her writing-desk littered with papers pursuing a slow and immensely elaborate system of household accounts.

The private education which Lady Strachey gave her sons and daughters was no less baffling and inconsequential. Though they remained uninstructed and, in the case of the daughters at least, completely unenlightened regarding the facts of life, she read to them all the works of the bawdiest and most rollicking Elizabethan dramatists, together with such novels as *Tom Jones*, evidently unaware that they might be expected to comprehend only a fraction of what was going on. Many years later, however, when Lytton brought up the question of Shakespeare's sonnets, she sent two of his sisters – then in their twenties – out of the room, while she argued in favour of Shakespeare's purity, explaining to her silent and disbelieving son that the poet entertained no sexual feelings for the man whom he was addressing. Degradation and horror had no place in her life, and she somehow avoided coming into contact with the blood, lust and savagery of the Elizabethans of whom she was so fond. After all, she reasoned, it was only fiction; and between fiction and the facts of life there was, as everyone knew, a great salutary gulf for ever fixed. Her vivacious temperament responded automatically to their ribaldry, but they held for her no power of actuality. Similarly, she learnt long passages of Milton off by heart, and, enjoying the music of the poetry, paid not the least attention to the doctrines expressed in it. Despite being a freethinker, she liked to read South's sermons aloud to her children purely to give them an ear for rhythm in English prose. Literature, in short, might be an excellent serious recreation, but it could bear little intimate relation to her own and her family's lives. By the same token, for all the obvious pleasure she took in managing this large family, she remained extraordinarily ignorant of what any single one of them might be thinking or feeling. As a good and capable Victorian wife, she parodied on a smaller scale her husband's way of life, so that although she was keenly interested in public matters, together with Richard Strachey she presented a blank wall of unconscious indifference to the subjective problems of all her children.

3

ELEPHANTIASIS AND UNCLES

When Lytton was four years old the Stracheys moved from Stowey House to 69 Lancaster Gate, a rather rambling and portentous Victorian edifice just north of Kensington Gardens, where he was to spend the next twenty-five years of his life. 'My remembrances of Stowey House are dim and sporadic,' he wrote long afterwards in an unpublished essay which examines his early life in relation to the family and its heritage, '– Jim Rendel[1] with a penny in a passage – a miraculous bean at the bottom of the garden – Beatrice Chamberlain[2] playing at having tea with me, with leaves and acorns, under a tree. But my consecutive existence began in the nursery at Lancaster Gate – the nursery that I can see now, empty and odd and infinitely elevated, as it was when I stood in it for the first time at the age of four with my mother, and looked out of the window at the surprisingly tall houses opposite, and was told that this was where we were going to live. A calm announcement – received with some excitement, which was partly caused by the unusual sensation of extreme height, as I peered at the street below. The life that began then – my Lancaster Gate life – was to continue till I was twenty-eight – a man full-grown – all the changes from childhood to adolescence, from youth to manhood, all the developments, the curiosities, the pains, the passions, the despairs, the delights, of a quarter of a century having taken place within those walls.'

An essentially gloomy establishment, dark, badly planned, ugly both

[1] James Meadows Rendel (1854–1937), Chairman of the Assam Bengal Railway and an expert on Poor Law administration, who married Lytton's eldest sister, Elinor.

[2] Beatrice Chamberlain (1862–1918), the eldest daughter of Joseph Chamberlain and his first wife Harriet Kenrick, was a half-sister to Neville Chamberlain, later Prime minister.

within and without, Lancaster Gate[1] filled Lytton with depression and discontent. He felt submerged by its solemn and prodigious bulk. The most obviously remarkable aspect of the place was its physical size, which produced a lasting, nightmarish effect on the small child, difficult to convey in adult language. But it was not mere size alone which chilled him so, Lytton believed; 'it was size gone wrong, size pathological; it was a house afflicted with elephantiasis that one found one had entered, when, having passed through the front door and down the narrow dark passage with its ochre walls and its tessellated floor of magenta and indigo tiles, one looked upwards and saw the staircase twisting steeply up its elongated well – spiralling away into a thin infinitude, until far above, one's surprised vision came upon a dome of pink and white glass, which yet one judged, with an unerring instinct, was not the top – no, not nearly, nearly the top'.[2]

Besides being of such gigantic proportions the Stracheys' new home was preposterously designed. There were, considering the vast area of space occupied, astonishingly few rooms. Lytton's father was the only member of the family to have a sitting-room of his own; while his daughters led an oddly communal existence in a tiny miserable apartment behind the dining-room, far higher than it was long or broad, and styled the 'young ladies' room'. For the boys there was not even this doleful sanctuary to withdraw into, and they enjoyed only the most precarious and infrequent privacy. The house contained altogether seven layers of human habitation: a basement, a ground floor, and a drawing-room that filled out almost all the first floor and above which were placed four further floors of bedrooms. These were all small, of enormous height and, except for one on each floor which looked out on to the street, very dark, since there was no garden or even courtyard. So lugubrious indeed was the outlook from the two back rooms that the windows of most of them were made of pink and frosted glass, and their occupants never saw out of them at all. Borrowing an idea from her husband's office in the City, Lady Strachey had had 'reflectors' put

[1] Today 69 Lancaster Gate is much altered. Though the shell of the building remains the same, the interior has been fused with the houses on either side and is unrecognizable. Since May 1959, the Stracheys' old home has been part of Douglas House, the large American Forces Club which now occupies Nos. 66–71 Lancaster Gate.

[2] Lytton's unpublished autobiographical essay 'Lancaster Gate', written in 1922 for the Memoir Club, traces the influence of this house on himself as its long-term inhabitant. It is an attempt to spin out the web on which the pattern of his existence had been formed, and should be read as a truthful reconstruction not from the point of view of an estate agent's prospectus, but of his own psychological reactions to the place. He was always given to dramatic exaggerations of the circumstances of his life – as of other people's – and his magnification of Lancaster Gate (in contrast with which the proportions of every other house he lived in seemed tiny) came probably from an hysterical origin.

up – vast plates of glassy material, slightly corrugated, which hung opposite the windows from chains. The actual windows themselves were so huge and cumbersome that no one could force them open, and little circular ventilators, working by means of cords and pulleys, had to be cut in the panes. All this created a weird impression on the young Lytton as he sat in his bedroom, dwarfed by its sombre, towering altitude, or in the schoolroom at the end of the passage on the ground floor – the mammoth windows of pale ground glass with their complex machinery of string and ventilator, and a dim vision of discoloured yellow bricks, chains and corrugations looming through the London fog outside.

Apart from the universal height and darkness, there existed other alarming inconveniences. 'There was the one and only bathroom, for instance,' Lytton recorded, 'perched, with its lavatory, in an impossible position midway between the drawing-room and the lowest bedroom floor – a kind of crow's nest – to reach which, one had to run the gauntlet of stairs innumerable, and whose noises of rushing water were all too audible from the drawing-room just below.'

Already, by the late 1880s, it was obvious that the family was in decline. Their heyday had been a generation or two earlier, when Sir Henry Strachey was on friendly terms with Clive, and Edward Strachey with Carlyle. Now, as the Victorian age tottered towards its exhausted conclusion, and the first grumblings of serious reaction made themselves heard, they looked about and for the first time found themselves out of touch with the rising mood. But within the arid and forbidding precincts of Lancaster Gate everything remained as before, unchanged and unchangeable. Being invited there for the first time was an odd, sometimes even alarming experience, like stepping into another age, perhaps another world. The first chill was cast upon one by the butler who drew open the massive mahogany portals. Mercifully, there was more to him than met the eye. Uncouth and quite unpresentable – the promoted gardener's boy of Stowey House – Frederick was a kind and gentle creature whose fearsome appearance, accentuated by a great mouth ill-concealed beneath a straggling moustache, belied his inner excellence. Later, he was replaced by a figure even more characteristic of the subtle *dégringolade* – Bastiani – 'a fat, black-haired, Italianate creature', as Lytton described him, 'who eventually took to drink, and could hardly puff up the stairs from the basement, and exuded . . . an odour of sweat and whisky into one's face. He disappeared – after a scene of melodramatic horror – to be replaced by Mr Brooks who, we could only suppose, must have been a groom in earlier life, since all his operations were accompanied by a curious sound of *sotto voce* hissing.'

As the evening wore on, a conviction would sometimes seize the less adaptable guests that time had not simply remained stationary within those immeasurable spaces of yellow marbled wallpaper but was actually in the process of moving backwards. 'At dinner,' recalled Leonard Woolf, 'someone might casually say something which implied that he remembered George IV (which he might) or even Voltaire or Warren Hastings. . . . The atmosphere of the drawing-room at Lancaster Gate was that of British history and of the comparatively small ruling middle-class which for the last 100 years had been the principal makers of British history.'

Hardly surprising then that the unprepared visitor would sometimes wonder whether he had strayed into an isolated colony of some remote, undiscovered form of civilization, an Erewhon or Zuvendi. Conversely, the child who was brought up within this drab mausoleum of a place took it for granted that here was the only world in existence. Indeed, Lytton hardly understood that anything else could be, though sub-consciously he was aware that something was wrong with this world – that it was an unpleasant shape. An incubus descended upon his spirit as, gradually, the advanced state of decomposition infected the growing boy. His cheerfulness ebbed slowly away, his animation faltered, his health mysteriously deteriorated. The disintegration of the home seemed to cast a physical and emotional spell on him.

The focal point of Lancaster Gate, which came to represent for Lytton the crowning emblem of a large family machine, was the monu-mental drawing-room. This great assembly hall, with its lofty eminence, its gigantic door, its glowing *portière* of pale green silk, its adumbrated sofas, instilled into him an almost religious awe. 'The same vitality, the same optimism, the same absence of nerves,' he wrote, 'which went into the deliberate creation of ten children, built the crammed high, hideous edifice that sheltered them. And so it was inevitable that the most characteristic feature of the house – its centre, its summary, the seat of its soul, so to speak – should have been the room which was the common meeting-place of all the members of the family: the drawing-room. When one entered that vast chamber, when peering through its foggy distances, ill-lit by gas-jets, or casting one's eyes wildly towards the infinitely distant ceiling overhead, one struggled to traverse its dreadful length, to reach a tiny chair or a far-distant fireplace, conscious as one did so that some kind of queer life was clustered thick about one . . . then in truth one had come – whether one realized it or no – into an extraordinary holy of holies.'

Here, amid countless groups of relations and their friends, Lytton first grew mesmerized by the riddle of the Victorian age being played out before his eyes. If the drawing-room was a temple erected to the enigmatic spirit of Victorianism, its altar was undoubtedly the large, elevated and elaborate mantelpiece, an expanse of painted wood, designed by Halsey Ricardo, with pilasters and cornices and various marble and multicoloured tiles. Having reached this citadel through the waves of persons ebbing and flowing around it, one could see, from the vantage-point of a mottled hearth, that this was in no sense a romantic room. And yet there was something, not quite analysable, which continued to fascinate Lytton. It was not the size, or ugliness or absurdity of it alone which exerted so potent a spell upon his imagination, but the subtle way in which it expressed the whole complicated state of things. Like the age whose history will never be written, it was incredibly familiar to him yet at the same time even a little surprising, as though withholding perpetually some secret essential to his real understanding. 'Up to my last hour in it,' he later confessed, 'I always felt that the drawing-room was strange.'

By character and usage it was primarily a family room, built to contain not only Sir Richard and Lady Strachey and their ten children, but also all the other branches of the clan, in particular a large quantity of paternal uncles. The most senior of these, Sir Edward Strachey – the third baronet and father of four children including St Loe Strachey, future editor of the *Spectator* – seldom left the fortified manor of Sutton Court, behind whose walls he laboured gallantly at his *Materials to Serve for a History of the Strachey Family*. The second of Lytton's uncles, Colonel Henry Strachey, who had explored Tibet with Sir Richard and whose redoubtable tenacity was to carry him through to his ninety-sixth year, would, though blind, make his way up more frequently from Sutton Court, where for some time he acted as agent, and talk over old times with his brother. He was a very polite old gentleman, Lytton later remembered, and 'very dim, poor man, but his shoes exquisitely polished'. Yet another uncle, Sir John Strachey, who as finance minister to three successive Indian viceroys had fostered a measure for the introduction of metrical weights throughout India – a Trollopian edict which was never put into effect[1] – and then, after

---

[1] The moving spirit behind this measure was in fact Lytton's father. See *Memorandum on the Introduction of Metric System in India* by Pitamber Plant, with a Foreword by Jawaharlal Nehru (Indian Government Publication, 1955). On the first page of this manual, the author remarks that Colonel R. Strachey's 'brilliant notes and memoranda (Appendices B1, B2, B5), in particular his Minute of Dissent (B2) are classic in their quality, imbued with scholarship, practical wisdom and above all a noble earnestness which not only invokes admiration but inspires. No aspect of this complex subject has escaped his notice and none has received but the most patient and careful treatment. With ninety years separating his writings from now, it is remarkable that they are as much relevant and enlightening today, during our present consideration of the problem, as they

disastrously underestimating the cost of the war with Afghanistan, left India for England, visited Lancaster Gate regularly in the summer months from his house in Cornwall Gardens. He had by this time become a philosophic radical after the style of Mill, while, as an ardent supporter of Garibaldi, he spent his winters in Florence.

But perhaps the general state of decomposition which encompassed and pressed in on Lytton as a boy was most strikingly embodied by his two junior uncles, William and George. Though both had shown signs of practical gifts when younger, their vein of pure eccentricity which, as an offshoot of thwarted creative talent – or the flower, perhaps, of originality gone to seed – was present in so many of the Stracheys, overran in time all traces of true ability. George, the youngest of all Lytton's uncles, had once possessed some aptitude for journalism and diplomacy, serving as H.M. Minister to the Court of the King of Saxony at Dresden. In his later years he spent much of the time reconstructing the special relationship which existed between the family and Carlyle; and he also contributed many articles to the *Spectator*, all of them decked in so richly prolix and ornamental a style as to be virtually unreadable. In the drawing-room of Lancaster Gate he presented Lytton with an exceedingly peculiar and unprepossessing spectacle, 'bent double with age and eccentricity, hideously snuffling and pouring out his opinion on architecture to anyone who ventured within his reach'.

The oddest uncle of all, however, was William Strachey. Born in 1819, he remained all his life a bachelor, travelling out to India as a journalist at the age of nineteen, returning five years later and then resigning from service while still in his twenties. Notwithstanding his having lived in India for a considerably shorter duration than his brothers, and his association with the British Empire having been slight and undistinguished, he persevered in upholding Eastern customs with a far greater rigidity and finer disregard for common sense than any other member of the family. Having once visited Calcutta, he

---

were when the subject was in his care.' See also pp. 8, 20, 53–104. The combined labours of Sir John and Sir Richard Strachey had a strong and lasting influence over the policy and the constitution of the Indian Government in every department of affairs. Celebrated jointly in a Kipling poem, the two brothers had unrivalled opportunities, through a long course of years, of obtaining knowledge regarding India. In the Preface to the third edition of *India: Its Administration and Progress*, Sir John Strachey records that 'for many years we took part, often in close association, in its government, and it would be an affectation of humility to profess that this part was not an important one. There is hardly a great office in that state, from that of Acting-Viceroy, Lieutenant-Governor, or Member of Council downwards, which one or other of us has not held, and hardly a department of the administration with which one or other of us has not been intimately connected.'

became convinced that the clocks there were the only reliable chrono-
meters in the world, and in consequence kept his watch resolutely set
by Calcutta time, organizing the remaining fifty-six years of his life
accordingly. The results were often disconcerting for his friends and
family in England. He breakfasted at afternoon tea and lived most of his
waking hours by candlelight. On visits to Sutton Court, his strange
nocturnal habits earned for him among the embedded Somerset folk an
immense reputation in astrology. At Lancaster Gate, his behaviour was
equally memorable. During his youth he had been something of a gay
man about town when, as he was probably well aware, his idiosyncrasies greatly enhanced his social prestige – though by now they were
no longer assumed but had corroded their way into the very substance
of his personality. He had been well known, too, at Holland House in
the middle of the century, and having once exchanged the time of day
with Palmerston, was now, in his later years, immoderately fond of
attributing his own opinions to the late prime minister, introducing
what he had to say with sentences commencing: 'I well remember Lord
Palmerston once told me . . .' At the age of seventy he impressed
his nine-year-old nephew Lytton as being an utterly fantastic
figure, dressed always in spats and a coat and waistcoat of quaint
cut and innumerable buttons – the very same that he might have
worn in the 'forties – and, whatever the season or the prevailing
weather conditions, attired in a pair of galoshes. One other distinction
he possessed; he was one of the very few Stracheys of his period who
did not add to the swelling plethora of historical documentation on
the lineage and past exploits of the family. When he died in his mid-
eighties, he left Lytton a legacy consisting entirely of unworn and
prettily coloured underclothes including 'some exquisite drawers
or "pants"'.

But Lytton also owed much, in his tastes and capacities, to the
Scottish side of his family. The Grants of Rothiemurchus traced their
ancestry back to John Grant, Chief of Grant, who in 1539 had married
Lady Marjorie Stuart, thereby making Lytton a potential claimant to
the Scottish throne. The laird, Lady Strachey's eldest brother John
Peter Grant, was rather remote from Lytton's London existence, but
numerous other uncles and aunts often visited Lancaster Gate. Lytton's
favourite was Uncle Trevor, a very friendly and uncomprehending
fellow, married to a dusky native of India, Aunt Clementina, who was
said to make chupatties on the drawing-room carpet. Together they
brought up a large unfortunate family, the most unfortunate member
of which ended his life being hugged by a bear. Besides Uncle Trevor,
there was Uncle Bartle, a military gentleman who, on periods of leave

from his regiment, edited a famous cookery book and compiled a learned volume on the orchids of Burma; Aunt Hennie, a most prominent and original figure who had been dropped on her head when an infant; and Uncles Charles and George who both had sons named Pat. 'White' Pat was presumed by the family to be a good character, 'Black' Pat a bad one, until, years later, 'White' Pat ran off with 'Black' Pat's wife. But most spectacular of all these maternal relations was 'Aunt Lell', the wife of Sir James Colvile. Two years older than Lady Strachey, she was utterly dissimilar to her – very aristocratic and sophisticated, a close friend of Robert Browning and a capable musician who had learnt the piano under Madame Schumann. Whenever Lady Strachey was away, Lytton would be left in the care of Aunt Lell, whose well-conducted social life, ebbing and flowing about her smart Park Lane house – so different from the knock-about régime of Lancaster Gate – immensely impressed him.

There was always at Lancaster Gate a large influx of these uncles, their wives, children and friends, and of the other branches of the family in all their various combinations and permutations. But it was on Sunday afternoons, a time when the Victorian hostess particularly delighted to invite her guests and when Lytton's mother was invariably at home, that the family atmosphere, reinforced from without, reached its most intense and bizarre pitch. 'Then the drawing-room', wrote Lytton, 'gradually grew thick with aunts and uncles, cousins and connections, with Stracheys, Rendels, Plowdens, Battens, Ridpaths, Rowes. One saw that it had indeed been built for them – it held them all so nicely, so naturally, with their interminable varieties of age and character and class.' Since most if not all of the Stracheys possessed peculiarly penetrating voices, and Lady Strachey's children inherited from her all the Scottish love of argument and discussion, the general volume of noise, the degree of turmoil and excited chatter on these weekly occasions was always terrific, and, though taken for granted by the family itself, bewildering for some of the more staid and fastidious visitors. Despite the chaos and confusion which reigned over these gatherings, the British Raj was still very much in the air, while the multiplicity of sons and daughters, nephews and nieces, fathers and mothers and uncles and aunts was beyond computation, their striking resemblance to each other giving an effect of nightmare to the whole proceedings. On one such afternoon Bertrand Russell, whom Lady Strachey had met as a fellow member of a committee designed to secure votes for women, was invited to call. 'All the children', he records, 'were to my unpractised eyes exactly alike except in the somewhat superficial point that some were male and some were female. The family were not all assembled when I arrived, but dropped in one by one at intervals of twenty minutes (one of them I afterwards discovered was Lytton). I had to look round the room carefully to make sure that it was a new one that had appeared and not merely one of the previous ones that had changed his or her place. Towards the end of the evening I began to doubt my sanity, but kind friends afterwards assured me that things had really been as they seemed.'

At least as startling were the unannounced customs and the general running of the house, to which all Stracheys, however sharply differentiated outside, unthinkingly conformed. With the exception of her time at Stowey House – to which she had become greatly attached and where she remained eleven years – Lady Strachey's domestic life had been largely unsettled. Never before had any house acted as her headquarters for more than two consecutive years, and she had moved to Lancaster Gate with great regret. 'My ideal life', she once confided to Virginia Woolf, 'would be to live *entirely* in boarding houses.' And all the homes which she did inhabit rather resembled these establishments. When one of her sons or daughters invited a friend back to lunch, no one would pay the guest the very least attention. Innumerable Stracheys would sit in solemn silence round the dinner table, Sir Richard wrapped in a shawl at the centre of them reading a novel, and everything would proceed with a mysterious absence of human communication. Then, once the meal was completed, uproar broke out again.

The crowd of visiting relations was at its largest at about six every Sunday, and then it gradually thinned away. As at Stowey House, only the minimum of an appearance was kept up, and unless someone of importance stayed on, none of the family troubled to dress for the long and serious family dinner which followed at eight o'clock. The butler of the moment, assisted by a liveried boot-boy, waited upon them during these formidable sessions. 'At the end,' Lytton wrote, 'the three mystic bottles of port, sherry, and claret were put at the head of the table and solemnly circulated – the port, sherry, and claret having come from the grocer's round the corner.'

The rigours of formality and the excesses of communal inconsequence might be increased if, as often happened, someone did stay on – Sir Frederick Leighton, maybe, with his Olympian features and imposing manner of address, or Nina Grey with her faded airs of Roman Catholic aristocracy, or Fanny Stanley with her lodging-house garrulity, or even Mabel Batten, 'with that gorgeous bust on which the head of Edward the Seventh was wont to repose' – all of them carefully observed by the quiet, odd-looking youth whom they can seldom have noticed. With such a constant stream of callers Lytton naturally saw a good deal of life at Lancaster Gate from his earliest years. Apart from these regular at-homes, there were repeated dinner-parties, and frequent musical entertainments at which celebrities, like the mythical George Grossmith of *The Sorcerer* and *H.M.S. Pinafore* – whose advent filled Lytton with extreme excitement – were sometimes invited to sing or play. The grandest of these musical occasions, given jointly by Lytton's mother and one of his aunts, was much later, and featured Joachim and Piatti playing in their quartet.

One of the most habitual visitors to Lancaster Gate during these early years, Sir William Ward, was himself musical, and the memory of his several performances remained very vividly with Lytton all his life. Besides having been Governor of the Straits Settlements he was, Lytton explains, 'an executor, of astonishing brilliancy, in pianoforte. Pressed to play, he would seat himself at the piano and dash off a Chopin waltz with the verve of a high-stepping charger, when suddenly a very odd and discordant sound, rising and falling with the music, would make itself heard. It was something between a snore and a whistle, and nobody could think what it could be. But the mystery was at last explained – the ex-Governor suffered, in moments of excitement, from a curious affection of the nose. While the family listened, a little hysterically, to this peculiar combination of sounds, all at once yet *another* sound – utterly different – burst upon their ears – the sound, this time, of rushing water. There was a momentary shock; and then we all silently realized that someone, in the half-way landing upstairs, was using the W.C.'

This admixture of heavy punctilio and extenuating farce, which made up the routine of life at Lancaster Gate, was unsettling to a sensitive boy such as Lytton; but it would be ridiculous to suggest that he was permanently and actively miserable. To all outward appearances he was the very reverse, and his sisters remembered him as full of fun and laughter, 'giggling fairly continuously from the age of three to nineteen'. 'He indulged in all the customary jokes of childhood,' according to Pernel and Philippa Strachey, 'fanciful nicknames, endless conversations in dog French, acting, ragging, playing jokes on visitors, not practical but subtle and disconcerting. The round of fun was hectic and delirious, and Lytton's inventiveness seemed endless.' Yet, as in later life, his laughter and jokes were curiously segregated from the main tide of his feelings; they were cerebral, cut off from his darker emotions. His spirit bubbled brightly, but were cold to the touch. For beneath the bright surface of his fun and gaiety, the clouds of tedium and aridity had already begun to thicken. 'It was not a question of unhappiness,' he explained, 'so much as of restriction and oppression – the subtle unperceived weight of the circumambient air.' The damp of the nineteenth century had entered into and warped his soul, causing a malady susceptible of no outright cure, but only a temporary relief when the mists of pessimism and loneliness would suddenly, miraculously, dissolve, the sun shine through and flood all his world with warmth and light. 'And then', he wrote, 'there were moments, luckily, when some magic spring within me was suddenly released, and I threw off that weight, my spirit leaping up into freedom and beatitude.'

4

MARIE SOUVESTRE

The most free and pleasurable periods of Lytton's childhood were those he spent up in the Scottish Highlands. For many years his mother made a practice of taking her children up to the Doune,[1] the Grants' family home in Rothiemurchus, during part of the summer or winter holidays. These were always happy excursions for Lytton, who found a deep satisfaction and relief in escaping from the dank physiological oppression of Lancaster Gate, without any compensating chills of insecurity. He was like a bird suddenly released from behind the bars of its cage. Newly alive, he could go where he liked, do what he wanted. The old London life which had clung to him damply seemed to have crumbled to pieces like an old shell, a dried-up mould.[2] He emerged from the dark recesses of Lancaster Gate like a butterfly liberated from its chrysalis, fluttering in the breeze over a fresh, wonderful universe of nature and sunlight. He never forgot this buoyant sense of liberation, and to the end of his life remained highly susceptible to the beauties of Rothiemurchus – 'its massive and imposing landscape, its gorgeous colouring, its hidden places of solitude and silence, its luxuriant vegetation, its wilderness of remote and awful splendour'. Though surrounded as usual by hordes of Grants and Stracheys, he could secure for himself here a modicum of privacy, and he loved to take himself off for solitary, day-dreaming walks among the pine-woods

[1] The Doune was the home of the Grants and of Mrs Smith of Baltiboys, authoress of *Memoirs of a Highland Lady*. Her brother, Lady Strachey's father, Sir John Peter Grant, had modernized the house in the 1870s.

[2] See *Pending Heaven* by William Gerhardie (Collected Uniform Revised Edition, London, Macdonald, 1948, pp. 216, 217).

and the mountains.[1] Many years afterwards he quoted in the *Spectator* a passage from a book, *Rothiemurchus* by the Reverend Hugh Macmillan, describing the silence of its primaeval forests which brought back vividly the wonderful, quiet independence of these childhood wanderings: 'In its gloomy perspectives, leading to deeper solitudes, there seem to lurk some weird mysteries and speechless terrors that keep eye and ear intent. You have a strange sense of being watched, without love or hate, by all these silent, solemn, passionless forms, and when most alone you seem least lonely.'

An early diary shows Lytton on one of these summer holidays in Rothiemurchus playing on the grass with one of his cousins, eating strawberries ripe and fresh from the garden, riding ponies, dancing, playing cricket and robbers, vaulting streams and climbing the slopes of the near-by Cairngorms. Altogether his time there comprised the mode of open-air, carefree and youthful living which he was to enhalo as an adult. In more easily recognizable and sedentary moods he would listen to his mother as she recited to him extracts from the *Iliad*, and to his sister Dorothy reading from Walter Scott's *The Abbot*. And at other times he sat sketching the mountain scenery or working out the puzzles which always fascinated him and with which his mother had a hard job to keep him supplied.

On other occasions, and more frequently as time went on, the family would rent a large country house for the summer in one of the Home Counties, Surrey or Essex, and here, amid a babble of young Stracheys, Lytton would play croquet and take an enthusiastic part in the amateur theatricals for which his mother and all her children cherished such an inordinate passion. But though he often enjoyed these country parties, they never cast the same happy spell over his imagination as the untamed hills and corries of the Highlands.

In the summer of 1886 Lytton was sent, in company with his younger sister Marjorie, to the Hyde Park Kindergarten and School at 24 Chilworth Street. Here he remained for some eighteen months, making excellent progress in all subjects, especially in arithmetic. All his reports

[1] In his memoirs, *The Good Old Days* (1956), Lytton's cousin Patrick Grant wrote: 'During the summer months the house was packed, often with the whole Strachey family, my first cousins. Inspired perhaps by having read that famous book *The Fifth Form at St Dominic's*, Lytton Strachey and I decided we must produce and edit a magazine. Being almost unable to pronounce Dominican, I called it "The Domican". I have it still, and it represents, I think, Lytton's very first attemp[t]s at creative writing. Little did we guess that in the days to come he would become a famous author. His sister Pernel, afterwards I believe the Head of Newnham, was kind enough to write it out for us, and everyone, even including the butler, wrote stories or verses for it. Lytton's father, old Sir Richard, even painted a picture for us, but though it was a great success there was never a sequel to the first number.'

were good; he took a keen interest in his lessons and gave his teachers complete satisfaction. All in all he appears to have been a model pupil, and in the words of the headmistress, Miss E. Fisher Brown, 'worked exceedingly well and was very intelligent'.

In one of his earliest preserved letters, dated 7 May 1887, Lytton wrote to his mother: 'I have just begun French, it is very exciting. I know the French for Lion – it is Lion but pronounced differently. Marjorie smudged this letter.'

Lady Strachey, an ardent francophil, was delighted by this news. 'I am very glad you like French,' she answered; 'the further you go the more exciting you will find it. There are beautiful stories and books of all sorts in it.'

During the subsequent years Lytton's enthusiasm for French, and for the literature of France especially, grew under the active encouragement of his mother, who helped him to write French verses and often presented him on his birthdays with a volume of traditional French songs, or a copy of La Fontaine's fables, or another such classic. She also saw to it that the first educational establishment which, indirectly, was to play a leading part in Lytton's early life and to help in shaping the course of his career, was a French girls' school near Wimbledon.

This unusual state of affairs had come about in the following way. Many years earlier, while in Italy, Lady Strachey had met a French-woman of great culture and distinction. Her name was Marie Souvestre, a daughter of the French Academician Emile Souvestre – author of *Un Philosophe sous les Toits* – and she conducted a celebrated and fashionable school for girls at Fontainebleau, called Les Ruches. So impressed had Lady Strachey been by this woman's charm, stimulating intelligence and determination – so close to her own vicarious ambitions – that those under her care should later go on to make their mark in the world, that soon afterwards she had sent her two eldest daughters, Elinor and Dorothy, to Les Ruches when they were each aged about sixteen. And when, shortly after Lytton was born, Marie Souvestre left France and became the headmistress-proprietor of Allenswood, at a little place named South Fields, not far from Wimbledon Common, both the younger Strachey daughters, Joan Pernel and Marjorie, were in due course entered there, while Dorothy was employed on the teaching staff, giving lessons on Shakespeare.

A brilliant and irreligious woman, Marie Souvestre was intimate with many of the radical and free-thinking set – John Morley, Joseph Chamberlain, Leslie Stephen, the Frederick Harrisons and numerous others. 'A remarkable woman,' Beatrice Webb described her in a diary entry for March 1889, 'with a gift of brilliant expression, and the charm of past beauty and present attractiveness. Purely literary in her training, and without personal experience of religious feeling or public spirit, she watches these characteristics in others with an odd combination of suspicion, surprise, and what one might almost call an unappreciative admiration. You feel that every idea is brought under a sort of hammering logic, and broken into pieces unless it be of very sound metal. If the idea belongs to the religious sphere and is proof against ridicule, it is laid carefully on one side for some future hostile analysis.'

The relationship between the Stracheys and Marie Souvestre during the 1880s and 1890s was very close. Comings and goings between Lancaster Gate and Allenswood were frequent, and sometimes the whole Strachey family spent part of their holidays at the school. Lytton, of course, was never enrolled as an official pupil of Marie Souvestre, but her influence on him, as Professor Charles Sanders has noted, was immensely important. During later adolescence, at a time when Lytton was bitterly critical of all mankind, 'cette grande femme', as he referred to her, was almost unique in that, throughout his often drastic and belligerent correspondence, he never once mentions her in a derogatory manner.

Of a naturally forceful personality, often galvanized with the unqualified enthusiasm of a child into sudden, impulsive action, Marie Souvestre was approaching sixty when Lytton first got to know her, and was obliged to pay a certain amount of attention to her health. She was watched over with loving care by Mlle Samaia, a very tiny, dynamic woman who had been with her at Les Ruches, and whose adoration now took the practical form of seeing to it that she always breakfasted in her bedroom and was never vexed by having to look after the business side of running the school. Marie Souvestre was already by this time white-haired and rather stout. Her head was strikingly impressive, with clear-cut features, a strong almost masculine face, noble forehead and dark piercing eyes which hypnotized her pupils into imagining that she always knew exactly what was going on in their minds. She never married, appearing to find her emotional fulfilment in looking after her girls, many of whom served her well by distinguishing themselves in their later careers. To them she ga' the whole of her emotive being, transforming the school into the very nucleus of her life. But she was by no means a typical headmistress, at least not by English standards. She entertained no especial or obsessive veneration for outdoor sports, and proficiency in such pastimes left her cold. Games were encouraged at Allenswood solely as methods of exercise, designed to keep the body reasonably healthy. That was all. Unable to comprehend a deity who would pay any regard to such insignificant creatures as human beings, she was a declared atheist, a humanist and, in politics, fervently pro-Boer. And though she did not attempt to indoctrinate Lytton, it was not in her nature to conceal her strong feelings before adults or children.

Nor was Marie Souvestre scrupulously impartial in the attention she paid to her girls. Mrs Eleanor Roosevelt, who was a student at Allenswood during the 1890s, recalled that 'she had a very soft spot for Americans and liked them as pupils. This was not surprising as a number of her pupils turned out to be rather outstanding women.' In particular she was drawn to girls who were intelligent, attractive in appearance, or who possessed an instinctive taste and appreciation for literature. Her voice, like Cordelia's, was 'soft, gentle and low, an excellent thing in woman', and she employed it with great feminine effect when reciting poems, plays or stories in French. Sometimes she would make the children read passages back to her. For her favourites, sitting on little chairs on either side of her library fireplace, the walls behind them lined with books and the room filled with flowers, and gazing forth on the wide expanse of lawn outside partially shaded from the heat of the sun by tall trees, these were moments of pure ecstasy, as they listened breathlessly to her voice and strove to imitate it. But those who were not similarly gifted would watch her striding up and down the room brandishing her pointer, and endure tortures as they waited with clammy hands and dry throats to make fools of themselves.

As the young and intelligent son of Lady Strachey, Lytton found himself automatically occupying a favoured position in Marie Souvestre's esteem, and he benefited enormously from the best that she, as the very embodiment of French culture, had to offer. The impression she produced on him was considerable and long-lasting. In the grace, the quick and witty brilliance of his literary style can be seen some reflection of her own peculiar charm and mental agility; while his views on public school education, his anti-religious convictions and his special feeling for French writers, in particular Racine, can be partly traced to her early influence. Under his mother's direction he had learnt to speak, or at least to understand, French quite well before the age of ten, and in collaboration with Marjorie he made up little booklets of bilingual verse which were submitted to Lady Strachey for approval. But that his interest in French literature survived and even blossomed beneath the beam of such attentive maternal encouragement was directly due to the presence of Marie Souvestre, whose spirit and personality permeated the whole family, and whose unique qualities recharged the core of his literary enthralment. Dorothy, his elder sister, has given a vivid evocation of the emotional response which this ageing woman could still engender within a sensitive adolescent mind such as Lytton's, in her anonymously published novel, *Olivia*.[1] In this memorable book, Marie Souvestre is portrayed tenderly and with realism under the name of Mlle Julie, the joint principal of a girls' boarding school in France, Les Avons. On the first occasion that Mlle Julie makes her appearance, she is described giving a remarkable reading from Racine's *Andromaque* – an interesting choice in view of the famous essay on Racine which Lytton was later to compose. 'I have heard many readers read Racine, and famous men among them, but I have not heard any who read him as well as Mlle Julie,' wrote Dorothy. 'She read simply and rapidly, without any of the actor's arts and affectations, with no swelling voice, with no gestures beyond the occasional lifting of her hand, in which she held a long ivory paper-cutter. But the gravity of her bearing and her voice transported me at once into the courts of princes and the presence of great emotions.'

After analysing the emotional excitement liberated in her by this characteristic recital, Dorothy concludes: 'What is certain is that it gave me my first conception of tragedy, of the terror and complication and pity of human lives. Strange that for an English child that revelation should have come through Racine instead of through Shakespeare. But it did.'

From another autobiographical passage in the novel, the reader is made to feel very forcibly the intoxicating enchantment which Marie Souvestre conveyed to all the Strachey family, and to understand the essential contrast in quality that lay between the influence of Lady Strachey – which, unsupported, might have led on to a subsequent reaction against literature in Lytton – and that of the French

[1] *Olivia* by 'Olivia' (1949), the title of which was suggested by the Christian name of Dorothy's sister who died in infancy. The picture of Lancaster Gate and of Sir Richard and Lady Strachey which is given by Dorothy in the opening pages of this novel should be read with some care. Though outwardly friendly, there was a degree of antagonism between mother and daughter which arose from the fact that Dorothy had turned down several eminent offers of marriage and then become the wife of the indigent French artist Simon Bussy. Comparing Lady Strachey with aunt E. (Aunt Lell) who 'was sensitive to art to the very finger-tips of her beautiful hands, and successfully created about herself an atmosphere of *ordre et beauté, luxe, calme et volupté*', she presents her mother as being without taste, artistic or otherwise, and responsible for that solid comfort within Lancaster Gate from which 'the sensual element was totally lacking'. Her view, too, of Lady Strachey being 'perhaps incapable of the mystical illumination' and of her home being purely intellectual, may partly have been brought about by the fact that, alone of the family, Dorothy had no ear for music. So, when all the rest of them trooped off to a Joachim Quartet concert at St James's Hall, she was left alone in the house. The trouble continued: Simon Bussy was also unmusical, and so, perhaps as a result, was their daughter Janie. There was no piano at their home and no sound of music till fifty years later the radio set in, coinciding, oddly enough, with a late birth of musical interest.

headmistress, which offered him further exciting adventures, and the revelation of a new heaven and a new earth. Despite her shrewdness and good sense, Lytton's mother had an extraordinarily ramshackle mind. The fashionable but limited social code under which she had originally been brought up remained a permanent obstacle to her capacity for absorbing any fresh ideas or unconventional emotions. Marie Souvestre, on the other hand, was pleasantly free from any such inbred inhibitions, and she gave Lytton the promise of new, unknown aspects of life, appealing to something latent and undeveloped within him, something which lay crushed beneath the heavy, impersonal atmosphere of the family home. When she entered the drawing-room there and began to talk, everything changed and took on an added dimension, so that Lytton for the first time became consciously and coherently aware of what he had always instinctively felt – that there existed somewhere beyond the boundaries of his home and his present knowledge an entirely different environment, far more congenial to his nature.

'I had no doubt been accustomed, or ought to have been accustomed, to good talk at home,' wrote Dorothy Strachey, comparing the atmosphere of Lancaster Gate with that of Les Ruches and Allenswood. 'But at home one was inattentive. . . . When one did listen to it, it was mostly political, or else took the form of argument. My mother and my aunt, who was often in the house, had interminable and heated discussions, in which my mother was invariably in the right and my aunt beyond belief inconsequent and passionate. We found them tedious and sometimes nerve-racking. My father, a man, in our eyes, of infinite wisdom and humour, did not talk much. . . . As for the people who came to the house, many of whom were highly distinguished, we admired them without listening to them. Their world seemed hardly to impinge upon ours.

'How different it was here! Mlle Julie was witty. Her brilliant speech darted here and there with the agility and grace of a humming-bird. Sharp and pointed, it would sometimes transfix a victim cruelly. No one was safe, and if one laughed with her, one was liable the next minute to be pierced with a shaft of irony. But she tossed her epigrams about with such evident enjoyment, that if one had the smallest sense of fun, one enjoyed them too, and it was from her that I, for one, learnt to realize the exquisite adaptation of the French tongue to the French wit.'

This description of Marie Souvestre's talk and personality might well serve as the basis for an appreciation of Lytton's mature prose style, and it conveys something of the infectious ardour and enlivening zest with which she must have touched the growing boy. Her wit and cultivated intelligence 'capable of points of view, fond of the stimulus of paradox', communicated to him a burning literary exuberance never to be extinguished. 'To sit at table at her right hand', Dorothy summed up, 'was an education in itself.'

5

SPELLBOUND

Most of Lady Strachey's family inherited something of her love of letters; but in Lytton she soon recognized a boy of exceptional literary promise. Together the children composed copious quantities of verse, and Lytton would bring out programmes for the plays produced by his elder brothers and sisters, and illustrate their notebooks and magazines. His own first recorded quatrain was written at the age of five; and two years later he was busily engaged on a lengthy and ingenious piece of poetry entitled 'Songs of Animals, Fishes and Birds'. He responded eagerly to his mother's inspirations, and with unusual application copied out the lyrics from Shakespeare, Marlowe and Blake which she taught him.

Versification was encouraged among the children as a game or hobby, and their best, most representative poems, which Lady Strachey collected together in a family book, are almost all playful, decorative pieces. But from among these many pages of light-hearted rhyming, one of Lytton's verses, written in April 1890, strikes an oddly discordant note. It is more sombre and enigmatic than amusing, and, by any standards, expresses a strange and unconventional sentiment for a boy of nine or ten – especially when one perceives that it is addressed to his sister who died in infancy.

> To me Life is a burden
> But to thee
> The joyous pleasures of the world
> Are all a gaiety.
> But if thou did'st perceive my thoughts
> Then thou would'st sigh and mourn,
> Olivia, like me.

As in many large families, the children were encouraged to work in couples, and Lytton was usually paired off with his younger sister Marjorie. At one time or another he collaborated with her in producing a literary magazine, *The Gazelle Gazette*; a book of songs, *Carmina Exotica*; the beginning of a French comedy; and a play with a sea captain and a detective. A photograph of him taken at about the age of three shows a small figure gorgeously attired, chubby and with long dark locks reaching below his shoulders. For many years his mother dressed him in petticoats because she thought them prettier and less absurd than knickerbockers. In appearance he consequently resembled a girl more nearly than a boy, a peculiarity which is brought out by another photograph of the whole family, taken probably a year later, in which the likeness between Lytton and Marjorie is very striking.

Except for his mother and his sisters there was no one towards whom he might turn for sympathetic companionship. The men in the Strachey household were either too old, too eccentric or too remote and self-absorbed to have much direct or intimate personal contact with Lytton as a child. His elder brothers were seldom at Lancaster Gate. Richard John Strachey,[1] the eldest of all, and soon to make an advantageous marriage to the daughter of a field-marshal, was a commissioned officer in the Rifle Brigade, while Ralph Strachey,[2] having failed to get into the army owing to defective eyesight, ultimately became chief engineer in the East Indian Railway. The third son, Oliver Strachey,[3] was away for much of the year at Eton. In his day-dreams, Lytton longed for a time when he, too, could play some part in these active, masculine spheres of life, and for several years he kept a map on which he charted every movement which his brothers made about the world.

At home he still worshipped his father from afar, and was jubilant when, during the holidays, the old man occasionally took him to the circus, or to the Royal Naval Exhibition of 1891, or the Crystal Palace to see 'The Wonderful Performance of Wild Beasts', or even to inspect the *Stracheya tibetica* and other lesser botanical specimens at Kew. Sometimes on these expeditions, and greatly to his son's delight, Sir Richard Strachey would descend from his godlike silence into an abrupt but charming extravaganza of tomfoolery. Yet Lytton's filial veneration only emphasized the closer, more intimate relationship for which he longed in vain, and which, as an adult, he later tried to make good, tending in his friendships even with much younger men to become

[1] Richard John Strachey (1861–1935) became a colonel in the Rifle Brigade. In 1896 he married Grace, daughter of Field-Marshal Sir Henry Norman. They had no children.

[2] Ralph Strachey (1868–1923) married Margaret Severs in 1901. Their first son is the novelist and writer of children's books, Richard Strachey. Their second son, John Strachey, is an artist and now lives in Antibes. Their only daughter, Ursula, who married Cyril Wentzel, an actor and barrister, was herself on the stage, and now works in the Foreign Office.

[3] Oliver Strachey (1874–1960). Musician, Civil Servant and joint-author with his second wife, Ray Strachey, of *Keigwin's Rebellion* (1916). For his work in the Foreign Office and the War Office during both World Wars, where he was employed as their expert code-breaker, he was in 1943 awarded the C.B.E.

unnaturally submissive and dependent. Ironically, in his eagerness to attain a satisfactory companionship of mind and emotion, he would frequently act as his mother did towards himself – and with similar results. For he lavished on his most esteemed friends such a passionate intensity of adoration as to infect them with a feeling of guilt and inadequacy, even embarrassment, so that they shied away from his suffocating, alternately maternal and filial attentions. Years later, just before going down from Cambridge, he was to write a letter to Maynard Keynes describing the total lack of affinity which then existed between himself and Professor Walter Raleigh. After recounting the events of a certain evening they had spent together – Lytton in typical silence, Raleigh in blank boredom – he summarized their want of intellectual sympathy thus: 'He [Raleigh] might be one's father.' The deplorable failure in human relationships could not, he felt, be expressed in more eloquent terms.

The prevailing atmosphere of femininity in which he grew up produced a definite retrograde effect upon Lytton's emotional development. While his mental faculties advanced swiftly, even precociously, his emotions were preserved in an almost static condition. An ingrained element of caution was nursed into a shrinking sense of shyness by the claustrophobic rigmarole of hushed literary dedication which was erected around him. He longed to join Oliver playing cricket, or teasing the peacock at the Doune, but his health, he was repeatedly reminded, was too fragile to permit anything so strenuous. His resistance to illness was certainly weak, and he was plagued by a constant and unremitting succession of disorders throughout his life. But no one ever seemed to know what, fundamentally, was the cause of these maladies. As a child he was subjected to a variety of cures, each one more unsuccessful than its predecessor. At one time he was obliged to consume at every meal a plate of porridge; at another he was dosed with glasses of port; and for several months he was fed, forcibly and almost exclusively, on raw meat. But, perhaps because his bad health was partly self-induced and not the result of a purely physical indisposition, no remedy, however far-fetched, was to secure his lasting improvement.

When he was nine years old Lytton was told by his mother that he was to be sent out of London to continue his education at a small private school on the south coast. The prospect filled him with a strange conflict of emotions – intense excitement and trepidation. He pined for the affection and comradeship of boys of his own age, and he yearned to escape from the onerous gloom of Lancaster Gate. Yet at the same time his pleasure was qualified by an opposing undercurrent of apprehension. Subconsciously, he already felt towards his family home something of the contradictory impulses of dependence and constitutional dislike. This ambiguous and divided response remained with him and became more coherent throughout his life – even after he had left Lancaster Gate for ever. In the unpublished paper read to the Memoir Club in 1922, he reveals that during his adult years he persistently dreamt that he was back there again with all the family. Everything is unchanged. 'We are in the drawing-room, among the old furniture, arranged in the old way and it is understood that we are to go on there indefinitely, as if we had never left it. The strange thing is that, when I realize that this has come about, that our successive wanderings have been a mere interlude, that we are once more permanently established at number 69, a feeling of intimate satisfaction comes over me. I am positively delighted. And this is strange because, in my waking life, I never for a moment, so far as I am aware, regretted our departure from that house, and if, in actuality, we *were* to return to it, I can imagine nothing which would disgust me more. So when I wake up . . . I have the odd sensation of a tremendous relief at finding that my happiness of one second before was a delusion.'

The contrasting layers to his feelings which he describes in the recollection of these dreams exactly match his somewhat ambivalent attitude towards the Victorian age at large. Lancaster Gate, which became for him a personal symbol of Victorianism, also produced within him a deep sense of security. Its grim recesses inspired him neither with unqualified disapproval nor with real affection, but with an involuntary fascination comprising in part horror and in part an attachment which he never outgrew. A strong awareness of this redundant, rationally objectionable heritage was early ingrained into him. The huge, towering mansion exuded a faintly musty air of superannuated traditionalism; and many of the family embodied it – something indefinably antagonistic to youthful enjoyment, edifying, no doubt, yet contrary to nature, twisting and concealing the young boy's tastes and instincts.

It is only when a tradition is bankrupt that its efficacy is unduly insisted upon. The Stracheys of the late nineteenth and early twentieth century, many of whom displayed a tendency towards degeneracy and an increase of hereditary defects, schooled themselves in the past history of their family, placing special emphasis on those times when its prestige had stood highest – a practice which Lytton Strachey himself was for a short time to emulate. Some of his earliest letters, written at the ages of nine and ten, question his mother concerning details of the family pedigree. And she, after punctiliously filing this correspondence for posterity, would deal with each query at proper length.

The young tendrils of Lytton's creative spirit naturally sought the light of complete freedom and independence; but a combination of poor health and early unpropitious environment, superimposed upon this background of stultifying and unnaturally preserved ancestral heritage, formed too great an obstacle for him clearly to surmount. The conventional domestic society of the nineteenth century which had eclipsed his mother's artistic potential also cast its long last shadow over his own dawning imagination.

'What had happened', he told the members of the Memoir Club, 'was that a great tradition – the aristocratic tradition of the eighteenth century – had reached a very advanced state of decomposition. My father and my mother belonged by birth to the old English world of countryhouse gentlefolk – a world of wealth and breeding, a world in which such things as footmen, silver and wine were the necessary appurtenances of civilized life. But their own world was different: it was the middle-class professional world of the Victorians, in which the old forms still lingered, but debased and enfeebled, in which Morris wallpapers had taken the place of Adam panelling, in which the swarming retinue had been reduced to a boy in livery, in which the spoons and forks were bought at the Army and Navy Stores. And then, introducing yet another element into this mixture, there was the peculiar disintegrating force of the Strachey character. The solid *bourgeois* qualities were interpenetrated by intellectualism and eccentricity. . . .

'Disintegration and *dégringolade*, no doubt, and yet the total effect, materialized and enormously extended, was of tremendous solidity. Lancaster Gate towered up above us, an imperturbable mass – the framework, almost the very essence, so it seemed, of our being. Was it itself perhaps one vast filth-packet and we the mere *disjecta membra* of vanished generations, which Providence was too busy or too idle to clear away? So, in hours of depression, we might have unconsciously theorized; but nevertheless, in reality, it was not so. Lancaster Gate vanished into nothingness, and we survived.'

But while it lasted, the notion that this régime would, in the course of things, come to an end was for Lytton unthinkable, a dreadful idea and one not to be contemplated – like death itself. By the time the family's diminished income eventually brought about this catastrophe, it no longer mattered. The house had already cast its inextinguishable mesmeric spell upon him, so that, wherever he might travel, the same dream, only slightly varying in its details and always transporting him back within the sombre walls of Number 69, recurred with a curious iteration. Even at the age of nine the chance of moving beyond its encircling orbit was faintly disturbing. What lay beyond? What would, what *could* happen, when he went away from Lancaster Gate?

CHAPTER II

'Funny Little Creature'

'At school, friendship is a passion. It entrances the being;
it tears the soul. All loves of after life can never bring its
rapture, or its wretchedness; no bliss so absorbing, no
pangs of jealousy or despair so crushing and so keen!
What tenderness and what devotion; what illimitable
confidence; infinite revelations of inmost thoughts; what
ecstatic present and romantic future; what bitter estrange-
ments and what melting reconciliations; what scenes of
wild recrimination, agitating explanations, passionate correspondence; what insane sensitiveness, and what frantic
sensibility; what earthquakes of the heart, and whirlwinds of
the soul, are confined in that simple phrase – a schoolboy's
friendship!'

Benjamin Disraeli –
Coningsby

I

SEA AIR

Lady Strachey was determined that her sons and daughters should all
distinguish themselves in their chosen careers, and much of her exceptional energy was directed towards the practical realization of this ideal.
Yet, in spite of her lifelong addiction to literature, she remained, in the
words of her daughter Dorothy, 'strangely devoid of psychology and
strangely unconscious of persons'. Nowhere were these defects more
incongruously expressed than in her conscientious efforts to arrange for
Lytton an expedient education. She appreciated that, as a boy delicate
in health and of a sensitive and impressionable mind, he might need
special treatment and attention. But what that treatment and attention
comprised she was never really sure. She seems to have been partly
swayed in her judgement by the educational history of Lord Lytton,
Lytton Strachey's godfather, whom she had first met in India a few
years prior to her son's birth. Their common love of literature had
initially brought them into close contact, and as time went on they had

become on increasingly confidential and affectionate terms. In an attempt to analyse her great admiration for him she once wrote: 'He was extremely unconventional, and not having been brought up at a public school, or in ordinary English society, was quite unable to understand the importance attached to conventionalities by the ordinary English public.' Undoubtedly she wanted Lytton to enjoy a similar unconventional enlightenment, and even to pursue a career comparable to that of the great Indian viceroy and poet. But the methods by which she sought to fulfil this ambition – the product of rather abstract educational theories held by an emotionally shy parent – were, in their cumulative effect, very far from successful.

Lytton was first sent, probably in the summer term of 1889, to a Mr Henry Forde, who took in a few boys for private teaching at his house at Parkstone, on Poole Harbour in Dorset. Here he was coached for the entrance examinations to the ordinary public school, one of which, it was thought, he might attend once his stamina had sufficiently improved. His mother appears to have strongly believed at this time in the beneficial effects of Victorian 'sea air', and during the holidays, when the family did not go up to Rothiemurchus, she would make sure that Lytton visited some seaside resort, usually Torquay or Dover and once to Broadstairs where Lytton 'taught the waiter how to fold a napkin!' He remained at Parkstone, with one interval spent in travelling abroad, until the summer of 1893, and although he must have inhaled more recuperative ozone during these four years than throughout the rest of his life, no remarkable improvement in his general condition resulted from it.

Henry Forde was a rather pretentious, Dickensian character, extravagantly obsequious and literary-minded, but capable occasionally of flashes of perception. He was harried continuously by an invalid wife, Grace, who resented the rival claims of her husband's few pupils to ill-health. 'What a trial the boys are, Henaree!' she would complain to him. 'Why don't you *whip* them?' The school reports which were sent to Lady Strachey during these years sometimes contain more information about their own son who, in contrast to the sickly Lytton, was, they boasted, 'roughing it' at a boarding school at Tonbridge. A few of Henry Forde's comments on Lytton, however, are of interest. 'I do not consider Giles behind the average of the ordinary boy at his age,' he wrote (December 1890) to Lytton's mother, who was worried lest his repetitive illnesses and inability to study for long consecutive periods might prove too great a handicap to his scholastic progress, 'indeed I think he is rather in advance of it; but he is much behind what a boy of his powers should have reached, *if* he had had health.'

Most of the coaching which Lytton received at Parkstone was devised specifically to enable him to answer the type of question posed by the average examination paper of those days. Generally speaking, though he did not excel in the Classics as Henry Forde had thought he would, and though he developed a faculty for rapidly forgetting the technicalities of grammar, his progress was very satisfactory. In spite of the academic limitations imposed on his studies, many of the stylistic qualities later to characterize his biographical and critical writings were already in the process of being formed, and his literary flair soon made itself apparent. 'It would not at all surprise me, if he were to become literary,' Henry Forde told Lytton's mother shortly after his twelfth birthday, 'I do not mean merely fond of letters – that he is sure to be – but a contributor to them, a writer. He has an ear for, and a knack of hitting off queer and picturesque phrases and turns of expression, and I could quite easily fancy his developing a marked style of his own in the future, and one that would "stand out". He is a distinctly unusual and original kind of boy; and I should think had best be let develop his own way; his education should be chiefly directed to giving him help to evolve himself, not to forcing him into ordinary moulds. Owing to his bid-able-ness and – one must at present say – his timidity, he might be easily moulded after the average standard, with the result I believe of docking and thwarting what is special in him.'

Despite often looking pale and tired, Lytton seemed in good spirits for much of his time at Parkstone. He got on well with the other boys, and was usually glad to see them again after the holidays were over. He must have presented them with a curious spectacle on first acquaintance, and one not easy to accept. Tall for his age but terribly thin, he was habitually reserved in his manner. To match his odd appearance he had moreover inherited more than a fair quota of the Strachey eccentricity, which he was already quite capable of exploiting both in what he did and what he wrote. This was soon recognized even within the family itself. 'When I read James the superscription of your letter,' Lady Strachey wrote to him on one occasion (1892) referring to his five-year-old brother, 'he said, "I know that's from Lytton, he's always so absurd"; and when he heard the contents he exclaimed, "He *is* a funny little creature!"'

While at Parkstone, Lytton entered clamorously into all the small school's activities. In his letters home, there are accounts of 'delightful bathes . . . I can swim a little' (9 July 1893); of sailing in a big boat called *The Lulu*, striking a rock in the sea, and being stuck there till rescued at nine o'clock at night; of watching 'Mr Gladstone in a tug-boat going to pool. They actually rang the church bells!' (16 June 1889);

of playing a 'lovely game of going round the room without touching the floor; it makes one get into a fever' (15 December 1889); of listening politely to Mr Forde as he read *Gulliver's Travels* – 'it is rather sickening but it can't be helped' (2 February 1890); and of starting 'a Small Naval and Military Exhibition which I hope will be a success' (7 June 1891).

He seems to have been particularly striking in the school's plays, which included a boisterous production of *Blue-Beard*, and several Shakespearian tableaux – Lytton playing Romeo in one, while in another 'I was Othello with my face blackened and a pillow and Cecil in bed being smothered'. His impersonation of female parts was especially convincing and sometimes well exploited in real life, as a letter to his mother on 27 March 1892 – written like an entry in *The Diary of a Nobody* – relates:

'On Sunday Dora was going to the Thompsons so she dressed me up in her short skirt and Mrs Forde's fashionable cape, bonet and she also put her boa round my neck wich hid my short hair behind we then went to the Thompsons and I was introduced by the name of Miss Miller – a friend of Dora's. After a little Mrs Thompson recognized me but as Mr Thompson had not come in yet so I was arranged with my back to the light. Soon Mr Thompson came in with a friend of his called Mr Pike, he is very frightened of ladies, so when the two entered I was introduced to them they were both unaware of what was going on. Soon the *whole* room was in suppressed laughter and the *unfortunate* Mr Pike didn't know what to do he grew redder and redder in the face and from red to purple and from purple to – I don't know what at last Miss Webb, perceiving his embarrassment said, "I think you'd [better] examine Miss Miller more carefully" – so he did – and then of course he recognized me.'

Though Henry Forde reported that Lytton 'eats with capital appetite' and did some 'spirited painting', his mother was disappointed with his continuing infirmity, and became fearful that he would fall behind in his work if he stayed too long at Parkstone. During the summer holidays of 1892, which the whole family spent at Holywell House near Wrotham, she told Lytton that she was arranging for him to go on a five-month voyage to Gibraltar, Egypt and the Cape of Good Hope, so that he would be able to inhale deeper and stronger quantities of 'sea air' and, even more important, escape the worst part of the English winter. He returned to Parkstone in September full of suppressed excitement which he communicated in a more ebullient form to the other boys.

This voyage did not in fact commence until nearly four months later,

when, two days before Christmas, he and his sister Dorothy set sail on
board the *Coromandel*. A diary which he now started tells how he began
to feel seasick a few miles out of port, but effectively cured himself by
drinking champagne – a tip given to him by his father before embarking.
Soon they reached Gibraltar, and Lytton noted that 'with the aid of
spectacles I could see what the place looked like. All the houses were like
toy houses scattered about the rock and to complete the smallness, the
water became filled with little toy boats.'

Having 'affected a landing successfully', they went to live for the next
month with their uncle, Charles Grant, a captain in the Black Watch;
his wife, 'Aunt Aggie'; and their son, 'Black Pat' – a 'horribly snouted
and absurdly mendacious' little boy of about the same age, with
whom however he got on very well. 'It is perfectly lovely here,' Lytton
informed his mother. 'All kinds of flowers are in bloom, there are
roses and oranges!' Together the two boys spent a delightful time,
driving around the place in a cab 'like a four post bed', going to
parties, playing bezique, climbing trees, inspecting the guns in the
public park, watching football matches and the soldiers parading about
the barracks, and being taught the Highland Fling by a Scottish piper
named Smith. In company with Pat's mother and father, the two
boys also crossed over into Spain where they visited an empty but 'most
interesting' bull ring, after which they would play each morning at bull
fights – 'We squat on the ground,' Lytton explained to his mother,
'and charge against each other.'

At the end of January the Black Watch was moved to Egypt, and
Lytton travelled with the regiment on board the troopship H.M.S.
Himalaya, reading and playing quoits for most of the passage, and
attired in a diminutive variant of the Highland costume which occasioned favourable comment from the officers and men. At Alexandria,
which Lytton disliked, they disembarked, travelling on by train to
Cairo. The three weeks they spent here were among the happiest of the
whole journey. The unfamiliar carnival atmosphere appealed enormously to Lytton's romantic imagination. The streets and buildings
seemed like illustrations from some fabulous story book suddenly and
mysteriously brought to life. 'It is a delight here,' he told his mother
(6 February 1893). 'We don't know what is going to happen to us.' He
explored the bazaars, the museums, the tomb of the Mamalukes, the
Citadel Mosque, and Joseph's well, down which he and Pat dropped
stones. The two boys went everywhere on donkeys which were even
more novel and exciting than four-post-bed cabs. 'The donkeys flew
and I greatly enjoyed myself,' Lytton noted after his first ride. 'These
donkeys would be priceless in England, they hold their heads up and

never think of stopping till they are told to and even then sometimes they won't.'

One of the sights which Lytton had been particularly anxious to see were the Pyramids. 'Vast and grand and towering above all things near them, they rose against the blue sky solemn and majestic,' he wrote in his diary; but with the perverse taste of all children he appeared much more impressed by the modern hotel near by at which he stayed for a time – 'the most beautiful in the world' as he described it. His good opinion of the Pyramids revived however after a hectic expedition which the party made to inspect them close at hand. 'We were surrounded by Arabs,' he narrated, 'and one seized each arm and hauled me up the pyramid. The steps are from three to four feet high. My two Arabs helped me along very well and I rested two or three times during the ascent. . . . Coming down was easier than going up I thought, but other people didn't. I simply jumped from step to step, the Arabs holding my hands.'

Almost immediately after this perilous ascent they were off again, this time to examine the Sphinx, whose feline, enigmatic expression, impenetrable as God, and obviously superior to all the mean, oppressive tribulations of the commonplace world, fascinated Lytton. The account which he gave at the time of this excursion is especially interesting, since, being less well integrated than his adult writing yet containing many of the same essential qualities, it shows the various individual strains which went to make up the composite pattern of his mature literary style – the wonderfully comic vision; the dramatic narrative gift; and the romantic and rhetorical rhapsodizing which, slightly overpitched, never quite brings off the ambitious effect for which it strives. 'Aunt Aggie', he recounted, 'said she thought it would be a good idea to go to the Sphinx on camels, directly she mentioned this word fifteen camels were on us, all making the most awful noises when sitting down. We were all seized by at least four men who pulled us in four different directions. I got to a Camel and an Arab said it was a lady's one, which it was not, so I was husseled off and two men came and lifted me into the air and put me on a camel, at this moment the sheik interfered and I got on to the one that was supposed to have had a lady's saddle. It was a rather ghastly sensation when the camel got up and you thought you were going to tumble off. We walked on our camels to the Sphinx where we dismounted and walked to a place just opposite its face. Although its nose had entirely gone it looked as if all its features were there. What an exquisite face it is – how solemn – how majestic you look, your eyes looking out into the desert with that beautiful expression always on your face, so collosal and so perfect. You, who have been there for

thousands and thousands of years, you, who have gazed and gazed at
that endless sea of sand ever since you existed, tell me, oh! tell me how
to look with that sublime expression on your face at all that comes and
all that goes, careless of everything for ever.'

This single visit to the Sphinx seems to have produced a lasting, if
somewhat juvenile, impression on Lytton's imagination. As he gazed
up into the staring eyes of this strange, eminently bland idol and
wondered at the incalculable mystery which lay behind them, the first
whisper of a poem went through him. Not composed in its final form
until several years later, 'The Cat' remains the only one of his many
verses to have been posthumously anthologized.[1] Looking into the
great cat's eyes, he subsides into a demi-dream and is filled with a
sense of exquisite enchantment, an almost mystical heightening of
awareness:

> An ampler air, a warmer June
> Enfold me, and my wondering eye
> Salutes a more imperial moon
> Throned in a more resplendent sky
> Than ever knew this pagan shore.
> Oh, strange! For you are with me too,
> And I who am a cat once more
> Follow the woman that was you.

Towards the end of February Lytton left Cairo and returned by train
to Alexandria. 'How interesting it's all been,' he commented in his
diary. 'How glad I am I came to Egypt and saw all these wondrous
sights.' To his great satisfaction he remained in Alexandria only twenty-
four hours, and then, on 27 February, embarked once more on the
Himalaya, arriving during the afternoon of the following day at Port
Said. By 1 March, his thirteenth birthday, he was sailing along the Suez
Canal, suffering under the intense heat but thoroughly relishing the
sensation of celebrating a birthday at such an unexpected place. 'My
birthday today,' he wrote, '– how odd – a birthday in the Suez
Canal. . . . Every now and then we pass a little red-brick house with a
brown roof and green trees growing round it, they look so pretty. At

---

[1] 'The Cat' was first printed on 12 June 1902 in the Supplement of the *Cambridge
Review*, p. XXIII, and signed 'G.L.S.' Subsequently it was reprinted in *Euphrosyne*
(1905), an anthology anonymously compiled by Clive Bell. It has appeared more recently
in Mona Gooden's *The Poet's Cat* (1946), and in *A Dictionary of Cat Lovers* (1949), an
exhaustive symposium edited by Christabel Aberconway, containing scholarly notes on
the 'Cat in Ancient Egypt', and on the belief in the sun and moon's influence upon the
eyes of the cat. In these later publications, the word 'pagan' in the opening line of the
second stanza quoted above, has been changed to 'northern'.

4 p.m. we arrived at Suez, a wee town on the edge of the desert. We couldn't have the birthday cake today as it was not iced.'

The *Himalaya* stopped long enough at Suez for Lytton to watch a cricket match, collect some shells and ride a few more donkeys. Then they were all off again, this time to Aden which they reached in the second week of March. Here Lytton occupied himself by wandering through the exotic camel market 'crowded with camels in different attitudes', throwing stones at an octopus and coins into the water for the little black boys 'who dived down and brought up the sixpences in their mouths; they swam exquisitely and were quite as at home in the water as in their boats'.

The party then continued its journey on to Mauritius, putting up at the town of Carepipe for two days of incessant rain. Lytton was not impressed. 'The hills', he recorded, 'were most extraordinary, they looked as if they were going to fall down every minute, they were not at all grand, but looked drunk and misshapen.'

Cape Town, on the other hand, where the *Himalaya* arrived on 23 April, was properly symmetrical, altogether better balanced and more pleasing. 'It is a most magnificent place,' Lytton decided, 'with palacial buildings and shops worthy of Bond Street but it is very small, everything is next door to everything else.' The six weeks which he now spent in Cape Town were tremendously exciting. His days were passed in climbing the slopes of Table Mountain which was 'exquisite and looked just as I'd expected it to be', setting off on fishing trips, playing croquet and billiards – at which he considered he had done exceedingly well whenever he failed throughout the entire course of a game to rip the cloth – and, helped by his cousin Pat, bringing out with the utmost industry an illustrated magazine, *The Comet*, which, he declared, was 'a great success, with poems and stories'.

Lytton's natural gift for treating grown-ups as his equals caused him to be made the hero of a farewell party given by the officers of the Black Watch, with whom he had spent so much of the voyage.[1] On 12 May, shortly before he was due to return to England, both he and Pat received an invitation to dine at the Mess. Lytton was attired for the occasion in 'my best Etons and a white waistcoat and a black tie'. Neither of them was allowed any alcoholic drinks throughout the evening, except to toast Queen Victoria's health, and so had to content themselves with lemon squash. After the Queen's health had been drunk, and much to the two boys' astonishment, the officers rose again to their feet. 'We did not know in the least what was happening,' Lytton confessed, 'and were going to follow their example, when they told us to sit down.

[1] Dorothy Strachey had returned to England several weeks earlier.

Capt. Gordon then said, "I beg to propose the health of the Rt. Hon.
Prime Minister Lytton Strachey and Field-Marshal Sir Patrick Grant!"
"Hear, hear" was heard from several voices. Soon afterwards we went
into the anteroom.

'. . . Then it was discovered that it was very late and that if we did
not hurry we should miss our train; so we hastily put on our coats and
dashed out, Arthur Marindin accompanying us. As we left we were
cheered by the officers! We ran with all speed to the station, my tie
streaming in the breeze!'

A few days later Lytton sailed for England. He had thoroughly enjoyed coexisting in close proximity to a regiment of soldiers for such a
long time, and being privileged to peep behind the scenes of military
life.[1] Altogether his five months abroad, with their aura of heat and
their perpetual stimulus of fresh excitement and companionship, comprised a carefree liberating interval in the dull and sickly routine of
childhood – one which he always recalled with pleasure and which
helped to quicken his lifelong passion for travel. 'I enjoyed the voyage
very much indeed,' the final entry in his diary runs, 'it was so entertaining and interesting – oh! it is like some beautiful dream.'

2

'GLAD DAY, LOVE AND DUTY'

It was not long before Lytton was dropped back again into the greyness
of his customary prosaic existence. After a fortnight spent at Lancaster
Gate, the bright luminescence of his travels had faded into a spectre,
confined to the realms of his romantic imagination and utterly un-
connected with his everyday life. In the second week of June, he returned to Parkstone, where rumours of his adventures about the world
had already made him a hero with the other boys. But for himself, the
novelty was over, and the subsequent re-entry into the alternating
routine of home and school palled on him. Mr Forde soon noticed a
marked change both in his state of health and of mind. 'He certainly
does look grown in every way: his cheeks are quite plump,' he wrote to
Lady Strachey. 'I am rather surprised to see that he is not at all tanned
by the suns and seas of his journey. He bears his return to humdrum
work and life like the philosophical boy he is; set to at his Virgil this

---

[1] A few weeks later, Lytton became highly indignant on learning that his uncle was
resigning his commission and returning to civilian life. 'I am most disgusted with Uncle
Charlie for leaving the army,' he announced to his mother.

morning as if he had only left off the day before, and is taking the ovation the boys are giving him – and which seems likely to continue for days, like a Roman Triumph – with dignity and as if it too were quite in its place and to be expected, and altogether is possessing his soul in blandness and calm. He is a most admirable boy.'

Lytton's mother had also observed a general toughening in her son's physique and a consolidation of his air of quiet and compact self-reliance. She was now determined that he must be removed from the educational backwaters of Parkstone and sent off to a larger, more cosmopolitan institution where, she believed, his new stamina and invigoration should help in promoting a permanently healthier circulation of life-energy. By August she had made the necessary arrangements, and informed Henry Forde that Lytton would not be returning to his care. 'We are very, very sorry to part with Giles,' he replied; 'we have all grown really fond of him. *I* also think it will be best for him, as he has grown so much stronger, to try his wings in a wider sphere, and more robust air. . . .'

Lytton himself was not sorry to leave. Though he liked and got on well with some of the other boys, he had no great opinion of Henry Forde, and still less of his sickly complaining wife. Parkstone, it appears, was not much of a place. 'There is a dead mouse under the schoolroom I think, because of the dreadful smell – so bad we can't write our letters there!' After almost five years he was bored with it all, and looked forward to joining a real school. Had he known, however, the type of rigorous and unrelenting character-building to which he was shortly to be subjected, he might have viewed this new phase in his life with more alarm.

The New School, Abbotsholme, to which Lytton was sent in September, described itself as an advanced 'Educational Laboratory' which aimed at producing wholesome, healthy citizens by what was known as 'the natural method'. Despite the well-publicized modernity, no day-boys were admitted within its sacred precincts since, it was believed, they tended to befoul the moral climate of a school. For similar reasons it was not thought proper to develop the place as a co-educational academy, and it was modelled, for the most part, on nothing much more adventurous than the public school tradition. Founded only four years previously by Dr Cecil Reddie, it originated what for a time was known as 'The New School Movement', and was the progenitor of the better known Bedales, and the Landerziehungsheime Schule of Germany, respectively under Dr Badley and Dr Hermann Lietz, both of whom were temporarily assistant masters at Abbotsholme. Among its indirect but conspicuous offspring were L'Ecole des Roches, Salem and Gordonstoun.

For Lytton, Abbotsholme was a strange, wholly unwise choice, and one that ran contrary to the excellent advice proffered some years earlier by Henry Forde.[1] For here, if anywhere, he ran the risk of being moulded after the average standard. Innovations there were in plenty, but they were more naïve than enlightened. The prospectus issued that year should in itself have sounded in Lady Strachey's ears an ominous warning. 'The aim,' one passage ran, 'is to provide an ideal home and life for the sons of parents who can afford to have the best for their boys' physical, mental, and moral welfare, and who realize that Education spells Empire.' The fee amounted to about fifty pounds a term, but added charges were imposed on those parents whose children were found to possess certain deficiencies. These extra sums were in the nature of vicarious penalties, fines levied against parents as a reminder that 'the School is intended for boys who are in all respects normal'.

It seems likely, however, that Lady Strachey was persuaded in favour of Abbotsholme by the strong and hypnotic personality of Dr Reddie himself. She was introduced to him by Charles Kegan Paul,[2] a mutual friend who, after serving as an assistant master at Eton, had been appointed one of the trustees of the New School. As founder and head-master of Abbotsholme, Reddie was in all ways its moving spirit. A dynamic figure of sturdy proportions, stern, with piercing eyes and a thundering flow of talk, he was worshipped by many of his pupils and held in extreme terror by others, including the teaching staff, none of whom – except the biology master – was permitted to marry. He was six foot tall, but rather stocky, owing apparently to his legs, which were shorter than they should have been. His autocratic assurance of manner and fierce idealism concealed from many the naïvety and crankiness of his schemes for remoulding national life, and producing from the gymnasium at Abbotsholme a higher type of human being. He was a man, or so he believed, whose mission was to rescue late Victorian England from degeneracy, by repopulating the country's key positions with Old Abbotsholmians. Lytton must have seemed poor material for

---

[1] There had been some question of sending Lytton to Eton, but Lady Strachey decided against this partly, it seems, because of her elder son Oliver's failure there, a love-letter from another boy having been discovered in his rooms. As an adult, Oliver was completely heterosexual and something of a womanizer – 'the most orthodox of all of us', as James Strachey described him.

[2] Charles Kegan Paul (1828–1902), had been Vicar of Sturminster until 1874, when he was converted to publishing. He translated a number of books from the German and French, edited the letters of Mary Wollstonecraft and wrote a Life of Godwin. His last publication was a volume of memoirs. In 1856 he had married Margaret Colvile, and was related, through marriage, to one of Lady Strachey's sisters.

Sir Richard Strachey, 1902: portrait by Simon Bussy

Lady Strachey

Ancestral home of the Strachey family, Sutton Court, Somerset

Lytton's birthplace: Stowey House, Clapham Common

such a grandiose plan of social reconstruction. But Dr. Reddie, still in the experimental stages of building up what he defined as his 'organization of a normal tertiary (higher secondary) school for English boys of eleven to eighteen belonging to the directing classes', was anxious to amass the references of as many influential parents and guardians as possible, so that even the most unlikely specimen from a distinguished Anglo-Indian family was for him a welcome prize.

To appreciate exactly what Lytton experienced at Abbotsholme and how this may have contributed to his strong views both on the public-school system and on the genus of stern educational reformers – as later exemplified by the third essay of *Eminent Victorians* – something of the particular methods instigated by Dr Reddie should be explained. Initially he had based his ideas of a reconstituted society on the writings of Disraeli, Carlyle and Ruskin. But it was in Germany, he confessed in his familiar regal style, that 'notwithstanding our English prejudices, we at once observed strong evidence of superior intellectual life and social order'. In Germany, too, he had first decided to put his theories of citizen-training into operation. As a schoolmaster, he had made a thorough study of 'Boy Nature' and convinced himself that he could divert the downward course of England's national life by incorporating with the ground plan of the public-school system those influences which modern culture and the up-to-date needs of society had shown to be desirable. By these far-seeing means, he was convinced that he could mould the pattern of a new English master race. Though many of the innovations which he planned were thought to be scandalously *avant-garde*, the main concept of his educational scheme was not progressive but reactionary – to resurrect the legacy of earlier, more wholesome and puritanical days.

Dr Reddie was, in short, a Utopian, and the Abbotsholme of his dreams largely an empty fantasy. His ideal boys were to be cultural athletes, glorified all-rounders, who cast no shadows in the real world and who were divested of everything which vexes the spirit in its partnership with the flesh. Yet there was a morning light on his miniature experimental colony which gave it a pastoral charm lacking in most of the clinical Utopias that are constructed to appease their inventor's desire for adult passion without its disillusionment and for action without risk of indignity. To keep alive this glow, reflected from the pure flame of his idealism, Dr Reddie sought out an idyllic setting: 'We must place first and foremost,' ran his opening manifesto, 'the magnificent position of the school amid unparalleled scenery – mountains and sea, woods and fields, and gorgeous skies, with its spectacle spread out before us of one of the loveliest cities in the world. Next we must place

the spacious grounds and stately buildings, an atmosphere of dignity
and culture, and a free and open life. Such was the place.'

But it was within the building, and especially within the chapel, that
Dr Reddie's spirit of sternly checked emotionalism was most faithfully
echoed. Here the corbels were carved with the heads not of saints but of
redoubtable men of action and vision – Nelson and Shakespeare –
while from the wall shone a five-pointed star, Solomon's seal, the sign
of wisdom. Behind a simple altar cross (and in these more modest and
self-conscious days concealed by curtains from the public gaze) stood the
statue of a naked youth transfixed in a Blakean pose. 'It was Dr Reddie's
attempt to express something of his faith in his boys,' writes the present
headmaster, 'of their power to rise to great heights by truth and self-
dedication.' In more secular matters he endeavoured to encourage these
latent qualities by what he described as 'natural methods'. These 'natural
methods' permeated the school, influencing even the most necessary
and inevitably natural functions of the boys. For on the question of
lavatorial procedure, as on everything else, Dr Reddie held decided
views. He dispensed with the sophisticated and decadent water-closet
altogether, and reintroduced what he conceived to be the more natural
method employed by the beasts of the field. Some concessions, however, were made to the higher status of the human being. The essential
primitivism was modified by a degree, a not too exaggerated degree, of
applied aesthetics. As they sat in a long military row, the boys looked
over a neat dismal garden, flowerless but well-weeded.

When Lytton went to Abbotsholme the school numbered just over
forty boys. The School House itself had an imposing exterior, being a
large country mansion in the Elizabethan-Victorian style, and surrounded by orchards and gardens. Altogether the Abbotsholme estate
covered some one hundred and thirty acres, and was set on the western
slope of Dove Ridge in Derbyshire, overlooking the river Dove. The
country round about was remarkably fine and open, and, being nearly
all permanent pasture, resembled a vast park. There were no towns
close by, and the nearest village – about a mile away – was Rocester,
once a Roman camp, and later the seat of the Abbey from which Abbotsholme took its name.

Lytton's ordinary day, during the winter term of 1893, was divided
into three main sections. His morning was devoted mainly to class-
work indoors; his afternoon to physical and manual work out of doors;
his evening to music, poetry, art and social recreation. Every morning
reveille was sounded at five minutes to seven (in summer it was ten
past six), and after a cold bath Lytton would fall in on the parade ground
for military drill and work with the dumb-bells. From here he would

hurry off to the chapel for a ten-minute thanksgiving service where he was able to recover a little before breakfast at twenty to eight. Twenty minutes later he was upstairs again standing by his bed while the dormitory was inspected by the masters. After dormitory parade, there came the first class of the day which was called Second School – First School in the summer being at six forty-five. These lessons differed from those of the ordinary public school in two respects: few of them exceeded three-quarters of an hour; and in the teaching of languages priority was given to German and French over the dead tongues, Latin and Greek. The classes which Dr Reddie took personally were often astonishing. Many a period supposedly given over to, say, physics or chemistry was sure to be occupied by the subject of hygiene, in which the importance of mental as well as bodily cleanliness was severely emphasized. 'On one occasion,' wrote Stanley Unwin, 'in a state of fury at our incompetence, he broke the pointer across the table and said that if we did not learn to think and to take more pains we should end by blacking the boots of the Germans.'

At midday the first of the outdoor activities commenced. Dr Reddie himself had been only moderately proficient at the usual English forms of sport such as cricket and rugger, and so the physical training at Abbotsholme consisted not just of mere games but also of useful manual labour which, he believed, promoted a less restricted social feeling than that enshrined by the traditional team spirit. As an exponent of what has been called 'the Gospel of Potato-digging' – originally conceived by Edward Carpenter – he strove to impress the minds of his pupils with the 'panoramic reflex of nature', and to banish from them the notorious psychological troubles afflicting those who lacked a hard and steady occupation employing body and mind together. This aim was to be secured by the muscular work involved in the agrarian occupations he set them, together with an indispensable programme of tonic exercises. Only these pursuits, Dr Reddie claimed, could 'stimulate the healthy growth of the body in supple grace and compact symmetry, and promote that frank, hearty, and instinctive appreciation of its beauty, which is essential to the true education. Moreover, to render the body strong, clean, and lovely is a religious duty. Therefore the claims of athletics will in no respect be ignored, but rather extended and rendered less artificial and mechanical.'

From twelve to one o'clock, when studies were interrupted by a brief lunch and a lengthy piano recital, and again from two o'clock to half-past four, Lytton was subjected to a variety of strenuous and unexpected tasks. Among the less arduous pastimes which were prescribed for these periods were drawing, carpentry, basket-making and bee-culture.

In addition to this, and in order to rouse in him a manly interest in the subject of clothing and its proper relation to the human body, Lytton might at times be coached in the processes of boot-making and tailoring, or alternatively instructed in the preparation of butter so that he could acquire a sound knowledge in matters which directly affected his health. Simply to obviate the dangers of loafing, some Rugby Union football – Dr Reddie's own favourite team game– was also obligatory, as was a large minimum quota of digging and tree-felling. Opportunity, too, was afforded him almost daily to learn on the near-by farm lands the rudiments of agriculture and food-production. Bringing in the potato harvest, damming the streams in the Dingle, erecting pigeon houses, Lytton was said to be gleaning the ways of nature at first hand, benefit-ing from a true though little regarded culture, and availing himself – should it prove necessary – of a sound preparation for colonial life.

Afternoon school lasted from half-past four till six o'clock, when the boys had their tea. This was followed by thirty minutes of freedom preparatory to the final part of the school day given over to artistic training. Since Dr Reddie himself admitted that he possessed 'neither talent, time, nor taste for literary composition; but on the contrary, feels a growing conviction that words and books, less by quality than by quantity, exert an exaggerated influence in our lives, producing new perils to body, mind, and character', Lytton's literary gifts received scant encouragement. Music, as the most social of the arts, was given the highest priority, and from seven to seven-thirty Lytton indulged in compulsory convivial glee-singing under the tuition of the heavily bearded German professor of biology, his voice, by this stage of the day, being described as 'rather weak'. The hour's artistic training which succeeded this period, in so far as it was literary, was designed to stimulate his dormant aesthetic sensibilities by the simple process of making him learn off by heart those stirring incidents of history immortalized in verse. Each evening, too, the boys would assemble in Big School to meet the ladies, masters, and any visitors who might have arrived, and learn to behave and amuse themselves in a sensible adult fashion. The day ended with a second ten-minute thanksgiving service in the chapel; and then, at ten minutes to nine, Lytton was at last allowed to go off to bed.

On the question of moral and religious instruction the New School took very high ground indeed. On Sundays, Lytton was permitted to rise as late as half-past seven. Before breakfast he was obliged to attend a twenty-minute chapel service, and after the usual dormitory inspection and a period set aside for writing letters home, he would fall in at the full-dress Church Parade. This ceremony lasted until almost midday, and was followed, when the weather was wet, by a corollary in the form of a further three-quarters of an hour's celebration in the school chapel. This chapel was in fact seen as the source from which all other activities took their illumination. The services were intended to condense all the most elevated incentives of the place, by proclaiming to the captive congregation definite maxims of conduct associated with the actions of ideal figures, the whole series of illustrations being grouped round the Person and Life of Jesus Christ. Readings, however, were by no means confined to the Bible, but followed an individual pattern laid out by Dr Reddie in a publication of startling prolixity: 'The Abbotsholme Liturgy, with Special Services for Christmas, Good Friday, Easter, the Ascensions, Whit-tide, Trinity; also for Waterloo Day and Trafalgar Day; also David's Lament for Saul and Jonathan, the Seven Beatitudes, the Ten Laws, and a number of Canticles and a large number of the Psalms, all retranslated, pointed and noted; also part of the anthology in the school chapel.' No boy, were he Protestant, Catholic, Hindu or Mohammedan, was permitted to escape the frequent rigours of these Abbotsholme Services conducted under the strict regimen of their headmaster.

Dinner, at one o'clock, was followed by an organ recital, while the remainder of the afternoon was left officially free. In practice this was not the case for Lytton. As a contribution to its religious purpose, the school was segregated into Fags, Mids and Prefects, and as a new boy he naturally came into the first category. This system, he might have been surprised to learn as he busied himself about his unofficial duties throughout the long afternoon, had been set up by Dr Reddie, in a special effort to educate the boys' affections towards one another. All boys 'are *trained* to understand their relation to one another', Dr Reddie explained in his prospectus. 'At Abbotsholme this natural relation of boys to one another is recognized and carefully organized.' To assist in this natural organization and training the prefects were empowered to beat the fags. The masters also, Dr Reddie continued, 'catch the same spirit and learn to use the same methods. The result is greater operation in the teaching and greater harmony in the boys' deportment. Both are humanized.' In this way Abbotsholme was conceived as a family unit, with Dr Reddie himself as God the Father hammering home the school motto: 'Glad Day, Love and Duty'. Involved in terrifying grandeur he ruled from above, yet was an omnipresent force. During his time at Abbotsholme Lytton must certainly have witnessed, if not actually been the subject of, one of the occasional floggings administered, with full Arnoldian gravity, by Dr Reddie before the assembled school. These were awful and solemn ceremonies which impressed themselves for life on the more sensitive boys.

At a quarter-past five the so-called free time ended and Lytton would join with the other boys in chanting retranslated canticles and hymns from Dr Reddie's anthology; while after tea he received an hour's religious instruction consisting, for the most part, of learning by heart portions of the Gospels and selections from the Psalms. There followed yet another hour's service in the chapel, before supper and lights out.

By this system of all-round modern and religious instruction, based upon the high-flown principles of educational science, and adapted to the special needs of the English cultured classes, did Dr Reddie aspire to instil in Lytton a lofty, self-reliant and immaculately disciplined moral character. The immediate results were not encouraging. After the protective custody of Lancaster Gate and Parkstone the physical toughness needed to stand up to such a sentence of hard labour proved altogether beyond him. Something of the strain and exertion imposed by Dr Reddie's curriculum comes out in his letters home. 'I enjoy myself greatly on the whole. Of course there are some things which I don't much like, such as cold baths and paperchases! – but still I'm sure I shall get used to them' (5 October 1893); 'Yesterday [18 November] we had a run because we could not play football as it was snowing. So we sallied forth – oh! it was dreadfully cold, and the wind and the snow hit you – and altogether it was most unpleasant! . . . I had my first round of boxing on Wednesday in which I was knocked flat on the ground!'; 'The baths *were* cold, I assure you! Everyday we change entirely into jersies and flannel knickers. One is allowed to put on as many jersies as you like – but no shirt or vest or draw!' (1 October 1893). 'I think you will get used to the cold bath in time,' his mother wrote to him hopefully. But already by the time her letter arrived at Abbotsholme, Lytton was in bed with a high fever. From this he recovered after some ten days' sedation, only to faint away with a spell of weakness and dizziness, being carried unconscious from the chapel back to the sick-room. His pulse became unusually rapid and he quickly lost weight. At this time he seems to have completely outgrown and overtaxed his strength, being already five feet two inches tall, but weighing only a few pounds over five stone. By December he had made a second recovery and, attired in a 'lovely' dress and wearing 'a beautiful yellow wig', gave a memorable performance as Hippolyta, Queen of the Amazons, in *A Midsummer Night's Dream*.[1] 'I remember you very well,' Dr Reddie wrote to him twenty-eight years later; 'I still

---

[1] Earlier that term he had acted another female role in a school production of *My Turn Next*. 'I had on a beautiful red silk dress with flounces,' he proudly told his mother.

have that photograph of you as "a fascinating female" in the little play we gave, as we sat in the conservatory.'

From the term report which Lady Strachey was sent at Christmas two interesting points emerge. First, Lytton was extremely eager to succeed in this new, masculine environment. He made a special effort to do well at athletics, drill and farming, but in each case lacked the necessary force and stamina. Secondly, Dr Reddie, in his anxiety that Lytton should not be removed from Abbotsholme, understated the physical ailments and deficiencies from which he suffered, and, so far as was consistent with his elevated principles, sheltered him from the full rigours of the New School's Spartan syllabus. Lytton's work was dismissed rather cursorily as 'good', and his health was cryptically described as 'fair'. 'I have not pressed this boy,' he wrote. 'He neither needs it nor can he safely stand it. He has been twice ill this term, once when most were suffering from similar feverish colds in October, and again lately during the *hot weather* feeling faint for two days. He has otherwise been in good health and in excellent spirits – I believe the climate suits him – As regards work and general development, nothing more can be desired.'

Lytton returned to Abbotsholme in January 1894, when life proved even harder. Dressed only in shorts and a jersey he was expected during the most Arctic conditions to carry cheerfully on mending fences and gates, tarring railings, cleaning out the cowshed, wood-cutting and other endless jobs on the estate. 'He is not in the picture captioned potato digging,' one of Lytton's contemporaries at Abbotsholme, Gerald Brooke, told the author. 'It was a bitterly cold day with a wind from the snow-clad hills driving over the valley. It nearly put me out! Strachey was probably talking to matron in the sick-room.'[1]

Lytton was very anxious to make some close friends from among his companions at the school, but they almost all regarded him as something of an outcast. 'He was', another pupil, G. Lissant Cox, recalled, 'a strange bird from my point of view.' And this appears to have been the general verdict. 'My recollection of him is that he seemed to be older than I was, with a very grown-up air for a boy. He must have lived with grown-ups,' another Old Abbotsholmian remembered. 'I think he must have been much above the school average in taught knowledge. He could talk to anyone who would listen to him but not to me. I was only interested in bird's-nesting and outdoor activity which meant nothing to him. I remember seeing him talking about the play while he

[1] 'Sometime ago we have all been digging up potatoes in the field, we had to work pretty hard, because they all had to be got away before the frost came on' (Lytton Strachey to Lady Strachey, 29 October 1893).

washed, then turning round stark naked to continue the discourse. He was circumcised but quite unconscious of the fact that he did not look like all other boys in the dormitory.'

During this, his second term, Lytton's health collapsed completely. It now became impossible to overlook his physical incompatibility with the bracing climate of the place. Before the end of the term he was removed altogether from the school and sent back home. His failure to endure the austerity of Abbotsholme threw him right back within the circumfluent effeminacy of Lancaster Gate. As in later life, his affability and sense of humour depended largely on his personal success, which liberated him from morbid self-preoccupation and enabled him to focus his mind upon external objects. In failure, he sank into an abysmal hypersensitive awareness of his own insignificance and isolation, from which the only satisfactory outlet was hostility. When older, he would sometimes speak with intense dislike of the Abbotsholme régime, but secretly he would have loved to excel there, and it is perhaps significant that he never entirely broke off his connexions with the school. When at Cambridge he attended more than one of the annual Old Abbotsholmian dinners given at Christ's College, and received several personal visits from Dr Reddie himself, who always seemed dazed by the great height of his ex-pupil.

'Teachers and prophets', Strachey wrote in *Eminent Victorians*, 'have strange after-histories.' That of Dr Reddie was no exception. After Lytton had left, the fortunes of Abbotsholme were constantly bedevilled by sinister plots and counter-plots, the strain of which brought out in Dr Reddie the more tyrannical symptoms of paranoia. Weighed down by complex worries and responsibilities, he shed much of the high spirits that had formerly animated him during the holidays and made him unrecognizable to those who knew him only as a forbidding headmaster. Suspicious of everyone, he once dismissed five masters in a single term, convinced that they were conspiring to take control of his miniature kingdom under the leadership of a mysterious bankrupt Dutchman who, escaping from the bailiffs out of the window of a near-by building which he had hoped to set up as a rival establishment to Abbotsholme, fled to Holland and was heard of no more. The greatest blow of all, however, fell with the declaration of war. Many parents who had previously supported the Germanic mode of school life now hurriedly withdrew their sons until at last, tenacious and perverse as ever, Dr Reddie was left in sole charge of two pupils. Various schemes were implemented by the old boys, to which Lytton faithfully contributed, in order to reinstate the school. Though he did not send his old headmaster a copy of *Eminent Victorians* for fear that some passages in the pen-portrait of Dr Arnold might offend him, Lytton did forward him *Queen Victoria* and was warmly complimented for his courage in praising at such a time the Prince Consort, a German.

By the late 1920s a group of old boys finally persuaded Dr Reddie to sell the school, and under Colin Sharp it became more successful than ever before – and more orthodox. At this time Lytton contributed generously to an annuity given to the ex-headmaster on strict condition that he did not go near Abbotsholme ever again. It was a bitter pill for an ageing but still fiercely idealistic man to swallow. His stature declined noticeably, and during his few years of retirement he became a figure of increasing pathos and peculiarity. While his reputation and self-esteem shrank, so, symbolically, did his very name. As dr cecil reddie, a leading 'member of the league for abolition of capital-letters to save everybody's eyesight and to simplify education', he retired to welwyn-garden-city in hertfordshire, from where he wrote 'dear giles' a number of letters complaining of the invalid female relatives he was now forced to look after. He died, worn out but still undaunted, within a few days of Lytton himself.

3
'SCRAGGS'

'At school I used to weep – oh! for very definite things – bitter unkindness and vile brutality.' So wrote Lytton in a letter to Leonard Woolf, comparing the intense unhappiness he experienced as a schoolboy with his vaguer, more generalized feeling of sadness at university. The brazen religiosity of Abbotsholme, which so devastatingly inflamed his natural timidity and weakened his health, was soon succeeded in the summer of 1894 by the more traditional philistinism of Leamington College, then ranked as one of the minor public schools. At an age when the adolescent boy is growing increasingly aware of the physical side of his being, Lytton's painful awkwardness and distinctly odd appearance, were at once seized on by his new companions and brought home to him with all the directness and malevolence at the disposal of the average schoolboy. Just as his younger brother had thought him 'absurd' and described him as a 'funny little creature' – comments which his mother had seen fit humorously to pass on to him on more than one occasion – so his schoolfellows immediately singled out his awkwardness and oddity for their special attentions. Enveloped by an atmosphere of unkindness which no discipline could dispel, he was given the nickname of 'Scraggs' and made a victim of the most brutal and savage bullying. 'I am not getting on very well at present,' he admitted, 'as on[e] of the boys (Phipps) as well as talking nasty things is rather a bully, which is rather painful.' The masters offered him little protection against this treatment, partly by reason of their ordinary human laziness and partly in the vague abstract belief that a totally uncivilized atmosphere, far from having any harmful effect, prepared a boy very adequately for the turmoil of the adult world awaiting him.

Something of the distress and mortification which Lytton felt is expressed in one of the letters written to his mother at the beginning of June, just after he had recovered from a bout of illness. Naïvely and ambiguously phrased, hinting at rather than complaining of bullying, the picture of life at Leamington which emerges between the lines caused some alarm and misconception back at Lancaster Gate where Lady Strachey, feeling that the situation was moving beyond her province, placed her son's correspondence before her husband. In the answering letter which he addressed to Lytton on 4 June, Richard Strachey discloses some rather mixed feelings on the matter – a somewhat weary anxiety that his son should not have to be transferred every few months from one to yet another unsuitable school being counterbalanced by a very proper apprehension lest various dire and unmentionable atrocities might in the meantime be perpetrated against him. 'I am glad to hear that you are now off the Sick List and beginning again to get on to your work,' he wrote. 'If you steadily stick at this you will find it in the end the best protection from annoyances such as you seem to have to submit to, from what you have written to your mother. I shall try as soon as possible to come up and see you, when you can explain if necessary more exactly what you have to complain of. Of course it is a very disagreeable position for a boy to be placed in to have to ask for protection against other boys, but there are some things which should not be put up with. If anything occurs that you feel any difficulty in writing about to your mother let me know or merely say that you think it better that I should see you and talk about it and I will come. As to mere petty bullying you may be able to grin and bear it – but certainly on no account put up with any absolute acts or attempts at indecency such as is well known are not unheard of at schools. You may feel quite confident that we will protect you completely against any unpleasant consequences to yourself if you resist all evil influences to the best of your ability, and do not hesitate to let it be known that you will not submit to what you feel you should resist.'

Lytton was both grateful and amused by his father's letter, which provided him with a much-needed sense of security and a resilience against his afflictions. What he wrote in reply shows clearly the extent and nature of this gratitude, intermingled with some slight irony – as a refuge from humiliation – and other sentiments, possibly a hangover from Abbotsholme, the biblical overtones of which Dr Arnold himself might have approved:

My dear Papa,

I think mine is a case of 'petty bullying' so I will to the best of my ability grin and bear it, which, I think, is the only thing to be done.

As to the other matter all I know is that conversations frequently take place without any regard to decency, but whether it is carried on further than this I do not know as I have only been here such a short time. But I hope that matters will clear up, and that I will have a happy issue out of my difficulties. . . .

Your letter cheered me greatly for you see I am not *very* happy and its so nice to feel there's a place from where I can be sure of help in time of need.

After his first term the bullying diminished and Lytton was able gradually to integrate himself with the continuing flux of school life. Soon we hear of him entering chess competitions, joining 'a glee society and on Saturday evenings we sing glees, which is rather amusing' (21 October 1894), and being dragooned into the choir – 'every Sunday – arrayed in a white robe I stalk into the chapel – feeling most grand!' And he reassures his mother: 'Yes, things are getting smoother now which is a great comfort.' In particular the amateur theatricals, which he had always enjoyed and which enabled him to exploit his idiosyncrasies to popular effect, presented him at Leamington with a welcome means of self-escape. His correspondence home gives pictures of him at one time or another acting in Sheridan's farce *The Critic* ('I come in at the end as Tilburina, stark mad in white muslin, accompanied by my confidant stark mad in white calico'); and in a production of *The Frogs* by Aristophanes ('The Scene is Dionysus and his slave being rowed across the Styx by Charon, who I am'). But even on the stage he was liable to be brought abruptly back to a state of painful self-awareness, as when, one Speech Day, a parent-member of the audience, startled by his first entrance, exclaimed loudly: 'What terribly thin arms he's got!' However, his acting ability coupled with his freakish appearance could sometimes prove useful. Once when he was walking with his sister Philippa who had come down to visit him at the school, a strange man approached them and began making alarming advances towards her. Realizing that he was no match for the man in physical combat and hating to make any humourless exhibition of himself, Lytton decided that ingenuity would be the better part of valour, straightway dropping into the role of a dangerous lunatic, and playing the part with such a pageant of convincing jabber and gesticulation that the stranger fled in terror.

Although Lytton's spirits greatly improved in the three years he spent at Leamington, various illnesses continued to plague him. During the notoriously cold winter of 1894-5, he was allowed to miss early school at seven o'clock and stayed comfortably in bed until breakfast an hour later. 'I also have milk and cod-liver oil at all hours of the day,' he told his mother. Despite these precautions his health again broke down during the following winter, this time so completely that he had to be taken away for the whole of the 1896 Easter term. After this setback he was only allowed by the family doctor to return once extra special arrangements had been made for his welfare. These included extra food ('My luxurious tea', he reported happily, 'is eyed by my fellows with looks of covetousness.') and indoor classes restricted to the morning so that he might inhale fresh air every afternoon to dispel the vapours. About this time, too, he learnt to ride a bicycle 'with some fluency though I have not yet mastered the art of mounting', and in the latter part of the day would go off for long solitary excursions about the countryside. On one of these afternoon bicycle trips he caught sight of a figure who was to play a minor part in his *Queen Victoria* and recorded the encounter in mock-Pepysian fashion: 'I also went to see the Prince of Wales, who had been on a visit to the Warwicks,' he wrote to his mother (21 May 1895). 'His Royal Highness was so gracious as to take off his august hat to me, and I returned the compliment. My lady Warwick looked very pretty but it struck me that her hat was not of quite the latest fashion.'

These regular absences from lessons acted as a serious handicap to Lytton's academic progress. Considering the number of classes he missed over the years, his scholastic achievements are impressive. His reports show him to have excelled in mathematics, French and English; to have been fairly good at Classics, but quite useless at science. In the late summer of 1895, when he was fifteen and a half, he took the Oxford and Cambridge Lower Certificate Examination, passing in seven subjects altogether and being awarded First Classes in arithmetic and English. Lady Strachey, who had been in a great state of anxiety as to how he would emerge from this, the first major test of his academic abilities, was delighted with the result. 'The Exam is for boys of sixteen years of age and a First or Second Class is given in *each* subject,' the headmaster explained in a letter notifying her of the good news. 'I am very pleased to say that Lytton obtained a First Class in Arithmetic and English, and a Second Class in Latin, Greek, French, Additional Mathematics and Scripture Knowledge – thus passing in seven subjects while five are only necessary for the Certificate. I think the result is highly satisfactory, and is due to the steady way in which he has worked. If he had been a stronger boy and able to bear more pressure, he might have got a First Class in other subjects. I think he might work for this next year and take the Higher Certificate the year after.'

Within twelve months of going to Leamington, Lytton had settled down quite comfortably into his own individual routine. Much to the relief of the whole family, the occasional letters which Richard Strachey received from this time onwards contained nothing more alarming than bulletins of the latest botanical developments taking place in his son's window-box, while Lytton's correspondence to his mother tells of cricket matches, plays, natural history expeditions which were 'distinctly unnatural and could never become history', and all the usual topics of school life, including, not surprisingly, editing the school magazine. Many of his comments and observations reveal also his inability to enter into the boys' more hearty and athletic pursuits. He did, however, learn to skate and 'Now,' he informed his sister Philippa, 'I am certainly able to fly at a descent rate, but occasionally falling, when performing the most brilliant feats.' At most of the other forms of sport his failure was less spectacular if quite as complete, and he spent much of his free time instead composing an Ibsenesque tragedy 'which is not only blood-thirsty, but dull, so dull that I cannot read it myself'. Nevertheless he was obviously better suited to such sedentary occupations, and these, together with his fondness for using lengthy, out-of-the-way words, made him an object of contempt, amusement, surprise and sometimes even admiration to his contemporaries. In general, he was less at home with the boys than with the masters, some of whom he would occasion-ally invite to supper in his room.

Lytton's passage up the school hierarchy from this time on was very rapid. He gave up studying science, but finished in the latter part of 1896 top both of the Classical School and of the Mathematical Sets. Already, by the autumn of 1895 he had been made head of his house and showered with a multitude of rather empty privileges: he was entitled to wear a tin mitre on his cap, to sport a walking-stick, and empowered to take roll-calls and read the lesson in chapel – his faltering and falsetto maiden performance, taken from the First Epistle of Paul the Apostle to Timothy, being an exhortation to widows. 'The agility of my voice', he wrote to Philippa, 'is not particularly convenient in this respect; as at one moment it is plunged in the depths below, and at the next is soaring with the lark at Heaven's gate – much to the alarm of the congregation.'

Lytton's house at Leamington College consisted of some thirty pupils. As head boy, he was one of its five prefects, and allowed a room of his own.

'My four colleagues', he confided to his mother, 'are *not* specimens of great brilliancy. Gaitskill is quite a fool.

'F—— is not so bad, but, I should think, devoid of all moral qualities.

'Clarke is mild and inoffensive.

'P—— is a thick headed lout ——

'And then there is myself!'

It was characteristic of Lady Strachey, an avowed agnostic, to ensure that her son went to schools where a special emphasis was laid on Christian teaching. The religiosity of Leamington, however, was mercifully of a less muscular variety than that of Abbotsholme. The school visitor was the Lord Bishop of Worcester; three of its vice-presidents were also of the higher clergy; the headmaster, described by Lytton as 'somewhat of a crock', was the Very Reverend R. Arnold Edgell; while of the half-dozen assistant masters two had seen fit to take orders. For this ecclesiastical body of men Lytton had not a good word: with one exception, the Reverend (later Bishop) E. J. Bidwell – 'an excellent man as well as being a clergyman' – who soon perceived that the young Lytton was pleasingly different from the average, boy.[1]

The upshot of being encircled for so long by representatives of the Church of England, whose pompous mummery and faked emotions jarred incessantly upon him, was that Lytton, while still at Leamington, discarded his mild, unreasoning acceptance of orthodox Christianity, and embraced a rather hostile and high-principled form of agnosticism. His letters home are sprinkled liberally with bitter and contemptuous

[1] In a letter to *The Times* (25 January 1932, p. 17), four days after Lytton's death, Bishop Bidwell wrote: 'It is stated in his obituary notice that Lytton Strachey was educated "privately". As a matter of fact, he was a pupil of mine when I was chaplain and a form master at old Leamington College, which then ranked as one of the minor public schools. I never saw or heard of him after he left till upwards of two years ago, when, seeing my name and address in a communication to your columns, he wrote me a most delightful letter, of the sort that gladdens the heart of an old schoolmaster. He said that he had been wanting to express his gratitude (I am afraid little deserved) for years, but had lost track of me when I went abroad. He describes himself as my "somewhat way-ward pupil". He certainly was, as I quickly perceived, different from the average boy, but my recollections of him as a boy are entirely pleasing, and I deeply regret his pre-mature passing.' In his letter replying to Lytton (11 April 1929), Bidwell had written: 'I cannot tell you how pleased I was to get your letter. It is comforting to be remembered after all these years. Yes, *I* recall you perfectly as a boy, but mea maxima culpa I never identified the youth I knew with the celebrity of today.'

references to the men of God whose arduous business it was to guide and instruct him. A few examples of these passages, sometimes a little priggish or over-extravagantly aimed at farce, will convey clearly enough the tenor of his mind.

7 October 1895

'We've had rather a painful missionary down here, converting us to the true faith! He religiously presented me with tracts, which I religiously presented to the waste paper basket! . . . The general opinion here is that the man has done more harm than good by making the boys think of things they would never have before, and which they'd do very well without.'

31 May 1896

'Two of the masters are engaged to be married – one of them Mr Jones, the mathematical wallah – is engaged to a sister of one of the boys. The other Mr Suthery (classics) to an unknown. I am sorry to say the latter is going to be a clergyman – not so the former.'

10 November 1896

'Mr Suthery, the master who has distinguished himself by becoming a clergyman, preached on Sunday, not remarkably.'

23 November 1896

'Yesterday a special clergyman, very much like a goat, came to preach on Foreign Missions. He meandered through many a path of idiocy, and then quite suddenly – and luckily – stopped. I think he was seized with a sudden desire to go to Thibet and begin converting Grand Lhamas, or we would be listening with rapt attention to his bland remarks e'en now.'

Lytton's mother accepted such critical and uncharitable outpourings without comment, slightly apprehensive that her own politer agnosticism should be taken up and given such a satirical and facetious twist. But when he turned his strong anti-Christian bias from life to literature she was more responsive. It was now, for the first time, that Lytton began to read Gibbon, whose literary style delighted him as much as his celebrated dislike of religion. During his last term at Leamington he concocted an amusing parody of Gibbon's balanced Corinthian rhetoric, which is nicely overweighted by the triviality of the fairy story to which it is applied: 'The Decline and Fall of Little Red Riding Hood.' In this tale, Lytton's most considerable piece of writing up to the age of seventeen, Red Riding Hood is shown, having been warned by her mother against the savage and terrible beasts of the forest, setting out for her grandmother's house. She has not gone far when all at once she is terrified to behold 'the crafty eye, the sinister jowl, and the gaunt form of a wolf, aged alike in years and in deceit'. The crafty and malign creature soon banishes her fears, however, by chivalrously offering her flowers, and then, learning of her destination, conjures up a scheme of astonishing evil – 'as harmless in appearance as it was diabolical in reality'. He races off to the grandmother's cottage and there enters into a battle from which he quickly emerges victorious:

'At last, having traversed twice as quickly as Red Riding Hood a road twice as short as that which she had taken, he arrived in triumph at the house of the redoubtable though comatose octogenarian. History does not reveal the details of the interview. It can only be gathered that it was a short and stormy one. It is known for certain, however, that the wolf obtained at the same moment a victory and a meal, and that when Little Red Riding Hood entered her grandmother's abode, the arch deceiver, occupying the bed, and arrayed in the nightgown of his unfortunate victim, was prepared to receive the child with a smile of outward welcome and of inward derision.'

Once Red Riding Hood arrives at the house, the celebrated dialogue, amusingly recast, between her and the wolf leads swiftly on to the climax of the story. Having made the girl exclaim with innocent wonderment: 'What big teeth you have!' Lytton polishes off the ending with a single short paragraph couched in his rotund imitation-Gibbonian prose:

'"The better," answered the wolf, seeing the culmination of his plan coincide with the humour of the situation, "the better to eat you with, my dear!" Suiting the action to the word, he leapt out of bed and with incredible savageness threw himself upon his victim. Then he divested himself of his borrowed raiment and slipped quietly out of the cottage.'

Although this early penchant for the classical historian – whose writing was to influence so noticeably his mature literary style – is interesting, a far more significant taste in Lytton's reading habits was for the works of Plato. Here alone was he able to discover something which tallied intimately with the passionate and mysterious emotions which, from the age of fourteen, had secretly risen up within him. Once he had relinquished Christianity, Plato's *Symposium* became for him a new Bible. In this dramatic dialogue he found a philosophy of love, at once sympathetic yet strict, which seemed wonderfully pertinent to his own confused state of mind. A short diary which he kept during part of November 1896 shows him reading the *Symposium* 'with a rush of mingled pleasure and pain . . . of surprise, relief, and fear to know that what I feel now was felt 2,000 years ago in glorious Greece. Would I had lived then, would I had sat at the feet of Socrates, seen Alcibiades, wondrous Alcibiades, Alcibiades, the abused, but the great, felt with them all!'

The love affairs which excited Lytton at Leamington were almost certainly platonic and inconclusive. Yet they stirred within him feelings of so violent and complicated a kind that the memory of them persisted for ever in his mind where they came to represent for him the ideal, limitless, intimate companionship which he sought to recapture in adult life. In this sense, these schoolboy infatuations may be said to have conditioned nearly all his later love relationships. Without any natural power of ingratiating himself within ordinary human society, he enhaloed those who seemed to sail through the heavy seas of life, untroubled by ugly apprehensions, calm, graceful and self-assured. This, indeed, was how he would like to have felt and appeared – splendidly handsome, immediately popular and magnificently un-perplexed. But since he could never bring about any such miraculous metamorphosis to transform his nervous spirit and sickly body into this vision of his ideal self, he did the next best thing: he endeavoured to mislay his remorseless sense of self-contempt in the all-embracing, all-absorbing contemplation of someone near to him with whom he could identify his romantic day-dreams, and even, for short ecstatic periods, assimilate his own being. While still in his first year at Leamington, he conceived a dumb, idyllic devotion to one of the larger, older boys, whose celestial image, by coming before and partly eclipsing Lytton's own personality as the foremost object in his mental and emotional horizon, induced a state of temporary self-oblivion, and cast over his world an incredible, twilight aura of happiness. Magically, he felt him-self released from the prison of his own hateful physique. This was his first real passion and it involved what he always considered to be his purest and best emotions – admiration, adoration and worship all wreathed and encircled by a wondering, inarticulate state of mind – 'that good kind exquisite abolition of oneself in such a heaven-born hero', as he subsequently described the sensation to Leonard Woolf. '. . . Part of it, don't you think, came from what we certainly can never get again – that extraordinary sense of corporal hugeness of our God? To be able to melt into a body literally twice as big as one's own.'

At the age of sixteen Lytton experienced another such delirious passion – 'the second of my desperate businesses at school', as he later called it. In many essential respects this relationship was similar to the first – unrequited and focused upon someone utterly different from himself, who for a time dominated his life and dissipated his morbid introspection. Lytton's weak constitution – a bodily expression of the fissure which seemed to be opening up between his intellect and his emotions – cut him off from the athletic pursuits of youth, and stimulated his desire to enshrine those who practised them with ease and efficiency. His choice of hero on this second occasion fell on a dashing young batsman, head of the averages, a rather plump, amiable boy named George Underwood, very freckled and with red hair which intoxicated Lytton during the bright summer months. Owing to his mathematical rather than his sporting talent, Lytton succeeded in getting himself appointed as scorer to the cricket eleven, travelling round with them to the near-by opposing schools, and lying in the long tickling grass under the sun amusing himself, and proudly assessing the quantities of runs, while the glamorous Underwood amassed, with consummate ease, extraordinary totals. Altogether it was a rapturous affair, entirely one-sided, which left him with a strong feeling of nostalgia in after-years. As late as September 1931, some four months before his death, Lytton recalled this romantic friendship in his diary with a sharpness of detail which suggests that the vision of it had often reappeared before his mind's eye.

'I was old and enormously devoted and obsessed,' he wrote; 'he was very sweet and very affectionate, but what he really liked was going off somewhere with Ruffus Clarke and the chic older boys, while I was left in the lurch, ruminating and desperate. How I loathed Ruffus Clarke! – a biggish, calm, very fair-haired boy, wicked and irresistible. I based my objections on purely moral grounds. I was a romantic prig, and the only wonder is how poor Underwood put up with me for a moment....

'Ruffus Clarke and Fell! I can see them with absolute distinctness. Both with that curious softness which some boys of about seventeen seem to be able to mingle with their brutality. Fell was handsome dark and slightly sinister, though not nearly so sinister as his younger brother, who, sandy and hatchet-faced, had devilry written all over him. Ruffus Clarke didn't care about prestige or anything else. As for me, I never knew what really happened – nobody told me – I couldn't even guess.'

From the early comments which he made about Plato's *Symposium*, Lytton appears to have been drawn most sympathetically to the character of Alcibiades – the man who, unlike Socrates, was never

harmoniously composed in his striving after a rather abstract and intellectual beauty, but who, while sensitive to the appeal of this disciplined
philosophy, was also susceptible to carnal pleasures and the lure of
political ambition. Like Alcibiades, Lytton was of a fundamentally
divided nature. Emotionally he might be fired by enforced restraint,
deriving a masochistic thrill from the subservient and passive role that
he was obliged to adopt in the various passionate friendships he formed.
Since these early affairs were not translated into physical terms, Lytton
was protected from slow disillusionment and made free to indulge
himself in pleasantly will-less broodings, enlivened with a highly
romantic turn of morality. Intellectually, however, he viewed the
situation in a different light, realizing that the type of boy to whom he
was fatally attracted tended to despise him, as indeed he despised himself, for being weak – though he might be kind and patient with his
weakness. The hero accepted his submissive devotion; he took without
thought his tremulous, abject offering, mixed with contempt as it was
in his mind. And when the infatuation had faded into nothing, this
contempt remained, cold and real inside Lytton, reinforcing the agony
of his own self-contempt, and forming in its residue the very fuel of
his ambition.

This repeated pattern of alternating submission and mortification
produced within Lytton a poison of accumulating resentment which
was to find its most powerful and successful outlet in *Eminent Victorians*.
A ludicrously ineffectual schoolboy, he remained outwardly timid as,
inwardly, his spirit grew more anarchical and embittered. Even as an
adolescent, the lustful germ of ambition fretted within him, making him
restless, discontent. By the end of 1896, being no longer in love with his
cricketer, he was eager to quit this 'semi-demi public school'. That
holiday, there was much excited bustle and activity at Lancaster Gate,
where preparations were in full swing for a family performance of
Ibsen's *John Gabriel Borkman*, of which William Archer's translation
had just appeared. Lytton himself played the part of Vilhelm Foldal, the
ageing government clerk, with great success. This minor triumph
added to his confidence and strengthened his determination to leave
Leamington once and for all. Without great difficulty he prevailed upon
his mother to write to the headmaster and inform him that her son
would not be returning after the Easter holidays.

Arnold Edgell was appalled by Lady Strachey's sudden decision, and
did all in his power to change her mind, even persuading the school
doctor to support his plea on the grounds that an extended stay at
Leamington would benefit Lytton's health. But Lady Strachey was
adamant, no doubt detecting that the headmaster's arguments came very

largely from a simple wish to add to the school's rather meagre list of scholars and exhibitioners.

Lytton himself was delighted. The years were moving on and he was resolved not to be left behind. At Leamington now he was only wasting his days, marking time. On 1 March 1897, his seventeenth birthday, he wrote to his mother: 'I am quite appalled by my great age. The man who instituted birthdays was a criminal.'

The following month he left Leamington for the last time, prepared to enter a new, challenging sphere of life, in which he was determined to excel, and where those who had despised him in the past should be forced to acknowledge his sovereignty. Yet because the main flow of his emotions was away from the direction of his mind, sovereignty and the possession of power would never be enough. He would always push through curtains to privacy and want some whispered words alone. Therefore he went, dubious but elate; apprehensive of intolerable pain; yet, so he felt, bound in his adventuring to conquer after huge suffering, bound surely to discover in the end his twofold desire for ascendancy and perfect, fulfilled love.

CHAPTER III

Liverpool

'The truth is I want *companionship*.'
Lytton Strachey –
Diary (April 1898)

I

PREPARATIONS

For six months after leaving Leamington College Lytton prepared himself both physically and academically for the university life that awaited him. Every week he would go off to perform isometrics before a Scottish doctor who had devised an elaborate system of weights and pulleys to develop his muscles. He also pursued his studies under the tuition of his sister Dorothy, the part-time mistress at Allenswood, who coached him especially in English, History and French.

There were times during these months when he bitterly regretted his decision to quit school. He missed the comradeship, the endless activity, colour and excitement. Now, buried alive in the towering edifice of Lancaster Gate, a vague and universal feeling of unhappiness preserved him dimly, like a dried-up flower on a pad of blotting paper. In the blackest moments of depression, his general air of sadness thickened appreciably, and a sickening sense of his own miserable weakness and inadequacy would rise up high into his lungs and stifle him. From the critical age of puberty, his emotions had turned inwards and now fed on themselves. Even the splendours of Rothiemurchus no longer eased his dissatisfaction as once they had. Nature was too vapid, too vegetable. She had only sublimities and vastitudes and water and leaves. His desires were for something more intimate and personal: for affection, for the right of an answering smile, an eye that understood, for the limbs of one person.

The impression which Lytton felt that he communicated to other people at this time was far from amiable. He was tortured by a need and inability to impress people. To those who did not succeed in drawing him out and proving their intellectual sympathy, he was cold and hostile. Mistrustful of all strangers who, he suspected, might be laughing at him, he felt their presence like a separating wall; and so as to avoid becoming vulnerable to their disapproval he retreated into a limbo of remote absorption, forbidding and unconciliatory. He hated what he considered to be the smug and trivial mediocrity of most people. What right had they, his obvious intellectual inferiors, to feel so self-satisfied? He did not admire them, and he refused to compromise with their ways. Already, at seventeen, he longed to consume them all utterly, to make them squirm and twist in their seats with his derision. And even from his silence they felt the radiating scintilla of his contempt – and returned it.

Something of the impression that could be conveyed by his odd adolescent looks and undeveloped, critically apprehensive nature has been recorded by Graham Robertson, who first met him about this time and felt for him a strong dislike which, as he was aware, was equally strongly reciprocated. 'I so seldom actively dislike anyone that, when I do, the change and novelty are quite a little treat to me,' Graham Robertson wrote to a friend many years later, recalling the incident. 'This boon was vouchsafed to me in full measure by Lytton Strachey. This statement is really unfair both to him and to myself, as he was a mere boy of eighteen or nineteen when we came across each other, with all his laurels yet ungathered and his character (presumably) unformed, but in its unformed condition it was, to me, singularly objectionable, and we violently disliked each other – if violence in any form could be attributed to so limp and flaccid a being as was the Lytton of those days. As to the "strong, deep voice" mentioned by Max as reserved for his intimates, my meeting with him was during a three days' stay with his family . . . I suppose his parents, brothers and sisters must be reckoned among his intimates, but I never heard him address them otherwise than in a breathless squeak of an asthmatic rabbit. Voices were not the family strong point. I think they all talked so continuously as to have exhausted the small allotment of voice originally accorded to them.

'Lytton certainly made good later on and must have developed considerably in after years, but we never met again, I think by mutual consent, except once, when his charming father dragged the reluctant Lytton with him.'

In September Lytton took and passed the Preliminary Examination of the Victoria University of Manchester. To Dorothy Strachey, who had written to offer her congratulations, he replied jokingly: 'Let me add my congratulations for your admirable coaching, and also let me bring before you the fact that it is AGAINST MY PRINCIPLES to fail in an examination.'

Since Lytton was still rather young to go up directly to Oxford, his mother decided that he should first attend a smaller university where he could make good some of the time he had lost in illness and get used to undergraduate life. Luckily, the family had a special connexion with Liverpool University College (as it then was) through Lytton's cousin, Sir Charles Strachey, a civil servant and a man of formidable idiosyncratic scholarship, largely responsible for the creation of pre-Commonwealth Nigeria. Besides – like so many of his relatives – devoting much of his spare time to a reconstruction of the family history, he also pursued assiduously a series of investigations into the lives of gipsies, on unsuspecting bands of whom he would without warning descend, observing them from camouflage, then emerging into the open to cross-question them and set up his living-quarters in the nearest possible proximity. In a lucid interval from these hobbies he had found time, some five years previously, to marry Ada Raleigh, sister of that most spirited of professional critics, Professor Walter Raleigh. It was because of Raleigh's position as King Alfred Professor of English Literature there that Lytton was sent by his mother in October 1897 to Liverpool University College, where he was to remain for the next two years.

2

FIVE BURLY MEN

The subjects which Lytton studied at Liverpool were Greek, Latin, mathematics, history and English literature. 'Five burly men spend their days in lecturing me,' he told his mother, 'so I really ought to be well instructed.' The best lecturer of all these, he added, was Walter Raleigh himself, who taught him English literature: 'He is thoroughly good.'

Lytton soon grew friendly with Raleigh who, besides being his foremost lecturer, also became the chief and most influential figure in his life before he went up to Cambridge. His wife, too, delighted Lytton with her outspokenness and frank iconoclasm. 'What do you think of Mrs Raleigh?' he once asked a friend. 'Don't you like her brimstone and vitriol? Have you talked to her about [Bertrand] Russell? They hate each other like poison; he's a moralist, and she's an anarchist. And secretly I'm on her side.' Raleigh's own disposition was one likely to appeal to most young men of intelligence and literary sensibility. He came as a distinct relief from the more pedantic, fussy type of don. It was difficult to think of anyone less capable of that sort of pedagogic brutality which finds some place in all universities. There existed, also, much that was similar in their two temperaments. Both loved literature, but distrusted social culture and academic pedantry. Both admired men of action more than men of letters. Both, in spite of irregular and romantic imaginations, became scholarly classical critics.

In Raleigh's mercurial personality Lytton found much that tallied with his own mixed feelings towards the world. Now nearing his forties, Raleigh had already written books on *The English Novel*, on *Robert Louis Stevenson* and on *Style* – all of which the young Lytton had read and liked – and was now working on a study of Milton. His writing, however, though painstaking, intelligent and often charming, lacked ballast and real originality. He had the flair of the artist for a fine phrase, but tended to suppress his buoyant powers of imagination in the supposed interests of promoting sound literary instruction. In contrast to this rather sober application and practice, he nourished a secret inner faith, he once admitted, 'not in refinement and scholarly elegance, those are only a game, but in blood feuds, and the chase of wild beasts, and marriage by capture. In carrying this last savage habit into effect there would be an irresistible dramatic temptation to select the bluest lady of them all.'

This quotation, with its fanciful longing for a state of super-reality heightened with appropriately wry melodramatic side-effects, reveals the frustrated soul of a don; for in proportion as most dons feel themselves futile they admire the man of action. Yet Raleigh was a don with just a dash of genius, who had landed up in what was, by and large, his most equitable position in the world. Such an interpretation of his character he himself would have found quite unacceptable, even unrecognizable. Despite a fine professional career at Liverpool, and later at the universities of Glasgow and Oxford, he had induced within himself a sincere but totally fallacious conviction that, by virtue of his over-bold and audacious spirit, he was for ever being threatened with dismissal from one academic post after another. It was a psychological device by which he reconciled himself to his steady doctrinal career. On one side he recoiled in instinctive distaste from the remorseless insensitivity of the world at large; and on the other he rebelled inwardly against the miserably safe, cloistered existence to which he was forced to subscribe. In place of the crude and sordid extramural reality, he substituted a mental vision of some Elysian fairyland whose sportive joys were perpetually being denied him. His response to literature was genuine and personal, but it represented an inferior alternative to action, and he always believed that 'the word was cousin to the deed'. The self-contempt which rose up within him whenever he allowed his thoughts to centre on his own career took the literary form of debunking parasitic writing – the name by which he used to refer to his own criticism. Books on books, being disconnected or at least one remove from action, must by their very nature be too trivial and indirect, since the principal value of all literature lay in recording and paying homage to great exploits. In his clearer moments, though, literature meant more to him in itself than a means of purging his own sense of inadequacy, which, when it turned outwards and focused upon the lives of soldiers, sailors and airmen, was given a humility at once naïve and touching.

Up to this point the parallel between Raleigh and Lytton was close. Had Lytton become a don – as could well have happened – he might have produced a literary corpus very similar to Raleigh's. But Raleigh possessed one accomplishment which sweetened the otherwise bitter inefficacy of his career and lifted him high out of the troughs of melancholia. When alone, immersed in the dire, unenviable drudge of authorship, surrounded by dead and dusty volumes of reference, his freedom of expression faltered and grew intermittent; but in friendly conversation, with its continuous, lively interplay of thought and feeling, his delightful exuberance and wit were at once released and would flow from him freely and easily. He loved an audience and excelled before a good one, however large or small, for only then could he translate literature back into terms of the actual movement of life going on around him. Few people who heard him lecture ever forgot the gaiety, the sparkle, the keen and pervading subtlety of his performances. Raleigh was one of those rare people who can address a large audience or a single individual with the same magical effect. Even his mannerisms, so well known, never jarred. First one saw the spread of his ready smile announcing that he was coming out with something he knew to be good, and which enlivened the anticipation of all who recognized it; next, in a single sentence, he would deliver his observation, clever, epigrammatic, conclusive; and then he would stop suddenly, as if in a delighted astonishment at his own shrewdness and fluency, and would glance about him as though to compliment everyone near by for their cleverness in drawing out of him such unexpected depths: '*There! You've got it! That's the point!*' Lytton, whose appreciation of the stage was inborn, was delighted by these accomplishments. 'Uncle Raleigh's voice is well suited for Blank Verse. Deep and Booming,' he told his mother after a series of especially fine lectures, with readings, which Raleigh had given on Elizabethan lyrics.

The Raleighs took a special interest in Lytton while he was at Liverpool, and would often invite him round to dinner, or take him out to concerts and theatres. The dissatisfaction which both men felt in themselves acted during these years as something of a common bond. But Lytton was never able to struggle free from his restricting inhibitions into the warmth of ordinary social conviviality, and though there was nothing dismaying about Raleigh's fervent and genial temperament, Lytton often left his company reflecting on his own introvert wretchedness, his contrasting lack of charm and energy. This outward diffidence was swollen by an inwardly accumulating intellectual arrogance, which tended to rouse some hostility among the 'bloods', that class of popular sportsmen whom above all others he wished to impress or at least conciliate, while yet still affecting to despise them. His low vitality, squeaky voice and long, ungainly body preyed more than ever on his mind, and made him behave in public with inept and artificial self-consciousness. In the company of a single, intimate friend he could be relaxed and happy, affectionate and kind. But whenever two or more were gathered together he felt as if he were on show, being stared at like some queer zoological specimen. His morbidity would then intensify, and though he wanted desperately to shine superior even to Raleigh, to occupy, by unanimous acclaim, the very centre of the stage, he was still more moved by the fear of failure, of public humiliation, his vanity and lack of supporting conceit conspiring to paralyse him into long periods of motionless non-competitive silence.

Both in his letters to his mother and in an occasional diary entry Lytton gave thumb-nail sketches of some of the other dons whose lectures he attended. The most eccentric of these was undoubtedly John Macdonald Mackay, Rathbone Professor of Ancient History. 'Professor Mackay is very weird and somewhat casual,' he wrote shortly after arriving at Liverpool. 'The first difficulty is to hear what he's saying as he speaks in a most extraordinary sing-song. When that has been mastered the connexion must be traced between the lecture and Roman History. Lastly, but most important, to prevent and curb shrieks of laughter.' The professor himself, however, never scrupled to curb his own outbursts of merriment, and as he soon grew particularly friendly with Lytton – having been at Balliol with his cousin St Loe Strachey – his peculiar mannerisms became rather embarrassing. 'Mackay's lecture on Greek History,' Lytton noted later on. 'This was dull today. M is rather too much inclined to think himself funny and laugh at his own jokes. He *will* look at me when he means to be witty, which is most inconvenient as I feel that I must smile and yet do not like pandering.'

Another don, hardly less colourful, was Assistant Professor P. Hebblethwaite, whose lectures on Greek impressed Lytton as being penetrating and humorous. 'H is quite a character,' he observed, 'very stout and lame of a leg; with handsome features and grey beard and hair. His eye-glasses are a constant source of amusement to me; and his continual "Yes?" which is quite unintended to be answered.'

The other dons were men of more ordinary stamp, and Lytton's opinion of them seems to have varied according as to how much he liked the subject on which they were lecturing him. At mathematics he had always been proficient, and he described Professor Frank Carey, the mathematical don, as 'thoroughly good'. His least favourite subject was almost certainly Latin. He found these lectures were consistently dull, while Professor Herbert Strong, who delivered them, was, he informed Lady Strachey, the least likeable of all his five burly instructors.

3

THE MELANCHOLY OF ANATOMY

The two years which Lytton spent at Liverpool were among the most bleak and empty of his whole life. In his solitude he would often grow nostalgic for Leamington, and murmur to himself homilies on divine comradeship. Boredom and isolation engulfed him. He was quite unable either to excel as he had once dreamed of doing, or to find those few intimate friends whose presence would have rendered his lonely existence endurable. 'My life is a turmoil of dullness,' he confessed in his diary. 'My days are spent in a wild excitement over the most arrant details. The putting on of boots is thrilling; the taking off of a coat, hat and gloves more so; the walk to the College and back a very procession of agitations. And all carried on with a feverish haste, and a desire to be done with it. As for letters – the expectation of one, no matter from whom, is the subject of frenzy.'

His daily programme had about it a depressing sameness. Each weekday he rose at about eight o'clock and after breakfast he attended intermittently from half-past nine to half-past one his various lectures at the college, in between which he would snatch a hurried bun at the refectory. The afternoons were left completely free. With his allowance of one pound a month, given to him by his mother, Lytton hired a bicycle which he called 'the Graphic'. After lunch he would set off for prodigious rides far away from Liverpool out into the country, or else to explore some distant second-hand book shop, trying all the time to forget the misery and chilling routine of university life. In under a year he succeeded in travelling during these afternoons and the week-ends a full thousand miles on the Graphic. This feat – an eloquent testimony of his urge to escape from the place – was all the more remarkable since on Tuesdays, Thursdays and Saturdays he had to be back in Liverpool before half-past six to undergo a course of strengthening exercises under the direction of a certain Dr Blüm, who, Lytton explained, 'is a Swede, and decent enough. The system is entirely different from the Macphearson, and much more scientific. No pulleys, no weights, merely movements of the arms, legs and body, he presses in the opposite direction. Thus the resistance is regulated by the man himself.' Most evenings Lytton would spend alone in his room, writing up the day's lectures, and composing poetry; and at about eleven he retired to bed.

During his years at Liverpool, Lytton lodged at Number 80 Rodney Street – just across the road from where Gladstone was born. It was a sombre, dignified street of Georgian houses, full of rather sombre and dignified professional men with their middle-class families. Typical of this highly respectable and parochial district were Lytton's landlords, Dr and Mrs Alexander Stookes. At first they had been apprehensive of having a young student in the house, fearing that he would be rowdy and irresponsible. But contrary to their fears Lytton turned out to be a model lodger, quiet, unobtrusive and invariably polite in suffering himself to be introduced to all their uninteresting unliterary friends, the medical fraternity of Liverpool. Their relief and gratitude were manifest. 'The boy has proved a delightful companion and no trouble to either of us,' Dr Stookes wrote to Lady Strachey after Lytton's first term. 'We could hardly have imagined that it would have been possible to have a stranger guest with so little friction.'

With Dr Stookes himself – whom he straightway nicknamed 'Spookes' – Lytton eventually grew quite friendly. Together they would discuss literature, religion, sociology and all manner of other subjects. As an uncompromising admirer of Ruskin, Dr Stookes considered that Lytton's literary taste was not sufficiently catholic, mainly, it appears, because Lytton – under Walter Raleigh's influence – much preferred the works of Stevenson to those of Ruskin, whose endless over-emphasis he found tedious. The doctor was astonished, too, when Lytton gravely announced to him that, up to the age of sixteen, he had been a devout Christian. It was Dr Stookes also who first introduced him to some of the country's most urgent social problems, escorting him round a number of Liverpool's worst slums. 'Nearly every street is a slum in this town, except those with the fine shops,' Lytton recorded in his diary. 'There is nothing intermediate. Hardly anyone lives in the town if they can possibly help it. Pitt Street was painful to me in the extreme; it stank; dirty farriners wandered in groups over it; and a dingy barrel organ rattled its jargon in the yard.'

The sordid scenes he witnessed during these expeditions deeply offended his sense of the aesthetic and the humane, making on him a lasting impression which imbued his writing on the squalor and degradation of the Crimean War – composed many years later for his 'Florence Nightingale' – with an unusual simplicity and austere power. Sometimes he would venture out to these gloomy slums on his own, when the dirt and drabness of the atmosphere filled him with loathing, seeming as it did to mirror his own internal wretchedness. 'In the afternoon walked down to the docks and thence to the landing-stage,' one diary entry runs. 'The crowds of people were appalling. The landing-stage blocked; and *all* hideous. It gave me the shivers and in ten minutes I fled. My self-conscious vanity is really most painful. As I walk through the streets I am agonized by the thoughts of my appearance. Of course it is hideous, but what *does* it matter? I only make it worse by peering into people's faces to see what they are thinking. And the worst of it is I hate myself for doing it. The truth is I want *companionship*.'

In a vain endeavour to find this companionship Lytton joined several of the undergraduate societies. Tempted by the promise of light refreshments, he told his mother, 'I attended the University College Christian Union meeting, thus becoming acquainted with some of the students. A very good thing I thought, but why Christian? A prayer terminated the proceedings. The undergraduates are not, I think particularly enlightened, but as yet I have only spoken to the less advanced ones.' A little later in his first term he was elected to the debating society, where he had higher hopes of meeting some kindred intellectual spirits. The first gathering which he attended did not promise well. 'The subject is very dull,' he wrote to his mother, 'viz: "The Eastern Foreign Policy of the Government." So easy to attack; so tedious to defend!' For several months Lytton continued to go to these debates without ever taking an active part in them. Then, in March 1898, much to his dismay, he was scheduled to make his first speech, in defence of the use of slang. 'The day of the debate on slang,' he noted in his diary. 'I was alarmed, as I had only been able to scribble a few remarks by 2.30. The debate was at 4.30 with a tea at 4. I managed to put down some absurd notes and then, palpitating with horror, started off for the College. I arrived late of course. The tea was in the Ladies Debating Room which was a most charming apartment. I stood dumbly and swallowed a cup of tea. Then, after a long pause, while everyone else was talking, we adjourned to the literature room, which was soon pretty well filled. I was horrified to see the swells of the place such as Grundy, Burnett, etc., accumulated there.' Luckily Lytton's opponents in the debate opened the proceedings with the proposition that slang was undesirable, so that he spoke last, seconding a Miss Hoare, a lady with flaxen hair and a twang. For half an hour he sat there hardly hearing what was being said and excruciated with a dreadful fear until it was time for him to rise and address the meeting. Then, despite his trepidation, all went well. 'Fortunately for me,' he modestly explained afterwards, 'I have come to be considered a funny man, so that the audience began to laugh even before I spoke. Perhaps my appearance accounted for this however. I stumbled through my very short oration somehow, and was relieved that it should have gone down so well.'

After this initial address, Lytton delivered several other successful speeches to the society. But though the strangeness of his manner and personal appearance enhanced these oratorical performances on the debating platform, he experienced it keenly as a barrier to all that he most desired from life, lust and power, love and humanity. He wanted to be a superman, and he felt he was a freak. His humour, however, often came to the rescue, reducing into ridicule the superior adjustment of others to the humdrum and taking the sting out of his own humiliation. Even when his sense of estrangement from the common run of men was brought home to him with unexpected sharpness, he was able, retrospectively at least, to convert such incidents into harmless and amusing anecdotes. He was adept at anticipating and neutralizing the derision of bystanders, and, by the same token, minimizing to himself the shock he had sustained – transferring it even to other people. 'The other day as I was sitting in the drawing-room with my back to the light,' he narrated to his mother on one occasion, 'a lady visitor who had been to inspect the twins, suddenly entered. Rushing up to me she said, "Oh my dear Dr Stookes, I really must congratulate you on your *charming* children! So pretty; so sweet!" Without a word I slowly rose to my full majestic height and the lady, giving one gasp of horror, fled wildly from the room!'

Some companionship he did eventually find to relieve his solitude, though it was far from being the ideal, passionate union for which he yearned. One new friend was Lumsden Barkway, later bishop of St Andrews, a student whose intellect was set in rather a different mould from Lytton's. 'He is the son of a presbyterian clergyman, and is going in for that profession himself,' Lytton informed his mother. 'But he tries his best not to be bound down, and takes an interest in pictures and such. He is rather melancholy, and has hardly ever been out of the suburb of Liverpool where he lives.' Another friend whom he met at this time was a Miss Combe, the 'austerely flighty' headmistress of a large girls' school, whose sister had married Oliver Strachey's friend, Roger Fry. Miss Combe was – or of necessity became – an ardent cyclist with an inexhaustible fund of pastoral sagas (she would prattle on effusively about 'spring foliage' and 'autumn tints') and their friendship was conducted almost exclusively from two bicycles. Despite a number of long, unchaperoned and 'not altogether unsuccessful' bicycle trips together, Lytton did not really warm to Miss Combe. 'Women are such strange creatures,' he remarked. 'Miss Combe is not so pleasant. She appeared to me to possess the qualities of a groveller.'

The rather outmoded conventions of Liverpool society helped to sustain and intensify Lytton's morbid self-awareness. He longed to succeed triumphantly in human relations, but a mixture of intellectual arrogance and shrinking emotional diffidence prevented him from outgrowing this unhappy condition of adolescence, and added to his difficulties in attaining that partnership with a complementary nature which, by dispelling the encircling shades of his egocentricity, might have released him from what he felt to be an outcast state. Throughout his two years at Liverpool he met no one who responded intimately to his odd, secretive personality, no one who answered his innermost needs. 'Miss C is not good enough,' he concluded; 'besides I want someone who can go out for walks with me at any time. Barkway? Dear me, is that all University College can give me? If I could only make friends with Grundy or Bird![1] But my "habitual reserve" is too much for them. Well, well, well, perhaps I shall find someone some day. And then I am sure he – or she – will not belong to University College. Talking of shes, I think it is too much that one cannot speak to a member of "the sex" without being looked upon askance by somebody or other. If only people were more sensible on this point, half the so called immorality would come to an end at once. I wonder if I shall ever "fall in love". I can't help smiling at the question – if they only knew – if they only knew! But it is tragedy also.'

---

[1] Allan Wilson Grundy and Lancelot William Bird, two senior undergraduates who, in 1898, were both awarded B.A. degrees in the Faculty of Arts.

4

DIARIES AND DECISIONS

Ill-health continued to dog Lytton while he was at Liverpool, especially during the winter months. Early in his second term he was stricken down with a severe form of influenza and a series of agonizing headaches. He took to his bed where, looked after by Dr and Mrs Stookes, he subsisted for some days on a diet of beaten-up eggs and port. By February he had largely recovered, though he still felt weak, and his mother carried him off into the country for three weeks' convalescence. This time he spent reading Trollope and Beaumont and Fletcher, and doing a little preparation work for an examination which he was due to take later in the spring.

At the end of February he returned again to Liverpool and on 3 March, two days after his eighteenth birthday, he began a new diary, all his earlier endeavours, he confessed, having been unsuccessful. 'Many times before I have got a book and written in it my thoughts and my actions,' he explained. 'But my previous attempts have been crowned with failure; in as much as after 2, 3, or possibly 4 entries the diary came to an end. Another effort! God knows there is small enough reason for it. My other autobiographical writings were the outcome of excitements really quite out of the commonplace; but this is *begun*, at any rate, in the veriest dog days imaginable.'

This latest diary was also his longest and most successful up to date, covering a period of about six weeks. Though it contains some amusing sketches and episodes, many of its pages make depressing reading, being filled with much sentimental rhetoric and exuding a stagnant air of sick, nebulous resignation. One of the opening passages reveals elaborately Lytton's obsessive lack of confidence and of self-knowledge, and the wavering uncertainty he felt in the course of his own future. 'My character,' he wrote, 'is not crystallized. So there will be little recorded here that is not transitory, and there will be much here that is quite untrue. The inquisitive reader, should he peep between the covers, will find anything but myself, who perhaps after all do not exist but in my own phantasy.' Unable to contemplate directly his own hated image, he uses Shakespeare as a convenient looking-glass, Shakespearian criticism being for the most part an indirect mode of literary autobiography. 'Had Shakespeare any character? of his own, that is to say?' The answer, he goes on, is that he had not, and that Shakespeare was 'a cynic in his inmost heart of hearts'. Assumed superior cynicism, the endemic consolation of those spirits too shy to assert themselves in the

The Strachey family. *Back row:* Pippa, Dorothy, Richard, Oliver; *middle row:* Ralph, Lytton, Lady Strachey (holding Elinor's daughter Frances), Sir Richard (with Marjorie between his knees), Elinor (holding her daughter Elizabeth); *front row:* Pernel (with racket) and Elinor's son William

Sons and daughters of Sir Richard and Lady Strachey: Marjorie, Dorothy, Lytton, Pernel, Oliver, Richard, Ralph, Pippa, Elinor, James

Lytton aged three

full company of others, is a condition of egocentricity most prevalent among adolescents. The usual front of envious contempt which accompanies this type of youthful disillusion is very clearly exhibited in the next passage from the diary, in which Lytton pretends to rejoice in his enforced isolation, preferring it to the loud and vulgar conviviality of the extrovert. 'Better so, perhaps; in fact necessarily so. And there are quite sufficient of the other sort.'

The purpose of keeping this diary was to redress the balance between the glamour of his private dreams and the degradation of the public spectacle he made, by administering to himself cryptic, palliative doses of reassurance to bolster up his self-esteem, and by scoring in secret off those who threatened to humiliate him, specifically or by implication, in the everyday routine of life. Within its pages Lytton was tortured by no fear of making an exhibition of himself, of boring others instead of impressing them. It was, he points out, 'a safety valve to my morbidity'. Although no longer bullied as he once had been at school, his sense of loneliness was more hopeless and overwhelming, for in the larger multifarious world of the university he remained unknown and disregarded. As always when deeply unhappy, his microscopic inward gaze could not avoid focusing sharply on his appearance, and he gave expression to his misery in terms of anguished physical self-disgust: 'When I consider that I am now 18 years of age a shudder passes through my mind, and I hardly dare look at the creature those years have made me.'

This feeling of wretchedness, which dominated so much of his time at Liverpool, was further deepened by his repeated failure to get any of the poetry he was now writing accepted by the university magazine, *The Sphinx*. The poems which he submitted – sonnets and epigrams – are less personal than his diary entries; they are sometimes competently done, but seldom really original. The first of his verses ever to be printed did not appear until he had gone up to Cambridge. But though eventually coming out in *The Granta* and not *The Sphinx*, they were in fact written while Lytton was still at Liverpool and belong to this period. Entitled 'On being asked for a description of a Roundel', this piece illustrates the commendable degree of metrical skill which Lytton, at his best and least ambitious, had by now attained.

> *A Roundel is a thing that's not*
> *So very irksome to compose.*
> *It's something that one throws off hot –*
> *A Roundel is.*

The first thing needful, I suppose,
Is some slight sentiment or plot,
Then start off with a fitting close
Add rhymes (with luck you'll find a lot)
And, my inquiring friend, – who knows? –
Perhaps you may have here just what
A Roundel is.

Not all Lytton's endeavours, however, were crowned with failure. At the end of March 1898, he took the Intermediate B.A. examination and learnt two months later that he had passed in all subjects – Mathematics, Ancient History, Greek, Latin and English literature. His mother, who as always was fearful that his regularly recurring illnesses might have jeopardized his chances of success, was delighted with this favourable result. That summer, with a view to improving her son's health, low spirits and his knowledge of the French language in which he was no longer being instructed academically, she arranged for him to spend some weeks with a French family, the Renons, who lived at Loches, about a hundred and thirty miles south-west of Paris, on the gently flowing Indre.

Early in June, with his baggage and his bicycle, Lytton set out, travelling first by train to Paris where he spent one night, and then on the next day via Tours, to Loches itself. Twenty-four hours after arriving there he wrote back a long letter to his mother describing all the adventures on this, his first journey abroad to be undertaken alone:

'Yesterday morning I sallied forth from the hotel, and, marching down the Avenue de l'Opéra found myself opposite the Hôtel du Louvre. . . . After making a tour of the building seven or eight times I found an entrance, and, giving up my umbrella to a gendarme, was soon lost among the majestic remnants of the Ancient World. I found it all too difficult to tear myself away. . . . But at length, seizing my umbrella, I dashed into a chabriolet which conveyed me successfully to Saint [indecipherable]. The price of a commissionaire to look after the luggage was 5 francs – too much – so I essayed the perilous task myself. What need be said of the wild journey through the metropolis of the great Republic, the fearful jolts of the vehicle threatening at every moment to snatch me from my bicycle which I still held clasped to my breast? Twice we were nearly killed; twice we escaped death by a hairsbreadth. We reached the Gare d'Orléans a quarter of an hour before time and . . . proceeded to Tours (changing at St-Pierre) where I had lunch, and took a walk in the town which appeared charming. Thence to Loches. I was met by a jeune homme aged 19, a son of M. Renon.

We then drove in an omnibus here – 6 miles – where I was received by the family circle with open arms. M. Renon, Madame, Mademoiselle (15 ?) et bébé (fils 10). The rest of the family I have not seen, and I am not sure whether they exist. The house is charming, quite small, with all the rooms opening out of doors. My room is on the ground floor, and can only be approached by a door leading into the garden. Everyone is as polite as peculiar – much more gentle (in its true sense) than in England in corresponding circumstances. I am lured on to talk, and can understand fairly well, though the speed distresses me. . . .'

Joining more readily than was customary for him in the casual but almost compulsory conviviality that went on, Lytton soon became acquainted with the rest of the family who were constantly in and out of the house, in particular M. Renon's jovial younger brother who lived with his wife two miles off at Persusson. 'Apparently he is the youngest of the brothers and the best off,' Lytton wrote. 'He has only one child I *think*; and cultivates the vine also.' Of several of the guests who were entertained by the Renons Lytton would make short pen-portraits which he then introduced into his letters home. 'On Thursday M. le Curé and les deux Anglais came to dinner. The Curé has white fuzzy hair, a red face, a black gown, and an ecclesiastical hat. Les deux Anglais are called Ross and Chamberlain. Ross is short, wears eyeglasses, and knows the whole of Bradshaw by heart. Chamberlain is the image of the rest of the family . . .'

The scheme of Lytton's life at Loches was happy and simple. He rose and went to bed early – seldom after ten o'clock – and spent most of the day reading Gibbon, walking for short distances in the cool of the day, composing a blank verse tragedy, catching frogs in the garden pond and, during the evening, playing cards. Every day, too, he repeatedly mislaid, until finally breaking altogether, his spectacles. He also inspected the dungeons at Loches where Louis XI confined his unfortunate friends, describing them as very terrible, 'most gloomy and ghastly, with the walls covered with the inscriptions of the prisoners'.

Despite his general mood of contentedness, the un-English way in which the Renons organized their time struck Lytton as eccentric and did not greatly appeal to him. 'Life here is more like that on board ship than anything else,' he explained to his mother. 'I rise from my couch at 8.30. At 9 I have a petit déjeuner of coffee au lait and toast and butter. At 11.30 Déjeuner, consisting of lots of vegetables, soup, a small quantity of meat and strawberries. At half-past six is dinner, pretty well the same as déjeuner . . . I don't much approve of the French system of meals which elongates the afternoon abnormally and abolishes the morning and evening. Before déjeuner I do "traductions" which are quite harmless and amusing. After déjeuner I sleep for one hour – the rarity of meals rendering a vast absorption necessary when there is one.'

On Sundays the programme was altogether different. After a rather later breakfast Lytton would go with the rest of the family at half-past ten to church. There, as a highly critical member of the congregation, he observed dispassionately the various Catholic rites and rituals, welcoming only those opportunities which the communion ceremony afforded him of augmenting his infrequent meals. Ill-satisfied, by and large, with the entertainment, he would later write up accounts of these services for his mother, some of which read more like theatre reviews of amateur musical productions in the outer provinces. 'I sat behind the altar, at the very back of the building. From this position the show appeared tawdry. The robes of the Curé were truly splendid, but the tinsel, and the sham marble wallpaper were incongruous. A young man played vilely on the harmonium and the singing rivalled that of an English village church. On the whole I was not impressed, though I ate the holy bread like a martyr.' As for the Roman Church in general, he was sadly disappointed with it. It was tawdry and vulgar. 'On the whole,' he reassured Lumsden Barkway, 'I think I shall remain protestant.'

Far more to Lytton's taste were the pagan and pleasure-loving festivities celebrated later in the day. Often during these Sunday afternoons in summer a fair was set up in the market-place at Loches where the whole town, reinforced by the floating population of several near-by villages, would assemble to enjoy themselves late into the long warm evenings. In marked contrast to the stilted and inept formality of the morning church services, the atmosphere at these gatherings was happy and spontaneous. The sight of all this carnival, holiday merrymaking exhilarated Lytton, who conveys much of the delight which infected him in his letters home. Yet in his descriptions of the revelry he is, however sympathetic and exultant, always the spectator, never an active participant. 'An awning had been erected beneath which the people were dancing to the sound of clockwork music. It was a most amusing spectacle. The paysannes with their white lace caps, and handkerchiefs tied round their waists to keep their dresses clean, hanging on to their partners with both arms round their necks. When the music stopped they kissed and parted! It was a great relief to see all this happening on a Sunday.'

It had been Lytton's original intention to spend a month or six weeks at Loches, but he found the gentle pace of life there so congenial that eventually he stayed on a full two months. 'France is not so bad as it might be,' he admitted to Lumsden Barkway. 'I was not so absolutely dumb as I expected to be; the country is charming and the people most kind and polite. The only drawback I have discovered as yet is in what I call the "sanitary arrangement". It is dark and dank, and full of blue-bottles! I hardly dare to venture in – most inconvenient.'

He returned to civilization in the early part of August, joining his family at Ardeley Bury, 'a really delightful country house' near Stevenage in Hertfordshire. Here he spent several pleasant weeks doing nothing very much except reading Lecky, Tacitus, Thucydides, Thackeray and *Paradise Lost* which, he told Lumsden Barkway, was 'the best thing in the English language!'

In the first week of October, Lytton returned once more to the dull routine of Liverpool. Having passed his Intermediate B.A. examination, he was now confronted with the decision of whether to read history at Oxford or at Cambridge. In the past the family had assumed that he would go up to Cambridge, but more recently his mother had decided that he should prepare himself for entry into the Civil Service, and that to do this best he ought to follow his brother, Oliver, up to Balliol College. 'If your object is the Civil Service,' she wrote to him (4 December 1898), 'you are likely to be better prepared for the examination at Oxford than at Cambridge. So we have settled it that way. Your father met Mr A. L. Smith – the Balliol tutor – at the Royal Society dinner, and he says you are to go to him and he will put you through your paces, and advise accordingly – which is his function; and this you will do during the Christmas holidays. We propose that you should enter at the next October term, and go up for the entrance exam before the Easter term.'

Although Lytton greatly preferred the prospect of studying at Cambridge, he acquiesced meekly enough in his mother's decision. At the same time Professor Mackay, learning that Lady Strachey was considering removing her son from Liverpool at the earliest possible moment and installing him at a private tutory, himself made a sudden dash up to Lancaster Gate and succeeded in persuading her to let him remain at University College for at least another two terms. He suggested, too, at this interview, that her son should take a Balliol scholarship in the following November. But to this Lady Strachey would not agree, and finally a compromise solution was reached: Lytton would take his Responsions in March and then, in June, try for a Christ Church scholarship which, if obtained, would automatically make him eligible for entry to Balliol in the Michaelmas term of 1899. Throughout all these shifting and involved negotiations Lytton – despite his strong feelings on the matter – seems to have been little more than a passive spectator.

These new arrangements for his academic future were communicated to Lytton at the start of the winter holidays. Not surprisingly he was very subdued, and his spirits were further depressed by the ordeal of a family Christmas at Lancaster Gate, which appears to have been celebrated by the Stracheys one day earlier than customary, and which was something that in later life Lytton always strove to avoid. 'My time has been spent as follows,' he informed Lumsden Barkway, '– Dec. 16th–Dec. 24th. Preparations for Christmas festivities, and visits to the National Gallery. Dec. 24th. Official Christmas (very terrible). Dec. 25th. My cousin Charles and his wife Ada (sister of Raleigh) came to dinner (at which I ate and drank *far* too much). They afterwards sang a charming song called the "Kensit Battle Hymn" written by Charlie and Raleigh. *Delightful!* Dec. 25th–28th. Severe illness resulting from Xmas festivities.' The next day some of the family left London and moved to the Bank House in the High Street at Guildford, which belonged to one of Lytton's uncles who temporarily went to fill the vacuum at Lancaster Gate. The exchange was made mainly because Lady Strachey herself needed a break from the contagion of London, where the gas had to be kept alight all day and the noise and bustle were incessant. Though they were not in the country, the move was generally felt to be an improvement, albeit with certain reservations. 'The house is over a shop,' Lytton explained to Lumsden Barkway, '– rather peculiar, isn't it? – but charming for all that, though the beds are rather short and hard.'

When he returned to Liverpool in the New Year, the course of his studies was altered so that he might prepare himself for the Christ Church scholarship in which his special subject was to be the Early Roman Empire, with eighteenth-century England thrown in as an extra. In view of the development of his own later prose style, the comments which he made at this time on Gibbon's method of treating Christianity are of particular interest. 'I have been reading the Great Gibbon lately,' he wrote to his mother in February, 'and have just finished the two chapters on Christianity. They are the height of amusement – his attitude throughout so unimpeachably decorous; but I can't help thinking it all rather unfortunate. If he had not been so taken up with his scorn of superstition, he might have paid some attention to the extraordinary change which was coming over the world, the change from the pagan idea to the christian idea, which, however unsound the doctrines that contributed to its success, was still dominating Europe (I suppose) at the time Gibbon wrote. He might at least have cast a glance at the old paganism that had gone for ever. But he never touches more than the externals. I suppose his mind was unable to appreciate the real spirit of Christianity. The whole subject of the

Roman Empire is so wildly and extraordinarily interesting that I am hardly able to contain myself when I think of it.'

On 21 March, Lytton travelled up to Oxford, spending four days in a bleak lodging house, No. 4 St John Street, while he took his Responsions. He hated exposure to public scrutiny, and in front of the Balliol tutor for Responsions, J. L. Strachan-Davidson, he cut a weirdly unprepossessing figure, accentuating the natural oddness of his appearance with a nervously unpredictable manner. This ordeal over, he returned for ten days to Lancaster Gate, bringing with him his Presbyterian friend, Lumsden Barkway, who had just won a scholarship to a theological college. 'I wish I were you!' Lytton told him. 'I have Oxford still before me. Alas.' The rest of this vacation was spent more happily with his cousin, Pat Grant, in Winchester.

By the end of April he was back at Liverpool for the Easter term. Three weeks later he visited Cambridge for a few days in company with Walter Raleigh, who 'gave a most witty lecture on Chesterfield'. The more rural and informal atmosphere of Cambridge appealed to him far more than Oxford, and he wished deeply that his mother had decided to send him here instead. Already he seemed to belong to its peculiar environment, to have assimilated himself with its community, and his letters home are full of social calls paid on friends and relations. 'On Sunday I lunched in Clough Hall where the Sidgwicks[1] were present, also the Freshfields[2] who were staying with them. On Monday I had dinner with Miss Stephen[3] in Sidgwick Hall. The Raleighs also came and paid Pernel a visit in her chamber.'

In the third week of June Lytton left University College Liverpool for the last time. Although his years there had not been happy or particularly successful, he felt little excitement at leaving, for he no

---

[1] Henry Sidgwick (1838–1900), the philosopher and free-thinker, who wrote textbooks on ethics and political economy, advocated higher education for women, and, in the words of John Maynard Keynes, 'never did anything but wonder whether Christianity was true and prove that it wasn't and hope that it was. He even learnt Arabic in order to read Genesis in the original, not trusting the authorized translators, which does seem a little sceptical. And he went to Germany to see what Ewald had to say and fell in love with a professor's daughter, and wrote to his dearest friends about the American Civil War.'
His wife, Eleanor Mildred Sidgwick (1845–1936), the Principal (1892–1910) of Newnham College, was a sister of Arthur Balfour, the Prime Minister.

[2] Douglas William Freshfield, mountain climber and author, and his wife Augusta, sister of Mrs Cornish and eldest daughter of the Hon. W. Ritchie, late Advocate General of Calcutta, were friends of the Stracheys. Their house in London was in these years a hub of cultivated society.

[3] Miss Katherine Stephen, a cousin of Vanessa and Virginia Stephen, became Principal of Newnham, where Lytton's sister Pernel was studying. Athena Clough, her successor and Pernel's predecessor as Principal, was then a tutor there.

longer faced the future with quite the same brave spirit which had infused his last days at Leamington. 'The thought of final departure is
indeed painful,' he wrote to his mother (12 June 1899). 'Packing will be
a sad business.' Paradoxically, Lady Strachey, who was happier at her
son's departure from Liverpool, felt generally well pleased with his
progress there. Most important of all, he had passed all his crucial
examinations, and this in spite of being persistently incapacitated by
sickness. It had been a very creditable performance. 'I think the Liverpool plan has been a success on the whole,' she told him, 'and I am sure
you have been better off than you would have been at a private Tutory.'

At the end of June, Lytton again went to Oxford, where he took the
Christ Church scholarship examination. From here he returned straightway to Lancaster Gate to spend a fortnight resting after some vaccina-
tions which his mother had arranged for the family doctor to give him.
Then, as soon as he was strong and well enough, he travelled up alone to
Rothiemurchus, where he stayed in lodgings, having meals with and
being looked after by one of his aunts, until early August. 'In the evening, when the sun is setting, one cannot help being a little sad,' he wrote
in the course of a rather stilted rhapsody addressed to Lumsden Barkway, but one which nevertheless does convey something of his very
genuine pangs of nostalgia, 'it is the sadness of regret. The days of childhood, with their passionate pains and pleasures, are with us; days nearer
to us, too, with their precious moments of bitterness and love; and the
present day that is fading beneath the hills for ever.' Also fading from
immediate prominence were the less aesthetic problems, the coarser
tribulations and worries of his contemporary existence. His examinations
no longer seemed so important, only slightly absurd. He idled pleasantly
through these summer days indulging himself in delicious retrospective
emotions, and soon he was feeling both happier and more philo-
sophically sad than at any time since leaving school. It was all very
satisfactory, to float along in a timeless chimera of recaptured sensations.
'Here, among the mountains,' he wrote, 'the Vision of Balliol itself
seems to dwindle and appear insignificant.'

The actuality of Balliol was also, unknown to Lytton, fast dwindling.
While he was in Rothiemurchus the result of his entrance examination
came through. In the course of a long letter to Lady Strachey, J. L.
Strachan-Davidson wrote:

'We have read the papers, and have come to the conclusion that the
Essay is decidedly promising, but that the Classical work is insufficient.
The Latin Translation was fair but the Greek was not up to the mark,
and the Latin Prose was bad.

'I am not sure that this disappointment will not prove all for the best.

I was struck by the extreme shyness and nervousness displayed by Mr Strachey, and much doubt whether he would be happy in a large College like Balliol. I am afraid that the pace would be too quick for him, and that he would find himself outside of the life and society of the place.'

Lytton would probably be happier, Strachan-Davidson continued, at some smaller college in Oxford. As a more suitable alternative to Balliol he suggested Lincoln College which, with his own special re-commendation, would almost certainly accept him. This college, he explained, consisted of about sixty-five undergraduates, most of whom had not passed through the great public schools, and its more modest and intimate climate would, for that reason, be far better for a boy like Lytton, silent, maladroit and of a literary turn.

Lady Strachey was both angry and bitterly disappointed at this exclusion of her son from Balliol, based, she felt convinced, more on a superficial and inaccurate estimate of his character than on the quality of his written work. She rejected absolutely the notion that Lytton would be happier or better placed at Lincoln College, and in her strongly worded reply to Strachan-Davidson she drew a shrewd and interesting analysis of Lytton's peculiar personality, giving due atten-tion to that hard but concealed inner core of his determination to pre-vail. 'I am sure you are mistaken in your diagnosis of his disposition,' she wrote, 'though I am not surprised at the impression produced. He has a very unfortunate manner which was no doubt at its worst in circumstances where a certain amount of nervousness is not inexcusable; but as a matter of fact it is more manner than anything else; he is both self-reliant and equable in a rather unusual degree. He has hitherto got on exceedingly well with other boys and young men wherever he has been placed, so that I should not feel very anxious about his eventually settling down comfortably in such a society as that of Balliol. At any rate, in sending him to College we look for the advantage to be gained by a larger, fuller life than would be obtained in one of the smaller colleges.'

Up in Scotland Lytton received the news of his non-acceptance by Balliol with mixed feelings. On first reading Strachan-Davidson's letter it seemed to him as if the 'comble des horreurs' had indeed arrived. He hated failure of any kind and, as he had told his sister Dorothy, it was AGAINST HIS PRINCIPLES to miss the mark in an examination. But once he ceased to brood over his personal lack of success and let his mind dwell on the possible life which, so un-expectedly, might now await him at Cambridge, he felt far happier than before. By this time his mother had made up her mind to send him to Trinity, which, with over six hundred undergraduates, was the largest college in Cambridge. The prospect delighted Lytton, and he wrote to assure her that 'the idea of Trinity is indeed pleasant'. As for Lady Strachey herself, once she had overcome her initial disappointment she was reconciled, even optimistic about the new plan. She could no longer see her son so clearly in the dual role of Lord Lytton, but perhaps, might he not just conceivably be another Lord Tennyson? 'I think you are to be congratulated on the change,' she told him, 'especially as it is a sign from above that you are to be a poet – the coming man in that line could never have been allowed to be anywhere but at Cambridge.'

Lytton returned to Lancaster Gate early in August and then moved down with the family to Selham House, near Petworth. There, surrounded by books and sisters, he spent his mornings preparing assiduously for the Previous Examination (then commonly known as the 'little-go'), and reading – in particular Swinburne, who was 'VERY GOOD', and Boswell's *Johnson* which he considered 'most delightful' – while the afternoons were usually passed bicycling in the country with his sister Pippa. Together they inspected the pictures at Petworth House, which Lytton pronounced to be 'excellent',[1] and visited Arundel Park – 'a most pleasant spot – very hilly and wooded. In the town of Arundel we were nearly arrested and thrown into jail for wheeling our bicycles on the pavement.' On another joint expedition they reached Witley, about fifteen miles off, where they called on Arthur Melville, the painter.[2] 'Mr M is painting what I daresay may be a chef-d'oeuvre – the crucifixion,' Lytton wrote to Lumsden Barkway. 'Most unlike anything you ever saw before on that subject – Realistic. Very bright colours on the top half, and shadow over the bottom. It is just the moment before the sun sets, and the crowd is coming away – the three crosses at the back – the Christ full in the light of the setting sun –

[1] The third Earl of Egremont's great collection of Turner's paintings, which he began in 1802. Turner often stayed at Petworth in the 1830s, working on his famous 'colour poems'. Sir John Rothenstein has written that 'at Petworth, the genius of Turner blossomed with an unprecedented brilliance . . . the last of the inhibitions that the busy world imposed on Turner were resolved, and he was free to see the world as light and movement. . . . Turner's sojourn at Petworth must ever be valued as one of the most fruitful episodes in the history of English painting.' There are, of course, many other things at Petworth besides the Turners. Lytton was particularly struck by two Holbein portraits – of Henry VIII and Edward VI.

[2] Arthur Melville (1855–1904), Scottish figure and landscape painter. He died at Witley of typhoid contracted in Spain almost exactly five years after Lytton met him. For a long time he had been a friend of the Stracheys. 'I remember him from at least 1893,' James Strachey told the author. 'In that summer when we had Syston Court, near Bristol, Arthur Melville made huge posters almost eight feet high of brown paper and other coloured paper in the most modern style to advertise "Mr Pecunia Sackum", a play written and acted by Lytton and Marjorie. He was a leading member of the Glasgow school – specially as a water-colourist in the impressionistic manner.'

his head forward – and *bright* red hair covering his face. It is rather magnificent and appalling I think. In the foreground in the crowd is a Roman Centurion on horseback. It is all very striking. There were some other most charming things – landscapes chiefly. He is a quaint man.'

But dominating all other thoughts during these weeks was the fearful, exquisite vision of Cambridge. 'As to Cambridge,' he admitted to Lumsden Barkway, 'I am looking forward to it with more dread than you. Though I am sure it will be charming in the long run – but the beginning I fear will be painful – as most beginnings are to me.'

Towards the end of September, Lytton left Petworth and, having in the course of the following month passed both parts of the little-go, he was admitted as a pensioner at Trinity. At about the same time, too, a letter from Walter Raleigh arrived at the college announcing that among its freshmen that Michaelmas would be a certain ex-pupil of his, an undergraduate of remarkable and unusual distinction.

CHAPTER IV

Fratribus

I think that in the chronicle of Age
The richest Chapter bears the name of Youth,
For in that fair and still unspotted page
Shines the incalculable jewel, Truth.

I think that Beauty, breathing on Youth's breast,
Alone can teach us what the Schools ignore
— How piled-up goods can never reach the Best
— How words are much, but eyes and hearts much more.

I think that with these Twain there ever dwells
Love, who for them with hands of gentle night
And deep, mysterious, and passionate spells
Has built a Heaven in this world's despite.

Lytton Strachey (undated)

I

A NEW ANIMAL

Now, for the fifth time in six years, Lytton had to face the terrifying ordeal of being a new member of a strange community. But on this occasion, owing partly to Walter Raleigh's thoughtfulness which helped to determine his immediate circle of friends, the agony of his isolation did not persist for long. At Cambridge he seemed to know from the first that he had entered a milieu which in many respects exactly suited him. The civilized sunny atmosphere was very wonderful after the damp breezes of Liverpool; and he was soon flourishing. Even his earliest letters home are unusually cheerful, almost jovial: 'Ho! Ho! Ho! How proud I was as I swept through the streets of Cambridge yesterday, arrayed for the first time in cap·and gown!' he wrote to his mother on 3 October. 'To my great surprise and delight the gown is blue! Lovely!' And again, a fortnight later, he was writing in the same ecstatic vein: 'I am enjoying myself deeply, though I have been here only a week and am just beginning to enter into things. Everyone is the pique of politeness and kindness.'[1]

Apart perhaps from Walter Headlam, the classical scholar, Lytton knew no one on arriving at Trinity until he came across his Liverpool friend Lumsden Barkway, who was studying near by at the Westminster Theological College. In these first weeks, before Lytton had made any new friends from among his fellow undergraduates, the two of them would go off on bicycle rides together, and have tea in Lytton's rooms. These rooms, like everything else at Cambridge, immediately delighted him. After an initial inspection he informed his mother that 'they are very nice – on the 2nd floor – the sitting-room facing the court [New Court], the bedroom the backs – with a beautiful view of weeping willows'. The following term he was transferred from these rooms to rather darker ones on the ground floor of New Court. These he did not care for so much and since, in the opinion of his mother, they were detrimental to his health, arrangements were made early in 1901 for him to lodge at a set of first-floor attics on Staircase K (where Byron had had rooms, in the topmost one of which he was said to have kept a bear) within the south-east corner turret of the Great Court of Trinity – 'nice and rather quaint with sloping roofs, etc.' Here, in what for unknown reasons used to be known as 'mutton-hole corner', he remained for almost five years.

Probably the only Cambridge phenomena which did not, even in these early days, meet with his approval were the dons. Many of them, it seemed to him, were too anxious by far to cloak their shrinking diffidence under a camouflage of arrogance and pretentiousness. His tutor at Trinity was J. D. Duff[2] whom he nicknamed 'Plum Duff', explaining to his mother that he 'cooes like a dove', and that he was fond of engaging him in long soothing talks 'chiefly about persons – ranging from Heine to Sidney Lee'. The professor under whom he learnt history, (Sir) Stanley Leathes – 'Mr Stand-at-ease'[3] – was, however, the reverse of soporific, 'rather severe, and hideously ugly, but very much on the spot'. Every week Lytton had to take him an essay which was read aloud while Lytton squirmed – altogether a most painful experience, but one which he later turned to good use, adapting it as a sensitive aural means of checking his literary compositions.

[1] Lytton first went up to Trinity at the end of September to take his little-go. This was presumably after the beginning of the Michaelmas term, but before the beginning of 'full-term'.

[2] Duff was an Apostle. He was devoted to Lytton and on his account, James Strachey told the author, 'put up with my subsequent unsatisfactoriness'.

[3] This name originated from his having been so announced by the butler at the door of the Lancaster Gate drawing-room.

With his long limp body, his congenital short-sight, startling pale complexion and rather prim secretive manner, Lytton was certainly a formidable-looking undergraduate, and one, from say Kipling's point of view, utterly unsatisfactory. 'His impact upon Cambridge when he came up was of a man from a different planet,' Professor H. O. Meredith told the author, 'human, but not of our humanity, who belonged in his speech, gestures, poses and opinions to no recognized category of adolescence or maturity. The Strachey "voice" (which became so deservedly famous: faint echoes of it are still discoverable in contemporary society) was only one of his "differentials". His ways of standing, or sitting in a chair, or helping himself to bread and butter – briefly everything about him differentiated him from the crowd. The impression was *not* however (*at least not primarily*) one of originality: there was about him not much suggestion of a genius and still less of a crank. He gave rather the feeling of one who brought with him the ways and manners of an unsurmised and different civilization.'

Inevitably such a man charmed some and irritated others. Though a few of the 'bloods' were actively annoyed by his freakish, affected personality and on one occasion attempted to duck him in the fountain, their numbers were never very great. Nor were the charmed numerous. The most usual reaction was to be more or less strongly intrigued: here was a new animal in their midst, alien yet inoffensive, whom it was not easy to accept and quite impossible to ignore.

Despite the initially weird and disturbing sensation he produced there, the Cambridge community, with its high proportion of vocational bachelors, accommodated Lytton far better than anything he had hitherto experienced. Within a few short weeks he had already struck up several new and permanently valuable friendships; and during the six years he was resident there, the number of his friends increased as his personal prestige and influence within the university steadily widened. These often lifelong companionships – similar in some respects to those of Edward FitzGerald – were, as Desmond MacCarthy once observed, more like loves. And for this reason, part at least of his career at Trinity is best seen in relation to those who were closest to him.

2

ONCE UPON A MIDNIGHT

Among the freshmen at Trinity that Michaelmas were three with whom Lytton soon became closely associated: Clive Bell, Leonard Woolf and Saxon Sydney-Turner. Early in Lytton's second term, and together with one other undergraduate, A. J. Robertson,[1] these five marshalled themselves into a small society which, in the opinion of Clive Bell in whose rooms it met, formed the original source of the celebrated Bloomsbury Group. 'The Reading Club consists of 5 members,' Lytton wrote to his mother soon after its formation (February 1900). 'Myself, Robertson, Sydney-Turner (very distinguished and with immense knowledge of English Literature), Bell (a curious mixture of sport and reading) and Woolf (nothing particular). Last night we read J[ohn] G[abriel] B[orkman] – my Foldal being considered very life-like. I died of internal laughter every 5 minutes. Last time we did The Return of the Druses and next time we do the Cenci – so you see our taste is catholic. They are all very amusing and pleasant.'

With Robertson, whom he originally described as 'a most entertaining personage . . . very tall, with a round cherubic face', Lytton's friendship did not develop far after he made the discovery that his father was a clergyman. But he quickly introduced into the group a sixth member, Thoby Stephen, who, he informed his mother (18 October 1899), 'looked a charmer, and the image of the others.[2] He has rooms in Whewell's Court. . . . He is rather strange but I think sensible and the best I have yet met.'

Only an unremittingly earnest band of young men could have survived such an arduous overture to lifelong friendship. They called themselves the Midnight Society since it was their custom to assemble each Saturday night at twelve o'clock. A number of them belonged to another society which met earlier in the evening, though it was probably a youthful craze for originality rather than any considerations of practical necessity which accounted for this dramatically inconvenient hour. Having first strengthened themselves for their late-night marathon 'with whisky or punch and one of those gloomy beef-steak pies which it was the fashion to order for Sunday lunch', Clive Bell recounts, they would proceed 'to read aloud some such trifle as *Prometheus Unbound*, *The Cenci*, *The Return of the Druses*, *Bartholomew Fair* or *Comus*. As often as not it was dawn by the time we had done; and sometimes we would issue forth to perambulate the courts and cloisters, halting on Hall steps to spout passages of familiar verse, each following his fancy as memory served.' Finally, feeling as though a poetic apocalypse had opened, they would disperse in silent awe and weariness, and wander back to their cosy, masculine rooms.

[1] A. J. Robertson was a brother in the flesh (i.e. as opposed to an Apostolic brother) of D. H. Robertson, the economist and father of James Robertson, the conductor.

[2] For two generations the Stracheys and the Stephens had been on cordial terms, and had a number of friends in common.

Perhaps the most unlikely member of the group was Clive Bell himself. 'A gay and amiable dog', as Maynard Keynes retrospectively described him, and a 'bubbler' in the opinion of Frank Swinnerton, he was full of boyish high spirits. His features and his fortune harmonized well with his richly colourful personality. Rather ample in stature, he was naturally athletic. His hair was golden-brown and covered his scalp with a waving luxuriance. The large, spacious, pink and polished face was fresh, though a little moonlike, and his forehead even now, before baldness had begun prematurely to set in, was intellectual in its smooth and lofty elevation. When he came up to Trinity from Marlborough most of his confrères had belonged to the affluent hunting and shooting set; and on the first occasion that the ascetic Leonard Woolf caught sight of him, he was strutting through Great Court arrayed in full sporting finery down to the hunting horn and the whip carried by the whipper-in.

In many ways Clive Bell was the exact converse of Lytton: a man of tremendous physical vitality, brought up by *nouveaux riches* parents amid the philistine world of sport, and nourishing a secret passion for intellectual pursuits. When he was his natural, breezy self, speechifying on about the hunt or the shoot in his unreflecting 'so-happy-that-I-don't-care-whether-I-impress-you-or-not' sort of mood, Lytton was swept off his feet and thought him splendid. But whenever he recollected himself and set out to play the part of the literary gentleman, he struck Lytton as more than slightly ridiculous. These literary and artistic pretensions were erected on the grandest scale imaginable. In due course Clive Bell planned to deliver himself of a *magnum opus*, the magnitude and importance of which seemed to justify the eternal postponement of its composition. Entitled *The New Renaissance*, this work was to deal with nothing less than every significant aspect of the age and so establish the cornerstone to a new and enlightened way of life. The magnitude of such aspirations astonished and displeased Lytton, whose own romantic ideals they seemed to parody: 'He's really rather a mystery,' he told Leonard Woolf (July 1905), '– what can be his *raison d'être*? He takes himself in deadly earnest, I've discovered, as Art Critic and litterateur. Very queer – and he likes, or says he likes, such odd things – Gluck, Racine, Pope and Gibbon. If it's mere imitation of us, the question remains – why the dickens should he imitate us? For he's not under our control, like Lamb.[1] He's even independent of the

[1] Walter R. M. Lamb, the elder brother of Henry Lamb the painter, was appointed Secretary of the Royal Academy in 1913 and later knighted. He was also author of *The Royal Academy* (1935). At this time he was anxious to be elected to the Cambridge Conversazione Society, to which both Lytton and Leonard Woolf belonged, but he was in fact never chosen.

Goth.[1] His stupidity is of course gross, yet he can be occasionally almost witty.'

Booming and rubicund, Bell was a good talker, though he sometimes spoke with a little too much self-satisfaction for every taste. Yet Lytton, a prey to parallel uncertainties, was not deceived: 'He's modest and retiring,' he explained to a friend; 'he's also quite unrestrained in general conversation.' In short, Bell's was not an easy character to understand, and one's feelings for him were always fluctuating according to his mood. Eventually, after knowing him for some five or six years, Lytton concluded that (1 July 1905) 'his character has several layers, but it is difficult to say which is the fond. There is the country gentleman layer, which makes him retire into the depths of Wiltshire to shoot partridges. There is the Paris decadent layer, which takes him to the quartier latin where he discusses painting and vice with American artists and French models. There is the eighteenth-century layer, which adores Thoby Stephen. There is the layer of innocence which adores Thoby's sister. There is the layer of prostitution, which shows itself in an amazing head of crimped straw-coloured hair. And there is the layer of stupidity, which runs transversely through all the other layers.'

Though naturally vivacious, the forced assertiveness and energetic congestion of Clive Bell's prose style – 'full of quotations from the classics', as Lytton described it, 'and curious Gibbonian sentences' – was to contrast oddly with his manner, especially his high voice and cackling laughter which, one of his friends remarked, was 'always trying to run away with him'. This disparity goes some way to endorsing what Lytton always sensed about him: that he was seldom as at ease among his literary and artistic acquaintances as he liked to make out. It was one of those curious and instructive cases of mistaken vocation. If only he had been content with the part for which nature had so palpably intended him – the country magnate, destined to marry an ugly wife and die at the age of eighty-four having spent his life doing excellent work prodding up his turnips in Wiltshire. But no; he *would* be an art critic!

Clive Bell had first got to know the other members of the group through Saxon Sydney-Turner, whose rooms happened to be near his own, and he soon became friendly with Thoby Stephen, who was also fond of riding and hunting. Certainly the reassuring presence within this bleak intellectual fraternity of someone like Thoby Stephen, with his disdainful athletic prowess and love of the open air, must greatly have facilitated Clive Bell's first bold, faltering footsteps in the mysterious new world of the *literati*. The two of them would smoke cigars and discuss points of hunting, watched by the others who,

[1] 'The Goth' was Lytton's nickname for Thoby Stephen.

struggling between envy and disapprobation, deemed them both very
worldly. 'Lytton, however, liked us for that,' Clive Bell shrewdly
observed; while Leonard Woolf noticed that 'in those early days, and
indeed for many years afterwards, intellectually Clive sat at the feet of
Lytton and Thoby'.

Thoby Stephen, the most mundane figure in the society after Clive
Bell, was the eldest son of Sir Leslie Stephen. His family background
was far closer to Lytton's than Clive Bell's, the Stephens belonging to
that same powerful and cultured stratum of the upper-middle class
as the Stracheys, and having distinguished themselves in many similar
spheres – scholastic, legal and military. In Thoby Stephen several of
these hereditary talents seemed inextricably mixed. He had come up to
Cambridge from Clifton, and while being quite at home in philosophical
and literary discussions, could also more than hold his own among the
bloods. Over six feet tall and of a somewhat ponderous build, he was not
ungraceful. He gave the impression of a sublime physical magnificence
which put some of his friends in mind of Samuel Johnson, without the
Doctor's infirmities yet with the same monumental brand of common
sense, the same depth of character. But perhaps the single quality which
above all others endeared him to Lytton was his natural and wholly
unselfconscious charm. So vividly did this charm affect all the members
of the Midnight Society that it called forth in them an element of hero-
worship – romantic feelings which were prolonged and even heightened
by his tragic death from typhoid at the age of twenty-six. 'His face was
extraordinarily beautiful and his character was as beautiful as his face,'
wrote Leonard Woolf some fifty years after he had died, and continued: 'It [his charm] was, no doubt partly physical, partly due to
the unusual combination of sweetness of nature and affection with
rugged intelligence and a complete lack of sentimentality, and partly to
those personal flavours of the soul which are as unanalysable and
indescribable as the scents of flowers or the overtones of a line of great
poetry.'

To someone who did not have the advantage of his friendship, and
so does not fall directly under the potent spell of this charm, there seems
to have been something rather turgid about Thoby Stephen. A photograph taken of him at this time shows a pair of fine, light eyes, but his
face, with its long nose and thick sensual mouth, is a little heavy. It was
really his strong masculinity both of appearance and manner, coming as
a relief from the bashful, disembodied intellectuality of the Cambridge
élite, which particularly enchanted Lytton, who saw him as 'a heroic
figure'. In a letter (1 July 1905) written to an Oxford undergraduate,
B. W. Swithinbank, he gives the fullest description of his admired

friend and unfolds something of the idolatrous feeling which Thoby inspired: 'He has a wonderful and massive frame,' Lytton wrote, 'and a face hewn out of the living rock. His character is as splendid as his appearance, and as wonderfully complete. In fact, he's monolithic. But, if it were not for his extraordinary sense of humour, he would hardly be of this world. We call him the Goth; and when you see him I'm sure you'll agree that he's a survival of barbaric grandeur. He'll be a judge of great eminence, and, in his old age, a sombre family potentate. One day we composed each other's epitaphs. He said that mine should be "The Universal Exception"; and mine for him was "The Forlorn Hope".'

Despite a strong sense of humour which helped to differentiate him from the usual muscular Christian or 'ape', as Lytton first described him to Pernel, and despite a fluent easy style of conversation and of writing, Thoby's mind was not especially quick, and afforded an excellent foil to any clever wild Stracheyesque exaggeration. Lytton venerated and idealized Thoby more than any other of his friends. Different in almost every respect from himself, he represented what was finest but for ever unobtainable in life, the perfect human specimen; and as an aesthetic ideal, Lytton deified him. 'Don't you think that if God had to justify the existence of the world,' he once asked Leonard Woolf, 'it would be done if he were to produce the Goth?'

In Leonard Woolf the Midnight Society had someone of an altogether different background, being neither recently affluent nor yet descended from a long line of illustrious forebears. The son of liberal Jewish parents, he was one of nine children brought up in London. His father, Sidney Woolf, an intelligent, hard-working, rather highly-strung man, had risen to become a successful Q.C. Later in life Leonard decided that he had always closely resembled his father; but certain aspects of his mother's more rosy, unimaginative temperament were also translated into his character – though in a far more intellectualized form – and gave rise within him to a peculiar blending of acute intelligence and little obvious sensitivity.

When Leonard was only five years old his father had died, and the family, from being reasonably prosperous, had overnight become financially insecure. This abrupt reversal of fortune had produced in the young boy an over-developed sense of high seriousness and an unchild-like feeling of responsibility. Despite all this, he seems to have enjoyed a pleasant enough childhood, though his exaggerated realism often shattered his mother's more romantic notions, causing much maternal distress and a morbid conviction in the boy, as their disunion gradually widened, that she cared for him less than for her other children. To some extent he felt more at home at his various schools than with his family.

Since he was naturally proficient at lessons, the general inefficiency of
the masters at Arlington House, his private school, could not prevent
him from winning a scholarship to St Paul's at the age of fourteen. But
before leaving he had already given irrefutable evidence of a severely
disciplinarian streak of puritanism, by dealing the low moral tone of the
place an edifying blow from which it must have taken several terms to
recover its normal equilibrium. The toughness and Spartan austerity of
public school life proved more to his liking, and he did well both at
games and work. During these years he was tutored by a fanatical
High Master, F. W. Walker, whose ambition it was, by means of an
intensive cramming of Greek and Latin composition, to turn any pupil
of rudimentary intelligence into an apparently brilliant classical
scholar. As a result of these battery methods, Leonard won an exhibition
to Trinity which he later converted into a foundation scholarship of a
hundred pounds a year.

As a freshman he was, so he later confessed, in a curious psychological
state. Having inherited a highly-strung intellect from his father, and
rejected his mother's squeamish sentimentality, he had grown up into a
rather dry, nervously unemotional young man, in appearance lean, with
a long predatory nose and pale ascetic lips. His humanitarian principles
were symptomatic of the repressed sensitivity which, in moments of
stress, found an outlet in the involuntary trembling of his hands. As
with the majority of men who appear to be guided by exclusively
rationalistic motives, the pendulum of his expressed emotions swung
through a fairly small arc. He understood the complexities and pre-
dicaments in other people's lives not so much from the imaginative echo
of his own feelings, but by laboriously deducing and evaluating them
through a process of ratiocination. To Lytton's delight, he never
actively believed in God, considering the whole paraphernalia of
prayer as 'one of the oddest freaks in human psychology'. For him the
pathos and the beauty of religious supplication was always to strike a
dumb note on the piano; and he was correspondingly deaf to other
such emotional appeals. His humanitarianism had a social, economic or
political emphasis which effectively divorced it from the immediate
affairs of the individual human being. At the same time, indications of
his subdued and latent sensibility are everywhere to be seen in the pages
of his memoirs, notably in the fine etchings he made of his friends.

In his dealings with women, the puritan self-discipline of his early
years brought out a repressive fastidiousness which applied the final
stranglehold to that genuine poetic element within him vainly struggling
to free itself. With his strong ethical feelings, he fitted well into the thin
intellectual gatherings at Cambridge, and it was he whom Lytton

singled out from among his new friends to act as his confessor, the one man to whom, during his first three years at Cambridge, he confided almost all his secret thoughts and passions. Such an outlet to his feelings would, Lytton felt, provide the relief which his early diaries had failed to give him. For diaries, as he now knew, tended to redouble one's self-preoccupation. Through some communion with a sympathetic but objective friend, he might, on the other hand, succeed in transferring – perhaps even permanently – some part of that onerous burden of isolation which afflicted him. The reasoning was sound; but the choice of Leonard Woolf was only partially successful. He had, of course, much to recommend him – a good brain, a lack of doctrinal religious prejudice, a detachment of manner. But his puritanism stood out as an insuperable obstacle to complete and spontaneous confidence. Often Lytton would tease him about it, suggesting that he should join a League for the Advancement of Social Purity, or refusing to send him 'an Etude quasi sadiste' which he had written, 'as I'm afraid you might think it improper'. Leonard Woolf always reacted indignantly to such jibes: Lytton's remark about a League for the Advancement of Social Purity was *not* amusing; of course he must send him the poem. But whenever Lytton tested him with some especially spicy or obscene piece of gossip, he would sense Leonard's fractional yet automatic and uncontrollable recoil. No amount of teasing or criticism could bring about that spirit of absolute unrestricted toleration and enlightenment for which he sought: 'It is hopeless,' he told his brother James, his next confessor but one, '– what can one expect in even a remote future, when *Woolf* thinks that people ought to be "punished" for incest.'

The remaining member of the Midnight Society, Saxon Sydney-Turner, in several respects resembled Lytton more closely. As undergraduates, both were retiring, scholarly and widely read, their minds, like protective antennae, cautiously exploring every inch in their immediate vicinity. But the periodic inclination felt by Lytton to withdraw from the boisterous vulgarity of life overcame Sydney-Turner to a far more extravagant and unqualified degree. During his first term up at Trinity he had shown himself to be charming and animated. But then, for no specific reason that his friends were able to ascertain, he suddenly broke down, relinquishing almost all interest and participation in what went on around him. As Lytton himself once remarked, he was still-born into the Midnight; it was only in those first months that he had really lived. 'When I first knew him he was a wild and unrestrained freshman,' he told B. W. Swithinbank, 'who wrote poems, never went to bed, and declaimed Swinburne and Sir Thomas Browne till four o'clock in the morning in the Great Court at Trinity. He is now . . .

quite pale and inanimate, hardly more than an incompletely galvanized dead body.' Those who had not known him early on usually found him a colossal bore, a sort of automaton of a man. But Lytton remained staunchly loyal to him, albeit – as was his habit and the fashion of the times – denouncing him mercilessly to his other friends.

Since, unlike Lytton, he entertained few romantic illusions about the world, Saxon Sydney-Turner felt no compulsion to excel in it. Whereas Lytton was skilled at reading aloud, Sydney-Turner was even more accomplished, since literature provided him with a complete system of vicarious living. From early childhood Lytton had been fascinated by puzzles; Sydney-Turner was still more adept at solving them, for they represented a deflexion, absorbing and consolatory, from the indissoluble pain and perplexity of the adult world, involving his mind without assaulting his emotions, and effectively diminishing the proportions of worldly problems to the neat dimensions of a crossword. There was always some part of Lytton's nature which rebelled against the need he sometimes felt for academic reassurance; in Sydney-Turner there was no such division, little compensatory yearning for the fulfilment of human love or individual supremacy. There seemed consequently something ghost-like and insubstantial about him. He moved quietly, indecisively, amid the shadows. Until the last years of his life, when in retirement from the Treasury he took dramatically and disastrously to gambling, his presence to many was either unendingly boring or unobtrusively dull, depending upon the company he was in. Tête-à-tête with Lytton or another confrère of the Midnight Society he would talk interminably on the most uninteresting subjects imaginable – cricket shop, or the technique of Wagner, or the use by Tacitus of the dative case. By strangers he was paralysed completely, languishing into long indefinite silences. From his early twenties, he seemed intent upon suffocating his soul, quietly, efficiently, and without even a brief struggle. Everything around him was kept in a static, monochromatic condition. The furniture in his room never varied, was never moved. He ate little, without relish and at unpredictable times. This slow process of self-murder was given physical expression by the increasing number of ailments which afflicted him and which were entirely symptomatic of his state of being, not, as was partly the case with Lytton, causative.

Signs of the self-destruction which he was determined to perpetrate seemed to be reflected in his fading appearance: short, thin, with an anaemic pallor and pale, straw-coloured hair. A portrait of him painted by Vanessa Bell in 1908 shows a sombre, precise figure, seated slightly bent before a pianola, and peering through his spectacles at some sheet of music with an expression of rapt, self-oblivious concentration. Small, bloodless and *effacé*, he might, Lytton always felt, have been a tragic figure on the grand scale, *if only he appeared aware of his tragedy*.

Nothing stands still; yet Sydney-Turner wholeheartedly, and Lytton fitfully, wished that it did. At times indeed, when his will-power began to crumble, Lytton felt that he might go under in precisely the same way as his friend. 'It would never do to become Turnerian,' he wrote to his brother James (October 1912), 'and I feel it's a danger that hangs over all of us.' And to Saxon himself a few years earlier he had written: 'Time and Space for you do not exist, and perhaps not for me either, who feel myself fleeting towards your philosophy. What this is you have never told me, but it occurred to me the other day, and though it made me feel very ill, perhaps I agree.' Even in his most wretched and pessimistic moments, however, Lytton never collapsed as Sydney-Turner had done.

With Lytton in particular, and the other members of the Midnight Society, Sydney-Turner did not retire absolutely into himself, for he still needed a minimum of human communication. He would listen to their talk for a time, occasionally interpose an indefinite observation, then wander off and ruminate at length and in solitude over what had been said. After a week or two spent chewing the cud in this manner, he would re-emerge from contemplation usually with some cryptic conclusion for his friends. 'He was right!' he might announce; or 'No, it won't do!'; or even, triumphantly, 'Her name was Emily!' And only after prolonged cross-examination could the others succeed in relating back what he had uttered to some far-off, long-forgotten dead discussion.

Probably he was the most exact and scholarly-minded member of the Midnight; and despite his taciturn, laconic nature, his Cambridge friends remained fond of him, showing by their continued affection that though he had tried to smother his soul out of existence, he had only succeeded in burying it alive. And occasionally Lytton and the others might catch a glimpse of the Saxon they had first known and who now lay entombed beneath a meticulously constructed carapace. 'He looks sometimes', wrote Leonard Woolf, 'like a little schoolboy whom life has bullied into unconsciousness.' And Lytton observed that 'he looks like some puzzled night-animal blinking in the unaccustomed daylight. Sometimes, even now, for a few moments, one realizes as one watches him that he still possesses a mystical supremacy and a sort of sibylline power' (1 July 1905).

One other friend Lytton made during his first months at Trinity, never so close but of almost equal value. This was George Trevelyan, the historian, who was some four years older than himself. Often he would be invited over to Trevelyan's rooms for breakfast and a lengthy walk; and when, on one occasion, he inquired whether – owing to another engagement – he might have the food without the exercise, he was curtly told: 'No walk, no breakfast.' Lytton found him very earnest, 'and somewhat patristic towards me', as he told Pernel. '... On Thursday I went to Breakfast – painful meal – with George Trevelyan. He is indeed eager – also somewhat piteous I think – and very virulent. I am to go again tomorrow! This although I insulted him by saying that I thought anyone who had been a Home Ruler was a fool!'

At other times the two of them would go off on bicycle rides to-gether, Trevelyan talking most of the time about Cromwell, Milton, the scenery, Oxford, Cardinal Newman, and the Early Christians. 'He is most friendly and kind,' Lytton wrote to his mother (March 1900), 'and very like what I imagined his father to be.'[1] But in time, this kind-ness, with its overtones of heavily affectionate, avuncular authority – so welcome when he still felt lonely and unknown in Cambridge – began to pall on him. It was excessive, patronizing. And even tedious, too, when, for instance, Trevelyan chose to explain that the pleasure which people derived from dancing came, not from the mere exercise, but from the legitimate physical contact it afforded partners of the opposite sex. Lytton did not like dancing, but it was hopeless to try and explain that his tastes lay in a different direction. 'He is very – I think *too* – earnest; and paternally kind,' Lytton wrote to his mother in the spring of 1900. And in subsequent years his opinion does not seem substantially to have altered.

3

PALPITATIONS, FRENCH AND ENGLISH

The Midnight Society temporarily folded up in the autumn of 1900, owing to Lytton's invalid health. He had come through the previous winter, for him, remarkably well. No chances, however, were taken, and, during the Easter vacation, he was sent, with his sister Pippa as chaperon, to the Albion Hotel, Broadstairs, where the bracing sea-climate, Lady Strachey felt, should do much to pull him round. Although in no way seriously ill, he there took on the air of a patient recovering

[1] Sir G. O. Trevelyan (1838–1928), nephew and biographer of Lord Macaulay, was an eminent historian and parliamentarian. His works include *The Early History of Charles James Fox* (1880) and a history of the American Revolution in six stupendous volumes (1899–1914). He was also an Apostle.

from some major operation – convalescent teas in the hotel lounge followed by slow, hypochondriac parades along the front to examine the sea.

'Broadstairs itself is charming,' he reported (19 April 1900). 'The sun has been out all day and the wind is easily avoidable. . . . I feel already revived. . . .

'The trippers are not as yet aggressive though somewhat amusing. We took a slight walk along the sands this evening.'

Later that month he returned to Trinity for the Easter term, during which, and from this time onwards, he was excused all chapel services – though whether owing to conscience or health is not certain. For other reasons too this was a happy term. Spring was in the air, and the world revolved merrily. There was always something going on. He went to listen to Stephen Phillips declaiming his *Paolo and Francesca*[1] in a sonorous monotone which hushed into expectancy the rustling lace and jangling ornaments of his almost exclusively female audience, but sent Lytton himself off to sleep. Less soporific, though rather more disagreeable, was a Newnham lecture which he attended, given by Edmund Gosse on Leigh Hunt. 'Law! He *did* think himself clever!' Lytton wrote to Pernel. 'After 3 sentences he suddenly said, "I was never in such a draught in the whole course of my life!" Katherine [Stephen] and Sharpley ran forward and screwed ventilators (apparently). And after a long time he said, "Oh, it really doesn't matter." Grossly rude, I thought.' This term, too, every Wednesday and Thursday, he went to lectures on Early Florentine Art given by Roger Fry. 'They are very interesting and good though somewhat abstruse,' he commented in a letter to his mother (15 May 1900).

When the summer vacation came he joined his family at a country house they had rented at Kingston Lisle Park, Wantage. 'The place here is lovely', he told Lumsden Barkway, '– in the Berkshire downs near the White Horse – a beautiful park and beautiful country.' It was while on holiday here during the hot weather of July that he was attacked by violent palpitations of the heart, which lasted intermittently until early September. A doctor was immediately called in to examine him, but could ascertain no specific physical cause for these attacks, which he put down to 'nerves'.[2] Sir Richard Strachey was also laid up

[1] At that time Stephen Phillips's *Paolo and Francesca* had not been publicly performed. It opened under George Alexander at the St James' Theatre in February 1902.

[2] It seems possible that he was suffering from what is called paroxysmal tachycardia. The cause of this condition is not accurately known, though it is probably of nervous origin and can be aggravated by physical wear and tear. The symptoms are sometimes very alarming, but it is not considered in itself dangerous, and may be treated with quinidine sulphate tablets.

at the time, and two nurses moved into the house, which was converted into a rather rough-and-ready sanatorium. Doses of digitalis and bromide were prescribed for Lytton, who was advised to rest for two or three months and, whenever practicable, to travel abroad during his future vacations. 'The disease is mysterious', he explained to Lumsden Barkway from his sick-bed, '– of no very definite nature – fainting and general weakness. Nothing is radically wrong say the doctors, but it has been settled that I shall not go back to Cambridge next term so as to make a complete recovery. This is I suppose the wisest thing – but I am very, very sad at the thought of it.'

Instead of returning therefore to Cambridge for the Michaelmas term he remained at home, attended by a train of female relatives, who forbade him the least exertion, even reading. 'Everyone and thing missed you last term,' wrote Leonard Woolf, to whom, in his letterless condition at darkest Lancaster Gate among eternal women, Lytton had cried out for the lifeblood of Trinity gossip, 'and I am sure the temporary death of the Midnight Society might have been avoided if we had had you to back up those members who are not afraid of late hours.'

By the middle of October Lytton already felt much improved. He had been moved to a nursing home in Queen's Gate Terrace[1] where Dr Roland Brinton, the family physician, gave him a thorough examination before reporting to Lady Strachey (18 October 1900) that 'he is more jovial and takes his food really well. I told him he could have a little light literature – after the business of the day is over – and before it is time for him to settle down for the night. He still has occasional attacks of palpitations – and his heart certainly has a tumultuous action – but I can find no reason to think that there is any structural disease there. So I feel fairly confident that all his uncomfortable sensations will disappear.

'He likes a little claret – but a pint bottle lasts him two days – so there is no excess.'

After six weeks of alternate resting, eating, drinking and professional massage, Lytton's weight increased from nine to eleven stone, and his mother was obliged to order an entirely new outfit, since his old clothes now failed conspicuously to meet across his manly chest. 'I feel much stronger', he assured Lumsden Barkway (23 November 1900), '– but not yet quite natural or ordinary – something of a portent or monster still . . . last Summer still remains a nightmare.'

By the beginning of December he felt well enough to travel to St-Jean-de-Luz, near Biarritz, in the Basses Pyrénées. His mother went

[1] This was what used to be called a 'Rest Cure' – invented in the 1880s by an American doctor called Weir Mitchell.

with him so that the journey should not be troublesome, and they stayed a night with some French friends in Paris. Then, having deposited Lytton in the Hôtel d'Angleterre near the shores of the Atlantic, and introduced him to some cousins living near by, she returned again to England.

The other residents at the Hôtel d'Angleterre Lytton found sufficiently tedious, but the countryside, round which he journeyed on his bicycle, was charming – 'blue sea and fresh air,' he told Leonard Woolf, 'and heat enough for anyone. The country is Basque and rather strange, with bullock-carts and things at every town – flooded with English of course which makes it more or less unpleasant. The only man of amusement (barring a decayed millionaire and a gouty Baron) is an Oxford person who teaches little boys and in intervals writes poems for the *Spectator*. . . . He gives me his poems to read (bad enough), and good advice (rather worse) and his views on Shakespeare (quite ridiculous). We talked the other day of people we should like to meet – I mentioned Cleopatra. He said, "I should rather see Our Lord to anyone else." I had to reply, "Oh, I put him on one side as inhuman."

'The people at the hotel are more than fearful. I often wish I was a snake and could wriggle on the ground. I have cousins here, whom I lunch with, and so manage to exist.'

The hotel was extraordinarily dull, especially at meals, when the few residents would seat themselves in order at a long table and stare hopelessly into a looking-glass opposite. On the table stood tall pots with some strangled, artificial chrysanthemums peeping out of the top, tall napkins and a few bleak cruet-stands. More dismal still was the conversation. Besides the tireless subject of Christianity, Lytton would listen daily at breakfast, lunch and dinner to monotonous golf and social gossip in appalling French. 'I have no one on my right,' he wrote to Lumsden Barkway describing the other inmates, 'on my left an old Irish squire of sorts – dull as ditchwater but good-natured enough – as I suppose all dullards are. He repeats indefinitely, and I dare say winds himself before he hops into bed at night. Next him an old maid – thin, and rather pitiful, then her two nieces – vulgar, *very* good, and *very*, *very* stupid. Poor people! At the head of the table a Captain (Caulfield by name) in the Navy – but *I* believe the Marines – or even Horse Marines. Terrible! Impossible to mention anyone who is not his bosom friend. As conceited as a cock-a-doodle-do, and as brainless. These are the English inhabitants of this house. Oh! I've forgotten one – Miss Roper, who looks like a governess, but who isn't, and wears curious tails to her jackets, and talks sensibly enough. I fear I am rude to some of them sometimes. I often want to make faces, and sometimes do –

when nobody's looking. Oh dear me! I live in hope of someone rich
and strange walking in at the door.' To lend further substance to this
hope he joined the English Club, where there was a fire, a few
papers and a good many more Anglo-Saxon dullards, drinking and
golfing.

The town itself, with its old narrow streets, its quay, its square, and
the ancient galleried church where Louis XIV was married, enchanted
him. But nothing happened there, or it seemed, ever had happened.
Increasingly, Lytton would escape into the delightful country. 'Imagine
the colouring of late autumn,' he wrote, 'the warmth of midsummer, and
the fresh air of early spring.' Often he went for long walks to surrounding villages and 'once I got on to a merry-go-round at a fair and
revolved to my heart's content'.

His happiest hours were spent bicycling among the hills and trees and
streams. He loved the wide expanse of sea and the mountains, both, it
seemed to his youthful romantic imagination, the chosen voices of
liberty. One day he went to Biarritz which, as a fashionable seaside
resort, was more towny and parady, though with a splendid sea-front
with magnificent waves coming up in a continual procession. 'Their
thunder was enormous, and their foam beautiful,' he wrote to Lumsden
Barkway. 'Have you noticed the resemblance between them and
Beethoven's music? I heard a Symphony by that great man the day
before I came here – oh! marvellous! – but appalling is the only word
to describe it properly – it grinds you to powder. I shudder with
emotion while I hear it – and so you see it is like the ocean. Talking of
great volumes of sound, isn't it extraordinary that some poetry really
makes as much noise as anything else? I mean Milton for instance – the
quantity of sound appears to me often as vast as that of a full symphony
of Beethoven or the enormous roaring of the sea. . . .

'Coming back in the train the sunset was miraculous – hardly
credible – dark purply grey – rose – pale saffron – altogether with the
mountains an effect of great peace. I wondered why all the heads I
passed were not turned towards it – but nature grows familiar and
so I suppose contemptible to country-dwellers – and this is one
of the advantages of travelling – one is woken up to the marvel of
things.'

Lytton's day-to-day existence was made much more congenial by the
hospitality of his cousins, Mrs King[1] – Lady Strachey's first cousin –
Irish and gay and bright, and her daughter Janie – married to a young

---

[1] Annie King was the daughter of Elizabeth Grant of Rothiemurchus (Mrs Smith of
Baltiboys). Her granddaughter, the daughter of Janie mentioned above, is Dame
Ninette de Valois, the founder of the Royal Ballet Company.

Irishman named McGusty[1] – an attractive and amusing girl with black polished hair, an olive-green complexion and a rather skull-like but youthful face. In the course of his stay they introduced him to some of the inhabitants at St-Jean-de-Luz, most of whom were far more interesting than the temporary English residents. There was a fat Dutch-Englishman called Boreel, with a made-up pseudo-handsome wife; and several bachelors – 'or people who ought to be bachelors – generals, bankers, loungers of all sorts. The man of business is Bellairs – half French and half English – talks French with an English accent, and English with a French, as Janie says, lays down the law on everything, says "damn it my dear fellow" a good deal, and is altogether a windy but not unimaginative fool. . . . Have I mentioned Mr Penny? a commercial gentleman staying here with a wife and child. He has, as he says, "knocked about all over the world", and now I suppose is settling down. His wife leads a sad life I fear, for even to us he is liable to give long lectures on the Roman Catholic religion and how to drive an omnibus. He is a Master of Platitude.'

Most interesting of all these new acquaintances were the Lilburnes, an amusing old Englishman and his Spanish wife, deformed and fascinating. Regularly once a week, and chaperoned by his cousins, Lytton went off to gamble at their roulette table, an occupation which he described as 'very soothing'. The chief attraction of these sessions was the opportunity which they afforded his social curiosity and powers of sharp, comic observation. On one occasion a note of keen excitement was introduced into the party by the unexpected arrival of ex-Queen Nathalie of Servia, at that time living in retirement near by. Lytton noted with keen-eyed and amused disapproval the ripple of thrilled obsequiousness produced by her regal entry into the Salle de Jeu: 'As the game was proceeding, suddenly "la Reine" was whispered, and everyone rising to their feet, Her Majesty, accompanied by her suite, entered the apartment. She looked pleasant and stupid – rather bulky and well-dressed – stayed for so long that I was late for dinner and consequently fined a franc and relegated to a side-table. People kissed her gloved hand when saying How-do-you-do, and curtseyed and shook hands at the same time on her leaving. I must say if I were a retired sovereign I should give up such airs and graces, and try to slip into a room like an ordinary mortal.'

By the end of the year Lytton had entirely recovered from the

---

[1] 'The two families live in a block of three villas one of which is empty – but you never know which one, so that you very often ring and knock in vain until a head, poked out of the window, tells you to go to the next (or next but one) house. Peculiar!' (Lytton to Pippa Strachey, 30 November 1900.)

palpitations and misery of the summer. He spent a mild Christmas dining with his cousins off turkey, champagne and plum pudding, held up a pine tree in the hotel, and received a novel present from his mother in distant England – 'a *minute* Milton (2 inches by 3) complete, on India Paper – and too charming for words. I carry it in my pocket, so that I may take it out and admire it at intervals.'

On 9 January 1901 he travelled back to London by himself, and a little later returned to Trinity, where the Midnight Society once again resumed its nocturnal readings, Lytton taking the part of Cleopatra in *Antony and Cleopatra*. In the months and years which followed, Lady Strachey was scrupulous in carrying out the doctor's recommendation, seeing to it that some part at least of every vacation Lytton spent either abroad, in the country, or by the sea. During March she took him down to the Belvedere Mansion Hotel, in Brighton, where he was visited for a few days by Saxon Sydney-Turner.[1] Much of this holiday was spent collaborating with his sister Marjorie on a long, incredibly involved but harmless literary composition entitled *Lachrymae Ostreorum*. This piece was made up from alternate lyrics, transcribed in red ink and called pearls, and blue-black chunks of blank verse on which the coloured lyrics were strung and which were termed cables. The lyrics were all written jointly in the usual way of a collaboration, but the cables were stitched separately in sections. An additional complication in structure and in the texture of the poem, revolved round the three languages in which it was written, only one of them – English – containing any meaning whatever. The verses cast in mock-Italian and mock-German were never intended to carry any real sense, but simply to sound as if they did.

In the intervals between working at this collaboration Lytton read Walter Pater, whose laborious and anaemic refinements of scholarship and taste, achieving only an imitation of true literary style, he greatly disliked. 'As for Pater,' he wrote to Lumsden Barkway, 'though I have not read much of him he appears to me so deathly – no motion, no vigour – a waxen style. . . . And after all does he say so very much that is worth hearing? In short I do not like the man.' In the evenings his mother would read out to him from *The Ring and the Book*, which engrossed him far more. 'What a work!' he commented. 'No one but R B could ever have dreamt of writing it.' About Henry James, whose early novels Lady Strachey was also very fond of reading aloud, he was even more intrigued, opening one of his letters to Leonard Woolf in imitation of the master: 'In settling the great question, at any rate, is there more than one answer of the many which, as a serious solution,

[1] Saxon Sydney-Turner's father was a doctor who lived permanently in Brighton.

can add more than nothing to an after all admitted ignorance? Do not, in their hubbub, the thousand vociferations only succeed in missing the failure by which they are self-condemned by satisfactorily proving even to the least experienced auditor the correctness of the one? Will you not agree that boredom is, essentially, life? Sleep, I think, and death are the only states of which a limited consciousness can speak without it.'

Brighton, with its integrated mixture of charm and vulgarity, fascinated Lytton, who tended to represent it as some strange Anglo-Saxon Venice. 'This place is most peculiar,' he informed Lumsden Barkway, 'rather oppressive, and very bracing. A regular metropolis on the sea – powdered boatmen, carriages in pairs, fashions and frivolity. Such a parade! two piers with kiosks and mosques, and I don't know how many theatres, music-halls and Alhambras! Of such things I have only explored one – an Aquarium where I went with my small brother who comes down for week-ends. The fishes and things were amusing and weird enough – it was all underground and there were various terrible side-shows – such as the "Strange Lady" with pale individuals trying in vain to attract the attention of passers by. Some of them rang bells I believe – but in vain.'

With the determinedly unexotic Belvedere Mansion Hotel, however, he was very far from delighted. The cold, antique surroundings here grated incessantly upon him. 'Brighton I dare say is killing me,' he complained to Leonard Woolf. 'The waits between the courses are so long and the courses themselves so exceedingly scrappy. This all round. Easter thick upon us with its attendant horrors. Everyone appears to be fat, smug, happy and *bourgeois*. They roll, of course, in money. Beasts!'

The summer holidays that year Lytton again spent with the family, this time at Cuffnells, a country house with vast and spacious gardens, near Lyndhurst, ten miles from Southampton and nineteen from Bournemouth. Much of this vacation was occupied in writing an essay on Warren Hastings for the Greaves Prize at Trinity, and in attempting to learn German. For a week in August he invited Saxon Sydney-Turner – 'pale and somnolent' – to stay with him, and found in his mute, unobtrusive presence a relief from the loud monotony of the assembled family, despite his friend's obstinacy in sitting down every day at the piano to strum out melodies from Wagner – a composer whose swelling themes were too overblown for Lytton's taste. In his solitary moments he was 'reading Keats in raptures' and going off for long walks in the warm summer countryside, of the beauty of which he seems to have been made more sensitively aware by the slow-moving, pictorial verse, steeped in desire and regret. His state of happiness and general contentment over these weeks was increased by the presence of the Stephen family, including, of course, the radiant and adored Thoby, whom he saw several times, once at a near-by fair where he was sporting himself very splendidly among village boys and coconuts. 'Here it is delicious,' he told Leonard Woolf, 'the New Forest – beautiful trees and weather. The Goth within five miles with his family. It is a school they live in, and the Goth at night retreats to the dormitory where he magnificently sleeps among the small surrounding beds.'

Once or twice, to his great delight, he was invited across by Thoby to the Stephen schoolhouse where, for the first time, he met his two aloof and lovely sisters, Vanessa – later to marry Clive Bell – and Virginia – who subsequently married Leonard Woolf – together with Adrian, their brother, and the awe-inspiring, patriarchal Leslie Stephen – 'quite deaf and rather dangerous' – who insisted on Lytton repeating all his falsetto remarks down a formidable ear-trumpet.[1] 'It is a nice though wild family,' Lytton wrote to Leonard Woolf, '– 2 sisters very pretty – a younger brother Adrian, and Leslie with his ear-trumpet and tam-o'-shanter. What is rather strange is the old man – older than he really is – among so young a family. He is well kept in check by them, and they are well bustled by him. They know each other very well I think.'

During the Christmas vacation of 1901, fearing that the cold, damp climate of England might be too much for him, Lady Strachey sent Lytton off to the south of France in company with two of his sisters, Dorothy and Marjorie. The three of them travelled down by train, breaking their journey for a few exciting days in Paris where they rushed about continuously, saw the Louvre, Luxembourg, Théâtre Français, the Opéra (*Lohengrin*), Notre Dame, the Sainte Chapelle, and snapped up a few books on the *quais*. They then resumed their progress south, and arrived shortly before Christmas at Menton. Here they put up at a comfortable Victorian house, Villa Himalaya, which had been rented by Lady Colvile, Lady Strachey's elder sister.

The blue sea, the sky and the land were all so enchanting that he dreaded returning to England and winter. He was perpetually occupied

---

[1] In an unpublished fragment, Virginia Woolf later recalled that she had been taken across to see the Stracheys by her father. 'Lady Strachey was in high glee. She had been routing about among the books, and had discovered a first edition, I think of Ben Jonson. "Look at that, Sir Leslie! Look at that!" she exclaimed, thrusting the book before him and pointing to an inscription on the title page, "Ex dono Áuctoris". My father looked and admired, but a little grimly I thought and on the way home he said to me, "I didn't like to tell Lady Strachey, but the accent should be on the second syllable of auctoris, not the first".'

in a most civilized and enjoyable manner – two *déjeuners*, one at ten and the second at twelve; expeditions of all sorts and at all hours; reading and writing scattered in between. 'This place is more charming than can be imagined,' he delightedly told his mother soon after arriving (29 December 1901). And on the same day he wrote off to Lumsden Barkway: 'This is heavenly! Yes, heavenly! The best of what one imagines the Riviera! . . . The country is of course perfect. Mountains! Yes! And some with snow! They tower! The sea glows and shimmers and swells! The sky is a marvel! . . . we continue our rounds of pleasure – among which I don't think I mentioned to you the fascination of food. Omelettes! Wines – sparkling and sweet like ginger-beer! Rolls! All quite absolute! Especially after one has been toiling on legs or donkeys up precipitous paths under tropical suns. One falls on food voracious as lions.'

A more leisured, gentle note is struck in another letter written to Leonard Woolf: 'One sees villas here with boats going out – and idleness is the first necessity. To work is to die – I always think. It's the very admission of time and space – our fearful limitations – but to dream! Italy is at hand too. Roman arches come upon one. Boys play in gardens. I turned the Cape the other day, and there was Monte Carlo. One wouldn't go there.'

His attitude to Monte Carlo, examined from a cautious distance, was somewhere between that of a very old maid and a Wordsworthian poet. 'Monte Carlo with its abominations in rococo architecture,' he wrote, 'painted women, and stay-laced men, goes down to perfect seas and is backed by magnificent mountains. Nature is best – the natives next best – when they're young, with complexions which you never see in England, recalling Brittanyan shrimps.' In short, it was a study in incompatible contrasts – breath-taking scenery and hideous, cheap modern buildings. He went there several times (despite the *caveat* to Leonard Woolf), gambled and lost a little, listened to the orchestra, wandered through the Royal Palace with its charming garden, and saw the delicious orangeries, the trees crowded together on bright grass, the stark drop of the wall to the sea a thousand feet below. With his sisters he also attended a luxurious New Year's garden party given by Sir Thomas Hanbury, a wealthy benefactor of the neighbourhood, at his ornate Italian villa – balconies in all directions and commanding every view – marble floors – bronze statuettes – and a celebrated garden going down in terraces inevitably to the sea. 'It was most pleasant wandering about,' he wrote to Lumsden Barkway. 'A band played and there were ices – imagine – New Year's day – Aerial summer!'

Despite the necessity for idleness, Lytton spent some of his leisure hours writing a dramatic three-act tragedy to be performed by the Midnight Society in the Lent term. In such an atmosphere, work did not come easily. 'The air is strangely lowering,' he told Leonard Woolf who had inquired after the progress of the play. 'I write the tragedy and walk – either strollingly or up steep hills to absurd villages.' The particular village to which this passage indirectly refers was Eze-en-haut, which hangs dramatically from a cliff top between Cap Ferrat and Monte Carlo. 'Dorothy and I made an expedition the day before yesterday to a place called Eza or Eze,' he wrote to his mother (29 December 1901), 'which is a minute village perched on the very top of a perpendicular hill. There are the ruins of a Moorish Castle there, also the foundations of a temple to Isis, now converted to a Church to the Holy Virgin.' One other village also caught his imagination. This was Castellar, 'in the depths – or heights? — of the hills. Very small and pleasant. With 4,000 children all shrieking and yelling – also a damp, tinsel R.C. Church – also one room of a mediaeval palace belonging to a family whose last descendant was hung from its own window in the time of the Revolution.'

Although, as Lytton once informed a friend, he had always nursed an obsession for paganism – outraged by the re-conversion work done at Eze – he generally preferred it to be Greek rather than Roman. He crossed the Italian border only twice during his stay at Menton, and on the first occasion detected no change between the two countries except that 'Italian roads are worse than the French – and that's the only difference'.

But on his second crossing, the brutal mediaeval paganism of the ancient Romans suddenly seems to have communicated itself to him with unexpected force. A few hours later, once this strange and insidious chill had passed and he was back in twentieth-century France, he tried rationally to analyse the peculiar sensation which had come over him. For the amusement of Leonard Woolf, he also set the story down on paper, the romantic variations and facetiae in his description acting as a defence against the risk of being thought absurd. Together with Dorothy and Marjorie, he told his friend, he had reached Ventimiglia, 'an old Roman post, with a high mound which was once an amphitheatre commanding views up to snow-mountains through a valley, and on the other side the long Provençal shore. Italy pleases me – and this is still to a great extent it. But everything is strange, almost lurid with contrasts, and the sense of abounding life. Coming down a winding hill-road through a valley, we heard the other day the noises of a butchery. The surroundings were so bathed in country peace, the sky was so blue, the vegetation so green and florid, that the sound struck as a horror. I imagined, in some recess, whence – believe it! – rose shouts of fiendish human exultations, an obscene and reeking sacrifice to a still remembered pagan god. Above us perhaps loomed (beneath the walls of Madonna's edifice) the hoary temple of Isis; who knows whether through the remoteness of these secluded years some worship had not lingered; some mystic propitiation and reconciliation of the hideous mysteries of life and death.'

Lytton returned to England in mid-January and, having maintained a very reasonable standard of health, went back a few days later to Trinity; where his dramatic tragedy was declaimed in the early hours of one morning by the approving members of the Midnight.

4

CHARACTERS

The permanent death of the Midnight Society[1] was eventually brought about by the regular week-end visits from London of three former undergraduates, Desmond MacCarthy, Bertrand Russell and E. M. Forster, all of whom got to know Lytton well during his early years at Cambridge. After the company of MacCarthy, especially, it was difficult to carry on with the solemn formality of a prepared literary reading. He would bring along his friend, the philosopher G. E. Moore, not primarily to debate questions of philosophy but to play with vigour and abandon upon the piano, and to sing. And after the musical entertainment, MacCarthy himself would come forward with a string of stories, often, admittedly, unfinished, but always specifically designed so as to delight his particular audience. There was a natural and easy world-liness about him that was tremendously refreshing in the rarefied

---

[1] This statement is based upon an account given by Clive Bell in his memoirs, *Old Friends*. It is possible that he may have over-emphasized the significance of the Midnight because of his extreme bitterness at not being elected to the Apostles. In the present chapter, the author has used the Midnight partly for aesthetic purposes, and partly because it was the first society to which Lytton belonged and, for a year or more, the chief one. After he had been introduced into the Apostles by R. G. Hawtrey in 1902, the Midnight completely ceased to exist. But even before this, its place had already been taken by the X Society – a play-reading club that met earlier on Saturday evenings. Leonard Woolf, Saxon Sydney-Turner, Thoby Stephen and Clive Bell belonged to it, together with a lot of miscellaneous characters such as Walter Lamb, D. S. Robertson (later Regius Professor of Greek), Hubback and Philby (the Arabian traveller and father of the 'Third Man' in the Burgess-Maclean affair). This group was still going strong after 1902 – 'I know because I went to a meeting much later,' James Strachey informed the author, 'when I was up for a week-end from St Paul's and they read *Love for Love*, much to my excitement.'

university atmosphere; and when he and Moore had done with their cabaret performance, the volumes of Swinburne, *Bartholomew Fair* and *The Cenci* would frequently remain unopened.

MacCarthy's reputation as a brilliant raconteur was rooted more in his skill as a practised listener than in his versatility as a speaker. In these late-night gatherings he achieved the difficult feat of talking just enough to suggest a flow of beguiling conversation. So winning and un-egotistical was his personality that many of his new friends were mesmerized into attributing to him their own most witty remarks, like men inebriated with selfless generosity. He was at his best with people to whom he owed no special obligation. On these Saturday visits to Trinity, the apparent play of his soft Irish humour, the seeming grace and pertinence of his speech, cast about him an aura of warm, social well-being.

Yet there was a reverse side to the coin. With his family – his mother, for example – and in dealings which called for a dutiful rather than a spontaneous display of feeling, he was less reliable. In later years, as literary editor of the *Speaker*, the *New Quarterly* and the *New Statesman* he was punctilious in giving Lytton and other of his personal long-standing friends the commissions that they needed. At the same time other, less intimately known reviewers for these papers were sometimes reduced to a state of impoverished despair by his vague, invariably courteous procrastination; and one of them, A. G. Macdonell, was eventually moved to retaliate by drawing a satirical pen portrait of him as Charles Ossory in his celebrated, overrated, comic novel, *England, Their England*. Like Oscar Wilde, another Irishman who radiated an even stronger impression of magical and benevolent charm on almost everyone with whom he came in contact, MacCarthy shied away from what threatened to be unpleasant or in any way tiresome. Significantly, he was often at his most enchanting with mere acquaintances, employing his elegant blandness as a gently applied brake against furthering any friendship to the point of supreme intimacy at which it might suddenly become complicated by a wearisome sense of duty, tarnished by implied or habitual obligations.

As he seemed to like everyone, so everyone liked him. He soon took to the shy, remote figure of Lytton and began to draw him out. But it was a long business. At first Lytton remained stubborn and suspicious, unused to such attentive, genial treatment. He had, moreover, an auto-matic feeling of disdain for those who could command instant popularity, and he did not feel really at home in MacCarthy's vague and expansive presence. In due course he began to thaw out, responding to the older man's charm and endearing sartorial eccentricities – thick-lined suits, a flannel shirt and large blue tie. 'I liked him much better than before,' Lytton was able to tell Leonard Woolf by December 1904. 'He seemed to understand a good deal, and want to be liked.'

But in general conversation, MacCarthy only superficially represented his elusive self. Since his skill lay in subtly impersonating his audience, his stories, while they lasted, both amused and soothed Lytton. But when they trailed off, and MacCarthy had left, he again felt the burden of his solitude, now even more severely reasserted. 'The curious thing', he observed, 'is that when one's with him [MacCarthy] it all seems very amusing, and that afterwards one can only look back on a dreary waste.' And in a letter to Maynard Keynes, he later (18 November 1905) described the same bewildering paradox. 'He's a curious figure – very dull and amusing. Also rather desolate.' This feeling of desolation is understandable once one appreciates that talking with MacCarthy meant little more than carrying on an animated dialogue with oneself – in Lytton's case the one person from whom he wished to escape. The temporary euphoria induced by MacCarthy's succession of stories was like that caused by a series of mixed drinks – immediately intoxicating, filling one with an artificial *amour propre*, and swiftly succeeded by a hangover of redoubled self-abasement. For MacCarthy did not need anyone *in particular*, only the stimulus of *any* reasonably illuminating companion to bring him alive, to retrieve his chameleon personality from the dark of a featureless oblivion. And in the sombre light of Lytton's rather passive company, his mind glowed as a bright though indistinct reflection.

As an entertainer MacCarthy was unrivalled. On more personal matters, Lytton found that he could never confide in him, seldom expose to his sympathetic understanding, so vague and universal, so soft and hazy, his own poignant, unique secrets. Despite his brilliance as a raconteur, he could be rather tiresome on more serious subjects, when his will struggled to assert itself and interfered with the elegant, easy variations of his mind. 'The thing is to keep him off literature,' Lytton once explained to Virginia Woolf, 'and insist on his doing music-hall turns: if only he'd make that his profession he'd make thousands. Can't you see him coming on in a macintosh?'

To the end of Lytton's life, MacCarthy remained a loyal and useful friend. Yet much of the pseudo-intimacy of their relationship, especially in these early years, depended upon the illusion that they closely resembled each other, whereas in truth their natures were greatly dissimilar. While Lytton had been influenced by a deeply rooted family tradition, MacCarthy was bound by an ever-present and seductive atmosphere of genial, well-mannered orthodoxy, a lax and unobtrusive

conventionality. Educated at Eton and Trinity, he perhaps found that
everything was made too easy for him during the formative years of his
life. His charm attracted numerous friends; he was seldom alone; a
heavy blanket of popularity suffocated his talent. The strength of the
Eton education – which he retrospectively recommended for Lytton –
lies, then as now, in the comparative freedom it allows the boys; its
weakness is to be found in the dogged and insensitive lack of encouragement given to any pursuits other than team games, and, in a more
diluted form, the odd esoteric scholarship examination. Both the
strength and weakness of this system conceal for the boy of developing
imagination subtle dangers which lurk like rocks under the calm surface
of the water. MacCarthy was impaled inextricably at the harbour mouth
within sight of land and of the open sea beyond. His faltering individuality was not resilient enough to withstand the tide of his pleasant
vices. He was plagued by a rueful sense of disappointment at never
having progressed further, a feeling which in itself became something
of an indulgence. 'One of Nature's Oppidans', as John Davenport once
called him, he grew into the kind of person many take to be a typical
Etonian of the best variety – intelligent, diplomatic without being
obviously dishonest, rather indolent by temperament, indulgent, and
passionless. His volumes of literary and dramatic criticism reflect
genuine catholicity of taste, but as in the rooms of an old house
illuminated throughout by a low voltage, there are no memorable
highlights. We may peer at the magnificent pictures suspended from the
walls, but all too little penetrates the consoling twilight. What might
have been vivid is vague. One longs to have the picture presented in
clear, sharp focus, to escape from the impression of gently dissolving
uniformity. By contrast, Lytton – a born rebel tug – is all simulated
sparkle and brilliance. Here one moves nearer the portraits to inspect
them more closely in all their glorious striking colours, and then –
phut! – the lights fuse altogether. And by the time they flash on again,
one is being hurriedly conducted through to the next room where, in
due course, the same process of exhilaration and anti-climax will repeat
itself.

Bertrand Russell, who used to travel down with MacCarthy, was of
an altogether different stamp, and his differing attitude to Lytton sheds
new light upon his character. Small and thin, with a pleasant, slightly
dry smile, his luminous intelligence seemed to shine directly through
his large dark eyes. Some of his near-contemporaries, notably D. H.
Lawrence, were to dismiss him as being all 'Disembodied Mind'. But
though his passions appeared to come to him in the form of ideas, so
that he passed from one to the other instead of from one co-ordinated

experience to another, there was something more positive and substantial to him than mere donnish fastidiousness and lack of Lawrentian
animal zest.[1] A totally unpsychological thinker, he was always a bad
judge of people. Like Lytton, he observed the general human predicament with absolute clarity. Even though he knew that life was carried
on in the most complex and irrational of fashions, he held that the
remedy was simple – namely, to carry it on more rationally. To this
end, and often with great courage, he quixotically crusaded, in contrast
to Lytton, who – even when his opinions exactly coincided with
Russell's – generally disengaged himself from the muddle of topical
controversies and essayed to impose upon them an ordered, retrospective justice.

Russell greatly appreciated Lytton's sense of humour, and on reading
Eminent Victorians in Brixton gaol, recorded that 'It caused me to laugh
so loud that the officer came to my cell, saying I must remember that
prison is a place of punishment.'[2] At the same time it struck him as
significant that while he himself was incarcerated for his humanitarian
beliefs, the feebly romantic Lytton – though ostensibly sharing these
beliefs – should be employing his secluded leisure to fabricate, after the
outdated rhetorical style of Macaulay, literary compositions largely
irrelevant to the current crises, and which, though clever and amusing,
were also palpably exaggerated and imbued with the sentimentality of
a stuffy girls' school. Russell's own mind was far more speculative than
Lytton's, but his vision, though wonderfully sharp, was restricted in
depth of focus. He could always understand an academic better than a
simple man, for the limit of his wisdom was marked by his inability to
account for prejudice and stupidity.

Something of the acuteness and over-simplification of Russell's mind
was evident in his qualified dislike of Lytton. While MacCarthy
apparently had a genius for discovering only the best in others, Russell,
being outwardly far more dispassionate, judged people by altogether

---

[1] 'By the way, do you bring out the fact that Bertie has the most marvellous mental
apparatus, perhaps, ever? I mean as a mere machine. Lawrence's view of him, incidentally, was extraordinarily obtuse. Bertie was full of *passionate* emotions (which led
him into trouble of all sorts).' (James Strachey to the author, October 1966.)

[2] On 20 May 1918, Lytton wrote to Lady Ottoline Morrell: 'I sent a copy [of *Eminent
Victorians*] to Alys [Russell], and oddly enough next morning had a letter from Alys
saying how much she had enjoyed it. If it pleases him as well, I think it really will suit
all tastes.' Bertrand Russell's reaction to the book was reported to Lytton by Ottoline a
few days later. 'Thank you very much for passing on Bertie's message,' he replied (26
May 1918). 'I am delighted that he should have liked the book, and that he found it
entertaining. If you're writing will you thank him from me, and say that I think it a
great honour that my book should have made the author of *Principia Mathematica* laugh
aloud in Brixton Gaol?'

different standards. He found Lytton's unexpected wit hilarious, but his amusement did not blind him to other facets of his character which he could only deplore. Russell was less objective than he liked to make out, and several personal reasons for his antipathy suggest themselves. In later years he and Lytton may be said to have temporarily been rivals for the friendship of Lady Ottoline Morrell. Russell, in the opinion of Gerald Brenan, considered Lytton to be fundamentally unpractical and frivolous over most major political and sociological issues, an attitude which he took to denote the essential shallowness of his mind. It may also have been, as James Strachey believed, that Russell resented the greater influence exerted over Lytton as an undergraduate by the author of *Principia Ethica* than by the joint-author of *Principia Mathematica*. G. E. Moore and Russell admired the power of each other's intellect, but their friendship never grew really easy or close. According to Frances Partridge, Moore sometimes rebuked Desmond MacCarthy for inviting Russell to his select reading parties during the Cambridge vacations, since he felt that his own patient, inquiring method of analysis was seriously disrupted by Russell's quick-fire, censorious and – so Moore sometimes felt – invalid arguments. Russell, indeed, must have been aware of this coolness in his colleague, for, as Alan Wood recounts, he once asked him: 'You don't like me, do you, Moore?' Moore deliberated with characteristic conscientiousness for several minutes, and then replied in a single pregnant monosyllable: 'No.' After which the two philosophers went on chatting amiably enough about other matters. Certainly Russell never actively disliked Moore – no one could – but he seems to have returned Moore's cerebral disapprobation, to some extent resenting the great esteem in which his rival was held by Lytton and other disciples. This indirect aversion was aggravated by moral considerations in the particular case of Lytton who, he considered, had perverted Moore's original doctrine so as to condone and even exalt his own homosexuality.

The increasing eccentricity that Lytton was, in the opinion of Russell, to exhibit at Cambridge had a debilitating effect upon his genuine talent and ability, while his growing affectation overlaid what was honest and truly admirable in his personality. Russell thought he saw clearly that Lytton's basic failure as a literary artist lay in the emphasis which he tended to place not on truth, but on dramatically appealing and often rather obvious effect. He disliked, too, the lordly and arrogant tone which the young Lytton sometimes chose to adopt towards human affairs in general, as when he expostulated: 'I can't believe people think about life. There's nothing in it.' Yet Russell condemned such an outburst from the particular context in which it was delivered, as a disembodied sentiment, without apprehending the personal impulse from which it sprang. After years of loneliness and dissatisfaction magnified by a deep sense of personal inadequacy, Lytton felt it imperative to establish some strong, easily remembered impression upon those around him. He desired more than ever to occupy the centre of the stage, and his ineradicable self-consciousness was best exploited by theatrical means. There was an underlying pathos, too, in his mannered behaviour, of which Russell and many of his other friends were unaware. By making his voice squeak with more deliberate inconsistency and affectation, by dressing rather oddly, by encouraging 'a small rather dismal moustache',[1] he may have hoped to convey the notion that his idiosyncrasies were not innate but arbitrarily chosen, not ugly but amusing.

These undergraduate moods and mannerisms were often disconcerting, especially to E. M. Forster. Forster liked Lytton, but found him a formidable and alarming young man, in whose presence he was for many years unable to feel at ease. His long unresponsive silences, which he spread like an airless eiderdown on all frivolous chatter, and the piercing little shrieks with which he would greet any vaguely mystical or other observation that he considered to be patently absurd, slightly unnerved Forster, who felt that he placed perhaps too high a value on boredom. He neither warmed to Lytton with the spontaneous bon-homie of Desmond MacCarthy, nor disapproved of him with the didactic heterosexuality of Bertrand Russell; for both he and Lytton possessed too oddly esoteric natures to respond freely and openly with one another. Indeed, Forster's contact with all the members of the Midnight Society seemed only intermittent, for already he was, as Maynard Keynes aptly described him, 'the elusive colt of a dark horse'. Of middle height and ivory pale complexion, the grave and modest sincerity of his manner, and his mild, implacable courtesy suggested at times that he was more intent upon self-communion than on conversation with his Anglo-Saxon friends, and provoked in some of them an exaggerated, if impotent, boisterousness, generated in a desperate effort to ferry over the moat of invariable social calm around him, or perhaps only connect with his remote, perpetually retiring, personality. Naturally withdrawn, even in his twenties, he seemed to combine the

---

[1] This description appears in an essay which Desmond MacCarthy wrote in about 1934, and which is included in the sixth volume of his collected essays, entitled *Memories*. James Strachey, however, took issue with this statement. 'What do you think you mean by this? What can you mean? A wispy moustache which grew with difficulty? One like Hitler's? It certainly wasn't like Sir Gerald Nabarro's. Not an R.A.F. moustache. Nor a cavalry moustache. But, as you might see from photographs, a thick one, not in the least straggly. In those days far from unusual. This is a good example of your unceasing desire to run Lytton down – in this case to make people think he was impotent – which, believe me, he wasn't.'

bashful demureness of a spinster with the more abstract preoccupations of a don. The tortuous literal integrity that he generally employed not for solving actual problems but for erecting fictional obstacles which he would subsequently just fail to surmount, was hardly conducive to everyday conviviality. Where fools habitually rushed in, he, prudently, refrained from treading. In the middle of these Cambridge discussions, he was apt to retreat completely into himself to examine in a mood of gentle, fussy romanticism, the problem, say, of whether he possessed an adequate reserve of personal courage to place friendship before patriotism, should the country call upon his services in such a manner as to render this predicament excruciatingly urgent.

But despite his discreet evasiveness, Forster's sensibility and subtle intelligence were clearly apparent to those who knew him best, and he reacted towards Lytton with the wariness and unspoken intimacy of one intelligent man to another. In some of his letters to other, mutual friends, Lytton sometimes criticized Forster rather uncharitably -- his quaint timidity, his amiable, prematurely old-maidish liberalism, and so on. But it is clear that what he really objected to was having a mirror held up to reflect the more negative features of his own image. 'Excessive paleness is what I think worries me most,' he wrote to Leonard Woolf. 'The Taupe [Forster] in his wonderful way I imagine saw this about me, and feeling that he himself verged upon the washed-out, shuddered.'

Forster was by no means the only person severely castigated in Lytton's correspondence as an undergraduate. No one escapes, and almost all his new friends are slated at one time or another without mercy. For though these carefully composed epistles of his Cambridge years contain many items of real amusement, they are not the writings of a happy person, but of someone hypersensitive and still insecure. The feeling which they induce is one of acute depression. He was more apprehensive than the average child. The over-protection of his mother, so abruptly succeeded by the bullying which at school he almost inevitably drew down upon himself, had left him with the instinctive feeling – which his intellect nevertheless rejected strongly – that he was safe only by her side, and that the rest of the world's population was potentially dangerous. Timid and self-conscious, yet at the same time absolutely determined to correct the effect of these shortcomings, he met people with a mixture of distrust and hostility, so that even now, surrounded by many new well-disposed friends of about the same age, he could still never be certain that they *really* liked him. For this reason there is often something unnaturally forced and artificial about his human relationships. He is too impatient for intimacy, seldom prepared to allow his feelings to ripen gradually, for fear that procrastination will ruin everything and merely help perpetuate his sense of deprivation. His life, after coming up to Trinity, was for the most part dominated jointly by two types of people. First, there was the man who approximated to the ideal and who excited his lust and adoration; secondly, there was the person to whom he confessed these feelings, and whose maternal sympathy, commiseration and encouragement, he could never do without. In some cases the borderline between these two is not absolutely distinct; but despite several variations within this pattern, the theme always remains essentially the same. Thus his emotions and his intellect, his imagination and his will, were kept separate, never fused together, so that for many years his loves and friendships brought him more division and disillusion than real happiness.

During this period of his life Lytton habitually tried to forearm himself against disappointment by stressing prematurely and with exaggeration the shortcomings of others, thereby deceptively elevating his own self-esteem. Before comparative strangers he thought it quite fatal to admit anything short of omniscience, and for some half-dozen years the highest word of praise which he was likely to bestow on any living person was 'tolerable'.

Among others who share the somewhat risky distinction of appearing in his correspondence at this time were C. P. Sanger, a gnomelike figure, universally loved, with bright sceptical eyes, rather older than Lytton, who had shown exceptional promise at Trinity and was now a brilliant barrister; Walter Lamb, rather short and conceitedly obsequious, whom Lytton nicknamed 'the Corporal' and who, he said, was 'like a fellow with one leg who's not only quite convinced that he's got two but boasts of his walking exploits'; R. C. Trevelyan (usually referred to as Bob Trevy), the whimsical, bookish poet and elder brother of George Trevelyan, whose writing Lytton thought tedious and whom he described as 'amusing but vague to a degree'; and J. E. McTaggart, the redoubtable Hegelian philosopher, whose rooms Lytton, in company with Leonard Woolf, Saxon Sydney-Turner and a few other chosen undergraduates, would visit every Thursday evening. A brilliant lecturer, severely neurotic and a sufferer from agoraphobia,[1] McTaggart completely bowled over Lytton before he came under the still greater force of Moore. As a character, he was intimidating and

[1] In the first volume of his autobiography, *Father Figures* (1966), Kingsley Martin writes: 'McTaggart was an extraordinary figure in my day. He suffered from agoraphobia, and walked with a strange, crab-like gait, keeping his backside to the wall, as if afraid that someone would kick it – and maybe they did at school. He talked very quickly and was very hard to follow.... He invited questions, but answered them so sharply and decisively that few were encouraged to ask another.'

shyly eccentric, his rapt capacity for silence and immobility being apparently limitless. But for his brand of philosophy – so far as it could be ascertained beneath the fathomless profundity of his inanimation – Lytton eventually seems to have had little use, and after hearing him lecture on the nature of good and evil, he soliloquized:

> *McTaggart's seen through God*
> *And put him on the shelf;*
> *Isn't it rather odd*
> *He doesn't see through himself.*

5

BALLADS AND COUNTERBLASTS

Lytton's taste and knowledge of literature expanded enormously while he was at Cambridge. He read widely and was continuously writing poems, epigrams, essays. The strange dichotomy of his character found an interesting parallel in the contrast that soon developed between his susceptibilities as a reader and his performance as a writer. 'My ideal in writing is the non-flamboyant – unless one's Sir Thomas Browne,' he wrote to his sister Dorothy (1905), 'but I'm annoyed to find that every time I write I become more flamboyant than before. It's so difficult to be amusing unless one does plunge into metaphors, "paradoxes", "brilliant epigrams", etc., etc., etc. – unless one's Swift.'

For Lytton, Swift was always one of the absolute masters of English prose. Sober, unemphatic and simple, 'the only ornament in his writing', he later wrote, 'is the rhythm, so that, compared to the decorative and imaginative prose of such a writer as Sir Thomas Browne, it resembles the naked body of an athlete beside some Prince in gorgeous raiment'. On the whole he preferred the stark and subtle vigour of nudity to the splendour of glowing colour and elaborate form. The classical authors were his natural favourites. Yet his persistent dread of boring others, and of being bored himself, drew him some way towards the more facile entertainment of romantic literature, and helped to create a catholicity of literary appreciation which operated on two distinct planes. But in his response both to the classical and romantic, the same wish to minimize or attractively embellish the disordered crudity of real life (and in this process diminish his own disfavoured personality, extinguish the last beams of morbid introspection) is clearly present. He loved the Elizabethans for their verbal felicity and dazzling variations upon formal, as opposed to subjective, sentiments. Sir Thomas

Browne, with his flaring opulence of splendour and passion which overlaid the strange mystic murmurs of his spirit, was at this time his best-loved seventeenth-century prosodist; while the eighteenth century, with its infinite delicacies and refinements of social intercourse, seldom disturbingly profound, always so pleasingly civilized, its calm and elegant carapace unruffled as yet by the invention of a communal conscience, fascinated him more completely than any other single epoch. Among Victorian men of letters, Swinburne was undoubtedly now his choice, preaching a paganism less offensively muscular and robust than Meredith, less despairing than Edward FitzGerald, but at the same time more excitingly romantic and alive than Walter Pater. On those early Sunday mornings as the Midnight Society was breaking up and its members wandering back to their rooms, the cloisters of Nevile's Court would re-echo to the wild, masochistic rhapsodies, the inspired efflorescence which Swinburne had poured out to those erotic phantoms, his imaginary mistresses.

On a different level was Lytton's youthful interest in Donne and Henry James. In neither did there exist this highly coloured romanticism, sensuous appeal or vivid, visual imagery; but instead an intricate and complex stylistic technique which absorbed his intellect. The mental processes of Donne were erected over and above the emotional content of his poetry, and so far from clarifying the poet's inner feelings, tended to abandon them altogether in a cerebral labyrinth. For Donne, like Lytton, had been at odds with his age and sought in these metaphysical acrobatics some relief from the oppression of his emotional self-interest. The attraction of Henry James was of a similar nature. 'I have been reading Henry James in large quantities,' he notified his mother (2 May 1901). Just as, when a child, he had lost himself in the disentangling of complicated puzzles, so now he quickly became fascinated in pursuing James's eternally prolonged and qualified meditations. In June 1901 he composed a long and amusing parody of James's style entitled 'The Fruit of the Tree'. Taken as a whole, the danger of such a parody is that it reflects only too faithfully the fearful tedium of the prose which it attempts to caricature. Something of its quality however may be seen in an extract taken from the opening preamble:

'For you who understand there can (with one exception) be nothing in what follows there ought not to be. My story, if I have one (and in that very speculation there seems to be so much of it), must, after all, be clarity itself to those from whom it is written, who are so exactly not those who would hesitate or boggle at a meaning. It's as right as anything – to you; for the one exception to its rightness, which may be, precisely, my way of telling it, I must make, in advance, both an apology and an explanation. If I could leave on you just the impression it left on me, oh! I should be thoroughly contented. It was deep; deeper, you know, a good deal than I was, or even am; so that, in the end, I found and perhaps still find myself swimming upon an ocean whose profundity it is altogether impossible to gauge. What he found – or whether he found anything at all – are questions which, though they add immensely to the complication – might perhaps eventually lead to a solution of the whole thing. At any rate it is certain that whatever interest my story has centres round just two persons, two characters, two phases. Its fascination is that it holds a perpetual antithesis between two such wonderful contraries. That one of them was he and one of them was I is really the least that can be said; there was (and I want to show it you) such a great deal more underneath. If I succeed you may have a glimpse of a conflict; the powers of good and the powers of evil you may see ranged as in *Paradise Lost* upon the one hand and the other: if I show you that I shall be happy; what I shall never show you, and what, even more, I shall never show myself, is, in the clashing of opposites, exactly which was which.'

Through a rigid application of such abstract literary devices, Henry James was able to transform normal people into extraordinarily involved psychological specimens, in which dismembered, inanimate condition they might be examined with the mind alone. His characters were no longer living men and women, but cold artificial entities, without the terror of flesh and blood. In reading his novels Lytton entered a world of emasculated beings incapable, unlike those around him, of causing real pain. What he gained, both from the recondite abstractions of Donne and the plots and subterfuges of Henry James, from the pro-longed formalities of the Elizabethans and the involved mannerisms of the eighteenth century, was always a diminution of his own internal apprehensions and sense of conflict. Like crossword puzzles, like the higher ethical dilemmas of G. E. Moore, such literature was removed alike from the humdrum and the vulgar, and posed an absorbing com-plex of abstract and oblique equations, capable of neat satisfactory solutions. To some extent literature was, and remained for him, a window closed tight against the racket, the noisome fumes and pandemonium of rushing and shuddering which, as he could clearly see from his snug retreat, filled the outside thoroughfare from end to end in one loud, excruciating traffic-stream. But though literature was to act partially as a refuge from, rather than a revelation of, reality, his sharp eye for salient facts and his needle of delicate feline malice, which are freely displayed in his most characteristic writing, were to pierce the soft cushioning of antiquated literary conventions and bring the reader momentary peeping glimpses of actuality and pathos. He was a born artist, but one who sometimes played for safety and directed his gifts to the professional task of becoming a perfect craftsman. Occasionally the mere hack-work of verbal carpentry, however accomplished, loses its power to hold him, he turns against it and produces a tiny gem of creative sculpture. But the revolt is followed, as it were, by a recoil of fear; and like a diver who has sunk too far into the gloomy depths of the ocean, he returns quickly and with palpitating heart to the smooth bright surface of things.

Another writer of whom Lytton became very fond at Cambridge was Pope, whose appeal was more directly personal. As a result of his pronounced bodily infirmities, Pope had nursed throughout his life a hypersensitivity which he reserved almost exclusively for himself and his own misfortunes. Though also extremely sensitive, Lytton, especially in his later years, was of a rather more kindly and humane disposition than Pope, whose feelings, he once commented, 'were far more easily roused into expression by dislike than by affection'. Because Lytton was particularly appreciative of Pope's similar vein of feminine delicacy and wit, and responded to his painting of the more subtle shades and undercoats of fervent emotion, he seems at this time to have overrated the quality of Pope's more obscure poems, so many of which show off an entirely ephemeral and malicious triviality that can hold no great interest for today's reader. Part of the reason for this overvaluation may be traced to his interest in the biographical aspects of Pope's literary career. For there was a special lesson to be learnt from the proper study of this miserable little man who, as potentate of letters, overcame his physical disadvantages to such a degree that even the most eminent and respectable members of the cultured classes came to live in fear of him.

Lytton's own wit, like that of many celebrated humorists, had been cultivated in private as a defence against anticipated hostility and ridicule in public. While at Cambridge he sharpened up his style by formulating nearly a hundred aphorisms. 'I occupy myself by writing Réflexions in the manner of the French,' he wrote to Leonard Woolf in July 1903. 'It is a very pleasant summer amusement, I find, and you shall see the result. The advantage is that one need never think about one subject for more than 5 minutes at a time, and one need never give one's reasons.' Many of these aphorisms deal with the adolescent subject of love and point to Lytton's obsessive preoccupation – most fully exhibited in his letters – with the genital and excremental functions of the human body. Perhaps the best are concerned with the problems of literary style and contemporary manners. Others are avowals of his paganistic objections to Christianity. Among the least successful are those which assume a cynical mood of worldliness. A number of examples, taken from his notebooks, will convey the variety and quality of these 'Réflexions'.

'It is as impossible to talk of a lady as if she were a man as to talk of her as if she were a prostitute.'

'It is always easier for a lady to fall in love with her footman if she is deaf.'

'A woman sometimes gives her love to her husband only when she has nothing else left to give him.'

'Our vanity is sometimes hurt even more by the admiration of those we disdain than by the disdain of those we admire.'

'It is easier to believe in reason than to be reasonable.'

'The excitement in conversation which is given by champagne is present of its own accord in the most exciting conversations.'

'It is possible to have good manners and to be vulgar; and it is possible to be refined and to have no manners at all.'

'We find it easier to reflect on the actions we have performed than to act on the reflections we have made.'

'We are never given time to think of the great things we have done by the little things we are doing.'

'It is a point of difference between prose and poetry that prose demands perfection of form and poetry can do without it.'

'There are a few common words – *rose*, *moon*, *star*, *love* – which are so beautiful both in themselves and in what they express that their presence insensibly heightens a bad piece of writing, but makes a good one more difficult to compose.'

'Civilization loves the truth and Barbarism tells it.'

'Some people are as much ashamed of their God as of their genitals, and blush when you mention either.'

'When a Christian is dying it is not the fear of Hell that disturbs him, but the fear of Death.'

Lytton also gave some epigrammatic expression to that inverted Wordsworthian feeling of self-obliteration which, in all his passions literary and emotional, brought with it such a sense of unburdening relief: 'We are so unimportant that whether we think we are or not hardly matters.' Many of his aphorisms are elaborately unspontaneous, concocted in the form of parables too long and commonplace to quote, and carrying with them the faint, musty aroma of Oscar Wilde's more affected fairy tales. Others are shorter and more trite. To become fully aware of the flatness of the worst of these one has only to contrast the urgent cry for companionship uttered in his Liverpool diary with a corresponding Cambridge aphorism: 'Our best and most beautiful pleasure is love.' In general, these maxims are not distinguished by any very penetrating insight or extraordinary wisdom, but consist of rather self-conscious experiments in style which convey much of the devitalized, waxed inefficacy that he himself found so deathly in Walter Pater. Some, however, are acute and one or two aptly sum up the whole business of writing epigrams:

'A witty thing is sometimes said by accident, but never a stupid one.'

'The maxims we write in our youth we correct in our maturity, and burn in our old age.'

'There are few things more difficult to write than a good aphorism; and one of them is to write a true one.'

In contrast to the artificial refinement of many of these aphorisms, Lytton was fond of expressing a degree of grossness in his verses which, like the indecencies of Swift, had its origin in the disgust felt by a confined, frustrated spirit at the dual nature of man. 'The best and worst parts of us are the secrets we never reveal' runs one of his aphorisms. On the whole, these love poems reveal the worst part of Lytton, though he occasionally, and without great conviction, represented them as his finest, most original contribution to English literature, still as yet far ahead of the times. Today, sixty years later, they remain largely unpublishable, for they are without true poetic value. There is little pathos in them, little tenderness and no humour. The ones which he himself prized most highly make up a sonnet sequence and were probably addressed to (Sir John) Sheppard. Written at a time when the Oscar Wilde scandal was still very much present in many people's minds, they are experimental in stated emotion rather than in any literary form, and their interest is mainly psycho-sociological. Lytton's compulsive preoccupation with the male reproductory and excretory organs was the outcome of and reaction to an age of excessive prejudice against sex – and in particular homosexuality – and while ostensibly these poems look forward to an epoch unfettered by uncomprehending and fearful puritanism, they convey above all else the intense morbidity of Lytton's mind during these years. Nevertheless, he remained convinced that his – as opposed, say, to R. C. Trevelyan's – was the only method of writing real poetry; that is, without an immediate eye to publication. It was, he felt, the only way of telling the whole truth; yet in moments of depression he was forced to concede that his poems were too wordy, too unintellectual.

What Professor Charles Sanders, with romantic *sang froid*, has described as 'the abandonment and ribaldry of a young satyr', consists of little more than various frequently reiterated expressions of hopeful, melancholy lust (more often than not depressingly rhymed with 'dust'), of vain invocations to 'Cruel Fate', and elegiac descriptions of 'laughing limbs', 'purple locks', 'cold lips', etc., and a truly phenomenal amount of copulation. What strikes one about these poems is the incongruity between their highly traditional and respectable form, and their obsession with sex, which Lytton refers to again and again as if in the mere repetitious penning of those unspoken words which describe the ordinary biological activities of mankind he was automatically thrown into some ravishing intoxication. 'But it's the extraordinary question of the naked body which really fascinates and absorbs,' he explained to Leonard Woolf. 'Heavens! it's mysterious and splendid! Terrible, melancholy and divine – those strange, inevitable, silent operations of nature! The lust and the strength of youth! Death!' Such moments of ecstatic delirium were usually followed by a sickening return to flat, inescapable common sense, when he seems to have comprehended in full the wide discrepancy which lay between the happiness he really sought and the dead quality of his versifying.

> *My love is larger than the universe*
> *Yet lies for ever coffined in my verse*
> *As in a pompous ineffectual hearse.*[1]

Among the published verses belonging to this period, one of the earliest, completed on 24 October 1899, was entitled 'I like the maiden of the Farm', and comprises a more or less formal rendering of the self-contempt which so often overwhelmed him:

> *She cannot hear me when I speak*
> *She thinks that I'm absurdly weak;*
> *She thinks that I'm a dreadful fright*
> *On all occasions – and she's right.*

[1] With the author's treatment of Lytton's Cambridge poems in the above two paragraphs, James Strachey was in vigorous disagreement. 'I have been positively staggered by some of your ethical judgements on the subject of sex and religion,' he wrote. 'Your remarks about Lytton's poems astound me. I can quite understand your saying that they're very poor poems and also that you can't quote them. But the impression you give of holding up your hands in shocked horror at their fearful obscenity makes me wonder whether you've ever come across a young human being. . . . When I read these passages I wonder why on earth you ever set out to write this book – and I feel inclined to want the whole thing thrown out of the window. The whole of Lytton's life was entirely directed to stopping critical attitudes of the sort that you seem to be expressing . . . in order to account for Lytton's quite ordinary youthful excesses, you have to cook up over and over again your stale Adlerian explanation. Things are really more complicated than that . . .'

Others of his poems, a number of which appeared in the *Cambridge Review* and elsewhere, show that he was already most proficient at imitating the metaphysical school of poets, as well as Pope, Dryden, Swinburne and Tennyson – 'a concoction of pretty verses', as he subsequently described the more sentimental compositions of the latter, 'flavoured to the taste of atrophied females'. Because his verse is so derivative, one of his most successful achievements was in direct parody. 'After Herrick', which came out in the *Cambridge Review* on 12 June 1902, has a neatness and simple control of metre that his other, more ambitious pieces often lack:

> *Wheneas I walk abroad by Night*
> *And Heavens-ward cast up my sight,*
> *The Luminaries of the Skies*
> *Make me think on Julia's Eyes.*
>
> *But when I take my walks by Day*
> *In flower-deckt field or garden gay,*
> *I see the flaming of the rose,*
> *And straightway think of Julia's Nose.*

Among his unpublished, but publishable, verses are several which exhibit a pleasing mastery of simple metrical technique. The art of composing this sentimental sort of poetry consists of laying down a certain fixed and regular pattern, and then producing small, harmonious variations on it – an exercise which Lytton could accomplish with charm and skill. A number of his compositions are cast in song or ballad form, with a repeated chorus at the end of each stanza. Others are more terse and epigrammatic, and lead on to a contrived twist held back to the last line to give point to the whole piece. The following two examples illustrate well his degree of proficiency in this field. The first is dated January 1900; the second, undated and without name, was probably written in 1903.

> ### By the Pool
>
> *Love, your body's very white,*
> *   May I touch it with my finger?*
> *(See, the day sinks into night)*
> *   Softly, softly shall we linger*
> *   By the pool we love so well.*
> *   Mirabel, oh Mirabel,*
> *Let me touch you with my finger.*

Love, your mouth is very red,
    May I pluck it like a cherry?
(See, the day is nearly dead)
    Who would be or sad or merry
        By the pool we love so well?
    Mirabel, oh Mirabel,
Let me pluck you like a cherry!

Love, your eyes are very blue
    May I gaze on them forever?
(Bid the day a last adieu)
    No rough hand us twain can sever
        By the pool we love so well
    Mirabel, oh Mirabel
Let me gaze on you forever.

Nature in jewels is so rich
She fills with diamonds every ditch,
Bright pearls o'er all her flowers she flings,
Gives the small beetle emerald wings,
With amber drops she decks the trees,
Adorns with sapphire the broad seas,
And so, complete in every part,
She fashioned out of jade your heart.

In his last two years at Cambridge, Lytton began to write book reviews, contributing half a dozen to the *Spectator* and rather fewer to the newly formed *Independent Review*. He also composed for various occasions a number of interesting essays – the literary form which above all others suited his peculiar talent. One of the earliest of these pieces, about thirteen thousand words in length, was 'Warren Hastings', a subject which attracted him by virtue of his family's association with India, and their traditional defence of Clive's and Hastings's colonial administration. He completed this essay on 26 September 1901, and submitted it for a Trinity award, the Greaves Prize. Despite the enthusiasm of Stanley Leathes, who thought it the best composition of its kind that he had ever seen, it did not win the award. There were, it would appear, several valid reasons for this failure. Though it is un-doubtedly a knowledgeable and thorough piece of work, aesthetically, as an essay, it is disappointing. The rather concentrated and uncolourful historical commentary – full of dates and information concerning the size of armies – which forms the backbone of the paper does not fit in with the romantic biographical portraiture and interpretation which is arbitrarily grafted on to it. As so often when he set out to conform wholeheartedly to the familiar traditions of the Stracheys, there was something forced and dissembling about his performance. In his anxiety to vindicate Hastings, he bombarded his enemies with a surfeit of invective and abuse, inflating the principal figures to the outsize proportions of Hollywood villains. For all his rhetoric and indignation they remain celluloid concoctions, beings without real substance, against whom Iago would appear to be a man of mixed intentions and redeeming vices.

The blackest of these knaves, and Hastings's evil genius, we are told, was Philip Francis, who 'could boast of a great reserve of malignity, of meanness, and of unscrupulous ambition. His personal enmities were distinguished by a ferocious and relentless cruelty, and his public opponents usually became his private foes. He was as crafty as he was false, as arrogant as he was selfish. In his private life he gambled and drank and seduced his neighbour's wife.'

In short he was thoroughly *bad*.

Like Iago, Francis, as depicted by Lytton, is little more than a puppet, whose dramatic function it is to force the unqualified idealist, the tolerant and enlightened hero – in this case Hastings himself – to see his conduct from the opposite standpoint, which explains every action in terms of self-interest. In this he is aided by a band of ignorant political enthusiasts among whom 'the figure of Burke is a supreme one, towering in all its superb error, in all its deluded grandeur, far above the stage sentimentality of Sheridan or the forced-up furies of Fox'.

But it is in its direct interpretation of Hastings as the best-abused personage in the whole course of history that the weakness of this total vindication becomes obvious. He will hear no word of censure against his hero, a man of fine deeds rather than empty words, of practice rather than quibbling theories, who brings out in him his own most romantic and unreasonable literary vein. Hastings was one of the gods, an ideal figure set in the same imperishable mould as the magnificent Thoby Stephen. The concluding paragraph of 'Warren Hastings' brings unblushingly into the open that all-consuming admiration which flared up within Lytton, like a schoolboy's infatuation, at the spectacle of this deathless, immaculate being:

'The final word on Hastings must perhaps be that he was a superman. What weaknesses, besides the physical, he had in common with the mass of mankind, it is difficult to see. His very passions took the form of devotion to the public weal; he never descended to a fault or even to a foible; he was perfection as a statesman, a husband, a friend; he soared.'

Most of the essays which Lytton wrote at Trinity were composed for the Sunday Essay Society which met every week in the rooms of Professor Bevan. The most notorious of the papers he read out to this Society was entitled 'The Ethics of the Gospels'[1] (February 1905), an attack on Christianity which delighted some and outraged others, and which in later years he was sometimes prevailed upon to deliver again. It is a painstaking and well-finished piece of work, but its assumed tone of detached clinical inquiry is very obviously sham – a stylistic device employed so as to exaggerate the devastating effect and findings of the paper. Its main aim purports to be an impartial consideration of the value of Christ's teaching, chiefly through a detailed examination of His commandments. By means of a rigidly austere, literal interpretation of meaning, and by ingeniously setting scripture against scripture, he leads his audience logically and infallibly on, deeper and deeper into a bewildering tangle of obscurities and confusions from which it can only reasonably conclude that Christ, as represented in the Bible, put forward 'no statement of the principles upon which feelings and actions ought to be guided'.

Another, earlier disquisition, entitled 'The Colloquies of Senrab', was on approximately the same theme, and also created something of a sensation. 'Senrab' was the backward spelling of Barnes, a brother of the future bishop of Birmingham, who had previously delivered a paper on 'Intellectual Snobs', directed against Lytton and the other members of the Midnight Society. Written as a parody of the uninspired, stereotyped sermon, Lytton's scathing rejoinder was regarded by many – including Maynard Keynes, a member of the audience, at that time personally unknown to Lytton – as 'a most brilliant satire on Christianity'. Lytton himself grew a little apprehensive at the rumpus to which it gave rise. 'I read yesterday (to the Sunday Essay Society) a scurrilous paper on the subject of Christianity,' he wrote to his mother (10 November 1902). 'I hope I shall not be sent down like Shelley in consequence. But the world has changed – and even Shelley was not at Cambridge.'

---

[1] In a letter to G. E. Moore (21 February 1905), Lytton wrote: 'I read a paper at the Sunday Essay last Sunday on the Ethics of the Gospels. It was considered unfair – a mass of quibbles, etc. [D.H.] MacGregor was heard to say something at lunch next day about the difference between Philosophy and Casuistry. [F. E.] Bray and A. C. Turner maintained a strict silence after the paper was read, until [Erasmus] Darwin begged some Christian to give his point of view. Bray's was that Harnack did not come to the same conclusion as the writer of the paper, also that the love of beauty was not good. A. C. Turner embarked on an enormous sentence, which no one ever heard the end of.'

Some of these early lucubrations anticipate, in argument, the artistic theories which he was later to put into practice in his own books. In 'Art and Indecency' he makes a witty and impassioned plea – reminiscent once again of Oscar Wilde[1] – for the divorce of ethics from aesthetics: 'It would be absurd to praise a locomotive for its virtue, or to condemn a soup as immoral; and it seems no less absurd to discuss the ethics of a symphony. Conversely, it is ridiculous to introduce aesthetic considerations into moral questions; the Kaiser's delinquencies have really nothing to do with his moustaches; and, while it is probable that some at any rate of the 11,000 virgins of Cologne were not good-looking, their holiness remains unimpeachable.'

Another paper, 'The Historian of the Future', may be regarded as a forerunner to the celebrated Preface Lytton wrote many years later to *Eminent Victorians*. But what is perhaps most noticeable about all these pieces is their distinctive style, which speaks eloquently of the great personal influence exerted over him at Cambridge by the philosopher, G. E. Moore. A single quotation taken from the last-mentioned essay will show readers of the *Principia Ethica* that Lytton's manner of argument reads in places like an unintentional parody of Moore's minutely detailed question-and-answer method of breaking down statements into their component parts in order to discover what they *really* meant and what evidence existed to support their meaning: 'The theory I want at present to discuss is, briefly, the theory that History is a science. What that phrase precisely means is certainly doubtful, and it is just this very doubt which makes me particularly inclined to discuss it. What do we mean by History? What do we mean by science? What, if you like, do we mean by "is"? These are all interesting questions, and questions which, considering their importance in any discussion of this sort, are singularly rarely asked, and even more rarely answered. Nevertheless it seems to me that to answer them is in reality a quite simple matter, and that having once accomplished this the true answer to the more complex question "Is History a Science?" will follow naturally and of its own accord.'

By far the best of Lytton's Cambridge essays are appreciations of English literature. From these, two stand out as supreme. 'Shakespeare's Final Period', originally delivered to the Sunday Essay Society on 24 November 1903, and published the following August in the *Independent Review*, was written as a counterblast to the theory, made fashionable by several respected critics of the day, that Shakespeare's last years – during which he wrote *Cymbeline, The Tempest* and *The Winter's Tale* – were passed in a saint-like state of tranquillity,

[1] See the Preface to *The Picture of Dorian Gray*.

ultimately benign and docile, and infused with a joyous spirit of universal forgiveness bordering on the senile. By the ample use of quotations which display a coarseness and brutality of language totally incongruous with the gentle, cosily idealistic fancies of Professor Dowden, Sir Israel Gollancz and a number of other noted Shakespearian commentators, Lytton demonstrated convincingly that there was little real evidence to sustain so improbably academic an interpretation. These critics, he pointed out, had naïvely relied on the happy endings to Shakespeare's last plays, those final scenes of 'forgiveness, reconciliation and peace', and Lytton is at his best and most assured in refuting this particular contention. Set in the style of traditional fairy tales, the conclusions of which were preordained by ageless convention, these plays, he believed, really illustrated Shakespeare's lessening hold on reality. He is in his second childhood, and his eyes, no longer fixed unblinkingly upon the actual world, are filled with a fairyland vision of wonder and enchantment. Yet this felicitous dream only holds him intermittently. Each time it fades and the shadows of his turbulent nature sweep across to darken the smooth unruffled surface of his fantasy, the dream plunges into nightmare, and Shakespeare's sudden terror bursts out in childish rage and petulance.

Lytton's understanding of Shakespeare's character had deepened since he wrote in his Liverpool diary five years previously that Shakespeare was 'a cynic in his inmost heart of hearts'. But 'Shakespeare's Final Period' still shows some latent uncertainty and obvious misinterpretation. He makes good use of the unabashed sentimentality of the established Victorian critics as a lens through which to bring his own contradictory view of Shakespeare into focus, to sharpen the contours of his figure. But once he strays from the perversely guiding commentaries of these critics and relies on his own unaided perception, a measure of his assurance falters, he confesses his lack of confidence in reconciling the work of any author with his personal character, and concludes that Shakespeare was 'bored with people, bored with real life, bored with drama, bored, in fact, with everything except poetry and poetical dreams'. As a piece of literary criticism this statement is hardly less sentimentalized in its own way than the theories of Dowden and Gollancz. What Lytton chose to call boredom was almost certainly complete exhaustion. It is at least as difficult to equate such an abyss of ennui as he imagines with the rage and fury of Shakespeare's outbursts (alternating with that pathetic, flickering unreality of his last wistful day-dreams) as it is to discover in these passages the ordered workings of a pedagogic mind conditioned to some state of serene and elderly self-possession. Boredom, which comes from a deficiency in imaginative and emotional experience, is a malady most incident to youth; exhaustion, the cumulative outcome of a surfeit of personal experience and physical activity, generally afflicts the old. The outward symptoms of both maladies can often appear similar, and Lytton's confusion of one with the other provides an interesting pointer towards his own state of mind.

The longest and best of all the prose pieces he wrote at this time was on the 'English Letter Writers', which he completed shortly after his twenty-fifth birthday and submitted in the hope of winning the Le Bas Prize for an English essay[1] – though that year no award was finally made. Over twenty thousand words in length, Lytton composed it, almost in its entirety, during a single week. The subject was well chosen and suited admirably his literary temperament. 'Perhaps', he was to write some fifteen years later, 'the really essential element in the letter writer's make-up is a certain strain of femininity.' In 'English Letter Writers' his own feminine strain of elegance and directness was consequently working in an ideal medium, and can be seen at its most enjoyable and illuminating. In their mixture of triviality and intimacy the letters with which he dealt formed an expression not of the innermost complexities of human nature – with which Lytton was seldom quite at his ease – but of the glamorous highlights and flourishes of the individual personality, the odd historical quirks and vivid characteristics which chiefly fascinated and diverted him. The theme of his disquisition was therefore not too exacting, and required just that blending of literary susceptibility and intellectual shrewdness with which he was so well equipped.

The essay is divided into six chronological chapters. In the first of these, which examines the Elizabethans, Lytton wrote: 'The Elizabethan age was pre-eminently an age of action, and some of the finest of its letters were written with the object of forwarding some practical end.' Elsewhere, too, the letters are analysed less as reflections of their correspondent's personal temperament than as microcosms of the age in which they were written. Lytton's sense of history, a subject which he had been officially studying now for many years at two schools and two universities, is as sure and well-informed as one would expect. 'An eighteenth century letter', he explains with assurance in his second chapter, 'is the true epitome of the eighteenth century.' His reading of character throughout succeeding epochs is less fluent. Of Pope's letters we are told simply that they do not reveal his true nature as does his

[1] This essay was not printed during Lytton's lifetime, but was first published posthumously by James Strachey in *Characters and Commentaries* (1933), and later reprinted in *Literary Essays* (1948).

poetry. The correspondence of Addison shows us merely a 'charming, polished, empty personality'; that of Steele, only an exhibition of fine manners; while we are introduced to Swift with the bland announcement that 'it is not our purpose, however, to discuss the colossal mind of the great Dean of St Patrick's'.

Passing on to his third chapter, Lytton considers first the letters of Lady Mary Wortley Montagu, whose 'wit has the quality which is the best of all preservatives against dullness – it goes straight to the point', but to whom life seemed little more than a game of whist; and secondly to the redoubtable figure of Lord Chesterfield, whose correspondence with his son provides a fitting counterpoint to Lady Mary Wortley Montagu's with her daughter. He is especially good when discussing Lord Chesterfield's letters, immediately putting himself in the place of the shy, bullyable, gawkish Philip Stanhope, with whose unremitting persecution by post he feels a profound commiseration. To Lytton's mind the scheme of conduct propounded by Chesterfield in these classic manuals of deportment was wholly odious – blindly, stupidly, vulgarly, patronizingly, absolutely conventional. The fanatical earnestness with which he strove to implant culture and an accomplished code of manners in his lonely, inarticulate son, only succeeded in stimulating to an unnatural extent a perfectly natural tendency to boorishness – a reaction which so incensed Chesterfield that he himself soon forgot his own manners, most improperly relinquishing his sophisticated self-possession and a number of those other social virtues which he felt such an ungovernable desire to promote in his stuttering, ungainly pupil. Though Lytton's indignation clouded in places the lucid, humorous relish he felt for this ludicrous tragi-comedy, the curious nature of Chesterfield's relationship with his illegitimate son greatly interested him, and he saw quite simply what so many more pretentious and masculine critics have missed: that, completely and irrevocably, Chesterfield was a bore of gargantuan proportions.

The fourth chapter of the essay is devoted entirely to the letters of Horace Walpole, to whom Lytton was often to return in the course of his career. His enduring interest in Walpole underlies much that was similar in their lives. The sons of ambitious practical men who had risen high in public life, both were closer to their more sensitive and emotional mothers, and managed with great control to reconcile these two inherited strains in their nature, following careers more akin to their maternal temperament though in such a way as to make them eventually as celebrated in their own fields as their fathers had been. As a result of their persisting fear of insecurity, they each remained emotionally rather immature, morbidly vulnerable to the least pinprick of ridicule. They subsisted as eternal though unorthodox bachelors, preoccupied for much of the time with escaping into the tranquillity of the past – 'into centuries that cannot disappoint one'. Both, in their later life, were reassured by pleasant, comfortable surroundings, a leisured and not too exacting routine, disliking, as shy, caustic and fastidious eccentrics, the rowdy, disconcerting presence of children. Above all, they practised the art of letter-writing with a grace, wit and highly cultured elegance seasoned with a dash of sharp, cat-like malice. But of the two, Lytton's absorption in the soothing shades of the past was far less complete. For he possessed a finer intelligence and humanity than Walpole, and, having once attained a measure of critical detachment, could never be so easily satisfied by purely social or historical meditation. At the same time, he felt a particular gratitude to Walpole for having produced, through the years, an encyclopaedic correspondence so perfectly composed as to elevate his cautious mediocrity to a point of literary skill where it became aesthetically engrossing and stimulating. In these letters there were no terrifying heights, no resounding chasms; everything was reduced to an evenly chiselled alabaster surface. The wilderness of nature had been tamed, and in its place Walpole had laid out the symmetrical and well-ordered precision of a formal garden. Lytton's response to this type of writing points, once again, to the duality of his temperament, for he never quite approves intellectually of what, he admits, attracts him emotionally. In short, he derived enduring enjoyment and solace in the contemplation of a voluminous correspondence written by a man whom he judges to be second-rate. Each time he picked up these letters he was allured and fascinated, following the figure of Walpole as he minced upstairs and downstairs and no further, daintily rearranging the china cups in the closets of Strawberry Hill. But then, on closing the book, the spell dissolved; and he would reflect critically on how little all this exquisite frippery amounted to.

The correspondence of Cowper and Gray was more personal, yet also more reticent. He probably read Cowper only in selection, for he misses altogether those tragic and lowering undertones of his epistolary style, the tortured pessimism of his subconscious apprehensions. As far as Cowper's letters go, he wrote, 'they are perfect, but they hardly go anywhere at all. The gold is absolutely clear; but it is beaten out into the thinnest leaf conceivable. They are like soap bubbles – exquisite films surrounding emptiness, almost too wonderful to be touched.' In the case of Gray, Lytton experienced a deeper and more immediate appeal. Was it, he asks, Gray's refinement, the breadth of his sympathies, or perhaps his quiet, compact sense of humour that so charmed his devotees? On reflection he decides that it was chiefly none of these qualities, but Gray's deep and abiding melancholy which sounded in his own heart such a sure echo. Had he himself been seduced into remaining all his life at Cambridge, been able permanently to drink in the calm and sunny peace from its soft Elysian fields, from those slow streams where meditation quietly shelters and thought ripples gently on,[1] it is possible that he might have come to share with Gray something of that same subdued note of tender regret, instead of developing that peculiar, off-beat counter-tenor, the straining, over-contrived exclamatory voice which can be heard in his more romantic writing. Lytton seems to have realized that he and Gray were partly of the same mettle, and their latent similarity is nowhere more implicit than in his final paragraph: 'His spirit seems still to hover about Cambridge. Those retired gardens, those cloistered courts, are as fitted now for his footstep and his smile as they were a hundred years ago. It seems hardly rash, when the midnight fire has been piled up, when sleep has descended upon the profane, when a deeper silence has fallen upon the night, when the unsported oak still stands invitingly ajar, to expect – in spite of the impediments of time and of mortality – a visit from Gray.'

The sixth and final chapter covers the letters of Byron, Shelley, Keats and Lamb. Of these Lytton appreciated the last three most. He offers neat epistolary quotations to display the individual merits of each correspondent, but has little really illuminating to say about any of them as human beings. With Byron, on the other hand, whom he disliked, the rays of his imaginative insight converted and focused upon the man who stood behind the letters. He is not blind to Byron's vivid appeal – 'The cumulative effect of Byron's vigour', he wrote, 'acts upon the reader like a tonic or a sea-breeze; he himself begins to wish to throw his ink bottle through the window, to practise pistol-shooting in bed, to scatter his conversation with resounding oaths' – but he found what he describes as 'the peculiar masculinity of his style' highly uncongenial. Though he knew only too well that all good letter-writers are egoists at heart, only Byron is taken to task for his egoism. 'Unfortunately,' he wrote, 'Byron's character was marred by a defect only too common to men of this particular type: he was a complete egoist. And round this fault a multitude of others naturally clustered – narrowness of interests, lack of real enthusiasms, vulgarity, affectation. His letters are concerned with one subject and one alone – himself.' Yet Lytton's strongly felt aversion did not rest simply with this general condition of egoism as he maintained, but sprang largely from one

[1] See William Gerhardie's *Memoirs of a Polyglot*, p. 263.

particular manifestation of it which he instinctively believed was the whole truth behind the wicked Byronic myth – the sordid, unaffectionate and incestuous affair he carried on with his sister. The contrast between Lytton's picture of Byron and the vaguer more blurred impressions of Shelley and Keats is convincing evidence of how, in much the same manner as Pope, disfavour could sharpen up his sense of reality. His discriminative powers crystallize round Byron and produce not just the embodiment of a romantic age or movement, but the living outline of a real if rather distasteful human being.

What makes 'English Letter Writers' such a good essay is the very authentic and familiar appreciation which Lytton obviously feels for his subject-matter, and which he charmingly conveys in a prose that is for the most part economical but never austere, and studded throughout with short, well-chosen quotations. Himself an extraordinarily prolific correspondent, he is well-qualified to show us that, though the best letters may have many distinguishing qualities – a deftness of touch, ease of expression, an unforced brilliance and gentle pervading amiability – yet, for true excellence, they must always succeed in suggesting that the personality of the letter-writer is even more attractive and unforgettable than the correspondence itself.

The theme of this essay was neither arbitrarily selected nor officially laid down, and unlike so many stereotyped competition pieces it is far from being just another laboured exposition of some humourless student thesis gravely compiled from the libraries at Trinity and the British Museum. As with many of the finest literary essays, the subject seems to have arisen naturally from the enjoyment of the author's everyday reading. Though the design of his later essays was more skilful and elaborate, and the pattern less obviously balanced, 'English Letter Writers' proves beyond question that Lytton's powers of selection and keen critical acumen, his mature taste and general knowledge of English literature, were already remarkably well advanced by the age of twenty-five.

6

BLANK, BLANK, BLANK

Because of his wide range of interests and literary predilections, Lytton's academic performance at Cambridge was conspicuously uneven. After matriculating in the Michaelmas term of 1899, he was made in the following year an Exhibitioner. In between prose and verse

compositions, and the meetings of the Midnight and other societies, he
was reading history in a rather desultory manner, and in June 1901 he
took the first part of his History Tripos. 'My tripos begins tomorrow,'
he wrote to his mother (21 May 1901), 'and lasts till Thursday. I am
calm and with the aid of chocolate will I hope weather it.' To the
general disappointment, he only obtained a Second Class. 'It was
exactly what I expected', he wrote to Lumsden Barkway, '– and I think
on the whole inevitable.'

The next year was, academically, Lytton's most successful. Early in
the Lent term he embarked on the longest and most complex exercise
in verse that he had hitherto undertaken. Entitled 'Ely: An Ode', the
piece is without poetic value or direct personal interest, and was
written specifically for the Chancellor's Medal which is awarded each
year for the best ode or poem in heroic verse and of less than two
hundred lines submitted by a resident undergraduate. 'Ely' is an
impeccably executed versification set in the strophes, antistrophes and
epode of the difficult Pindaric mould. The subject of Lytton's entry
was the near-by cathedral of Ely, and throughout the composition one
feels that he is on his very best behaviour. It is, in fact, the only
Cambridge poem in which he addresses God with a capital 'G'.
Characteristically he left himself very little time to complete this ode.
'Ely, if it is, will have to be written by next Saturday,' he told his
mother (26 January 1902). 'I think of making a pilgrimage, and dream
of strophes, antistrophes and epodes.' But all went well and a week later
he was able to write: 'Ely was sent in yesterday! I fear too hurried. But
beautifully arranged with strophes, antistrophes and epode!' The next
month Lytton learnt that he had won the award, narrowly beating (Sir)
John Sheppard of King's into second place.[1] 'I could dance with joy,'
his mother wrote to him from Lancaster Gate, 'and we are all in the
greatest delight.' And on 2 June the family delight was further increased when they came up to Cambridge and heard Lytton read his
winning ode in the Senate House, upon the occasion of a congregation
for the conferment of honorary degrees before an audience of distinguished personages, many of whom were visiting England in connexion with the imminent Coronation of King Edward VII.

Meanwhile, after passing another examination in the early spring, he
had been admitted as a scholar of Trinity in company with Thoby

[1] In a letter to his mother, Lytton wrote: 'I am going to get for my prize Merivale's
Roman Empire (bound and stamped) and Swinburne's works – au naturel. This will be
rather more than £10 – but I thought the magnificence of twenty-nine volumes was not
to be resisted.' There was no collected edition of Swinburne's works in those days.
Besides these twenty-nine unbound separate volumes, Lytton finally bought an obli-
gatorily bound two-volume edition of Shelley.

Stephen and some others. 'The ceremony was not particularly impressive,' he commented in a letter to his mother (28 April 1902), 'in
fact particularly absurd. We all had to be dressed in black with white
ties and bands – mystical articles which much increased the ludicrosity
of the performance. We all assembled at the Lodge first, where the
Master received us in his usual charming method. We then proceeded
to Chapel. Various grinning dons occupied the pews. Each scholar
advanced and read aloud his name in a book, and then knelt down on
both knees before the Master, placing his hands between his, while he
(the M) said in latin, "I admit thee a scholar of this College." But the
whole thing was hurried over as quickly as possible – no pomp or even
pomposity.'

This summer of 1902 marked the climax of Lytton's scholastic career
at Cambridge. Towards the end of July a seal was set on his triumph by
one of his father's now infrequent letters.

My dear Lytton

As I wished to make you a present as a token of our pleasure at your
recent success at Trinity College – and especially on your getting the
Chancellor's Medal, I thought that no more appropriate gift could be
found than a portrait of your mother to whom so much of your literary
training is in truth due.

                                        Your affnt father
                                        Rd. Strachey.

In view of his having been made a scholar of Trinity, it was generally
expected that Lytton would obtain a First Class in Part II of the
History Tripos and then go on to become a Fellow of the College.
Already, by the autumn of 1902, he had a particular Fellowship dissertation in mind and asked his mother to find out from Sir John
Strachey – his uncle and the author of *Hastings and the Rohilla War*
(1892) – whether he considered Warren Hastings and the Begums of
Oude a good subject; and whether, too, should he embark on it, there
existed any opportunities for original research work. Lady Strachey
herself thought the subject a fine one; the only drawback, so far as she
could see, being that it would involve Lytton spending a lot of time at
the British Museum. In October she wrote off to Sir John Strachey who
promptly replied that he was sure that Lytton could make a most
valuable monograph out of Hastings's encounter with the Begums.
'Lytton's idea seems to me an excellent one,' he wrote back. 'With the
exception of Stephen's *Nundkomar*[1] and my own Rohillas there has

[1] *The Story of Nuncomar and the Impeachment of Sir Elijah Impey* (1885) by Sir
James Fitzjames Stephen.

been, in my belief, little or no original research into the history of these times. I never looked into the great mass of Hastings's papers at the British Museum or the India Office Records for any time after that with which I was concerned, but there can be no doubt that they are a mine out of which a vast amount of knowledge can be dug. Unless someone unknown – which is not very likely I suppose – has been at work since my time nobody I believe, except myself, has ever seriously examined any part of the British Museum papers . . .'

But first there was the second part of the History Tripos. Lytton took this in the early summer of 1903, and once again, to everyone's dismay, he obtained only Second Class Honours. In a personal letter to Lady Strachey (30 June 1903), J. D. Duff described the result as a great disappointment and a complete surprise to him. 'That he is a First Class man is a point on which I feel no doubt at all,' he wrote. 'Of course I have never seen his work, except an Essay on Warren Hastings some years ago; but I judge from our personal intercourse, and say that in quality of intellect he is superior to any pupil I have had in my four years; and I have had dozens of Firsts and Double Firsts.

'Nor do I think it was a matter of health. He was not pressed for time: most men have only one year for the second part of that Tripos: and he kept well during the two years and I don't think he suffered during the examination.

'From what he has said to me, I believe the real reason to be that his Tripos involved a good deal of task work, books to be got up and definite facts to remember, and that he did not do this work. I had no notion of this beforehand, though perhaps I should have found it out.'

Though Lytton himself affected not to care overmuch about this Tripos result, his failure did entail one serious and very practical danger: that a Double Second might in due course prejudice the Fellowship Electors against him. They were a body of about sixteen dons representing all subjects, and all keen for their own candidates. Two, probably, would represent history; but all heard the evidence for each candidate before voting. 'I think Lytton might do so good a Dissertation as to overcome this prejudice', Duff told Lady Strachey, 'but it will undoubtedly be felt and expressed.'

Lady Strachey was also anxious lest Lytton's indifferent degree should act as an impediment against his entering the Civil Service, her original choice of career for him when he was applying to Balliol, and one which she now enthusiastically revived. Cambridge at this time trained a large proportion of its undergraduates for careers in public service, and several of Lytton's friends at one time or another

Marie Souvestre

dr cecil reddie

Queen of the Amazons: Lytton as Hippolyta in the Abbotsholme production of *A Midsummer Night's Dream*

were conscripted into some branch of the Civil Service – A. R. Ains-worth, Ralph Hawtrey and Robin Mayor going to the Education Office; Theodore Llewelyn Davies and Saxon Sydney-Turner to the Treasury; Maynard Keynes for a couple of years to the India Office; and Leonard Woolf, for seven, to the Ceylon Civil Service. But competition was keen and most of Lytton's associates were awarded Firsts or Double Firsts. 'Personally,' wrote G. M. Trevelyan to Maynard Keynes, 'I think it most distressing the way the civil service swallows nearly all the best Cambridge men.'

Lytton would have agreed with this opinion, for he felt no great urge himself to join any particular branch of the Civil Service – though this general disinclination was slightly qualified by a vague, rather romantic sense of social ambition. His mother however was determined that he should join the Board of Education, as it was then called, and Lytton once again appeared to fall in with her wishes. For the next few months she waged an energetic campaign on his behalf. After several abortive attempts she succeeded in arranging a confidential interview with J. W. Mackail, who had worked in the Education Department for some twenty years and had recently been made an assistant secretary. He assured her that the lack of a First Class degree was by no means an insurmountable obstacle to appointment, since these things were still largely arranged by private influence.

Now the campaign began in earnest. While both his parents sent off letters to their various influential friends and relations, Lytton busied himself getting testimonials from the dons under whom he had studied. The letters of recommendation written by them for this occasion are naturally enough all very flattering. But, after all allowances are made for the goodwill, generosity and spirit of helpfulness normally motivat-ing such testimonials, they do show that he was held in unusually high esteem among those of an older generation. J. D. Duff, more well-meaning than well-informed, wrote again along the lines of his earlier letter to Lady Strachey:

'I have known Mr Strachey well during his four years of residence. His character has always been excellent; and in point of intellect I consider him not inferior to any among the two hundred men who have been my pupils during the last four years.'

Stanley Leathes, who had been an examiner for both parts of the History Tripos, wrote of him as an undergraduate whose abilities deserved a higher place than that recorded in his official examination results:

'He is a man of unusually wide culture, of considerable originality, and unusual literary gifts . . . he is in every sense a well-educated man, and worthy to rank with first-class men, as is shown by his being elected to a Scholarship at Trinity. I think that his intelligence, wide reading, versatility, and cultivation would render him a good public servant in the Education Department. His intellectual capacity is far above his University degree.'

From the University of Glasgow, where he was now Professor of English Language and Literature, Walter Raleigh added a more personal note in support of Lytton's application:

'I have known Mr Strachey for years and I cannot think of anyone among my numerous past pupils, whom I should prefer to him for work requiring ability, tact and judgement. He has a mind of rare power and distinction, a character of great decision, and a temper so reasonable and gentle that it is a delight to work with him. I hope that he may be successful in obtaining the appointment that he seeks, where I am sure he would quickly gain the confidence and esteem of all who should have to do with him.'

Appropriately enough the briefest and most ambiguous of all Lytton's testimonials was contributed by a doctor of divinity, the Reverend William Cunningham,[1] later archdeacon of Ely, who managed on this occasion to discharge his responsibilities in a single sentence, which apparently recommended the man he was later to reject outright as a Fellow of Trinity, and which was remarkable for its unambitious wording:

'I have known Mr G. L. Strachey well during his period of residence at Cambridge; he has impressed me as a man of *unusual* ability, and I believe that he *might* be thoroughly trusted to discharge the duties of a responsible position with earnestness and accuracy.' (Emphasis added.)

Not long after Lytton had successfully canvassed these opinions, Lady Strachey got in touch with Sidney Webb, who was at that time especially influential as chairman of the London County Council's technical education board; and he in turn introduced her at a dinner given on 18 November to Sir Robert Laurie Morant, Permanent Secretary of the Board of Education. As a result of a talk they then had together, Morant agreed to interview Lytton once he returned to London for the vacation. Lady Strachey was jubilant. Her efforts seemed at

---

[1] Dr William Cunningham (1849–1919), familiarly known as 'Parson Bill', a pioneer though rather indifferent historian, who, in October 1901, had succeeded Stanley Leathes as Lytton's director of studies. 'William Cunningham was an imposing figure as he passed slowly across the Court in the shadow of his great archdeacon's hat,' wrote G. M. Trevelyan, 'looking like some high personage of Trollope's Barchester; but his capacious mind was evolving the new science of Economic History as an academic study, which has since grown to such great proportions.' His best-known work is *The Growth of English Industry and Commerce*.

last to have led to the very brink of a successful outcome. 'I believe I have done the trick,' she wrote to Lytton the day after meeting Sir Robert Morant. '. . . I have little doubt that if he finds you satisfactory he will give you an appointment when there is a vacancy. He asked me every detail concerning you and said you were very young. He said he preferred to have in the office men who had read for the bar, but that is not essential.'

What exactly transpired at Lytton's meeting with Sir Robert Morant is not now known. All that can be said with certainty is that he did not at any time join the Board of Education and that afterwards Lady Strachey once and for all abandoned her idea of a career for him in the Civil Service. Moreover, the similarity between this unsuccessful petition and his previous, equally fruitless application to go up to Balliol is very striking. In both cases it is his mother who, as the originator and driving force behind the scheme, brings it as near completion as is within the power of a third, not directly involved party. Though there exist marginal academic obstacles, both plans ultimately depend upon the personal impression created by Lytton himself at a single confidential interview. And though, as the written testimonials from his various tutors show, he was capable of producing over a period of time a highly favourable impression on older people occupying positions of authority, it was without doubt the uninspiring, maladroit figure he cut in these interviews that finally damned his chances of being appointed to vacancies that he was not, from the start, notably keen on filling. Pure shyness or a subtle, obstinate line of subterfuge? Either would account for these failures, and both reactions could be characteristic.

Whatever the reason, the practical consequences were irrevocable. With the possibility of a career in public service gone, Lytton now prepared himself to pursue yet another of his mother's vicarious schemes – a Fellowship. Once again he was not entirely pleased with the prospect laid out before him. He had no great desire to metamorphose into a don, to enter that faded world of weak bodies and spent minds, that half-life passed in accumulating knowledge which would be of no use to others, and only of use to himself in so far as it might numb his discontent with existence. He would, he liked to imagine, rather enjoy the high seas of life

> Than sit, with eyes grown spectacled and smug
> Hands soft, feet planted slippered on the rug,
> To note, infer, insinuate and opine!

But Cambridge itself he loved as no other place save perhaps the wild, natural beauty, open skies and riotous vegetation of Rothiemurchus. And with rooms at Trinity he could escape the ponderable gloom of Lancaster Gate. Besides, what assured future *could* there be for him beyond the university?

'After Cambridge,' he wrote to Leonard Woolf, 'blank, blank, blank.'

CHAPTER V

Beetles and Water-spiders

'I feel I should go mad when I think of your set, Duncan
Grant and Keynes and Birrell. It makes me dream of beetles.
In Cambridge I had a similar dream. I had felt it slightly
before in the Stracheys. But it came full upon me in Keynes
and in Duncan Grant. And yesterday I knew it again in
Birrell – you must leave these friends, these beetles.'
    D. H. Lawrence in a letter to David Garnett (19 April 1915)

'I can see us as water-spiders, gracefully skimming, as light
and reasonable as air, the surface of the stream without any
contact at all with the eddies and currents underneath.'
                   John Maynard Keynes –
                         'My Early Beliefs' (1938)

I

ANARCHISTS AT TALK

During his full six years in residence at Cambridge Lytton joined
several clubs within the university apart from the Midnight and the
Sunday Essay Society. There was, for example, the Shakespeare Society
at Trinity to which a number of his friends – Walter Lamb, Thoby
Stephen, Leonard Woolf and others – also belonged. And there was the
Union Society, at whose debates he remained for the most part silent.
'I, I fear, am no orator,' he explained to his mother.

The most celebrated of all the university societies, to which he was
elected in his third year up at Trinity, was the 'Cambridge Conversazione Society', better known as the 'Apostles' or simply 'the Society'.
Unlike the Midnight, the X, and all other such groups, the Apostles
were not confined to Trinity: they covered the whole university, and at
that time particularly King's. Lytton had hardly known any King's
men before he was elected. But from this time onwards, his circle of
friends expanded noticeably. For the Apostles differed from the usual
undergraduate societies in the fact that members did not cease to belong
once they had graduated or gone down. Although they had no say in
the elections, many of the older brethren would still regularly attend

their meetings, and it was as a result of this that Lytton was able really to get to know people such as Desmond MacCarthy, C. P. Sanger, Bertrand Russell, G. E. Moore, Goldie Dickinson and others. If one takes the spring of 1902 as a watershed, one begins to find a change in his writings and in the views he held. It wasn't simply a question of these Apostolic meetings. Almost every week-end one or two of the older brethren would turn up. Lytton would meet them at tea or dinner on the Saturday – and Sunday breakfasts were always an event. This contact with older people of a special sort was bound to have its effect, as can be seen in the various papers he wrote after this date.

Since its original foundation almost a century earlier, the Apostles had been – and still are – a 'secret' body, though only in the more journalistic sense of the term, which accounts for their having unerringly attracted to themselves a far greater volume of publicity than could ever be bestowed on less perseveringly clandestine fraternities. At the same time, there was a quite practical reason for this concealment. Although it was known to readers of memoirs, practically none of the under-graduates realized that the Society still existed. Consequently, the Apostles were protected from those who aspired to be elected and would behave in peculiar ways to achieve this end.

Lytton jubilantly proclaimed his election, which officially took place on 1 February 1902, in a heavily marked 'Private and Confidential' letter to his mother – who already knew much of the eminence and mystique of the Society, and was overjoyed at the news.[1]

'My dearest Mama – This is to say – before I am committed to oaths of secrecy – that I am now a Brother of the Society of Apostles – How I dare write the words I don't know! – I was apparently elected yesterday, and today the news was gently broken. The members – past and present – are sufficiently distinguished. Tennyson was one of the early ones. But I shall know more when I visit the Ark – or closet in which the documents of the Society are kept. It is a veritable Brotherhood – the chief point being personal friendship between the members. The sensation is a strange one. Angels are Apostles who have taken wings – viz, settled down to definite opinions – which they may do whenever they choose. I feel I shall never take wings. This has once occurred with the apparent result that the Ap. was eventually transported for life! Another person whom I don't know called Sheppard (King's) was elected at the same time as me. We meet each other tonight! . . .'

---

[1] Lady Strachey had also been told something of the Apostles by various friends and relations – Walter Raleigh, Sir Henry Maine, James Fitzjames Stephen and Arthur Strachey, all past members – and had grown fearfully keen that Lytton should be elected. Before he went up to Cambridge, she had passed on to him all she knew of the Society.

The Society had been founded as a small, comparatively humble and unpretentious debating club in St John's College. But during the 1820s it fell under the control of two formidable undergraduates, F. D. Maurice and John Stirling, who transferred its rendezvous to the larger and more fashionable Trinity. Once established in this new head-quarters, the nature of its business soon underwent radical alteration. Its members, from now on selected only with the extremest caution, met behind locked doors on Saturdays, when, after tea and anchovy toast, they would read papers, often on moral topics, and hold troubled, militant discussions.

'The society', wrote Sir Roy Harrod, friend and hagiographer of Maynard Keynes, 'was very skilful in its choice of members.' Tennyson, who describes it in canto 87 of his *In Memoriam*, was, as Lytton had told his mother, an early member, and so was Arthur Hallam. But Tennyson's association with the Society was unhappy, and when his turn came to read a paper on 'Ghosts' embarrassment so overcame him that he tore the paper to pieces, the evening's entertainment ended in disaster, and he was summarily removed from the favour of the *élite*. Among other near-contemporaries Kingslake, Edward FitzGerald and Thackeray were not admitted into the circle; while Kemble, an authority on Anglo-Saxon, Sunderland, who died insane, and Venables, who failed to achieve any form of distinction whatever, were prominent at its gatherings. The Society was, continues Sir Roy Harrod, 'remark-ably successful in preserving its characteristics throughout the genera-tions'. And certainly the system of strict Apostolic succession which the brethren so resolutely exacted did ensure among its members a stern consistency. The suspicion with which, for example, the more monastic adherents regarded Maynard Keynes's excursions into the open world of politics was given ample and exact precedent. 'He will end up as an old Civil Servant,' Lytton once said of Keynes during the course of a passionate denunciation,[1] 'and will regret that he never was able to go into the House of Commons, for then he could have ended up as an old parliamentary hand.' Over sixty years earlier the tone might be less aggressive but the attitude was identical, as is shown by a letter sent in 1830 from Blakey to Thompson – the Master of Trinity – in which the writer expresses a similar anxiety over the disturbing weakness ex-hibited by the nineteen-year-old Hallam, who 'was not well while he was in London', we are told; and who, moreover, 'was submitting him-self to the influences of the outer world more than (I think) a man of his genius ought to do'.

The inner world of the Apostles was sacrosanct. Accounts of its

[1] 'Shall we go the Whole Hog', a paper delivered before the Society on 25 February 1905.

workings given by two nineteenth-century brethren, Dean Merivale and Henry Sidgwick, 'show that its nature and atmosphere have remained fundamentally unaltered throughout its existence', wrote Leonard Woolf, who was elected in the same year as Lytton. Dean Merivale, a contemporary of poor Tennyson, describes its activities as follows:

'Our common bond has been a common intellectual taste, common studies, common literary aspirations, and we have all felt, I suppose, the support of mutual regard and perhaps some mutual flattery. We soon grew, as such youthful coteries generally do, into immense self-conceit. We began to think that we had a mission to enlighten the world upon things intellectual and spiritual. We had established principles, especially in poetry and metaphysics, and set up certain idols for our worship . . . we piqued ourselves on the name of the "Apostles" – a name given us, as we were sometimes told, by the envious and jeering vulgar, but to which we presumed that we had a legitimate claim, and gladly accepted it. We lived, as I said, in constant intercourse with one another, day by day, meeting over our wine or our tobacco; but every Saturday evening we held a more solemn sitting, when each member of the society, about twelve in number, delivered an essay on any subject, chosen by himself, to be discussed and submitted to the vote of the whole number. Alas! alas! what reckless joyous evenings those were. What solemn things were said, pipe in hand; how much serious emotion was mingled with alternate bursts of laughter, how everyone hit his neighbour, in-tellectually, right and left, and was hit again, and no mark left on either side; how much sentiment was mingled with how much humour!'

The testimony of Henry Sidgwick, a close friend of the parents of Maynard Keynes, who was elected in 1856–7, shows only too clearly that, some three decades later, though their intellectual pugilism, their weird cerebral shadow-boxing, could be just as exhaustive, their collective sense of humour had become no laughing matter:

'Absolute candour was the only duty that the tradition of the society enforced. No consistency was demanded with opinions previously held – truth as we saw it then and there was what we had to embrace and maintain, and there were no propositions so well established that an Apostle had not the right to deny or question, if he did so sincerely and not from mere love of paradox. The gravest subjects were continually debated, but gravity of treatment, as I have said, was not imposed, though sincerity was. In fact it was rather a point of the apostolic mind to understand how much suggestion and instruction may be derived from what is in form a jest – even in dealing with the gravest matters.'

This unencumbered sincerity and funereal merriment formed part of the close bond which continued to unite Apostles of the mid-nineteenth century and later, long after they had gone down from Cambridge, and which was given elevated expression by several of the elect. Jack Kemble announced that the world was one great thought, and he was thinking it; while his colleague, Venables, would often extemporize with genuine amazement on their good fortune at being exalted so far above the general rank and file of humanity, and wonder why in heaven they had been gifted to such excess over 'those cursed idiotic oxford [they spelt the hated word with a tiny "o"] brutes'. And Lytton, too, felt something of the same fiercely partisan convictions, lamenting over the rival university like Christ over Jerusalem. 'It's all or nothing with us,' he wrote on one occasion to Maynard Keynes (4 November 1905), 'Oxford's the glorification of the half-and-half.'

This denunciation of Oxford had a serious meaning. Under Gerald Balfour,[1] brother of the prime minister and himself a senior politician, Alfred Lyttelton,[2] a Conservative cabinet minister, and Henry Cust[3] the distinguished art-historian, the Apostles had for a time gradually evolved into a more sophisticated and urbane group, and it was only in about 1890, with the election of Goldie Dickinson, Robin Mayor[4] and McTaggart, that it had finally reacted against this 'top hat epoch' and reintroduced more austere doctrines. By the time Lytton and Sheppard joined, the principles and aims were once again well-defined. They sought to establish a rival influence to that of the eclectic, worldly climate of Benjamin Jowett's Balliol.[5] Above the splendour and prestige of political advancement they venerated solitary self-development, and held abstract contemplation to be of more value than direct action.

[1] Gerald Balfour (1853–1945) was a Fellow of Trinity and member of Parliament for Central Leeds (1885–1906). Among the appointments he held were Chief Secretary for Ireland (1895–1900) and President of the Board of Trade (1900–1905). A popular man of great social charm.

[2] Alfred Lyttelton (1857–1913), lawyer, statesman and popular socialite, who was head of the Colonial Office (1903–5) but whose chief eminence was as a cricketer. His play, remarked W. G. Grace, was 'the champagne of cricket'.

[3] Sir Henry Cust (1859–1929), the plump and ebullient director of the National Portrait Gallery, who married Alfred Lyttelton's sister Sybil, collaborated for ten years with Roger Fry as joint-editor of the *Burlington Magazine*, and, in his capacity as surveyor of the king's pictures, was responsible for the rehanging of pictures in the various royal palaces. His books include a rather inelegant *History of Eton College* (1899) and an exhaustive study of Van Dyke.

[4] Robert John Grote Mayor (1869–1947), Old Etonian, Fellow of King's and a prominent Civil Servant. Married Beatrice Meinertzhagen (1912), was assistant secretary at the Board of Education (1907–19) and became principal secretary (1919–26).

[5] Benjamin Jowett (nicknamed 'the Jowler'), Master of Balliol from 1870 to 1893, who said that he wanted to 'inoculate England' with his college alumni, and who became one of the supreme influences in Victorian England. Arrogant and temperamental, with a shrill voice, squat figure and owl-like features, he was famous for his succinct rudeness and pithy conversational rebuffs. A formidable if erratic scholar and divine, he was Regius Professor of Greek at Oxford and responsible for a frigidly asexual translation of Plato.

Lytton warmly approved of this philosophy, but by temperament he was never wholly akin to it. He honestly believed that a lust for fame contaminated the pure search for truth, that a love of power distorted human affections. Yet personally he was not altogether unambitious, only unconfident. He therefore welcomed a way of life and standard of conduct that discouraged for all the worldly success he secretly cherished but felt he could never attain. If others, more fitted for social and political triumphs, disdained such prizes, then his friendships might never be poisoned by envy. Self-effacement did have an authentic appeal for him; but obscurity was a constant irritant. He was never truly Apostolic as men like Ralph Hawtrey,[1] G. E. Moore, Lionel Penrose, Frank Ramsey, C. P. Sanger, W. J. H. Sprott and James Strachey were, but, in Apostolic jargon, slightly 'tinged with the phenomenal'. He revered the Society, and considered the values they upheld to be the real ones. But world-wide renown was later to make him a happier, more beneficent being. He was right to be ambitious. Fame suited him. For only when he was famous could he effectively carry out his real ambition – the education of the public to more humane views.

A few days after their election Lytton and Sheppard attended their first formal meeting and inscribed their names in the official society ledger. 'I am number 239,' Lytton informed his mother (10 February 1902). 'We have previously inspected the ark in which the papers and books of the Society are kept. It is a charming cedar-wood chest – presented by Oscar Browning.[2] A paper of Arthur's[3] is preserved in it – also a speech by Uncle Raleigh. The minute books are very amusing. The procedure is as follows. A subject is chosen on which the next paper

[1] Sir Ralph Hawtrey (b. 1879), economist at the Treasury (1904–45) and author of many books. President of the Royal Economic Society (1946–8). Married Hortense Emilia D'Aranyi – one of the musical sisters. 'I retain a vivid recollection of him [Lytton Strachey] and of his personality,' he wrote to the author (23 April 1963). At Cambridge he was chiefly known as a mathematician, and had great arguments with Moore, Russell and Harry Norton on metaphysics (logic and epistemology).

[2] Oscar Browning, C.B.E. (1837–1923), historian and historical biographer. Educated at Eton and King's College, Cambridge. In 1859 he had been made a Fellow of King's, and the following year took up a post as assistant master at Eton. Returned to King's in 1876 as lecturer in history. Hugely fat, he was a notorious socialite and 'character', a 'genius flawed by abysmal fatuity', as E. F. Benson once called him. His last years were spent in Rome, where he was appointed president of the Academy of Arts. Among his many friends was Oscar Wilde. 'Do you know Oscar Browning?' he asked Robert Ross (circa 13 October 1888). 'You will find him everything that is kind and pleasant.' There is a biography of the legendary 'O.B.' by H. E. Wortham, called Victorian Eton and Cambridge (1956).

[3] Sir Arthur Strachey (1858–1901), the second son of Lytton's uncle, Sir John Strachey. At Trinity Hall he had taken a degree in law, after which he went out to India and was made Chief Justice of the High Court at Allahabad. He died in Simla.

is to be read; but as a matter of fact the paper need have nothing to do with the subject chosen. . . . Everyone speaks (though in a purely conversational way) in turn after the paper is read. There were a good many distinguished persons present – among them Goldie Dickinson – and I, being the last elected, had to speak last. They seemed fairly amused.[1] We then voted on this (which, though you wouldn't expect it, seemed to be the main point at issue) – Shall we be anti-vivisectionists? Most I think (including me) said no. Sometimes people add notes to their negatives or affirmatives – and this is what makes the minute books amusing . . . everything's so mysterious, one doesn't always know exactly the thing that's wanted. What at present alarms me is the thought that I, as junior member, will have, at the annual dinner in June, to fulfil the function of Vice-President, and return thanks for the health of the Society proposed by the President, who will probably be either Sir Richard Jebb or the Earl of Carlisle!'

The papers which Lytton read out to his fellow Apostles during the first two or three years of his membership illustrate something of a discrepancy. At their best these Apostolic addresses dredge up to the light of day the sour effluence of a bitter and repressed revolutionary spirit. Probably the most outspoken of them was 'Christ or Caliban?' (25 October 1902), a Swinburnian essay in which Caliban symbolized freedom from all restraint, and Christ the bleak and barren plane of modern civilization. In essence it is a tract against the kind of unenlightened, hide-bound Victorian society which had turned its back on his own deepest problems and silently decreed that he should be branded a misfit. This old rule still persisted, merciless and uncomprehending, still enforced its senseless restrictions upon the free play of the human spirit. And while it remained, a strange feeling of revolt bubbled and surged up dangerously within him.

Yet even before his fellow Apostles, Lytton could not speak all his mind. The true gist of his meaning can only be interpreted between the lines of his speeches; and it is not quite clear how fully aware he was of the conceptions which lay at the root of some of them. The absurd overtones of a piece like 'Christ or Caliban?' with its Lawrentian enhaloment of the 'savage races' is to some extent offset by a vein of slightly self-conscious humour running through it. At the same time the repressed, crusading spirit which informs his words is as real as Rousseau's passionate call to mankind to throw off its chains and revert to the natural primitive life. As real and as romanticized. Like Rousseau, Lytton did not have a truly speculative mind; he was not really interested in religious, philosophical or even historical theory, and his

---

[1] Lytton's paper was entitled 'Dignity, Romance and Vegetarianism'.

papers have the same network of sentimental fallacies and inconsistencies, saved however from ultimate absurdity by the unanalysed force of feeling which thrusts its way through every line – a belief in the superabundant importance of the individual, his dignity and his rights. 'Christ or Caliban?' contains little of Rousseau's paranoiac fire and morbidity, but it is written with a pallor and execration of its own. The iron chains of Rousseau are replaced by *démodé* elastic braces, and the whole fulminating composition unwittingly lends itself to a series of cartoons in the style of Max Beerbohm – Lytton as Greek slave, Roman gladiator, or British flyweight. For example:

'I, at any rate, would be willing with all the alacrity in the world to put myself back into one or other of those more violent ages where railways and figleaves were equally unknown. – "But if you were a slave?" I would be willing to risk that, for I should perhaps creep in to see the first performance of the Birds, or I might be doorkeeper at the Globe, or with some luck I might get to a Gladiatorial show. – How terrible! But supposing you were a gladiator yourself. You wouldn't enjoy that! – Perhaps not; but at any rate I should die a violent death . . . at least I should have no braces. . . .

'We still have our field sports, we still hunt; and if I had ever been allowed to choose my life anywhere in my own age I should have been a stout athletic boxer. . . .

'But if external help is lacking, is there no chance of some swift internal disintegration? Is there no possibility of a break-up so general and so complete that the entire reorganization of society would be a necessary sequence? Personally, I welcome every endeavour, conscious or unconscious, to bring about such an end. I welcome thieves, I welcome murderers, above all I welcome anarchists. I prefer anarchy to the Chinese Empire. For out of anarchy good may come, out of the Chinese Empire nothing.'

Several of his other Apostolic harangues strike the same fiercely iconoclastic note. 'Shall we be Missionaries?' (undated) was an attack on imperialism: 'I believe, indeed, that some Englishmen do sincerely hold that if England conquered the whole world the greatest possible amount of good would be produced.' Another paper, 'Is Death Desirable?' (January 1903) reaffirms his settled agnosticism: 'It is no longer, for me at any rate, either interesting or profitable to pretend to believe in the immortality of the soul . . . immortality has been relegated simply to the position of a mere possibility, absolutely devoid of any particle of probability.' In other papers which ignore metaphysics and concern themselves exclusively with the benefits of *this* life, such as 'Will it come all right in the end?' (undated), a distinctly sybaritic tone is adopted: 'It *is* lust that makes the world go round.' And in line with this emphasized anarchical hedonism is an amusing take-off of prudery in art and morals, 'Ought the Father to grow a Beard?' (10 May 1902), where Lytton feigns horror at the growing fashion of naked chins, the failure of so many modern young people, even of quite good family and schooling, to wear a decent covering of whiskers over their stark fleshy faces. 'And that rounded chin, that soft repletion of flesh and fat, is it not more hateful than ever was the bristling and curling hair? More bare, more vile, more loathsome, more incomparably lewd?'

But in contrast to all this belligerence and declared apostasy, the papers which Lytton read out on the subjects of aesthetics and human relationships are orthodox, even diffident. In company with Clive Bell he had begun to develop by this time a rather literary appreciation for the visual arts, but his taste was, and always remained, conservative. In 'Ought Art to be always Beautiful?' (undated), one of his earlier papers, he spoke out against Manet and the Impressionist school of painting, arguing that although it was theoretically possible for good painting not to treat a subject inherently beautiful in itself, in practice it must always be otherwise. His aesthetic concepts on the art of the theatre are sounder, but hardly revolutionary, as another paper, 'When is a Drama not a Drama?' (undated) illustrates: 'My theory is that the essential point about a drama is that it should be composed of two parts, during the first of which the states of mind of the characters should be entirely different from their states of mind during the second. The transition from the first part to the second is the culminating point of the drama – the climax.' Such a well-tried theory of dramatic art was not unknown even in the Greek theatre, and probably represented what he was endeavouring, rather academically, to put into practice in a three-act Euripidean tragedy on which he was working at about this time.[1]

But perhaps the least revolutionary of all his papers are those which deal directly with human relationships. Altogether different from so much that he wrote in private letters to his closest friends, these personal reflections are qualified, mild, almost apologetic. In 'Does Absence Make the Heart Grow Fonder?' (19 November 1904), he wrote: 'I cannot help confessing that if I had the chance of marrying in quite the ordinary way the person whom I wanted to, I wouldn't hesitate for a

---

[1] In November 1903, Lytton had read a translation of *Iphigenia in Tauris*, and written to his mother: 'I long to write the tragedy as sketched by him [Euripides].' Preserved among his papers are two undated plays in manuscript, 'Iphigenia in Aulis' in three acts, and 'Iphigenia in Tauris', a fragment of one uncompleted act.

moment.' But the chances of this actually happening, he felt, were remote. For as he admitted a year later – 'Shall we take the Pledge?' (December 1905) – 'My acquaintance among women is small; I know very few with anything approaching intimacy; and I must confess that I have never been in love with one.'

There were altogether only some half-dozen undergraduate members of the Society when Lytton and Sheppard were elected. For them, the greatest delight of belonging to the Society was the freedom of speech which it not only allowed but actually encouraged. At last, after years of silent constraint, one might say out loud something of what one felt and thought; and this was a marvellous release from the polite and decorous suppressions of Victorian 'mupple-class' deportment, a sudden expanding joy not so easy to appreciate these days. 'It was a principle in discussion that there were to be no *taboos*, no limitations, no barriers to absolute speculation,' wrote Bertrand Russell in his autobiography. 'We discussed all manner of things, no doubt with a certain immaturity, but with a detachment and interest scarcely possible in later life.'

Truth – that was what they were after; and truth they knew could never be beguiled by mere mental ingenuity. Above all they must be candid, speak their minds openly, confess their doubts with sincerity and irreverence, and generally behave with the rational good sense so lacking in ordinary mortals. 'We were at an age', wrote Maynard Keynes in My Early Beliefs, a paper delivered in 1938 to the Memoir Club, 'when our beliefs influenced our behaviour, a characteristic of the young which it is easy for the middle-aged to forget.' And so, twenty-five years later, it may have appeared. But in practice there is no age at which a statement of beliefs directly and straightforwardly anticipates or even succeeds human action. For a man's opinions are almost always intuitively evolved as the natural corrective force counterbalancing his psychological state of being and the opposing everyday habits of his behaviour conditioned by his environment. Countries such as England, languishing for so long under the yoke of a puritan tradition which dams up and perverts the natural emotions of the individual until they rise to an unnaturally high pressure, produce as adjacent cells to their coercive societies a profusion of pocket utopias, protective coteries. These miniature ideal worlds are usually either social or religious in their framework, depending primarily on whether they exist merely to administer solace and consolation, or to stimulate more active reassurance and sedition.

If one looks into it, the whole system of the Apostles appears curiously analogous to a religious system; clearly is, in fact, a parody of religion. One can perceive without difficulty the distinctive character-istics of all religions in the dogma, the ritual procedures and unspoken faith which made up the nucleal sanctity of the Society. Not to be Apostolic was not to exist. The formalities of a meeting and of an election were designed to caricature all the mystique of a religious service. There was no pulpit, but the hearthrug fulfilled a similar func-tion and was spoken of in exactly the same respectful fashion. In place of a blessing the brethren used a curse. There was, too, an impressive mumbo jumbo, secret words and secret meanings of words – 'whales', for instance, which referred to the sardines now consumed in lieu of the original anchovies, and which were held to have been the object of some fantastic law of transubstantiation. And there was a complete mystical hierarchy from 'embryos' – those who were in the running for election – up the scale to 'angels'.

A religious secrecy, also, full of paradox and mystery, fed their legend. Theoretically, they wanted everyone to be Apostolic; yet very few there were who were admitted to the Cambridge Conversazione Society. For the uninitiated, it was terrible, fascinating, exciting, to imagine exactly what these latter-day Apostles were up to, each Saturday night, behind those locked and bolted doors.

2

FATHER FIGURES

Although the Society had not altered much over seventy years, some minor changes of emphasis had gradually evolved. During the nine-teenth century the congregation of brethren were frequently uplifted by transcendental politics. But by the turn of the century the debates had become the battleground of the younger Cambridge philosophers, J. E. McTaggart, A. N. Whitehead,[1] Bertrand Russell and G. E. Moore. True, there was still a small political element within the group, but it was very far from being in the ascendant. The ethical and metaphysical speculations which dominated their discussions were too elevated and immaterial to preserve any very solid contact with the mundane affairs of party politics. And, at the beginning of the Edwardian era, this philosophical influence so overshadowed all other preoccupations that

[1] Alfred North Whitehead, O.M., F.R.S. (1861–1947), mathematician and philo-sopher. Colleague of Bertrand Russell, with whom he wrote *Principia Mathematica*. Author of many distinguished books on mathematics and science. In his later days he was chiefly famous for his philosophical writings.

fierce radicals like George Trevelyan and Nathaniel Wedd[1] would sometimes doze off to sleep during the involved proceedings; while Leonard Woolf's anxiety to make arrangements for G. E. Moore to be appointed president of the Board of Education found little active support among his confederates and none at all from Moore himself, who was the last person to be offered, let alone to accept, such an appointment. For Lytton, politics was little more than, in Keynes's words, 'a fairly adequate substitute for bridge'.

Lytton spent as much of his time as possible in the company of other Apostles, his 'new and important friends' as he described them in a letter to Lumsden Barkway. In the Easter vacation of 1902 he was invited to a reading-party at Ventnor on the Isle of Wight, with a select band of brothers, including Charles Sanger, Robin Mayor, Desmond MacCarthy – who turned up late – G. E. Moore and his future brother-in-law, A. R. Ainsworth.[2]

Lytton was looking forward to the Isle of Wight, so pleasantly small, with lots of sea all round and chalk downs. The party stays at the Blackgang Chine Hotel, where rooms are to be had at two guineas a week; and there they follow a daily Apostolic programme of work and entertainment. The mornings are consecrated to serious writing and reading – Moore pens philosophy; Ainsworth reads Plato and *Anna Karénine* in French, and Lytton *Père Goriot*, *Madame Bovary* and then Montaigne's essays, Swinburne's poems and Webster's plays – the afternoons are usually given over to walking to Carisbrooke, Freshwater and elsewhere, and the evenings to amusements – conversations on philosophy and literature, or games of jacoby or picquet. This is the most peaceful part of the day – Moore at the piano singing Brahms in his low German tenor, the tall, bespectacled Bob Trevelyan, with his craggy face and nebulous mind, standing by him swaying vaguely with the melody; MacCarthy in front of the fire deep in a rocking chair, his feet on the mantelpiece; Ainsworth still poring over his *Anna Karénine*; Lytton himself perfectly motionless, hovering on the interminable brink of some illness, of some precipitate and complete loss of temper.

'Can you imagine the scene?' he writes to Leonard Woolf. 'We have

---

[1] Nathaniel Wedd, Fellow of King's College, where he was for many years Classical Lecturer and Assistant Tutor. Also member of council of Newnham College. Lionel Trilling, in his study of E. M. Forster, writes that 'the decisive influence on Forster was his classics tutor, Nathaniel Wedd, a cynical, aggressive, Mephistophelean character who affected red ties and blasphemy'.

[2] Alfred Richard Ainsworth, C.B. (1879–1959), who after leaving Cambridge took a job as lecturer at Manchester University (1902–3) and then at Edinburgh University (1903–7), later becoming a Deputy Secretary at the Board of Education.

a sitting-room to ourselves – a table in the middle, very uncomfortable red plush chairs, pictures of whores on the walls, a piano (at/on which Moore plays and sings) a marble mantelpiece, and 43 red and yellow glass ornaments. . . . We are all very nice and happy I presume – though sometimes your humble servant sinks into demi-depression.'

These troughs of melancholia are occasioned by a succession of unforeseen calamities. Frequent attacks of indigestion interrupt his reading during the mornings and eventually reduce him to a noisome diet of bread and milk. In the afternoons he is regularly chilled to the bone as, together with the rest of the party, he makes his way joylessly across the cold blustery countryside, along twisting hillocks and sunken Victorian villages. And finally, over the course of several evenings he nearly quarrels with Ainsworth – 'I don't like the personification of irrelevance' – and waxes especially angry on being told by him that George Trevelyan shares Bernard Shaw's low opinion of Webster. 'My view of the world', he tells Leonard Woolf, 'becomes black when I think of it.'

Between such fits of darkest anger and discomfort, Lytton wastes away in a gehenna of boredom, and is soon looking forward to his eventual departure. The tedium and 'utter drivelling imbecility' of the party, however, moderates just before the end, when Goldie Dickinson and Roger Fry turn up. 'The latter – as of course you know – is a sort of art-critic,' he reminds Lumsden Barkway. 'He began as a scientist but threw up that for painting. His quaker relations were a good deal agitated and fussed, and his father offered to increase his allowance by £100 if he'd promise not to study from the nude. But the charming offer was refused.'

Among the general un-Apostolic population of the world Lytton felt increasingly ill-at-ease. In July 1902 he went with some of his family to Oxfordshire to stay with three sisters, Ianthe, Ina and Angelica Homere – 'my Greek Lady friends' as he used to call them – who had lived next door to the Stracheys in No. 70 Lancaster Gate, but who now subsisted in moderate comfort on the wrecks of a fortune lost by their father in earnest speculation on the stock market. After the old man's death, his three daughters – the severely practical and embittered Ianthe, the nondescript Ina, and Angelica, a nymphomaniac of great beauty apparently infatuated with the dazed and cautious Lytton – had moved to a modest house between Kingham and Chipping Norton – quite close to Oxford, and with far-stretching views on every side – into which they took paying guests. The peaceful routine of life at Kingham rapidly provoked in Lytton an intense lack of feeling. The enveloping feminism and absence of all intellectual excitement was monotonous in the extreme. 'For me I dribble on among ladies, whom I *cannot* fall in love with,' he complained to Leonard Woolf (July 1902). 'One of them is beautiful, young, charming – oughtn't I to be in love with her? We go for walks together, read each other sonnets, sit out together at nights, among moons, stars, and the whole romantic paraphernalia – oughtn't I to be in love? We talk about it. Oughtn't I? It's *my* disease, I'm afraid, not to be.'

His existence grew fractionally more tolerable when, at the end of the month, he visited Walter and Lucie Raleigh at a quasi-farmhouse abutting on the village green of Stanford-in-the-Vale, in Berkshire. 'We sit out of doors and bicycle,' he wrote to his mother (3 August 1902. 'Uncle R writes his book in the morning – on Wordsworth. It is chiefly to deal with the technical points – poetic diction and such-like – so it ought to be very interesting to those who like such questions. We have been to two Clergyman tea-parties. One to Mr Cornish of Childrey, who so far failed to know who I was as to ask me whether I too was a Scotch Professor.' But even with the Raleighs things were not quite as they should have been. The general air of clergymen and bicycles reminded him unpleasantly of Liverpool. Uncle Raleigh, of course, was very brilliant; his talk bubbled away like champagne. Yet something was wrong. Raleigh, after all, was an Apostle, but with an important difference; he was a *Victorian* Apostle, and for this simple reason curiously out of date, tuned in, as it were, to some foreign wavelength from Lytton and his undergraduate friends. What was this difference between the opposing generations? They, the older generation, were altruists and enthusiasts; he was a disillusioned egoist. Their high-minded integrity seemed somehow theoretical, their idealism insensitive. They were always so eager to offer up real suffering individuals for the sake of some noble abstraction, some nice point of principle. How fond they were of sacrificing the actual here and now to some invisible, un-get-at-able future! Yet Raleigh was one of the best of them. '*He* is very eminent, but frantically taken up with a book on Wordsworth,' he told Leonard Woolf (August 1902), 'and at other times paralysing conversationally. She jabbers *sans cesse* – rather amusingly – altogether conceitedly – of persons more than things.' To complete Lytton's dismay he found that the farmhouse also contained four children. Like most fundamentally shy persons he liked to avoid all contact with '*le petit peuple*', though on this occasion he was pleased to note that one of them was 'most inviting' – a future embryo perhaps?

A week later, he was a critical spectator along the route of Edward VII's much-postponed coronation. In his present iconoclastic mood the procession to Westminster Abbey failed to rouse within him a proper degree of zeal. Plush ceremonies and gorgeous trooping always appealed to his romantic imagination. Parades of this sort were a kind of civic ballet in the streets, not a dogmatic assertion of militarism or power. Yet he was not in the festive vein. He admitted of no false sentiment.

'Their Majesties of England had the honour to be cheered by me on Saturday,' he informed Leonard Woolf (11 August 1902). 'A purely mechanical stimulus. Kitchener looked almost absurdly proud. Roberts of course absolute. To have been in the Abbey would have repaid. My mother reports sumptuosities of dresses and trains unspeakable – also other things.'[1]

The last weeks of this summer vacation were spent at Verdley Place, a country house near Fernhurst in Sussex, rented by the Stracheys. Here Lytton read Renan and Gibbon, played a little gentle croquet 'with a personage called Pearsall Smith – a literary, American gent – Bertie Russell's brother-in-law, who lives near by', and finally, before a select congregation presided over by an 'oily young clergyman', went through a ceremony of Christian confirmation. 'It was truly edifying,' he told Saxon Sydney-Turner, 'taking the body and blood of our Saviour into one's tum-tum. I assure you I felt a better, wiser, and happier man.'[2]

In the Michaelmas term his devotion to the true religion was handsomely rewarded on being elected secretary to the Society. 'The position is eminent and interesting,' he proudly wrote off to his mother (15 November 1902), 'as the S. has to keep a good many of the Society's papers, and generally arrange matters. I have got a book begun by Harry Wilson of biographies of brothers, which I hope to go on with. Much is mysterious and difficult to find out about the beginning part (1820, etc.). There is also a photograph book which we want to make as complete as possible.'

The special advantage of belonging to the Society was that, as a young undergraduate, Lytton might get to know some of the older members. In particular he encountered two distinguished Apostles who are reputed to have influenced his mind considerably and with whom he remained closely associated for some years after leaving

[1] This almost certainly refers to the surprising presence in Westminster Abbey of a number of Edward VII's favourites, past and present – among them Sarah Bernhardt, Mrs George Keppel, Mrs Hartmann, Lady Kilmorey and Mrs Arthur Paget.

[2] Although Lytton describes this confirmation ceremony, it may be an apocryphal event, since no one else has recorded it or has any memory of it. His nephew, Richard Strachey, was born and christened at Verdley Place (now owned by the Imperial Chemical Industries). 'One of the sights was seeing the General (who for some reason had to function as a stand-in Godfather) being asked by the Vicar, as part of the service: "Do you believe in God the Father Almighty, maker of heaven and earth? And in Jesus Christ his only Son our Lord? who was, etc., etc.," and answering at the end "I do". His face was a sight.' (James Strachey to the author, October 1966.)

Cambridge: Goldsworthy Lowes Dickinson and George Edward Moore.

The influence exercised by an older man upon a younger is very often no more than the sign of some latent natural similarity of temperament already existing between them. The similarity between Lowes Dickinson and Lytton is in several respects striking. Like Lytton at Abbotsholme and early Leamington, Lowes Dickinson had hated his schooldays at Charterhouse, where his physical unfitness had made him an object to be despised not only by the other boys but also by himself. At Cambridge, however, where he could choose his companions with more freedom, he had been happier; and later, as a Fellow of King's, he was able to observe the barbarous panorama of life from a more comfortable distance. Yet the self-contempt originally generated at school still lingered on. For a time he struggled to purge this unhappy feeling by setting himself up in the outside world as a citizen of some public value, a social servant propagating through example and precept the virtues of good citizenship. His endeavours to become immersed in a manly and active occupation and to attain thereby a state of reputable self-respect lasted only a few years during which he laboured on a co-operative farm, lectured in the provinces and studied medicine with the view to becoming a doctor. Back at Cambridge again he resigned himself to his unavoidable destiny with a sense of relief, leaving the community to make out as best it could. Here, secluded and safe, he should have been in his natural element, for, as one of his critics put it, 'his hatred of school had not sprung from any aversion to the young of his own sex'. But even now a simmering self-contempt continued to fret and ruffle his academic retirement. At first he sought through political journalism to appease this unrest, being a Conservative Unionist in the 1890s but growing progressively more left-wing as time went on. At the onset of the 1914–18 war he was to sketch out the idea of the League of Nations and in the following years devoted most of his energies to the furtherance of this scheme designed to establish a better-behaved Europe. But these activities, towards which, in his papers to the Apostles, he already showed signs of moving, could only lead on to eventual disillusionment. He was trying to create a world modelled after the disciplined and cloistered pattern of Cambridge, to expand a form of Apostolicism into an international world society, only to find that, on a far greater and more horrific scale, it was already set irremediably after the savage ways of Charterhouse.

In women Lowes Dickinson took no serious or sustained interest. His misogyny was indeed celebrated, and he used to say of the female graduates who attended his lectures that he could never tell them apart:

they all resembled cows. A congenital bachelor and almost perfect example of the academic millenarian, he was a pleasant thoughtful and sincere man, whose best and most genuine presence was appreciated not by the great world of action and affairs, but by his personal friends, who were devoted to him. Politically naïve, he was socially kind, and even, in a cautious docile manner, rather romantic; his gentleness, generosity and pathos eliciting from those nearest him a love and admiration amounting, in some cases, to hero-worship. In the opinion of his bed-maker at Cambridge, Mrs Newman, 'he was the best man who ever lived'; and his biographer, E. M. Forster, comments that these were the 'truest words about him'.

Though exasperated sometimes by his mellowed sentimentalism, Lytton respected Lowes Dickinson; G. E. Moore he admired deeply. The one, a wonderful, sympathetic listener, acted as a perfect con-versational foil, bringing out the latent brilliance of those around him; the other was a far more palpable and salient figure, whose Socratic method of thinking forced its way into the very blood-stream of his audience. Of a more dynamic intellectual disposition, Moore felt no tortuous urge to enter the realms of practical politics. 'What a brain the fellow has!' Dickinson wrote of him in a letter to R. C. Trevelyan. 'It desiccates mine! Dries up my lakes and seas and leaves me an arid tract of sand. Not that *he* is arid – anything but: he's merely the sun. One ought to put up a parasol – I do try to, one of humour, but it has so many rents in it.'

As a boy, Moore had been of a less dominating personality, reserved, and a little overshadowed by his brother, Thomas Sturge Moore, the poet, who was, he later admitted, 'a far readier talker than I and far more fertile of ideas'. One of the junior members of a large Victorian family, his early years were comparatively sheltered and uneventful. Both his father, Daniel, and his grandfather, George, after whom he was named, had been physicians. Daniel had married twice, producing one daughter by his first marriage, and three more daughters and four sons – of whom George was the second – by his later marriage to Henrietta Sturge. The Sturges, an old Gloucestershire family, had through four successive generations figured as prominent Quakers until, according to hearsay, Henrietta's parents were expelled from the local Friends' meeting, the members of which objected to the marriage of cousins. In any event there were no residual elements of orthodox Quakerism in George's upbringing to condition his unworldliness as a man; and he spent his childhood at Hastings Lodge – a detached, typically middle-class and suburban red-brick house on Sydenham Hill, Upper Norwood – enshrouded by an atmosphere of devout

Baptist puritanism. At the age of twelve, however, he had passed through an ultra-evangelical phase, waxing for a time so zealous as a Jesus-lover that he went about preaching to people on the highway, until his brother Thomas was obliged to take him sharply in hand and convert him to agnosticism.

After leaving Dulwich College, where he and his brother were educated as day boys, Moore went up in 1892 to Trinity College, and was later elected to a Prize Fellowship given unconditionally for a period of six years. Lytton initially got to know him well on his own election to the Apostles when the philosopher was twenty-nine, some seven years older than he. From the first, Moore inspired in him a reverence that was profound, and which arose from a recognition of the scrupulous, uncompromising sincerity which illuminated every facet of his character. Though they saw a lot of each other, Lytton seems always to have preserved a rather awed, if not humourless, respect for Moore, and never to have developed any really close familiarity with him. In a letter to Leonard Woolf (April 1905), he describes Moore as 'quite inaccessible on his cold, restrictive searchlight heights'. For some time he cherished the hope that Moore might marry his sister Pippa. And many years later he told a friend that of all the eminent people he had encountered in the course of his life, only Moore impressed him as being, without question, really great.

'About the greatest men', one of Lytton's aphorisms reads, 'there is always something incredible.' In the case of Moore this was especially true. To an extraordinary degree the philosopher fulfilled Lytton's ideal of genius. The passionate incandescent purity of his thought seemed to imbue and transfigure his countenance with a sublime beauty. He was still young enough to share many of Lytton's own enthusiasms, yet he appeared to feel no need of the protective social and cerebral carapace which the more youthful Apostles tried so assiduously to acquire. While they continued scrutinizing themselves with meticulous care for signs of superficial ostentation or turgescence, Moore went his way apparently unconscious of the risk of ridicule, and without a trace of intellectual arrogance. A philosopher by divine vocation, he was sincerely perplexed less by the extraordinarily intricate problems of ethical analysis than by the ordinary day-to-day *mores* and shibboleths of society, with which he was sometimes inevitably obliged to come in contact. Among those whom he did not know well, he was shy and naïve. Even the ordeal of penning a simple, chatty letter in answer to one of his friends would fill him with impotent, baffled despair. 'The reason I haven't written, in spite of wanting to, is that I don't know what to say,' he once confessed in belated reply to Leonard Woolf. 'I have begun three letters to you already before this one; but I wouldn't finish them because they were so bad. I'm afraid I have nothing to say, which is worth saying; or, if I have, I can't express it.'

Moore's inability in this context to find anything to say was the simple result of his possessing no natural powers of fancy or invention by means of which he might elaborate with elegant sophistication on phenomenal affairs that neither interested him nor struck him as being of any intrinsic importance. In conversation he was neither witty nor brilliantly quick. Every word uttered in his presence was pondered over and subjected by him to an astringent linguistic analysis as part of the cumulative process of formulating an accurate interpretation of the complete sentence. An incorrectly employed word or an ambiguously distended infinitive, Leonard Woolf recalls, would draw from him a gasp of astonishment as at some shocking obscenity; he was incredulous, scandalized; he gazed at the speaker as if one or other of them must surely be mad. And later he would confess hopelessly: 'I *simply* don't understand *what* he means!' If a man could not define *exactly* what he meant, then he must be presumed to have meant nothing at all. Moore's attitude in this respect illustrates the converse of Blake's dictum, for if a clever man persists quite so tenaciously in his cleverness, he becomes a bit of a damn fool. Instead of drawing his conclusions in the ordinary way from the association of any opinion with the mood and disposition of its author, and thus interpreting it in a personal light, he insisted upon applying a uniform and absolutely literal method of semantic deduction. In ludicrous contrast to this articulate, grammarian slowness was the lightning speed of his intelligence. He responded with immediate delight to Lytton's impeccable snake-like witticisms and highly individual stiletto stabs of humour. 'There was no question of his being shocked,' records Sir Roy Harrod in the course of an analysis of Moore's paramount influence over the Apostles, 'and the young had no inhibitions in his presence. When Strachey made one of his subtle, perhaps cynical, perhaps shocking, utterances, the flavour of which even his clever undergraduate friends did not at first appreciate at its full value, Moore was to be seen shaking with laughter . . . the veneration which his young admirers accorded him almost matched that due to a saint.'

Happy and at ease amid the congenial company of his Cambridge friends, Moore joined in whatever they were doing with wholehearted passion. Whether it was the evaluation of ethical dogma, or the singing of a Beethoven song, or an energetic game of fives, or just a tide of pure uncontrollable laughter, he would be caught up into it with a breathless total concentration, the sweat pouring from his face, enthralled as a boy, oblivious to all else. An interesting line of argument always claimed his rapt attention to the exclusion of more mundane matters, and when he was with Lytton, Maynard Keynes, Desmond MacCarthy and Bertrand Russell, his pipe, alternately gripped in his hand and clenched between his teeth, would remain unlit all evening, though he might have exhausted a full box of matches in repeatedly burning his fingers. Lytton and the other Apostles were charmed by such endearing traits – his wonderful unselfconscious freshness, sudden captivating passions, the strong radiating beam of his mind – and they responded spontaneously to his simple and unworldly temperament. Many of them, notably Leonard Woolf, have testified to the enchanting sweetness of his personality, the aura of 'divine absurdity' which emanated from his commanding presence and shone most powerfully from his amazingly beautiful face, with its high domed forehead, its ethereal expression, its delightful and infectious smile. Guileless and sensitive himself, he could never comprehend guile and cynicism in others. His thought had the absolute directness of a child, both its strength and limitation, its muddle, its sudden tender sensibility and ruthlessness.

Still slim in those days, Moore seemed indeed not of this miserable and wretched planet, but a prophet nourished with wisdom and goodness from some far-off mysterious source, enhaloed with transcendental illumination. And in 1902, while his apostles watched and waited to be directed by this Messiah towards their new promised land, Moore himself was hard at work on the book which, the following year, was to make his name and match and even exceed his admirers' greatest expectations, the celebrated *Principia Ethica*. Meanwhile: 'One has a few moments that are tolerable,' wrote Lytton, '– one breathes, as it were, again; one remembers things, but one hardly hopes. I hope for the New Age – that is all – which will cure all our woes, and give us new ones, and make us happy enough for Death.'

3

A ROSE-WATER REVOLUTION

Early in the year 1903, Lytton's attention was temporarily diverted from the affairs of the Society by a family event which shook the régime of Lancaster Gate to its foundations. A destitute though talented French painter, Simon Bussy, who had arrived in England the previous year with a letter of introduction from Auguste Bréal, taken a studio near by in Kensington, and become a frequent visitor at the Stracheys' home where he did portraits of several of the family, suddenly announced his engagement to Lytton's sister Dorothy. Before the death of Queen Victoria such undesirable unions were traditionally brought off by secret elopement or not at all. But Lady Strachey was a woman of greater enlightenment than the stereotyped Victorian matriarch; and besides, the more reasonable and tolerant climate of the Edwardian era had already begun to invade the country, carrying with it a slight thaw in the frigid moral and social code of the nineteenth century. No one denied that Simon Bussy could paint very nicely; nevertheless, the advanced liberalism of his future mother-in-law faltered and finally broke down altogether at the sight of him *actually cleaning up his plate with pieces of bread*. Dorothy was almost forty at this time, and it was thought proper tactics to employ an unspoken adult censorship with her in place of any more aggressive form of persuasion. But all the silent disapprobation in the world was to no avail. With what Lytton later called 'extraordinary courage' she remained adamant. She was absolutely determined to marry her penurious French artist and no amount of maternal embarrassment could alter her determination. Disapproving, resigned, yet not without some impartial humour, Lady Strachey broke the catastrophic news to Lytton in a letter dated 8 February 1903:

'You will doubtless be more astonished than pleased to hear that Dorothy is engaged to marry S. Bussy. She is very much bent on it, and of course must do as she chooses, and we must all do our best to help her with it. The terrible feature of the case is the smallness of means, but this will doubtless improve as years go on. If you ever have occasion to mention him do say he is an artist of genius, one of the rising young painters of the modern school in France – which is strictly true . . .

'P.S. Oh la! la!

'P.P.S. I now understand the expression in her portrait.'

By the very same post Lytton received a letter from Dorothy herself announcing the same news in rather a different fashion:

Dearest Lyt,

Please give me your fraternal blessing. I am going to marry Simon Bussy. Most people I am afraid will think it exceedingly wild, but in reality it is an action of the highest wisdom. (vide Maeterlinck.)

We shall have 2d. a year but we shall be very gay and sensible – and live if possible in a minute house near Roquebrune.

Lytton found it hard at first to get on with his future brother-in-law. To begin with there was the language barrier: Bussy could speak little English, and Lytton refused altogether to utter a word of French. And

then, of course, like most Frenchmen, the poor fellow had no brain.
No doubt he painted pictures very charmingly, but as everyone knew,
artists had no need of brains – they never knew what they were doing
anyway. What, he wondered, did his astounding sister see in this
Frenchman? He was very *spirituel*, had a great deal of *esprit*, and –
bouffe! – nothing more that he or anyone else could detect. Still, on
principle, he supported Dorothy rather than his mother. Her act was a
significant step in the disintegration and *dégringolade* of Lancaster
Gate, a break-through of supreme importance in the Strachey an-
thropology. Parental dismay was made manifest at the marriage later
in the year, when, under a feeble plea of difference of nationality, a full-
scale wedding ceremony was dispensed with, and the family merely
forgathered instead at a stiff and uneasy party in the mammoth
drawing-room.[1]

Despite the revolutionary nature of this development – a cut clean
across those fetters of convention which had held their parents' generation prisoners – life for Lytton was at first to carry on very much as
before. In preference to returning home during the Easter vacation, he
goes off with another of Moore's reading-parties to Penmenner House,
at the Lizard in Cornwall. Among other Apostles who attend are
Leonard Woolf, C. P. Sanger and Desmond MacCarthy – who turns
up late. 'Others expected later,' Lytton informs his mother (3 April
1903), 'including Bob Trevelyan, whose play[2] has just come out. I have
read it – it is, I'm afraid, sad stuff. Moore has also brought the last
volume of Charles Booth's new book – on religion in London.[3] It
looks very interesting and full of details – which are the charming
things.

'The country is at present grey. We are quite close to the sea. The
house seems very comfortable. We have two sitting-rooms. There is
another party of young gents from Oxford in the house.'

Lytton much prefers the Lizard to the previous year's Isle of Wight.
Every outward circumstance conspires to make him healthy and
contented. By the second week in April the weather has actually become
quite hot: the sun shines, the blue sea stretches away in almost every
possible direction, Moore sings and laughs as seldom before, the

[1] Sir Richard Strachey in fact turned out to be extremely generous to the Bussys. He
bought La Souco, a fine villa in the South of France, and gave it to them as a wedding-
present.

[2] *Cecilia Gonzaga.*

[3] *Life and Labour of the People of London. 3rd Series. Religious Influences, volume 7.*
Part of an eighteen-volume social survey – one of the first of its kind – compiled under
the direction of Charles Booth, a philanthropic shipowner. He and his wife, Mary
Macaulay, were close friends of Beatrice Potter before her marriage to Sidney Webb, of
whose socialism they disapproved.

Oxford gents leave and all is very pleasant, comfortable and lazy – no illnesses, no arguments and no necessity to shave. On most bright days the brethren take themselves off for communal strolls along the coast, eating sandwiches among the rocks, while a few of the more intrepid ones paddle. And one afternoon they walk to Mullion, a village about seven miles away, to watch Desmond MacCarthy and Bob Trevelyan play in a football match for the Lizard.

Back the following month at Cambridge, Lytton was obliged to start studying more seriously for the second part of his Tripos. It was a bleak and lifeless term. Trinity seemed absolutely dead, though in other parts of the university the fierce academic radicalism of George Trevelyan – heralding the more fashionable wave of socialism which was to capture the undergraduates of two or three years later – stirred within him an amused though severely non-partisan curiosity. 'The only excitement is at King's,' he wrote to his mother (19 May 1903), 'where the whole college is racked by the social work and agnosticism question – viz, it wants to do work among the Poor, but can only find Clergy to help it to do so. But it doesn't like Clergy, so that it's in a quandary. I don't like Clergy, but then I don't want to do work among the Poor.

'Cambridge is flooded by so-called "working-men" imported by George Trevelyan for the day, who have to be entertained at various meals.'

By the second week of June his Tripos was over, and he was able to plunge into dissipation – two garden-parties at Newnham and a visit from his cousin, Duncan Grant.

The summer vacation that year was distinctly un-Apostolic. While he waited for the result of his Tripos and, a little later, of his application to the Board of Education, he spent July with the Homeres at Kingham, August with two elder brothers and a sister-in-law at Swift's Place at Cranbrook in Kent – the house, he told Leonard Woolf (who came to visit him there), being named after the bird and not the bard – and finally, September at Lancaster Gate. Seldom had his family seemed more tedious and remote. 'I find them a little difficult and on the whole a little dull to talk to', he wrote to Leonard Woolf, ' – I'd always rather be doing something else.' Every day for a fortnight he walked to the British Museum, looking through the Hastings papers. 'My life depends on what I find there,' he told Saxon Sydney-Turner. Fortunately, his initial researches were encouraging, and in October he returned again to Cambridge to work on his Fellowship dissertation.

And so began what, very distinctly, was to be the second part of his university career.

4

THE GOOD LIFE

By far the most significant event of the year 1903 for all Apostles was
the autumn publication of G. E. Moore's *Principia Ethica*. Its impact
was enormous. Moore's views on moral questions had, of course, been
known for some time, but the algebraic passion of his book came as a
revelation. Discussion of its ethical concepts dominated, for a time,
everything else. The effect on Lytton personally was instantaneous. He
saw Moore as another Plato, and *Principia Ethica* as a new and better
Symposium. On 11 October he wrote a long, rhapsodic letter from Lancaster Gate, which conveys something of the tremendous enthusiasm
which swept over him:

Dear Moore,
    I have read your book, and want to say how much I am excited and
impressed. I'm afraid I must be mainly classed among 'writers of
Dictionaries, and other persons interested in literature', so I feel a sort
of essential vanity hovering about all my 'judgements of fact'. But on
this occasion I am carried away. I think your book has not only
wrecked and shattered all writers on Ethics from Aristotle and Christ
to Herbert Spencer and Mr Bradley, it has not only laid the true
foundations of Ethics, it has not only left all modern philosophy
bafouée – these seem to me small achievements compared to the establishment of that Method which shines like a sword between
the lines. It is the scientific method deliberately applied, for the
first time, to Reasoning. Is that true? You perhaps shake your head,
but henceforward who will be able to tell lies one thousand times
as easily as before? The truth, there can be no doubt, is really now
upon the march. I date from Oct. 1903 the beginning of the Age of
Reason.
    The last two chapters interested me most, as they were newer to me
than the rest. Your grand conclusion made me gasp – it was so violently
definite. Lord! I can't yet altogether agree. I think with some horror of
a Universe deprived for ever of real slaughters and tortures and lusts.
Isn't it possible that the real Ideal may be an organic unity so large and
of such a nature that it is, precisely, the Universe itself? In which case
Dr Pangloss was right after all.
    . . . Dear Moore, I hope and pray that you realize how much you
mean to us. It was very pleasant to be able to feel that one came into

the Dedication.[1] But expression is so difficult, so very difficult, and there are so many cold material obstructions, that the best of Life seems to be an act of faith.

This is a confession of faith, from

your brother
Lytton Strachey.

From the language which he employs, it is obvious that this letter is very far from being mere flattery, and that it constitutes an attempt at giving some coherence to the extraordinarily optimistic but as yet unsettled emotions to which *Principia Ethica* had given rise. Since there was no object in flattering a man such as Moore, this 'confession of faith' is in no way overpitched. For once, all Lytton's correspondence to other friends strikes exactly the same eulogistic note. 'The last two chapters – glory alleluiah!' he exclaimed in a letter to Leonard Woolf (October 1903). 'And the wreckage! That indiscriminate heap of shattered rubbish among which one spies the utterly mangled remains of Aristotle, Jesus, Mr Bradley, Kant, Herbert Spencer, Sidgwick and McTaggart! Plato seems the only person who comes out even tolerably well. Poor Mill has, simply, gone.'

To account for this unstinted, sweeping approbation, and make some assessment of the extent to which it was justified, one must first trace the main outlines of *Principia Ethica*. From its pages the unmistakable, highly individual qualities of Moore's mind and personality can be felt with transparent clarity. At the beginning of the twentieth century ethics had been chiefly metaphysical, and were dominated by Bradley's Hegelian idealist theory. Moore himself, for a short time during the 1890s, had been converted to this way of thinking by the redoubtable J. E. McTaggart, whose influence among the Apostles then eclipsed all others'. But subsequently he had reacted against Bradley, the idealists, and, so it seemed, metaphysical ethics in general – a change of mind which was to anticipate the whole future course of moral philosophy.

Moore was the Homer, not the Einstein, of modern ethics. His *Principia Ethica* is known to philosophers for its initial chapters; but to Lytton and the younger Apostles it was for the delicate uplift of the conclusion that it came to be especially revered. Compared with the unworldliness of its last pages, Keynes once observed, the New Testament was a handbook for politicians. The final two chapters – which

---

[1]Doctoribus Amicisque Cantabrigiensibus
Discipulus Amicus Cantabrigiensis
Primitias
D. D. D.
Auctor.

Lytton singled out in his letters to Leonard Woolf and to Moore himself – 'Ethics in Relation to Conduct' and 'The Ideal' – are certainly different in tone from the rest of the book. The rigmarole of meticulous and muddled argument, of cross-examination, assertion and counter-assertion, becomes less concentrated, while, particularly in the last chapter of all, the judgements grow more frankly personal, and Moore's forceful and passionate spirit shines through with ever-increasing vividness. Moral conduct, or duty, is defined as the obligation to select that action which will achieve more good than any alternative action. In so far as the goodness arising from the probable results of any specific act should be calculated in advance of that act being performed, this concept of moral conduct may be summarized as the intelligent prediction of practical consequences.

In the final chapter of all, 'The Ideal', Moore presents those things which, to his mind, are intrinsically good. In a crucial passage he writes: 'By far the most valuable things, which we know or can imagine, are certain states of consciousness which may be roughly described as the pleasures of human intercourse and the enjoyment of beautiful objects. No one probably, who has asked himself the question, has ever doubted that personal affection and the appreciation of what is beautiful in Art or Nature, are good in themselves.' This personal if rather haphazard choice of good things, together with an equally arbitrary list of what is bad – love of ugliness, hatred of beauty and the consciousness of pain – is defended by means of an argument to the effect that since good and bad are familiar to us through intuition, and since these particular qualities strike Moore's own intuition very obviously as being respectively good and bad, then it follows that they must be so.

It is only thus in the last resort that Moore appeals directly to the intuition. His mind was purely literal and speculative, not richly imaginative, and it operated along a straight, two-dimensional plane in tackling problems which were essentially multi-dimensional. It is as if Newton had been entrusted with the composition of Blake's prophetic writings; one is aware of a truly remarkable and powerful mind at work, but the achievement is in some respects terribly inadequate. The questions which Moore's remorseless probings unearthed could only be answered satisfactorily by a type of highly subjective psychology which had not yet been very far developed in this country. Again and again in the course of his book he emphasizes that the matters with which he is dealing are *not* fallacies, but *material, real*. Yet, despite this repeated assurance, the cast of his mind and tenor of his argument were irrefutably pedantic. His world was largely a conceptual one, almost a verbal one at times, and he handled words as a mathematician uses symbols and formulae. To explore the sort of issues which so fascinated him, one must of necessity take as the basis of one's perceptions and experiments the single real unit which exists in this life – the individual human being. Though in the last instance Moore was compelled to relate his search for truth to his own being, his basic unit as a philosopher comprised a network of impersonal linguistic principles upon which, with fine precision, he spun his closely reasoned theories. Anyone not possessing his incorruptible integrity and unassailable tenacity of purpose would have led himself into a morass of confusion before completing a dozen pages of a book which attempted to express the soul of a poet by means of the rigid mental apparatus of a logician. To the end of his life Moore retained this strait-jacket of wholly dialectic and objective ratiocination which increasingly hampered his freedom of communication. As time went on he was to experience greater and greater difficulty in transforming, diminishing and breaking up his valid intuitional promptings into clear, static components of philosophical jargon. The more he laboured the more fantastically complex the problems which confronted him loomed.[1] For he was like a man endlessly, impossibly, engaged in trying to explain immortality in terms of a sequence of time, or to reduce eternity to an orderly chronological progression of feelings and events.

Moore's influence upon Lytton and the younger Cambridge Apostles can be categorized under three distinct headings: the philosophical, the literary, and the personal. Despite its wide reputation as a source-book of ideas and ideals among the Bloomsbury Group, the actual philosophical content of *Principia Ethica* exerted little precise influence on Lytton. But to a limited extent it does seem to have acted as a guide to 'good-as-an-end' and 'good-as-a-means' or the means to good, which clarified the whole subject and, being theoretically sound, was of some realistic and even practical help to him in life. The literary effect of this book upon him was more negligible, though it certainly did exist for a time and is well illustrated by the style of some early papers he wrote for various university societies. His later critical and biographical prose, with its alternating flow of rhetorical queries and bright responses, reads

[1] After his second book, *Ethics*, was published, Moore sent Lytton a disarming letter (20 September 1912) that proclaims something of the chaos and bewilderment which were overcoming him. 'I feel very grateful for your remarks about my Ethics,' he wrote. 'I've been longing to hear something about it, and haven't heard a single word yet, except for one sentence from Sorely the other day. All your criticisms seem to me perfectly just, except that the particular passage which you say you found so baffling, doesn't seem to me so very difficult. But there were others in that chapter which I couldn't follow myself when I read the book through. I was fearfully bothered for want of space towards the end. If it hadn't been for that, I think I really should have brought out the main points more clearly and also made a better thing out of the last chapter.'

in places like a facile parody of Moore's insistence that the thinker's first logical step was to formulate clear questions in order to establish clear answers.

Undoubtedly the main effect which *Principia Ethica* produced on Lytton was of a personal nature, and he may be said to have seen in Moore's philosophical writing an extension, minutely expounded and defined, of his beguiling personality. The doctrines expressed in Moore's work served not to unify the Apostles but to differentiate one from another. Each one measured off from this hedonic calculus a different point. Maynard Keynes, for example, accepted what was for him the religious attitude of *Principia Ethica* as practised by the older Apostles, but ignored Moore's views on moral consequences. Leonard Woolf later adapted and applied Moore's method of defining duty to an historical and political purpose, believing that the historian, by investigating the communal psychology of the past, might attain an understanding which would enable him to forecast the results of future policies. Lytton, in paying particular attention to the final chapter of *Principia Ethica* with its elevating accent upon the merits and virtues of human intercourse, turned his back upon ethics in relation to conduct. The impact which Moore had on him was pre-eminently not one of morals but of morale. By absorbing 'The Ideal' he could allay if not actually co-ordinate those two ever-disparate sides of his nature, the romantic and the classical or intellectual. For Moore employed a severely rationalistic argument to support what Lytton felt to be an entirely sympathetic emotional appeal. No wonder he announced that the Age of Reason had at last dawned. He saw in Moore a supreme cerebral force, simple yet subtle and effective, which severed at one stroke the umbilical cord binding art to orthodox morality, which gave the arts a free and independent life, which refuted the old Victorian cant and hypocrisy that had enveloped the country by insisting with re-invigorated emphasis that, in Bishop Butler's words, 'everything is what it is and not another thing', and which, finally, pointed the way to a new dawning psychology, in the line from Dostoievsky to Henry James, to Freud.

Principia Ethica lit up for Lytton that remote region of the soul where morals melt into aesthetics. In the New Age which this book heralded, his own physical and psychological peculiarities would count for little. Indeed, in such a world they might be counted attributes. Moore was the prophet of that divine companionship for which he so urgently longed. Above all else *Principia Ethica* spelt out one word to Lytton: *friendship*. And it is not perhaps surprising at a time of criminal intolerance and incomprehension that it especially meant to him the

Goldsworthy Lowes Dickinson

G. E. Moore

Harry Norton

Desmond MacCarthy

Bertrand Russell

Clive Bell

glorification of that friendship which, throughout the Victorian Age of Unreason, had dared not speak its name. On several occasions he was on the very point of asking Moore whether he ever experienced any homosexual feeling; but in the end could never quite pluck up the courage. 'Dear Moore,' he had written, 'I hope and pray that you realize how much you mean to us.' Moore, however, seems to have been characteristically quite unaware of the personal interpretation which Lytton and some other Apostles elected to place on his work. He was the prophet: the crusaders must be other men, Lytton himself and more like him – Maynard Keynes, for example. 'Our great stumbling-block in the business of introducing the world to Moorism is our horror of half-measures,' Lytton once wrote to Keynes (8 April 1906). 'We can't be content with telling the truth – we must tell the whole truth; and the whole truth is the Devil. Voltaire abolished Christianity by believing in god. It's madness of us to dream of making dowagers understand that feelings are good, when we say in the same breath that the best ones are sodomitical. If we were crafty and careful, I dare say we'd pull it off. But why should we take the trouble? On the whole I believe that our time will come about a hundred years hence, when preparations will have been made, and compromises come to, so that, at the publication of our letters, everyone will be, finally, converted.'

Such highflown, semi-serious predictions are in fact less valid forecasts of the future than eloquent reminders of the Victorian past. Lytton turned a blind eye to the puritanical element in Moore's teaching, and extracted from it a message answering his own most imperative needs. Expressed as an equation, this was: aesthetic experience + personal relations = the good life. For him the book was a foretaste of a liberated existence where the generally acknowledged virtues were to be largely coincident with his own mental attributes and emotional predisposition.

Lytton was a natural disciple as a young man. But because he did not efface himself and respond at a very profound level to those who in turn dominated his life, because he was as much fascinated by their position of authority as by their actual creeds, an undercurrent of resentment flowed against the stream of his intense but immature hero-worship. He did not like himself, and by the same token tended to despise those who thought highly of him. His early passionate surrender to people older than himself – Marie Souvestre, Professor Walter Raleigh, and even Goldie Dickinson – usually cooled off after a relatively short time. He set each one up as an intellectual and cultural god, and as gods they failed him. And, anxious himself to attract prestige and authority, he was always half-exultant, half-fearful of emancipating himself from their immediate dominion over him. Moore was really the last and greatest of these deified intellectual human beings. From Moore he gained a sense of reassurance which compensated in some degree for his invalidism, and gave him a prophetic hope of happiness and the success he so coveted. Frail and unprepossessing though his body might be, he was now confirmed in his ownership of a subtle and agile mind which was in itself a considerable weapon. There were many times when he exulted in thin but intense high spirits, of forced-up Rabelaisian rhetoric, when the pressure of his ideal longings mingled with his physical desires and banished all other feelings. 'I think I am now only excited by physical desires,' he once told Moore (5 February 1909). But these moments were interspersed with others, during which he demanded from his friends only the strictest intellectual standards.

Like a cripple who has just learnt to walk with sticks, Lytton sometimes needed but no longer sought for someone to aid him after Moore. From this time onwards, though he was to be absorbed by various other trends of thought, though he always remained *emotionally* dependent upon stronger, younger men, he felt no wish to adopt another intellectual mentor. At last he was gaining enough outward confidence to stand up for himself, to forge, in due course, his own place in human society and ultimately in the pantheon of literature.

5

HASTINGS'S CREATURE

Lytton's friendships among other undergraduates may be conveniently segregated into two chronological halves. During his first three years at Cambridge most of his close friends belonged to his own college, Trinity. In his last three years he made so many excursions into King's College that when, some time after he had gone down, one of the university papers published a reproduction of Henry Lamb's early portrait above the caption 'Lytton Strachey (*King's*)' hardly anyone was aware of the error. All the members of the original Midnight Society had gone down long before Lytton himself left – Thoby Stephen to set up house in Gordon Square with his brother and two sisters after the death of their father; Clive Bell to shoot at animals in British Columbia, and subsequently to work at a dissertation in Paris on British policy during the Congress of Verona; Saxon Sydney-Turner to an attic in Somerset House; and, last of all, Leonard Woolf to the Civil Service station at Hambantota, Ceylon, where he became as Lytton put it to Moore 'absolute Lord there of a million blacks'. His own college now depressed him. 'Trinity is like a dead body in a high state of putrefaction,' he wrote in his last year there. 'The only interest of it is in the worms that come out of it.' And so he turned for companionship to the other colleges, especially King's.

One of the most intimate of his new friends was (Sir) John Sheppard, later provost of King's, who had been elected to the Apostles at the same time as Lytton. With his white hair and diminutive frame, Sheppard often gave the impression of being prematurely middle-aged, but there was always something light-hearted and theatrical about his manner which at once delighted Lytton. By leaning on a stick and affecting a slight limp he could appear positively senile at times, yet his vivid conversation and cherubic features always contrasted ludicrously with his performance. The zest and whimsicality of his character were memorably caught, too, in his infectious laughter which he produced as a nasal, high-pitched blast, a sort of gasping preposterous explosion which held in it a note of mingled protest and incredulity. He could never be relied on to present himself as only twenty-four hours older than on the previous day. 'He is generally, I think, about his fifteenth birthday,' wrote one interviewer from *The Granta*, 'but sometimes he has just passed his hundred and fifteenth.' Though less obviously brilliant, less quick and supple in articulation than, say, Maynard Keynes, also of King's, whose arrogance and contempt for fools was often too apparent in his irascible tone of voice, Sheppard was equally effective in debate,[1] and his acting on the stage was energetic and original.

There was much in Sheppard's personality to appeal to Lytton, and for almost two years he remained the chief figure in his emotional life. Together they used to go off to the rooms of a middle-aged widow, near Emmanuel College, to be instructed in the art of dancing. In turn each of them would solemnly circle the room in the arms of this unsmiling lady whose equally dismal sister sat in the corner strumming out sepulchral melodies upon the piano. These classes, however, were not a success; and on attending their first ball at Lancaster Gate,[2] both pupils were hopelessly outclassed by their partners, and obliged to retire early and ignominiously from the dance floor.

Sheppard had a fine scholarly mind, but appeared to do little work as an undergraduate, much preferring those athletic pursuits for which he possessed no aptitude whatever. Like Lytton he worshipped Thoby

---

[1] Sheppard became president of the Cambridge Union.

[2] Lytton and Sheppard had decided to take up dancing in order to equip themselves for a special Dance that Lancaster Gate was giving before Dorothy Strachey's marriage.

Stephen, and loved to chide him with being a 'muscular Christian', for which taunt he would be exquisitely chased round the Great Court at Trinity, or the fountain at King's. But Lytton, whose admiration for athleticism was more furtive and inverted, did not approve; and he rigorously set out to make Sheppard a person fit for his affection. 'If I hadn't liked Lytton,' Sheppard told the author, 'I couldn't have endured it.' His amiable sentimentality and vague disregard for things of the mind brought out the worst didactic side of Lytton. He alternately teased and scarified Sheppard for consorting with his intellectual inferiors. Friendship, he would explain, was all very well; but not friendship with *anyone*. He would grow jealously possessive, objecting to his friend going off on walks with other people, especially non-Apostles. Yet, unless removed entirely from temptation, Sheppard remained incorrigible, and ruthlessly tolerant towards people. He couldn't seem to help it; he actually *liked* everyone.

In the winter vacation of 1903–4 the two of them went down to the Mermaid Inn at Rye, where they spent a pleasant Apostolic week together, reading, talking, walking to Romney and Winchelsea and keeping an unavailing eye open for the legendary Henry James who lived at Lamb House, a few yards off. Surrounded only by retired field officers, clergymen, and the occasional antiquarian golfer, there was little chance that even Sheppard would stray towards other sympathetic companionship. 'The inhabitants of the inn seem to be mostly military gents,' Lytton wrote to his mother (17 December 1903). 'There is a parson who drinks champagne and plays billiards, but is otherwise the dullest man in Europe.'

This Christmas was, however, one of the last occasions on which Lytton and Sheppard managed to preserve any really close harmony, though they continued as more casual friends for many years. Sheppard was given up by Lytton as an impenitent sentimentalist, worse perhaps than Goldie Dickinson; so much so, in fact, that for a while he even displayed all the symptoms of falling in love with one of Lytton's sisters. There was no reasoning with him. In many of Lytton's letters to other friends from this time on, poor Sheppard is severely castigated for his lack of rigidly-applied high intellect, and for being hopelessly out of date. Lytton's enchantment had passed; and the one-sided infatuation once over was mercilessly purged. Already, by the following July, he told Leonard Woolf: 'I'm fairly bored by him, and as frigid as if he were a lovely young lady.'

Since the University Library did not stock several of the books which he needed for his Fellowship dissertation, Lytton spent part of the Lent and almost all the Easter term of 1904 up in London working at the

British Museum. 'I shall not be up,' he told Saxon Sydney-Turner, 'as the B. Museum and India Office are imperative. Whether I shall ever get to Cambridge next (Easter) term God knows. I suppose I shall somehow. I shall be a mere ghost till the damned dissertation is written.' He did spare some time, however, to enter into the family's town and country social life. In particular, feeling that the ceremony was an event not to be missed, he accepted an invitation in March to the wedding of George Trevelyan and Janet Ward. These solemn and obsequial celebrations, garnished with some unusual secular and religious rites, were staged in Oxford of all places, and did not in the least disappoint Lytton's most gloomy expectations. 'Have you heard of the arrangements for the Trevelyan-Ward wedding?' he inquired in a note to Pippa (9 February 1904). 'Bride and bridegroom wanted *Office*, Bride's mother [Mrs Humphry Ward] wanted *Church*; compromise arrived at – An Oxford Unitarian Chapel with a service drawn up by Bride, Bgroom, and B's mother – at present chiefly Emerson. The happy pair are to lead the Simple Life, and will go to Oxford in a special train.' Lytton himself travelled down from Lancaster Gate with several members of his family, and the following day wrote up an account of the proceedings in the course of a long letter to Leonard Woolf (20 March 1904): 'My mother said we were a "cultured crowd" and we were. Mostly matrons, in grey silk and hair – Henry James, Sheppard, Hawtrey, Theodore L. D.,[1] etc., filled in the gaps. The lunch was free, and at separate tables, but the whole train was inter-connected, so that there was a good deal of moving about. A High char-à-banc, with a horn, drove us from the station; flags were waved of course, and there was some cheering . . . Mr Edward Carpenter officiated. He began with an address composed of quotations and platitudes, during which, as Miss Souvestre said, the bride and bridegroom looked at the windows as much as they could. . . . On the platform going away, as Sheppard and I were talking, I turned round – and there was Cornford.[2] He was in the most antique of toppers, and was travelling third. I suppose I looked at the hat too much, for at last he said, "I thought it would do my top hat good to have an airing – I haven't worn it for 7 years." Then he looked at Sheppard's and added, "Yours looks comparatively new." "Yes," I just remarked, "but then you see Sheppard isn't quite as old

[1] Theodore Llewelyn Davies of the Treasury, a good-looking, austere, highly intellectual contemporary of Lytton's at Trinity.

[2] Professor F. M. Cornford (1874–1943), then lecturer in classics at Trinity and later Laurence Professor of Ancient Philosophy. Author of several works on the cosmology of Plato. Married Frances, the well-known poetess, and granddaughter of Charles Darwin. His most enduring work is perhaps a skit on university politics entitled *Microcosmographia Academica* (1908).

as you are." He positively blushed and stepped into his non-special train.

'The bride and bridegroom were almost completely hideous. But I suppose one must let copulation thrive. The service was practically all balls in both senses.'

Ten days later, in another letter to Leonard Woolf, he appended a postscript summarizing to his mind the whole *mésalliance*: 'I didn't tell you Henry James's *mot* on the occasion – "The ordinary service binds, and makes an impression – it's like a seal; this was nothing more than a wafer."'

At the start of the Easter vacation, Lytton went down to a reading-party at Hunter's Inn, not far from Lynton off the north coast of Devon, with Moore, Sanger, Ainsworth, Leonard Woolf, Desmond MacCarthy and a few other meticulously selected Apostles. 'This place is more like a hotel than an Inn,' he wrote to Pippa (4 April 1904). 'There is a large party of Oxford men with an elderly tutor; also an antique male and less antique female. The country is highly beautiful, the weather tolerable. We go for long walks, and usually quarrel about the way.' Apart from walking and arguing, Lytton spends some time writing a long review of Mrs Paget Toynbee's *The Letters of Horace Walpole*, 'something of a heterogeneous composition' which appeared the following month in the *Independent Review*.

Usually one of the more permanent members of Moore's reading-parties, Lytton is on this occasion unable to remain at Hunter's Inn longer than a few days, since he has previously agreed to spend three weeks of his vacation with Simon and Dorothy Bussy in the South of France. On 8 April he set off on his journey, leaving Hunter's Inn some time during the afternoon and following what he took to be a brilliant short cut across a vast and misty common, to arrive over an hour later, triumphant but lost, on a distant unknown road on the other side. After a long walk he at last encountered a group of three men sitting in a field skinning a dead pig. They seemed surprised when this lanky and lugubrious stranger, evidently held in suspense between curiosity and a sense of nausea, shouted across to them in a reedy, piping treble, to ask for the station. 'The tavern?' they queried. By the time Lytton eventually arrived at Woody Bay Station his train had already long since vanished. But there was a fire in the waiting-room where he sat for three hours dozing and dreaming of the interminable journey which lay ahead. 'For the next four hundred years,' he wrote morosely from this dreary railway waiting-room to Moore, 'I shall be voyaging.'

Early the next morning he collected his belongings from Lancaster Gate, and the following day he was in Paris, where at the Hôtel St

James he met Marie Souvestre 'bursting with Alfred de Vigny'. That evening he went to the Théâtre Antoine. 'The house was completely full, and very appreciative and quite stupid,' he wrote back to his mother (13 April 1904). 'The French bourgeois are I think on the whole more maddening than the English aristocracy; they are equally conceited, but infinitely more pedantic. An abbé and a vieille girl in the train here talked and colloqued together for several hours about education and classical literature with such a horrible wealth of platitude that I longed for cricket shop of the most degraded kind.'

On 12 April he arrived at La Souco, the little house in Roquebrune where the Bussys had recently installed themselves. Immediately he was enchanted with the place: so small, so pretty, so charmingly proportioned and coloured that it might have come from an illustration out of some children's story book. 'The house is perfectly divine,' he informed his mother (13 April 1904), who had not yet visited Dorothy since her unfortunate marriage. 'The pink of beauty reigns – marble staircases, Chippendale chairs, Louis XIV Cabinets, impressionist pictures, and the best view in Europe. . . . My bedroom looks out on to the neighbouring banker's and baron's garden, whose chief object is a gigantic red umbrella under which the bankers and barons sit.'

On the same day he wrote to Leonard Woolf with almost equal enthusiasm and in greater detail. 'It is a most extraordinary place. The house is 3 inches square[1] – and a dream of beauty. The floors are tiled with smooth red hexagonal tiles, and partially covered with matting; the walls are white, the furniture replete with every beauty. A few impressionist pictures are on the walls. If the whole place was taken up and plunged 400 miles away from everywhere and everything but the flowers and the frogs, I could live in it for ever; as it is there are too many Germans whirling past it through the air – too many terrific English driving tandems from Mentone just below and just above us.'

'I feel a little guilty to be here,' he wrote to another friend (18 April 1904), 'so, at any rate, physically happy. Today and yesterday have been really something superb in weather. English August but with a

[1] To anyone not having been brought up in Lancaster Gate, La Souco might have appeared quite a fair-sized villa. It had originally been built by the Roquebrune carpenter for his own occupation, but was bought for the Bussys before it was finished, and has been extended since then – one main addition being a garage. Visiting it in August 1964, the author was surprised to find that it had three spacious ground-floor rooms plus a dark and narrow kitchen, and three bedrooms, balconies and a bathroom upstairs. The villa lies just off the Grande Corniche below Roquebrune village, and looks directly across to Monte Carlo bay. It has a steep terraced garden, now wildly overgrown, a number of olive trees and one towering cypress. Adjoining the house are a large studio and a patio with muralled walls. La Souco has recently been bought by the Belgian ex-ambassador to Montreal.

peculiar serenity added.' In England, Lytton could be prevailed upon to speak precious little French; in France itself he seldom uttered a single word. Conversation with his brother-in-law was consequently out of the question. Besides, even if he did speak the language, what was there to talk about? From his sister, on the other hand, the rebel of the family, he expected great things once he had presented her with a copy of Moore's *Principia Ethica*. To his dismay, however, she informed him after reading through it that in her view the last chapter omitted all the difficulties, and was untrue. In addition she did not believe in the concept of 'good in itself' but was in favour of self-determination – or whatever it was called – as constituting the real 'good'. This, it seemed to Lytton, was most discouraging for posterity. If intelligent females could not recognize the underlying truth of Moore's teaching, then who could? Perhaps, though, they were too bound up these days with the feminist movement to see things steadily and see them whole. It was understandable. Naturally he too believed, if more tepidly, that women should be given the vote – the poor things wouldn't have much else before long. Yet Dorothy's failure to hold opinions and feelings coincident with his own irritated Lytton. Probably, he reasoned, stupidity was infectious, and she had caught a bad dose of it from her French husband. Their exclusive heterosexual contentment seemed to add insult to injury, and irked him to an unreasonable degree. How insensitive they must be, he thought, to feel so happy with each other. Their show of love and affection made him feel an outsider. What right had people without a tithe of his intellectual talent and 'goodness' of feeling to enjoy such felicity? Really, the world was too extraordinary. Only the dull, it seemed, lived happily. 'I must say that I am sometimes a little annoyed at their affectionateness,' he expostulated to Leonard Woolf (13 April 1904). 'Wouldn't you be? Two people loving each other so much – there's something devilishly selfish about it. Couples in the road with their silly arms round their stupid waists irritate me in the same way. I want to shake them.'

There was not much to occupy Lytton at La Souco and he was soon missing acutely the conversation of his friends. The Bussys were extremely poor and led a quiet retired life, so that, apart from an occasional lunch with his aunt, Lady Colvile, who was staying near by, Lytton was provided with little social *divertissement*. He went for plenty of long solitary walks, but in the evenings especially apathy and lassitude would descend upon him. Always highly susceptible to boredom, it was for him not merely a negation of excitement, but something more positive and overwhelming, infecting every particle of his being like a malignant cancer. 'This is a wonderful, fascinating country,' he told Leonard Woolf, 'but as for living in it –! I don't think I could live anywhere out of England – I should always be moving on.'

Turning from the euphoria of stupidity and the blank tedium everywhere around him, he soon resigned himself to working on his long dissertation. Almost every day he pressed resolutely along with it; but here too he was confronted by monotony and defatigation. The task of perpetually renewing his original enthusiasm, of elucidating in detail for the benefit of crass pedagogic examiners information already so stalely familiar to himself was unbelievably enervating. Depression and ennui ate into the very marrow of his bones. 'I am lost', he confessed, 'over Warren.' But still, day after day, he forced himself methodically to go on with it.

Early in May Lytton returned to England, dividing the next six weeks between Lancaster Gate and the British Museum. By the second week of June, he had completed the bulk of his research work on Hastings, and was free to go off for a few days' rest, staying at Ivy Lodge, near Tilford, three miles from Farnham in Surrey, with Bertrand Russell, his wife Alys and her brother Logan Pearsall Smith, who was then working on his *Life and Letters of Sir Henry Wotton*. 'Everyone talks without stopping on every subject,' he wrote to his mother (16 June 1904). 'Ping Pong S reads poetry aloud in a wailing voice, which is rather depressing. I believe he thinks all poetry should be mildly melancholy, and has no more idea of drama than a cow. Russell is writing a chapter on the Improper Infinitive.'

On his return he resumed for the next few weeks his work at Lancaster Gate, inching his way forward with the Warren Hastings thesis like a mole burrowing towards the light. 'My dissertation is assuming most unwieldy proportions,' he told Maynard Keynes (14 July 1904). 'You don't know how superb one feels – writing a real book, with real chapters.' In fact he had at this time been asked by Methuen, the publishers, to write another 'real book' on 'Holland House and its Circle', but refused the offer since he could afford to think of nothing but the Hastings, and felt that in any case Methuen were not willing to pay him enough money for what would be an arduous and risky undertaking.

On 15 July, he moved out of London to Morhanger Park, a country house at Sandy in Bedfordshire, within half an hour of Cambridge. He was pleased to leave behind the distractions of London, and now immersed himself completely in the final stages of his work. 'I want to see everyone very much,' he wrote to Keynes; all the same he could not spare the time to go into Cambridge, not even to hear C. P. Sanger read a paper to the Society on copulation: 'I feel', he told Keynes (21 August 1904), 'that if I left off writing for a single second all would be lost.' Instead, he invited a few of his friends, Sheppard, Moore and one or two others, to visit him at his retreat. But he begged them not to disturb him. Best of all they should emulate the unobtrusive example of his father. 'Be prepared for doing nothing but sit in the garden and read novels,' he warned Moore (8 August 1904). 'Won't you like that? I am ploughing on with my dissertation; it's now very boring! But it looks beautiful all typewritten out.' Painfully and painstakingly he laboured on, though by this time it was distressing for him even to have to think of Warren Hastings. As each sheet was finished it was passed to his sister, Pippa, who typed it out neatly on foolscap pages. At one point the table on which Lytton was working, bent low by the accumulation of reference books, collapsed with a bang, distributing the unnumbered papers all over the floor and giving rise to a general panic and pandemonium. But the chaos was soon sorted out by a cluster of female relatives, and the slow dispiriting progress again resumed.

The side issues of his work seemed at times to interest him more than the thesis itself. As he struggled along he began to observe and note his alternating moods and the physical responses to which they gave rise with all the devotion of a true introvert and hypochondriac. 'I am in a fairly hellish state which makes me seem rather magnificent to myself,' he wrote and told Leonard Woolf (July 1904). 'Horrible illnesses attack me, and I sometimes think all's lost. But really perhaps the only supremacy is the supremacy of effort. I feel occasionally like an unchained tiger. . . . But by God! one does have hours of hideous collapse! Also, I find, of a sort of wonderful, sublimated sentimentality. . . . I have it often at breakfast when my stomach is all wobbly with being up so early. I don't know – I seem to have a physical feeling in my abdomen of spiritual affection. But perhaps it is merely lust.'

Despite prolonged hard work, he had left his final concentrated effort rather late and now had serious doubts as to whether the thesis would be completed in time, especially since it was turning out to be longer than he had originally planned. 'I have become involved in endless coils of controversy and conjecture and general hallucination,' he told Leonard Woolf in the second week of August. 'I have already had to make Chapter III into Chapters III and IV, and now I think I shall have to make Chapter IV into Chapters IV and V. At this rate you see I'm done for. And of course I'm now hopelessly bored. I have a fortnight in which to finish everything. God forgive us all!' From this time on he could afford neither to see nor even to write to his friends, making only one exception to ask Maynard Keynes for a copy of Rosebery's *Life of Pitt* in a pale wan scrap of a letter which, he admitted (21 August 1904), 'should have been part of Chapter V, with quotations from Sir Eyre Coote, and information upon William Markham – hush! – I think he *must* have been Hastings' creature – and the police of Benares.'

With a couple of days to spare the dissertation was finished, and Lytton went off until the end of the month to join C. P. Sanger[1] in Caernarvonshire, passing the final hours going through his typescript and making a number of minor corrections and emendations. Sanger's company, as always, suited him very well, but never more so than now in his rather exhausted, anxious state. For Sanger's penetrating intellect, with its swift bird-like flashes, never diminished or obtruded upon his natural gift for friendship; in a unique way his acute and critical mind was coupled with a warm, unambitious temperament to make up a truly sweet personality with which Lytton could relax and yet be entertained. To a rather lesser degree Lytton responded to Sanger as he did to Moore; he had something of the same beneficence, the same mystic fusion of heart and mind. Refreshed by this short holiday in Wales he returned to Trinity on 1 September to assemble with the other Fellowship candidates. 'I handed in my Dissertation all right, having corrected everything – with one exception remembered afterwards – and added a note on the spelling of proper names,' he wrote to his mother (2 September 1904). 'I find that there are about seven other people going in for fellowships, which is fewer than usual, and that there will be perhaps four fellowships – which is more than usual. There are very few people up, and those who are seem to be declining into perpetual melancholy.'

When he returned a few days later to Morhanger Park Lytton was in a state of well-concealed, hopeful expectation. Although the opposition likely to be encountered from the scientists was stiff, his chances of obtaining a Fellowship would never be better. But for the moment, being utterly sick of Warren Hastings and the whole subject of Anglo-Indian politics, he tried to turn his mind away from all the complicated historical issues which had been occupying it so unremittingly during the previous months. Compulsory reading that autumn for all Apostles was the posthumously selected essays of Henry Sidgwick, who, half a century ago, had refertilized and revived the spirit of the Society in a fashion similar to Moore's. From these miscellaneous papers Lytton returned again to Sidgwick's *Methods of Ethics* to which Moore had paid

[1] C. P. Sanger, the barrister and conveyancer, author of *The Structure of Wuthering Heights* and a highly erudite edition of Jarman *On Wills*.

generous acknowledgement in his *Principia Ethica.* But Sidgwick's arguments, Lytton found, were never so pointed or so formidably marshalled as Moore's. 'He [Sidgwick] seems to make hardly any false propositions, and the whole thing seems to be extraordinarily weighty and interesting,' he told Leonard Woolf (September 1904). 'But Lord! What a hopeless confused jumble of inarticulate matter. It is a vast vegetable mass of inert ponderosity, out of which the Yen[1] had beaten and welded, and fused his peerless flying-machine. Don't you think Sidgwick contains the embryonic Moore?'

In the third week of September, Lytton returned once more to Trinity to compose an essay for the Fellowship Examination in the form of a dialogue between Johnson, Gibbon and Adam Smith on the uses and abuses of universities, and to dine at the Master's Lodge with the other candidates. It was now that the awful news was broken to him that the electors, headed by a don with the sinister name of Moriarty, had referred his dissertation to a clergyman! – none other than that high-minded Tory Divine, the Rev. William Cunningham, the doctor of divinity who had the previous year provided him with such a cryptic testimonial for the Board of Education. It seemed a disastrous omen.

He was sure by now that all was lost. Ten days later he arrived back at Trinity to be told by Cunningham that, as suspected, he had failed to win the Fellowship. 'Things are less satisfactory than I think might have been hoped,' he wrote off to his mother (12 October 1904), whom he had earlier forewarned of his likely lack of success. 'Cunningham's main objection to my dissertation was that its subject did not allow sufficient scope for original treatment. That is to say, the main point of view from which it is proper to regard H's administration has now been satisfactorily established by James Fitzjames and Uncle John, and hence all that a subsequent worker has to do is to follow along the line which they have indicated. This, Cunningham thought, I had done exceedingly well; but he saw no evidence to show that a man who was not first class might not have done the work which I had done. . . . The Reverend Doctor was very kind, and persisted strongly that my work was well and thoroughly done – but he thought that it had not brought out the qualities which were to be looked for in a fellowship candidate.'

The restrained tone of this letter, with its impartial unemphatic wording, gives no indication of the terrible despondency that now engulfed him. He believed that Cunningham's objections to his dissertation were trivial and confused: his work had been absolutely original in that it gave for the first time an account of the complex and involved Benares incident as it had actually occurred, with his personal reasons –

---

[1] The Yen was Lytton's nickname for G. E. Moore.

supported by new and unpublished evidence – for believing that everything had happened as he described it. What could be more original than that? He did not, however, make it clear to his mother – or even apparently admit to himself – that Cunningham's objection was not simply to the effect that his dissertation carried on a line of research already begun by Sir James Stephen and Sir John Strachey – a purpose that was *prima facie* logical and justifiable and did not necessarily exclude originality – but that the affair of Cheyt Sing – especially when (as in this instance) severed from that episode concerning the Begums of Oude – was considerably less important and less difficult of treatment than those of Nuncomar and the Rohilla War. Nor had it ever aroused anything approaching the storm of controversy excited by those two matters.

Lytton had worked harder on his dissertation than he liked to admit to his friends. He wanted to be elected as a Fellow of Trinity almost, as it were, against his will, and certainly without any obvious or apparent effort. Besides, it was AGAINST HIS PRINCIPLES to fail in an examination. His immediate disappointment was so bitter that he could barely endure to remain a single day longer in Cambridge. 'My misery is complete,' he confided to Leonard Woolf who was himself preparing to leave Cambridge having done relatively poorly in the Civil Service examination. 'I have never felt more utterly desolate and now can hardly imagine that I shall be able to stick out the term. However, I presume it will at any rate never be worse than this, as there is absolutely not a soul or a cat in the place. . . . Shall we ever recover? Is this the end of all? Well, Lord have mercy upon us!'

And again later in the same letter: 'I have hardly the heart to say anything – only that we *must* have courage. This is only the first rebuff; how can we expect anything if we give up so soon.'

Leonard Woolf, for his part, felt less pessimistic, and he endeavoured to raise Lytton's spirits. After reading the typescript of his dissertation, he replied (October 1904): 'W.H., I thought, was enthralling, but I believe I see what those asses mean. It's too enthralling, and not enough like a dissertation. It's a little too graceful for them, and if you made it all seem more laborious and magnified all the points, they would have elected you.'

Lytton at once responded to this encouragement. It seemed obvious that he knew more about the original approach and treatment of history than his examiners. A letter which he dispatched about this time to Leonard Woolf illustrates very clearly that the crushing arrogance and absurdly infantile pride which many people found so offensive in him was no more than skin deep – a protective intellectual façade erected in the hope of raising his self-esteem and pulling himself out of the morbid troughs of melancholia which threatened, in times of misfortune, to overcome him utterly. It was the reverse side of the coin whose face was abject unhappiness. 'Yes; our supremacy is very great, and you've raised my spirits vastly by saying so,' he told Leonard Woolf early in the Michaelmas term. 'I sometimes feel as if it were not only we ourselves who are concerned, but that the destinies of the whole world are somehow involved in ours. We are – oh! in more ways than one – like the Athenians of the Periclean Age. We are the mysterious priests of a new and amazing civilization. We are greater than our fathers; we are greater than Shelley; we are greater than the eighteenth century; we are greater than the Renaissance; we are greater than the Romans and the Greeks. What is hidden from us? We have mastered all. We have abolished religion, we have founded ethics, we have established philosophy, we have sown our strange illumination in every province of thought, we have conquered art, we have liberated love. It would be pleasant to spend our days in a perpetual proclamation of our magnificence.'

So Lytton wrote at a time when his misery and disappointment were complete; for the more wretched he felt the more far-fetched and highfalutin had to be his claims to lift him above the abyss of failure. Read in its biographical context, this affirmation of supremacy shows itself to be little more than the whistling of an ambitious man, trying to keep up his spirits in the dark.

So fed up was he with Cambridge, its academic pedantry and restrictions, that a few days after Cunningham had pronounced his fatal verdict, Lytton decided to leave for the consoling wilds of Rothiemurchus. There, amid the trees, the lakes and mountains, the vast impersonal forces of nature, he could forget his petty troubles and frustrations, soothe his angry disappointed will. 'I have banished almost everything from my mind,' he wrote to Leonard Woolf (October 1904) after only a few hours there. Following this oblivion, his appetite for life returned. Something, he reasoned, might still be constructed out of the ruins. Cunningham had told him that there would probably be very few Fellowships next year and that it would be an outside chance if he got one. But at the same time he had urged him to go on with the work he had already done – remould his account of Benares and add to it a reconstruction of the Begums of Oude incident. To do this would certainly be more worth his while than beginning again on some other subject. If he pursued his researches, Cunningham had said, the result would be most useful to future historians, and even if it didn't win him a Fellowship, the thesis ought to be published

Methuen were already interested in it. Besides, what else could he do? There seemed no alternative. He must try again. 'On the whole,' he wrote to his mother (12 October 1904), 'I believe this is the best thing I can do.' Perhaps, one day, G. L. Strachey's 'Warren Hastings' would be acknowledged as a magnum opus – a fine revenge for the disregard of the Trinity electors.

Also, there was always that outside chance.

6

A VERY QUEER GENTLEMAN

The dissentient who persists long and steadfastly enough in his unconformity at length dictates the norm of behaviour. When he first went up to Trinity Lytton was a lonely, frail creature, so he felt, ashamed of his own awkwardness and freakish appearance. But in his final two years he had grown to be so much of a fashionably intellectual force that his influence is said to have left its mark on at least three generations of undergraduates, who strove to tune their voices in with the Master's high-pitched glandular key.

Anxious not to be forced into the shades of oblivion by his physical and emotive peculiarities Lytton was determinedly outspoken, above all on matters of religion. He would go about the streets and rooms of Cambridge exclaiming 'Damn God!' and other daring oaths and blasphemies, waiting in complacent disbelief for the Old Testament Lord God of Hosts to do his stuff and hurl down a thunderbolt. It was an infantile way of going on, and an example of the ludicrous postures into which an unnaturally restrictive and superstitious society can distort an otherwise highly intelligent human being. With many, of course, it produced the desired effect – that of offending the unthinking self-satisfaction which seemed to become an Edwardian undergraduate's station in life, of shocking him out of his traditionally accepted code of manners and beliefs. Some he converted; many more were banished from his awful presence. His ferocious agnosticism affected those whom he knew only indirectly: 'I cannot endure the people I meet in your rooms,' a fellow scholar and friend wrote to Leonard Woolf. 'Either they or I had to go, and as I was the newest and alone I waived my claim to the older friends and the majority. Strachey . . . &c. are to me in their several ways the most offensive people I have ever met, and if I had continued to meet them daily, I could not be answerable for anything I might do. . . . I am not what is known as religious, but I was not going to associate with people who scoffed and jeered at my religion: fair criticism given in a gentlemanly way I do not mind. But the tone of Strachey and even you on matters of religion was not gentlemanly to me. . . . I have never been in your rooms without someone coming in whom I do not like, usually Strachey. . . . I always spoke to you as a friend to a friend, except when Strachey was with you. Silence is then safer.'

To all Lytton's behaviour – some of it on the surface disconcertingly flippant – there was an extremely serious object. He was, even now, seeking to jolt people out of their automatic conventional morality and persuading them to accept more personal, enlightened attitudes. It says an immense amount for the amazing power of his personality that, as Noël Annan has pointed out, although he showed no signs of publishing anything except the isolated book review, he was recognized by so many as an arbiter. He was unauthorized, but taken as an authority, and his influence became extraordinarily wide. 'My own view is that Lytton's Cambridge years had an important effect on the subsequent mental life in England: especially on the attitude of ordinary people to religion and sex,' James Strachey told the author. 'The young men in my years (though also interested in socialism) were far more open minded on both those topics than their predecessors – and I believe they handed on what they derived from Lytton, and this (taken in conjunction with Freud, who was totally unknown till much later) is, I think, what has resulted in the reform of the general attitude to sex.'

Undoubtedly Lytton was the nucleus of that revitalized anti-religious group which now sprang up within the university. Clear evidence of his potent influence upon other undergraduates is provided by their letters to him, in which they studiously aimed at hitting off the same style of brash, pornographic pessimism. Beyond his own set and around Cambridge at large his sinister reputation for pagan decadence and wickedness spread alarmingly. 'You must be careful next term for "the College" is really enraged with us,' Leonard Woolf wrote to him in the summer vacation of 1903. 'They think you are a witch and given up to the most abandoned and horrible practices and are quite ready to burn us alive at the slightest provocation. One of Barlow's acquaintances, a scholar of the college, it is now a well-known fact, once went to tea with you and came out white to the lips and trembling. "The conversation," he said, "was too horrible! And the pictures and atmosphere."'

Lytton was secretly delighted. At last his presence was being felt; at last he was considered someone worthy to be reckoned with. The authorities, his foes, were being encouraged by nothing more aggressive than the force of mere words to adopt an attitude of transparent mediaevalism that must, he reasoned, forfeit them much support. Nor was the cautious Leonard Woolf exaggerating that mysterious evil prestige which hung around him and aroused such loathing and hostility. Some confirmation of what he had written in his letter is recorded by a humorous article in *The Granta* – one of a series entitled 'People I have not met' – based on his by now notorious heathenism. The imaginary interviewer finds Strachey reclining on a sofa, robed in a négligé costume consisting mostly of silk pyjamas, with his eyes half-closed over the *œuvre* of some French poet. Several bottles of *absinthe* and similar concoctions stand near by, and from these he frequently and with trembling hands replenishes his glass. The room is wreathed in swirling clouds of smoke from the heavy black tobacco cigarettes at which he draws deeply in between drinks. 'As I came in,' the interviewer wrote, 'he directed towards me the listless gaze of his cold, glassy eyes, but made no attempt to simulate the least interest in my presence.' The fictitious colloquy proceeds quietly, with Strachey still lying on the sofa, his hands bright yellow and his cheeks white and hollow, until without warning everything accelerates to a sudden climax. Rising to his feet, Strachey is seen to dance about the room 'after the manner of a lunatic who imagines himself to be an inebriated Bacchante in a frenzy of Greek orgy, but cannot find any liquor of sufficient strength to give the necessary realism to his performance'. This exhibition of mild exercise quickly exhausts him, and he falls back mumbling that he has found what he has been searching for all his life, an original sin – 'a corkscrew to open the bottle of an hitherto untasted draught of life'. Finally, before relapsing into bad verse, he terminates the interview with a last cryptic utterance: 'Oh virtue, virtue, life's a squiggle.' From which it would appear, Clive Bell rather ambiguously commented, 'that his reputation was not purely literary after all'.

The scene brings to mind Oscar Wilde's rooms some thirty years earlier at Oxford. Their similar renown at university for picturesque, effete sinfulness was based partly on distinctive tastes which they held in common. As undergraduates each of them displayed a deep and lasting fascination for the stage; each won a much-coveted prize for rather in-different, insincere poetry; fell out with the religious authorities of the day, and eventually – despite a contrary reputation for brilliant intel-lectuality – failed to obtain a Fellowship. In both cases their homo-sexuality was tied to an exaggerated self-preoccupation which, with its accompanying passion for the applause of others, acted as the limiting factor in their creative output. They evolved ingenious aesthetic theories which were more fanciful than truly imaginative, and which, for all their craftsmanlike expertise, never convince one as being

profoundly original. Their strangely divided natures spoke through
two antithetical literary styles; the sugary, ornamental fairy-tales and
melodramas of Wilde, roughly equivalent to Lytton's own shrill thin
romanticism, were the weaker strain. Like Wilde, Lytton was usually
best at his most succinct; the crisp, spare irony of *Eminent Victorians*
is anticipated perfectly by Wilde's study in green, his memoir of
Griffiths Wainwright, *Pen, Pencil and Poison*.

In their lives, too, there is a parallel. It was the penalty of this dual
nature that their charm was entangled with an ugly thoughtlessness. In
the course of his life Lytton's unique and memorable personality, his
reserved, steely strength, stamped itself indelibly on a remarkable
number of people, sometimes altering the whole course of their lives
and inspiring in them an intense and enduring devotion. 'Je n'ai jamais
rencontré quelqu'un qui dominât la vie comme lui,' wrote Francis
Birrell of him. 'Souvent silencieux et morose, généralement en proie à
quelque malaise, il était constamment environné d'une atmosphère de
déférence.' For such people he represented the virtues of tolerance,
enlightenment and humanity. Yet at the same time, as a logical but
seemingly paradoxical result of his twofold temperament, the humanitarianism for which he stood was erected and maintained against a
scathing contempt for the mass of humankind – the ugly, the boring,
the stupid, the ambitious, the powerful and the ordinary. Towards these
classes of persons he sometimes reacted with the unselfconscious
brutality of a child, his rude and abrupt behaviour being quite as
extraordinary as the warmth and kindness he lavished upon those he
liked. From his deficiencies, his very lack of vitality, he had constructed
a character of astonishing force. By deliberately withdrawing his
personality from the reach of those around him he was able to cast a
withering blight upon any social gathering of which he disapproved or
which wearied him. Under the inspired tension of his silence the very
fires would seem gradually to fade into dead ashes, the room grow chill.
'How dull everyone is!' he once exclaimed in the middle of a picnic:
and even the birds on the near-by trees stopped their singing in discouragement.

To attract this displeasure was a dismaying, sometimes a terrifying
experience. He seldom scrupled to hide his boredom or the awful outward manifestations of his extreme shyness. Once, when with difficulty
he had persuaded Leonard Woolf – whom he was then visiting – to
invite a rather prosy and well-known literary man to dinner so that
they might be introduced to each other, he was so overpowered with
ennui after five minutes' conversation that he retired completely into
himself and, determined to take no further part in the proceedings, fell

into a deep tortuous silence, 'fixing his eyes upon his food or upon the ceiling and tying his legs into even more complicated knots than usual'. His habitual diffidence before strangers would sometimes blossom among mere acquaintances into a cutting callousness. 'Mr Strachey, do you realize it's five years since we met?' inquired Constant Lambert, then a clever, charming but rather noisy young man; to which he received the purring unexpected reply: 'Rather a nice interval, don't you think?' At parties he had no small talk whatever, and his grim, unremitting lack of response to any form of idle or trivial chatter was often devastating. Like most inhibited people he could, on occasion, be arrantly outspoken. At the end of a solemn, lengthy lecture delivered in candlelight by A. C. Benson on the critic and historian, John Addington Symonds, he swayed to his feet like a languid jack-in-the-box and piped up from the back of the hall: 'But tell me, had Symonds *any* brain?' His capacity for disturbing repartee was difficult to match. When a taxi driver, having driven him home, suddenly turned to him and expostulated, 'I should never have agreed to take you had I known *this* was the house you wanted,' Lytton did not trouble himself to ask what on earth the man could have meant, but simply retorted: 'Has anyone ever told you what a *bore* you are?'

A blatant display of stupidity often drew from him some lightning ironic rejoinder. 'Dances in Paris begin at midnight,' announced one blasé undergraduate who had just spent his vacation in France. 'And in Vienna', Lytton snapped back testily, 'they begin at two'; whereupon there was an awkward protracted pause, and the atmosphere grew electric. Any form of Christianity, which offended his intellect and oppressed his emotions, was of course like a red rag to a bull. Sometimes the religious and rationalistic debates waxed too earnest for him, the hot-house of ethical discussions too claustrophobic. 'I expect, Strachey, you would maintain that self-realization was the end of existence?' queried a certain young Christian intellectual striving to be fair and reasonable before an avowed sceptic. 'That', Lytton immediately answered, 'certainly would be the *end*' – a retort which impressed some admirers as being worthy of Voltaire. Humbug and grandiloquence he was especially swift to deflate, as on one notable occasion when he petrified a party of Highland sportsmen. A *Punch* artist had been pompously deprecating the practice of lynching Negroes and by way of a gentlemanly, worldly-wise comment, added: 'But you know what it is they lynch them for.' 'Yes,' replied Lytton. 'But are you sure the white women mind it as much as all that?'

This quick contemptuous temper was a natural outlet for his seething inner self-dissatisfaction, sharpened to a fine edge by continual ill-health.

Outward circumstances were sometimes less a cause than an excuse for his cynicism and offensiveness; for, like Samuel Rogers, he seems to have felt that, with his weak voice, he could only be heard when he said unkind things. He never exploded with anger or indignation, but with perfect cold control planted his dagger in the heart of a chosen adversary. Perhaps the most striking example of his unprovoked rudeness took place a few years after leaving Cambridge, and had as its victim the poet and Chinese scholar Arthur Waley. At that time Waley was suffering from defective eyesight and unable to read. To enable himself to play chess, which as a substitute for reading he very much enjoyed, he used to tie a label round the bishops so that he could distinguish them more easily from the pawn pieces. Entering a room where Waley was bent low over this chess board, Lytton glanced at the labels fluttering from the bishops and remarked: 'I see you're not only blind, Waley, but also half-witted!'

Many such remarks, intended as humorous sallies, were never meant to hurt, for at heart Lytton had a kindly nature. But, in these early days, he was often unaware of the diabolical effect his manner produced upon others. Whenever it was pointed out to him that he had un-wittingly offended someone, he would feel intensely remorseful, going to some lengths to apologize and set matters right again.

Although he had found a degree of happiness at Cambridge to dissolve some of those cares and vanities of his former existence, his new self-confidence was still aggressively precarious. Some still thought him guilty of searing intellectual snobbishness. But with the luminous example of Moore and others to encourage him, such criticisms were already less wounding. Naturally he was always in a minority; but it was no longer a minority of one. Like Wilde's dandyism and bold check suits, Lytton's sartorial devices, which later came to a head under the influence of Augustus John, were both a means of drawing attention to himself and of emphasizing in the most theatrical manner his departure from the conventions of the past. Yet his eccen-tricities were less easy-going than Wilde's. He had a devout horror of high fashion and during the autumn of 1904 was compelled sharply to rebuke such a close friend as Leonard Woolf for his brown boots and green collar. Since aesthetics were inextricably bound up with ethics in the public imagination, and many people judged others simply by their clothes, Lytton's unconventional views were often strictly and for-midably applied. Wilde had made an art of disconformity; Lytton set out to make of it an asset. He chafed against his own eternal adolescence – of which his unbroken teenage voice was a perpetual reminder – instead, like Wilde, of sinking complacently within it. In his last year or two at Cambridge, he made himself into something of a philosopher-clown. And for a time, his clothes became very unlike what most people would have expected the son of a Victorian general to wear. A farmer's wife who let lodgings told Bertrand Russell that Lytton had once come to her to ask whether she could take him in. 'At first, sir,' she said, 'I thought he was a tramp, and then I looked again and saw he was a gentleman, but a very queer one.'[1]

Cambridge temporarily became for Lytton the home from home for which he had been searching. Before going up there he had usually found himself an unwilling, embittered outsider, a rebel through force of circumstance. But within a single year at University he established himself as an integral part of a small but intimate community. The all-male society of Trinity and King's was a convenient niche, but it appealed, as he himself came to realize, only to the more timid and unadventurous side of his nature, those weaker elements within him which he was resolutely determined to overcome. Now, in the autumn of 1904, he reigned over a tiny kingdom; but it was not enough. He longed for – and dreaded – some wider sphere of activity. But what? Until he could decide upon a fixed course for the future, supremacy over a small university group was preferable to the role of a wandering nonentity in the world at large. Cambridge offered him a haven of static and protective custody where his intellect might be beguiled in the contemplation of human beings as diagrams which provided the basis for aesthetic and dialectical discussion.

As was the custom then, they all addressed each other by surname, never by Christian name, though nicknames were considered quite proper. With his heightened physical awareness Lytton, or rather Strachey, was responsible for inventing many of these nicknames himself. Maynard Keynes, to his evident dislike, was dubbed 'Pozzo', possibly, it has been suggested, on account of his figure, though probably after the devious Corsican diplomat, Pozzo di Borgo; Forster was familiarly known as 'the Taupe' because of his resemblance to a mole, in stature, in the snug richness of his apparel, and in the strength and silence with which he constructed his formidable works;

---

[1] James Strachey disagreed with the author that his brother was ever at all eccentric – an epithet which he interpreted as being purely derogatory. As an alternative to this, he took the view that Lytton was 'quite unshakeably rooted in commonplace sanity and reality', and that therefore a comparison with Oscar Wilde was unjust ('the only resemblance I can see is that they were both buggers'). His clothes, too, James Strachey wrote, 'were always perfectly conventional except during the rather short Lamb-Augustus [John] period. My own very rarely used Savile Row tailor (an old gentleman now) told me a couple of years ago of his pride in having persuaded Lytton to go back to ordinary smart clothes (such as you see him wearing in the photograph with the globe). I think you get this from Bertie.'

Thoby Stephen was rechristened 'the Goth' owing to his monolithic appearance and character; the inscrutable, far-seeing wisdom of G. E. Moore was suggested by 'the Yen'; the second-rate officiousness of Walter Lamb was implied by 'the Corporal'. Despite looks which lent themselves easily to caricature, Lytton's friends never gave him a lasting nickname, possibly owing to their understanding of his painful physical self-consciousness.[1] Such names expanded the general atmosphere of conviviality without really breaking the conventions of upper-middle-class reticence. In much the same spirit of prudent intimacy, of prim anti-puritanism, Lytton declared a little later that 'certain Latin technical terms of sex were the correct words to use, that to avoid them was a grave error, and, even in mixed company, a weakness, and the use of synonyms a vulgarity'. It is partly indicative of his undeveloped character, as well as of the indeterminate Edwardian age in general, that though sex was placed so high on the agenda of discussion, all deliberations should be carried on with the aid of a dead language.

Lytton gave as his reason for staying up a further year at Cambridge the need of the Society to be put back on its feet again. Its members were sadly depleted, and there seemed no one else capable of selecting desirable embryos. Moreover, the Michaelmas term of 1904 marked the end of Moore's six-year tenure of his Prize Fellowship. To the dismay of his admirers, the most elevated angel of them all showed no inclination to remain at Trinity, but retired in September with A. R. Ainsworth to live in Edinburgh. 'He has gone,' Lytton wrote to Keynes during the Christmas vacation (11 January 1905). 'The wretched creature said he had no intention of coming to Cambridge next term, but that he would have to in the May term, as he's examining the Tripos. This is rather disappointing, isn't it?'

Just as Moore had succeeded McTaggart as the dominating influence among the young Apostles, so now Lytton and subsequently Maynard Keynes supplanted Moore. And, by the same token, metaphysical speculation soon began to retreat as the popular basis for intellectual discussion before its bastard offspring, psychological gossip, in much the same fashion as political idealism had earlier given way to metaphysics. Although Lytton possessed a clear head for argument, his mind was not especially well adapted to contend with labyrinthine reasoning and the abstract circumlocutions of ethics. Some of the changes in thought and habit which were foisted on the Society while Lytton was

---

[1] For a short time at the beginning of the war, David Garnett used to call Lytton 'the Cowboy', because of the wide-brimmed hat he then liked to wear. But the name did not stick. And at Cambridge, Leonard Woolf called him by a shorter version of his surname – 'the Strache'.

one of the supreme undergraduate members are elucidated by Bertrand Russell in his autobiography. 'The tone of the generation some ten years junior to my own was set mainly by Lytton Strachey and Keynes,' he wrote. 'It is surprising how great a change in mental climate those ten years had brought. We were still Victorian; they were Edwardian. We believed in ordered progress by means of politics and free discussion. The more self-confident among us may have hoped to be leaders of the multitude, but none of us wished to be divorced from it. The generation of Keynes and Lytton did not seek to preserve any kinship with the Philistine. They aimed rather at a life of retirement among fine shades and nice feelings, and conceived of the good as consisting in the passionate mutual admirations of a clique of the *élite*. This doctrine, quite unfairly, they fathered upon G. E. Moore, whose disciples they professed to be . . .'

Owing largely to Moore's puritanical attitude towards pleasure, the prevailing mood of the Apostles had been one of serious and studied gloom. For hours they would remain, as Maynard Keynes describes the scene, 'sunk deep in silence and in basket chairs on opposite sides of the fireplace in a room which was at all times pitch dark'.[1] There, in the smoky obscurity they sat on interminably with their toes on the fender, talking about philosophy and God and their livers and their hearts and the hearts of their friends – all broken. Though it was only later in life that Lytton was to make a fetish of pleasure, he did during the last years or so of his time at Cambridge introduce a brighter note into these Apostolic proceedings. Occasionally the meetings got out of control and were enlivened by delicious, infantile pranks – cushion fights and thrilling games of blind man's buff. At Lancaster Gate, Lytton had been a fitfully gay and giggling child; and now, as an adolescent, he brought with him an element of fun and laughter. He loved puns and ingenious ribald jokes. Yet his high spirits seemed something of an artificial contrivance, largely detached from the conscious emotions of life, and his wit a magic fountain playing bravely and prettily amid the surrounding night, but from which no one could assuage a real thirst. Despite his joking and his inventiveness, the pleasure-loving mask which he assumed was more a distraction from the disappointments and

[1] Of the above passage, based on Maynard Keynes's 'My Early Beliefs', and the previous passage taken from the first volume of Bertrand Russell's autobiography, James Strachey frankly disapproved. 'Of course,' he wrote to the author, 'you swallow Bertie's jaundiced story without a word of hesitation. It's quite untrue that metaphysical and logical arguments were out. When I was a brother, Maynard, Norton and Hawtrey (who came up very regularly) had constant hard headed arguments about such things as sense-perception or truth or internal relations; and Whitehead, Sanger, Russell and Moore turned up often enough to affect the sort of conversation. . . . And equally of course you accept without reservation Maynard's forty years' later bleatings.'

tedium of existence than the manifestation of a genuinely happy nature, for his deepest convictions were still pessimistic. It was these convictions, these 'good states of mind' as they were now called, that he liked to ventilate in the company of his special friends. For in spite of all his discontent, his illnesses and unrequited affections, somehow, way down within him, the magic fountain played irresistibly on. It was curious, almost distressing, how in the face of such numerous complaints – his own deficiencies and the infuriating shortcomings of those near him – he still enjoyed himself so much.

In the opinion of Bertrand Russell and some others, the new note of gaiety that Lytton injected into the Society acted as a salutary antidote to the immature and over-solemn priggishness of some of the elder brethren. And there were other, more crucial departures from the past. The Apostles 'repudiated entirely', in Keynes's own words, 'customary morals, conventions and traditional wisdom. We were, that is to say, in the strict sense of the term, immoralists.' Bertrand Russell is even more specific. 'After my time the Society changed in one respect,' he records in his autobiography. 'There was a long drawn out battle between George Trevelyan and Lytton Strachey, both members, in which Lytton Strachey was on the whole victorious. Since his time, homosexual relations among the members were for a time common, but in my day they were unknown.'

From going through the Society's papers in his role as secretary, Lytton had become convinced that many past Apostles were in fact secret and non-practising homosexuals. But in those unenlightened times some of them had not even been fully aware of their predilections, while other more introspective brethren had steadfastly suppressed all such inclinations and lived out lives of miserable, twilight celibacy. Now, in the new uninhibited age of reason heralded by Moore, all this was to be altered. From his personal influence on his contemporaries, Lytton hoped to ease forward the gradual advance of civilized opinion in the country as a whole. Reconstituting the Society was a first essential step along this road. But he was not alone. In Maynard Keynes, who had been elected an Apostle during February 1903, there existed a worthy if rather more cautious lieutenant. Within the voluminous correspondence which passed between these two during the next five years, Lytton expounds some of the special virtues and advantages of that love which passes all Christian understanding. Its superiority to the humdrum heterosexual relationship lay, so he believed, in the greater degree of sympathy and the more absolute dual-unity which it could command. Between opposite sexes there must always be some latent residue of doubt, ignorance, perplexity; so often intelligence was matched with stupidity, talent paired off with mediocrity. But through homosexual love, which aimed at duplicating or replacing the self rather than complementing it, one could inhabit the body and assume the personality of one's choice. And so, instead of extending, unsatisfactorily, the burdens of adulthood, one escaped into a vicarious existence at once stimulating to the intelligence and imagination, and nourishing for the imprisoned, frustrated will.

Of all Lytton's new friends at King's, Maynard Keynes was to play the most significant part. From his scholastic parents he seemed to have inherited an overplus of intellectual power. His mother was a formidable Mayor of Cambridge; his father, an ardent Nonconformist, lectured in old-fashioned deductive logic and political economy, but placed a greater significance on morality than on reason. Maynard claimed to be less concerned with moral issues – he considered Bertrand Russell, for example, 'too censorious' – but there persisted in his character a strong Nonconformist strain. At Eton he had been both scholastically and socially successful, impressing those who liked his company as astonishingly mature, and those who did not as regarding himself as a privileged boy with rather more than the standard quota of cerebral conceit. Though he commanded a beautifully modulated speaking voice, he was not handsome. A long spoonbill nose, slightly *retroussé*, which had earned him the nickname of 'Snout' at school, was surmounted by a pair of brilliant, amused eyes. Dark-haired, still fairly slim, with a receding chin and thick sensual lips partly camouflaged by a trim moustache, he looked infinitely and amusingly sly. He had, also, a tremulous, supple look. Like a cat in a bush, he watched everything, yet was very forthcoming too. There was something of Homer's 'Ulysses' about him. His extremely lively countenance conveyed great charm and animation; he was most ambitious and impatient. His own health, however, like Lytton's, was never good, and he suffered, too, from an unutterable obsession that he was physically repulsive. Like Lytton again, he could charm or dismay an audience with unusual power; but he showed his displeasure not merely by withdrawing into himself, but by projecting a terrible punitive ray which seemed to shrivel up all opposition. Along with this greater violence and more active ruthlessness went a higher degree of caution. After their first meeting Lytton described him as 'stiff and stern'; but under this reserved surface manner of self-possession and aloofness, Sir Roy Harrod has assured us, his emotions ran strong. During his first year at Cambridge especially, he felt the need of understanding friends, for he could not radiate that aura of disarming personal affection which breaks down the barriers of formality and attracts companionship quickly. In Lytton, who had previously experienced something of the same difficulties, he soon found someone in whom he might trustingly confide; for to the intellectual affinity which existed between 'Scraggs' and 'Snout' was added a deeper, secret communion of spirit. He discovered, also, that though Lytton was often brittle and affected in company, in private he could be far more relaxed and easy, and to those who were unhappy or victims of a condition of loneliness akin to his own he showed his best, most sympathetic traits – his kindness, gentleness and even sentimentalism.

Already, by the time he was elected to the Apostles, Keynes's cleverness was prodigious, and his intellect, in the opinion of Bertrand Russell, 'was the sharpest and clearest I have ever known'. In spoken argument only Russell himself could match the young undergraduate. Keynes, however, seemed colder, more detached and clinical. Whereas Russell was prone to attributing motives of the blackest villainy to those who disagreed with him, Keynes merely dismissed his opponents as dismal idiots. And yet, for all the extraordinary speed of his brain, the lightning rapidity with which he sucked in and devoured information, there was some imaginative quality lacking in his make-up of which he himself seemed obscurely aware and to which he drew others' attention by his uncharacteristically humble prostration before the altar of the arts. His mind was so restless and quick that his more turgid, watchful emotions never caught up with it, were never quite in step. The brilliant, translucent sparkle of his writing is not superficial, but rather icy. Like a barrister, he was often bent on putting over a point of view at one remove from himself, and his stated opinions seemed on occasions to be oddly vicarious. He appeared almost frightened of a fusion between heart and mind, and in his anxiety to keep them segregated sometimes grew impatient or wilful, making and stubbornly maintaining, with an irritated air of bluff, judgements which were absurdly wrong-headed for a man of his capability. His retrospective exposition of an initially false premiss was sometimes brilliant, extending his ingenuity to the full; and round this central untruth the satellites within his orbit would spin brightly and with incredible velocity.

Bertrand Russell has confessed to wondering sometimes whether the degree of cleverness which Keynes possessed was incompatible with depth, but decided that his suspicions were unjustified since Keynes was perpetually so overworked that he had not the time to give of his best in his books. Yet Russell's intuition may be a surer guide to Keynes's character than his impartial reasoning. The constant overwork which pressed in on Keynes all his life did not create itself accidentally from without, but was attracted by some urgent, personal necessity. He went through life as if he had to fill an eternal vacuum within himself, and appeared scarcely capable of relaxing. Above all, he was stimulated not chiefly through his emotions, but by problems which acted directly upon his brain. With all his great charm, his view of things remained cold and almost mechanical. Sometimes, his computer-mind could be a source of considerable irritation to Lytton. Everything, even making love, he evaluated in statistical terms, and he was fond of making absurd mathematical comparisons between people's affections – one person was two point five per cent happier than someone else, and so on. For several years Lytton's intimate personal life was bound up with that of Keynes, so that it was not until after the First World War, when Keynes had grown into a more benign personality, plumper and balder, that Lytton was able to assess his character impartially. 'An immensely interesting figure', was his verdict delivered to Ralph Partridge in 1920, '– partly because, with his curious typewriter intellect, he's also so oddly and unexpectedly emotional.'

For some considerable time at Cambridge, Keynes's superficial aloofness repelled Lytton. Desmond MacCarthy once said of him that his object in life was to impress men of forty, and Lytton felt inclined to agree. 'I don't believe he has any very good feelings', he wrote to Leonard Woolf (December 1904), '– but perhaps one's inclined to think that more than one ought because he's so ugly. Perhaps experience of the world at large may improve him. He has been ill, and I have been twice to see him in Harvey Road.[1] Really the entourage is shocking. Old ladies call, and gossip with Mrs Keynes. He joins in, and it flashed upon me that the real horror of his conversation is precisely that it's moulded on maiden aunts.'

Despite Keynes's prematurely spinsterish manner, Lytton became increasingly friendly with him. 'Keynes is the best person to talk to,' he admitted to Leonard Woolf later that same month, 'for he at any rate has brains, and I now believe is as kind as his curious construction allows him to be.' When Woolf had sailed for Ceylon six weeks earlier, he had left vacant the role of confessor in Lytton's life. Keynes was an obvious possibility as his successor, and by the beginning of the Lent term of 1905 the substitution had been completed. 'You are the only person I can speak to,' Lytton now told Keynes. And to Leonard Woolf he wrote (February 1905), making amends for previous slighting observations: 'There can be no doubt that we are friends. His conversation is extraordinarily alert and very amusing. He sees at least as many things as I do – possibly more. He's interested in people to a remarkable degree. N.B. He doesn't seem to be in anything aesthetic, though his taste is good. His presence of character is really complete.

[1] No. 6 Harvey Road, Cambridge, was Keynes's home.

He analyses with amazing persistence and brilliance. I never met so active a brain (I believe it's more *active* than either Moore's or Russell's). His feelings are charming, and, as is only natural, in perfect taste . . . he perpetually frightens me. One can't be sentimental about a person whose good opinion one's constantly afraid to lose. His youth chiefly makes itself obvious by an overwhelming frankness, and of course often by a somewhat absurd *naïveté*.'[1]

The frankness which Lytton and Keynes exchanged in their letters from this time onwards seems, at a first reading, to uncover a state of affairs within Cambridge which would have provoked curiosity in Gomorrah and caused the inhabitants of Sodom to sit up and take note. A more careful examination, however, suggests that, especially during these early years, there was a good deal more talk than action. A special glossary is really required in order to reduce to some verisimilitude the actual meanings of the words so freely employed. To 'propose' would seem to indicate little more than the slight ambiguous pressure of one hand upon another; to 'rape' or even to 'bugger' usually means a peck on the cheek, or a dubious embrace. For, in a society which regarded homosexuality as more grave than murder, what Lytton and Keynes were looking for almost as urgently as love itself, was a discreet and sympathetic source of disclosure. For a time they found this in each other, and, not unexpectedly, made the most of what was for both of them something of a luxury. What does emerge very clearly from between the lines of this correspondence is that it was not the younger Keynes who appeared so absurdly naïve, who stood in need of experience of the world at large, but Lytton himself, since it never occurred to him until it was too late that they were not just secret confidants, but also rivals.

By the autumn of 1904 Lytton and Keynes had already established themselves in joint ascendancy over the Apostles. A visiting Oxford contemporary that Michaelmas term, J. D. Beazley,[2] recorded nearly fifty years later that 'when I went over to Cambridge at that time I thought Keynes and Strachey were the two cleverest men I had ever met; and looking back over the years, I still think they are the two cleverest men I ever met.' Sir Roy Harrod, to whom he was speaking, then asked him whether he received the impression that one was leading or dominating the other. 'No,' he replied, 'they seemed to me to be equals, peers, different and complementary.'

[1] 'My disease is that I am so frank that nobody believes me and takes it for wickedness.' (Maynard Keynes to Lytton Strachey, April 1905.)

[2] Professor Sir John Davidson Beazley (b. 1885), the distinguished archaeologist and author of many works on ancient sculpture, painting and pottery, who was at this time an undergraduate at Christ Church.

Although Lytton saw more and more of Keynes at this time, he was leading something of a solitary existence. A receptacle of confidences, he had none of his own to impart, only other people's. Now that all those with whom he had originally come up were gone, the place, life itself, seemed empty and listless. He felt strangely dispirited, 'sunk in every kind of sloth'. Cambridge had nothing fresh to offer him; he had seen it all. 'I have had practically every experience,' he wrote. 'Nothing can come to me new again.' And to Leonard Woolf he morbidly philosophized (January 1905): 'Illness itself haunts me, but I dare say that by being always on the edge of the grave, one manages to avoid falling into it. Our bodies are like Comets' tails, trailing behind us as we whirl towards the stars; when we lose them we turn into dead coals and drop into the earth.'

Towards the end of November 1904, just as the mists of depression seemed about to enfold him absolutely, a new star appeared on the Cambridge horizon which, as if by magic, dispersed the clouds and filled his whole world suddenly with its light. This was (Sir) Edgar Duckworth, known then as 'Dicker', a freshman at Clare College, which nestles, appropriately enough, between King's and Trinity, though more closely to the former. Here, so it seemed to Lytton, was the perfect embryo to fill that vacancy in his life created by Sheppard's stubborn vagueness and sentimentality. The Society – Lytton himself – was saved. 'Duckworth is fair, with frizzy hair, a good complexion, an arched nose, and a very charming expression of countenance,' he wrote to Leonard Woolf (30 November 1904). 'His conversation is singularly coming on, he talks a good deal, in a somewhat ingenuous way, but his youth is balanced by great cleverness and decided subtlety in conversation. He's interested in metaphysics and people, he's not a Christian, and sees quite a lot of jokes. I'm rather in love with him, and Keynes, who lunched with him today at Lamb's is convinced that he's all right... He was at Eton, but at 17 he insisted on going to St Andrews to learn medicine, which he does up here. This in itself shows a curious determination. But he doesn't look determined; he looks pink and delightful as embryos should.'

For some months the task of securing Duckworth's election to the Society occupied much of Lytton's time. There was among the Apostles a common practice, much commended by Henry Jackson, Regius Professor of Greek and one of the senior Fellows of Trinity, that no freshman might be admitted. Undeterred, Lytton went to see Jackson, who carried great weight in the Society, and persuaded him that this custom, like all traditions, needed the odd exception to establish its general efficacy, and that, in any case, 'two years at a Scotch

University' corresponded to a full year at Cambridge. Once this had been agreed, Lytton set about introducing the new embryo to other Apostles. To still others, less accessible, he dispatched letters. 'Our embryo Duckworth is still as satisfactory as ever,' he reported to Moore (13 December 1904). 'I had arranged that MacCarthy should meet him at lunch last Friday, but at the last moment that evil person telegraphed to say that he couldn't come. . . . I should like to talk to you. I feel rather like a buzzing Chimaera, but Duckworth is a *vast* encouragement.'

By the end of the Michaelmas term almost all Lytton's canvassing seemed to have been successfully completed. He retired from Trinity to Lancaster Gate, and, cut off from the delightful company of his new embryo, the mists of gloom began to descend about him once more. 'This place is a mere mass of fog,' he wrote to Keynes (17 December 1904). '. . . I manage to exist.'

Most of this winter vacation was spent working at the second part of his Hastings dissertation. But in the late afternoons he would put his writing to one side and have tea with Goldie Dickinson and Sheppard in the purlieus of the British Museum, all three of them disputing heatedly as to the wisdom of electing a freshman to their circle.

For a moment, however, Lytton's attention was diverted from this absorbing affair by the dramatic emergence of a figure from his past. 'Marie Souvestre – the eminent woman – is ill with no one knows what,' he wrote to Leonard Woolf (21 December 1904). She refuses to let any doctor examine her – no one knows why – but they guess it may be because she's afraid she's got cancer – and writhes in agony. They think she hasn't got cancer – but can't tell. It would be a sad loss if so eminent a person were to die.' In fact her instinct was surer than that of her doctors, and within three months she was dead. All her friends, the Stracheys included, visited her in these last months, and though the hand of death showed on her face, she seemed quite as passionately alive in spirit as ever. 'Veracity, an undeviating directness of intelligence, faithfulness and warmth of affection, were her most delightful qualities; dignity of manner and brilliancy of speech her chief ornaments,' wrote Beatrice Webb in her diary for 31 March 1905. 'An amazing narrowness of vision for so intelligent a person; a total inability to understand religion; a dogmatism that was proof against the spirit of scientific investigation; a lack of charity to feelings with which she did not sympathize – in short, an absence of humility was, perhaps, the most disabling of her characteristics. It narrowed her influence to those whom she happened to like and who happened to like her.'

Shortly after the new year, Lytton left London and went to stay with his brother Oliver, G. E. Moore, and a contemporary of his at Trinity, (Sir) Ralph Wedgwood – 'a sort of railway person'[1] – at Howe Hill, near Harrogate. Oliver, rather peremptorily removed from Balliol, had been hastily sent on a tour round the world under the tutory of Robert Bridges, the poet. On his return, he successfully persuaded his mother to let him study the piano under Leschetizsky in Vienna, where he had been one of only two Englishmen at Brahms's funeral. From Vienna he returned once again in disgrace to England, his piano playing not being up to concert standards, and was at once dispatched to India, to join the East India Railway. Recently he had returned home yet again, this time with a Swiss wife,[2] and set up home with Ralph Wedgwood, who had procured him a job. This was Lytton's first visit to their house, where Moore was a frequent guest. Despite some very violent arguments leading directly on to a correspondence between Oliver Strachey and Bertrand Russell, which considerably influenced the latter's philosophical views, Lytton remained mostly sleepy and almost bored. Compared with the illuminating reality of Duckworth, who would be elected in a few short weeks, all these dialectical discussions seemed rather dim and remote.

'The household consists of Oliver and Ruby and Julia[3] (his wife and child), and Wedgwood,' Lytton wrote to Leonard Woolf (January 1905). 'Moore has been here since Saturday, and I expect he goes to Edinburgh tomorrow. Wedgwood is a quasi Goth, large, strong, ugly, and inordinately good natured. He is rather stupid, but argumentative and jocose; and much better than it's possible to convey in description. His face is often positively wreathed in kindness of a strange fatherly sort. He likes music and has no perceptions. Moore has been much the same as usual, and of course rather wearing – especially with his damned Turnerisms. He has sung a good deal and played very violent duets with Oliver. I find it rather difficult to talk to him, and he has said nothing of much interest to me. Tonight he came out in a grand discussion with W and O with all the usual forms and ceremonies – the groans, the heaves, the tearing of hair, the startings up, the clenching of fists, the frowns, the apoplectic gaspings and splutterings.'

---

[1] Ralph Wedgwood became chief general manager of the London and North-Eastern Railway, 1923–39, then chairman of the Railway Executive Committee, 1939–41. He was knighted in 1924, and created a baronet in 1942. His daughter is Dr C. V. Wedgwood, the historian.

[2] Ruby J. Mayer.

[3] Julia Strachey, who married Stephen Tomlin, the sculptor, and subsequently Professor Lawrence Gowing, the painter. She is the author of *Cheerful Weather for the Wedding* (1932) and *The Man on the Pier* (1951).

Nevertheless, in spite of Lytton's general lapse into paralysis, the party seems to have been sprightly enough. Moore and Oliver play Schumann pieces with great verve and abandon, and in between tea and dinner everyone takes part in playing games of Pit, the infant Julia joining in the yells. Domestic calamities are numerous. The pipes freeze, and both the water and the gas have to be turned off. But no one – except Lytton – appears perturbed by the damage and inconvenience. 'The vagueté is undoubtedly too great,' Lytton comments. 'Wedgwood, however, does a great deal, I expect, in the way of taking steps.'

The Lent term of 1905, to which Lytton had so impatiently looked forward – which was to witness the glorious, unprecedented election of a freshman and mark, perhaps, the consummation of a new and perfect friendship – in fact turned out to be the most volcanic of his entire six years up at Cambridge.

The first shock exploded in his face during the last week of January. Lytton was sitting quietly and composedly in his room reading the *Essays of Elia*, when the secretary of the Shakespeare Society came in and, handing him a card, murmured something indistinct about one of the visitors that night being unable to attend. Automatically and without interest Lytton inquired who and why. 'Oh,' came the answer, 'a man called Duckworth smashed himself up last night on a bicycle.' What strength Lytton possessed drained away from him and he was hardly able to ask for any further particulars. In any case, the secretary could tell him little more than that Duckworth had been run over by a cart full of bricks and had injured a leg. When the man had left, Lytton remained sitting inert, and hours seemed to elapse before he summoned up enough nerve to cross-examine his bed-maker as to the dangers, generally speaking, of this type of accident. She, however, was re-assuring. So, venturing out, he hovered about the Great Court for a time, then at last plunged into Duckworth's room. He was in bed, being read to by a friend. In answer to Lytton's frantic questionings he declared that the doctor had been and pronounced him to be only bruised. 'Oh dear!' Lytton wrote to Keynes (2 February 1905). 'The appearance. He was flushed, embarrassed, exquisite. I fled after three seconds, cursing everything and everybody . . . and wondering how soon the news would spread abroad, and how many people his bedroom would be able to hold. These thoughts still agitate and blast me. I am consumed by terrors. We live upon a cataract; and at any moment, while we are yawning at the Decemviri, or maundering at McT's, the Hope of the World may be crushed to smithers by a cart in Trinity Street.'

After tottering back to his own rooms, weak with shock, Lytton gave expression to his turbulent emotions throughout the long night in verse:

> *O the darkness! O the stillness!*
> *All our world is closed in sleep.*
> *I in sadness, you in illness*
> *Solitary vigil keep.*
>
> *You, with happy head and tired,*
> *Lie around your silent room,*
> *Feel your heart still vaguely fired*
> *Paint with splendour all the gloom . . .*
>
> *Ah! You bring to gentle sleeping*
> *Smiles that once were my smiles too;*
> *Now I smile no more, but weeping,*
> *Lonely, write these songs for you.*

This incident, the prelude to a far greater shock, immediately circumstantiated the strength and fervency of Lytton's feelings towards his new embryo, whipping them up to an unprecedented pitch. But the second unforeseen event, more profound in its effects and itself the overture to a later, even more dynamic disaster, was to prove equally clearly that these feelings were not returned. Quite by accident Lytton stumbled upon the fact that his friend and confidant, Maynard Keynes, was also enamoured of Duckworth. At once a bitter rivalry broke out which took the outward form of a struggle to determine which of them should act as sponsor for his Apostolic election. All, it is said, is fair in war, and Lytton's half-hearted guile proved no match for the greater ruthlessness of Keynes. By the third week of February it was all over. Keynes, in victory, embraced the new Apostle, and Lytton was left to brood abjectly over 'my own unutterable silence – my dead, shattered, desiccated hope of some companionship, some love'.

Never, it seemed, had his loneliness, his desire for affection, been so violent as in the next few weeks. 'Duckworth . . . was duly elected last Saturday,' he wrote to G. E. Moore (21 February 1905). '. . . Oh Moore! I feel like a primeval rock, indifferent and venerable. I am too old ever to take wings. The only passion I have left me is the Black Rage. My stomach struggles through endless sloughs of dyspepsia. Alas!'

Some relief he did obtain by channelling his despair into a series of unhappy love poems after the style of John Donne – 'The Conversation', 'The Speculation', 'The Situation', 'The Resolution', 'To Him', 'The Category', 'The Reappearance', 'The Exhumation' – which examined the whole affair in detail and from every possible angle. Like many of the poems he composed in later life, they are written for the most part in a strain of subdolorous insipidity, the hazy, unspecific language seeming at the same time to record and conceal the secret moments of his emotional life. Common to several is a peculiar, pervading fascination – partly made up from a sense of revulsion – for the cruder sexual actualities of life, which is offset to some extent by an ecstatic longing for some unknown, delirious state of self-oblivion. Of those which emanated directly from his unhappy infatuation for Duckworth, probably the most interesting is 'The Two Triumphs', in which he contrasts the immediate joys of lust with the final unsullied triumph, the masochistic rapture, of unrequited love. Writing in the first person, Lytton imagines his rival tasting the sweet fruit of carnal passion to its bitter core. In this 'wrong world' lust has always been triumphant; but his own purer and more spiritual love is not blotted out. On the contrary, it flourishes in platonic adversity:

> *Yet listen – you are mine in his despite.*
> *Who shall dare say his triumph mine prevents?*
> *My love is the established infinite,*
> *And all his kisses are but accidents.*
> *His earth, his heaven, shall wither and decay*
> *To naught: my love shall never pass away.*

In the final verse Lytton drifts into a mood of erotic mysticism, not uncommon to many of the most rationalistic humanists, momentarily consumed by the fires of intense feeling. Also, in several of the other poems belonging to this sequence, Lytton's semi-aversion from sexual intercourse, mixed with phrases which bear witness to a thorough classical education and to its dubious benefits in the context of twentieth-century poems, is repeatedly exemplified. The theme running through them all is the decay of physical love. In 'The Exhumation', for example, the once beautiful body is seen as a corpse, and sexual desire is equated with death and the grave. Here, too, as in 'Knowledge' and other verses, the word 'lust' is significantly made to rhyme with 'dust'.

For some two months following the election of Duckworth, Lytton was filled with an almost demented hatred of Keynes. On 25 February, only a single week after the election, he launched an extraordinary onslaught upon Keynes before the assembled Apostles, an onslaught which, for all its fury, still preserves the anonymity of a Christ denouncing Judas: 'For it is one of his queer characteristics that one often wants, one cannot tell why, to make a malicious attack on him, and that, when the time comes, one refrains, one cannot tell why. His sense of values, and indeed all his feelings, offer the spectacle of a complete paradox. He is a hedonist and a follower of Moore; he is lascivious without lust; he is an Apostle without tears.'

By March he was still racked with animosity and revulsion. He could endure neither to see nor to speak to Keynes. Their correspondence had faltered and broken off. 'He repels me so much,' he wrote to Leonard Woolf that month, 'that I can hardly prevent myself ejaculating insults to his face.' But soon this harrowing antipathy underwent a subtle and curious change. All at once, and somehow in spite of himself, he was conscious of feeling closer to Keynes than ever before. The disgust which he had felt for him was perhaps only a variation of the contempt which he so often lavished upon himself. They had, after all, fallen in love with the same person; and he began to realize just how much they had in common. So it was not altogether surprising that when Duckworth drifted apart from Keynes, Lytton should experience a genuine sense of commiseration and sympathy for his late rival. 'That episode is over,' Keynes wrote to him at the end of April, '. . . I swear I had no idea I was in for anything that would so utterly uproot me. It is absurd to suppose that you would believe the violence of the various feelings I have been through.' And so, by confiding to him all his troubles and suggesting that he had not been unscrupulous but devastatingly honest and direct in his behaviour, Keynes won back Lytton's trust. Their parallel miseries over Duckworth intensified their feeling for each other, both of intimacy and of dislike, which alternated for some years often in response to rather trivial incidents.

'Poor Keynes!' Lytton wrote that spring. 'It's only when he's shattered by a crisis that I seem to be able to care for him.' This was just the beginning of a new lease of friendship. Soon their correspondence started up again and their reciprocal affection grew for a time increasingly warm. Indeed, so close was their spirit of companionship that they sometimes wondered whether they might not, just possibly, be in love with each other!

7

SALE VIE AND A GLIMPSE OF HEAVEN

During both terms and vacations, Lytton was all the while working steadily at the second part of his mammoth dissertation. 'My history has been – perpetual labour, interspersed with an occasional Symphony,' he wrote at the beginning of April. Three weeks later he left London for Moore's Easter reading-party, to be held this year at the Crown Hotel,

Pateley Bridge, near Middlesmoor in Yorkshire – 'A Godforsaken village inn,' as he describes it, 'eight miles away from a station, and a hundred from anywhere else.' In the company of Ainsworth and Moore himself, Lytton arrives here late one night in a blinding snow-storm. The three of them are joined in due course by Bob Trevelyan, C. P. Sanger, Crompton Llewelyn Davies[1] and, eventually, Desmond MacCarthy. After a cold disastrous beginning, the party settle down to their pleasant if unspectacular routine, Lytton growing progressively more healthy, bored and lonely as the days pass by. In this comatose, unresponsive mood he takes little part in the conversations, finding even Moore inaccessible. Occasionally Ainsworth will turn towards him, observe complacently, 'Strachey, you look unhappy,' and return to the general talk. As so often when there is no illness or pending infatuation to absorb his attention, he has sunk into the sloughs of tedium. Perhaps it is only in heaven that one is never bored when other people are talking. 'Isn't it ridiculous,' he writes to Leonard Woolf, 'that after a week one should find one's dearest friends quite unsupportable.' But boredom, he notes, stimulates his appetite, and each day he devours 'vast slabs of salt bacon, chunks of mutton, plates of "tea-cake" (at breakfast) pints of foul "ale" and hot jam pudding, deluged with cream. It's sickening in the abstract; but I manage to look forward to every meal. . . . We don't laugh much, and we play two games of jacoby every evening. This is a tolerable life for a fortnight.'

Early in May, he returned to London, spending a few further morn-ings at the British Museum, and the afternoons or evenings at various concerts or plays. 'On Thursday afternoon I went to You Never Can Tell, which was charming,' he wrote to Moore (16 May 1905), 'es-pecially as I could look during the intervals (from the Pit) at [Edward] Marsh[2] (in the stalls) talking to a simply incredible lady.'

The Easter term at Cambridge was already well advanced by the time Lytton returned to Trinity. It was late spring, and punts and panamas and iced drinks reigned along the banks of the Cam. The

---

[1] A solicitor, and brother of Theodore Llewelyn Davies.

[2] Sir Edward ('Eddie') Marsh (1872–1953), private secretary and close friend of Win-ston Churchill; scholar, wit, inveterate bachelor and 'the greatest friend that our painters and poets have found in the twentieth century' (Raymond Mortimer). Among the painters he helped were Mark Gertler, Ivon Hitchens, John and Paul Nash, Stanley Spencer, Graham Sutherland and Christopher Wood. Edited *Georgian Poetry*, wrote a personal memoir of Rupert Brooke, and translated the *Odes of Horace* and *The Fables of La Fontaine*. A tremendous first-nighter and diner-out, he was at the centre of the cultural, political and social scene for half a century. He also wrote an autobiography, *A Number of People* (1939), though much the fullest record of his life is given in Christopher Hassall's official biography (1959).

laburnum and lilac were out on the backs; the roses bloomed again on King's Chapel; the early peaches dropped from the walls of the Senate House; the scorpions reared their heads once more in the sunlight of the Great Court and all Cambridge came alive with the sweet scents and pale colours of an English summer. It was to be, as Lytton must have realized, his last term. The fresh yet familiar beauty of each street and building, the glamour and high spirits of youth seen through an idealizing myth, stirred in him feelings of tremulous nostalgia. 'I am restless, intolerably restless, and Cambridge is the only place I never want to leave,' he wrote, 'though I suffer there more than anywhere else.'

The first news affecting his future which reached him after returning to Trinity was not encouraging. His 'English Letter Writers' had failed to win the fifty pounds which went with the Le Bas Prize. 'That devil the Vice Chancellor[1] had awarded the Le Bas prize to – no one,' he wrote to Leonard Woolf (May 1905). 'So here am I penniless after my titanic efforts.' Still gloomier rumours and prognostications were to follow. 'I also gather that my chance for a fellowship is now merely nil – for 2 reasons. i, There are only two to be given, and ii, Laurence[2] is to be my examiner. Amen!' Vere Laurence, a lanky bearded history don at Trinity, was pretty well as unpropitious a choice, Lytton felt, as Cunningham had been the previous year. They had never been friendly. But hopeless though the prospects seemed, he had no alternative but to continue struggling on with his work. 'I try to write my dissertation, and fail,' he told Keynes (7 July 1905). 'I die daily, as the Scriptures have it. But then I die in so many different ways.'

By June, after an Apostolic debate on 'Is Life Worth Living?' Lytton had returned again to Lancaster Gate. It was the end of the Easter term, and three months' hard labour awaited him on the Hastings dissertation – to be crowned with almost certain failure. Unavoidably, he was wasting his time. Life seemed more wretched and pointless than it had ever been. On this occasion his pessimism and enervation were not simply the outcome of some transitory unsuccessful affair; they came as the natural culimination of everything. Life, as he now knew it, was certainly *not* worth living. 'Oh lord, lord, lord!' he wrote to Leonard Woolf (June 1905). 'I do feel that I'm extraordinarily misty – a sort of coloured floating film over the vicissitude of things. The mere business of carrying on one's life seems something so overwhelming

---

[1] Edmund Anthony Beck, a Trinity Hall don.

[2] R. Vere Laurence, then much under the influence of G. M. Trevelyan, in those days an austere teetotaller. Laurence himself was addicted to drinking and smoking, and before he died in 1934 had become an alcoholic.

and exhausting that it's all one can do to get along from hour to hour. One sleeps, washes, dresses, eats, forths, reads, eats, walks, talks, eats, reads, eats, despairs, yawns, and sleeps again, and all one's energies have been used up, and one is exactly as one was before. If one were a disembodied spirit there'd be some sort of hope . . .'

In mid-June, he visited Balliol College, Oxford. Here he was the guest of an undergraduate, Bernard Swithinbank, who, 'tall and handsome', we learn from Sir Roy Harrod, '. . . an elegant, even exquisite schoolboy', had been Keynes's closest friend at Eton. Keynes, in fact, had introduced him to Lytton, who began to cultivate his friendship soon after Duckworth's election to the Apostles. This he seems to have done not with any motive of personal revenge against Keynes – to whom he was now again confiding his thoughts and inner feelings – but out of an instinctive sense that should their friendship happen to develop automatically on to a more intimate level, then some natural law of justice would be properly fulfilled. He was particularly anxious to get on well with Swithinbank, who was himself obviously in correspondence with Keynes, and felt apprehensive lest his natural reticence should give his new friend a false impression. 'I want to tell you that I enjoyed my visit to Oxford more than I've enjoyed anything for ages and ages,' he wrote the day after returning to Lancaster Gate (20 June 1905). 'I hope you'll believe this in spite of what I'm afraid may have seemed appearances to the contrary. It's almost impossible ever to express one's feelings properly, so that when I say that I shall always remember your rooms with pleasure, will you make allowances for my inadequate statement? It was really exciting to meet the people whom I met there.'

By the same post he sent off a letter to Leonard Woolf in Ceylon, describing his new Oxford friend who, it seems, was probably as shy as Lytton himself. They must have made an odd, rather pathetic pair. 'In appearance he's tall (taller than me, I believe) and rather large footed and essentially solid; but by no means looks a strong and bulky person, his face is pale, ill and intellectual. The expression is often cat-like – the eyelids droop, and the mouth broadens; the features are all well-shaped, the nose arched. His hair is fair and thick, his voice rather shrill and boyish. The general impression he gives is undoubtedly one of vagueness. One sees at once that he's kind, nervous and impractical; and one's a little inclined to think that that's all. But it by no means *is* all. To begin with, there's his humour, which is always faultless and always wonderfully his own. Then his character is a real character. It's poetical – untrammelled. I mean by actualities; and quite unafflicted by contortions and affectations; it shines with a pale sincerity.'

Life at Lancaster Gate during the next few weeks consisted of slow, grinding research work interspersed with a few glittering social events – a brilliant Joachim concert; *Phèdre* with Sarah Bernhardt ('Do you know the play and the lady?' he asked Swithinbank. 'Lord! But one can't expatiate. C'est Vénus toute entière à sa proie attachée'); a visit from Desmond MacCarthy who read aloud, in his half-asleep, tumbling way, pages of Landor, and occasionally succeeded in making Lytton laugh; and an introduction, through Desmond, to Harley Granville-Barker, who, like most people, made him yawn with boredom. 'I live in the bosom of a large and vivacious family,' he informed Swithinbank (1 July 1905). 'I spend my days in the British Museum; and my nights are diversified by an occasional tedious dinner-party, or by conversations with the relics of my Cambridge friends.' Together with some of his and the Stephen family he also spent a week-end at the end of June with the Freshfields, parents of Elinor Clough, down in Sussex. 'Their house is incredibly vast and new,' he wrote to Swithinbank (1 July 1905), 'and packed with priceless cabinets, rugs, china vases and pictures. I was horribly depressed by the magnificence, and by the conversation, which was always on the highest levels. We discussed Henry James and Cymbeline and the essence of Architecture from morning till night.' From the other guests he singled out one as possessing exceptional qualities – Virginia Stephen. Their reaction to the house seemed to coincide exactly, and she put into words what was for him the true cause of his depression about the place, when, in mock-horror, she exclaimed: 'There's not an ugly thing in it!' Lytton could only add: 'Except the owners.'

These weeks were largely impregnated with thoughts of Swithinbank. He wrote to his new friend, received an immediate reply, and straightway wrote off again boldly suggesting a walk in Richmond Park. 'So today I went, and we punted (or rather he) up to Twickenham, had tea there, and came back,' he notified Keynes (7 July 1905), to whom Swithinbank was also reporting back the news. 'It was perfectly charming. I said very little and he a good deal. When I left him, I was in a condition. Lord, lord. I didn't know one could have such affection without lust. But there it is. He's unique – exquisite. Only I'm jealous of anyone else thinking so, almost. I only know one other work of the Creator equally beautiful as an aesthetic whole – the Goth. And heavens, what a difference!'

Lytton had always found it difficult to work in London and was thankful when, in the third week of July, he was able to move down to a large country house, six miles from Kettering, which the Stracheys had rented that summer. Great Oakley Hall, as it was called, was a typically Tudor mansion, with gardens, bowling-greens and box-hedges, all encompassed by magnificent elm trees. Inside, the rooms were complete with family portraits, carved doors and sliding panels; and there was also a large, insignificant library which on close inspection was found to contain several yards of collected sermons, the State Trials, and an edition of Pope's Homer. The spacious and leisurely air of comfort fitted in with Lytton's temperament very well. He took to the place at once, though regretfully noting one serious drawback to it: 'The Church is on the croquet lawn,' he explained to Swithinbank (15 July 1905), 'so I'm afraid our games may be interrupted by psalms and sermons. I expect there's a family pew in the church, which my mother will occupy in state, as she insists upon going to Church in the country, in order to keep up (I believe) the Established Religion. This seems a queer form of atheism, but harmless. As for me, I think I am a Christian, who never goes to Church, in order to encourage Freedom of Thought.'

Every day of the six weeks which Lytton now spent at Great Oakley Hall was passed in hard and exacting labour over the second part of his Warren Hastings. 'I work like hell, and live a regular life,' he wrote to Leonard Woolf, but he added, 'I have no hopes' (July 1905). To Clive Bell also he complained of his life of hopeless work (28 July 1905): 'My dissertation oppresses me horribly,' he admitted, 'but I cast it off as much as I can. I read Sir Charles Grandison in the intervals between wishing I were alive and wishing I were dead.' For recreation he promenaded delicately among the flowering rose bushes, perused the back numbers of *Punch* and gossiped about Clive Bell's unsuccessful proposal of marriage to Vanessa Stephen, which he was keen one day to make the basis of a comic novel. In his leisure moments he began to read John Ford and Diderot, preferring the former, and he also made one exciting literary discovery – Benjamin Constant, whose little masterpiece of exquisite art and charming, subtly-blended psychology enchanted him. 'I'm here, in the ordinary condition of exhaustion, and doomed to death though fated not to die,' he wrote to Keynes (18 July 1905) in a letter the frequent spelling mistakes of which emphasize very nicely the wraith-like and incompetent condition into which he had drifted. 'I cannot write the English language, and spend my time doing nothing else . . . Have you read Adolphe? It's superb. The point of view is original – i.e. that of the lovee. Don't you think rather a good idea? He's so dreadfully bored, and yet likes and doesn't want to give pain. It's wonderfully done – all in epigrams.'

Encompassed about by his family with all their high-strung enthusiasms and lack of inner comprehension, and involved perpetually himself in a hellish treadmill of scholasticism, Lytton was overcome for much of this summer by hopeless melancholy. 'I feel like a condemned criminal awaiting the chaplain's visit,' he told Saxon Sydney-Turner. And to Clive Bell he wrote (28 July 1905): 'The country has closed in upon me, and I'm gasping in the vacuum. Quelle sale vie! Nothing but village school treats on the lawn, and rectors to lunch, and not a word about any part of the body that happens to come between the waist and thighs.' Maynard Keynes, whom Lytton had once convinced of the dangers of unvariegated overwork, invited him to come and stay at Cambridge where he was living with his parents preparatory to a few weeks' holiday in Switzerland. Lytton's reply, written on 27 July and almost exulting in his wretchedness, conveys very strongly the empty pessimism by which he was now entangled:

Dear Keynes
    Total cash – 1/3½
    „   hope – ditto. i.e. hope of finishing dissertation, of ever seeing you again, of learning how to spell correctly, and of being in anything but a damned trance. I spend hours, days, and weeks in simply staring at blank sheets of paper – hopeless, helpless, utterly incompetent, completely vague, absolutely comatose, physically, morally and spiritually, DEAD. Oh my brethren! Take warning by this sad spectacle of a ruined soul. Such are the results of moral looseness. Cambridge, with its sad atmosphere of paradox and paederasty, is doubtless much to blame; but it would be idle to pretend that the fault does not mainly lie with a perverse intellect which has wantonly squandered the talents supplied by an all-wise Creator.
    Lord! This garden is wreathing and writhing with a school treat. It keeps on blowing motor horns, or things like motor horns, whose blasts pierce my entrails like so many swords. This is the quiet of the country. All I can say for it is that it gives me an excuse for not pretending to go on with my dissertation; but I don't know – my nerves are now so jangled that I doubt whether I'll be able to finish this.
    I have no news, except that the rector is married, that yesterday there was a flower show at Rockingham Castle, that today we had haddock for breakfast, and that tomorrow I shall stab myself . . .
    Friday. Suicide postponed. I shall risk all, and come tomorrow – so please expect me sometime or other. Also, please consider this. Shall I stay at King's? Is it against rules? Wouldn't it be much better for talking, etc. . . .

In another letter written that same month to Swithinbank, Lytton examines his own marked and ever-recurring low spirits rather less theatrically and with a more earnest introspection. The contrast in mood and tone illustrates what is perhaps in any case well enough implied, that beneath the flippant and amusing banter which makes up so much of his correspondence – always for him the freest, easiest mode of communication – there exists a very real, baffling undertow of misery and isolation. 'Is it merely bad health, or is it the feeling of one's hopeless incapacity, or is it one's horrible loneliness?' he asked (15 July 1905), and then confessed: 'I don't know – I so often feel that all is absolutely lost. The Lord knows I take no pride in this; I'm not Byronic. I'm not even decadent; it's only the truth.'

After a pleasant week-end interval at Cambridge, Lytton applied himself once more to the self-disciplined routine at Kettering. Each morning he breakfasted at eight. From ten o'clock to half-past one he worked at Warren Hastings. Then he would have lunch. During the afternoon, between three and half-past four, he usually went for a walk in the country among the elms and roses; and then, after tea, he would settle down to two hours' further work. At half-past seven he attended the family dinner, and between ten o'clock and half-past eleven he went back for a final period of writing his dissertation. He retired to bed regularly each day at midnight. It was, especially for a man of little natural stamina and of fragile health, an exacting routine. Had any of his friends ever heard of such scholarly application? He rather thought not. But it paid dividends, and in one week alone he completed over seventy large pages of manuscript.

At the beginning of August, Lytton was partly seduced away from this exigent programme when his cousin, Duncan Grant, arrived for a stay of two or three days. 'He's wonderfully nice, and nice looking,' he informed Leonard Woolf. All thoughts of Swithinbank were abruptly annulled. The lanky, shy Oxonian friend of Keynes had only been a convenient substitute for Dicker. With his diffident, nervous manner, his pale and fading countenance, his body so stalwart but frail, his expression so cat-like and comatose, his voice so shrill, he approximated far too closely to Lytton himself. A companion in loneliness rather than a means of escape from it, his company had provided consolation, not vivacity. To fall in love with him would have been like preparing for a journey to the ends of the earth – and then moving next door. But with the handsome, talented Duncan Grant, an affair might lead any-where. Of all his associates Lytton chose Maynard Keynes to whom to confide his secret rejuvenated hopes, at once so wonderful and so agonized: 'As for me – I don't quite know what I'm doing – writing a dissertation presumably,' he told Keynes (3 August 1905). 'But I've managed, since I saw you last, to catch a glimpse of Heaven. Incredible, quite – yet so it's happened. I want to go into the wilderness of the world, and preach an infinitude of sermons on one text – "Embrace one another." It seems to me the grand solution. Oh dear, dear, dear, how wild, how violent, and how supreme are the things of this earth! – I am cloudy, I fear almost sentimental. But I'll write again. Oh yes, it's Duncan. He's no longer here, though; he went yesterday to France. Fortunate, perhaps, for my dissertation.'

The rest of August passed without any major deflections from work. Duncan Grant's failure to reply to his letters was the cause of some self-pity, but when at last he did receive an answer it brought on a wild, violent and supreme attack of indigestion. At the same time he was shocked to learn of the tragic death of his friend Theodore Llewelyn Davies, drowned while bathing. The two incongruous events, coming together, almost prostrated him. But apart from this, his leisure moments were made up solely of trivial incidents of the ridiculous and amusing sort that always diverted him and which he loved to describe in his letters, as in his essays and books. 'There have been no particular adventures here – except one, as we were driving with Beatrice Ch. to Kirby,' he wrote to Duncan Grant (15 August 1905). 'Three bicyclists were seen approaching; two passed us safely; then there was a shriek, and a vision of a sprawling female. Shocking ! We leapt out, and found it was a young female who didn't know how to ride, out with her uncle and aunt. "For Gawd's sake, Maria," said the aunt, "don't tell your mother." She had dashed into the back wheel of our carriage, but fortunately seemed not to be hurt. We transported her to Corley station and left her reposing in the waiting-room. Of course dear Beatrice was very much to the fore. But in spite of her reassuring presence, it was an awkward affair.

'Madam Fischer arrived the other day to inspect her daughter. She is French, and both her sang-froid and her bottom are tremendous. (I think the two things always go together, don't you?) The two ladies left for Liverpool today. . . . I spend my days in a horrible treadmill of Begums, etc., but hope to be out of it all in a week's time. Every day I take a stroll among the elms, and down the rose-walk.'

This dissertation forecast proved rather too optimistic, for no sooner had Lytton sent off this letter than he encountered a number of un-usual difficulties, the solution to which occupied every spare moment of the next fortnight. Meanwhile, family affairs whirled and eddied around him almost totally unheeded: his mother fell ill with lumbago, his aunt Kate had a heart attack which temporarily robbed her of the power of speech, his sister Pernel withdrew into convalescence with mumps; meanwhile, Marjorie, his younger sister, departed for France, Ruby and her daughter Julia Strachey came to stay, and so did Lytton's eldest military brother, Richard, with his wife Grace. Only one fleeting appearance distracted his attention for a few brief hours – that of Duckworth, who, since he happened to be passing near by, came to lunch with the Stracheys. By now Lytton was able to observe him with a good deal of cynical detachment. He was as vain as a woman, he noted with bitter disillusion, and obviously had feelings of the wrong sort altogether. On the whole his short visit was chiefly amusing for the effect it produced on Lytton's family – one of dazzled fascination. 'Everyone bowed before him, and talked to me after he'd gone about his hair,' he informed Keynes (7 September 1905). And to Duncan Grant he wrote (30 August 1905): 'You can't imagine how he charmed everyone. I was a good deal amused at the sight. He was as vague as usual, and I felt, as usual, that he thought I adored him.' After lunch they sat out on the lawn together and Lytton noticed that he looked rather pale, and that he also complained as usual, though not perhaps more than usual, of constipation. For much of this time they discussed, in the abstract, the question of physical love. 'Poor thing,' Lytton lamented to Keynes after he had gone (7 September 1905), 'he doesn't seem to understand much! He says he's repulsed by it – what can one reply? All the same he understands more than most.'

On 30 August, Lytton completed once and for all his encyclopaedic dissertation on Warren Hastings and dispatched it to Cambridge by the last possible post. 'The weight is now off my spirit,' he wrote to Leonard Woolf (31 August 1905). 'The last week has been one of the most unpleasant of my life. Perpetual constipation, nervous irritation, headaches even, utter boredom, desperate hurry, incapacity to think – all the most sordid nuisances the flesh is heir to. I am now more or less happy, and at any rate lazy, though a good deal wrecked.'

'Warren Hastings, Cheyt Sing, and the Begums of Oude' covers in typescript some four hundred large foolscap pages, and, at nearly one hundred and twenty thousand words, is the longest single work Lytton ever produced. It is, as might be expected, a thoroughgoing piece of scholarship, far better balanced, far less arbitrary in its conclusions than the essay which had failed to win him the Greaves Prize four years previously. The ceaseless animosity of Philip Francis, for instance, is much more credibly conveyed; yet the ultimate aim of both compositions was the same – to vindicate the reputation of Hastings as a colonial administrator. In outlining the peculiar difficulties that confronted him, and refuting the misinterpretations of Burke – the ignorant enthusiast – and in particular of Mill, the arch-culprit on whose false statements Macaulay had based that brilliant essay which was to become the bed-rock of the popular, evil conception of Hastings, Lytton's writing is at its best. Indeed, as he states it, the uphill task of rectifying those original errors which had been repeated and given palpable life by Macaulay's sweeping narrative was similar to that which he himself was later to impose on Catholic biographers of Manning, fervent educationalist admirers of Thomas Arnold, and imperialist and feminist hagiographers of Gordon and Florence Nightingale.

'There can be no doubt', he wrote in his Introduction, which was written partly to forestall the particular line of adverse criticism he anticipated from the dons, 'that the popular conception of Hastings is based upon the view of his career and his character expressed with consummate skill in Macaulay's brilliant sketch. The great historian has lavished upon his subject all the resources of his art – his incisive clarity, his powers of splendid description and masterly narrative, his easy wit, his vast knowledge, the rhetoric of his darkest and most dazzling colours; and he has produced a picture which, once seen, is seen for ever. To the ordinary Englishman, uninstructed in Indian history, the figure of Hastings stands out as Macaulay painted it – a Satanic embodiment of wickedness and power, a creature endowed with a mighty intellect and an indomitable will, who perverted these noble qualities to the hideous uses of violence, rapacity, ruthlessness and fraud. The portrait is a masterpiece; but it is a masterpiece of imagination, and not of history. Under the clear light of impartial inquiry, the fascinating spectre which Macaulay conjured up vanishes into air, or rather takes its place, once and for all, among the villains of romance. Nevertheless, the impartial inquirers have very little to boast of. For one man who reads the results of their researches there are a hundred who read Macaulay. In general, books are read solely for the pleasure that they give; and the mixture of a lie doth even add pleasure. Macaulay will triumph, until there arrives a greater master of the art of writing, who will choose to invest the facts of Indian history with the glamour of literature, and make the truth more attractive than even history itself.'

On this occasion Lytton did not attempt to rival Macaulay as a master of the rhetorical art of writing, though the above passage indicates how such a challenge could stimulate him. He does not blame the great essayist for the downright falsehoods which he accepted second-hand and popularized; on the contrary he enhaloes his literary skill, so brightly attractive when seen against the kind of pale, unread researches to which he himself was now obliged to contribute. Instead therefore of clashing swords with Macaulay in open combat, he endeavours to cut the ground from beneath his feet by illuminating in microscopic detail the sober and punctilious deceptions of Mill's history. From the minute examination of evidence which follows, Mill emerges not as a deliberate liar, but as a man blinded by preconceived theories and obsessed by the *a priori* belief that all methods of government except his own were infamous. By these means Lytton is able partly to exonerate the literary artist, Macaulay, whom he rather admired and whose style helped to influence his own, and shift the blame on to the shoulders of the dull, unattractive historian.

'The blame for having given currency to a totally false view of Hastings does not rest with Macaulay alone,' he concluded. 'The great criminal was James Mill. Every important statement in the Essay is taken from Mill's work; and it is clear that Macaulay entertained no doubts as to the value of the authority upon which he so implicitly relied. The truth is that no historian appears more certainly to deserve it. In style Mill's history is the precise antithesis of Macaulay's Essay. It is crabbed, cold, and dull; and the general impression which it produces is that the writer has sacrificed every grace of language and every audacity of thought for the sake of a meticulous accuracy. Yet the more Mill's work is examined the more delusive this general impression turns out to be: its dryness is nothing more than the cloak for a multitude of errors. And inaccuracy is not the only fault of which Mill is guilty. It has been clearly shown that his transgressions were far more serious, that he misrepresented facts, that he suppressed material evidence, and that the whole treatment of his subject was impregnated with acrimonious prejudice.'

Something had already been done before Lytton started his dissertation to correct the faults to which Mill had given, as it were, an official *imprimatur*. Professor Wilson, in his edition of the History, had drawn attention to Mill's gravest errors in a series of notes. But the true nature of Mill's transgressions had not really become obvious until the publication of Sir James Stephen's work on the Trial of Nuncomar and the Impeachment of Impey. Then, in 1892, Sir John Strachey did for the Rohilla War what Sir James Stephen had done for the Trial of Nuncomar, and another part of Hastings's administration was put in its proper light. But these two books only dealt with a relatively small portion of Hastings's full career; the rest lay still involved in the Cimmerian darkness of Mill's malevolence. Meanwhile the current biographies of Hastings, though they did not subscribe to the calumnies of Mill, had an almost equally serious defect; for – except in their accounts of the Rohilla War and the Trial of Nuncomar – they were not founded upon any scientific or original examination of the facts. Thus, the only history of Hastings's administration which was confessedly based on documentary research had to be rejected as worthless, while the entirely contrary view of Hastings's career as propounded in the modern biographies was unsupported by adequate evidence. The object of Lytton's dissertation, in so far as it related to two important sections of Hastings's Indian administration, was to remedy this anomalous state of affairs.

Since neither of the two incidents which Lytton selects to implement this purpose involved in themselves any significant development of colonial policy, they are perhaps of more moment to the political moralist than the true historian. To both Cheyt Sing and Oude, Lytton allots seven long chapters which develop his line of argument along roughly parallel paths. But the first part, which gives an authentic account of the relations between the affluent Rajah of Benares and the British Government in Bengal, is, if not the more interesting of the two, the more successful as a piece of vindication.

In this part especially he succeeded in disposing of Mill's charges of gross inhumanity against Hastings, showing how the historian misquoted and misrepresented the facts. But in order to accomplish this once and for all, he was obliged to do more than state his own conclusions. It was necessary to refute in some detail the most authoritative pronouncements of Mill; and it was necessary, also, to lay before the examiners the grounds upon which he based his own account of Hastings's acts. With both these ends in view, he inserted into his narrative a great number of quotations from contemporary documents, suitably juxtaposed with the corresponding passages from Mill's history. These quotations – from the Hastings papers at the British Museum, the Bengal Secret Consultations preserved at the India Office, Hastings's own account of the insurrection, the nine volumes of the minutes of written and parole evidence taken at the impeachment of Hastings, and the speeches delivered at the impeachment by the managers and Counsel – as Lytton himself wrote in his introduction, 'form an essential part of my work. To have paraphrased them, or to have relegated them to footnotes, would have been to throw into obscurity those very portions of my composition to which it was most necessary that attention should be drawn.' This then was the principal reason for the great length of his dissertation, whose structure sometimes resembles a site on which a new edifice is erected while excavation work is being simultaneously carried out.

Lytton's investigation of Hastings does exhibit in particular two special qualities – a real talent for controversy and a considerable ingenuity of deduction. The former is displayed at its most brilliant in his able and convincing denunciation of Mill's specific charges against

Hastings. He exposes Mill's dishonesty in 'smuggling the sunnud out of sight, and converting the resolutions at the council table into a treaty'; he reveals Mill's trick of paraphrasing an important authority in such a way as to suppress its most significant statement; he conducts a lucid discussion of the circumstances connected with Cheyt Sing's present to Hastings of the two lakhs of rupees; and he refutes decisively Mill's assertion with reference to the good government of Benares by Cheyt Sing. Finally, he concludes: 'You cannot acquit a man upon every count, and condemn him of the whole indictment.'

Lytton's aim and achievement were not, as Cunningham had rather implied, merely destructive; he had not simply attempted to expose the shortcomings of Mill or the treachery of Francis. On the contrary, he had set out to write an account, based upon the evidence of original records, of the actual conduct, the actual motives, and the actual policy of Hastings in an important episode of his controversial Indian career.

The plan of composition which Lytton adopted in the second part of his work closely resembled his treatment of Hastings's dealing with the Rajah of Benares. The Begums of Oude had been his initial idea for a dissertation when in the autumn of 1902 he had asked his mother for Sir John Strachey's advice. But his early researches had led him to suspect that Hastings's despotic conduct – possibly the result of frayed nerves – was less easily justifiable in this affair. Further research only endorsed this suspicion, though he did not abandon the Begums in 1904 simply because of his uncertainty, but because a rather excessive amplification of the Cheyt Sing theme had left him with no time – and no inclination – for another complicated study.

As in the Cheyt Sing incident, Lytton is able convincingly to show that the ends which Hastings had in mind were sincere and quite possibly, in a political sense, valid. The quantity and the consistency of evidence establishing the Begums' complicity in the revolt of Cheyt Sing, whom they were aiding with their treasure, could not be ignored. The declared object of this rebellion was to root the British out of India; thus, so long as the Begums' power continued to exist, Lytton's argument ran, good government was an impossibility. Above all else Hastings desired a strong united government in Oude, so he insisted upon the Vizier divesting them not only of their vast domains, but of the treasures of the State upon which they had seized. Up to this point Lytton was confident of having demonstrated what he later called 'a consistent and admirable line of policy'. But precisely at this point he began to falter. One factor which tended to confuse a clear understanding of the whole issue was that Hastings's policy involved the liquidation of a large debt to the East India Company. Though doubtless an added political point in favour of this policy, such an immediate practical end gave rise to the view that the mainspring of Hastings's action was the desire for plunder, and not, as Lytton's thesis would have it, responsible administration. The true bearing of the whole affair, Lytton felt, had been fatally obscured – beyond lucid clarification – once again by Mill's candid and impartial manner of concealment, by Macaulay (whose fondness for seeing in situations of this sort only the vivid clash of personalities had hurried him into unjustifiable extremes), by Sheridan (whose love of the stage was greater than his love of reality), and above all by Burke (whose conduct throughout the Hastings business was a prime example of the fatal results of a mixture of enthusiasm and ignorance). Yet Lytton very properly differentiates between Sheridan's mellifluous fustian and the passionate oratory of Burke. The former he discounts as insincere, defining his speech as a piece of highly theatrical, self-intoxicated dramaturgy. Burke, on the other hand, responded to public matters as intensely as other men feel their private joys or reverses. 'It would, of course,' Lytton wrote, 'be senseless, and worse than senseless, to suppose that Burke's conduct was actuated by any motives save the purest and best . . . The press and passion of his most resplendent qualities let loose a wild beast in him, which drove him headlong into the paths of frenzy and folly; so that he would willingly turn away our eyes from the spectacle of such virtue brought to such a miserable pass.'

What beams of light Lytton was able to introduce into this dark obscurity illuminate details of what was in its essentials a rather squalid affair. The degree of violence which was employed in carrying out Hastings's policy of seizure and confiscation was almost impossible to ascertain. Upon the later treatment of the eunuchs, Mill's hasty assertions seem about as implausible as Lytton's scholarly qualifications and academic doubts. The diffidence and the uncertainty with which he approached this controversial subject are well explained and conveyed in the following short passage:

'The precise nature of the pressure which was applied is a little doubtful, owing to the fact that Middleton, whose verbal evidence is practically our only authority for the whole of these transactions, steadfastly refused at the Impeachment to answer any questions which might tend to incriminate himself. There is, however, reason to believe that the treatment which the eunuchs underwent at the time was not more severe than that involved by a very rigorous imprisonment. They were put in irons, and their diet was restricted; and they suffered these distresses for about a week.'

If, as Lytton suggests and as is probably the truth, no flogging was administered, this leniency was probably due to the mildness of Middleton, which Hastings himself considered excessive. In actual fact the eunuchs were in irons for altogether longer than a single week, though in any case the relatively short term of their punishment hardly attests convincingly to its lack of severity. As for Lytton's phrase 'their diet was restricted', this refers to Middleton's order that the eunuchs should be kept 'from all food, etc.' But whatever the precise circumstances of this episode, the authoritative employment of personal severities under the superintendence of British officers, in order to extract money from women and eunuchs for the alleviation of the Company's finances, was by any standards an ignoble kind of undertaking. Lytton once again urges that Hastings's motives were sincere; but then, in another context, so undoubtedly were those of Burke. He also maintains that there was no practical alternative to this policy, which was absolutely necessary to avoid any worse disaster and to establish the type of subordinate conduct needed for the good government of Oude. But one feels throughout this piece of special pleading that Lytton is putting forward a point of view thrust on him by the awkward nature of his thesis, and which does not spring from the heart. His closing words give some indication of the difficulties into which he had been led, and partly contradict his previous plea of absolute historical necessity:

'Though he [Hastings] had been able to initiate measures admirably calculated for the future good government of the country, he had not solved the problem of Oude. . . . His measures were but the prelude for a long series of difficulties and disorders, ending at last in annexation. But, for Hastings himself, these problems and these agitations were at an end. Within six months of his departure from Lucknow, he had left India for ever.'

Except when he turns his attention to the various historical and literary commentators on the Hastings impeachment, Lytton was far more concerned with reconstructing, minutely, a series of complicated and controversial events than in depicting individual character. Thus, the reader never gets to know the personality of Hastings at all intimately, and is left to deduce for himself the degree of peculiar self-deception and almost mystical self-righteousness which ran through his character. Because of this muted and unexplored aspect, one can only faintly discern between the lines that Lytton's personal response towards Hastings had undergone some alteration, not as a result of any new biographical information that he had uncovered, but owing to certain psychological changes gradually taking place within himself. When writing 'Warren Hastings' for the Greaves Prize in 1901, he had been swept off his feet by a rather schoolboy admiration for this magnificently robust and stoical type of man. But, imperceptibly, during the course of the next four years at Cambridge, the direction of his feelings had begun to veer until he now, if still hesitantly and intermittently, venerated artists above men of action. It was a change of heart that was to affect for a time both his writing and his private life. He felt increasingly that the character of a man such as Hastings did not accord at any very real or profound level with his own – for all his splendid romantic attraction. A complete and irrefutable exculpation of Hastings was perhaps, in any case, not possible. And some five years later he conceded in an anonymous article that 'in the popular view Hastings is, and will probably long remain, a man of mixed motives and doubtful honesty, whose brilliant services can hardly be balanced against his unscrupulousness and hardness of heart'.

Since the time of its writing the dissertation has been privately consulted by at least one historian of British India and has indirectly helped to form the now widely accepted assessments of two intricate and interrelated events. Today it is largely out of date; not because any of its findings have been proved wrong, nor because any significant amount of new material has been unearthed, but because the incidents which it examines have now been thoroughly researched in a way that makes its original, punctilious aim largely obsolescent. It is, in short, the scale and scope of Lytton's treatment and not his conclusions which, in its unedited state over sixty years later, tend to invalidate the work. In 1905 there was still a real need for such a definitive investigation. The current biographies of Hastings were either too short to present an adequate view of his career, or were merely compilations from well-known printed sources. In subsequent years, however, several exhaustive studies have been produced, so that it is now no longer possible to claim, as Lytton did, that the great mass of original materials which throw light on Hastings's life and work remain almost entirely unexplored.

Lytton's eventual completion of the two-part thesis which had occupied him on and off for some two and a half years was a tremendous invigorating relief. The spell of grinding apathy was broken and he felt all at once a new energy creeping through him. Whatever the electors might decide, there was nothing more he could do about it. To all practical purposes he was at long last free from all its worries and entanglements. 'The Begums have at last been vanquished,' he wrote triumphantly to Duncan Grant (30 August 1905), 'and today they were dispatched to Cambridge, where they may rot at ease till the judgement day. Your letter came just in time to see the tail ends of them, whisking out of Great Oakley like so many witches on broomsticks. The result is that I am now considerably re-animated.'

A week after sending off his dissertation he left Kettering and went, via Oxford, to stay with the Homere sisters again near Chipping Norton, where he enjoyed a peaceful and uncomplicated twelve-hour-day routine – up at eleven, croquet in the afternoon, and back to bed again at eleven. In the third week of September, he returned to Great Oakley Hall and was visited for a few days by Keynes. 'My existence here is pretty comatose,' he informed Clive Bell (5 September 1905), 'but less shattering now that my wretched dissertation is finished and done with.' He was especially keen to see Duncan Grant and conjured him to leave all, leap on a train, and come for the last few days of the summer – if not to see him again then at least to meet his great friend Keynes, whom he was sure to like. 'I think I am very disgracefully behaved not to have written before to you in answer to your invitation to stay,' Duncan Grant replied (24 September 1905). 'I am afraid I cannot manage it. . . . I should like to have seen Canes (?) very much.'

Two days later Lytton set off for Trinity, and the following evening attended, in company with the other fellowship candidates, his second ceremonial dinner with the examiners. As luck would have it he sat next to his own examiner, R. Vere Laurence, that rather prim and austere Irishman. 'Laurence was wicked as usual,' he wrote afterwards to Leonard Woolf. 'I thought at times obviously hostile – well, well. What's so curious, I find, when I talk to these people is that I simply roar with laughter at my own jokes. I suppose it's to encourage myself.'

The fellowship decisions were not to be announced for another week and in the meantime Lytton rejoined his family who had by now moved back to Lancaster Gate. The days passed listlessly, and he spent much of the time recording the trivia with which they were filled, chiefly for the amusement of Duncan Grant: 'This afternoon [2 October 1905] I visited the Times Book shop in New Bond Street. It's an awful institution. One of the lady assistants was so polite to me that I very nearly proposed.'

When the Fellowship results were at last published, Lytton had returned yet again to Trinity. 'I could see everything,' he wrote to Leonard Woolf (25 October 1905), 'and Rosy's[1] enraged disappointed red face told me at once all was over.' Although his failure did not come as a shock, he was nevertheless more dismayed than he cared to admit. His disappointment was easily understandable. The quality of writing and research in 'Warren Hastings, Cheyt Sing and the Begums of Oude'

[1] Rosy Haigh, Lytton's bedmaker.

would seem quite up to Fellowship standard. Officially, the reasons given by the examiners for their rejection were exactly contrary to the type of adverse criticism – 'readable but inaccurate' – which was to be most often levelled in later years against his famous biographies. The dissertation, they said, gave evidence of conscientious work and of persevering endeavour to arrive at the truth by means of a thorough scrutiny of original records. But the style and arrangement were respectively obscure and ill-ordered. The examiners ignored altogether the specific reasons which Lytton set out in the Preface for quoting rather than paraphrasing his sources. They felt that the force of his argument was frequently spoilt by the close juxtaposition of extracts of patently unequal interest. Any extract which did not possess intrinsic significance should, in their opinion, have been briefly paraphrased or even reduced to footnotes instead of appearing verbatim. Otherwise the really telling extracts lost their effect. Moreover, the incessant breaking up of the narrative by these verbatim quotes of secondary importance rendered the whole piece unnecessarily confused and tedious to read. Some of the most telling points were so successfully buried in a mass of subordinate matter as to be only discoverable by an expert in this field of research. It was these defects that led the examiners to a verdict that Lytton's dissertation 'cannot be regarded as possessed of special excellence'.

The tone of this verdict indicates that possibly a number of ancillary matters had reduced beforehand the likelihood of Lytton's success. In the first place it is not very usual for someone who has won only Second Class Honours to be elected to a position where he may be required to urge other students to excel where he has previously failed. Lytton certainly appears to have thought that Vere Laurence disliked him personally, and, whatever the foundation was for this particular belief, it does seem possible that his unsavoury reputation as a leading decadent at Trinity – the 'brilliant wicked Mephistophelean myth' which had arisen round him – may have had an adverse effect on his chances of being admitted as one of his College's reputable Fellows. In addition, he met with unusually stiff opposition from the scientists that year. It was, moreover, rather unfortunate perhaps that, while the examiners were reading his dissertation, two new books on Hastings incorporating fresh, unpublished information should have happened to be published. Neither Sir Charles Lawson's *The Private Life of Warren Hastings* nor *The Letters of Warren Hastings to his Wife*, transcribed and annotated by Sydney C. Grier from the originals in the British Museum, actually contradicted anything that Lytton had written, but they took the edge off his scholarship and emphasized the personal aspect of Hastings's character, which the dissertation had tended to ignore.

In the long run, however, it was certainly to Lytton's advantage not to settle down at once into an academic society which had exalted the poetaster at the expense of the creative essayist by rewarding such an abstract, linguistic exercise as 'Ely: an Ode' with acclaim, while disdaining a far more remarkable composition like 'English Letter Writers'. As James Strachey was to express it, 'the Cambridge authorities had enough foresight and self-restraint to spare my brother the corrupting influences of an academic career'. But the immediate blow, however much he had previously tried to discount it, was severe. Once again, AGAINST HIS PRINCIPLES, he had failed in a vital examination and encountered a set-back to his precarious self-confidence. 'But when Cambridge is over,' he had written to Leonard Woolf (April 1905), 'when one has been cast into the limbo of unintimacy, of business, of ugly antiquity – is there any hope? . . . Supposing London kills me!' Cambridge, he felt, was his spiritual home; the only place where he had been reasonably happy and successful. As it slowly became populated by his special friends, it had acquired almost a magic quality, unique and wonderful. 'Body and spirit, reason and emotion, work and play, architecture and scenery, laughter and seriousness, life and art – these pairs which are elsewhere contrasted were there fused into one,' wrote E. M. Forster. 'People and books reinforced one another, intelligence joined hands with affection, speculation became a passion, and discussion was made profound by love.' But hardly, it seemed, had Lytton begun to taste this sweet, comprehensive unity, when he was rudely expelled, forced to return to the portentous edifice in Lancaster Gate, and start up the old alien life there all over again.

Lytton's writings over the next twenty-five years are sprinkled with nostalgic, bitter-sweet references to Cambridge, 'whose cloisters', he remarked in *Eminent Victorians*, 'have ever been consecrated to poetry and common sense'. In an attempt to define the potent spell of Cambridge, its special atmosphere blended with personal associations, he contrasted his own university with Oxford, to the disadvantage of the latter. A foreign population of non-graduates had taken up its abode cheek by jowl with the most ancient of Oxford sanctities, he pointed out, so that the once amiable congruity of the place had departed for ever. At Cambridge the peaceful academic purity of mood had been far better preserved, unclouded by the introduction of corrupt and purulent matter. Huddled by the river and protected from intruders, Cambridge afforded its inhabitants a serene privacy, undisturbed by the cruder infringements of extramural activities. The university had formed itself into a self-contained nucleus of civilization, sealed off from outside, where one could escape from 'the weariness, the fever and the fret' of the modern town. Summarizing his thoughts and feelings, Lytton concluded: 'The real enchantment of Cambridge is of the intimate kind; an enchantment lingering in the nooks and corners, coming upon one gradually down the narrow streets, and ripening year by year. The little river and its lawns and willows, the old trees in the old gardens, the obscure bowling-greens, the crooked lanes with their glimpses of cornices and turrets, the low dark opening out on to sunny grass – in these, and in things like these, dwells the fascination of Cambridge.'

Lytton had vainly hoped that this feeling of fascination might permeate and form the integral part of a new and happier period in his life; that the congenial beauty of Cambridge might supersede charmless Lancaster Gate as his home. But it was not to be. 'The wicked dons of Trinity have refused to make me a fellow,' he wrote to Duncan Grant (9 October 1905). 'I'm sorry, but resigned. I had imagined so many splendid things for us, if it had come off. Poverty, drudgery must now be faced.'

Before the start of the Michaelmas term, Lytton quitted his rooms on staircase K in the Great Court of Trinity, and returned to London. It must have seemed to him that the companionship for which he had so desperately longed at Liverpool and cherished so deeply at Cambridge was now in danger of being forfeited altogether. For six years he had eagerly frequented doctor and saint, and had heard great argument, but finally, like FitzGerald's Khayyám, had gone out by the same door as in he went. His departure from Trinity marked, so he felt, the end of his youth, and the premature onset of a dull and dusty middle age. At twenty-five, nearly twenty-six, he was back almost where he had been at the age of eighteen, and in much the same style as his diary entry for the spring of 1898, his thoughts turned inwards. Infinitely elevated with long spidery legs and arms, a large nose, mild eyes, a thick moustache and calamitous equine teeth, he felt himself to be handicapped by a hideous appearance that immensely inflated his inner misery: so that he expressed his sense of failure partly in terms of physical self-denigration and disgust: 'You don't know what it is to be twenty-five,' he told Duncan Grant (11 October 1905), 'dejected, uncouth, unsuccessful – you don't know how humble and wretched and lonely I sometimes feel . . . Oh God, these are wretched things to be writing.'

PART II

'The middle-aged fill me with frigid despair –
they have so little to recommend them – really
only their vague sense of the past. I feel that I am
dimly dwindling into that terrible condition – a
sort of dying process. One struggles – but one
sinks.'

Lytton Strachey to Maynard Keynes (21 January 1906)

CHAPTER VI

Post-Graduate

'I feel desperately homesick – but for what home?'
Lytton Strachey to Leonard Woolf (1905)

I

BUBBLES, OYSTERS AND POTATOES

During the autumn of 1905, and for several succeeding years, a solitary young man, the son of an English general, was to be seen journeying between London and Cambridge. His striking figure, long and limp, with its half-languorous, half-drifting motion, gave him the aspect of an adolescent, which contrasted oddly with the mature darkness of his hair and his brown moustache. There was a similar contrast – enigmatic but unprepossessing – between his pallid complexion – the hue of a seasoned scholar – and the large brown eyes with their look of almost childlike innocence and alarm. To the intellectual inquirer he would explain, in a high, musical voice, that he was engaged in elucidating two problems – the kind of things that ought to exist for their own sake, and the kind of action we ought to perform. He believed, indeed, that he possessed the solution to these problems, as a reference to some passages in the book he was carrying would show.

This singular person was Lytton Strachey, and the book was reputed to be his bible, *Principia Ethica*.

On his arrival back at Lancaster Gate that autumn, Lady Strachey had given over to him a bed-sitting room where he was to do much of his writing over the next two years. 'I am established in a room here,' he wrote to Leonard Woolf (25 October 1905), 'with a folding bed, and all my books ranged in 2 bookshelves. It's pretty dreary, and when I'm to do any work heaven alone knows.' In this desolate upper chamber he sat, bent over a hissing gas fire, trying vainly to imagine himself back in Trinity Great Court, while beyond the steamed-up pink and frosted window-panes, the dreary enthralling life of London ebbed past unheeded. His heart and mind still dwelt amid the enchanted lawns and cloisters of Cambridge– yet after only a week, he was thinking of it all as strangely impalpable, a fantastic, remote place like Prospero's island, half real, half fairyland. 'I find Cambridge already hardly more than a vision,' he told Keynes (13 October 1905). Like his Shakespeare in the final period, Lytton found himself partly charmed by retrospective visions of beauty, partly bored to death. On the one hand he was inspired by fancy to the composition of sentimental verses, and on the other he was urged by a general resentment and disgust to burst out occasionally through his torpor into bitter, violent speech. He must, he felt, be getting old.

'The refusal of the persons of Trinity to give me a fellowship has left me here, nominally a journalist, really, as far as I can see, a complete drifter, without any definite hopes, and the New Age as far off as ever,' he wrote summing up the position in a letter to Leonard Woolf (25 October 1905). 'If I were energetic – but it's so absurd – how can one be energetic over reviews? I pray to God, though, that I may miraculously take a turn towards the practical – for a year or two – which I believe would be enough. But it's all very dull and vague and quasi-infinite.'

As always when discussing his own work, Lytton was inclined to understate the amount of conscientious effort he put into it. There was something ridiculous and undignified about hard work. Besides, he liked to encourage among his friends the notion that any piece of his which they might happen to read was thrown off lightly, thereby disarming censure. But easy writing's vile hard reading, and the consistent readability of Lytton's essays attest to the minute concentration he gave to his narrative. His overall output at this time, however, was not large. In his last two years at Cambridge he had contributed about half a dozen essay-reviews for the *Spectator* and *Independent Review*. During the following two years, that is until he was taken on to the regular staff of the *Spectator*, he produced, on average, about one article every six weeks. Although these were all of a very reasonably high standard, the labour of reviewing other people's books was far from his liking – searching about in the roots of things at three guineas a piece: all exertion and no fulfilment. 'I spend my days here trying to be a journalist,' he gloomily informed Swithinbank (15 October 1905), 'but I seem to lack the conviction and energy which I feel are necessary. Other things are much more interesting than reviews! But daily bread must be obtained somehow . . .'

Yet in some respects his existence at Lancaster Gate was not so odious. Part of the horror of giving up Cambridge was simply the actual process – which vanished once it was over. Life, at any rate, did not automatically stop, but trickled on in approximately the same old unsatisfactory way as before. He still had his friends. Above all others came Duncan Grant. He was also seeing now quite a lot of the Stephen family, gazing in rapture at the magnificent unapproachable Goth, and with curiosity at the enigmatic Virginia. Then there was Clive Bell – hopelessly, it seemed, in love with Vanessa Stephen – who had returned from Paris, and having failed to obtain a Fellowship himself, assured Lytton with robust confidence that he was well out of Cambridge. Perhaps, though, matters might have turned out very differently, Lytton reflected, had he been able to continue directing the affairs of the Society. 'It's shocking about Cambridge,' he confessed to Keynes (8 November 1905). 'I've been having tea with Bell[1] – very dim and decadent in a blue dressing-gown in his wonderful Temple chambers– and he tells the same story. It shows how far things have gone that Lamb should be the most eminent person in Trinity. What's of course chiefly lacking is intellect, and that's lacking in Oxford too – only they make up for it by culture and indecency.'

Almost every day now he was writing to Keynes about the affairs of the Society. He was hungry for Cambridge gossip which, after extracting from Keynes, he would pass on to Leonard Woolf in Ceylon. 'The freshmen sound most exciting,' he replied to Keynes after a few days at Lancaster Gate (16 October 1905), 'and I can hardly contain myself – I burst with impatience and curiosity.' And again, the following month (27 November 1905): 'You are my only Evangelist, and I watch the posts for news from the Only Place.'

At first the most exciting new discovery seemed to be a freshman by the name of Goodhart,[2] whose wild temperament and lack of control thrilled Lytton. The grandson of Lord Rendel, and cousin of Lytton's eldest brother-in-law, Goodhart was reckoned to be 'possibly a genius, certainly remarkable and almost certainly nice', in Lytton's words to Leonard Woolf. 'Even James was excited when I saw him, about a "wonderful" conversation they'd had, after which Goodhart had fallen back with spasms and palpitations and had had to send for a doctor. He's violently musical and wildly architectural, he talks in torrents, and believes in mediaeval Christianity.' But all this excitement soon turned out to be a South Sea bubble. Goodhart was taken up by the Society like an oyster, and then, almost immediately, damned and

[1] Clive Bell, in fact, was never a member of the Apostles.

[2] Harry Stuart Goodhart-Rendel (he assumed by Royal Licence the additional name of Rendel) had a distinguished career both in musical and architectural fields. Among his many official appointments were Slade Professor of Fine Art at Oxford, Governor of Sadlers Wells, president of the Architectural Association and president of the Royal Institute of British Architects.

dropped again like a hot potato after it was discovered that his Christian beliefs were not confined to mediaeval times. But there were always new embryos to take the place of the duds – the young Charles Darwin,[1] for example, whose election Lytton supported; and Dillwyn Knox,[2] one of the famous brothers, whom Keynes had recruited, but of whom Lytton did not approve: 'Did I tell you that I took a pretty violent zid against Knox?' he asked Keynes. 'He seemed to me too gravely inconsiderate, in the regular damned Etonian way. It's impossible not to dislike someone a little, who so obviously dislikes one so much.'

But among the freshmen was another less obtrusive Old Etonian, Harry Norton, destined to become a close and permanent friend of Lytton's. During his first term at Cambridge the impression which Norton produced on the Apostles was not particularly favourable. His casual, rather condescending manner struck them as indicating an inadequate respect for their own superior station in the university hierarchy. 'I'm sure he has a very good logical kind of mind,' Keynes gravely reported to Lytton (15 October 1905); 'his own view, however, is that he is cultured – and he is incredibly. His whole person is girt about by a writhing mess of aesthetic and literary appreciations, which I have – so far – discovered no means of quelling. He's very proud of all this, but it's really rather nonsense: what saves him is his strong comprehension – I hardly ever caught him really stupid.

'There is nothing to say about his appearance – ordinary public school.'

A public school appearance was evidently not very attractive. Norton's face was round; he had a fine forehead, a short straight nose. He was tall, but owing to short shin bones he minced along with ludicrously tiny steps. Through the spectacles he always wore after his first term at Cambridge, his eyes stared out at the world with ever-diminishing optimism. Among his Cambridge friends it was held that he possessed a remarkably 'pure' intelligence. His first years at Trinity were marked by the most violent high-spirits imaginable. He talked incessantly, rattling along with loud intermittent yells of laughter. He had, too, a gentleness and sweetness of disposition, mixed, not with any sham sentimentality, but with a genuine cerebral power

[1] Charles Darwin, seven years younger than Lytton, a younger brother of Gwen Raverat, the authoress and artist, was a grandson of the great scientist Charles Darwin. He married Katherine Pember, while his younger sister Margaret became the wife of Maynard Keynes's younger brother Geoffrey. These Darwins were the children of Sir George Darwin, Plumian Professor of Astronomy at Cambridge, and a particular friend of Lytton's parents.

[2] A. D. Knox, the second of the four Knox brothers, a brilliant classical scholar, afterwards Fellow of King's College. In later years, Lytton became very friendly with him.

that endeared him to Lytton. 'He's an Etonian,' Lytton wrote to Leonard Woolf after his first meeting with Norton (October 1905), 'and created some sensation there by being observed to read Russell's book. He's very cultured and reads poetry by the yard.' After their second meeting he recorded his impressions as follows: 'He's undoubtedly nice, though very young and rather ugly. He's obviously open and honest . . . talks in fact too much because of an innocent ignorance of what other people think, but talks without restraint and is quite vaguely and ingenuously indecent. As to his intelligence it seems to me doubtful, but I could hardly tell.'

Norton was in fact suffering from what is technically known as hypomania, and this, after some years, turned over into a quite opposite mood – one of severe depression which eventually paralysed his mental processes and led to a nervous breakdown. 'He had an extremely high-grade mental apparatus,' James Strachey told the author. 'He was one of the only three or four people I have ever known in the same intellectual category as Russell – with whom he was perfectly able to argue on equal terms.'

Lytton hoped that Norton might be able to draw out his younger brother James, an enigmatic and impassive character, much given, it was felt, to mental and physical laziness. But to his dismay, James began to associate more with the much-vilified Walter Lamb, while Norton was seen on more than one occasion talking to that 'blind confused charming affectionate creature' Sheppard. As for Lytton, he was powerless to do anything about it himself, for any definite act of interference, any proffering of unsought advice would be, by Apostolic ethics, to commit the unforgivable Sin of Parentage.

There were, also, other potential drawbacks to Norton. Being an undergraduate of considerable means, he sometimes adopted a tone of unworldliness which the others, hoist with their own philosophical petard, found hard to match. 'D'you think there's any danger in his becoming absorbed in the phenomenal?' Lytton anxiously inquired of Keynes, who thought on the whole that there was not. In later years Norton gave Lytton crucial financial help until, with the publication in 1918 of *Eminent Victorians* – which is dedicated to Norton ('To H.T.J.N.') – Lytton was able to reimburse him in full. A mathematician of very great ability, Norton was elected to a Fellowship at Trinity in 1910. But to many of his friends he appeared to lapse into a state of dispirited inertia, and most of them were not surprised to learn when he died at the age of fifty that his work on the Cantorian theory of numbers was still unfinished. Yet he had continued in his unobtrusive way to labour intermittently at it, and his papers, even in their fragmentary conditions, were found to have made important advances in a branch of pure mathematics.

Of all the new friends whom Lytton met that autumn and who were eventually elected to the Society, perhaps the most interesting was Rupert Brooke. Some seven years younger than Lytton, he had attended Hillbrow, the same private school as James Strachey, and had later gone on to Rugby with Maynard Keynes's younger brother Geoffrey.[1] His father, William Parker Brooke, was the housemaster of School Field, the house at which Rupert was entered and where every hour, he later said, was 'golden and radiant'. Good alike at work and sport, charming, debonair and with unusually good looks of a type which are at their height in the late teens and early twenties, he was immediately successful at whatever he put his hand to. He seemed, indeed, almost too good to be true, and, like some mythical deity, attracted extreme adulation from almost all those in his vicinity. Lytton had heard much of Brooke before meeting him in September at Kettering,[2] and though his curiosity had obviously been roused, he was more than prepared to dislike him. In fact, he found this legendary schoolboy quite pleasant and inoffensive. 'He has rather nice – but you know – yellow-ochre-ish hair, and a healthy young complexion,' he wrote to Duncan Grant (5 September, 1905), who had also known Brooke at Hillbrow. 'I took him out for a walk round the Park this morning, and he talked about Poetry and Public Schools as decently as could be expected.' Brooke, for his part, rather took to Lytton: 'Lytton Strachey I found most amusing,' he wrote to Geoffrey Keynes, 'especially his voice.' And for some years subsequently, as Christopher Hassall has shown and as Brooke's own letters testify, Lytton's influence worked strongly upon him.

Lytton's attitude towards this golden-haired young Apollo is interesting. Some of the rather nonchalant indifference with which he writes of him may be assumed – a reaction from the admiration of everyone else, in particular his brother James. But while he was not

[1] Sir Geoffrey Keynes (b. 1887), later to become a surgeon of the first rank and our foremost Blake scholar, whose *Job* he converted into a ballet, choreographed by Lytton's cousin Ninette de Valois, and with music by Vaughan Williams. His bibliographies include volumes on the writings of John Donne, Sir Thomas Browne, Rupert Brooke and Siegfried Sassoon. He was Trustee of the National Portrait Gallery (1942–66) and Chairman of the Board (1958–66).

[2] Lytton and Rupert Brooke had in fact met before. In the summer of 1898, the Stracheys had rented a country house called Ardeley Bury, near Stevenage. During that time Rupert came to stay with James. They were both then aged between ten and eleven, and James remembers Lytton reading *Paradise Lost* aloud to him in the garden. They met again in Brighton during the Easter holidays of 1900, but the encounter was of no significance and neither of them appears to have remembered it.

The Visigoths: Vanessa (*above*) and Virginia Stephen

Professor Walter Raleigh

Rupert Brooke in *Comus*, 1908, showing legs

insensible to Brooke's personal appeal, he certainly did not respect his intellectual capabilities. He may possibly have thought his looks too sugary, and on occasions he suspected that Brooke, for his part, regarded him as too avuncular. At any rate, though Brooke was then hesitating between going up to Oxford or Cambridge, Lytton did not appear very anxious about the matter one way or the other. After he had left Kettering, he wrote to Maynard Keynes (7 September 1905): 'Rupert Brooke has been with us. I wasn't particularly impressed. His appearance is pleasant – mainly, I think, owing to youth – complexion, hair, etc. Of course he's quite incredibly young, so it was rather difficult to talk. I felt he wanted to attack the subject of Platonic Love, etc. but the whole thing seemed so dreadfully commonplace that I couldn't manage it. He's damned literary, rather too serious and conscientious, and devoid of finesse. The Cambridge-Oxford question still hangs in the balance. I didn't make any great effort to obtain him. The decision rests with Dr [H. A.] James, the H. Master of Rugby.'

This lukewarm response was partly due to the lack of common ground in their background and early years. Lytton's schooldays had been overshadowed by failure; Brooke's were spent basking in the limelight of popular and academic success. 'The genius at school is usually a disappointing figure,' Lytton was to write in his essay on Beddoes, 'for as a rule, one must be commonplace to be a successful boy. In that preposterous world, to be remarkable is to be overlooked.' Rupert Brooke had never been overlooked. From the various comments which Lytton passed on Brooke in his letters to friends, it is not clear to what extent he may at times have felt envious of the younger man's triumphal progress through life. But it is certain that he considered him, despite his poetic appearance – his long hair, silk shirt and loosely knotted foulard tie– to be fundamentally unremarkable. Because of the reverence felt for him by their respective younger brothers, Lytton and Maynard Keynes spent a good deal of time assessing Brooke's character – especially since he later became an Apostle. At this early stage, on the basis of an hour or two's acquaintance and an examination of some of Brooke's letters to James, Lytton found him to be below the line of medium capacity – to adapt a phrase of Beatrice Webb's – mainly on account of his 'vile diction', feeble epigrams and jokes and general aesthetic tinge. He was irritated, too, by what he judged to be Brooke's 'complacent egoism'; but added, in mitigation, that he seemed to have an acute sense of character and situation, a general innocence, and an interest (though not perhaps a deep one) in interesting things. These saving factors encouraged him to believe that 'something might be done', though he remained doubtful.

Shortly after Lytton's meeting with Brooke at Kettering, Geoffrey Keynes came up to Cambridge from Rugby to try for a scholarship at Pembroke. With him he brought Brooke, who had decided to stand at the same time for a scholarship at King's. Both of them stayed with the Keynes family in Harvey Road, and Maynard's letters to Lytton reveal the fact that Geoffrey was deliberately effacing himself so that this radiant schoolfriend should shine at his most brilliant. Both of them succeeded in obtaining their respective scholarships, and next year were whirled up into the undergraduate high life.

Brooke had left Rugby with honours thick upon him. During his time there he had assumed a literary cult reminiscent of Beardsley and Dowson. This pose had considerably impressed his schoolfellows, but at university all such dandyism was by then right out of fashion, and it failed to win him the usual acclaim. Consequently, during his first year at Cambridge he was uncharacteristically plaintive and discouraged. King's was devoid of amusement. He liked nobody. Everyone seemed dull, middle-aged, and ugly. 'I'm filled with an hysterical despair,' he wrote in his first long vacation.'I hate myself and everyone. . . . Go back to Cambridge for my second year and laugh and talk with those old dull people on that airless plain. The thought fills me with hideous *ennui*.'

Yet even at Cambridge things do not stand absolutely still. A wave of Fabian socialism was soon sweeping over the new undergraduates, and politics, not psychological literature, became the principal topic of conversation among the intelligentsia. This new tide caught up many of Lytton's friends – including James, Maynard Keynes, and Brooke himself.[1] As president of the university Fabian Society,[2] Brooke was to feel more at home discussing through the night and until dawn the teachings of the Webbs with his colleague, Hugh ('Daddy') Dalton.[3] He also took part in the social life at King's, and with his namesake, Justin Brooke,[4] formed the Marlowe Dramatic Society. Despite his feeling for poetry and his enthusiasm for the theatre, Rupert was neither

[1] So far as the Apostles were concerned, Fabian socialism had no impact, except on James Strachey. Maynard Keynes always despised the Fabians, and Norton remained quite unimpressed. The really influential figure at Cambridge was Ben Keeling, who converted Hugh Dalton from a Conservative tariff reformer. It was only after the First World War that communism became a topic of discussion within the Society.

[2] Rupert Brooke became the third president of the Cambridge Fabian Society in 1909.

[3] Hugh Dalton (1887–1962), later prominent in the Labour Party. Chancellor of the Exchequer 1945–7. He preceded Brooke as president of the Cambridge Fabian Society.

[4] Justin Brooke of Emmanuel College was no relation to Rupert Brooke.

a good speaker of verse nor even a competent actor – he never appeared natural – and the Marlowe Society's performance of Milton's *Comus* was treated by Lytton to a rather unflattering anonymous review in the pages of the *Spectator*. Both Brooke and Lytton were fascinated by the stage, but whereas Lytton was always endeavouring to rearrange the painful disorder of living into the pattern of a neat intriguing theatrical performance, for Brooke life had seldom been anything else. This staginess enveloped him like a cocoon, through which he eventually burst to be fatally poisoned by his contact with rude actuality. Assured self-dramatization had begun with him as a child, whereas Lytton had slowly acquired it as a defensive equipment against failure and loneliness. In a letter to a friend Lytton wrote of 'Rupert *en beauté* in the stalls', a phrase which, Hugh Kingsmill commented, 'conjures up Brooke in the high summer of his triumph as the toast of King's . . . [and] the hollow-eyed and desiderious Strachey whom I picture peering down from the front row of the dress circle'. Brooke, indeed, always seems closer to the stage platform than Lytton. He was like the playboy son of some fabulous financier, cashing in on a happy series of speculations, strangely determined to press his facility and good fortune beyond the furthest possible limit; while Lytton, through one or two brilliant but carefully considered investments, just succeeds in keeping the duns from the door while his once tiny capital slowly and surely accumulates.

Like most of his contemporaries, Lytton thought as little of Brooke's early poems as of his acting ability and 'Grantchester' he later dismissed as 'a bloody affected concoction'. It has been suggested by Desmond MacCarthy and by Raymond Mortimer that the change in diction and inflexion of Brooke's verse was directly attributable to Lytton's enthusiasm for Donne and seventeenth-century poetry, and even perhaps to those poems of his own which he used to declaim to his closest Cambridge friends. Without admiration for his versatile talent, it was hardly surprising that Lytton's feelings for his young friend were so mixed. After his first mood of casual indifference had passed, it was partly replaced by a latent, nagging element of disapproval which fretted the complicated compound of his emotions and which on one or two occasions exploded in violent outbursts of temper. To some extent he was susceptible to Brooke's picturesque charm, but found him altogether too improbable, too insubstantial a personality – the sort of glorified legendary figure, with sinister undertones of puritanism, who, in other circumstances, he might have made the subject for a short, ironical pen portrait. 'Rupert Brooke,' he wrote to Virginia Stephen in April 1908, 'isn't it a romantic name? – with pink cheeks and bright yellow hair – it sounds horrible, but it wasn't.' And he continued in much the same fashion as a latter-day Tennyson might have described those dull and dreadful meetings of the Apostles, lit up by the magic presence of Arthur Hallam. 'The conversation is less political than you think, but I dare say you would have found the jokes a little heavy – as for me, I laughed enormously, and whenever I began to feel dull I could look at the yellow hair and pink cheeks of Rupert.' Nice to contemplate as a mythical decoration, he seems to have concluded, but Lytton *knew* he must have feet of clay, weak knees – both probably. Virginia Stephen, of course, also met Brooke herself. 'He was very keen on living the "free life",' she told William Plomer and Stephen Spender. 'One day he said, "Let's go swimming quite naked."'

'And did you, Virginia?' asked William Plomer.

'Of course. Lytton always said that Rupert had bandy legs. But I don't think that was so.'[1]

2

THE LIMBO OF UNINTIMACY

On leaving Cambridge, Lytton's rooms were rather violently re-decorated in apple-green and taken over by his younger brother, James. 'The room is grotesquely changed – an *art nouveau* symphony in green and white,' Lytton described it to Leonard Woolf, 'with James, very prim and small,[2] sitting in the extreme corner of the sofa, which is covered with green sack-cloth.'

Though Lytton had chosen the room's new decoration himself – a fact which he omits in his description of it to Leonard Woolf – the atmosphere seemed to him now much more louring than ever it was when he had lived there. But what chiefly dismayed and maddened him was the sight of his brother, a preposterous caricature of his past self, sitting there silent, contemptuous, utterly ineffectual, impotent and dull – a mere reflection of a reflection which went by the name of Walter Lamb, whose air of wheedling superiority James seemed to prefer to Norton's Etonian culture. It was dreadful to see him so alone and unhappy, unable to take an interest in anything, dismally submerged by the flatness of the world. But perhaps the Society, as soon as he was elected, would have a good effect, would widen the field of his en-

[1] Fresh evidence on this subject was recently made available to the author by James Strachey. 'Rupert *had* bandy legs, all the same.'

[2] 'In fact,' James Strachey pointed out, 'in our stockinged feet, we were both, at our best, exactly 6 ft. 1 in. tall.'

thusiasms and make him generally more cheerful. One could only hope so.

James's withdrawn nature and youthful appearance soon earned for him the name of 'the Little Strachey', while Lytton now figured as 'the Great Strachey'. At Lancaster Gate, James had been known as 'Jembeau', and even 'Uncle Baby' by some of his nieces and nephews considerably older than himself. But such nicknames were exclusively family matters, and it was owing to the difficulty of differentiating in conversation between himself and his younger brother, who now, for the first time, was fully entering his world, that Lytton suggested to his friends that they should in future address each other by Christian names. This recommendation, which was universally accepted, did not therefore constitute, as has been made out, a measure of deliberate social implication – a breaking down of formal, hidebound Victorian conventions – but was a matter of practical convenience and common sense. All his life Lytton actually preferred pet-names or nicknames to either surnames or Christian names. 'The pomposity of real Christian names', he once wrote to Duncan Grant, 'is too grinding.'

The presence of a younger enigmatic brother in his old rooms at Trinity acted as a powerful catalyst to Lytton's post-graduate reputation. 'I see you're rapidly becoming a kind of distant, eminent brilliant wicked Mephistophelian myth,' Maynard Keynes wrote to him (5 November 1905). And Lytton at once replied with a touch of prophetic foresight: 'It's rather alarming to find oneself a myth. I feel as if I ought to wear very peculiar clothes – à la Tennyson – so that people like Goldschmidt[1] shouldn't be disappointed if they happened to see me. Perhaps a fur tippet in the Verrall[2] style, a fur cap, and eyeglasses at the end of a stick. But of course the first necessity is a beard!'

The everyday commonplaces of his existence in London were very far removed from the fantasies of such a myth. He wrote the occasional review, went to a series of Joachim concerts, had an interview on the subject of Warren Hastings with (Sir) Algernon Methuen who 'looks like one of those dreadful Leonardo drawings, so that I wasn't surprised

---

[1] Ernst Goldschmidt was a freshman of sinister reputation, lately arrived from Austria. For a time Lytton and Keynes considered electing him to the Apostles, but finally decided on a more appropriate measure – an introduction to Oscar Browning. In later life Goldschmidt became a leading member of the Bibliographical Society and the author of *England's Service* by 'Sarpedon'.

[2] Arthur Woolgar Verrall (1851–1912), Greek scholar and Fellow of Trinity. A remarkable lecturer with a rich shrill voice, he was one of the first dons to treat the classics as works of art. A memoir of him by F. M. Cornford and reminiscences by Eddie Marsh (on whom he acted as a great influence) are included in *Collected Literary Essays* by A. W. Verrall (1913). His chief claim to celebrity was his *Euripides the Rationalist* – the best kind of detective story.

to get nothing out of him,' and saw a performance of Ibsen's *Wild Duck* which 'was superb – shattering in the extreme – terrible and pathetic. At the most tragic parts the audience had uncontrollable fits of the giggles.'

Clive Bell had once again left for France, and during the late autumn and the winter Lytton saw more of Duncan Grant and Desmond MacCarthy than any of his other friends. He would sometimes have lunch with the former at his new studio in Upper Baker Street, which appealed to his bohemian notions of how a painter should live – an almost completely bare room, ornamented solely with his sketches and drawings. 'They're superb,' he told Keynes after his first visit there (24 November 1905), 'and I've no doubt of his supremacy qua artist. He made an omelette in a frying-pan over the fire, and we ate it on the bare wooden table with bread and cheese and beer. After that we drew our kitchen chairs up to the fire, and smoked cigarettes and talked . . .'

A less romantic figure, Desmond MacCarthy was of more practical use to Lytton. He had recently become dramatic critic of the *Speaker*, and arranged for Lytton to contribute unsigned book reviews. Whenever they met, MacCarthy liked to read out loud to Lytton, who sat beside him, a languid, unappreciative audience. 'I've rarely been read aloud to so much,' he complained in a letter to Leonard Woolf, '– and have rarely heard anyone read aloud so badly.'

To one of these early articles he wrote for the *Speaker* there attaches some biographical interest, foreshadowing a later development in his career. In 1904 he had entered for the Harness Prize, the subject for that year being John Lyly. The prize, however, was won by another undergraduate, John Dover Wilson, who 'worked like a nigger' for it, as he later recorded, 'succeeded, and gained far more than the prize itself in the friendship of three men'. The first of these was Lytton, 'at that time quite unknown except to his small circle of friends, my exact contemporary, who had himself written an essay on Lyly, far more brilliant, I have no doubt, than anything I sent in, but not supported by the same amount of industry. And of course what dons like is industry.' After the result was declared Lytton wrote a little letter to the winner disclosing that they had been competitors and suggesting that they might become friends. The letter concluded with an invitation to coffee in his rooms. 'He liked being original,' Professor Dover Wilson told the author, 'and he made his coffee as the chemists conduct their experiments, with a series of glass tubes standing on a table. The process was striking; the coffee was cold.'

Through Lytton's gesture of generosity, Dover Wilson soon obtained entry into that charmed circle which included Keynes, Sheppard, the Stephen brothers, and others. In particular he was inducted into one of their various secret societies where, he wrote, 'the discussion formed perhaps the best education that I found at the University'.

The first of Lytton's contributions to the *Speaker* was a review of Dover Wilson's *John Lyly* which he called 'a thoroughly scholarly piece of work . . . it contains no irrelevance and no bad taste'. But it is the comments with which he qualifies this praise, and from which one may deduce the lines along which his own essay on John Lyly had been conceived, that are perhaps most interesting. He could not agree that Lyly had been a great influence on English literature. In his view the future of English prose had stemmed not from *Euphues*, as Wilson contended, but from Sidney's *Arcadia*. Lyly's example, too, in tightening up the structure of drama had produced little significant effect on the later Elizabethans. When one thought of the loose construction of most Elizabethan plays, he observed, Lyly's influence in this field seemed merely 'of the kind that a doctor has when he kills his patient'. Lytton believed instead that the essence of Lyly's drama lay not in its construction but in its dialogue, to which he cheerfully sacrificed character, intrigue, and action. 'Lyly was not the discoverer of a new Pacific; he was the explorer of a blind alley. . . . For what other writer is there who is at once so youthful, so happy, so ridiculous, and so infinitely dead?' Yet this divine gift of youthfulness, which Wilson had seemed to miss, was for Lytton the saving factor, and did something to preserve Lyly's work. 'It is this quality which gives charm to his lyrics,' he wrote, 'which puts something almost like life into one or two of his dramatic monologues, and which, for all the portentous mass of rococo ornament overlying it, pervades the pages of *Euphues*. Indeed, the very rigidity of his decoration is a sign of youth. He is stiff and formal as a schoolboy is stiff and formal when he goes into high collars and begins to be a gentleman.'

In his own existence there appeared to be no saving factor; youthfulness had departed for ever. Over everything hung the awful brooding régime of Lancaster Gate, which exerted itself ever more potently as the weeks passed and dissolved into months. It was not that he disliked any of his family, but that regular family life corroded family affection. 'I have a sister-in-law – she's now in the house – Lord!' he wrote to Maynard Keynes in despair (9 December 1905). 'She talks incessantly balderdash of the lowest description. She tries to flirt with me. She ogles, and wonders what I can possibly mean. If you come on Thursday she'll be here to flirt with you.' Such minor disturbances and irregularities seemed to emphasize his premature middle age, to convince him that his youth had belonged to Cambridge and was irretrievably left behind there. The world was a muddled worry. 'I don't believe I shall ever get back what I seem to have gained so easily and lost so vaguely,' he confessed, '– the happy state of premonitory, half-conscious, summer passion, "the tender eye-dawn of auroran love". I wonder what it is that divides me, infinitely and eternally, from those innocences and those delights. . . . The best things come to us before we know they are coming, and vanish before we know they have come. One lives a thousand ages without ever realizing what it is to live, and then, in the moment of discovery, one finds that one's already dead. . . . Oh dear! are we really so antique?'

These mortuary reflections express the pessimism which his physical incarceration within Lancaster Gate were prompting within him. On every possible occasion he struggled to escape, to spend even a single night elsewhere. He thought enviously of his brother Oliver, who was on the point of departing again for India: 'How he hates it!' Lytton exclaimed to Keynes. 'How he longs to stay! Ah! how much I'd like to go instead of him.' Frequent less ambitious trips away from Lancaster Gate, however, he did manage. During the course of the Michaelmas term he visited his brother twice at Cambridge, and was introduced by Keynes to all the new embryos. But the great days of the Apostles had passed – even Keynes himself admitted so. Christianity, like a pernicious weed, was springing up everywhere again. Nevertheless, after London, the air of youthful decadence was extreme. 'The whole place seemed to me more depressed and more sodomitical than usual,' he told Swithinbank after another stay there in the Lent term (4 February 1906). 'If things go on at this present rate, I shudder to think what our sons may or may not be doing twenty years hence. But perhaps by that time the fashion will have changed, and they'll all be womanizers. Well, it will be a great triumph to be thought indecent by one's son.'

Early in November he went to stay in Oxford with the Raleighs, who took him to hear a performance of the Brahms Requiem in which one of his sisters was singing. Walter Raleigh was charming and brilliant – at the same time quite unable to talk about anything that interested Lytton personally. 'Here I am, a little shattered,' he wrote to Keynes (2 November 1905). 'Last night I spent with the Raleighs, partly at a rather dull concert, and partly listening to his consummate brilliance. It's so great that it practically amounts to a disease. But in any case he belongs to the age before the flood – the pre-Dickinsonian era – which is really fatal. He's not interested in the things which absorb us – result, dead silence on my part, and blank boredom on his – though of course there are compensating moments.'

From the Raleighs, he moved across to Balliol to spend a few days with Swithinbank. And here, at last, he seemed more in tune with his surroundings. 'The amusement has been and continues great,' he told Duncan Grant (3 November 1905). 'Life here swims through a beautiful sea of gentleness and *politesse*. I was not surprised, when the door opened and someone who looked like a freshman glided in, to hear him addressed as Gabriel. The angel Gabriel, I thought, of course.' He peered at many of Swithinbank's friends – including Daniel Macmillan[1] and J. D. Beazley – went to the Union, and attended a meeting of the Pleiads – a society of seven ('perhaps too many') members founded by Swithinbank – where he heard a paper read on 'Les amours de Chopin et de George Sand'. But in comparison with the proceedings of *the* Society it seemed pretty feeble stuff. The paper itself was just dully constructive and informative, gleaned from text-books specially for the occasion, while the discussion which followed seemed hopelessly vague – questions from anybody to anybody, and developing into scattered smut and small-talk. As to Oxford in general, its cultivation and impropriety mixed made up a peculiar charm, at once gentle and cerebral, which Lytton had found lacking in the more fervid, revolutionary spirit of Cambridge.

But even here there were disappointments in store for him. He would have liked to establish a close and affectionate relationship with Swithinbank, who, he instinctively felt, would cause him less pain and depression than Duncan Grant. But the more he saw of him, the more he came to realize the unlikelihood of any really intimate friendship such as he desired. Swithinbank was too shy – too *intellectually* shy. He needed to be drawn out by a degree of tactful insinuation, obliquely and patiently applied, which was alien to Lytton's astringent and hasty temperament. 'There are awkward silences,' he reported apologetically to Keynes (2 November 1905); 'you see we really do at present have very few topics in common – I mean easy topics; though very often it's charming, and we can giggle without restraint. But what I think is the chief horror is his incapacity to analyse. He seems almost frightened and sheers off. Is it education or nature or what? This evening I pressed him hard – on the subject of Raleigh's character. He hedged for some time, and then made some quite good though rather muddled remarks. I went on, and he seemed to collapse completely – a sort of tormented resignation.'

Later in November, Lytton again succeeded in escaping from Lancaster Gate, this time to visit Bob Trevelyan and his Dutch wife Bessie for a few cold days at Holmbury St Mary, near Dorking. But it was an

[1] Daniel Macmillan (1886–1964). Elder brother of Harold Macmillan, later prime minister. A scholar of Balliol College, he subsequently became chairman and managing director of Macmillan and Co. Ltd, the publishers.

aimless, unsatisfactory life he was now leading. 'I feel', he wrote, 'like the Israelites who wandered in sight of the Promised Land for forty years.' His tenuous connexion with the Only Place was still being preserved primarily through Keynes, who was 'certainly now', he informed Leonard Woolf (November 1905), '– though I hardly expect you to believe it – the most important person there. He maintains a curious aloofness.' There was, in many of his references to Keynes about this time, an undisguised note of aversion. 'Keynes sits like a decayed and amorous spider in King's,' he wrote to Clive Bell (17 January 1906), using the very imagery which he was later to apply to King Philip of Spain, the spider of the Escurial, 'weaving purely imaginary webs, noticing everything that happens and doesn't happen, and writing to me by every other post.'

The truth was that their respective circumstances had changed much since Keynes was first elected to the Society. Then Lytton had been indisputably the major figure of the two, listening to the younger man's confidences and putting at his disposal the benefit of all his magnanimous understanding. But the quick and eager Apostle soon began to develop a confidence and dominating personality of his own. Prince D. S. Mirsky has suggested that Keynes might have grown into 'a rather dangerous rival' in the world of letters. Undoubtedly Keynes's phenomenal, un-Apostolic successes aroused in Lytton some feeling of disdain, made bitter by sexual jealousy. Whereas his own influence at Cambridge was literary, moral rather than ethical, and did not extend far beyond the inner circle of Apostles and the intimate friends at Trinity and King's, the more catholic Keynes became not only a leading Apostle, but also president of the Union and of the University Liberal Club – a person of wide authority. Lytton had only obtained Second Class Honours; Keynes, with a minimum of hard work, had won a First. Lytton half-heartedly failed to be accepted by the Education Board; Keynes went on to pass the Civil Service examination with some ease. Lytton was not elected as a Fellow of Trinity; Keynes was awarded a lectureship and then a Fellowship at King's. And when, in time, the fashionable conversation switched from metaphysics and literature to economics and political philosophy, Keynes could still more than hold his own, while Lytton, despite laughing enormously at jokes he found a little heavy, remained something of an outsider. This steady and complete reversal in the pattern of their fortunes set up an undercurrent of strain and stress which ran contrary to the flow of their old comradeship. He felt a genuine unadulterated appreciation for Keynes's intellectual powers and for the raciness of his conversation. But although he admired the author of *The Economic Consequences of the Peace*, he despised the mechanical salt-butter rogue who treated his love-affairs statistically and took the doings of the Liberal Party with great seriousness. These two attitudes persisted all through their relations. Lytton's feelings of sexual jealousy were something separate, which nevertheless magnified at times his critical judgements. What he particularly minded in his own life during these early years was lack of money combined with a lack of comfort of all kinds. The room he had been given at Lancaster Gate (it had previously been Dorothy's bedroom) was quite remarkably squalid and miserable – enough, it seemed to him, to depress anyone. The comparison with Keynes's happier and more prosperous circumstances irritated him, and it was only when Keynes suffered momentary set-backs and could no longer be considered an object of superficial envy, that their former intimacy was re-established.

The path which their gradual, limited estrangement was to follow can be traced between the lines of those letters which passed between them in the period soon after Lytton left Cambridge. This alienation, though it only once boiled over, simmered perpetually below the outer crust of their continuing friendship. Hating London, Lytton is ever thirsty for information about Cambridge youth, anxious to absorb himself in their activities, but Keynes replies casually and with a disconcerting echo of Lytton's own exact sentiments a year earlier: 'I really believe I would leave Cambridge and come up to London at once – but for one reason. I suppose the Society must be put on its legs again – or at any rate one has to try.' Lytton's letters expatiate, often movingly, on the twists and turns of his own shadowy passions and preoccupations. Keynes writes at length of his new satisfactory successes in economics, the flattering remarks on his papers, and his intention to study ethics for the Civil Service examination. Lytton answers with mixed feelings: 'I suppose it doesn't matter very much whether you get into the C.S. or not, does it? If you didn't, wouldn't you get a fellowship, and take rooms in the Temple? That you might do in any case – very charming. Oh dear me!' Deliberating on his course of action Keynes wonders whether he should stay on at Kings's as an economist. 'I could get employment here,' he writes, 'if I wanted to.' But Lytton, who hopes to leave Lancaster Gate and set up home with his friend somewhere in London, is appalled at the notion. 'Oh no, it would be surely mad to be a Cambridge economist,' he replies. 'Come to London, go to the Treasury, and set up house with me. The parties we'd give!' Soon, however, Lytton realizes that Keynes has no intention of getting a flat with him in town, and reflects that in these altered circumstances his rooms in King's might continue to be very useful. But already it is too late. Keynes, without Lytton's apprehension of the unknown, is determined to quit the deadening, stagnant atmosphere of Cambridge and embark on the adventure of life in London as soon as possible. He will conquer the metropolis as he has the university. He even confesses himself a little taken with Ray Costelloe,[1] who was later to become Oliver Strachey's second wife; he takes up mountaineering in the company of Geoffrey Winthrop Young[2] (recently sacked from his post as a master at Eton), and is immediately successful. Lytton's consternation rises and he sadly admits to Duncan Grant that he has no faith in Keynes's power of penetrating below the surface of life.

In due course the result of the Civil Service examination comes through. Keynes is second. 'A wonderful achievement,' his father noted in his diary. But Maynard, who has worked only intermittently, is furious – and writes to Lytton at length to tell him so–[3] whereupon Lytton sorrowfully confesses to Duncan Grant: 'I used to tell Keynes everything, but his commonsense was enough to freeze a volcano, so now I've stopped.' At this point, however, Keynes encounters a period

[1] Ray Costelloe was the daughter of Logan Pearsall Smith's sister, who later married Bernard Berenson. Ray's sister Karin married Adrian Stephen, and her aunt Alys was the wife of Bertrand Russell. An acknowledged leader in the Woman's Movement, she was the author of many books, including *Millicent Garrett Fawcett* (1931). She and Oliver Strachey had two children, Barbara, who joined the administrative staff of the B.B.C., and Christopher, now one of the top computer wizards in Britain.

[2] Geoffrey Winthrop Young, poet and mountaineer. On leaving Eton, he had taken up a post as one of H.M. Inspectors of Secondary Schools (1905–13). Later he became renowned for scaling Alpine peaks after having lost a leg in the battle of Monte San Gabrielle.

[3] Lytton celebrated the occasion with some witty verses entitled:

'In Memoriam J.M.K. Ob. Sept. 1906.'

Here lie the last remains of one
Who always did what should be done.
Who never misbehaved at table
And loved as much as he was able.
Who couldn't fail to make a joke,
And, though he stammered, always spoke;
Both penetrating and polite,
A liberal and a sodomite,
An atheist and a statistician,
A man of sense, without ambition.
A man of business, without bustle,
A follower of Moore and Russell,
One who, in fact, in every way,
Combined the features of the day.
By curses blest, by blessings cursed,
He didn't merely get a first.
A first he got; on that he'd reckoned;
But then he also got a second.
He got a first with modest pride;
He got a second, and he died.

of adversity, and is re-admitted as the sympathetic repository of Lytton's emotional problems. For the next two years, 1907 and 1908, Keynes works in the India Office, but even before his first twelve months are up he is already consumed with ennui and thinking about moving on again. 'I'm thoroughly sick of this place,' he writes to Lytton in September 1907, 'and would like to resign. Now the novelty has worn off, I am bored nine-tenths of the time and rather unreasonably irritated the other tenth whenever I can't have my own way. It's maddening to have thirty people who can reduce you to impotence when you're quite certain you are right.' Lytton, at once responding to this familiar blend of boredom and arrogant frustration, is enthusiastically sympathetic. It is more like old times again. 'I feel it's a great mercy,' he wrote later, 'having you as Brother Confessor.' How pleasant it was being able freely to divulge what he felt! For his feelings were now centred strongly round Duncan Grant, to whom he had succeeded in introducing Keynes in the very first month of his return to Lancaster Gate. And he had much to divulge.

3

DUNCAN GRANT AND HIS WORLD

Duncan Grant was some five years younger than Lytton. His father, Major Bartle Grant, Lady Strachey's youngest brother, had married Ethel McNeil, a beautiful but penniless Scottish girl, and Duncan, who was born in Rothiemurchus, was their only child. His early years had been spent out in India where Major Grant was serving with his regiment. But once the boy was old enough to attend preparatory school he was shipped back to England, spending his holidays with the Stracheys at Lancaster Gate. Destined for a military career, he had in due course been entered with James Strachey as a day boy at St Paul's, where he was placed in the army class and instructed in such subjects as mathematics, of which he understood nothing. He could see no purpose whatever in learning how to multiply, add or even subtract large quantities of money when he neither possessed nor expected to possess anything remotely comparable to such sums. But Lady Strachey, aware of her nephew's true artistic potentialities, at length succeeded in persuading his parents to let him study at the Westminster School of Art. 'The great excitement is about Duncan,' she wrote to Lytton in December 1901, 'who appears likely to turn out a genius as an artist, at least so the experts say. But what to do with him is the difficulty.' For, in the traditional style of genius, Duncan seemed to benefit little from orthodox teaching and eventually failed to gain admission to the Royal Academy School.

From his father, Duncan Grant had inherited a love of music and an aesthetic sensibility; from his mother, as a self-portrait painted in 1911 clearly shows, his beauty. 'His face is outspoken,' Lytton wrote to Leonard Woolf (October 1905), 'bold, and just not rough. It's the full aquiline type, with frank gray-blue eyes, and incomparably lascivious lips.' As a young man among the Cambridge exiles and 'Bloomsberries' to whom Lytton soon introduced him, he appeared refreshingly un-hampered by the paraphernalia of a pedantic classical education, though the unsophisticated way in which his artistic imagination tended to operate was sometimes misinterpreted by conventional people as rather naïve stupidity. As a youth he often wore a dirty collar, usually upset his afternoon tea, and never knew what time it was. When he spoke he blinked his eyes, and generally carried on in such an irresponsible fashion as to convince his uncle, Trevor Grant, that he was a hopeless and possibly certifiable imbecile. His pleasing appearance, however, was matched by a correspondingly attractive personality for those who knew him well. He was entirely natural and unconstrained in manner, possessed a lively entertaining mind, was keenly observant, but, less happily perhaps, given to practical jokes, which were nevertheless in his case not malicious in character, but merely the outlet of a rather impish precocity.[1]

Lytton's feelings for Duncan Grant were very far from being just skin deep. In fact he disapproved of affiliations formed solely by physical appeal. 'I know there's a sort of passion,' he wrote, '– an animal feeling, a passion without affection, which is merely bodily pleasure, and doesn't count.' It was certainly not this that he desired, but rather an ideal union in which lust did not destroy companionship, and where genuine affection and friendliness did not diminish passion. Only through such an immaculate relationship could the disparate elements within his own nature, the conflicting will and imagination, be satis-factorily integrated; only thus could his strange, immaterial spirit of fantasy and romance be heightened, his nagging ambitions assuaged vicariously.

In these first years of exile from Cambridge, Lytton wished above all else to be an artist – a literary artist it would have to be – yet he was

[1] In D. H. Lawrence's *Lady Chatterley's Lover*, Duncan Grant appears under the name of Duncan Forbes: 'that dark skinned taciturn Hamlet of a fellow with straight black hair and a weird Celtic conceit of himself'. For an account of the meeting which took place between Lawrence and Grant, see the letter Lawrence wrote to Lady Ottoline Morrell on 27 January 1915.

racked by profound and agonizing doubts as to his capabilities. The man of action was beginning to seem too remote and immature a vision of perfection, and as it slowly faded so it was replaced by a different breed of hero, the painter, the musician, the creative literary genius. But fears of his own inadequacy pressed in on him as he laboured over his book reviews. 'Perhaps', he wrote, 'the truth is that I'm not an artist. But what the devil *am* I?' In his perplexity he looked for someone on whom to centre his complicated emotions, and towards whom he might escape from the tightening ring of his deflated egocentricity. And it was on Duncan Grant that he fastened.

In all his infatuations, even those at school, Lytton was endeavouring to relinquish his own personality and assume in its place that of the person loved. It was therefore only to be expected that he should now fall in love with an artist. 'Let's both be great artists and great friends,' he exhorted Duncan Grant. 'Je t'embrasse de tout mon coeur.' Once he had succeeded in establishing himself as a literary exponent in the arts, the direction, though not the nature, of his desires would accordingly change, aiming once more for the impossible. After *Eminent Victorians* he would again venerate social and physical splendour, and worship blue-eyed rowing Blues and handsome young Old Etonians. But these days were still far off. For this reason, however, there was always something ingenuous and adolescent about his love-affairs, a quality of most extreme urgency within the aura of ethereal day-dream, where a sort of divinity seemed to clothe his senses.

Now, while his self-confidence was at such a low ebb and he followed an aimless, lonely existence, haunted daily by the thought of failure, the figure of Duncan Grant seemed to exemplify in dazzling fashion the very reverse of all his own personal shortcomings. He was a star shining miraculously in the black vault of the heavens, to which Lytton would hitch his battered and decrepit wagon. For in his view Duncan Grant was undoubtedly a genius, and destined to triumph in one of the noblest creative spheres known to man. 'He sees everything, you know,' Lytton told Keynes excitedly (18 November 1905), 'and he's probably better than us. I have a sort of adoration. When I hear people talking about him I'm filled with a secret pride.'

The obverse of this adoration was an exultant self-abasement. All his life Lytton tended to gravitate naturally towards the role of victim. At school he had attracted bullying; and he sometimes magnified his illnesses to extract from them a rarefied contemplative pleasure – though he hated sickness in others as the dreaded evidence of mortality and decay without their more delicious symptoms. In his adult love-affairs something of this pattern repeated itself, for he manœuvred himself without fail into acute distress. Sometimes his complaints were well-founded, sometimes they were delusions; but almost always he himself was their own architect. Duncan Grant was genuinely fond of him, but Lytton's intensive emotionalism produced in him the terror of an affection greater than he could absorb. Being of a reasonably self-sufficient composition himself, he felt overloaded by Lytton's hyper-sensitive attentions, his kindnesses, his claustrophobic possessiveness. For it was not simply that Lytton longed to assimilate his body, but to take, as it were, vacant possession of his very soul. Duncan, on the other hand – and he was unlikely to have attracted Lytton's attentions had it been otherwise – felt little wish to intermingle or even surrender his own identity. The responsibility for supporting Lytton's own emotionalism was too excessive, and he set about erecting a network of defences to demonstrate that he could not be taken over in this fashion. In order to evade the full flow and rigour of Lytton's love he went to work presenting himself as a person totally unfitted to receive such romantic affections. He tried to cut the very ground from beneath Lytton's feet by reversing the current of eulogy and self-abasement. Lytton, he wrote, was 'too good, too true, too great'. He despised him-self 'for not being of the fine clay that could fly with you into limitless space for ever,' though, of course, he still felt for him 'a very great friendship and the utmost regard'. Over and above this modest degree of fondness, he suggested, Lytton's sentiments were wasted. As for himself, he was little better than a brute; his affection was on a lower level – nothing more than a perverted form of calf-love; he could never match the wildness and nobility of Lytton's passion.

But to all these evasions and dissimulations Lytton had a ready answer. Duncan, he explained, had overestimated the wonder and supremacy of his emotions simply because he, Lytton, was better able to give expres-sion to them. It was merely a matter of being older. And all the while he seemed, partially at any rate, to thrive on this self-induced ill-treatment; it gave him such an emotional kick and, above all else, it preserved intact his adoration. For Duncan Grant's tactics to dilute the strength of Lytton's infatuation, though subtle, were unconvincing. Towards anyone who was absurd enough really to think highly of him or hold him in great affection Lytton automatically felt less. He returned admira-tion with something of a diminution of feeling. After all, he despised himself so utterly that he could not think well of a person who was taken in over so vital a matter in human relations. What, in a sense, he demanded from those on whom he fixed his love was a contempt so powerful as to blast and obliterate his own personality without trace. He laments repeatedly that Duncan Grant is stand-offish, unkind, indifferent: and at the same time he worships him all the more. 'Duncan tortures me. But a crisis must happen soon. I find him perfect,' he wrote. He was in a torment lest the unbearable torture should cease; lest he should fall out of love, and back into nothingness. How pale and un-profitable would all the uses of the world seem after such a catastrophe as that!

In the intervals between these painful spasms, he reflected lingeringly on his own heightened reactions to everything around him. He was, even in the ordinary course of things, of a highly sensitive disposition, prone to dizziness whenever he was swept by any sudden gusts of emotion. At concerts and in the theatre he invariably sat at the end of the row in case he should faint; for any excess of feeling always threatened to overwhelm his fragile body. This risk of losing conscious-ness naturally increased when he felt himself to be in love – a condition to which he was extremely susceptible, since the image of his love was so powerful that it often betrayed him into aiming at it when the reality was not there. While in these infatuated states of mind he became hyper-emotional to an astonishing degree. Describing the sensations which would consume and ravage him, Lytton frequently couples together the words 'dim' and 'intense', to indicate that any overplus of violent feel-ings automatically brought about a fading away of his physical aware-ness. From boyhood onwards, it was precisely this wretched, hateful self-awareness that he sought to eradicate. To transfer it from his own body to that of his partner was the logical apotheosis of all his passions, and one which he never fully accomplished. Half-way he does seem to have reached – expelled out of himself but injected into no one, and so wasting away into the thin air between. Exhilarated, semi-conscious, he would float like some astral projection of himself, suspended pre-cariously *in vacuo*, a luminous, misty and insubstantial phantom hover-ing on the edge of an unimaginable re-incarnated paradise – *Lytton Strachey in love*. But always, after each crisis of dizzying emotional high tide, he would be sucked down again into the sickening depths of his own, ultimately inescapable personality.

Lytton's friendship with Duncan Grant lasted many years, but it was probably never more intense – at least on Lytton's part – than during the winter of 1905–6. 'I have fallen in love hopelessly and ultimately,' he wrote to Clive Bell (17 January 1906). 'I have experienced too much ecstasy, I want to thank God, and to weep, and to go to sleep.' While Duncan, on the other hand, persisted in acting 'almost as though he were afraid of me, of my affection – as if he didn't dare to face something he couldn't reciprocate', Lytton grew more and more deeply obsessed with the idea of being in love with him. The affair prompted his most romantic and highflown vein: 'One feels that one might, by some extraordinary twist of the will, make everything all right; and one comes against an adamantine and irrevocable rock which no power under heaven can move. Shall one dash oneself against it? That's the only question. I generally seem to do both, which is the worst solution.' Yet this did provide some sort of temporary solution, for it kept in a state of perpetual animation the repressed vehemence of his exultation – a state in which radiant happiness and delirious misery were so strangely intertwined. 'He [Duncan] is the full moon of heaven. I rave, and you may judge of my condition when I tell you that it's 4 p.m. – the most utterly prosaic hour of the day,' he confided to Maynard Keynes (8 December 1905). '. . . At the present moment I feel capable of achieving every wonder, of rising to incomparable heights! Good heavens, last night my despair was too absolute.' Lytton's admiration for Duncan Grant developed in double harness with a corresponding dislike of himself. 'I am sometimes miserable,' he ended another letter to Maynard Keynes, 'I am often desirous, I am usually unconscious, and I am always your G.L.S.' As the ardour of his affections strengthened so he felt himself liberated from the husk of G.L.S., pushed by the sheer pressure of his emotions into a strange, new multi-dimensional existence. 'I live in a mist,' he wrote to Keynes on 21 December '– perhaps a golden one – where most ordinary things are fluctuating and dim. My nerves have quite gone. I seem to be in direct and mystic contact with the Essence of the World. The air is full of divinity, and the music of the spheres enchants me as I walk.' And in another letter describing the occult perceptivity shed upon him by his emotional excitement, the breaking out of his egocentricity, he writes: 'I feel that as long as I keep up my spirits all will be well. But we do live in a queer eminent world. Perhaps – I don't know – a trifle unreal.'

Towards the end of December an event occurred which seemed about to change the dream into a living reality. This was nothing more devastating than a 'Grand Conversation' in which Duncan Grant explained his feelings to Lytton, and convinced him of his genuine affection. Lytton was at once overjoyed, and wrote off to Keynes the next day to delineate his fresh onrush of passion: 'My own crisis – oh lord God! I hardly know what to write. All that's obvious and before my nose is that he's absolutely mine. I haven't the nerve to think of the future; and, for the present, though I'm cheered, happy, proud, perhaps even rejuvenated – I'm too battered and pale to feel the high supremacies of joy. I don't know – I can hardly believe – is it possible? . . . We have reached the reign of Affection – but one can't expatiate; one can only accept.'

The swift reaction away from this new enthusiasm was characteristic. Lytton and Duncan had been invited by Lady Colvile to spend the first week of January at her home, Park Cottage, at Ledbury in Hertfordshire. By all that was strictly rational Lytton should have been delighted. But he was not. Everything was going rather too well for his taste. On the face of it, he had to admit, he was in luck. What could be more pleasant than the prospect of Ledbury with Duncan? But then it was sure to be all sham – *mere* enjoyment, mere blind, spurious, moonstruck ecstasies. His accustomed role was as the victim of some bitter and hopeless passion, and any other part made him uneasy. Besides, Duncan could not have much of a brain if he in fact thought so well of him – as it really seemed he did. Either he was a fool or a consummate liar. The infatuation began to ebb, his jubilation to become marred with doubts. Love was like faith – one didn't like to lose it until one had, when one couldn't understand why one ever wanted it. 'I begin to wonder whether his [Duncan's] intellect is satisfying enough,' he confided to Maynard Keynes (31 December 1905). 'I can imagine myself bored. We're to go to the Cottage at Ledbury on Wednesday, and I almost dread five days tête-à-tête.' He was beginning to suffer the pangs of requited love.

Lytton's fears, however, proved to be unjustified. The days at Ledbury were full of turbulent and unpeaceful happiness. It was impossible not to offend someone in Lytton's tense, supersensitive condition, someone, moreover, who almost cherished persecution. 'Nothing definite has happened,' he reported back to Keynes at one stage. 'I was blissfully happy till suddenly he said something which brought it over me in a sudden shock that he didn't care for me, and wanted to escape.' On the instant Lytton relapsed into a 'wretched state'; he despaired of everything and gave himself up to thoughts of death. Duncan, in response, complained of his moodiness, of the wild incoherent terrors that afflicted his soul. And all at once Lytton was head over heels, madly infatuated again. No question of boredom now. He laments of pouring out his affection into a bottomless pit, of Duncan's total lack of reciprocation; and he reflects with terror on the possibility of their friendship coming to an end. Yet the self-torture, on this occasion, was largely gratuitous. Without Duncan he felt he was nothing. The voluntary nightmare and the dream merged into a blissful, self-obliterating fantasy: 'But how often didn't I feel that it was he who was the great person and that I was a mere ineffectual shade!' he wrote to Keynes a few hours before leaving Ledbury (9 January 1906). 'His mind! – I didn't realize before what it was – the audacity, the strength, the amazing subtlety. . . . But please remember – he's a *genius* – a colossal portent of fire and glory. His feelings transcend all – I have looked into his eyes, and the whole universe has swayed and swum and been abolished, and we have melted into one indescribable embrace. His features were moulded by nothing intermediary, but by the hand of God itself; they are plastic like living marble, they clothe a divinity, a quintessential soul. I rave; but I weep too. Looking at his face, I imagined last night the marks of Time upon it. I saw the lines and the ruins and the desolations of Age, I saw Death too, and the face composed in Death; and I prayed that the whole world might stand still for ever.'

In the second week of January, Lytton returned reluctantly and alone to London, stopping at Bristol on the way, and also spending a night with his cousin Edward Strachey at Sutton Court. Back in Lancaster Gate, he took up the bare threads of his old existence again. On the surface, life during the next month was full of variety. He was writing articles for the *Independent Review*, the *Spectator* and the *Speaker*. He went to the occasional theatre and concert, and also to a dance given by the Ridpaths, which amused him as sophisticated and expensive parties always did, with their endlessly flowing champagne, processions of bright youths, and their invariable and utter absurdity. He dined with Isabel Fry[1] and met for the first time Hilton Young[2] – 'very dull and pompous'. He visited the Stephens; he saw a lot of Harry Norton, Saxon Sydney-Turner, Charles and Dora Sanger in their little set of rooms at Charing Cross, and Desmond MacCarthy (recently engaged to Mary Warre-Cornish, daughter of the Vice-Provost of Eton) who used to invite him round for 'evening meals' that always consisted of more conversation than food. And every minute of these weeks was documented in one, two, even three letters a day to Maynard Keynes.

Lytton tried hard to be cheerful during this time. His pessimism and the agitations of his spirit only upset Duncan Grant, the one person he wished to make happy. But it was little use; he was 'a damned morbid selfish idiot'. Sometimes he even welcomed minor illnesses, which enabled him, for the benefit of others, to trace his defects to a definite cause. People who experience a kind of tension over nothing, or at least nothing they can pin down, were, he knew, the ones who suffered most. It was something of a relief to be able to attach some temporary physical diagnosis to his complaints. 'I'm pretty ill,' he explained to Duncan Grant on succumbing to a cold in the head, 'and in the very highest

---

[1] The fifth child of Sir Edmund Fry, and sister of Roger Fry. An educationalist of outstanding brilliance, she inaugurated a new method of teaching language structure.

[2] Hilton Young (1879–1960), poet and politician, brother of Geoffrey Winthrop Young and father of Wayland Young, the author and member of Parliament, was then at Trinity. In his political career he was Financial Secretary to the Treasury (1921–22) and Minister of Health (1931–35). Created first Baron Kennet in 1935.

spirits.' But the cold passed and the symptoms of debility persisted. He felt that he would like to go away by himself and forget everything for a few weeks. The long, unsatisfactory dragging on of his affair with Duncan was a sort of painless torture. In his numb and listless condition he thought of visiting the Homeres at Chipping Norton, but could not bring himself to creep away. Each week he saw Duncan once or twice, no more; just enough to revive and exhaust his passion. 'I like seeing him so much, and I'm so horribly unhappy when he goes away,' he told his Brother Confessor. But perhaps the worst part of all were the blank periods between these meetings, days of lassitude, nights of agonized introspection, twilight moments of terrifying, senseless indifference. Duncan seemed so unpredictable, too; at times charming and expansive, on other occasions secretive and off-hand – more friendly, even, towards Lytton's brother James.

As the days crawled by, bringing no solution to his problems, Lytton's preoccupations concentrated inwards, and he grew pitifully maudlin: 'Don't think of me, please, as perpetually unhappy,' he implored Duncan (25 January 1906), ' – only as a muddle-headed, well-meaning, weak-kneed creature, who generally manages to get along better than one might expect, but who sometimes stumbles and lapses.' Ledbury seemed a hundred years away. By the beginning of February he despaired of ever attaining the ideal love after which he was seeking, and sank into 'a sort of utter melancholy at the hopelessness of attainment, the impossibilities of ever reaching the complete, the absolute, the adored. One's love seems to be sometimes so far above oneself – one despairs.' The vision of a mystic reincarnation had faded and disappeared, and he was sucked back into the prison of his own feeble, ugly frame. Everything now revolted him, was tainted with his own disgusting putrefaction. 'The whole world stinks in my nostrils,' he cried out to Maynard Keynes (1 February 1906). 'I stench in my own nostrils.'

4

MEN IN LOVE

Describing himself as 'a little shattered' in the months after leaving Cambridge, Lytton seemed to nourish no real appetite for life. He felt no desire to enter the roar and turmoil of the London circus on just *any* terms; he wanted to excel, to impose upon its vivid animal chaos the kind of manufactured coherence that is to be found in his best books and essays. His ambitions, like his love, were rooted in a sense of personal insufficiency. Just as his passions came to him as an imaginative form of envy, so his quietly assertive will fed on frustration and was reinforced by his inability to escape from envy through fantasy and infatuation. Like many homosexuals, too, he felt somehow outside the common social run of humanity, and this sense of dissociation stimulated his determination to succeed.

But in 1906 he was unknown. The busy metropolis passed him by, and he hated it. London was a hideous, unaesthetic muddle; the grotesque existing in such close proximity to the plain, squalor rubbing shoulders with overloaded luxury, a lack of all reasonable satisfying order, a disconcerting unnatural alternation of beauty and shabbiness, and running through it all the senseless tempest of noise, corruption and vulgarity. It was not simply a matter of architecture and acoustics. London presented to him a spectacle of the adult world, the complexities of whose relationships appalled and terrified him. He shrank from all its heedless, cruel confusion. Even Bethlehem, and all it stood for, was preferable to this raucous, twentieth-century capital, for at least Jesus Christ hadn't been a typical city hypocrite, a brutal money-maker and womanizer. 'I want to go back to childhood,' he confessed to Duncan Grant (5 February 1906), 'to be two years old, like Ethel Melville's baby, who has been lunching here, and as exquisite, charming and divine. Talk of the feelings of dogs! Pooh! All goodness seems to me to dwindle into nothing when I look at a child of two. I'm willing to forgive our friend J.C. for all his delusions, stupidities, and wickednesses, because he really did understand so thoroughly that *they* are Heaven itself.'

Like many men who suffer from recurrent ill-health, Lytton loved at all times to travel. His dislike of London was strengthened by the uneasy state of his family life, which was responsible, he believed, for much of his desperate morbidity. But the most prominent source of this depression – which he was later in life to revere as a divine condition of youth[1] – was, of course, the tortured relationship with Duncan Grant. In his feverish commotion of mind, Lytton found it almost impossible to work. All through December he had struggled with an essay on Sir Thomas Browne which had given him far more trouble and taken up far more time than any such composition ought to have done. 'I feel that the only chance for my doing anything in the way of work,' he

[1] 'You know there is really something divine in some forms of depression and discontent – for one thing they are often signs of youth. . . . All decent people remain young for an incredible length of time and suffer accordingly.' (Lytton Strachey to Roger Senhouse, 16 January 1929.)

wrote to Maynard Keynes about the situation, 'is either that we should live together or else apart.'

The first, and most exciting of these solutions, was impossible, since Duncan had recently been given by his aunt, Lady Colvile, a hundred pounds for his twenty-first birthday, and with this sum he proposed to continue his artistic education in Paris. Staying on at Lancaster Gate while Duncan was enjoying himself on the other side of the Channel was, for Lytton, a pretty bleak prospect, and he secretly hoped that, to make this separation easier, Lady Colvile would invite him down to her villa in Menton.

Early in February Lady Colvile did write to Lady Strachey suggesting that Lytton should pay her a visit. 'I'm going to the South of France in a few days,' he wrote happily to Swithinbank (4 February 1906). 'This I feel to be wicked, as I've positively no excuse, and I can't see why I should bask in sun and roses, and other people not. However I suppose the world is arranged on these principles.' Yet, although Lytton felt that his flight to Menton might, as he put it to Keynes, 'save me from utter death', his mood was not one of unmixed elation. He knew, of course, that he must in any event part temporarily from Duncan, but as the date of their departure drew nearer he was filled with fresh agitation. 'I'm sad because I'm so futile and incompetent,' he explained to his cousin (5 February 1906), 'and because the thought of parting from you is a dull agony. I feel like a schoolboy at the end of his holidays, who knows that tomorrow he must go away from home. How dreadful to be an exile!

'. . . I don't see that there's anything to prevent my going as soon as possible. I think it may save me. Sun, flowers, Dorothy, and comparative comfort! Don't you think so? Please be sympathetic, for I am very sad, almost in tears.'

Before leaving for France Lytton spent a last week-end down at Cambridge seeing many of his old friends, and his sister Pernel[1] at Newnham. Among the other people he met were Thena Clough, and the redoubtable Mrs Fawcett, 'a lady with indistinct features and a practical mind, [who] . . . talked about land reform, small holdings, etc. – I daresay, as I was a man, she thought I followed her'.

Since both Duncan and Lytton were going to France, Lady Strachey decided that the two of them had better travel together. Accordingly

---

[1] Joan Pernel Strachey (1876–1951), after being educated at Allenswood, Newnham and the Sorbonne (it was through her, while she was in Paris, that the connexion with Simon Bussy had been made) had become a lecturer in French at Royal Holloway College. In 1905 she gave up this post, returning to Newnham as a tutor. Later (1917–23) she was Director of Studies in Modern Languages at the college, and then, from 1923 to 1941, Principal of Newnham.

they set off on 18 February by train to Paris, and stayed one night at the Hôtel de l'Univers et du Portugal. The next day, Lytton left Duncan 'up 42 flights of stairs in the hotel', a little alarmed, but glad to be in France, and continued his gloomy journey south, alternately sleeping and writing long regretful letters back to Paris. 'It's very nice now – gliding along by the shore in a demi-trance. I often turn round to say something to you; why aren't you here?'

On his arrival at Menton, Lytton was met by Lady Colvile and Trevor Grant, 'a dowager aunt and a vagabond uncle', as he described them to Swithinbank, '(they're brother and sister not husband and wife)', who took him up to their home, Villa Henriette. 'This is a very small house,' he wrote to his mother (20 February 1906), 'but charmingly placed, the front rooms looking over olive-trees to the sea.' As so often, the sea-climate and scenery acted as a solace to the wear and tear of human affairs. The landscape seemed to blend into and become a condition of his spirit. Basking under the sun he could dissolve and quite forget the enervating confusion of his emotional life, could submerge himself beneath the mighty impersonal forces of Nature. The rocks and mountains appeared to draw out and absorb his personality, which evaporated into the quivering, fathomless air above. It was far from being the ideal process of bodily transubstantiation to which he would always aspire, but it was restful and recuperative. 'The sun and general exhilaration is wonderful,' he told Maynard Keynes immediately after his arrival (21 February 1906). 'I have high hopes of regaining health . . . I can hardly believe anything any more, I pass along in a dream, looking at peacock-blue seas, and talking to imbecile dowagers, and eating artichoke omelettes . . .'

And so the first days passed slowly by in health and apathy. He bought himself a rather dashing pair of green-yellow gloves and a very splendid and very cheap Monte Carlo hat, and would sit for long motionless hours on the terrace looking at the blue blur of the sea and sky through palms, olives and cypress trees. In a sense he almost ceased to exist as a separate entity, losing all count of space and time, and becoming part of the fixed, lunatic landscape. 'Imagine, if you possibly can, my infinite silence,' he wrote to Keynes. 'I've become at one with the rocks and trees. I respond if I'm spoken to, I give out reciprocal sounds; voilà tout! I've lost count of everything, the day of the week, the number of reviews I ought to be writing, the length of time I've been without seeing Duncan, the name of the founder of the Society – all, all has gone. I can only think of whether the Protestant Church ought to have a new organ loft, and of how much Mrs Trollope loses per week at bridge. The word reminds me – I believe I was once – I have some memory – I don't know though – *was* I once at Cambridge? Are you there now? I wonder. No, no, I think it must be the colour of the sea that I'm thinking of – if it really is sea and not scene-painting. – But after all, what can one expect of one's state of mind when one's reduced to reading the works of W. W. Jacobs? – "The captain turned in his chair and regarded his daughter steadily. She met his gaze with calm affection.

' "I wish you were a boy," he growled.

' "You're the only man in Sanwick who wishes that," said Miss Nugent complacently.'

Lytton was as happy during these early days as it was possible for him to be, cut off from Duncan Grant. He thought about him constantly. The brief, agonizing rejuvenation which this affair had brought about now faded mildly away, and he awaited in a detached, contented way his journey home, when he should be able to stop off again for a few days with him in Paris. They would be the happiest days of his life. Meanwhile his happiness was suspended, lying remote in the back of his mind. 'Now that I've sunk into middle-age,' he wrote to Maynard Keynes (7 March 1906), 'a quiet married life is all I look forward to, for myself, and for everyone else.' And he assured Swithinbank (9 March 1906) that 'if you were here, I should insist on walking with you into the mountains, which are very charming, though their shapes are usually hideous. As it is my furthest walk is to the bandstand, where I sit surrounded by Germans listening to Meyerbeer.'

But as his 'shattered nerves' mended, so his latent discontent began once more to mount. The sky and the sea were all very well, but after a while they grew infinitely tedious. Together they might form a beautiful background, but as things stood, it remained a background for nothing in particular, an empty stage. He missed his youthful talented friends and felt a good deal in the wilderness, discovering no one at Menton to take their place. The local boys, too, were rather disappointing. Their olive complexions and bare necks looked at first sight promising, but on closer inspection they nearly all turned out to be too dirty and too stupid to be tolerated. 'I have seen no one of even respectable looks for almost a week,' he complained to Keynes (24 February 1906), 'and I am becoming a little impatient . . . I suppose I ought to be thankful for what I've got – sun, comfort and plenty of books – and I am, but Lord! the flesh is weak, and it's difficult not to think sometimes of what *might* be. However, it's no good talking.'

Some distraction was provided by the antics and the eccentricities of Lytton's aunt and uncle, both of whom were, by all his accounts, highly extravagant characters. About Lady Colvile, a figure apparently of

Elizabethan force and colour, rich, musical and refined, he would recite stories in his letters to Duncan Grant – the kind of amusing trivia which always appealed to his curiosity and sense of the ridiculous. 'La tante Elinor has so far been fairly well under control,' he reported back during the first week of his visit. 'There is a wretched imbecile of a French maid called Nina whom she worries at meals rather, but that's all. I relapse into the pathetic silence of a delicate youth, whenever I see anything like a crisis approaching. This has an excellent effect, and Nina (who deserves it), is immediately blown up for serving the currie before the rice, or for not putting the Oriental Pickles on the table.' But a week or two later 'Aunt Lell' began to suffer from *twinges* and retired to her bed. Even in illness she struck Lytton as quite magnificent: 'Aunt Lell is exquisite – perhaps tragic,' he wrote (6 March 1906). 'Her hands are enough in themselves to prostrate one; and even her face I find absorbing. I saw her the other day in bed, without her wig. You can't conceive the difference. She looked terribly old.'

As a result of Lady Colvile's sickness, Lytton was thrown together rather more with his uncle. Trevor Grant was an ex-Indian civilian, vague, well-intentioned and somewhat cranky. To keep out the heat he wore an enormous overcoat (even in winter) and spent most of his waking hours in all seasons noisily draining down cups of coffee, reminiscing about the past, and reading the day before yesterday's copy of *The Times*. Lytton was half fascinated, half repelled by this grotesque spectacle and he described his uncle in the terms of some freakish zoological specimen. 'We get on pretty well,' he assured Duncan Grant, '– he talks, and I do my best to listen appreciatively – it's not very difficult, as it's all about old Indian days, and fairly amusing. . . . He's rather trying in some ways. He makes the most disgusting swilling and squelching noises when he's eating, and I sometimes feel that I shall shriek if it goes on for a second longer. It does, and I never do – such is my virtue, or cowardice. The truth is that he is a vagabond, not an ordinary civilized human being accustomed to live in houses, behave at table and so on. He ignores all that, and floats dimly on in his dim self-centred way. Sometimes I see him at dusk prowling along the sea-shore in his long flapping overcoat – a mystic solitary figure. What can he be thinking of? His sons? His photography? Old Indian days? Clementina? Death? Nothing at all? . . .'

Not long after Lytton's arrival in Menton, Trevor Grant returned to England, and his place at the Villa Henriette was taken by another of Lady Colvile's brothers, George – the complete antithesis of Trevor, very spruce and haughty and English. Removed from his natural habitat to the South of France, he seemed pathetically out of place, and no one – certainly not Lytton – could find anything to say to him.

Presently another member of the family joined the household. This was a cousin of Lytton's, Alfred Plowden, a magistrate of Marylebone Police Court.[1] Most of his holiday was spent at Monte Carlo, where he went for the sake of the tables and his smart friends, all of which Lytton austerely deplored – though it is evident that at times he felt something of the thrill and attraction of this bright tinsel life. 'Everything there [at Monte Carlo] is made out of painted cardboard,' he told Swithinbank (9 March 1906); 'the palm-trees are cut out of tin, there is always a band playing, and one feels as if one ought to be in tights and spangles.' As for Alfred Plowden himself, he struck Lytton as being one of the silliest creatures he had ever come across – 'a sort of hopelessly non-existent character who simply walks about on the stage and vanishes into space when no one else is there', he described him to Duncan Grant (7 April 1906). 'A Personnage de Comédie, I think, pure and simple.' And in a letter to Maynard Keynes he remarked (2 April 1906): 'It's really quite painful to feel as superior as I do to him. He even feels it himself. Poor man!'

Shortly before Alfred Plowden left, a rather absurd incident which took place on the railway platform suggests that the glimmerings of some mute sympathy might have arisen between them. 'I saw him to the station the other evening,' Lytton recounts (8 April 1906), 'and as we waited for the train the fearful noise of the croaking frogs made him say, "I wonder what they can be doing?" I couldn't help bursting out with, "I think they *must* be copulating." The Police Magistrate did smile.'

Undisturbed by the comings and goings of his various relations, Lytton preserved an invariable daily programme during his stay. 'I spend the days here pretty lazily,' he informed G. E. Moore (28 March 1906), 'though I have breakfast at a quarter to eight. I write a few reviews, and spend the rest of the day having tea with ladies of sixty.' In fact he wrote just two pieces for publication in these weeks – his essay on Blake which appeared in the *Independent Review*,[2] and a long

---

[1] Alfred Plowden, a first cousin of Lady Strachey's, was a tremendously celebrated figure in the popular press during the early years of the century. Like Mr Justice Darling, he was famous for the jokes he made in court, and readers of the halfpenny papers could find them quoted almost every day. His daughter Pamela, a great beauty and the first love of Winston Churchill, married the second Earl of Lytton who was for a time acting-viceroy of India.

[2] Published in May 1906. On 7 April, Lytton wrote to Duncan Grant: 'With some difficulty and agitation I finished my review of Blake. It is for the Independent, and will I hope appear in the May number. It annoys me to think of the poor result of so much effort. After it was finished I felt worn to the bone – a 'poor, pale, pitiable form', as he says himself. But I'm now more or less cheerful again. My dear, he's certainly equal to the

review of Augustine Birrell's *Andrew Marvell* for the *Spectator*. Much
of his morning was given over to the writing of letters – to G. E. Moore
on Society matters, filial and fraternal letters to the family assuring them
that Dorothy Bussy, then about to bear her first child, was being
properly looked after, patriarchal letters reassuring his aunt, Ethel
Grant, about the supposed degenerative influence of Paris on her son
Duncan, affectionate letters to Duncan Grant, and letters about affectionate letters to Maynard Keynes. But perhaps the most surprising
part of his correspondence on this holiday was with Edmund Gosse.
Lytton's critical essay on Sir Thomas Browne, which had given him so
much trouble to compose during December, had been based on a
volume of Gosse's, recently issued in the 'English Men of Letters'
series. In January he had written a second anonymous review of this
book, rather more disparaging to Gosse, for MacCarthy's *Speaker*. It was
the substance of these two articles that formed the basis of their ensuing
correspondence. In Lytton's view Browne's works, unlike those, say, of
Byron, were not of the kind which needed, in order for them to be
properly appreciated, a biography of the author to serve as commentary.
'The Glasgow merchant who read through *Don Juan*,' he wrote, 'and
asked at the end whether the author was a married man was surely in
need of some enlightenment.' For writers like Browne, on the other
hand, it was sufficient to know that they had lived, and Gosse's book
would have gained if it had told its readers 'a little more about Sir
Thomas's style and a little less about his sons'. Chronologically,
Browne belonged to the seventeenth century but his idiom had much in
common with the Elizabethans. What could be more futile, then, than
to seek for simple constructions and homely words in the pages of
Browne's prose? In attempting to do just this Gosse, so Lytton maintained, had attacked the central principle of Browne's style, 'its employment of elaborate and gorgeous latinisms'. Gosse was like a man
who admired the beauty of a butterfly but did not care for the wings:
'To the true Browne enthusiast, indeed, there is something almost
shocking about the state of mind which could exchange "pensile" for
"hanging" and "asperous" for "rough", and would do away with
"digladiation" and "quodlibetically" altogether. The truth is, that there

---

greatest of poets – though I somehow failed to say this properly in my damned review.
His poems are the essence and sublimation of poetry.

> *Poor, pale, pitiable form*
> *That I follow in a storm;*
> *Iron tears and groans of lead*
> *Bind around my aching head.*

Isn't it a triumph? And almost too much?'

is a great gulf fixed between those who naturally dislike the ornate, and those who naturally love it.'

As a correspondent Lytton found Gosse no less uncongenial than as a critic. Perhaps the most interesting aspect in their letters is that Gosse, in defending the use of biography as a legitimate aid to literary criticism, seems to be upholding a far more enlightened principle, which is nevertheless partly contradicted by the example of his own too tactful life of Browne and partly by his over-polite and somewhat cloying epistolary style; while Lytton, dealing deftly with all points of the controversy, writes in a livelier, more amusing and up-to-date manner in order to defend a notion which is incomplete and, in the most deadly sense, academic. In the end perhaps Gosse had the best of the exchange, if only because each of his letters, its contents dull as night, was written on House of Lords cream-laid, extra thick, imperial octavo notepaper, and brought with it an excess charge of fifty centimes. 'I think of replying on an unstamped postcard,' Lytton told Keynes after paying out several francs in instalments, '"this correspondence must now cease."'

Besides writing reviews and letters, Lytton did a lot of reading, sometimes for his work, sometimes for pleasure, but always with the curiosity and fastidiousness of a born bibliophil. 'I'm now reading Lockhart's *Life of Scott*, Blake's poems, and the Correspondence of Voltaire,' he wrote to G. E. Moore (28 March 1906). 'It's a frightful mixture – but if one's a JOURNALIST what can one do? I read the first because I want to have read it, the second because they do me good, and the third because I like it – or because I think I might. How charming it would be to "tear the heart out" of books, like Dr Johnson! That's to say, if one liked hearts. I think I prefer the spinal marrow.'

Of these books, and indeed of all the books he read during this time, his favourite was Voltaire's Correspondence. Letters, he once told Lady Ottoline Morrell (31 October 1916), were 'the only really satisfactory form of literature', because they gave one the facts so amazingly and drew one right into the world from which they had been written. The kind of enjoyment he derived from Voltaire's letters, the gossip and illuminating if often petty idiosyncrasies which brought to life the figures from the past, is well conveyed by a *risqué* passage in one of his own letters to Maynard Keynes (27 February 1906). 'I'm reading Voltaire's Correspondence,' he wrote, 'which is the greatest fun to me imaginable. There's a poor Abbé Desfontaines whom he hated like hell because he criticized his wretched tragedies, and he works himself up into a splendid fury. At first he merely says the Abbé had been in prison; then that it was for Sodomy; then that it was for Sodomy with a chimney-sweeper's boy for Cupid – and so it goes on in letter after letter. At last there comes a little poem describing the rape, and how the Abbé was seized by the police in flagrante delicto, stripped and birched – 20 strokes for sodomy and 30 for his bad verses. It's really all very scandalous; and I think it's pretty clear that Voltaire himself had had affairs.'

One other book which he read during these two months deserves mention. This was *Henry Sidgwick: A Memoir* by A. and E. M. Sidgwick, which had just then been published and was the main subject of conversation among all Apostles. Their impatience with the lack of intimacy in its tone, of boldness in its thought, and of lucidity and crispness in its style, epitomized the dawning twentieth-century revolt against the approved standards of the nineteenth. The free-thinking Sidgwick was certainly a most eminent Victorian, and the Apostles' sharp revaluation of him as man and philosopher has been seen by some as a key to the general change in attitude among all thinking people at about this time. Yet, perhaps because the break with the Victorian age was not complete, the *Memoir* provoked an involuntary fascination in most Apostles. 'I have never found so dull a book so absorbing,' Keynes told Swithinbank. The same note of profound, paradoxical interest is more elaborately sounded by Lytton in a letter to G. E. Moore: 'My last great intellectual effort was the perusal of Sidgwick's life. I wonder if you've read it. I found it extraordinarily fascinating – thought I can't think why, as *every* detail was inexpressibly tedious. I never realized before what a shocking wobbler the poor man was; but my private opinion is that his wobble was not completely honest – I believe he did it because he wanted to, and not because he thought it reasonable. Really his ethical reason for postulating an Almighty is a little too flimsy, and I don't see how an intelligent and truly unbiassed person could have swallowed it. His letters irritated me a good deal – but perhaps you wouldn't find them so. The conscientiousness and the lack of artistic feeling combined occasionally drove me wild. Also the tinge of donnishness – however, I suppose one must forgive a good deal quia multum amavit.'

With Maynard Keynes, who had already read the book and written to him about it, Lytton felt freer to discuss its full implications, the peculiar remoteness which it lit up of those past times from their own new age of reason. Sidgwick was, of course, very Apostolic, but how different he was from them! Obviously Victorianism had incapacitated him. 'What an appalling time to have lived!' Lytton exclaimed in horror. 'It was the Glass Case Age. Themselves as well as their ornaments, were left under glass cases. Their refusal to face any fundamental question fairly – either about people or God – looks at first sight like cowardice;

but I believe it was simply the result of an innate incapacity for penetration – for getting either out of themselves or into anything or
anybody else. They were enclosed in glass. How intolerable! Have
you noticed, too, that they were nearly all physically impotent? –
Sidgwick himself, Matthew Arnold, Jowett, Leighton, Ruskin, Watts.
It's damned difficult to copulate through a glass case.'

After mornings spent reading and writing, Lytton would pass the
rest of the day in more social pursuits. 'Both Aunt Lell and Uncle
Trevor apparently live in a whirl of tea-parties,' he wrote to his mother
in the first week of his holiday. 'Uncle Trevor I believe adores it,
though he pretends to groan and moan.' Lytton, too, while groaning and
moaning quite as loudly, seemed to derive some amusement from this
whirl of social activity, and like a well-conducted person allowed himself on every possible occasion to be taken to all the tea-parties, lunches
and picnics. He went almost daily to the Bussys at La Souco, where he
had stayed two years before, and the house seemed, if anything, even
more delightful. 'You can't imagine how exquisite their tiny garden is –
all intricacies, covered with every variety of growing things,' he wrote
in a letter to Duncan Grant (5 March 1906). 'There are brilliant orange
and lemon trees quite close to the house, and a large cluster of large
white daisies, and clumps of wallflowers. Too divine, and all seen at a
glance in the brilliant sun.'

The Bussys themselves appeared radiantly happy. But Dorothy's
pregnant state disgusted Lytton, and he was vastly relieved once he had
successfully been delivered of a niece, Jane Simone, in the first week of
March. He had always liked and admired Dorothy, though he had not,
until now, thought very highly of her husband. The sudden reversal in
his attitude was another instance of that feeling which so influenced
these post-graduate years – a veneration of the true artist, accompanied
by a complementary abasement of himself as an instinctive yet hopelessly unfulfilled artist. This new response, quite different from anything he had felt in the spring of 1904, is most clearly conveyed in a
passage from one of his letters to Duncan Grant, a passage which also
reveals by implication the twin source of his envious admiration for the
unlettered man of action – another form of self-contempt which had
been paramount at school and university, and would rise again in later
life. 'I admire Simon very much,' he wrote (25 February 1906), 'and I
wish I could speak to him. I think he thinks me lazy – and I am – and
he can't bear the idea of people being lazy. He urged me to begin a
great work. It was a curious moment or two, in the twilight, at the
window, looking out over the splendid Monte Carlo bay. I didn't know
what to do, I couldn't speak French, and, even in English, what could I

have said? – "Allons, Lyttone, allons!" – He was superb, and I was perfectly out of my depth. How could I explain – oh! what I can hardly explain to you – my utter inability to take "art" and "literature" and the whole bag of tricks seriously?[1] . . . I nearly burst out to him – "Je suis obsédé! Obsédé par les personnages!" Only I didn't, because it couldn't have done any good, and the French seemed more than doubtful. So it ended up in an awkward silence and I went away half in tears.'

With Simon Bussy, too, he discussed in detail the problem of whom Duncan Grant should elect to study under in Paris, and how he should plan his year there. It was as a result of their deliberations that he became a pupil of that excellent teacher, Jacques-Emile Blanche.

Before the other inhabitants of Menton, Lytton could resume his mask of incredulous superiority. The English residents in particular used to give him many fits of the giggles. In a mad helpless sort of way, the congregation of 'characters' struck him as really too grotesque – fit only for the pages of Flaubert. Never had he come across such an appalling corporate mass of dullness, especially at those tea-parties which the dowagers of the place gave twice an afternoon with unfailing zest. As if unable to credit his senses, he went again and again, and even extracted a soothing, soporific contentment from their unvariegated repetition. Perhaps he was 'seeing life'; perhaps it might all prove good material for some dramatic comedy he would later compose and which would carry all before it, making him and his friends millionaires.

'Oh heavens!' he wrote to Duncan Grant after staggering away from the first of these gatherings (25 February 1906). 'All the females were so much alike that I hardly knew whether I was talking to complete strangers or to the Countess [Pallavicino] or Harriet [Codrington] herself. Mrs Hodgson is a relief, as her nostrils are apparently amputated, so that I can recognize her pretty well. But Miss Scott, and Miss Egerton, and Miss Duparc! – They have all long red noses, they are all 45, they are all hopelessly respectable and insufferably cheerful.' Most eccentric of all these bright-nosed quadragenarians was Lady Dyer, a cross between a vicar's wife and an ex-governess, invariably dressed in a long velvet cloak with fur edges and a round yellow straw hat trimmed with pale mauve chrysanthemums. Lytton rather recoiled from the forceful personality which went along with this bizarre uniform, and 'came to the conclusion finally that she is a complete vulture. Her red

---

[1] In a later part of this letter, which was written the following day, Lytton added a significant amendment. 'I find that I didn't quite say what I meant last night, about my not taking "art" seriously. I suppose I do, in some way or other, though not in the way that "artists" do. But I can't quite make out what exactly I mean.'

Lytton Strachey reading *State Trials*: portrait by Duncan Grant, 1909 (*The Tate Gallery*)

James Strachey: portrait by Duncan Grant, 1910 (*The Tate Gallery*)

Lytton and Pippa at Rothiemurchus

Giles Lytton Strachey

pointed nose and her moulting fur added to the effect.' But from out of this matronly gynaeceum, it was Miss Egerton – 'a pretty terrific female, 38 wishing to be 28, with a long red nose which shoots triumphantly over the abyss' – who finally established herself as the most formidable. She took to reading Lytton's palm, and to conducting him on 'bracing expeditions' or forced marches along the coast. Having heard of, though not read, Bernard Shaw, she soon confessed to being cleverer than most people in Menton, and graciously allowed that Lytton might be almost as clever as herself. This, however, may only have been flattery, since she had written an article on the 'Holy Land' which she had illustrated with photographs of her own, and she hoped with Lytton's aid to get it accepted by the *Strand Magazine*.

The men of Menton were even odder than the women – mostly plain, old, paralysed majors. By far the most redoubtable of this troupe were Mr Bax Ironside, a distant cousin of Lytton's nicknamed 'Mr Iron Backside'; a doddering inhabitant by the name of Stainforth who collected spiders; and Major Horrocks who, though blind, always spotted the lurking figure of Lytton from the very opposite end of every crowded drawing-room, and compelled him like some infinitely decrepit Ancient Mariner to listen to descriptions of his many diseases, eczema especially. Lunacy among the men though was not confined to the English residents, but extended, in an amiable inarticulate fashion, across the Italian border – or so at least Lytton deduced from an encounter with an Edward Lear-like character on one of his few excursions into Italy: 'I strolled into Italy the other day – I honestly believe there's something different in the atmosphere over the border,' he wrote to Duncan Grant (5 March 1906). 'At any rate it's a great change to go from the dreary respectable villas of this side to the cabarets, guitars, singings, and dancings of the other. The comble was reached when I met a highly respectable personnage in overcoat and felt hat, who suddenly drew up in the middle of the road opposite me, and began to jump. The dear man! I really believe I should have joined him, if I had happened to have the wherewithal.'

When he was not flirting with virgins of fifty or encompassed by the military, he took himself off for solitary patrols along the shore, side-wise, like a crab, with his face to the sea and his back to the mountains. At other times he would lie out on the terrace at the Villa Henriette, gazing blankly over the still, blue limitless Mediterranean – 'any colour from peacock to an incredible *pâleté*' – in a state of the merest collapse and too lazy even to feel ashamed of himself. Below, in the bay, he watched a huge steam yacht belonging to the Rothschilds, and dreamt of owning it himself, of christening it *La Belle Espérance* and floating out in it over purple seas for ever and ever, with his chosen companions, reading Voltaire and drinking champagne. How abominable that it didn't belong to him; how mean life was. His weariness with humdrum reality and with the humdrum people round him quickly stimulated his appetite, which, once gratified, brought on recurrent attacks of dyspepsia. 'I can think of nothing nowadays but the next meal,' he confessed to Keynes; yet after only a boiled egg and a cup of coffee he suffered acutely. Nevertheless he showed himself resolute in risking further discomfort, and never permitted himself to miss even the most lugubrious or unappetizing luncheon- or dinner-party. Though his general health had certainly improved since leaving London, his digestive system, for no obvious reason, remained 'indescribably infamous'. He enjoyed good food tremendously, yet he was now meticulous as to what and how much he ate, even to the point of giving up the delicious French coffee which he loved so much, for cocoa, which he did not like and which, in addition, did him no good. In fact none of his gastronomic sacrifices seemed to help. Indigestion stubbornly persisted. Each morning he woke starving, and at night went to bed famished.

This vicious circle of tedium and sickness, which held him tightly in its grip for several weeks, aggravated his moods of loneliness. Though life was sometimes dreary without those 'quasi-intimate pseudo-crises' which used to fire him with nervous, thrilling spurts of energy, there was, he told himself, no case for falling into despondency. Yet it was difficult not to when one had no digestion. 'I shudder to tell you that I am 26 today,' he wrote to Duncan Grant on 1 March. 'Can you bear it? I hardly can, but I shall do my best to disguise the truth. I should like to be your age, and I really don't think there's much difference between the me of now and five years ago.'

In his brooding state, Lytton grew hungry for more Cambridge gossip, eager to exert some distant influence, revivifying to himself, on the Apostles. His letters to Keynes, Ainsworth, Moore and others are written as from an imaginary outpost to the central point of Reality. Yet despite this anxiety for news, he felt little wish to quit the torpid amenities of Menton for the cold, Christian shores of England. 'I gather from the papers that it's snowing in England,' he wrote to Keynes on 14 March. 'Why does anyone stay in that blasted country? I have had to draw my chair under the shade of an olive tree, for fear my complexion might be ruined. Venez, venez vite!'

Keynes, in fact, was then on the point of leaving England. Both he and Lytton had been invited by the Berensons to 'whirl through Italy in a motor-car' and to put up at their villa, I Tatti, at Settignano. Lytton had 'judiciously declined', but Keynes accepted with alacrity, and the two of them arranged to meet for a few preliminary days in Genoa before Keynes went on to join his hosts. And so, in the third week of March, Lytton boarded a steamer at Monte Carlo, which, he told his mother (20 March 1906), 'was packed with Germans who talked at the tops of their voices to each other without intermission; but there was an old American who came up and talked to me, telling me his life history, etc. How he had made his pile, and was now travelling with his wife and daughters. He told me that he thought Europe was a very interesting place, and that he reckoned the Mediterranean was one of the oldest seas on this planet. I agreed; but when he went on to say that in his opinion the gambling rooms at Monte Carlo exemplified Our Lord's saying as to the danger of building houses on the sand, I felt obliged to demur. His final conclusion was that I was "a lord in disguise", and I didn't deny it.'

The only completely satisfactory moment of the whole expedition was, in Lytton's retrospective judgement, the steamer's entrance into the harbour of Genoa, the weather being brilliant and the spectacle very splendid and gay. For the remainder of the time the wind blew and blustered and the rain poured down incessantly, so that he was especially glad to have Keynes to talk to in the dark interior of the Hotel Helvetia, where they spent many hours together. On the whole Lytton preferred these hours to the hours of sightseeing, feeling that he would have been quite content to stay for ever in those Helvetian recesses, eating omelettes – which he was now able to digest properly – and discussing ethics and sodomy with Keynes. Some sightseeing, however, was deemed compulsory. 'The palaces were simply écrasant,' he wrote to Duncan Grant (26 March 1906). 'We felt like miserable marionettes, beneath their vast and endless bulks. The staircases were particularly incredible. I tried to imagine Marchionesses, etc., sweeping up them, but could hardly believe that they'd ever reach the top. The pictures were mostly of the Bolognese school, and they certainly didn't come up to the Roger Fry level. But among the 40,000 that we saw in the 40 palaces that we went into there were about 6 which it would have been delightful to have.'

These few days in Genoa with Keynes rather unsettled Lytton. On his return he felt more keenly than before the limitations of his life at Menton. Silence and dimness prevailed in such a manner that he seemed to have become immured himself in one of those appalling Victorian glass cases. Everything was so negative and spinsterish. He made up his mind to work – and did nothing. Accompanied by his invalid aunt he was solemnly driven round the 'Battle of Flowers', was pelted by every hand, and pelted back as hard as he could. But it was a depressingly chaste affair. All the while he gazed out eagerly for a decent-looking boy, and saw not one.

About this time he received an invitation to join Moore's Easter reading-party which was to take place later that April in the Peak district, but, though longing to see Moore, MacCarthy, Sanger and the others again, he reluctantly decided to remain in France, chiefly for the sake of his health. If only he could empty Villa Henriette of his relatives and fill it with friends and Apostles! That would be ideal – to hold the reading-party under the roof of blue Ionian weather. What talks, what stories, what laughing and singing there would be! And when the stars came out and it was time to be romantic, what adoration, what tears and ecstasies under those warm Aegean nights with nothing to think about but Beauty and Love! But all this, of course, was hopeless day-dreaming. The reading-party would foregather in the wind and the rain – and he would not be there. 'I have now decided to stay on here till the beginning of May, so that I'm afraid it's impossible,' he replied apologetically to Moore (28 March 1906). 'The sun and the Dowagers of Mentone have proved overpoweringly attractive; also, I am here, and the strength of inertia contributed to hold me rooted. How could I make up my mind to face the snows and whirlwinds of the Peak, with the peacock-blue Mediterranean spread out under my nose? The die is cast; I have "extended" my return ticket; so that I am no longer a free agent – a mere pawn in the vast and weaving strategy of Messrs Cook. I hope other people will be less faithless. Will you write and tell me what happens – where you go, and who goes, etc.? I long to hear all about it.'

No sooner was his decision irrevocably made than he began to regret it. The prospect of another month at Menton with his aunt weighed heavily on him, though he had no choice but to go through with it now. 'I begin to talk to myself as I believe prisoners do in solitary confinement,' he confessed to Keynes (8 April 1906). The only conversation he could enjoy was through letters; and of these there were all too few. Without the correspondence of his friends, he seemed to withdraw altogether from the living world. Above all he longed in vain for some warm words from Duncan Grant, and felt increasingly depressed at not being able to do anything himself but express his sentimental affection by post. For all this, there was only one compensation: the calm, ominously unsensational routine of his life must, he felt convinced, be doing him a power of good. Like all restorative medicines, the taste was unpleasant, but the cumulative effect would be most welcome. The absence of all active emotional strain and stress was so excruciatingly dull that it *had* to be beneficial.

That was how matters stood when, early in April, Duncan Grant did write. It was a short letter, but it had something cataclysmic to communicate, which 'I suppose I must blurt out as fast as possible. Duckworth as you know has been staying here and I have fallen in love with him and he with me.' This, he hurriedly went on, made no difference to his friendship with Lytton, and he hoped that Lytton himself would not feel differently. He signed himself 'your ever loving Duncan'.

The immediate shock numbed Lytton. He knew that Duncan wanted to be reassured about his reaction, but he secretly believed that this mad, totally unforeseen development would in fact make a real difference to their friendship. It was true, of course, that they could like each other as before, and even go through, as before, the dreary phantasmagoria of desire. But they could never be *alone* together. In what he described twenty-four hours later as 'a hysterical letter', he wrote back to Duncan Grant: 'I think you may think me cruel, or sentimental – or both; especially, I think, if the "you" is in the plural number. – No, no! Don't be angry! Think of me, please, as a poor damned daffed human being, but a human being still, who would give his ears to be talking to you. Good heavens! I occasionally burst into fits of demoniac laughter to think of the incredible muddle of everything and everybody.'

At first Lytton appears to have been overcome more by wild, incoherent pandemonium than actual unhappiness. He wrote at once, of course, to Maynard Keynes to break the news to him in a letter which is longer and even more excitable than the one to Duncan Grant sent by the same post. 'I'm still gasping,' he admitted. 'I don't know what to feel – I only have the sensation of the utter unreality of everything, and even this blessed landscape, when I look at it, seems to waver in a wild mirage. God forgive us all! What a hideous muddle! – I have wept and laughed alternately and at the same time, wildly, hysterically, ever since I read it. Oh, how I long to talk to you! I think what I mainly feel at present is a sort of stupor. I have subsided; I'm waiting to see what will happen next.'

For some days this stupor persisted. He still didn't know what to think. Perhaps it was altogether too bizarre to take very seriously, a mere insane episode signifying no more than an added twist in the grotesque abortion of their lives, which would make no palpable difference to anything or anyone, unless, that was, he became simply a maniac in jealousy. In any case Dicker and himself hardly figured as rivals. The notion was too ludicrous. Or was it? At times he felt as if he knew nothing, as if he was losing his head. The whole thing seemed lunatic from beginning to end, more vicious and chaotic than anything that ever happened in the world before. He felt as though he had heart disease. His pulse beat deafeningly through his body, and rocked him to the very spine like the recurrent vibration of a pneumatic road drill. It took his breath away. He wanted to laugh and cry simultaneously – why he scarcely knew. 'As I walk along the road here I want to collapse among the passers-by in one heaving ruin of laughter,' he wrote to Keynes; 'and sometimes I do burst out. They stare, but if they could only know the whole story – the whole incredible, impossible, inexhaustible complication – well I suppose they would collapse too.'

But after a few days this precarious, artificial euphoria slumped, and Lytton was overpowered by a purgatorial hangover. The whole affair now sickened him. It occurred to him that it really was a drawback to the 'New Style' of love that the chance of complications should be exactly doubled. No doubt Christians would hold that this was the right and proper punishment for unnatural emotions. However, perhaps the added amusement made it worthwhile. He still burst into uncontrollable fits – but there was little happiness in his laughter, only a stunned incredulity. For really there was no sense in any of it. At this rate no one would be able to remember off-hand who was meant to be in love with whom, or whom, indeed, they were supposed to be in love with themselves. The permutations and combinations in the constantly changing molecular structure of this kind of loving were without limit or logic. But what hurt more than anything else was the realization that Duncan Grant, who he had thought really loved him in his own strange, undemonstrative fashion, in fact felt no more for him than an amiable attachment, though this was in itself so good that it almost made up for everything. And his depression was deepened by the discovery that Duncan's more intense feeling was directed towards someone of whom he, Lytton, disapproved.

Duncan's revelation plunged Lytton back again into the baffling intrigues of human affairs from which he had originally escaped to the South of France. At one blow the soothing dullness of Menton was exploded. 'This place is so vilely relaxing that I believe it's undermining my health,' he explained to Duncan. 'I get tired very easily, and the other night I had the most horrid palpitations.' In a half-hearted sort of way he was longing to see Duncan in Paris again, especially since Duckworth was returning to England. But he did not know whether his arrival would embarrass Duncan, and in any case doubted whether he had the courage to tell his aunt that he wanted to leave. Two days later, however, his physical and mental condition had deteriorated so markedly that it provided a legitimate excuse for his return. 'My health is completely shattered,' he wrote to Keynes (15 April 1906), 'and I cannot stay here in relaxation and solitude. . . . Anyhow it is now *certain* that D is not and was not in love with me. I dare say in our old age we'll come together again. His charmingness in his letters is incredible, and I love him à l'outrance.'

Later that same week Lytton left Menton, but on the train northwards his fever rose dramatically. On reaching Paris he got off and dragged himself round to the Hôtel de l'Univers et du Portugal, where he at once retired to bed and summoned a doctor who prescribed quinine in large doses to bring down his soaring temperature. 'I am here,' he announced to Keynes after a few days in bed (23 April 1906), 'I think recovering, but I have been very ill. How I got here I hardly know; my weakness was complete, and my depression almost absolute. I fear my health may be appallingly weakened. But at the moment I'm better.' Nevertheless he looked so wretchedly ill that his sister Pippa was sent for to escort him back on the remainder of his journey home. No sooner were the two of them ready to depart, however, than a railway strike crippled the whole of Paris, and they were obliged to stay on a further week.

This was for Lytton a time of uninterrupted torment. He woke up each morning in tears, wondering what he had to live for. The Society? It was a poor substitute. Sometimes his frail, supine body was convulsed with a terrible anger when he reflected on the way things had turned out; and sometimes he lay there too exhausted to be angry any more. In his fevered state, he thought a lot about Dicker, and wondered what there could be in him to damage everyone so devilishly. There was something aphrodisiac about the role he had played in all their lives – a grain of love-powder that worked hell. And once again his circling imagination was drowned in a sea of horror – his own rich ineptitude and Dicker's rewarded folly. But why think of him? Duncan was doing enough of that. But even as he attempted to expel these sick and infected wanderings from his mind, an unexpected letter arrived from Dicker in England. It said nothing much; but how the handwriting shocked Lytton, rekindling his excitement when first he saw it on a letter addressed to himself. What a muddle it all was! What a muddle!

Each day Duncan would come up to his room, sit at the foot of his bed, and talk. He was kind, amusing, gentle, considerate – everything up to the very verge of what Lytton wanted. But it was not the Duncan he used to know – the boy in the orchard at Great Oakley, or during those wonderful few days at Ledbury, or the young painter in his romantic studio in Hampstead, or even, less than two months back, up those forty-two flights of stairs in this same hotel. He seemed larger and stronger, irradiated no doubt with visions of Dicker. Never could

Lytton have believed that he might actually come to fear his presence, and long to escape from it. How ironic it was that every evening at Menton he had looked forward to these few days in Paris! They were, so he recalled, to have been the happiest of his life!

But abruptly his mood would change. And 'then I know what a fool I am, what a miserable fool, for why should I be distracted and humiliated and lost? Why should I madly beg for strange unwilling kisses, and be happy for a moment amid that warmth and that diminutive sweetness? Why should I cast you from me with horror and mortal anguish, and with unsatiable adoration, and with intolerable desire? Oh yes, I know you are Duncan still.'

By the first week of May, Lytton and Pippa were at last free to return home. 'I'm rather wrecked, and fear all sorts of doctorings and wretchednesses may be necessary,' Lytton wrote to Keynes shortly before leaving. At the Gare du Nord Duncan came to see them off, and was given an embrace by Lytton. They travelled by easy stages, spent one night at Dover, and the next day were re-engulfed into the noise and gloom of London.

5

INFLUENCE FUNESTE

The doctorings and wretchednesses that Lytton had predicted continued for about three weeks, during which time he seldom, if ever, moved beyond the portals of Lancaster Gate. The family physician, after examining him thoroughly, came up with a new diagnosis and course of treatment. 'My health is I think improving gradually,' he was able to report by 16 May. 'Poor old Roland seems to be doing his best. He says that my disease is that there is not sufficient room in the lower part of my torso for my lungs, liver and lights, so that they are liable to press in an inconvenient way upon the heart, which is in itself superb. The cure is to be a course of terrific "exercises" of the most ghastly and depressing type, which it is hoped will expand the frame to a more reasonable size. I haven't begun this yet, but in the meantime am allowed to drink nothing at meals, as liquid'll do nothing but wash away all the nourishing matter. . . . My depression is usually pretty heavy, but I suppose it will improve with health.'

But the recovery of health did not automatically bring about a rise in his spirits. The worst aspect of these weeks was not so much his physical ailments as the continual incarceration with his family and their friends. Family life, he told Swithinbank, was very bad for the nerves. He did

not feel at one with them – they were too violently 'outside', as he
called it. For in his leisure time he had evolved a new theory to the
effect that there were two sets of lines in life – the inner and the outer.
The outer was safe and dull; the inner was exciting and dangerous. On
the inner circle were such figures as Blake, Leonardo da Vinci and, a
good deal more than was comfortable for him, Lytton Strachey. On the
outer circle were Holbein, Pope and the rest of the Strachey family.

Much of this spring was spent in bed. Between the drinkless meals
and terrific exercises he tried his hand at writing a short story, but his
enthusiasm quickly cooled, and the piece was never completed. He
wrote copiously to his friends, some of whom were able to come and
visit him. But he was more amicable on paper than in person. When
Desmond MacCarthy offered to introduce him to Max Beerbohm, he
declined on the grounds that he had no wish to be infinitely bored.
Maynard Keynes also came and visited him, staying a couple of nights
at Lancaster Gate. But Lytton was critical of his friend, and when
Pippa remarked that she thought Keynes was growing old too rapidly,
he felt inclined to agree with her. 'I'm afraid,' he wrote to Duncan
Grant with a hint of prophetic foresight (16 May 1906), 'that in three
years I may find it impossible to speak to him [Keynes].' As yet,
however, there was no one remotely suitable to take his place. 'You are
the only person I can speak to,' he assured Keynes again in October.
'Pippa is unconscious. And my mother!'

In the final week of May, as soon as he felt robust enough to get up
and go out, Lytton dashed off to Cambridge where he felt sure that he
could count on some scandal to revive his spirits. Whenever he stepped
into that train at King's Cross, he was reminded of some lines from
Baudelaire:

> *Je m'avance à l'attaque et je grimpe aux assauts,*
> *Comme après un cadavre un chœur de vermisseaux.*

At Trinity he spent five heavenly days with all his old friends and
associates – Harry Norton, Dillwyn Knox, Walter Lamb, his brother
James and Maynard Keynes who appeared in a rather better light
against these more amiable surroundings. Indeed everything seemed
more enchanting than before. Cambridge was more beautiful now than
ever it had been when he was an undergraduate. But then it was always
fatal to live in a place: one must keep continually on the move. At one
point during this visit he caught sight of Dicker, looking, he thought,
rather unhappy. Altogether, it was an entirely satisfactory week, and he
enjoyed himself immensely. 'It was delightful to feel conscientiously
lazy,' he wrote to Duncan Grant (31 May 1906), 'and to glide about in

the canoes among the lilac and laburnum and horse-chestnuts, and to watch the cricket, and to eat strawberries, and to talk about whatever one liked.'

He was now working again, too, at his essay on Johnson, a review for the *Spectator* of J. C. Collins's *Studies in Poetry and Criticism*, and, for MacCarthy's *Speaker*, an article based on J. E. Farmer's *Versailles and the Court under Louis XIV* – which, wrote the Indian scholar K. R. Srinivasa Iyengar, 'concludes with a description that could have only been inspired by a personal visit'. Lytton had found this book waiting for him on his return to Lancaster Gate and after glancing through it, wrote off to Duncan Grant: 'I have been sent rather a fascinating book to review – on Versailles and the court of Louis XIV. It is full of plans and pictures, and I think it ought to be amusing to write about. I hope, with the aid of your descriptions, to be able to make it appear that I have constantly been there. The poor deluded public!'

Health and spirits, he had reported from Cambridge, were good. It was far easier, he had discovered, to concentrate on his work at Cambridge, and he returned there in the second week of June, following this up with a brief spell at Oxford. By the middle of the month he was back again in London. 'I lead a mostly unconscious life,' he told Swithinbank (4 June 1906), '– I think it's the effect of summer in London, which appears to me purely phantasmagorical.'

There was something reanimating about each sally forth from London. On 21 June he set out again, this time in company with his sister Pernel, to stay at Thena Clough's house, Burley Hill, in the New Forest. Also staying there was the brilliant A. W. Verrall who lectured at Cambridge on English and mediaeval literature, and who, Lytton wrote to Swithinbank (22 June 1906), 'talks almost perpetually with wonderful animation; it's more champagny than Raleigh's though I think less supreme; and one only has to listen and put in an occasional word'.

Once more he bobbed back to Lancaster Gate, and once more he was off again on another tour – first to Cambridge where he was 'able to finish Versailles quite comfortably', and then on to visit Bertrand Russell, at Bagley Wood, Oxford. 'We have been, of course, amazingly brilliant here,' he informed Pippa (9 July 1906). 'The only other guest is an American lady literature professor (also Quaker), who is nice, cultivated, etc. Bertie informs me that he has now abolished not only "classes" but "general propositions" – he thinks they're all merely the fantasies of the human mind. He's come to this conclusion because he finds it's the only way in which to get round the Cretan who said that all Cretans were liars.'

By this time he had been sent by the *Spectator* a new book to review – *Pastoral Poetry and Pastoral Drama* by W. W. Greg – and so, instead of returning again to London, he proposed to go once more to Cambridge. 'With luck,' he told Pippa, 'I think I ought to be able to manage a *Spectator* review while I'm at C. I find it easy to write there, and the conversation is encouraging.' The disadvantage of this plan was that, not being in London in the second week of July, he would have to miss Desmond MacCarthy's marriage. It was not that he would particularly have relished this performance, but that he feared MacCarthy might feel offended by his non-appearance. To mitigate this risk he determined to send him an especially acceptable wedding present – a beautiful warming-pan – but at the last moment his courage failed him: it seemed so utterly useless.

That summer the Stracheys had rented Betchworth House, near Dorking, a large country mansion with a magnificent long gallery, and standing in park lands which enclosed a trout stream, golf course and tennis courts. Here Lytton lingered for seven painfully domestic weeks, surrounded on all sides by his family, visited by Maynard Keynes and Harry Norton, and working on his essay 'Mademoiselle de Lespinasse' for the *Independent Review*. Another of his friends was now getting married – Lumsden Barkway, who wrote to invite him and Lady Strachey to the wedding in London. His letter brought back a great many old memories of the Liverpool and early Cambridge days, and 'I couldn't help reflecting', he replied (21 July 1906), 'that, though there are many bitter and horrible things in life, there are always one's friends to make up. I write nonsense, but you understand and agree.' In this case there was obviously no chance of honourably avoiding the ceremony by means of an expensive present, all the more so since Lady Strachey would not leave Sir Richard who, now in his eighty-ninth year, felt uneasy whenever his wife was absent. Besides, as a companion Lytton had that rare and endearing gift of remembering the past, and rather looked forward to seeing Lumsden Barkway again, even at his wedding. His single day in London, however, was the only excursion he made away from the family during these summer weeks.

The thought of being drawn back to Lancaster Gate again to spend there, without interruption, the darkening autumn and winter months, was full of the usual horrors, and Lytton eventually decided to make a peregrination into the extreme north of Scotland, staying with Clive Bell and his family who had gone up there to fire off guns at Scotch animals. At least this would be a month's break from the gloom of Bayswater, an invigorating if not particularly lucid interval.

He set out from London on 9 September and stopped off for a day and a night in Edinburgh, staying with G. E. Moore and A. R. Ainsworth at 11 Buccleuch Place. 'Moore', he reported, 'was quite cheerful, and played most of the Eroica with the greatest verve.' The next day's journey north to Lairg, his eventual destination, was not without terrors. The train was so late at Inverness that there was no time for lunch, and he was able to eat nothing but a bun and a banana between breakfast at Perth, and dinner at Lairg itself. He had also given up all hope of finding his luggage, which had disconcertingly vanished at Inverness, but which, to his incredulous relief, was magically waiting for him as he rolled into the Lairg platform. He was met at the station by a gay and wonderfully golden-bearded Clive Bell, sitting, like Toad of Toad Hall, at the wheel of a dangerous-looking motor-car;[1] and together they whirled away for twenty tremendous miles over breakneck roads through absolute deserts, lakes, mountains and sunsets. 'The motor drive was somewhat terrific,' Lytton afterwards wrote to Pippa (11 September 1906), '– the road is decidedly dim, and one bumps and leaps and shrieks as I imagine one might on a buck-jumper. But the fascination of the movement is intense, and I am glad to say that every journey has to be made on it.'

The Bells appeared to be camped in a tiny 'shooting-box', set loftily on the edge of Loch Merkland. As for the family itself, Lytton's first impression of them was that they were all hearty, dumb, deaf and, except for shooting, quite blind. Yet, curiously enough, he felt that the long journey had been abundantly justified. 'We are on the edge of a loch, high up, on Ennick heights, with nothing but moors and mountains for 20 miles in any direction,' he wrote to Pippa the day after his arrival. 'Lairg is 22 miles away, and there is only one house between here and it. The country is exquisite, with vast long lakes streaming one after the other, and beautiful pale hills. It is quite unlike Rothiemurchus – far less distinguished of course, but also far more completely remote and inhuman. The house is quite small, mostly made of tin, and entirely lined with pitch-pine walls, floors and ceilings . . . I intend secretly to have a shot at a stag, or at any rate to try to, before I come away. Everyone is very "hearty", and one's appetite is too.'

After ten invigorating days at Lairg, Lytton travelled south to Feshie Bridge, to join Maynard Keynes, Harry Norton and James Strachey for what has been called 'a last wild excess . . . of talk upon the old subjects'. Here, in a cottage about six miles south of Inverdruie, the four of them had found rooms, from which they would set out on terrific excursions into the mountains – one of them, to Ben Muich Dhui, being

---

[1] Professor Quentin Bell tells the author that Lytton was probably inexact in giving this description. Clive Bell never did and never could drive a car.

at least a twenty-five-mile walk as well as a stiff climb. Lytton also hoped to undertake a comprehensive tour of the Western Highlands, but none of his companions were keen, and he was forced to abandon the scheme. 'I could find no one adventurous enough to share the perils,' he complained to Moore, 'and what are perils unshared?' Early in October therefore he returned to England, breaking his journey again at Buccleuch Place.

Presently he was back at Lancaster Gate, and his old routine of life re-asserted itself at once – an occasional theatre, a general state of debility, and frequent encounters with his friends, chiefly MacCarthy, Norton and Sanger. 'What a vale of desolation is No 69!' he exclaimed in a letter to Keynes; but there seemed no further way of escaping it. He quickly resumed his essay-reviews – on Walter Scott for the *Speaker*, on W. P. Ker's *Essays on Medieval Literature*, and Sidney Lee's *Shakespeare and the Modern Stage, with Other Essays* for the *Spectator* – and at the same time recommenced his shuttling back and forth between Cambridge and London. 'I have been to Cambridge once this term,' he wrote on 12 November to Moore, whom he had agreed to accompany to the great annual feast, Commem, 'and am going there again next week. The Society seems to be going on all right. Keynes is constantly there. No very promising embryonics seem to have appeared yet, though I have some secret hopes of the young Charles Darwin.'

The even tenor of his life was abruptly shattered, when on 21 November he read an announcement of Thoby Stephen's death in *The Times*. 'I am stunned,' he wrote immediately to Keynes. 'The loss is too great, and seems to have taken what is best from life.' The following week he was invited by Vanessa and Virginia Stephen to their home at 46 Gordon Square and told all the details: how Thoby on holiday in Greece had been suffering from what was supposed to be pneumonia, but how his illness had turned out to be the fatal typhoid. To all three of them, who had known him so very well, such a fate seemed even now impossible. The monolithic, the immortal Thoby dead – it did not, despite their certain knowledge, ring true. But Maynard Keynes, who had known Thoby mainly through Lytton's legendary accounts of him, wrote: 'He seems to me now, I don't know why, the kind of person who is doomed to die.'

Lytton was now seeing a lot of Keynes, who had just come down from King's convinced that he was far and away superior to the examiners who had dared to place him only second in the Civil Service examination. At the end of November he stayed a few days with Maynard and the Keynes family at their home in Harvey Road. The two Cambridge exiles planned to spend part of December together in Paris, where Keynes could get to know Duncan Grant better, but since Lytton would not receive payment for his last batch of reviews until January and Keynes had not enough money to pay for them both, they decided instead to go for a week to Rye, putting up at the Mermaid Inn where Lytton had some years previously taken Sheppard. 'The inn is comfortable,' Lytton wrote to Saxon Sydney-Turner, 'but the weather cursed cold. We go out for duty-walks in order to get up appetites for too-constant meals. I am halfway through the Brides' Tragedy; as you said, it's not a patch on the Jest Book[1] – but it has some superb things. – "I've huddled her into the wormy earth!"'

Shortly before Christmas, Lytton returned to Lancaster Gate. After finishing *The Brides' Tragedy*, he now turned for the first time to Charles Darwin, and was enthralled. During the next month or two he read nothing but the works of Darwin, whom he came to consider one of the greatest stylists in English literature. Huxley, whom they all praised so, was a signboard painter in comparison. 'I'm reading the Descent of Man,' he wrote to Duncan Grant on 30 December, '– it's most entertaining, with any number of good stories about Parrots, Butterflies, Capercailzies and Barbary Apes. The account of how the Peacock grew his tail is a masterpiece. But the chief charm is Darwin's character, which runs through everything he wrote in a wonderful way. I should like to show you some passages in his Autobiography – really magnificent! He was absolutely good – that is to say, he was without a drop of evil; though his complete simplicity makes him curiously different from any of us, and, I suppose, prevents his reaching the greatest heights of all.'

This discovery of Darwin was the single bright spot to a year which closed for Lytton in much confusion and anguish. His sickness during these final days of December came as the last and mildest of a series of indigestion attacks, palpitations of the heart, high fever and piles which had plagued him on and off throughout the autumn. These ailments seem to have been closely associated with his emotional upsets, the cause of them being, once again, the presence of Duncan Grant, who had returned to England for a few weeks' Christmas holiday. Lytton's feelings on seeing him again fluctuated wildly, he told Keynes, between '(1) Excitement, (2) Spiritual affection, (3) mere lust, (4) Intellectual interest, (5) jealousy, (6) Boredom, (7) Despair, (8) Indifference.' And of all these moods the most prevalent was despair. Although he saw Duncan fairly often, they were seldom if ever alone together. Nevertheless, at many of these meetings, Lytton felt that he showed with horrible

[1] *The Brides' Tragedy* (1822) and *Death's Jest Book* (1850), both by Thomas Lovell Beddoes.

transparency the repressed and surging effervescence of his emotions. He tried to speak to him about important things which concerned them both, but failed miserably. And all the time Duncan appeared utterly uninterested, perhaps even unaware of the hideous turmoil going on within him. From the cruel phlegmatic way in which he seemed to avoid his company, Lytton felt sure that he must still, after all these months, be enraptured with Dicker. He found it difficult to understand how someone of such intelligence could have lost his judgement so completely. His faith was being put to a severe test, and his hopes dreadfully postponed. But then, he reflected, perhaps he was wrong to think of it in this light. It was the nature of one's passions, not their object, that counted. Then, once more, his mood would shift, and such philosophical evaluations would appear superficial and irrelevant. Everyone seemed to possess some strange compound element within him, which baffled analysis and turned intellectual judgements into dreams. He and Duncan and Keynes were like characters in Shakespeare – the Hamlets and Cleopatras, whom no one could fix down with neat thumb-nail definitions.

As the days and weeks of autumn slipped by, merging into winter, the weather grew colder, the attacks of one illness or another more acute, the emotional frustration increasingly desperate, and Lytton felt that he had reached about the end of his forces. He was weak, and his torments of mind and body were more than a strong man could bear. He could neither sleep nor work, and physically he was reduced to a wreck. 'I am really ill,' he insisted from his sick-bed in a letter to Keynes, '– too ill to go round to you, as I should like to do. What will happen to me? My body was hideously bouleversé and still is. Oh God! I have suffered too much.' After each one of his visits Duncan would stalk out of Lancaster Gate without either a special look or word for Lytton, leaving him to brood with miserable indulgence on the traditional subject of suicide. Of course he didn't want to die, but how exactly was he to continue living as things were? That was the question. Possibly he was afflicted by a peculiar psycho-somatic condition – *rabies amantis* he would call it – which could be cured only by going to sleep for a long long time. That was what he would like to do.

'I have never known such anguish,' he told Keynes. 'What can ever make up for it?' But this question, as he admitted to himself, was without real meaning. Even in the lowest depths of his unhappiness he did not regret his feelings because they had brought him sorrow. That was the sin against the Holy Ghost – to blaspheme one's best affections, which were one's Holy Ghost. His outpourings to Maynard Keynes were cries for comfort from the agony of a paradise lost:

Me miserable! which way shall I fly
Infinite wrath, and infinite despair?

There was the true meaning of his question. How to extricate himself
from the seemingly inescapable trap into which he had fallen? His
infatuation flourished under a disillusion continually deferred. Duncan
Grant's elusive incuriosity and apparent coldness inflamed his unhappy
passion which was at some moments sublimated in renunciation, at
others overcome by a frenzied desire kept in circulation through
perennial restraint. His impotent wrath and despair intermingled and
formed the main content of his letters to Keynes: 'That that little devil
should despise me, and with justice, is my lowest infamy,' he wrote on
28 November. 'That he should register my tears, and dishonour my
abandonments, my failures, the miserable embraces I can't withhold! –
That he should say that he pities me perhaps! – I want to shake the
universe to dust and ashes! Hell! Hell! Hell!'

In dramatic contrast to the wild, stormy emotionalism which rose
behind the dams of his everyday self-discipline and flooded over the
pages of his almost everyday letters to Keynes, is the circumspect,
diffident moderation of his correspondence over these same weeks with
Duncan Grant himself. From these two concurrent and complementary
sets of letters one is given not only a reflection of Lytton's peculiar
duality, but also unequivocal evidence of the vain, obsessive shyness in
his outward manner which has helped to spin the popular misconception of him as a dry, passionless, sublimely detached cynic, someone set
aside from the current of life. He could never convey his love directly
by statement or expostulation to the person loved. Instead of railing at
his cousin's cryptic unresponsiveness, he merely expresses a vague and
somewhat timorous wish that he could talk to him more. Of course, he
adds hastily, it is no one's fault – the world itself is hardly made for talking.

Once this tone is set, the correspondence swiftly slides into a welter
of mutual self-recrimination. After one unsuccessful encounter – at a
family dinner at Lancaster Gate – Lytton writes to apologize in case he
may inadvertently have said something – anything – during the course
of the long dismal meal to offend his feelings. If he has been hurt,
Duncan must forgive his, Lytton's, insensitive stupidity; if not, then
he must forgive these superfluous and troublesome apologies. Whatever
the case, Lytton demands forgiveness. Duncan, however, doesn't
remember being pained, and is sure that Lytton would never hurt or
offend him. Perhaps, he suggests, he had failed to comprehend something. Incomprehension can, physiognomically speaking, resemble
pain – doesn't Lytton agree? In any event he himself intended to write
to apologize about his beastly behaviour the previous week at a picture

gallery they had visited together. He had felt out of sorts – and the pictures hadn't helped. But probably Lytton, with that incomparably generous nature of his, had already forgiven him. Anyway, it was of no special significance and Lytton must not, he begs, bother to answer this note.

Lytton's reply comes by return of post, expressing his gratitude both for the letter itself, and for the knowledge that his mania for inferences has led him astray. But he is horrified at Duncan referring to his earlier behaviour as beastly. On the contrary it was he, Lytton, who was at fault. He ought to have overcome his wretched sensitiveness – no, *selfishness* – and saved Duncan from feeling that he had been beastly. There had been nothing wrong at all except circumstances acting on his ridiculous nerves.

The tussle for forgiveness and for the onus of blame now warms up. Duncan at once counters Lytton's claim of selfishness with the plea that he himself is without a sense of humour. Not alone that, but he had got into the absurd way of crediting Lytton with special powers of telepathy, of knowing things automatically without being told them. This had, in fact, once led him to be enraged at a joke Lytton made about Dicker, with whom he was still hopelessly in love, but whom he was trying to forget. He saw now though that, even if Lytton had known the truth, it was foolish of him to have done anything but laugh. In his answer Lytton once again quickly shoulders all the available blame. He had got into the habit, he explains, of making jokes at serious things; it relieved (to his mind) the heaviness of existence; it was like the drops of lemon on a pancake. He was truly sorry for what he had said, and was pained at Duncan having been – legitimately – enraged with him. Was it only a blind tantrum? Perhaps the whole affair was more complicated than that. 'I'm afraid', he wrote, 'that it may have been something more – that you may have thought, perhaps, that I didn't really care. Your not being certain that I realized that you were still in love with him makes me think this too. I don't want you ever to think of my feelings, but I did hope that you simply *knew* how much I cared.'

The last unforgiving word in this particular series of exchanges belongs to Duncan Grant: 'My brutality was rather a bitter return for your perfect goodness. When I look back and see what I have ever given you in return for it, I nearly collapse at my perfect unworthiness. O! Lytton I really mean it, when was there anyone so unselfish and noble as you. If it weren't for you I am sure I should not be able to bear life now.'

The labyrinthine pattern of Lytton's emotional life seemed to be set irrevocably in the original passions and inspirations of the past. True, Thoby had gone – but his need for a distant pedestal-hero was now less urgent than before; and besides, Thoby would later be replaced by

George Mallory, the handsome mountaineer also fated to die young, who, so the unlikely story goes, once prevented the Trinity bloods from ducking Lytton in the college fountain. The brief reappearance in London of Duncan had proved to him, if proof were needed, that the other figures remained as dominant as ever – fixed points between which he was suspended, and the sudden disappearance of which could quite possibly bring about his own extinction. At any rate he could see no one as yet to take their place. 'What will happen to me?' he had asked Keynes; and so far as he himself could tell, the answer was, Nothing. He would continue living with the family at 69 Lancaster Gate; he would continue visiting Cambridge; he would continue his career as journalist, writing occasional articles and reviews for various papers; and, above all, he would continue revolving like a half-dead satellite round the far-off Duncan Grant and sending out irregular, incoherent messages to Keynes. That was all. What else could there be?

Duncan Grant had disappeared back to Paris on 19 January without saying good-bye. The next day Lytton wrote to him: 'Last night, when I came down to dinner and saw that you had taken away grandpapa's portrait, I knew that you had gone, and was utterly crushed. It was all I could do not to burst into tears at dinner, and afterwards Mama asked me if I was ill, and I nearly gave way altogether.' A few days later his misery, bewilderment and sense of loss arranged themselves into a sonnet, 'The Enigma', which he composed while walking between Piccadilly and the Charing Cross Road. It is highly characteristic of all Lytton's versifications in its form, rhetoric and the type of indeterminate outspoken innuendo which he was so fond of using to record the crises of his love life:

> *Oh, tell me! – I have seen the strangest things:*
> *I know not what: beginnings, threads and shears.*
> *And I have heard a moaning at my ears,*
> *And curious laughter, and mysterious wings.*
> *Have friends or angels tricked me? Oh, what brings*
> *This river of intolerable tears*
> *Over my soul? And all these hopes and fears?*
> *These joys, and these profound imaginings?*
>
> *Will no one tell me? Ah! Save me, it seems,*
> *The puzzle's plain to all. I am as one*
> *Who wanders in an unknown market-place,*
> *Through bustling crowds with business to be done.*
> *Vain are my words, and my conjectures dreams.*
> *I cannot greet the unremembered face.*

CHAPTER VII

Intentions

'The dangers of freedom are appalling!'
Lytton Strachey to Duncan Grant (12 April 1907)

I

JOURNEYMAN WORK

The year 1907 was to see the first successive links in a tightening chain of events that, during the course of the next eighteen months, would completely split apart Lytton's old routine. No sign of these dramatic changes, however, was evident in the quiet, predictable beginnings to this year. Soon after Duncan Grant had returned to Paris – 'that DAMNED TOWN' as Lytton called it – he himself left for the Homeres at Chipping Norton. The chief advantages of this move were two: first, he was less likely to be tortured by reminders of the absent Duncan; and secondly, he was afforded better opportunity to concentrate on a memorial essay which his mother had asked him to undertake on her old friend, and his godfather, the first Earl of Lytton. At Kingham he was given a little upstairs sitting-room where, alone with 'Venus',[1] he remained quietly working at the essay, his various *Spectator* reviews, and, of course, his correspondence to Duncan Grant, without whose 'incredibly kind' letters he felt he would fade away into nothingness. As it was, he had become little more than 'a doddering old hermit, . . . the Diogenes of Kingham – to whom Cambridge is a dream and even London no more than a tale that is told'. Why were dreams, he wondered, so much more heavenly than actual life? Crouching over the hot gas fire, carrying on his involved epistolary conversations with Duncan instead of pounding on for the *Spectator*, his spirit seemed to vaporize and re-form into someone else, someone who could do and say all the things a woman was able to do and say. If only he had been a woman! But alas . . . ! Yet, in these misty, androgynous trances he was perfectly contented. He wanted nothing else from the world, 'and I really think

---

[1] 'Venus' was the name of Lytton's fountain-pen, so called because, to make it write, he had to twist the bottom of it, which caused the nib to rise from the waves.

that if I had three wishes, I should wish for three fires – one behind me and one on each side of me – as hot as the one in front'.

His methodical seclusion at Kingham, however, was repeatedly invaded in the most unplanned and disturbing fashion. The Homere sisters, noticing his wistful, melancholy expression, straightway concluded that he must be unhappily in love with the beautiful Vanessa Stephen who, shortly after the death of her brother, had become engaged to Clive Bell. It was Ianthe – 'who always talks about interesting things' – who came out with their suspicions. Lytton shrilled with amazed laughter, at the same time secretly wondering whether it ought not to be as they imagined. But then, what was one to do? These distant meditations were soon brought up short by the passionate advances of Angelica Homere, the nymphomaniac youngest sister and a prime beauty, who, inflamed by a sudden, quite pointless jealousy, flirted with him so boldly that Lytton grew terrified lest she might get carried away to the point of actually launching a physical assault upon him. He was thus obliged to play an unaccustomed though ironically familiar role – that of Duncan Grant to her Lytton Strachey. Indeed, he believed that it was only by the most stringent severity that he managed to ward off a scene *à quatre diables*. Even so, the things she insisted on saying, despite his so visibly expressed fury! The dialogues he failed to avoid!

Angelica: Will you be in London when I'm there in March?

Lytton: I'm afraid I shall be in the country on a visit.

Angelica: Oh dear! I had looked forward to seeing you so much. . . . D'you know that you're perfectly beautiful?

Lytton (casual and unmoved): Of course. I've always known that.

Angelica (in tears): Do you hate me very much?

Towards the end of his stay in 'Homereland' he wrote to Keynes: 'I have done no work but my health has improved tremendously. I can't go to C. this week, as I must commit myself to my godfather with the utmost stringency. What a bore!'

While he was still at Kingham, a letter arrived from Desmond MacCarthy announcing that later in the year he expected to be appointed literary editor of a periodical to be called *The New Quarterly*. This was excellent news, and spelt out the first real change for Lytton in his career as journalist. He would, MacCarthy told him, earn about one hundred pounds a year from his commissions, and the work would be pleasant – that is, he would not have to write about anything or anybody who did not interest him, and there would not be much to do. The time, Lytton felt, might then come for a bold stroke – if he could muster up the courage. He wanted to sever altogether his rather loose connexions with the *Spectator* and, in the intervals between his *New Quarterly* contributions, devote himself to some major literary work. He would reconstruct his *Warren Hastings*, and, more exciting, compose a play – a tragic masterpiece on Queen Elizabeth. And then, of course, he would have to live apart from the family, on whom, at the same time, he must still remain to some extent dependent financially. The trouble was that the family prospects were in a worse way than they had ever been. The Secretary of State for India – 'honest John Morley' as Lytton sarcastically used to call him – had refused point-blank to grant Sir Richard Strachey a pension, and no one knew what was to happen. Things were certainly breaking up. Yet MacCarthy's letter, in spite of all the problems and obstacles which it spotlighted, cheered Lytton immensely. It was the starting-point of something new, something for which he must even now prepare himself. 'I am trying to shake myself free of most of my entanglements,' he wrote to Dorothy Bussy, 'and when I've succeeded in doing so – ho! for the chef-d'oeuvre! At times, though, I feel as if I shall never be free. My hope is to eke out a subsistence with the aid of a New Quarterly Review which MacCarthy is going to bring out, and by that means to have time for masterpieces in the intervals.'

Soon after his return to London, Lytton saw Desmond MacCarthy and they discussed in more detail the new paper which MacCarthy hoped to edit. 'It's probably to be called the London Quarterly,' Lytton wrote to Duncan Grant after this meeting (11 February 1907), 'and may possibly come out in July. I had a long talk with MacCarthy about it the other day, and I'm to lunch with him today for more. He's a very wild editor, but he's cheerful and seems to believe in me. The publisher is Dent, who will do it free of charge in order, MacCarthy thinks, to get the reputation of dealing with first-class literary gents.'

Although nothing was yet firmly settled, Lytton felt that he ought to inform St Loe Strachey, his cousin and editor of the *Spectator*, of these plans. 'I interviewed him in his office,' he wrote afterwards to Duncan Grant (21 February 1907), 'and told him that for the present I should not review any more books for him – the first step towards Liberty! He was most gracious, and said that if ever I wanted to begin again he'd be charmed to let me.' He also invited Lytton to call on him at Herbert House, his London home – a large, archetypal Victorian mansion, with faded carpets, red plush curtains and coloured glass chandeliers – where he lived with his wife 'Oriental Amy' and where he was visited by a *bourgeois* group of hangers-on including the 'dull and vulgar' Sidney Lee. 'Poor dear old St Loe strikes me now as a trifle *épuisé*,' Lytton commented to James shortly afterwards, 'with moustaches more than ever fading, and even spectacles (when no one's there). Amy is *une matrone* in blue silk with amber necklaces. . . . I went in some trepidation to call at their grand Belgrave Square mansion, but when I got there found such a *bourgeois* little group – Sidney Lee, and Mr and Mrs Skinner – all in laced boots, and hardly a frock-coat between them.' Finally, as a result of these meetings, it was mutually agreed that Lytton should, after all, continue his occasional reviews for the *Spectator* until his appointment as a regular contributor to MacCarthy's new paper actually came into effect.

2

CAMBRIDGE PEOPLE RARELY SMILE

As if to emphasize his new hopes of liberation and literary achievement, Lytton at once embarked on a succession of London gaieties – lunch at the Savoy, dinner at the Carlton and the Ladies' Athenaeum, a French play, a performance of *The Gondoliers* and *The Marriage of Figaro*. The hostess on all these occasions was that noble woman, Lady Colvile, who succeeded in introducing into Lancaster Gate while she was staying there this spring a new air of festivity. 'In the intervals of these orgies,' Lytton confided to Duncan Grant, 'I hope to finish my review of Lord Lytton for the Independent, but it's damned difficult. I lay on the butter as thick as I can – there's such precious little bread.'

The one topic of conversation among the Stracheys at this time was the first large-scale demonstration which the Society for Women's Suffrage was to stage in their nation-wide campaign for emancipation – three thousand ladies proceeding from Hyde Park Corner flanked by mounted police, to be harangued by leading zealots at Exeter Hall, in what subsequently became known as the 'Mud March'. Lytton's sister Pippa, who was later to win fame and distinction as the dynamic secretary of the Fawcett Society,[1] had succeeded in commandeering the services of both family and friends to assist with the organization of this parade.[2] James Strachey and Harry Norton were summoned from Cambridge to waft the ladies to their places in the hall; Keynes was conscripted to help marshal them in the park; and even the ineffectual

[1] For her work as secretary of the Fawcett Society, Pippa was awarded the C.B.E. in 1951.

[2] Mrs Fawcett was leader of the constitutional movement in favour of women's suffrage – a movement going back to John Stuart Mill. It was only fairly recently that Mrs Pankhurst and her supporters had started up a society which employed non-constitutional methods to gain the same objective. The Stracheys were old friends and colleagues of Mrs Fawcett, but they deplored the behaviour of Mrs Pankhurst and the Women's Social and Political Union.

Swithinbank was fetched up from Oxford to act as a supernumerary volunteer. Pippa controlled all, and interviewed the police at Scotland Yard daily. She actually persuaded the apprehensive Lytton to join the men's league for the promotion of female suffrage, even though he considered the whole thing rather a bane, and, at its worst, distinctly alarming. 'I believe the ladies will try to forbid prostitution,' he complained fearfully to James; 'and will they stop there?'

The grand procession was held on the second Saturday in February. As the crucial date approached, Lytton realized that he was not going to be able to face it, and fled away to Cambridge for the week-end. But here, too, he was solicited by inviting women, being asked to tea at Newnham with Mrs Sidgwick,[1] 'a faded monolith of ugly beauty, with a nervous laugh, and an infinitely remote mind, which, mysteriously, realizes all'. He also saw those of his friends who had managed to escape Pippa's vigorous enlistment – Sheppard, Walter Lamb, and Dilly Knox, about whom he had by now completely changed his mind. 'His beauty was transcendent, and his feelings seemed to me superb,' he wrote after seeing him just once during this week-end.

Under Pippa's astounding management the Suffrage procession went off without a hitch, and once it was safely over, Lytton felt safe to return again to Lancaster Gate. His quick, bird's-eye view of Cambridge had rather depressed him. He really must not allow himself to go there again until it was warmer. The cold had been preternatural – arctic nights, and days of frost and slush – he was not warm once the whole time. And the discomfort and untidiness of James's room which he occupied! – fires faint and few, draughts from every quarter, and the appalling sight of James's half-demolished breakfast with its broken eggshells and spilt tea over the table to greet him on arrival and again each morning when he rose at twelve from his icy bed. If only it were still his own room, the chaos would not have been so distressing. But it wasn't his, so that nothing was done for him, and, left unaided to put the coals on the fire, he was unable to find a shovel, the tongs broke, and he was finally obliged to bend down and prise out each black lump with his long, trembling fingers. It was a nightmare. Even the miraculous divinity of Knox had not atoned.

For once then he was happy to go back to London. The round of dissipations started up again with Aunt Lell, and for a short time Lytton was 'as cheerful as a Kangaroo'. Life could really be exciting! Those

---

[1] E. M. Sidgwick (1845–1936), the widow of Henry Sidgwick, who become president of the Society for Psychical Research, a body concerned with making scientific investigations of such phenomena as telepathy and seances. Though not a spiritualist, she eventually became convinced of the probability of survival after death.

waiters, for instance, at the Carlton! He almost fainted when they bent over to serve him with vegetables, brussels sprouts and peas and roast potatoes. Back at Lancaster Gate, however, everything was drab and dim. The lack of conversation grew increasingly overpowering, especially after the family dinner when there seemed no prospect ahead but silence until one tottered to an untimely bed. That silence, that grim, gray, arid silence, was so heavy that he was seriously tempted to make another mad dash for Cambridge. But the force of inertia and a sense of duty combined to keep him steadily at work. Result: a *Spectator* review on Herbert Spencer. Other disasters soon threatened. First the boiler burst making Lancaster Gate almost as cold as Trinity, and then his aunt Hennie arrived – 'a dreadful worry, but still a distraction'.

The subject of all this worry was the final, reluctant decision of the family to leave Lancaster Gate. The news left Lytton feeling curiously empty. Liberation had come too late. For twenty-five years the place had lain like an incubus upon his spirit until it had now become an indissoluble part of his whole scheme of things, interwoven with the very fabric of his nature. To leave Lancaster Gate and all that it stood for – such a thing seemed scarcely possible. As with the death of Queen Victoria herself, it appeared as though some monstrous reversal in the course of nature was to take place. He had never known a time when the great brooding mansion was not looming over him. But now he was simply told that the upkeep was too expensive for the family to sustain with their depleted fortunes – a common-sense explanation which hardly matched the significance of the change. Lady Strachey had decided that they should move later that year to a spacious, dilapidated house in Belsize Park Gardens, Hampstead. 'There is a basement billiard-room,' Lytton wrote to Duncan Grant after inspecting the new house for the first time, '– the darkest chamber I've ever seen in my life, and without a billiard table. Your mother, mine and I found ourselves locked into it, and thought we'd be discovered three crumbling skeletons – forty years hence. Fortunately I was able to leap a wall and attract a caretaker.'

Towards the end of February Lytton did return again to Cambridge, this time to spend some three weeks in the more luxurious rooms of Walter Lamb, who was away in hospital. He was determined to enjoy himself more than before, and looked forward especially to seeing Rupert Brooke, who, despite everything, was probably the best of the younger set – though this did not say much for them. As it turned out, however, he saw little or nothing of Brooke on this occasion, and a good deal of Harry Norton and Dillwyn Knox, whom he now nicknamed Adolphus, after Benjamin Constant's hero. Following several long conversations with the serious-minded Norton, he came to the conclusion 'that he's DOOMED. It seems to me that he lacks will (just as I do, of course, and James, only it takes us in a different way) and that the end of it will be simply the Solicitor's Office, a wife, and £60,000 a year. He hasn't the will to disentangle himself from his own webs – just as J. and I haven't the will to entangle ourselves in any web at all.' It was queer how helpless everyone was about everyone else. People were unimpingeable units whirling on fated courses, and one could no more deflect them than a ghost. Their souls were so solid that flesh and blood seemed shadows compared to them, and an outstretched hand in contact with a moving spirit melted to nothing.

In company with Knox, on the other hand, Lytton at first seemed to make contact with something more substantial. It was a relief to talk to him after the DOOMED Norton. Their conversations, of course, were pitched on a less elevated intellectual plane, but then what one actually articulated was really unimportant, since the only things that counted were so mysterious and impalpable that it would take an Ibsen or a Henry James to unravel them and get them down. What struck him immediately about Knox was his resemblance to Swithinbank; and he was confronted with all the same difficulties in their relationship – the embarrassments, the lack of keen cerebral grip, the tantalizing fascination. To take just one example: one evening they held a discussion on the relative merits and demerits of sapphism and sodomy – a fruitful subject, Lytton should have thought, under almost any circumstances. And yet, though it was taken up as the most natural thing in the world, it simply petered out after a time into a dim miasma. Knox was as charming as ever – but it just wouldn't do. Lytton could see his future all too clearly; he'd be elected a Fellow of King's soon, and waste away his life in blind academicism. It came to this: he simply wasn't *intellectual* – and even Bob Trevelyan, *even Walter Lamb* was that. It was a relief to talk to the DOOMED Norton after one of his discussions with Adolphus. What a dreadful business conversation was! So many remarkable contingencies were necessary to make it anything but intolerable that it was surprising it ever did come off. The worst of everything was that with advancing years (and he was twenty-seven now) it did not seem – to him at any rate – to grow easier or more amusing. Perhaps he should be thankful it did not grow less. As for seriously comparing Knox with Swithinbank, it was out of the question. He hadn't the same subtlety of feeling, the same divine discontent or cosmic dissatisfaction with life, or that wonderful impassioned atmosphere which sometimes transfigured Swithin. Although he did not command a major part in Lytton's life, it was agreeable to think of

Swithin occupying a supporting role – a role which, at least as yet, Knox had no chance of challenging.

Lytton's failure to strike up any new important friendships, or to extend the boundaries of his old associations during these Cambridge weeks, came as a serious setback. The world was one vast negative, he reflected, and he was its full stop. Why then did he still hang about Trinity? There was no startling new embryo, no Rupert Brooke. 'I linger on vaguely from day to day,' he confessed to Maynard Keynes (27 February 1907), 'partly in the dim hope of excitement, and partly from being too lazy to pack. I see now, though, very very clearly that nothing will ever happen, and that life is all a cheat.'

But if there existed no positive excitements, there was still a fairly continuous stream of activity. Apart from day-to-day conversations, some solitary writing, a few lectures by McTaggart and other old familiar figures, and lightning week-end visits by Charles Sanger, Bertrand Russell and others, Lytton prepared and read out before the Society two long papers. The first of these, 'Was Diotima right?', is a reasonably orthodox analysis of the relation of truth and beauty to the nature of reality, and demonstrates once again, that, though Lytton might be a revolutionary in sociological matters, he remained pretty conservative in his attitude to the arts. The same basic division is revealed, too, in his second and more interesting paper, 'Do Two and Two make Five?', in which he contrasts the Platonist and Aristotelian views of the world. Coleridge has held that every man is born an Aristotelian or a Platonist. He did not think it possible that anyone born an Aristotelian could become a Platonist; and he was sure no born Platonist could ever change into an Aristotelian. They were two classes of men, beside which it was next to impossible to conceive a third. Plato considered reason a quality or attribute; Aristotle considered it a power. With Plato ideas were constitutive in themselves; with Aristotle they were but regulative conceptions. He could never raise himself into the higher state which was natural to Plato, in which the understanding is distinctively contemplated, and, as it were, looked down upon from the throne of actual ideas, or living, unborn, essential truths. Dryden, says Coleridge, could not have been a Platonist – Shakespeare, Milton, Dante, Michelangelo and Raphael could not have been other than Platonists. And Lytton Strachey? He does not seem to have known Coleridge's dictum and goes some way to setting himself up as the third, to Coleridge inconceivable, type of man – the Aristonist or Platotelian. Strachey, the scathing iconoclast and anarch, came down firmly on the side of Aristotle, equating reason with power; Strachey, the delicate impressionist critic and biographical craftsman, favoured the more imaginative Plato. As William Gerhardie has advocated, the term 'Aristotelian' might justly and with literary advantage become pejorative; and since Lytton, too, never believed that the primary value of literature was to the state as opposed to the individual, the two irreconcilable attitudes continued in their uncertain joint possession of his mind. On the whole, however, since it is much easier – intellectually speaking – to be a revolutionary than an artist, his Aristotelianism predominated, though deep within him there lay obscure immortal longings – faintly echoed in his essays on Blake, Beddoes, even Gordon and elsewhere – which this ruthless, matter-of-fact creed never touched.

The sorrowful state of the Society reflected the general negation and decomposition of Cambridge life, with its switch from literary and speculative to Fabian political preoccupations. The Apostles had entered one of their usual phases of crisis. No unanimous decision could be reached about new embryos, and there seemed every likelihood of Norton and James being the only undergraduate members in the next year. It was a doleful prospect – the DOOMED Norton; and James, sunk in appalling gloom and radiating an atmosphere of apathy and oppression that ate into one's very bones. His fundamental disease, in Lytton's estimation, was that he could rouse himself to take no interest in anything but the few people he admired or was in love with – which, of course, was simple Death. Phlegmatic as a sponge, he just sucked up interminable pain and despondency. It was dreadful to visit him in his rooms, like coming across one's past self, horribly objectified and parodied. The poor creature seemed quite unable to think, or read or work at all. Instead he spent all his time dreaming over a solitary fire, which eventually went out because he was too dilatory to put on more coal. There was not much to deserve all this agitation, to Lytton's mind – he wished there had been! Yet how easy for good looks and fair hair to stir up passion, if one hadn't the energy to overcome it. Laziness had become an inveterate habit with James. The very contemplation of anything difficult was poison to his system and brought on a complete collapse. Already, at twenty, he didn't appear to have adequate stamina for the slightest exertion, and made no positive use – even as an analgesic – of his mind. It was at any rate a mercy, Lytton often reflected in his own moments of adversity, that one was not a mere machine of nerves, that one possessed, after all, something of an intellect. This, he felt, was the great stand-by, perhaps in the long run, when desire would fail and the voice of the grasshopper would become a burden, the *only* worthwhile thing – though one hardly liked to dwell on that.

It was all pretty sickening, and yet Lytton felt as if he could never drag himself away from Cambridge. The beauty and the sunshine and the comfort were entrancing. But perhaps the real fascination of the place lay in the endless possibilities of adventure which might come off – and never did. Probably he took too black a view of the New Cambridge, with all the fresh and likely young men taking up politics and leaving the Apostles high and dry. In any event the one significant effect on Lytton of this change in the university climate and of his failure to enter into the life of the freshmen with their open-air socialist zealotry, was to strengthen his determination to lead a new independent life of his own, a life of literary dedication. 'As for me,' he wrote to Keynes (16 March 1907), 'I am thinking of retiring, once and for all, into Private Life. I am going to pull down the blinds and put up the shutters, and commit my mind to the manufacture of chefs d'oeuvre. I shall appear sometimes of an evening, and make a jest or two very much à la Adolphe himself, and then I shall retire, as the clock strikes twelve, to my lucubrations. The truth is the Younger Generation is too much for me. I don't pretend to understand it any more, and it can do very well, I must imagine, without me. If I let my mind dwell on some things, I get into a state – I don't [know] what – I feel almost as if I . . . was out of date. However, it's very easy to pull down the blinds, and that's what I shall do. And it's not only easy, it's delightful. I am unimpassioned, I am free, I am Adolphus.'

At last, in the third week of March, Lytton tore himself away from Cambridge and went on for a few days to stay with Desmond and Molly MacCarthy in their country house, the Green Farm, Timworth, near Bury St Edmunds. This turned out to be a large farmhouse, partly uninhabited, with a somewhat decayed garden, and fine flat sweeping fields of turnips and cabbages all around. The newly married Mac-Carthys had only recently taken possession of the place so that things were not as comfortable as Lytton, in his luxury, had hoped and expected. The meals, for one thing, were never punctual; and the fires, for another, were always going out. It was exasperating – and yet somehow he managed to amuse himself. Poor dear Desmond, of course, was incomparably dim, but his affable company was pleasing enough for a short duration. They talked much about the new periodical, about Bernard Shaw, and modern poetry, and whether the *Nation* was better than the *Speaker*, and in the evenings they strolled round the splendid park near by, with its great lake and wood. This was the part of each day that Lytton enjoyed best, the domestic inconveniences forgotten amid the beautiful dream-like landscape – the wide stretch of water with the light on it, and the surrounding forms of trees vanishing away in haze. He was enchanted. His walks there during these warm, gentle evenings were like precious moments stolen from the rush of Time; and, being timeless, they would remain for ever in his memory.

Indoors there were distractions from boredom of a more trivial and humorous kind. Molly MacCarthy's mother, Mrs Cornish,[1] was also staying with them, a capricious eccentric of iron whim, some description of whom, Lytton reasoned, might amuse Duncan Grant. She was, he wrote (23 March 1907), 'incredibly affected, queer, stupid and intelligent. She flowed with reflections on life, and reminiscences of George Eliot, and criticisms of obscure French poetesses who flourished in 1850. She was damned difficult to answer though. What is one to say when a person says – "Ah, isn't it delightful to think of all those dear animals asleep around us?" Do you know her remark to an Eton youth when he was introduced to her? "Oh, Mr Jones, has it ever occurred to you how very different a cow is from a thrush?" I dare say she's mad, and I'm pretty sure she's a minx, and a minx of sixty. "Can't one tempt you to Eton, Mr Strachey? You'd find all Walpole's letters in the library, and a great many delightful boys." What was one to say to that?'

3

HEART OF DARKNESS

From the MacCarthys, Lytton hurried back to Lancaster Gate – but not for long. He was already deep in complicated negotiations with G. E. Moore about another Easter reading-party. The problems were endless. Where should they go? Yorkshire would almost certainly be too cold; Lytton could still vividly recall the snowstorms of two Easters ago, and those vast slabs of salt beef at the Crown Hotel. What about the Lizard once more? 'I long to see the charming place again,' he wrote to Moore. But Penmenner House had unfortunately been snapped up by a party of Christian young men, and so was quite out of the question. Eventually they engaged rooms at Court Barton, in the village of North Molton, near Exmoor in Devon. The intricacies of choosing 'the elect of the elect' were even more difficult than usual. Too many people would distress Moore; too few would distress the landlady. And they must be the *right* people. Moore would naturally bring Ainsworth, as always; and, as always, Lytton would bring James.

[1] Blanche Warre-Cornish, daughter of William Ritchie, was the author of two long novels and a rather tame monograph of R. H. Benson – Corvo's 'Bobugo Bonsen' – the Catholic writer and apologist.

But after that the composition of the party was uncertain. How could they make sure that Duckworth, for example, was given the impression – without any actual lies being told, which would be unethical – that there was to be no reading-party that year? How to ensure that Bob Trevy did not stay the full three weeks? Would MacCarthy come at the last minute? Then what of Saxon Sydney-Turner and Ralph Hawtrey? And how, on top of all these dilemmas, to fit in Norton and Keynes?

This last question was simply one of timing. Norton and Keynes could only join them for the last ten days, since they had decided to spend a week beforehand in Paris, together with James. Lytton thought this an excellent scheme. They ought, he said, to do the thing *en grand seigneur*, and put up at the St James Hôtel in the Rue St-Honoré. This would be comfortable, close to the Louvre, fairly cheap, and frequented by friendly English people. What could be better? Norton and James were silent, but Keynes gently demurred. Perhaps, he suggested, it might be even cheaper, even more comfortable to stay with Duncan Grant at 22 Rue Delambre near the Boulevard Raspail. And Lytton was at once enthusiastic. What a splendid idea! Why hadn't *he* thought of it? – especially since that very week he had written to Vanessa Stephen urging her 'to look up my little cousin, when you're in Paris'.

He saw the three of them off at Charing Cross station, and returned home to dream of the wonderful holiday they would be enjoying together. It gave him a stab of keen vicarious pleasure, this day-dreaming, heightened by just a shade of mild melancholy. He was particularly anxious that Keynes and Duncan should get on well, that Keynes with his dry, unimpassioned aloofness should not bore or irritate poor Duncan. What a party they might have! He saw visions of them all crowding through in the Louvre, or lingering among the fountains and the oranges, the bronzes and the marble gods which he had described but never seen at Versailles, or perhaps looking over the Pont Neuf at the Seine, or again, if it were warm and the sun were shining, wandering in the Tuileries Gardens where Mademoiselle de Lespinasse walked not so very long ago and in the evening went to hear the same *che farò* that they might hear that very night. Lytton's only fear, so he told Duncan Grant, was that they might fall into the hands of the police. If they did, then of course they must at once telegraph him so that he might busy himself collecting certificates of character and of good conduct from various people – Duckworth, Walter Lamb, himself and others. In any case Keynes, with his multifarious connexions, would be quite safe, as he could get the son of a bishop to swear to his exemplary behaviour while at Eton. Duncan would be let off as an artist; and no one could look at

James and find him guilty of any conceivable crime. So that poor Norton was really the only one of them in danger, and he, very probably, would be excused as an *Anglais fou*.

Such titillating speculations delighted him. Now that Keynes had quitted King's and was languishing on his stool at the India Office, Lytton certainly felt more kindly towards him. Poor old Keynes! It really was more like the old times now that he was suffering under adversity. He felt closer to him than for many months. Yet this was to be the last flicker of a largely extinguished affection. The check to Keynes's progress was only momentary, and soon enough good fortune was to shine down on him again. More successful mountain-climbing would follow, and, if that were not enough, more golf. By June 1908, when he resigned from the India Office to take up a lectureship at Cambridge, his role as Lytton's Brother Confessor had already been partly taken over by James. And before the following March, when Keynes was elected a Fellow of King's, the substitution had been completed. The triumph of Keynes was assured, and the old intimacy between the two friends never fully recaptured – another change in the pattern of Lytton's life that even now during this trip to Paris was, with amoeba-like slowness, gradually moving into place.

The reading-party at North Molton opens in the final week of March and lasts three weeks. Within its limitations – of comfort, warmth, good company but no love – it is one of the most agreeable gatherings Lytton has ever attended. 'Inconceivable, quite inconceivable, is the beauty of the weather,' he writes to Duncan Grant (1 April 1907). 'I'm sure the earth has given itself a twist, so that we've all become demi-tropical. I haven't seen a cloud for the last fortnight, it's been endless sun and splendour, and now that the habit has been acquired I really think it must go on. This country is in the region of Exmoor (except that there is no moor to be seen), and I like it, with its rolling hills vanishing away to the horizon, and its valleys with streams and trees in them, and its general air of health. We are in a farmhouse, touching a church, and there are some rather nice turkeys to be seen strutting about and gobbling outside my bedroom window, and there is plenty of Devonshire cream at meals, and there are a good many amusing (and instructive) books, and there is a piano which Moore plays in the evening.'

In short, the mild tranquillities of Court Barton are all that mild tranquillities can ever be – there is the happy certainty of a 'surplusage of beef and Devonshire cream' to be disposed of by country walks; there is a village shop with bull's-eyes in it; there are two sitting-rooms and a garden; and upstairs there are feather beds and books. Perhaps the

Apostles are made for mild tranquillities and second-hand regrets. Perhaps their business is to read novels and to go to sleep in the sun dreaming of masterpieces they will never create. 'In a few minutes we shall all be tramping through the sun. And then more cream, and then more beef, and then somnolence, and then bed – solitary bed.'

Lytton has taken with him to North Molton his Warren Hastings dissertation, intending to prepare the typescript for some future publication. It will, he hopes, form a solid, scholarly cornerstone to his new career in literature. On the average he spends, during these three weeks, one hour a day emending, polishing and re-writing parts of it – much less than he has originally planned. Some of the time which should have been allocated to this work is given over to composing verse, and among the pieces he writes is his longest if not most ambitious poem to date – of about a hundred lines. This composition, which is more readily enjoyable than many of his verses, relates a simple story with an ironic, Pope-like wit and point. Long ago, we are told, a great dearth of things to say afflicted the human race. The situation baffled human intelligence until one day a young quick-minded shepherd put forward a startling innovation. His empty volubility, which illustrates as he speaks the gist of the suggestion he is making, is nicely caught by Lytton.

> O mortals! Would you know the one sure way
> Of saying much when there is naught to say?
> Imitate me! Construct the flowing line,
> With numbers' art your syllables entwine,
> Swell out the pompous verse with stress and pause,
> And govern all by metre's mystic laws!
> Then shall your wandering words move sweetly on
> When the last shred of meaning has quite gone,
> Then empty feet transport you where you will,
> And simple rhythm waft you forward still,
> Then rhyme, self-spun, shall wrap you round and round
> And all your folly vanish in a sound.

This speech, Lytton recounts, was considered at the time to be rank blasphemy, and the shepherd was straightway hanged from the nearest tree by an angry crowd of righteous and indignant citizens. Generations later, however, an altar is erected where this tree stood to the poor shepherd's martyrdom. An amusing description then follows of the new, articulate religion which subsequently flourished there – a mock-exaltation of the staleness and concealed boredom to which Lytton always felt so personally susceptible – in lines which show his aptitude for non-romantic, satirical rhyme.

Here maudlin lovers seeking how to spin
Poetic cobwebs from their faint and thin
Imaginations, found inspirèd aid,
Murmuring nonsense in the holy shade.
Here many a pompous simpleton pursued
Through its dull coils the eternal platitude,
Found out that what was fated came to pass,
That mortal beings perished like the grass,
That all the world was subject to decay,
That he who gave might likewise take away,
That much was known to men, yet more was not,
And naught was certain in the human lot.
Here too would hired laureates fill their lays
With ever-fresh incontinence of praise,
Proclaiming in the same insipid breath
A royal birth, or victory, or death,
Then hymn aloud in strains as void as air
The copulation of a princely pair.

Whenever he is not versifying or labouring away at the Warren Hastings, he will write long letters to his friends describing, for their amusement, how the reading-party was being conducted. 'At this moment Keynes is lying on the rug beside me,' he tells Swithinbank (31 March 1907), 'turning over the leaves of a handbook on obstetrics which seems to keep him absorbed. Norton is next to him on a camp-stool, and it is he who is writing mathematics. Next to him is Bob Trevy, under an umbrella, very vague and contented, and planning out his next *chef-d'œuvre*. I should have mentioned that I am on a basket chair (with plenty of cushions in case of accidents), and that I am perfectly happy, as I am writing to you instead of doing what I ought to be doing, viz., composing a preface to Warren Hastings. . . .'

Most of the time during these first sunny days the party sits out in the garden, Lytton in a panama hat (also in case of accidents) and a flannel open-neck shirt, with a red beard half an inch long, feeling very hot and idle, glancing round him at the others and then continuing his interminable letters; Bob Trevy fast asleep dreaming of his opera on Bacchus and Ariadne which he has just written for Donald Tovey to set to music;[1] Ainsworth with a pair of blue spectacles to ward off the sun, reading Plato; Keynes under the umbrella, reading Galsworthy;

[1] It was at this time that Sir Donald Tovey began work on his only opera *The Bride of Dionysus*, the libretto of which was written by R. C. Trevelyan. Not completed until 1918, it received its first performance in Edinburgh on 23 April 1929.

Sanger, flat on his back on the grass, studying law; James Strachey crouched in the shadows, reading nothing; Norton for ever absorbed in his mathematics; and Moore, reclining full length on a rug, making pencil notes in the margin of Locke's *Essay on Human Understanding*.

So, for the first fortnight, the mild tranquillities drift along pleasantly enough, with Lytton reading Darwin's journal of his voyage round the world and re-reading Cowper's letters. Then, one day, everything breaks up. Keynes and Norton leave for London, the weather abandons its habit of cloudless, demi-tropical splendour and deteriorates into vile and ceaseless rain, Sanger retires upstairs to his feather bed with a severe and persistent cold, and James collapses with toothache. The world is a vale of tears again. Lytton is left huddled in the smaller sitting-room with Ainsworth and Moore, who, intoxicated by the surfeit of beef and cream, appears to be in the throes of an abstruse ethical revolution, from which he finds relief in declaiming out loud the novels of Captain Marryat. 'Has the rumour reached you of the astounding news?' Lytton asks Keynes. 'Moore has shivered his philosophy into atoms, and can't for the life of him construct a new one. He "doesn't know what to think" – about *anything* – propositions, eternal being, Truth itself! In fact he's pretty well chucked up the sponge. Isn't it shocking? Christ denying Christianity! Hegel gapes for him, and shuddering worlds hide their horror-stricken heads. He's a great man, and if he's not got water on the brain he'll come through, and soar to even more incredible heights. But has he got water on the brain? Shall we ever know?' Moore's volte-face is in fact the outcome of a succession of growing doubts and qualifications with which he has been wrestling since Christmas. But by the end of the reading-party he already seems to be moving onwards again out of his dire perplexity into the obscurely obvious. 'The Yen has discovered that when you say "So and so is so and so's father," the word "father" in the sentence has no meaning whatever. It's a rather important discovery; but I suppose it'll be blasted soon enough.'[1]

The reading-party dispersed on 18 April, and Lytton went off to spend 'one intolerable night' at Sutton Court where he hoped to examine some papers kept there relating to Warren Hastings. In fact he was not able to see them as his cousin, Sir Edward Strachey (later Edward Lord Strachie), had gone off to London taking with him the

---

[1] In an explanatory postscript to this letter, Lytton added: 'When you say "So and so is so and so's father", you mean "So and so occupies a relation towards so and so to which the word 'father' may be properly applied" – and that's all; you needn't (and probably don't) know what "father" means.'

only key to the box in which they lay. In his place, Lytton was entertained by Edward's younger brother Henry, the forty-four-year-old
artist and art-critic. 'It was on the whole a boring business,' he told
Duncan Grant (21 April 1907), 'though I was never bored to death, and
I liked seeing Sutton Court, and looking at his books and his re-
productions of pictures. But oh dear! he *is* a sad husk of a human being,
and very often there seemed so little to say that there was a distinct
gêne. I suppose you've never felt that, with your breezy manner, etc.
He was of course extraordinarily "nice"; but pray what is there to say
to him? He showed me his pictures and there seemed even less to say
to *them*. In the evening his wood-carving class arrived, but I stayed in
the other room, and didn't even go to look at them, for I felt that I
knew so exactly what they were like it wasn't worth while. Once or
twice I couldn't resist saying things that I knew would put him out,
such as that the colours in the Bacchus and Ariadne were too glaring, or
that art was more beautiful than nature. But it really wasn't much fun –
he could never cease to be polite.'

The next day he returned to Lancaster Gate. 'London is a shocking
place as far as people go,' he complained to James (May 1907). When he
wasn't dreaming as usual over his old gas-fire with the foggy rain
streaming down outside, or plodding along Kensington Gardens, or
dragging himself through everlasting family dinners, or suffraging,
or helping with the gargantuan arrangements of moving house, he
shuttled apathetically back and forth between Maynard Keynes's
service flat at 125B St James's Court, and 46 Gordon Square where Clive
and Vanessa Bell had set up house – finding little enough satisfaction
in either.

But a few distractions, mostly pictorial, did lighten the gloom, including an exhibition of Simon Bussy's paintings at Leighton House
which he advised Clive and Vanessa Bell to see – 'They are all pastels,
and most of them dreams of beauty' – also a private view at the New
Gallery more remarkable for the onlookers than the pictures – 'That
astounding creature Pinero[1] was there. . . . Large red face, immense
black eyebrows, rolling eyes, vast nose, theatrical manner, bandana
handkerchief, trousers creased *à la rigueur*, and patent leather boots with
brown fronts' – and finally, at the Carfax Gallery, 'a charming collection
of Max Beerbohm's caricatures – many of them really beautiful, and
some like Blake – all (to my mind) the height of amusement.'

During the spring and early summer Lytton did very little but read
the reminiscences and letters of Carlyle – 'a psalm-singing Scotchman

[1] Sir Arthur Wing Pinero (1855–1934), prolific playwright much influenced by Ibsen.
His best-known play is *The Second Mrs Tanqueray* (1893).

with a power of observation which knocks you flat' – and the novels of Joseph Conrad whom he described as 'very superb – in fact the *only* superb novelist now, except old Henry James, etc. – and Lord Jim is full of splendid things. The Nigger of the Narcissus is another very wonderful one, and perhaps the best of all is a shortish story called Heart of Darkness in a book called *Youth*.' Among recently published books there was his friend E. M. Forster's *The Longest Journey*. 'I don't think you know Forster,' he wrote to Duncan Grant (30 April 1907), '– a queer King's brother, and a great friend of Hom's.[1] He's just written his second novel, and there's a rather amusing account of Cambridge in it, and Cambridge people. One of the very minor characters is asked to breakfast by one of his friends and replies by putting his hand on his stomach, to show that he's breakfasted already. MacCarthy thinks that this is me. Do you? But the rest of the book is a dreary fandango. After the hero (who's Forster himself), the principal figure is Hom.'

As for his own writing, he was planning two major essays, one biographical, the other critical. The first of these, his final contribution to the *Independent Review* which had now re-formed under the name of the *Albany Review*, was on Lady Mary Wortley Montagu. The attraction which this subject held for him – something akin to an adopted filial pride – is very clearly indicated in a passage from another of his letters to Duncan Grant (13 May 1907): 'I am going to write an article on Lady Mary Wortley Montagu (Have you heard of her?) – a magnificent 18th-century lady, who wrote letters, and introduced inoculation into Europe. She was sublime, and no one knows it nowadays. I shall try and show that she was and how. She had only two tastes – intellect and lust. Imagine her pessimism! But her honesty and courage were equal to every emergency, and she never gave into anything or anybody, and died fighting. Great Lady Mary!'

The second of these essays reflects the complement of his enthusiasm for such splendid, prepotent females – a taste for men of vulnerable, superfine sensitivity. He had been introduced to the writings of Beddoes by Saxon Sydney-Turner, and soon became both fascinated by his personality and spellbound by his poetry. Like Lady Mary Wortley Montagu, Beddoes was an unjustly disregarded figure on the literary stage, a sad state of affairs that Lytton hoped to correct, by means of a long re-appraisal of his work in the opening number of MacCarthy's *New Quarterly*, now due out in the autumn.

There were other, more distant plans, too, in his mind for critical

[1] H. O. Meredith, known as 'Hom' among his Cambridge friends, a Fellow of King's who later became professor of political economy at Queen's University, Belfast.

and biographical essays. Meanwhile, 'I regret to say that I go to sleep after lunch more often than not,' he admitted to Duncan Grant (18 June 1907). 'The other day I actually did it after breakfast! But that undoubtedly was a sign of disease – I wonder, though, of *what* disease? – "The disease, sir, of sloth!" a vicar would probably say. But one need pay no attention to vicars.

'I am in my room. James is opposite, reading Chinese poetry. I'm sure I must have shown you the book – one of the most charming in the world.[1] I want to write about it, and so gain a little cash. And I want to write about Madame du Deffand,[2] and Baudelaire, and Beddoes, and Marivaux and God knows who. Why on earth don't I? "Sloth, sir, sloth!"'

4

NOTHING TO LOSE

On 22 May, Lancaster Gate was put up for public auction. Lady Strachey was determined that the place should not go for less than three thousand pounds, but Lytton, who liked to imagine that they could let it furnished for the season to some wealthy American 'and live on the proceeds in lodgings for the next ten years', thought this too unrealistic a price to ask, and his view seemed to be proved right when the auction came to nothing. However, it soon turned out that there was a prospective purchaser hanging in the wind, with whom Lady Strachey eventually succeeded in coming to reasonable terms – though, as a result of this man's hesitancy, the family, instead of occupying their new Hampstead home in June as originally intended, were obliged to postpone their move until September.

While these hectic and prolonged negotiations were being argued out, the ordinary day-to-day life at Lancaster Gate took on an even more chaotic air than usual. 'I now read through all meals steadily,' he told Maynard Keynes two days after the abortive auction, '. . . I think I may have spoken three sentences today.' And to Duncan Grant he grumbled: 'I really haven't the vaguest idea what I've done since I came back to London. The only certain thing is that I've done no work. Oh, devils! devils! – I've been to no plays, and heard no music, and hardly talked

---

[1] A collection of poetry translations from the Chinese made by Professor H. A. Giles of Cambridge, and originally published in 1898. Lytton was to write an appreciation of this book in the summer of 1908, printed that autumn in the *New Quarterly* and the *Living Age*.

[2] Lytton's essay on Madame du Deffand was not in fact composed until 1912.

to anyone but Keynes (and him I believe only twice). On Thursday I had dinner with Clive and Vanessa in Gordon Square. They seemed somewhat less insistent on the fact that they were in love with each other, which made it easier to talk to them, and I enjoyed myself pretty well.' Such a passage, with its grudging, almost unintentional admission of enjoyment is very characteristic of Lytton at this time. In fact his everyday life was, as he would say, fairly tolerable. He was now in reasonable health again, and his social activities were not so reduced or devoid of incident as he liked to make out. But his home was uncomfortable, and he was still impecunious. Also he felt keenly his failure to blaze a glorious trail through the world. Secretly impatient for success, he was fearful that his friends, insensible to the pulsing ambitions so long constrained within him, would underrate his discontent. It was perhaps to indicate the force of this discontent as well as to draw in the uncritical sympathy which he felt it demanded, that he exaggerated the circumstantial hardships of his existence.

Among the most interesting of his social engagements now, on account of the varying descriptions of it recorded by the parties concerned, was a dinner-party with William Rothenstein, his wife, and Isabel Fry, the younger sister of Roger, later to win fame as a brilliant educationalist. 'The dinner was remarkable,' Lytton wrote to Duncan Grant (13 May 1907), 'chiefly because Rothenstein and his wife were there. It was *the* Rothenstein – very Jewish and small and monkey-like; I believe the one who was at the Friday Club,[1] and who annoyed me, must have been his younger brother, because wasn't he rather podgy and hubristic? At any rate, I was annoyed almost as much this time – and by very much the same style of vagueness. I rather peevishly dissented, and I fear he was offended! He was nice, and extraordinarily meek, but oh! the rot he talked! Madam[2] was a blonde, somewhat devoid of [undecipherable], worshipping him, and enraged with me for daring to disagree with him! My philistinism was increased by the frightful fact that I alone of the party was in evening dress! A haughty and exclusive aristocrat was what I appeared to be, no doubt, trampling poor artists underfoot as if they were so many beetles! And I unfortunately let out that I lived in Lancaster Gate! "Horribly rich," I'm sure she murmured to him, or rather "Orribly rich". Shall I call on them, when we've settled in bijou residence in Hampstead, dressed in my third best brogalines and without a collar? But even then I should

---

[1] Vanessa Bell's Friday Club was not founded by her until June 1910. Lytton was probably referring to Virginia Stephen's 'Friday Evenings' in Fitzroy Square.

[2] Alice Knewstub, who had married William Rothenstein in 1899. According to her son, John Rothenstein, she was 'an inflammable compound of Toryism and anarchy'.

never be able to agree that Nature was only one aspect of Art, that Beauty was the expression of True Emotions, and that Music, Poetry, and Painting were the plastic embodiments of Life.'

William Rothenstein has also left a description of this encounter in his *Men and Memories*, which enables one to draw an interesting comparison between the impression which Lytton made and imagined he made on chance acquaintances – though the account here is somewhat qualified by judicious afterthoughts. 'Lytton Strachey's look in these early days was very unlike his later appearance,' Rothenstein recalled. 'Long, slender, with a receding chin, that gave a look of weakness to his face, with a thin cracked voice, I thought him typical of the Cambridge intellectual. . . . During one night with Isabel Fry, I recollect saying that poetry, usually regarded as a vague and highfaluting art by many, was in fact the clearest expression of man's thoughts. Strachey replied acidly. Who indeed was I to talk of matters with which I was not concerned? And I thought that here was the cultured University man, who lies in wait, hoping one may say something foolish or inaccurate, and then springs out to crush one, in high falsetto tones. But I was mistaken. Of course Lytton Strachey was much more than a cultured Cambridge man; he was to become a master of English prose; and with reputation came a beard, and long hair, and a cloak and sombrero, which gave weight and solemnity to an appearance previously not very noticeable. I think Lytton Strachey was of so nervous a temper, that he needed some defensive armour to cover his extreme sensitiveness, and a weapon with a sharp edge, with which to protect himself. He suffered fools less genially than Max [Beerbohm], to their faces at least.'

While preparations for the move to Hampstead were being made, Lytton felt obliged to remain in London.[1] But in the course of May and

[1] Among the plays he went to in these months was Herbert Beerbohm Tree's production of Wilde's *A Woman of No Importance*. 'It was rather amusing,' he told Duncan Grant (2 June 1907), 'as it was a complete mass of epigrams, with occasional whiffs of grotesque melodrama and drivelling sentiment. The queerest mixture! Mr Tree is a wicked Lord, staying in a country house, who has made up his mind to bugger one of the other guests – a handsome young man of twenty. The handsome young man is delighted; when his mother enters, sees his Lordship and recognizes him as having copulated with her twenty years before, the result of which was – the handsome young man. She appeals to Lord Tree not to bugger his own son. He replies that that's an additional reason for doing it (oh! he's a *very* wicked Lord!). She then appeals to the handsome young man, who says, "Dear me! What an abominable thing to do – to go and copulate without marrying! Oh no, I shall certainly pay no attention to anyone capable of doing *that*, and —" when suddenly enter (from the garden) a young American millionairess, shrieking for help, and in considerable disorder. The wicked Lord Tree, not contented with buggering his own son, has attempted to rape the millionairess, with whom (very properly) the handsome young man is in love. Enter his Lordship.

June he did manage to get away twice – for one week-end to Cambridge and another to Oxford. The Cambridge visit was particularly refreshing. The lilacs were in full bloom, the horse-chestnuts flowering, 'the backs and river pullulating with undergraduates in flannels, and prostitutes in tights and spangles – the whole thing really delightful'. The usual group of Apostles met in Sheppard's rooms to discuss Christianity – much to Lytton's amusement; but the chief event of this visit was the sight of Knox wearing heavy black spectacles. The shock was considerable, and one that could not be erased from Lytton's mind. From this time on Knox was eliminated from even a subsidiary role in his life. As for considering him a rival to Swithinbank – why, it was laughable!

Another shock awaited him on his week-end at Oxford. As at Cambridge, everything seemed very pleasant at first, and he was enchanted by the variety of the scene. He dined off cold duck and champagne with the governor of the Seychelles; he breakfasted with Granville Proby,[1] a fat, aristocratic Old Etonian friend of Keynes's, with Humphrey Paul,[2] 'a merry farceur, with four thousand anecdotes at his command', with Geoffrey Scott,[3] 'a bad character, all egoism and love of amusement and importance for their own sakes . . . clever, and amusing and extremely scandalous', with Dillwyn Knox's younger brother Ronnie,[4] 'a christian and a prig, and a self-sufficient little insignificant wretch!' and with James Elroy Flecker,[5] who made no

Handsome Y.M.: "You devil! You have insulted the purest creature on God's earth! I shall kill you!" But of course he doesn't, but contents himself with marrying the millionairess, while his mother takes up a pair of gloves and slashes the Lord across the face. It seems an odd plot, doesn't it? But it required all my penetration to find out that this *was* the plot, as you may imagine. Epigrams engulf it like the sea. Most of them were thoroughly rotten, and nearly all were said quite cynically to the gallery. Poor old Tree sits down with his back to the audience to talk to a brilliant lady, and swings round in his seat every time he delivers an epigram. The audience was of course charmed.'

[1] Granville Proby, later Clerk to the House of Lords and Lord Lieutenant of Huntingdonshire (1946–50).

[2] Humphrey Paul, son of the historian and biographer Herbert Woodfield Paul.

[3] Geoffrey Scott, the notable Boswell scholar, and author of *The Architecture of Humanism* and *The Portrait of Zélide*.

[4] The Rt Reverend Monsignor Ronald Arbuthnot Knox (1888–1957), whose biography has been decorously written by Evelyn Waugh (1959). Author of many books on Roman Catholicism, and of *Studies in the Literature of Sherlock Holmes*, a work that gave impetus to the Holmeseology 'which has since become rather tiresome'. Translator of the Vulgate. When Lytton met him he was up at Balliol College and reputed to be the wittiest president of the Oxford Union within living memory.

[5] James Elroy Flecker (1884–1915), poet and dramatist, who left Trinity College, Oxford, in 1906 with only a third in Mods and Greats, and returned the following year in an abortive attempt to live through writing. Agnostic and tubercular, he became an accomplished linguist, a great traveller and keen bibliophil. His finest poem is usually considered to be *The Golden Journey to Samarkand*, much admired by Eddie Marsh, but

particular impression on him; he lunched with Swithinbank on strawberries and cream, and saw Jack Beazley, resplendently beautiful with high complexion, curling red-golden hair and charming, affectionate manners; he had tea with the Raleighs, and met a professor of Greek and a doctor who had recently examined a notorious murderer. Everything was as entertaining and as agreeable as he could have wished. The beauty of the colleges amazed him. In the evening he strolled with Swithinbank round the Cloister Court of Magdalen, wondering at the strange mediaeval atmosphere. It was not difficult to imagine, where the Blues and Beazley and Swithin now walked among those dark old stones and brooding antiquity, monks and novices of the Middle Ages traipsing about with their *pater noster*s, their atonements, penances, secret preoccupations. How sinister it all was! Had he been alone there in the fading twilight he might have felt quite frightened. But he was with Swithin, at the sight of whom, if the Universe were conducted as it should be, Magdalen would vanish like a dream when the sun comes in at the window and one wakes up. Then the two of them wandered out into the light, back into the new age of reason and sanity, and history seemed no longer terrifying, but slightly ridiculous. And he could only reflect on how pleasant and civilized it was to walk with his friend in the evening sun; how lucky he was to have a friend like Swithin!

Then, out of the blue, Swithinbank announced that he had applied for the post of sanitary inspector in the Fiji Islands, a job for which, he believed, there was little ardent competition. Once he had been convinced that this was not some new style of joke, Lytton did all in his power to dissuade his friend from such a scatterbrained course. But Swithinbank was curiously adamant. 'He has taken it into his head', Lytton wrote to James with what, it seemed to him, was only slight exaggeration, 'that there is only one thing for him to do – viz. to become Inspector General of Brothels in the Fiji Islands. Did you ever hear of such a thing? Nothing will induce him to change his mind; and he hopes to sail in July!'

Lytton's consternation was all the greater since, by a freak coincidence of timing, the now heavily bespectacled Knox – the only possible successor to Swithinbank, waiting in the wings of his life while Duncan Grant still performed in mid-stage – had been eliminated as a competent understudy that very month. The absurdity of it was that Swithinbank

---

which D. H. Lawrence declared 'only took place on paper – no matter who went to Asia Minor'. His chief drama, *Hassan* (published posthumously in 1922), was produced with a ballet by Fokine and music by Delius. Reconverted to Christianity, he received communion on his death-bed at Davos in the first week of 1915.

could quite easily become a master at Winchester which he would thoroughly enjoy, whereas the drainage system of Fiji really *couldn't* please him. He only did it from sheer indecisiveness, yet there was, of course, every reason to suppose that he would be given the job. And that, so far as Lytton was concerned, would be the virtual death of him. Something must be done!

Hurrying back to London, he conferred with Keynes, and both agreed that here was a matter for decisive intervention and counterplot. After some debate they embarked on a bold policy. Lytton went off to see his cousin, Sir Charles Strachey, in the Colonial Office and asked him what he thought of Swithinbank's plan. After making certain inquiries and confirming that the post was very far from being considered a coveted one, he condemned the whole idea as being utterly absurd. Armed with this official verdict, Keynes then wrote off to Swithinbank's father, a clergyman, imploring him in the name of God to prevail upon his son not to go, and painting all the vices and horrors of Fiji in their most lurid lights. A silence followed, during which Keynes and Lytton waited in some trepidation. Then came a telegram from poor Swithin – 'Fijis are off!' And so the situation, for the time being, was saved.

While this crisis was being sorted out, another one affecting Lytton even more directly had arisen. Towards the end of June, St Loe Strachey wrote to Lytton asking him to join the *Spectator* staff. He proposed that, with effect from October, Lytton should review a book each week for a salary of one hundred and fifty pounds per year. It was a difficult and depressing decision for Lytton to have to make. The emolument was not great, but with MacCarthy's *New Quarterly* starting up at the same time, it would, at a single blow, amount to a livelihood. For a few days he deliberated. He asked Keynes, who advised him to accept: 'It is hardly possible to overestimate the importance of money.' He asked James, who was later to become a member of the *Spectator* staff himself, and who strongly advised Lytton to refuse the offer. Acceptance, he warned his brother, would be tantamount to selling himself to 'the Mammon of Unrighteousness'. Sooner or later pressure was pretty certain to be put on him to become a regular, full-time journalist – *et voilà tout*. Once he had started this kind of work, he would not be able to resist when the time came, and all his dreams of *chefs-d'œuvre*, plays, novels, even biographies, would have to be abandoned.

In the end Lytton accepted. 'It seemed on the whole the wisest thing to do,' he explained to Duncan Grant (25 June 1907), 'though I'm still not sure whether it wasn't simply the most cowardly. I had hoped to begin doing something worth doing, but the money, and the obvious fact that Mama wanted me to accept it, and the conceivable possibility that I might at least *think* of things, and the certainty that I could always chuck it when I liked – these considerations turned the melancholy balance, and shattered my dreams of ease and comedy. However, the splendid thing is that I shall be wonderfully rich next year (if I survive the stress and strain of composition!) and, as there's no particular reason why I should be pinned to London, I shall be able to travel.'

In July the only certainties ·for the future were increased wealth, decreased time, and no contractual compulsion to go on with reviewing if he found that he really could do nothing else. As for James's objection, Lytton hoped he had not sold himself but merely made friends with the Mammon of Unrighteousness. If pressure were applied in the way James had gloomily prophesied, then they would see who was right, whether he would have the strength to decline. One thing was definite. The *Spectator* appointment was another link in the chain pulling asunder his old, aimless and unproductive life. But was it at the same time forging another bondage for him? Only time would tell.

5

DUMB ASSUAGEMENTS

Three months of ease and comedy still awaited him, and Lytton was determined not to waste them. As soon as the *Spectator* appointment had been ratified, and his 'Lady Mary Wortley Montagu' completed, he began to make plans for spending a week with Duncan Grant at Versailles. This was something he had often dreamed of doing, and had indeed already done by proxy, but never, of course, in actual person. Now, before it was too late, before his freedom was too strictly curtailed, he would make his dream reality.

After some delay, he set off in the second week of July, and for seven idyllic days he lived with Duncan in La Bruyère's house, passing most of their time in the wonderful gardens – those of the Grand Trianon for choice, for they were more retired. Though he had been prepared for much, the beauty of the place took his breath away. 'What I want to know is why anyone lives anywhere else,' he wrote to Clive Bell. 'I suppose one wouldn't be up to it for more than a week or so at a time. The ghosts would begin to grow more real than oneself.'

Surrounded by these splendid gardens, and enchanted by the company of Duncan, Lytton was content to pass his days lazily. 'We spend most of our time beside a basin in the Trianon,' he informed James, 'but

one day was given to Paris, on which I looked at every picture in the
Louvre, and every statue, and then went off and had a blow out, and we
viewed a farce in the Boulevard Montmartre, and then we steamed back
to Versailles.'

He returned to London on 17 July and almost immediately left again
with James, Pernel and Marjorie for Burley Hill, which Thena Clough
had once more lent the family. Here all was silence, regularity and
health. After the wild exhilarations of Versailles, Lytton soon sank back
into a benevolent trance which must be 'middle-age, as I seem to be
remarkably contented', he told Keynes who visited him for a few days,
and who was, so he informed Duncan Grant, 'rather uglier than usual'.

When not out walking in the New Forest or labouring 'hours and
hours every day at my desk, signifying nothing', Lytton would sit
indoors reading, in particular – and perhaps not surprisingly after his
recent trip to France – the works of Saint-Simon, whose *Mémoires*
recapture the life at Versailles with such unrivalled vividness and
verisimilitude. He had transported the first volume of a vast edition of
Saint-Simon down with him to Burley Hill from the London Library –
'you never saw such a monument of erudition', he wrote to Clive Bell
(9 August 1907). 'I thought I'd read the text, and skip the notes, appendices, and excursuses; but lord, I read it every word, and have sent for
the next two volumes. If I stay here much longer I shall become a
scholar, and when we meet you'll think I'm Turner.'

Lytton stayed at Burley Hill for a month, during which time his
reading was confined almost exclusively to French literature. Besides
Saint-Simon, he read Laclos and Baudelaire, who, he wrote to Duncan
Grant, 'was the greatest man of the nineteenth century'. Whenever he
felt that family life was growing too much for him, he would prescribe
for himself a letter from *Les Liaisons Dangereuses* before going to
bed, and a Fleur du Mal the first thing in the morning. It seldom failed.
'I've just got a book,' he told Clive Bell (9 August 1907), 'in which
some notes by Baudelaire on the Liaisons Dangereuses are printed – do
you know them? They're really splendid – all his wonderful sanity,
precision, and grasp of the situation are finely displayed. He says, comparing modern life to the eighteenth century – "En réalité, le satanisme
a gagné. Satan s'est fait ingénu. Le mal se connaissant était moins
affreux et plus près de la guérison que le mal s'ignorant. G. Sand
inférieure à de Sade."'

But after some three weeks the bitter, controlled pessimism of
Baudelaire, and the general lack of quickening imagination which
characterized so much French writing despite all its virtues of style,
lucidity and order, began to deflate him, and instead of prolonging the

happiness of his idyll at Versailles, these books only consolidated his familiar English apathy. 'Is literature the dullest thing in the world?' he asked Swithinbank (21 August 1907). 'At the moment I can think of nothing duller. Let's all become painters and musicians, and embark for Cythera.'[1] But of course there was no escape. His romanticism fizzled out like a damp squib, and he was left feeling flat and sour, sick of almost everything in the universe. He wanted to engrave his mark upon the age, like a lion with its claw; but he had got nowhere, and looked like getting nowhere in the future. What on earth was he doing? Little more, it seemed, than twiddling his thumbs while his hair turned grey. And after all, wasn't that a just summary of all life – gradually, *contentedly*, to subside into a mummified state of motionless frigidity and putrefaction? How often were beauty, goodness, and splendour lost and forgotten! The human race grubbed along like hedgehogs, sniffing and snouting, and for ever turning up its pettifogging roots. Yet possibly this view of mankind, occasioned by his study of the French Swift of poetry, was unnecessarily dismal. Surely *somewhere* there was *something* that was enormously important, some divine solution beyond analysis? And if there were, then really everything was all right after all. It sounded almost religious, such speculation, but weren't they all religious *au fond*? Not, of course, Christians – whose social virtues of obedience to duty and self-sacrifice reduced all men to the proportions of ants and termites – but religious in the proper, intellectual way, with a faith or hope that their Unknown God would help them to devote their energies to something other than merely perpetuating the futile cycle of human existence – to irradiating and enlarging the ambit of individual awareness.

These reflections were stirred not only by his casual reading, but also by his daily struggles at Burley Hill to apply himself to some writing. 'I have been grunting and sweating over a filthy article on Beddoes the whole time,' he wrote to Swithinbank towards the end of his stay there. The conditions of authorship being what they inevitably were, the actual physical and mental processes of writing – as opposed, say, to those of painting – could hold few attractions. Why then write at all? It was surely not just a matter of vanity, of more blind hedgehog grubbing. The best answer would seem to be that the practice, however execrable and precarious, of the craft in which one found one's deepest fulfilment was to some extent a happiness, in so far as the denial of it

---

[1] This refers to *The Embarkation for Cythera*, a diploma piece painted by Antoine Watteau in 1712 for the Académie Royale de Peinture et de Sculpture. This painting, now in the Louvre, depicts an imagined voyage to a destined island of love and blessedness.

would be a misery. As a labour of love, the composition of his Beddoes was arduous and exhausting. At the same time his curiosity was more than usually provoked by the mysterious undertones in Beddoes's life. Here was a strangely distant character – a throwback to the Elizabethan age – yet in some ways Lytton felt remarkably close to him. For, as with General Gordon, he was not slow to perceive the special affinity which lay between them. 'I am trying to write on Beddoes,' he told Keynes (30 July 1907), 'and become daily more persuaded that he was a member of our sect. What do you think? It occurred to me yesterday that Degen[1] is probably still alive, and that we've only got to go over to Franckfort and inquire for a respectable old retired baker, aged seventy-seven, to hear the whole history! Won't you come?'

At the end of August, 'The Last Elizabethan', as he entitled his Beddoes essay, was finished and he left Burley Hill, not alas for Frankfurt but London. The family's furniture and luggage were now being transferred from Lancaster Gate across to 67 Belsize Park Gardens, and Lytton was temporarily billeted with his eldest sister Elinor's father-in-law, Sir Alexander Rendel, at 23 Russell Square. He could be of little practical use in the complex business of moving house, and so, after only a few days, he left London to spend a week at Hurst Court, in the village of Hurst near Twyford in Berkshire, which Harry Norton's family had rented that summer. This visit was not a success, but it did provide Lytton with some insight into the Norton *ménage* that was perhaps instructive as a warning of what might easily happen to himself. Before many hours had elapsed, he felt that he was literally expiring from boredom, that, before he could decently escape, he would be stifled altogether in the airless, domestic atmosphere. It was an ominous lesson in the debilitating effects produced over a long period by family life – something that he himself must at all costs struggle to avoid. Surrounded by his mother and sisters, his only respite the smoking-room and the last number of the *Mathematical Journal*, Norton was reduced to a condition of gibbering inanity. It was impossible to believe that, in the whole course of his life, he had ever addressed one single sensible word to them. In any case what would be the use? All of them indulged endlessly in aimless jokes and mad, trilling laughter which was sustained throughout a series of senseless meals repeating themselves ad infinitum, like something in the *Inferno*. And the cumulative coincidence of family ugliness! At moments during his stay Lytton began to despair of the whole human race. No wonder Harry was so pitiably crushed.

---

[1] Degen was the nineteen-year-old baker with whom Beddoes lived in close companionship for six months at Frankfurt.

'The poor fellow!' he lamented to Keynes (10 September 1907). 'Never did I see anyone so utterly done for – beyond reach of human aid. He's submerged in the ocean of stupidity and dullness which that terrible family existence of his has created. Oh! The horror of Sunday! And to see him appearing at breakfast, rather ashamed of being four minutes late, dressed in the complete vulgarity of "best clothes" with a dreadful fancy waistcoat and a revolting tie! Oh, oh! And then "church" – ugh! Fortunately no attempt was made to induce me to go – I think if there had been I should have said something gross. As it was, I hardly opened my mouth once. He is a weak-willed creature, very good-natured and very clever, but content to be his mother's puppet, and the rest of the family's buffoon.'

After his week was up at Hurst, Lytton fled to the Homere sisters at Kingham. By now he felt too exhausted to do anything but sit out in the more or less comfortable garden 'among my Greek ladies', Chopin in the distance, no reading, no writing. Middle age had descended upon him for ever. 'I have lost count of time, and have fallen into a sea of dullness, health, and decent conversation that's too shocking to think of,' he wrote hopelessly to Swithinbank (13 September 1907). 'I can dimly remember that I saw Keynes for a minute or two some years ago, but what he said to me or I to him, and why and where we met – swallowed, swallowed by the waters of female oblivion . . .

'. . . I can't help it. Could you, if you were where I am on a deck-chair (very uncomfortable) in a misty garden, looking at nothing but a tree or two, and listening to a Greek Lady (very fine and fat) practising scales on a grand piano ten yards off? I feel as if I were hardly more than a scale myself, or at least an arpeggio. Here comes a glass of milk for me, and a couple of rusks. I believe I am perfectly happy.'

On 20 September, he emerged from this contented, enervating seclusion to stay with Clive and Vanessa Bell at Curfew Cottage in Watchbell Street, Rye, close to the Mermaid Inn where he had put up with Sheppard and Keynes. He had always loved Rye, with the mysterious unseen presence of Henry James brooding over it, and it was especially enjoyable to be there among friends – real friends, that was, with whom one could do as one pleased – come down late for breakfast, go to sleep on the drawing-room sofa, and even succumb to fits of annihilation. Virginia and Adrian Stephen were also there. 'They *are* nice,' he told Duncan Grant, 'and Bell, too, really, if one isn't put off rather by a thick layer of absurdity.' As for Vanessa, now that she was safely with child, he felt that he could almost have married her himself.

While at Rye he shrugged off his lethargy and began writing once more – an essay on Rousseau which was not actually published until some three years later, and an eight-stanza poem, 'Knowledge', which was inspired by the prospect of seeing Duncan Grant, who had just returned from France.

> *For I have seen in half-extinguished eyes*
> *The dumb assuagements of immortal grief,*
> *Infinitudes of exquisite surprise,*
> *Looks beyond love, and tears beyond belief.*
>
> *And subtle transmutations I have seen*
> *Upon a dreaming face subtly unfold*
> *As when in autumn heaven's purpureal green*
> *Gradually melts to opalescent gold.*

After some five days in Rye, Lytton finally returned to London, moving in for the first time to the new family home in Hampstead. Number 67 Belsize Park Gardens was a smaller house than Lancaster Gate, but still quite fair-sized enough to cater for the rather depleted numbers of the family now living together. As before, Lytton was assigned a bed-sitting-room where he was to compose his reviews and articles. 'Rousseau and his bag of tricks have absorbed me,' he wrote to Clive and Vanessa Bell at the end of the month. 'I spend my days in the British Museum, and my nights in my Hampstead chamber, poring over Grimm, Madame D'Epinay, Mr John Morley, and Mrs Frederika Macdonald,[1] and trying to determine which is the silliest. It's a dreadful occupation, and I shall probably end by being the silliest of all.'

6

WILD MAN OF THE WOODS

Lytton's brief, full-time career as journeyman of letters began on 1 October, the date on which his duties for both the *Spectator* and the

[1] 'The Rousseau Affair' was based on a two-volume publication *Jean Jacques Rousseau: a New Criticism* by Frederika Macdonald (1906). The principal revelations of this work related to the *Mémoires et Correspondances de Madame d'Epinay* (1818), the concluding quarter of which contains an account of Rousseau's quarrel with his friends, written from the anti-Rousseau point of view. This hostile narrative, as Mrs Macdonald showed, was in effect composed by Diderto and the Baron de Grimm. Lord Morley had published an earlier biography of Rousseau, taking the accuracy of the *Mémoires* for granted. Lytton's essay (incorrectly dated as 1907 in *Books and Characters*) did not in fact appear in the *New Quarterly* until 1910. 'What is going to happen to that appalling paper?' he wrote to Desmond MacCarthy (7 June 1910). 'I was furious to see my old Rousseau hash served up in it, and I shall never speak to you again if you don't pay me for it. I am dead for want of money, so I insist on being saved by £5.'

New Quarterly commenced. Of these two jobs, the one for the *Spectator* occupied far more of his time, and in the next nineteen months he contributed to the literary section of the paper no less than seventy-five articles of one kind or another – mostly long book- and theatre-reviews.

At first he found this employment rather invigorating. It was something new; it helped to deflect his morbid inward gaze; and it gave some immediate point and focus to his existence. Once a week he called at the *Spectator* offices to collect some book or other, wondering desperately all the while whether he could possibly complete his piece on it in time. It was a straightforward challenge to his capabilities, and as such spurred him to new effort. Overcoming the hurry and the drudgery of hebdomadal journalism acted as a tonic to his system, imbuing him with a sense of practical accomplishment and a fresh feeling of confidence in his own powers. He could do it! And not alone that, he could do it better than most others. His apathy and premature middle age were temporarily shaken off. He was reinvigorated. 'I walk on the Heath pretty nearly every afternoon and feel amazingly young and cheerful,' he wrote to Keynes towards the end of October. 'I do really feel seventeen – with all the tastes of that age, and all the vices. Very queer indeed.'

But all too soon the inspiriting novelty of journalism wore off and the mechanical, habitual, devitalized nature of the job began to tell on him. After a month or two, once his first anxieties had been composed, he grew bored and fretful. It was no more exciting than taking up his weekly essays to the history tutor at Trinity. 'What a filthy life this is!' he complained to Keynes (14 January 1908). 'Full of such silly horrors, and enjoyments sillier still. A taximeter is about as near to heaven as one's likely to get.' Such contemptuous sentiments were not assumed but deeply felt, yet, since he could not bear to fail at anything, he did his job so well that before four months had passed he was already being tempted by the Mammon of Unrighteousness in just the sort of manner that James had predicted. To deny this temptation proved a comparatively easy matter. In a letter dated 18 January 1908, he wrote to James to say that he had been offered the editorship of the *Spectator*, and had refused on the grounds that his business was literature, not politics. St Loe had replied that on consideration, though he regretted Lytton's decision in the interests of the paper, he was bound to say that he considered it to be the right one. 'D'you think', Lytton asked James, '*le pauvre homme* realizes the depths he's got into, and wishes that he too had chucked it? I wonder. It's odd.'

With the money he was now beginning to earn, Lytton was able to repay various small loans which he had been given by Keynes and

Norton, and to take them to lunch at Simpson's in the Strand, for many years his favourite London restaurant, and conveniently placed just round the corner from the *Spectator* office in Wellington Street, almost on Waterloo Bridge. Otherwise life went on for the most part much as before – the odd play with MacCarthy, the periodic evening with Clive and Vanessa Bell, with Virginia and Adrian Stephen, the occasional week-end dash to Cambridge where James was endeavouring against odds to get Rupert Brooke elected to the Apostles, a brief visit from Ainsworth who had now moved down from Edinburgh to London and whom Lytton found more entertaining than Keynes, and from the benign and patriarchal Saxon Sydney-Turner who was less entertaining than almost anyone he had ever encountered. What had they ever found to talk about in those studious cloisters of Trinity, he and Woolf and Turner and the others? 'We reviewed old days, of course,' he wrote to Duncan Grant, 'as you may imagine, and said what we always have said for the last hundred years. Friendship is a queer business.'

The familiar and monotonous rigmarole of London life during these autumn months were once more overshadowed by the enigmatic presence of Duncan Grant. It was the old story: another resurgence of that rotating cycle of misery, rage and bewilderment that had welled up in Lytton a year ago. Almost at once the sorry deluge of letters started again, letters of flaring anger and abject apology, of self-pity and obsequious gratitude. Frightened of losing his cousin's affection altogether, he ricocheted from one overwrought mood to another. Sometimes he was reduced to utter despair, paralysed and incoherent, by Duncan's insouciance; at other times a wild exasperation swept over him; and then again he would wonder meekly whether, after all, everything was not his own fault. In one important respect however the situation differed from that of the previous winter. By now the figure of Dicker had faded altogether from the scene. So what could be the explanation of his present indifference? They had got on so well together at Versailles. And at Belsize Park Gardens Lytton had looked forward to seeing much more of Duncan, who was living with his family a few hundred yards away in Fellows Road. And yet, with the most implausible excuses, he continued to avoid him – or so it appeared.

Made crestfallen by this unforeseen turn of events, Lytton's anxiety of mind soon brought about a collapse in his precarious health. 'I'm in a most unholy state – ill and worse,' he wrote on 23 November. 'I'm really frightened sometimes, you've no idea of the horrible things. And then such nightmares as I had last night! Duncan, it's not you that's the cause. I have a devil inside me – perhaps seven. I occasionally feel that I'm done for, and that I shall really smash up, and "go under", as they say, like a decadent poet. It's my imagination, my awful imagination. I should like to go to sleep for ages and ages. Oh God, what a miserable thing is a human being! There's no hope for a human being outside love. That I shall never get now, and it's all I want.'

This whole hideous emotional *déshabillé* had coffined him – without hope, it seemed, of even visionary resurrection – in a shoddy, maudlin, shifting world of vanity and illusion. Beauty, truth, intelligence – these were mere trifles, he reflected, dimly expressive of the single inner truth of love; and all his activities, such as travelling, talking, scribbling, and so on, were no more than unsuccessful efforts to keep this truth suppressed, to render life liveable without it. The moment his desires failed to find someone on whom to fix, everything flew to dust and ashes, and he was swallowed up in a void of unendurable, self-centred tedium. Yet never for long. Each time, the cord attaching him to those points where his heart was focused drew him up out of these dull, vacuous caverns and re-established him as a prisoner of all the familiar longings for amatory reincarnation, so hopeless and unrealizable. Refreshed by the miraculously renewed surge of love and lust which flowed like an incoming tide over the dry sands of his loveless, corpse-like, solitary existence, the uprush of buried emotions would crush and desiccate him. In recoil from its unfulfilled unification with another being, his body felt as weak and unresistant to physical sickness as a baby's. Early in December he took to his bed, but did not send for the doctor. There was little, as he knew from past experience, that a doctor could do to assuage his symptoms. Besides, medical men were a dreadfully tiresome species. They seemed, somehow, always so moral, more insistently so, he often thought, even than clergymen. And then, of course, they actually did believe that good health was the *summum bonum*. But could anyone really be good and healthy at the same time?

After a few days in bed Lytton floated down to Brighton where his health and frame of mind were soon cheered up wonderfully. Notwithstanding Christmas, everything seemed more sanguine on his return. Duncan was in a more friendly vein, and they read *Mansfield Park*, went for walks on the Heath, and caught mild influenza together. This disease had struck down several of the Stracheys early in the New Year, and to avoid infection Lytton had gone to stay with his sister and brother-in-law, Elinor and Jim Rendel, at their Kensington home, 15 Melbury Road. But the illness had already caught up with him, and so as not to spread it still further, he moved to 23 Russell Square, where he could be isolated with comparative ease.

It was while convalescing here that he heard the news that his father had fallen very seriously ill. He returned home at once. A few days later, on the morning of 12 February, Sir Richard Strachey died in his sleep. Although Lytton had never succeeded in getting close to the old man, he had always remained extremely fond of him, greatly admiring his scientific ability. For a time he contemplated writing a biography of him. There were plenty of facts, especially relating to Sir Richard's Indian career, waiting to be regrouped and organized into a literary or documentary pattern. But the plan never materialized. It would have meant, he told James, writing the whole history of India in the nineteenth century. His father had been, and would always be, not so much a tantalizing enigma, challenging curiosity and interpretation, as a remote and shadowy personage with whom it was almost inconceivable to deal except on formal terms. Their close accord on the mathematical problems which were sometimes debated in their letters to each other, had marked the limits of their lifetime intimacy. And, in retrospect, Lytton came no nearer to this distant paternal spirit. Though he had long ceased to reach out to him as any kind of confidant or companion, his father's detached and silent presence in the house had acted as a loadstone, drawing him back from his frequent but never very long trips out of London. Now that magnetic power was switched off for ever. The focal point of the family, a rock of impregnable masculinity standing out from the eternal sea of females, had finally submerged and vanished. Somehow, and some time soon, Lytton resolved, he too must leave, and set up home elsewhere. Family life had always been incompatible; now it was frankly unendurable.

But first there was the problem of his mother and sister. Lady Strachey was herself ill with influenza, and Pippa, who had been looking after both her parents, was exhausted. Towards the end of February, once she had sufficiently recovered, Lady Strachey set out with her brother Trevor for the South of France. Lytton and Pippa accompanied them as far as Calais and saw them into their train. Then they went on to Boulogne where they remained for a few days at the Hôtel Bristol et Christol. The trip did them both good, especially Pippa, who needed a change and some rest urgently. Soon after their return to England, and while their mother was still abroad, they both went down for a short visit to St Loe Strachey's country house at Newlands Corner, near Guildford. 'A most gorgeous newly-painted scarlet motor-car took us to and from the station,' Lytton wrote to his mother (11 March 1908), 'and St Loe insisted on my wearing one of his numerous fur-coats, so I felt very grand. In the evening we all went to the Parish room in the village, where Amy's "Masque of Empire" was performed – mainly by village boys and girls. Amabel[1] was Britannia, which was the leading part. She looked nice but her acting was too much in the regular affected "recitation" style, which Pippa thinks she must have learnt from Amy. I can't imagine anyone acting so by the light of nature. . . . Amy was most affable and not at all prononcée. When I went she insisted on my taking away the Masque to suggest any improvements that might occur to me. It is in the main quite harmless – the chief blot to my mind is that at the end Britannia and all the Colonies and Dependencies fall on their knees, repeating R.K.'s poem "Lest we forget" and praying for mercy, etc. . . . One thing annoyed me. She talked of Queen Victoria as Britain's "greatest queen". I begged her to put "long-lived" instead – or any other disyllabic adjective – pointing out that that could only apply to Queen Elizabeth. But she wouldn't hear of it.'

By now it had become Lytton's chief object in life to escape on every possible occasion from the distractions of the new family régime. Its discomfort, its intense solitude without privacy, depressed him beyond measure, blighting alike all his attempts at work and pleasure. In numbers the family was greatly reduced. There was his mother, his sisters Pippa and Marjorie, and occasionally Pernel. Ever since the earliest Lancaster Gate days, Lady Strachey had been given to reading at lunch and dinner, not books, but copies of *Home Chat* and *Tit Bits*, from the pages of which, with cries of laughter, she would shout out jokes. Everyone deprecated this practice, and she would indignantly protest at the lack of enthusiasm with which these readings were greeted all round the table. The arguments between Lady Strachey and her daughters, in particular Marjorie, were high-pitched and continuous. Very sensibly, Lytton became in time a little deaf to all this din. But Marjorie's voice was especially raucous, and the noise was often nerve-racking.

Earlier in the year, before his father's death, he had declined an invitation from Moore to join his Easter reading-party, to be held this time in the Green Dragon at Lavington on Salisbury Plain, where for seven years Henry Edward Manning had lived as rector of the parish. But in the altered circumstances he now quickly changed his mind, and in the third week of April hurried down to Wiltshire. There, despite the magical charm of Moore himself – still 'a colossal being' as he describes him to Virginia Stephen – who plays the piano and sings in the

[1] Amabel Strachey (b. 1894), who later married B. C. Williams-Ellis, the architect and man of letters, was the eldest child of St Loe and Henrietta Amy Strachey. She is the author of many books for children, including *Darwin's Moon* (1966), a biography of Alfred Russel Wallace.

old inimitable way with the sweat pouring down his face, this gathering
of his friends only seems to add to his growing sense of isolation. The
topics of conversation are for the most part no longer those that deeply
interest him. Something of the distinctive, indefinable flavour of their
former comradeship is missing. Hawtrey, Sanger, Bob Trevy – it is the
same crowd as always; but, individually, they are changing. And perhaps he, too, is changing. The nostalgia he feels for Cambridge now
intermingles with a new bitterness, born out of three years' aimless
wandering in the wilderness of London. He has become more than
ever sharply critical of the dons, their dull caution and dry-as-
dust attitude to living; and only that month, in the columns of the
Spectator, has launched a slashing attack on the fifth volume of *The
Cambridge Modern History*, likening its learned authors – one of
whom is his old tutor, Stanley Leathes – to 'the barbarians of the Dark
Ages'.

In any event, whether it is he or his Cambridge companions who
have changed, Lytton feels himself left out of things – an estrangement
which comprised a vague and as yet obscure sense of rivalry with
Keynes, and hardly any contact at all with the younger undergraduates
headed by Rupert Brooke. Even his own brother, James, appears
'very mysterious and reserved, and either incredibly young or inconceivably old'. In retreat from the whole complex shifting problem of
human relationships, he spends much of his time re-reading Racine,
who, unlike the Apostles these days, occupied himself with the only real
and permanently worthwhile subject in the world – the human
heart!

'Oh, adventures! Does one ever have them nowadays?' he exclaims
in a letter to Virginia Stephen. '. . . Do you? Is the Atlantic enough for
you? I am the wild man of the woods, I often think, and perhaps inexplicable to civilized people . . .' Unfortunately Lytton's physique
is not up to supporting such claims, which are perhaps no more than
bluff and weary outward expressions of the nagging frustration
within him, that shifting ambition which burns and gnaws and con-
sumes him inwardly like a physical malady. Even these 'congregations
of intellect upon Salisbury Plain', as Virginia Stephen describes the
reading-party, proved too adventurous for him. He travelled back to
Belsize Park with a violent cold and once there confined himself to his
room, crouching over a fire 'snivelling and cursing and drinking
quinine'.

May was an atrocious month. All the constitutional complaints of his
life seemed to conspire and set upon him in unison, as though he were
some world-figure like Job, to be tested in the fires of adversity by an

Old Testament deity. For much of the month he lay ill in his room, and at no time could he find the opportunity or summon up the energy to slip away from the anxious cluster of female relatives. He was desperately overworked, too, with his continuing *Spectator* and *New Quarterly* articles. Sometimes he felt absolutely sick at the thought of going on much longer in the coils of this present phase. He detested the Hampstead régime, at least as much as Keynes hated the India Office; and alas, there was no King's to receive him. 'I am almost completely lost – for the time being,' he wrote on 8 May. 'DEATH has set in. Articles to be finished in the twinkling of an eye! Horror! Horror! . . . Don't come near me or attempt to speak to me for several days. No Simpsons I fear on Tuesday. Only rain and mortification.'

In addition to this regular work he had recently been asked by the Oxford University Press to write a long introduction to any book of his choice, to be published in the same series of reprints as *Blake*, which had been brought out in the previous year by Walter Raleigh – through whose personal recommendation Lytton had received this commission. For several weeks he racked his brains in vain for something that was both suitable and worth republishing, and after discussions with the publishers and with Raleigh he at last decided on *A Simple Story* by Mrs Inchbald. By May he should already have been well into this work, but could find no time to fit it in and was obliged to write off to the publishers begging for a short extension. Yet, whatever happened, the 'dreadful introduction' could not long be delayed.

And as if all this were not enough, Duncan had again been off-hand, immediately plunging Lytton down into the blackest troughs of despair. Would this torture and confusion never end? Only, he decided, when he could quit Belsize Park Gardens for good and live elsewhere ; for only then could he hope to face things calmly and see them in proportion. 'I am having an acute fit of family fever, and the world is black,' he wrote to James later that same month. 'Certes, plus que je médite, the less it appears tolerable to lead the sort of hole-and-corner, one-place-at-table-laid-for-six life I do at present. It's impossible to think and impossible to breathe. Oh! Oh! I have serious thoughts of flight. But how? Where? – Could I ever face poverty, journalism, and solitude? The whole thing's sickening. It's bad luck that Duncan should be so singularly hopeless as a companion – what a great difference a little difference would have made! And now, too, just now, when I seem to see clearly that I ought to go, Keynes makes up his mind to go too, so that that avenue is cut off from me. I've a good mind to take rooms at Cambridge next term.'

Since Keynes had now removed from his flat at 125B St James's

Court, preparatory to settling into King's where Alfred Marshall had offered him a lectureship in economics with a salary of a hundred pounds a year; and since Duncan was so vague and unreliable as a friend, with whom else could he possibly share a flat? To live alone was impracticable – unthinkable. But perhaps even now something might be worked out with one or other of them. Either would be preferable to his Hampstead home.

Some temporary respite from this problem came in June, almost all of which he spent in very pleasant rooms at King's. Between *Spectator* reviews, and when the weather was fine, he entertained himself with a variety of simple pleasures – gazing out of his windows at the divine Backs, or gliding up and down the river very slowly in a punt which James worked with a paddle, or eating too much, or just wandering along Trinity Street with a fixed lack of purpose. 'The only disadvantage of this place are the beauties,' he confided to Swithinbank (5 June 1908), 'who are everywhere and ravish one's heart in the most unpleasant manner. . . . I write a review a week for the *Spectator* . . . and spend all I get in reckless luxury. It's the only way of consoling oneself for the ruins of life.'

Among his old friends Lytton saw much of Sheppard and Norton, who seemed to revive whenever he was away from home for any length of time, and became particularly charming, amusing and on the spot. Of more interest though were his impressions of Rupert Brooke, with whom his relationship was complicated by the single-minded and depressing veneration of his brother. 'As for Rupert,' he told Duncan Grant (12 June 1908), '– I'm not in love with him, though it's occasionally occurred to me that I ought to be – but there really are too many drawbacks to him, though of course there are charms and pleasantries too. His self-conceit is *écrasant*, and his general pose merely absurd. He's also, I *think* – but I'm not sure – rather brutal to me, who'm an innocent friendly person, and no fool. Not the ghostliest shadow of a dream of a rapprochement. It's disappointing – a little – but certainly my heart's not broken – only rather pricked.'

Lytton was also encountering some of the other younger men now up at Cambridge – in particular Gerald Shove,[1] Hugh Dalton and James Elroy Flecker ('whom we now don't much like'), but with none of them was he able to communicate freely and intimately. How different it had been when he was up! In those delightful far-off days things were less ambiguous and therefore more exciting. One's soul could discharge

[1] Gerald Frank Shove (1887–1947), the economist, who became a lecturer in economics at Cambridge and a Fellow of King's, was at this time a keen left-wing socialist and syndicalist.

itself in covert glances, allusions, delicate hints. It was easy enough
to be personal, intimate, amused, even to make implications about
amours, when one was twenty, and life was an affair of plain sailing.
But when 'middle age', Spectatorial responsibilities and a ruined
digestive system combined to harness and perplex one, and when one's
mind was lost amid an eternal abyss of incertitudes and ghostly agitations, what could be expected? Perhaps his failure to make new and
rewarding friendships was due to the overall confusion of his mind.
Certainly it had enough to be confused about. 'My story is now quite
unfit for publication,' he wrote to Clive Bell (12 June 1908), '– not
because of its decency, but because of its muddles – it's aesthetically
very poor indeed. . . . So far my successes among the younger generation have not been remarkable. Am I altogether passé? But I occasionally
find myself shattered, and I *have* embarqued on various intrigues. But it
won't do, it'll none of it do. Beauty is a torment and a snare, and youth is
cruel, cruel! Today I drove in a barouche to the races with a select
assortment of undergraduates. Doesn't it sound romantic? But it was
merely rather nice. Yesterday I drank champagne from 11 to 1,
and discussed love and friendship, and the day before I went to the
A[mateur] D[ramatic] C[lub]. . . . and was bored – or amused? – I
really can't make up my mind.'

This mood of gentle nostalgia, of introvert but not unpleasurable
melancholy was nicely suited, Lytton felt, to his poetic muse. For long
hours he would sit closeted in a small inner sanctum working at his
verses, solitary but not altogether undisturbed. For so often he heard –
or seemed to hear – the door of the outer room open, and someone
enter, and – did he advance and come towards the inner door? Or was
it the bedmaker? Or the wind outside? Or simply imagination –
spectres from the old days? Lytton could not tell; only the inner door
never opened and he sat on alone and silent, listening, and then re-
applying himself to his work, striving to arrange in some poetic pattern
the vague, muddled and tormented moments of his past. Much of his
verse during the last three years was spun round the idealized figure of
Duncan Grant, and perhaps the most successful one – because it is
least pretentious – catches something of the shrouded, insubstantial
quality of their relationship.

> *One day you found me – was I there?*
> *Perhaps it was my ghost you found –*
> *I know not; but you found me fair*
> *And love was in my lips and hair*
> *And in my eyes profound.*

You kissed me, and you kissed me oft.
– Was it my ghost or was it me? –
Your kisses were so sweet, so soft,
The happy cherubim aloft
Wept that such things should be.

You vanished then – I know not why;
But that you vanished 'tis most true.
Yet did you vanish? – Till I die
Methinks I'll doubt (my ghost or I)
If 'twas your ghost or you.

But in view of the dramatic events now about to burst upon him, perhaps the most fitting comment and summary of the whole affair – implying all his peculiarly mingled incredulity, innocence and awareness – is contained in a couple of casual sentences which he had addressed earlier that year in a letter to Duncan Grant. 'The world is damned queer – it really is,' he wrote. 'But people won't recognize the immensity of its queerness.'

7

A POCKET HANDKERCHIEF ON MONT BLANC

On his return to Hampstead at the beginning of July, Lytton discovered that for some time past Duncan Grant had been deeply in love with Maynard Keynes, and that his affection was returned.

Of all the darkly amorous crises sprinkled throughout his life, this was perhaps the most wretched. It came as an explosive shock, a kind of death. Like the violent eruption of an earthquake which alters every feature in the surrounding landscape, this sudden revelation destroyed in a few moments the whole structure of his last three years. The two fixed points upon which his unstable emotional existence had been so delicately suspended were instantly rooted up. He could not be sure that he would ever recover from the calamity, though reason told him that he eventually must. Yet, overwhelming all this agony of bitter disenchantment and regret was the aching realization that he had been made to look impossibly ridiculous. As he retraced the pattern of events in his mind, it was this thought which harrowed and excruciated him most. How inconceivably blind he had been! No wonder he had felt swamped by so much muddle and confusion. Now that he knew the simple truth, everything slipped neatly and obviously into place. In the first instance it had been he who had driven the two of them together, almost against their will. And to think that all the time he had been confiding to Keynes about Duncan's childish irresponsibility and inexplicable elusiveness, and joking with Duncan on the subject of Keynes's irremediable lack of passion (*lack of passion!*), they could well have been comparing notes. How they must have laughed at him! And then, too, while he was cautiously meditating on the relative merits of living with either Keynes or Duncan, they had gone off – so he now discovered – and found accommodation together in Belgrave Road.[1] God! What a total fool he had made of himself. The world was indeed more immensely queer than even he had recognized!

There was nothing for it now but to put the best possible face upon it all. At any rate he resolved that by no word or action should he in any way swell his past accumulation of foolishness. To expend his mounting fury and remorse in pointless recrimination would only tend to emphasize all his previous stupidity and incomprehension. Nor must he break off diplomatic relations. For one thing this affair of Duncan's and Keynes's might still only be a brief flash in the pan; and for another, any pompous and humourless reaction could only make him appear even more inane – always providing, of course, that that were possible. Instead then he must treat it as a comparatively small incident, and so, by minimizing everything, reduce the magnitude of his own idiot cuckoldry. If supremely civilized, supremely controlled, his behaviour might win him back some of the esteem which he had shed, and at the same time prompt feelings of guilt in his treacherous friends.

Lytton's reaction was, or attempted to be, impossibly altruistic, like an overacted mimicry of Christ, a sentimentalized personification in some weird Passion play. To Keynes, whom he detested now more than at any other moment in his life, he wrote: 'Dear Maynard, I only know that we've been friends far too long to stop being friends now. There are some things that I shall try not to think of, and you must do your best to help me in that; and you must believe that I do sympathize and don't hate you and that if you were here now I should probably kiss you, except that Duncan would be jealous, which would never do!'

Keynes's response to this magnanimity was all that Lytton could have desired. 'Your letter made me cry,' he wrote back, 'but I was very glad to get it.' He wished very much to write something more, the letter

---

[1] After a short tenancy at Belgrave Road, they moved to 21 Fitzroy Square. Then, in 1911, they shared a house at 38 Brunswick Square with Adrian and Virginia Stephen, Gerald Shove and Leonard Woolf. Later still they moved to 46 Gordon Square which they shared with Clive and Vanessa Bell.

went on, but he did not know what to say. Might he come to Hampstead? This proposition, naturally enough, was the very last thing to appeal to Lytton, who was always far surer of himself on paper than in person. All sorts of disasters might ensue from such a visit. Keynes would eloquently put his case and make himself appear to be innocent and upstanding; the mere sight of him might well stir Lytton into losing his temper and making a further ass of himself. Far better to keep Keynes at some distance where he remained permanently at a disadvantage. He therefore replied saying that on the whole – if Keynes did not mind – he thought it best that he should *not* come and see him at present. He was still most horribly *accablé* with the Inchbald introduction, and this combined with the general chaotic situation had reduced him to such a state of ruin and confusion that he would really have nothing whatever to say at an interview. Soon perhaps he would be going away – he did not know where or with whom. He was rather ill, too.

But Keynes still pressed resolutely for a meeting and postponed his journey to Cambridge in order to force one. Would Lytton, he inquired, like to go with him to see *Isadora* Duncan dance, and forget the real Duncan, whom no one in the world could help but adore?

Lytton, however, ignored altogether both the pun and the invitation in his answer. He had, he wrote, sent Keynes a present of some books to adorn *his rooms at King's*. Doubtless they were waiting for him now. He asked his friend to examine carefully the binding which, he believed, was of a quality and type that he particularly admired. He hoped that Maynard would be pleased with this little gift; the book on walking-sticks was especially entertaining.

And so there was nothing that Keynes could do but concede a tactical defeat, quit London and pick up his books at Cambridge. They were delightful, he wrote back on his arrival there: 'Dear Lytton, why have you given them me? They show something you couldn't write, and they make me feel a great deal which you must understand without my saying it. Oh Lytton, it is too good of you to behave like this.'

To wrest from his opponent the very last trick of beneficence, there now only remained one final card for Lytton to play – he thanked Keynes lavishly for the letter thanking him for the books. 'Thank you,' he replied, 'dear Maynard, for what you wrote about the books. I'm glad you liked them, and it's very nice of you to feel what you say. Duncan is very kind, too. I'm sure of one thing, and that is that affection makes everything right. So I'm really extraordinarily happy now.'

In his simultaneous dealings with Duncan Grant, towards whom his attitude was more complicated, Lytton was unable to sustain the same high-minded and impassive front of dignity. He began, however, on quite the loftiest note of altruism yet struck. Duncan, he knew, was considering taking art lessons in London with a certain Dr Bach. What gesture could be finer than to offer to pay for these lessons? It was an inspired stroke, which drew from his cousin an almost identical response to that from Keynes. 'Lytton you're *too* kind,' he told him, 'you make me burst into tears; I cannot bear your being so completely good and generous. I think it cruel of you to plunge me into such contradictory emotions.'

And there, perhaps, Lytton should have been content to leave it. But he could not. Remembering the past – Ledbury and Versailles in particular – it was impossible not to believe that Duncan had once felt something for him, and that everything might so easily have turned out altogether different. Duncan had praised him now for his kindness, and he could not forbear to send off a somewhat rueful answer: 'Oh, Duncan, I have thought of unkind letters, unkind words – and heaven knows you may have them from me yet; but now it is not with that in my heart that I want to speak. It is not for you that I am feeling, but for myself; and I should like you to know my thoughts . . .

'Concealment would have been easier now too, as you may guess, since if I am to speak all it must be to one more than I want to speak to. He [Keynes] will tell you, no doubt, that I am wrong, that I am foolish because I am jealous, and that I am to be pitied because I am in love. I am ready to face even pity, even the pity of both of you, on the condition that Duncan knows my mind.

'There are things in me, I know very well, which are beastly; and there are things in you Duncan, which irritate me, which pain me, which I even dislike. If you understand that, will you understand this besides – that I am your friend? It would be irrelevant to say more.'

But once this much had been said it was impossible not to say more. The dams of absolute self-restraint had been opened a crack, and the voluble waters of self-pity, of anger, recrimination and humility cascaded through. On the evening of the day – 17 July – that Duncan received this letter, he called round unannounced at Belsize Park Gardens. Lytton could not refuse to admit him, but said very little and did not attempt to stop him when, after a brief, uneasy session, Duncan rose to leave. Later that night he sent off a short note, saying that he had thought it best that Duncan should leave when he did. Otherwise 'I might have been stupid'. Whatever happened, he concluded with a familiar refrain, they were still friends.

What really pained Lytton, however, was Duncan's ensuing silence. Unlike the persistent Keynes, he did not write for days on end to expatiate on his, Lytton's, angelic and self-effacing goodness. After the first, rather short letter, there was nothing – no consistently renewed and visible evidence of Duncan's contrition. What was he thinking? Lytton's imagination kept churning away until, after a fortnight of waiting, he could no longer contain his doubts. The urge to set down and to explain his own thoughts and injuries grew too strong for him to resist. But he was clutching at straws in the wind, begging for the kind of pity he professed so much to abhor – pity of himself, not for his grief. And so, though he painfully insists, yet again, that nothing need greatly have changed, that their sublimated friendship is still intact, the letter does not, significantly, conclude with a mere *à bientôt*.

67 BPG July 31st 1908.

Dearest Duncan

I want to say something, though I'm afraid it may annoy you, and I daresay I've said it already – but I feel an uneasy suspicion that I may not have made myself quite clear. It is this – though I like Maynard, I cannot think of him as you do, or else, I suppose, I should be in love with him too! The result is that I don't take your affair as seriously as you do either, and therefore imagine that you will some day or other return from Cythera. But that, I feel, is neither here nor there, and so long as you *are* in Cythera, I don't see why that fact should prevent my liking both of you as much as I always have. Please realize what I mean, if it's not too vilely expressed, and forgive me if it's all obvious and I'm merely harping on what you know. I can't bear to think that other people may think I think what I don't, and this must be my excuse for writing what I know will give you some pain. It looks rather bleak, and I wanted to say it, but there was no opportunity when you were away. When you write, it would be very kind if you would say that you understand – I'm sure you won't think I *feel* bleakly. Dear me, this seems to be about nothing but myself, which is so unimportant!

. . . Oh lord, lord, why do we live in such a distorted coagulated world? I feel all topsy-turvy and out of place, as if I were a pocket handkerchief that somebody had dropped on the top of Mont Blanc. It's all too preposterous, and what's worse, I'm well aware that I do very little but add to the preposterousness. But I believe that a just God – a *really* just God – would completely bear me out. Oh! You're laughing.

This is an absurd kind of letter, you must admit; I'll write again perhaps more sensibly, from somewhere or other. And you must write to me. It'll be forwarded. Adieu!

Your
Lytton.

Early in August, Lytton travelled up to Scotland on a voyage of recovery. Accompanied by James, who himself hoped to wear off the ill-effects of his 'dumb deaf and blind adoration' of Rupert Brooke, he went first to the Isle of Skye, putting up for a week at the Sligachan Inn. Sligachan was a strange and desolate place, some nine miles from Portree, the nearest centre of civilization. On all sides lay deserts of bumpy green morass, sea-lochs, and, farther off, distorted blunt black mountains bulging into the sky and wrapped in a pale wet mist – a magnificent but dehumanized spectacle that seemed to act upon Lytton as a recuperative force, at once conciliatory and life-enhancing. From the absence of all herded jostling humanity he derived a wonderful solace; while from the great vegetable processes of Nature going on all around he drew fresh incentive for a renewed existence. The miserable past was largely obliterated and he was remade. A new feeling of his separate, unique and indestructible identity flooded through him, finding its strength, paradoxically, from the recognition of his anonymity and entire submergence in some vaster, grander organism. There must, he thought, be something about this champagne-like air which helped to revive him, as from the anaesthetic for a partial amputation exorcizing his old injury, and stifling for ever the repercussions of pain and humiliation that arose from it. Of course, he was still feeble, still convalescent after such a major operation. The wound, though cleansed, had as yet to heal fully. But the climate seemed miraculously hygienic. Occasional blazing sunbursts would light up within him unsuspected reservoirs of hope and anticipation; and even the perpetual rain was soothing and merciful, like a gentle antiseptic washing away the stench and stagnation of human intercourse. His long sickness of living had now begun to mend, and nothing brought him all things.

Such was the amazing physical energy released in them, that the two brothers were able to make a couple of expeditions on foot and through the almost impenetrable deluge to Portree, which stirred in Lytton faint tremors of his old emotions. The youth of the place seemed to him resplendent – even the women were good-looking! After a week at Skye he felt ready, if not to be re-embedded in the horrors of London, at least to make his first step back south. He was beginning to grow more critical and complaining – a sure sign of improvement. The second trip to Portree convinced him that, far from being attractive, the population was uniformly ugly beyond his wildest nightmares. And the mountains, hotels and local inhabitants appeared to him to be all on a par – all highly eccentric. The Sligachan Inn was decent enough, but filled to bursting point with fat ladies, fishers and climbers, who canted endlessly on about fishing and climbing, and threw sly apprehensive

glances at the two thin-legged, bespectacled monstrosities sitting paralysed by the fire. After some days of torture in the smoking-room, the
pressure of continual scrutiny from this crowd of burnt and weather-
beaten Alpinists and fishers of fish drove them into a private sitting-
room, where they could relax by themselves in luxurious and intelligent
silence. So, at least, Lytton told Maynard Keynes. Yet even here, the
mounting curiosity which their presence seemed to excite telepathically
communicated itself through the walls to them, and they decided to
flee south to Rothiemurchus.

They arrived at Rothiemurchus in the second week of August and
for the next month put up in a tiny cottage with only one room and a
'cave' at their disposal. 'The "accommodation" is, as people say, rather
primitive,' Lytton explained to Swithinbank (13 August 1908), '. . . a
smallish sitting-room, where I have to sleep, and a sort of cave adjoining it, where brother James sleeps . . . and there is an exceedingly
amiable Scottish matron who does everything; and that's all.' Yet the
place was everything that could be desired. The beauties of the countryside were truly awe-inspiring. To be among them once again made
Lytton feel that life was definitely worth living after all. The beauties of
humanity were rarer, though the cottage – almost touching the road to
Loch an Eilein[1] – was in a strategic position for observing them. All
day and every day the world swept past his window in carriages, brakes
and motors; and as the road divided just in front of the house, many of
them stopped to ask the landlady the way to the loch, so that Lytton
could press his nose against the glass and stare his fill. It was, for the
time being, as close as he wished to be to mortal men.

While at Rothiemurchus Lytton continued to lead what was, for
him, a very healthy and virile life – unceasing walks and sittings-out
in the sunlight and brushing-away of flies. He was out of doors so
much that his nose soon grew red and raw as Bardolph's. It was all
very fortifying. On one boiling day he went so far as to make a brief,
unsuccessful return to savagery, plunged wildly into a mountain pool,
lost his eyeglasses and very nearly perished miserably of exposure. 'We
are tapis here (brother James and I)', he wrote to Clive Bell (13 August
1908), 'in a hut near a lake, like so many lop-eared rabbits. The beauties
of nature satisfy me (for the moment); I go out before breakfast in
pumps and brood over the lake; I walk in the heat of the day on to the
summits of mountains.'

[1] Loch an Eilein is a Gaelic place-name meaning 'the loch of the island'. A famous
beauty spot, it is incredibly romantic and much reproduced on tourist picture postcards.
The island-fortress in the middle of its placid waters was, as legend has it, the lair of the
notorious Wolf of Badenoch, who in fact died several years before it was put up. The
fortifications, now in ruins, were erected in the fifteenth and sixteenth centuries.

The Shakespeare Society, Trinity College, Cambridge. In the back row, Thoby Stephen is second from the left and on the extreme right is Walter Lamb. In the front row, on the extreme left, is Lytton Strachey, and on the extreme right Leonard Woolf

E. M. Forster in his rooms at King's

Roger Fry: self-portrait
(*National Portrait Gallery*)

Duncan Grant and Maynard Keynes

He was also writing again – things other than his *Spectator* reviews, which he had somehow managed to keep up throughout the crisis. Over these weeks, in a long series of letters to Maynard Keynes, he fabricated a highly ingenious and quite imaginary love-adventure – the most inspired of all his fictional compositions. Keynes – now passing two leisurely months in the Orkneys with Duncan Grant and working at *A Treatise on Probability* while having his portrait painted[1] – was by turns curious, amazed, *almost* incredulous. Then at last came the catharsis. Not a single word of it was true. Everything had been re-counted in the lightest, most amusing manner; but there can be no doubt as to the motive – deliberate or unconscious – behind this skilful and extraordinarily elaborate piece of invention, with all its enticing scandal and controlled melodrama. Keynes had been used as a Brother Confessor to something that never took place; his old role had been falsified, and Lytton had got a little of his own back in fiction for the way he had been deceived in fact. From now on, James, who had helped him each evening over their peat fire to concoct this plot, would be his confidant in real life.

During July, when the crisis first broke, Lytton had felt up to reading little except Voltaire's correspondence which, he told Swithinbank, was 'the only completely satisfactory thing in the world'. But it was another favourite volume he took up with him to Scotland – Professor Giles's anthology of *Chinese Poems*, in which he now entirely immersed him-self, writing a long appreciation of them for MacCarthy's *New Quarterly*. He had had a surfeit in the last weeks of high emotional drama and complexity, and his strength and stamina were seriously impaired. He wanted to get away from people, to avoid, even in his reading, anything that involved him too painfully in raw passion and direct suspense. Instead he looked for simplicity, tenderness, consola-tion – emotions faintly recollected in tranquillity. To allay his remorse, to escape from the self-consuming rage, the nausea and suffering which welled up out of his recent tribulations, he abandoned the bitter, in-consequent world of reality for the magic sphere of pure art, where every loose end, that weighs on the heart like a broken assignation, was satisfactorily tied up, where tragedy was smoothed and rounded into song, and love and lust were no more than a bewitching interplay of syllables. In Professor Giles's anthology he found just the perfect dreamy and pervading melancholy to chime in with that medley of old emotions moving beneath his usual carapace of frigid aloofness. The

[1] This portrait, which was exhibited at the Duncan Grant Tate Gallery retrospective exhibition of 1959, and again, in 1964, at Wildenstein's 'Duncan Grant and his World', now belongs to the Provost and Fellows of King's College, Cambridge.

peculiar enchantment of these poems, which caught, through a hundred subtle modulations, all the sadness in the fragility of human relations and transmuted it into something delicate and profound and lasting, was like a balm to his wounded spirit. Fragmentary, allusive, evanescent, they seemed to compel reminiscence and romance, to redeem all the horrors of the past, changing its sorrow and vanity, misunderstanding and sentimentality from pettiness into something universal and other-worldly. It was comforting to reflect that morbid affairs of the heart such as his had been going on for centuries, and had so often been overcome. And now he, in his turn, was weathering the storm and sailing into smoother waters. The old pain seemed finally to be assimilated into a philosophical calm, that was the last stage in that gradual metamorphosis from youth to dry, uninterrupted middle age.

Just how Lytton associated his own personal story and blended it in with the charm and antiquity of the Chinese poems can best be demonstrated by quoting the final long paragraph of his essay, which concludes not with a translation, but with some of his own verses:

'Our finest lyrics are for the most part the memorials of passion, or the swift and exquisite expressions of "the tender eye-dawn of aurorean love". In these lyrics of China the stress and fury of desire are things unknown, and, in their topsy-turvy Oriental fashion, they are concerned far more with memories of love than expectations of it. They look back upon love through a long vista of years which have smoothed away the agitations of romance and have brought with them the calm familiarity of happiness, or the quiet desolation of regret. Thus, while one cannot be certain that this love is not another name for sublimated friendship, one can be sure enough that these lovers are always friends. Affection, no doubt, is the word that best describes such feelings; and it is through its mastery of the tones and depths of affection that our anthology holds a unique place in the literature of the world. For this cause, too, its pages, for all their strange antiquity, are fresh to us; their humanity keeps them immortal. The poets who wrote them seem to have come to the end of experience, to have passed long ago through the wonders and the tumults of existence, to have arrived at last in some mysterious haven where they could find repose among memories that were for ever living, and among discoveries that were for ever old. Their poetry is the voice of civilization which has returned upon itself, which has achieved, after the revolution of ages, simplicity. It has learnt to say some things so finely that we forget, as we listen to it, that these are not the only things that can be said.

We parted at the gorge and cried 'Good cheer!'
The sun was setting as I closed my door;
Methought, the spring will come again next year,
But he may come no more.

The words carry with them so much significance, they produce so profound a sense of finality, that they seem to contain within themselves a summary of all that is most important in life. There is something almost cruel in art such as this; one longs, somehow or other, to shake it; and one feels that, if one did, one would shake it into ice. Yet, as it is, it is far from frigid; but it is dry – dry as the heaped rose-leaves in a porcelain vase, rich with the perfume of how many summers! The scent transports us to old gardens, to old palaces; we wander incuriously among forsaken groves; we half expect some wonder, and we know too well that nothing now will ever come again. Reading this book, we might well be in the alleys of Versailles; and our sensations are those of a writer whose works, perhaps, are too modern to be included in Professor Giles's anthology:

Here in the ancient park, I wait alone.
The dried-up fountains sleep in beds of stone;
The paths are still; and up the sweeping sward
No lovely lady passes, no gay lord.

Why do I linger? Ah! perchance I'll find
Some solace for the desolated mind
In yon green grotto, down the towering glade,
Where the bronze Cupid glimmers in the shade.'

The composition of this literary essay seemed to purge Lytton of much of that faintness and frailty which had eclipsed his being, especially during those first wet days at Sligachan. Rothiemurchus, he now felt, was an altogether more rational and civilized region than Skye, with its multitudes of imbecile mountains and eternal rain. 'This is such divine country,' he wrote to his mother (2 September 1908), 'that I feel as if I should never be able to tear myself away from it. I am enjoying myself very much, and am feeling unusually well.' And to Virginia Stephen he wrote: 'This place is, qua place, perfection. One begins to realize in it that Nature may be romantic and beautiful. I linger by lakes, and tear up mountains, all day long. The nights are spent over a peat fire writing endless letters which – it seems to me – are never answered . . .'

The only drawback to this peace and beauty was the encircling presence of his family. Pippa and Pernel Strachey came up to stay with Trevor Grant in Rothiemurchus, swelling the copious number of Lytton's relations already there. Their persistent and rather alarming propinquity during the four weeks of his holiday grew increasingly irksome to him. 'My only consolation', he wrote to Virginia Stephen, 'is that my health, as a matter of fact, is almost tolerable. I am sunburnt and I digest. Do write to me if you can. Pippa and Pernel are in a cottage half a mile away, and hundreds of dread relatives lurk behind every bush. They are of all varieties – countesses, country cousins, faded civil servants, and young heirs to landed property – and all eminently repellent. I think I shall make an Encyclopaedia of them. It would be enormously large.'

By the second week of September Lytton's only consolation was rudely snatched away from him, when he was attacked 'by a most disgusting internal disease which seemed to be a chill on the entrails', as he diagnosed it to Clive Bell. '. . . It was unpleasant, as you may imagine, struggling with this among the rigours of a Scotch summer and the sanitary arrangements of a Scotch cottage.' As soon as he was able to travel, he fled southwards on a journey which, he told Moore, 'very nearly killed me'. Moore had now moved from Scotland to a house at Richmond, and Lytton wrote to tell him, in words which reflect something of his own dilapidated condition on re-entering England, that he had visited his old home. 'I spent two nights in Edinburgh, and took a walk to look at Buccleuch Place – it seemed very deserted and grey.'

8

CUL-DE-SAC

'Deserted and grey' – this was certainly how Lytton saw himself on his return that September to the home influences of Hampstead. Looked after by his sisters and fed on a special preparation of meat-juices, he lay in hope of a quick recovery and a quick escape elsewhere. It was not a happy time. But he was well cared for and temporarily too sick to be actively discontented. 'I think I'm still rather ill,' he wrote to Clive Bell (17 September 1908), 'and I'm certainly lazy, but I have projects for an infinitude of things. I've begun to read Condorcet, and it's charming, and I should like to go straight through his two volumes – but the time! the time!'

As he became stronger, he again grew more adversely critical of things; and his change of mood appears this time to have been mirrored in his reading. No longer was he content to meditate dreamily over those gentle Chinese lyrics, which seemed in his more aggressive moments to be rather too insipid and over-polite. Instead, he now turned for the first time to the correspondence between Voltaire and Jean d' Alembert. In the militant reflections which these letters prompted, can be over-heard the distinct grumblings of that mood which was to develop and crystallize into the outward-looking anarchical period of his life, a period which found its culmination in the writing of *Eminent Victorians*. 'I've also read for the first time the correspondence between Voltaire and D'Alembert,' he wrote off to his mother (2 September 1908). 'Don't you think there's a good deal to be said in favour of a war à outrance with the infâme. I think France is on the whole a more civilized place than England, and it seems to me that may be the result of their having had their superstitions and prejudices rooted up once and for all by the philosophers. What a disgrace that the education of the country should depend upon the squabbles of nonconformists and anglicans! But what else can happen so long as everyone goes on taking these people at their own valuation?'

This spirit of simmering revolutionary ferment was as yet relatively infrequent, and Lytton soon returned obediently enough to the placid broken-down routine, as he rather too disparagingly put it, 'of a literary hack'. He attended second-rate plays; devoured solitary lunches at Simpson's where, he was pained to observe, the mutton that autumn was, rather more often than not, a little disappointing; visited St Loe and Charles Graves[1] to collect further consignments of books and to be assured that the *Spectator* was never complete when there was nothing by him in it; went by taxi to the London Library for more books to help him with these reviews; and divided his remaining hours between Hampstead and Bloomsbury. 'There are moments – on the Heath, of course, – when I seem to myself to see life steadily and see it whole,' he wrote to Virginia Stephen, who was in Paris with Clive and Vanessa Bell, 'but they're only moments; as a rule I can make nothing out. You don't find much difficulty, I think. Is it because you *are* a virgin? Or because, from some elevation or another, it's possible to manage it, and you happen to be there? Ah! there are so many difficulties! So many difficulties! I want to write a novel about a Lord Chancellor and his naughty son, but I can't for the life of me think of anything like the shadow of a plot, and then – the British public! Oh dear, let's all go off to the Faroe Islands, and forget the existence of Robin Mayor and Mrs

[1] Charles Graves, assistant editor of the *Spectator*, who had worked with St Loe on the *Liberal Unionist* and the *Cornhill*, and who was a contributor to *Punch*.

Humphry Ward,[1] and drink rum punch of an evening, and live happily ever after!'

Though he stayed at King's for one week-end late in October, Lytton did not visit Cambridge again during the final four months of this year. There were too many people there whom he had little inclination to see. 'Cambridge has become a complete myth to me,' he wrote to James in November, '– with all the mystery and importance of a myth. I imagine it such a wonderful place.' To preserve this illusion intact he continued to stay away, but the urge to leave London was strong upon him: he went for a few days to live with Moore at 6 Pembroke Villas, on the Green at Richmond; he made plans to visit his Greek ladies where, he told Clive Bell, 'I shall probably be loved'; and when Virginia Stephen returned from Paris, he arranged to go off with her and Adrian, her brother, not on a reckless expedition to the Faroe Islands, but quietly down to Penmenner House, at the Lizard in Cornwall, where he had passed some of his happier and more comfortable hours with Moore's special congregations of Apostolic intellect. After a few peaceful days together spent reading, walking and talking, the Stephens left, and Lytton, who wished to postpone his return to London for as long as possible, stayed on 'in extraordinary solitude, willing to sell my soul for a little conversation. How long I shall bear it I haven't the faintest idea. There have already been moments in the long evening when I've shuddered, but Saint-Simon supports me, wonderful as ever.'

He arrived back at Hampstead towards the end of November for the last time that year. It had been for him a bad, perhaps even his worst, year; but it was not over yet. Now, finally, the time had come for Swithinbank, the understudy, to step into the principal role in his life. For long he had been a mere auxiliary, a recruit; but this winter he should at last be promoted from the reserve to the Front Line. Lytton could at least congratulate himself on not being entirely deserted, for having successfully scotched that mad venture to the Fiji Islands, and for having groomed Swithinbank as a fitting companion. He wrote off to him an affectionate letter, only to receive in reply the news that his friend was making arrangements to take service in India. It was a painful shock, and Lytton at once exerted himself in order to change Swithinbank's mind again. The letter he now sent off (20 September 1908) was written in an unusually urgent and even earnest tone, and is

---

[1] Mrs Humphry Ward (1851–1920), popular novelist and author of *Robert Elsmere*. A niece of Matthew Arnold and a strong reactionary, her novels, especially the earlier ones, examined problems of faith and ethics with a solemn and unsmiling sentimentality that was taken at the time for high intellect.

particularly interesting in someone who, not so long ago, used to envy his brothers for their active, Anglo-India careers. 'I believe as strongly as I believe anything that you oughtn't to go,' he wrote. 'Have you thought enough of the horror of the solitude and the wretchedness of every single creature out there and the degrading influences of those years away from civilization? I've had experience – I've seen my brothers, and what's happened to them, and it's sickening to think of. Oh! You've got your chance – your chance of being well off and comfortable among the decent things of life, and among your friends.'

But this time there was no dissuading him from his folly. He had decided; and Lytton was forced to capitulate. 'But go away,' he exclaimed in hopeless irritation, 'and be a great man, and rule the blacks, and enjoy yourself among apes and peacocks.' From the official point of view, the point of view of *Who's Who* or the *Dictionary of National Biography*, Swithinbank's career was only just beginning: he rose to be Commissioner of the Pega Division of Burma from 1933 to 1942, and subsequently adviser to the Secretary of State in London – a reasonably distinguished and honourable life. But for Lytton, this departure – like that, apparently, of Leonard Woolf four years before – spelt out his final extinction, his DEATH. Their correspondence lingered on to the following year and then shut down altogether. And as for Lytton himself, he was temporarily flung back towards Duncan Grant. There was no one else. Not, of course, that he ever recaptured his former passionate intimacy; but he continued for a while to mouth and exchange the same, now fatally moribund, formulae of words and endearments, like some circus animal who has been taught a single trick for the public, and who persists hypnotically to play it in his cage long after the performance is over and the audience departed.

But no tricks or deceptions could conceal from Lytton his own abysmal failure, both in human relationships and in the advancement of his literary ambitions. Life is a synonym for desire, and all that he desired in happiness and success had eluded him, and now seemed farther off than ever. His few accomplishments appeared trivial when set beside his vague and limitless aspirations. The truth was that his move towards a new life had not been bold enough. The dangers of absolute freedom had proved too intimidating, so that he had merely replaced the chains of his past with the shackles of the present dim and misty existence. All that he had wanted fundamentally to alter remained in essence the same as before; all that he had wished to develop and perfect was destroyed and lay in ruins about him. The tumour of frustrated desire throbbed and swelled within his head. His buoyant faith in the ultimate, though perhaps distant, arrival of a Voltairian millennium of reason, had

locked in conflict with his devitalized apathy. Though no one could
deny that he had full cause for grief and pessimism, he simply could not
submit to the destiny of a mere journeyman. On the contrary, he would
do such things – what they were yet he knew not – but they would
be the wonders of the earth!

But for the time being his powers could find no all-absorbing purpose
to harness them satisfactorily. Oppression descended upon him like
an airless cloud. It had been a terrible year, and at the end of it, here
he was, left alone with projects for an obscure infinitude of things, but
no likelihood of bringing any of them to fulfilment. Deserted and
grey: the words which had come to him as he stood before Buccleuch
Place, dismal and uninhabited in the autumn wind and rain, epitomized
the predicament in which he had landed up after almost twenty-nine
years of struggle.

CHAPTER VIII

Independent and Spectatorial Essays

'It's a pity that writing should be nearly always such an intolerable process.'
Lytton Strachey to B. W. Swithinbank (13 August 1908)

'I suppose I shall worry through somehow – but how I loathe writing for money and against time!'
Lytton Strachey to David Garnett (23 August 1915)

I

BIOGRAPHIA LITERARIA

On 3 March 1903, Lytton had written to his mother: 'I have taken 5 shares in Trevelyan and Co's Review, feeling (1) it was the least I can do, and (2) that I rather wanted to as he [G. M. Trevelyan] says, every time he sees me, "There is a majority of Apostles on the Editorial Committee!" So there's room for hope at least that it won't be as fearful as its prospectus. They haven't yet thought of a name.'

Later that same year, this new intellectual liberal monthly was christened the *Independent Review*, and its first issue came out in October. The aspirations of its subscribers ran high, and when E. M. Forster purchased the initial number, he felt convinced that 'a new age had begun'. As it turned out, the review did not enjoy a particularly long life, though it elicited in its time many good articles. The consumptive Nathaniel Wedd, Lowes Dickinson and George Trevelyan were all associated with the paper's foundation and the laying down of its political policy – which was to combat militant imperialism, protectionism and Joe Chamberlain, and to advocate what they considered to be a constructive domestic programme. Since the type of qualified radical humanism which it favoured has always been a popular line among English middle- and mupple-class intellectuals, the *Independent*

Review soon attracted some of the most able men of letters of the day, including Lascelles Abercrombie, Hilaire Belloc, Wilfrid Blunt, H. N. Brailsford, G. K. Chesterton, Ramsay MacDonald and H. G. Wells. In April 1907 the name of the periodical was changed to the *Albany Review*, and several further distinguished persons were added to the list of contributors, among them William Archer, A. C. Bradley, Thomas Hardy, Andrew Lang, Gilbert Murray, G. W. E. Russell and Sidney Webb. Under both names the review ran from the autumn of 1903 to the spring of 1908, bringing out altogether some fourteen volumes, ten numbers of which include papers by Lytton. Yet though he remained a faithful contributor, Lytton did not wholeheartedly go along with the official policy, which he considered to be still too reactionary and illiberal. Several of his pieces which appeared in the review's columns were intended to be veiled attacks on the Liberal Party.[1] By adopting a controlled, diplomatic tone he contrived to jam over his powder so that even the editor would not notice the political import of what he was saying. But it was a tiresome business, and perhaps, he sometimes reflected, once it was successfully achieved the efficacy of the powder had almost disappeared.

These essays, together with those which were printed in the *New Quarterly* from 1907 to 1910, were written ostensibly as reviews of current books, and may be divided into three different categories: those in which Lytton indulged his liking and wide knowledge of French literature; those which may be regarded as an overflow from his original Cambridge essay, 'English Letter Writers'; and finally a few miscellaneous pieces set in eighteenth-century England – his favourite period in English history.

It was when contributing to this first category that Lytton seems to have felt at his most assured. The opening issue of the *Independent Review* carried in it his very first published prose work entitled 'Two Frenchmen'. For an undergraduate of only twenty-three it is an astonishingly impressive essay, displaying not just literary promise, but mature achievement. 'The greatest misfortune that can happen to a witty man', the essay begins, 'is to be born out of France.' And with his own style Lytton clearly exhibits his personal preference for aphoristic neatness. Each sentence is beautifully balanced and finely condensed, and the whole composition flows with perfect smoothness. But in places his fondness for the epigrammatic is overstrained to the verge of triviality, as, for example, when he announces: 'La Rochefoucauld, there can be no doubt, was the cleverest duke who ever lived.'

[1] See, for example, 'The First Earl of Lytton', *Independent Review*, XII, March 1907, and included in *Literary Essays*.

Dealing not only with the two Frenchmen of the title, Vauvenargues and La Bruyère, but also with a third, La Rochefoucauld himself, the essay is particularly interesting for the split it shows between Lytton's purely impressionistic criticism and his more analytical method of examination. 'Two Frenchmen' reads almost like the product of two men in good working collaboration. While one of them is intoxicated by the sheer minstrelsy of elegant literary variations, the other evidently stands in need of strong drink in order to face up with equanimity to the petty self-interest and meanness of the human beings who chant these mellifluous songs. Thus he responds to La Rochefoucauld's writing with rapture, comparing it to 'a narrow strip of perfectly polished parquet whereon a bored and aristocratic dancer exquisitely moves'. But a little farther on, when he is evaluating the achievement of Vauvenargues and no longer under the hypnotic spell of La Rochefoucauld's literary performance, he notes with aversion his (La Rochefoucauld's) 'paradoxical cynicism', and condemns him for his 'portrait of humanity restricted and distorted to the extent of being (for all the sobriety of the presentment) really nothing more than an ingenious caricature'.

That Lytton's partiality for French literature did not overwhelm his critical faculties – even where his heroes were involved – is convincingly demonstrated by his paper on 'Voltaire's Tragedies', published in April 1905. As with 'Two Frenchmen', the piece starts off with a pithy epigram: 'The historian of Literature is little more than a historian of exploded reputations.' There can be little doubt that during these first years of writing criticism, Lytton, with his heightened sense of the ridiculous, was acutely conscious of how easy it is to be ludicrously mistaken in one's literary pronouncements. The effect of this constant awareness was to promote that inbred caution which held pretty firmly in check his more romantic flair. Here he telescopes into a tightly-knit, dry résumé the highly complex and unrealistic plot of Voltaire's *Alzire, ou Les Américains*, revealing as if almost by accident the fatuity and insignificance of the whole counterfeit concoction. In its ironic compression, with all the emphasis and foreshortening of caricature, 'Voltaire's Tragedies' stands out as an early miniature example of Lytton's biographical technique.[1]

Also anticipating the form of his later books is the fine biographical

---

[1] This essay also provides what is perhaps the first example of what austere persons would consider an atrocity. '[Voltaire] is capable, for instance, of writing lines as bad as . . .' Lytton explained, and gave three quotations, the last of which – 'Vous comprenez, seigneur, que je ne comprends pas' – was never in fact written by Voltaire at all, but was a parody invented by Lytton's sister Marjorie. But then, of course, Lytton only says that Voltaire was *capable* of writing lines as bad as this.

pen portrait he drew of 'Mademoiselle de Lespinasse'. This was the eighth of his articles to appear in the *Independent Review*, by which time the struggle between his sober reliance on known facts and the attraction which he always felt for romantic speculation is more jauntily presented: 'Who was her father? According to the orthodox tradition, she was the child of Cardinal de Tencin, whose sister, the famous Madame de Tencin, was the mother of d'Alembert. This story has the advantage of discovering a strange and concealed connexion between two lives which were afterwards to be intimately bound together; but it has the disadvantage of not being true.' All the same, such disadvantageous truth was not to frustrate altogether the expression of romanticism, and where Lytton was unable to interweave it unobtrusively with the main thread of his narrative, he falls back on personal asides which stick out at intervals like frayed and gaudy strands. His overblown comment, for instance, on one of Mademoiselle de Lespinasse's letters, is pure romantic rhetoric belonging, in mood, to his *Elizabeth and Essex* period: 'Who does not discover beneath these dreadful confidences', he asks darkly, 'a superhuman power moving mysteriously to an appointed doom?'

But if Lytton's imagination was intermittently romantic, premeditating and seeking to evolve fanciful mysteries in preference to solving real and tedious problems, his critical intelligence remained strictly classical, paring the wings of his more conjectural flights, and saving him from the risk of flopping into rich absurdity. This classicism is best exemplified by his unrivalled ability to describe and reconstruct a highly involved factual situation with absolute, compact lucidity. In this task he is never wearisome, never superfluous or dull, since he always goes straight to the point, sharply illuminating what hitherto had been merely shadowy and ambiguous. It seems quite evident, too, that realizing full well how adept he was in this sphere, his enjoyment was proportional to his self-confidence. Today, his style still retains all its sparkle and power to enliven the reader. He is, for instance, sympathetic to Mademoiselle de Lespinasse, and depicts her as an undeserving victim of circumstance – the way in which he sometimes saw himself. Though this interpretation may not be deeply perceptive, nevertheless her life and adventures are sorted out and narrated with such vividness that a stronger impression of her true likeness is conveyed to one than can be directly accounted for by the slightly sentimental estimate of her which this essay specifically puts forward.

Written at a time when he was still searching for some home from home – an idealized, amiable community where he could rediscover the joys of Cambridge – Lytton evokes the salon of Julie de Lespinasse in language, the sad, breathless intensity of which suggests that he already had in mind some notion of the then gradually emerging Bloomsbury Group. 'Oh! It was a place worth visiting – the little salon in the rue Saint-Dominique. And, if one were privileged to go there often, one found there what one found nowhere else – a sense of freedom and intimacy which was the outcome of real equality, a real understanding, a real friendship such as have existed, before or since, in few societies indeed.'

This fascination which Lytton felt to disentangle and clarify the complex impulses that lay behind a love affair revolving so close to the vortex of some glittering sophisticated social scene had affinities with his attraction to the stage, and is equally pronounced in his essay 'Lady Mary Wortley Montagu'. The self-deceit, the appeal of social reputation masquerading as profound human love, the welter of ambition and egotism so deftly intermixed with protestations of selfless devotion, all this emotional machinery conducted at the forefront of fashionable society was aggrandized, for Lytton, from something sordid and mean into the rich and forgivable flamboyance of a picturesque spectacle. The aristocratic sugar icing sweetened and made deliciously appetizing to his palate the whole messy, tasteless dish; the action on the platform was transformed from a rude conflict of raw and ruthless impulses into a carnival decked with fine regalia. Written two years after his 'English Letter Writers', 'Lady Mary Wortley Montagu' reveals a rather deeper, more intricate understanding of human nature. In the Cambridge essay Lytton had been too greatly swayed by Horace Walpole's portrait of Lady Mary as 'Moll Worthless' and was content to represent only the superficial truth. But in this later composition he shows that there existed another side to her, and he is at pains to emphasize the pathos and tragedy of bitter disillusionment which underlay her sterile eccentricities and which gave humanity to the 'old, foul, tawdry, painted, plastered personage' whom Walpole saw in the last dreadful years of her life.

The occasion of this article was a newly published biography, *Lady Mary Wortley Montagu and her Times* by George Paston. In referring specifically to this book, Lytton states in strong and unqualified terms the disgust he felt at the quality of contemporary biography – which he was soon enough to alter so fundamentally by the example of his own work. 'The book,' he wrote, 'with its slipshod writing, its uninstructed outlook, its utter lack of taste and purpose, is a fair specimen of the kind of biographical work which seems to give so much satisfaction to large numbers of our reading public. Decidedly, "they order the matter better in France", where such a production could never have appeared.'

Another of his essays produced as a corollary to his 'English Letter Writers' was 'Horace Walpole'. Walpole, of course, was one of Lytton's favourite literary figures, and here he defends him convincingly from Macaulay's brilliant caricature – 'mopping and mowing, spitting and gibbering, dressed out in its master's finery, and keeping an eye upon the looking-glass'. Ironically enough, some of the features which are depicted in this gloriously burlesque portrait might be said to resemble Lytton himself. In a passage which Lytton ignores, Macaulay had written of Walpole's literary capacities in words which some later critic might apply to the essays of Lytton Strachey with almost equal justification: 'What then is the charm, the irresistible charm of Walpole's writings? It consists, we think, in the art of amusing without exciting. He never . . . fills the imagination or touches the heart; but he keeps the mind of the reader constantly attentive and constantly entertained. . . . If we were to adopt the classification, not a very accurate classification, which Akenside has given of the pleasures of the imagination, we should say that with the Sublime and Beautiful Walpole had nothing to do, but that the third province, the Odd, was his peculiar domain.'

By his mastery of graceful decoration and the perpetual process of his sparkling imagery, Walpole banished that arid sense of boredom to which Lytton was so acutely susceptible that he had attributed it to Shakespeare. He felt a special affinity with Walpole's deceptive and subtle character, and liked to see the incongruity between his own private and public self reproduced in the double personality of Walpole. So much is evident from a passage which comprises the whole essence of his defence against Macaulay's soaring banalities: 'But the truth seems to be, in spite of "those glaring and obvious peculiarities which could not escape the most superficial observation" – his angry, cutting sentences, his constant mockery of his enemies, his constant quarrels with his friends, and his perpetual reserve – that Walpole's nature was in reality peculiarly affectionate. There can be no doubt that he was sensitive to an extraordinary degree; and it is much more probable that the defects – for defects they certainly were – which he showed in social intercourse, were caused by an excess of this quality of sensitiveness, rather than by any lack of sincere feeling. It is impossible to quarrel with one's friends unless one likes them; and it is impossible to like some people very much without disliking other people a good deal. These elementary considerations are quite enough to account for the vagaries and the malice of Walpole.'

There is plain autobiographical interest, too, in 'Sir Thomas Browne', which was the first major piece of criticism Lytton composed after coming down from Cambridge. The swelling nostalgia he feels rises raw and undisguised near the conclusion of the essay, when he suddenly breaks in to exclaim: 'In England, the most fitting background for his [Browne's] strange ornament must surely be some habitation consecrated to learning, some University which still smells of antiquity and has learnt the habit of repose. The present writer, at any rate, can bear witness to the splendid echo of Browne's syllables amid learned and ancient walls; for he has known, he believes, few happier moments than those in which he has rolled the periods of the *Hydriotaphia* out to the darkness and the nightingales through the studious cloisters of Trinity.'

A less direct and articulate indication of the unhappiness and sense of loss that afflicted Lytton at this time is provided by the general tone and manner in which 'Sir Thomas Browne' is written. As one might expect, it is one of the most purely academic of all his literary essays. After cursorily admitting that Browne was a physician who lived in Norwich, Lytton quickly absorbs himself into a close study of his style, and except for a single oblique reference to the amount of self-confidence needed to indulge such a wealth of allusion and unrestrained ornamentation, he nowhere seeks to associate the extraordinary stylistic qualities of Browne's prose with the personality of its author. The esoteric vocabulary, the Latinisms, the 'elaboration of rhythm, wealth and variety of suggestion, pomp and splendour of imagination', which he describes with such awe are connected with nothing but themselves, and make up a vacuous, self-contained world full of sound and extraordinary charm, of abstract and elliptical patternings, half-grotesque, half-romantic and wholly imaginary. The 'subtle blending of mystery and queerness' which characterizes Browne's prose is the dreamland of Caliban, and, like Caliban, Lytton is comforted in his loneliness by the sweet airs that fill the place of his captivity, that promise to carry him elsewhere, and that, pending this paradise, compensate for those deficiencies in himself and in the hideous actuality of London where, as an exile from Cambridge, he was forced to go on living.

By its very nature any capital city will always suck into its orbit a number of eternal undergraduates. But the groves of Academe in London could offer Lytton precious little retrogressive shelter to hold him absolutely *in statu quo* as a Chekhovian perpetual student – 'Why is it', he once asked David Garnett (May 1915), 'that we are *not* Tchekhoff characters?' Despite his initial withdrawal under the shell of abstract literature, the personal and biographical element was soon reintroduced into his method of criticism. Published in the *Independent Review* during March 1907, and composed shortly after Thoby Stephen's death in the previous year, 'The First Earl of Lytton' contains a passage on the correspondence between Sir James Fitzjames Stephen and Lord

Lytton – his own godfather 'Owen Meredith' – which very obviously reflects on Lytton's past friendship with Thoby: 'The friendship', he writes, 'is remarkable for something more than its swift beginning: it was a mingling of opposites such as is a rare delight to think upon. Sir James Stephen was eminently unromantic. His qualities were those of solidity and force; he preponderated with a character of formidable grandeur, with a massive and rugged intellectual sanity, a colossal commonsense. The contrast is complete between this monolithic nature and the mercurial temperament of Lord Lytton, with his ardent imagination, his easy brilliance, his passionate sympathy, his taste for the elaborate and the coloured and the rococo. Such characteristics offended some of his stiff countrymen; they could not tolerate a man to whom conventions were "incomprehensible things", who felt at home "in the pure light air of foreign life", whose dress "was original, as nearly all about him", and who was not afraid to express his feelings in public. But the great lawyer judged differently. . . .

'The story which the letters tell has much of the attractiveness of a romance.'

And so as to cement still further the likeness between himself and the man on whom Lady Strachey had hoped Lytton might model his career, he points to qualities in 'Owen Meredith's' poetry which echo some aspects of his own writing – its graceful wit, its fancy superimposed upon its underlying, half-hidden mood of sadness. But in truth he did not think much of Lord Lytton as a man of letters, and had undertaken to write about him chiefly to please his mother.

In all these papers, a natural caution, enhanced by his awareness of the easy fallibility of critics, is in conflict with a desire to create some novel and striking effect. The greater part of his review of Austin Dobson's *Fanny Burney*, entitled 'The Wrong Turning', is given over to expounding and amplifying the paradox of Fanny Burney's immense reputation among the greatest intellects of her own day as an original and creative novelist – a reputation that, after her death, fell like a stone into insignificance. Again, in 'The Lives of the Poets', these two opposing strains are neatly brought together and crystallized into a single sentence: 'Johnson's aesthetic judgements are almost invariably subtle, or solid or bold; they have always some good quality to recommend them – except one: they are never right.' This criticism, with its carefully manipulated opening which appears not to detract from but actually to add emphasis to the apparently audacious conclusion that it builds up to and controls, is entirely just. For it is surely undeniable that Johnson's piety warped his sense of literature, that his avowed intention to furnish his readers with moral instruction stifled any eloquent expression of the beauties he could sense but not interpret in the poetry of Shakespeare and Milton. Yet Lytton's generalization, from which springs the whole theme of his essay, is again a deliberately narrow one, giving only the illusion of breadth. What of Dr Johnson's more positive attributes? After his defence of Warren Hastings and Horace Walpole, one might reasonably have expected Lytton to attempt a rescue of Johnson from Macaulay and Carlyle's one-sided portraiture, and to develop the view propounded by Leslie Stephen and Walter Raleigh that, notwithstanding the merits of Boswell's magnificent *Life*, a great deal of Johnson's character lay outside the biography's scope. Instead, he swallows this version whole, and can offer only one feeble answer as to why such a John Bullish personality could still be read with pleasure. It was, he explains, Johnson's *wit* which sanctified all his copious errors. 'He has managed to be wrong so cleverly, that nobody minds.'

This basic lack of appreciation of Johnson's salient qualities is the obverse of Lytton's relish for the elaborate architectonics of Sir Thomas Browne. In these immediate post-Cambridge days his interest in Johnson was restricted to an evaluation of him as a skilled exponent of English prose style who, like Horace Walpole, had found his linguistic exemplar in Browne. Yet in the essential dissimilarity between Johnson's relationship with life and letters, and his own, lay Lytton's real cause for disapproval. For though Johnson's writings contain less artistic organization than Lytton's, less response to the more recondite beauties of the English language, less dramatic balance, one can feel in their rough, abiding texture what is absent from so much of Lytton's work – the free gust of life itself, moulded into its own most natural form, which outlasts even the cleverest and most fluent of sterile, unsaturated literary techniques. Lytton's offspring are elegantly proportioned, but they are still-born in comparison with the very best of Johnson's, which, like himself, might be deformed, but through which the erratic pulse of life beats strongly.

At the same time Lytton cannot be dismissed by any means simply as an appalled and curious spectator of life. He was a partial participant. As a spectacle the world fascinated him. As an experience it filled him with a mixture of enthralment and revulsion. The ironic detachment which is larded over his prose style had a real purpose. It was something of a protective mantle – like Walpole's mannerisms – assumed so as to disguise his febrile and erotic vulnerability, his predisposition to unhappy, undignified infatuation. His unsteady and emaciated frame, so finely attuned, trembled on the brink of perpetual disaster. Cerebrally and emotionally he responded with a nervous, phrenetic abandon to life;

physically he responded less. And in this partial restraint, he sometimes felt, lay his saving factor. Although he had too much sense of humour to set up as an important, pompous personage, he flattered himself that, publicly, he could establish an impressive, even formidable figure, of which his oddly reticent and impeccable prose style was to form a destructive feature.

This peculiarly segmented taste for living – like a soft glutinous core held within a shell of glacial adamant – conditioned his appreciation and practice of writing. Lytton's response to the greatest poets and men of letters was real and sincere. His relation to their work touched the most profound springs of his being; yet he could not always hammer into words what that relationship was. The sharp abrasive bisection between his emotion and thought manifested itself as an artificial barrier which was erected between his obvious literary enjoyment and his powers of interpretation, a barrier which ran almost straight across the entire corpus of his criticism. Like the old Cavalier in *Woodstock*, he loved 'to hear poetry twice, the first time for sound, the latter time for sense', and the separation of these two qualities impeded his own depth of critical penetration. 'Words are to the poet', he once wrote, 'as notes are to the musician'; and he saw his first duty as a critic to point out what was best worth hearing in an author, supported by some testimony from the work under discussion. 'Hear how melodious such a passage sounds!' he exclaims with rapture, and plays a few bars for us to listen to. Then to this illustration he appends a rather pedagogic appraisal which seeks to analyse the properties of each note or phrase in isolation. Since, however, the sum of the properties of each isolated note seldom approximates to the cumulative, harmonious effect of the completed passage, Lytton is left to conclude that art is magic, a fabulous sleight-of-hand produced by the unconscious instinct of the artist-conjurer. Again and again he points in hopeless wonder and exaltation at the mysterious processes of literary creation. For so long as it remained inexplicable, literature could not be demeaned by common-sense definitions and made subject to the ordinary laws of the empirical world. Art, therefore, was removed from actuality, and far from irradiating the humdrum and painful everyday with fresh meaning and beauty, constituted a universe of its own, a land of fantasies and day-dreams which conferred on one the same benefits as falling in love.

Like a boy, Lytton expected and desired the marvellous and mythological in what he read. Much of his favourite reading was for him a spicy, unusual and vicarious concoction, an opiate in the drinking of which the encircling, documentary view of life faded back into a blurred oblivion. He shrank from relating art too directly with the natural order of things – a divorce which automatically gave rise to the mystery of its immaculate conception. Because the greatest poems in the language are not autobiographical, in the sense that though rooted in intense personal experience they rise to an impersonal significance, Lytton maintained that they were not to be associated with the 'particular griefs or joys or passions which give birth to them'. Poetry was a world on its own, self-contained, self-sufficient and safe, into which one might escape for short intervals whenever the pressure of outside events rose too high. But it follows that, if the actual source and original context of a work is cut off altogether from its literary qualities, then there remains little for the critical faculty to grapple with except the mechanics of literature – the grammar, the punctuation, the peculiarities and conventionalities of style – all of which is about as relevant as an analysis, in the appreciation of a piano sonata, of the wood from which the piano has been constructed. Lytton's two-stage critical formula, applied to all sorts and conditions of poets, led to a wide deviation in values, and synchronized with perfect grace and harmony only when matched with the highflown, romantic writers so beloved of academics – the rich, colourful prose-world of Sir Thomas Browne, or the wild rhapsodies of Swinburne, so languorous, dreamy and unreal. But in its application to men who drew their inspiration more directly through personal experience, the defects of this critical method, the incongruity between his passionate enjoyment and the dry, inadequate, scholastic comment, is often striking. Thus, with due seriousness, Lytton balances the merits and demerits of an adjustment of the time sequence in *Othello*; Gloucester's eyes are torn out in *King Lear*, he observes elsewhere, 'as a contributory means towards a general artistic purpose'; and again, after quoting some timeless, transcendental lines from Wordsworth, he adds: 'Who can doubt that the vague and vast sublimity of this wonderful description depends upon the Latinized vocabulary?'

Nowhere can the apprehension of ridicule that helped to spread this disharmony of heart and mind be more palpably felt than in 'The Poetry of Blake', an essay which Lytton contributed to the *Independent Review* in the spring of 1906. The sense and melody of Blake's poetry is so uniquely compacted together that to attempt any separation of the two is tantamount to reducing its meaning to a childish prattle and its music to the piano lessons of a backward and unwilling infant. Nevertheless, this is what Lytton, rather hesitantly, set out to do. As one might expect, he is fully sensitive to the awful loneliness, the power and the visionary, unselfconscious naïvety of Blake's lyrics, but the essence of these incomparable utterances, he goes on to explain, partly depends 'upon subtle differences of punctuation and of spelling'. Surely criticism of this nature is as narrow and unavailing as the most preposterous of Johnson's aesthetic precepts?

'It often happens', Lytton wrote in one of his *Spectator* reviews, 'that criticism is mainly interesting for the light it throws on the critic.' This dictum holds good for his own criticism of Blake. On first acquaintance, these pure, ecstatic lyrics seemed to open up regions of strange imagination and mysterious romance, a fancied world of fable and delight. But closer knowledge disclosed that such attractive surface qualities were singularly deceptive. Beneath the childlike charm there lay a forbidding austerity; the far-off fairyland proved to be a mirage which, on dissolving, uncovered a horizon of unearthly remoteness. For Blake's universe was not make-believe, but real: a visionary interpretation of human destiny. His short poems shoot like fearful stabs of lightning across the darkness of the sky, illuminating momentarily the quagmires and shifting sands of our sad, twilight existence. But these were sights that remained shrouded from Lytton's eyes. 'Nothing', declared Blake, 'can withstand the fury of my course among the stars of God and the abysses of the Accuser.' To Lytton the ring of such a sentiment was superb; but it was not practical politics. He almost preferred the cosier simplicity and directness of Mary Coleridge, or even the pastoral mysticism of Wordsworth, whose spiritual tenderness was more earthbound and countrified than Blake's 'inspired ravings', and whose habitual caution – finally to extinguish all his visionary dreams – Lytton significantly described as 'sanity'.

Nevertheless, though he could not follow Blake's meteoric flights, he did feel the force of their pull. 'We look,' he wrote, 'and as we gaze at the strange image and listen to the marvellous melody we are almost tempted to do likewise.' Almost, but not quite. For always his 'sanity' held him back and he translated the apprehension which assailed him whenever he contemplated such a journey about the heavens into a general condemnation of mysticism. 'Besides its unreasonableness, there is an even more serious objection to Blake's mysticism – and indeed to all mysticism: its lack of humanity. The mystic's creed – even when arrayed in the wondrous and ecstatic beauty of Blake's verse – comes upon the ordinary man, in the rigidity of its uncompromising elevation, with a shock which is terrible, and almost cruel. The sacrifices which it demands are too vast, in spite of the divinity of what it has to offer. What shall it profit a man, one is tempted to exclaim, if he gain his own soul, and lose the whole world? The mystic ideal is the highest of all; but it has no breadth.'

This view of mysticism as a strait-jacket creed donned voluntarily by inspired semi-lunatics is plausible, but entirely without real comprehension. Mysticism does not involve blindness to three-quarters of the world's objects and events, but an alteration in the focus through which one regards them. It is a product of the imagination, that blending of the emotions and the intellect which reconciles apparent opposites with a simplicity unobtainable from pure analysis or sensitive impressionism alone. Though he was attracted towards mysticism, Lytton, whose intellect and emotions were so permanently divided and who had confessed himself more of an Aristotelian than a Platonist, achieved simplicity in his own writing not by this stereoscopic fusion, but by a single-minded, selective concentration which often had the effect of blotting out latent discrepancies and impoverishing the rich multidimensions of a story. His partly preconceived literary patterns, however cunningly reorganized and skilfully arranged, do not carry somewhere within them the burgeoning seeds of tropical chaos which lie scattered about in real life. They are, in truth, *over*-simplified, for the order is largely imposed from without and not perceived to exist within the disorganized muddle and confusion of living.

Nor is inhumanity a necessary element of mysticism as Lytton fearfully suggests. The strident, ugly note in Blake, as in Beethoven, was not the result of his powerful imagination, but of his immense will. The more potent the imagination, the stronger must be the will that is needed to support it. But in those nightmare moments when doubt and terror overcome the mystic, when his imagination falters and his intuitive vision is distorted, then the volcanic power of his unimpeded will erupts and covers his transcendentalism with a crust of militancy and oppression. It is, thus, not the power of mysticism which brings about this ruthlessness, but its impermanence, its lost battles with the will to power.

Lytton's criticism of Blake, and of men of comparable stature, Shakespeare and Johnson, defines the limits of his own talent and points to the reason why, for all his excellence and discriminating literary sensibility, he never developed into one of the very few truly great creative writers himself. For Blake, as for Shakespeare and Johnson, the imaginative faculty was a means by which to transmute their deepest, most genuine response to life into the deathless anatomy of literature, to overreach the passing moment and shape the free current of their experience into indestructible, creative form. The pursuit of the imagination was for them love and truth; that of the will, lust and power. Through the imagination which yearns for union with another life, they sensed that man might apprehend a harmony which envelops though it does not penetrate our present existence. The will, with its passion to dominate and possess, destroyed this unity and left chaos and division.

For Lytton the imagination was something different – a magic carpet on which he set out for those impossible, dematerialized escapades away from the inhibiting confines of himself and the conventional pressures of society. In many of his essays he uses the word, and always in the same sense as when he writes of Johnson that he ' had no ear and he had no imagination'. The imagination, for him, was a symphony, every note of which found a place in his heart; and he was so weak and sensitive that it played upon him as upon an instrument. In this literary, more restricted sense, the imagination implies not *discovery*, but *effect*, measuring the purely musical quality of a work at one remove from the meaning which it happened to convey and which was itself made subject to the will. In short, he employed his own imaginative talent not so much to overhear the rhythm which underlies the discord of our lives, as to conjure forth a never-never land full of sweet, wistful harmonies which could drown such discord. Thus, in the critical writing, his imaginative power seldom penetrates to a sudden revelation of the hidden truth, but evokes, as he himself wrote in his essay on Racine, 'a beautiful atmosphere, in which what is expressed may be caught away from the associations of common life and harmoniously enshrined'. Again, in a letter which he wrote in 1909 to Virginia Stephen – showing, incidentally, how clearly he recognizes the imagination to be something quite set apart from brilliance or sheer cleverness – he writes as though it were an *inventive* rather than a creative faculty, something which, with a wave of the wand, produces a bolt-hole from the cheerless frustrations, the doldrums of the everyday – a wild infusion of joy and fantasy in which one willingly suspends one's rational disbelief. 'The French seem to me a melancholy race,' he wrote, '– is it because they have no imagination, so that they have no outlets when they find themselves (as all intelligent people must) *vis-à-vis* with the horrors of the world? There's a sort of dry desperation about some of them which I don't believe exists with the English – even with Swift.'

On less exacting themes Lytton's criticism is always interesting and acute, and never more so than in his essays on Beddoes and Racine which he wrote for the *New Quarterly* in the years 1907 and 1908. Perhaps his greatest quality as a critic was his capacity for appreciation, and in both these pieces he is conscious of dealing with the reverse of what had been the case with Fanny Burney – poets whose reputation in this country had never risen to the level at which they deserved to stand, so that the fallibility of other past and present literary commentators had created an opportunity for himself to make an original re-appraisal of their work, a chance of striking a novel effect with less risk of ridicule.

The only way to judge a poet, Wordsworth has said, is to love him. Certainly Lytton's love of Beddoes and of Racine was responsible for some of the finest literary criticism he ever wrote. His treatment here is far above the belletrist's mere invitation to enjoyment: it represents an attempt to define the individual quality of the work and to convey, with the exact image or similitude, the particular impression which it has made on him personally. Though Beddoes and Racine were extremely dissimilar poets, Lytton was able to detect in both some affinity with himself. Beddoes, of course, delighted in Elizabethan drama, and Lytton argues convincingly that, although born at the beginning of the nineteenth century, his proper place as a dramatist was among the Elizabethans: he was 'The Last Elizabethan'.

It is easy to understand the appeal which Beddoes held for Lytton. Eccentric, mysterious, brilliant, a figure as improbable as the characters in his own dramas, this strange personality fascinated him. What little he could discover about his life – the letters displaying his humour and vitality, the suicide – whetted his appetite for more knowledge. Most beguiling of all was his companionship with Degen, a handsome young baker. 'The affair Degen is indeed mysterious,' Lytton wrote to Duncan Grant while working on the essay (11 June 1907), 'but there doesn't seem to me to be much doubt about his having been in love with him, especially as there is a German passage in one of his letters in which he says in so many words that he's a lover of boys.[1] I believe if one could get hold of the MSS one would find all sorts of wonders – love poems to Degen, perhaps, who knows? They belong to Browning's son who lives in Florence.'

So skilfully are these few biographical fragments arranged, so generous and discerning is the criticism which runs alongside, that the effect of this essay is to re-create a living poet out of what had previously been an uneasy ghost. Lytton's apt quotations illustrate and convey the radiant intensity of that visionary world, full of unearthly pathos, of grotesque, ominous humour – like the mood engendered by the haunting symphonies of Mahler – in which Beddoes seems so much

---

[1] This phrase emanates from an inaccuracy of Gosse's. In one place he gives it, as Lytton reported it to Duncan Grant, as 'Liebhaber von Knaben'. But in another place he gives it, far more probably, as 'Liebhaber von Knocken' – a lover of bones. Beddoes was an anatomist as well as being absorbed by death.

more at home than in the towns and cities of England and Germany. In such a passage as:

> *I begin to hear*
> *Strange but sweet sounds, and the loud rocky dashing*
> *Of waves, where time into Eternity*
> *Falls over ruined walls.*

there is a sure echo of those dreamland instruments that so enchanted Caliban that, on waking, he cried to dream again. The death-wish which runs through Beddoes's life is the practical, embodied expression of this cry, a reaction to the sudden, sickening descent from the supernatural to ordinary environment, from the ecstatic realms of the imagination to the coils of the enfeebled will. In his disregard for the common actualities of existence, Beddoes gave full rein to that romantic tendency which, in Lytton, was held in check by an innate caution and good sense. Both wished to awaken the drama of their times by some presentation of the bold and extraordinary contrasts so dear to their hearts; yet their finished achievements are strikingly diverse since, in spite of similar proclivities, their temperaments differed widely. Notwithstanding his evident admiration for the poetry of Beddoes, Lytton considers it with fine critical detachment, balancing his positive accomplishments – the mastery of magnificent utterance, the power of his vast, strangely imprecise yet stimulating conceptions evoking unanalysable sensations within one, his simplicity and splendour – against his characteristic imperfections – the faulty construction, the unthinking inconsistency of his *dramatis personae*, his curious remoteness from the flesh and blood of human affairs.

The attraction of Beddoes's poetry for Lytton was partly that of psychological drama, partly mysticism. He was impelled equally by the boredom of continual safety and by the fear of solitary self-fulfilment, and he sought through literature to reconcile these two impulses, as it were, at second hand. Beddoes did not, like Blake, project that terrible blinding focus on everything; his energies were more dissipated, his poetry more uneven and diluted; and when his imagination faded he did not find sustenance in an awful, ruthless willpower, but sank into spiritless inertia – a reaction far more in keeping with the fluctuation of Lytton's own melancholic emotions. Like many imaginative persons Lytton felt at times a need to make the

> *flight*
> *Of the poetic ecstasy*
> *Into the land of mystery.*

But though he might respond to this dream of a transfigured universe in the poetry of Beddoes or Wordsworth, he never journeyed there himself, for his drive was not towards another world, but another personal existence in this world. In his love of literature, as in his sexual love of men, there existed some vague mystical consanguinity; but because he could not convert other people's experiences into his own, because he was after a sublime and magical analgesic rather than the revelation of a new heaven and a new earth, he could not accommodate poetic transcendentalism, despite the magnetic allure it held out for him.

Lytton's love of Racine was of an altogether different order. He could discover here no wondrous vision for the imagination to feed on, no exotic, spectacular vocabulary, no extravagant imagery, no bravura or wild fantasy to dazzle the mind and banish the cold, unfriendly regions of London from his awareness. Instead he found 'the beauties of restraint, of clarity, of refinement and of precision'. The source of his delight in these qualities lay partly in the nostalgia which they could call up in him, their formidable power of re-awakening some of the happiest and most exciting hours of childhood; and the aim of this essay was to arouse in his readers something of the same exhilaration, that thrilling tide of music and greatness that had swept over him when his mother and Marie Souvestre had first introduced him to Racine.

The means by which he set out to fulfil this purpose were subtle and effective.[1] How has it come about, he asks, that on this side of the Channel 'Racine is despised and Shakespeare is worshipped, on the other, Shakespeare is tolerated and Racine is adored?' In answering this question he uses as a foil to his own deeply rooted response the wide contrast that existed between a specific and typical French and English viewpoint, so that in the cross-current of *fâcheux* misunderstanding his own estimate of Racine emerges with added authority and elucidation. Only in one instance, when he relates Racine's work directly to his own adult experience, does Lytton momentarily falter. Having gone some way to establish Racine as a realist, he then instances what he calls his 'wondrous microcosms of tragedy', and contrasts them with our actual vague and untidy behaviour. For, he writes, 'in life, men's minds are not sharpened, they are diffused, by emotion; and the utterance which

---

[1] On 5 April 1908, while he was planning this essay, Lytton wrote to Desmond MacCarthy: 'I see that your favourite M. Lemaître is bringing out a book on Racine – do you think I might write on that? I might bring in also Mr J. C. Bailey's rotten book on French Poetry, in which he abuses the greatest poet in the world – just as you do. It wouldn't be particularly easy to carry the business off properly – but I think it *might* be done. If you could bear it, let me know – at any rate it would be more interesting – wouldn't it? – than the old rag-and-bone man Sir Henry Wotton.'

best represents them is fluctuating and agglomerated rather than compact and defined.' And so, he concludes, 'It would be nearer the truth to rank Racine among the idealists.' Lytton's view of the effect which a sudden upsurge of emotion produces within any human being strikes one immediately as being just, even obvious; it is plausible, it is rationalistic – but it is not true. A strong current of emotion passing through a man injects him, if only briefly, with a heightened awareness of reality, and charges his faculties with an electric, split-second sharpening of focus. Under such a shock, his powers of expression are often concentrated wonderfully, and it is only in retrospect that he will experience the diffusion to which Lytton alludes. So it is that someone undergoing a swift emotional upheaval will frequently utter words of absolute, pregnant simplicity and compressed significance such as Racine puts into the mouths of his characters, but immediately afterwards will echo the same sentence again and again in meaningless muddled repetition. Lytton is surely wrong in denying Racine a place among the realistic writers; for the realist in literature must telescope time into reality as opposed to converting time back into time by reporting, blow by blow, the chronological and documentary details of any incident.

But if this is a weakness, it is one only of classification. Throughout the essay Lytton has the full measure of Racine's genius, and although he makes an actual reference to Sarah Bernhardt, whom he had seen acting in *Phèdre* at the Royalty Theatre and elsewhere, perhaps in his most fervent passages we can overhear, too, the silent voice of Marie Souvestre, and feel within the child sitting at her feet the first great rent made in that veil which conceals the passions of men and women from the eyes of innocence:

'But to his lovers, to those who have found their way into the secret places of his art, his lines are impregnated with a peculiar beauty, and the last perfection of style. Over them, the most insignificant of his verses can throw a deep enchantment, like the faintest wavings of a magician's wand. "A-t-on vu de ma part le roi de Comagène?" How is it that words of such slight import should hold such thrilling music? Oh! they are Racine's words. And, as to his rhymes, they seem perhaps, to the true worshipper, the final crown of his art . . .

'. . . To hear the words of Phèdre spoken by the mouth of Bernhardt, to watch, in the culminating horror of crime and of remorse, of jealousy, of rage, of desire, and of despair, all the dark forces of destiny crowd down upon that great spirit, when the heavens and the earth reject her, and Hell opens, and the terrific urn of Minos thunders and crashes to the ground – that indeed is to come close to immortality, to plunge shuddering through the infinite abysses, and to look, if only for a moment, upon eternal light.'

2

MARGINALIA

It has always been difficult to place a literary article, as Desmond MacCarthy once complained, unless there is some arbitrary pretext for presenting it to the public. Between the essay-reviews which Lytton wrote for the *Independent Review* and for the *New Quarterly* there is a slight difference of tone arising from the degree of latitude he was allowed in each case. His choice of subject had been wide when writing for the *Independent Review*; he could make use of almost any book which had been published fairly recently as the basis for a long critical or biographical paper. But as a contributor to the *New Quarterly* he was even more fortunate, for the selection of theme seems to have been left entirely to himself. The bestowal of such freedom came, of course, from his friend MacCarthy, the literary editor, who greatly admired Lytton's talent and who, with a wisdom and courage rare among literary editors of periodicals, did not insist upon a cramping restriction to the topicalities of literary journalism. Consequently Lytton was at liberty to turn his attention to any subject that best suited his ability, and to compose essays neither connected with works just issuing from the press, nor confined to specific dates marking the celebration of centenaries.

It was Desmond MacCarthy, too, who commissioned a few anonymous book reviews from Lytton for *The Speaker* between December 1905 and October 1906. *The Speaker* had originally been founded to balance the *Spectator* after the Home Rule split in the Liberal Party. Its politics, similar to those of the *Independent Review*, were reasonably sympathetic to Lytton's outlook. Vigorously anti-imperialistic, the paper had, during the South African war, been the most emphatic organ of the pro-Boer minority in the country. Several of its regular contributors, besides Lytton, also wrote for the *Independent Review*, including Hilaire Belloc and G. K. Chesterton. In 1899 J. L. Hammond, the historian, had been appointed as its editor. He began employing MacCarthy in 1903 as an occasional critic and by December 1905, when Lytton's first anonymous review of John Dover Wilson's *John Lyly* appeared, MacCarthy had risen to a position of some authority on the paper. But in November of the following year *The Speaker* was converted into *The Nation*. The new editor, H. W. Massingham, promptly dispensed with the services of MacCarthy;[1] and so Lytton's reviews, the last of which had come out the previous month, ceased altogether.

He was already by this time writing for *The Speaker*'s rival, his cousin St Loe Strachey's *Spectator*. The political policies of this paper were less to his taste and he was accorded far less freedom in his choice and treatment of subject. It was, however, at this period the most widely read of all the political weeklies, though something of a laughing-stock among the intelligentsia, and especially among the younger Stracheys who, believing the main body of its subscribers to consist of clergymen, used to apply the epithet 'Spectatorial' to its more pompous pronouncements.

Between 1905 and 1910 Lytton contributed almost ninety long reviews for the *Spectator*, and considering that these pieces were usually the result of quick reading and hasty assimilation, their standard is remarkably high. His 'Shakespeare on Johnson', for example, written in the summer of 1908, is superior to his 'Lives of the Poets' composed two years earlier and included in both *Books and Characters* and the posthumous volume, *Literary Essays*, in the collected edition of his works. For the first time Lytton displays some real understanding of Johnson's merits as a writer, and balances his aesthetic limitations against the breadth and sanity of his outlook upon human affairs. Being moved more by the humanity than by the poetry in most passionate writing, Johnson 'was not in essence a critic of literature', Lytton explains, 'but a critic of life'. And his conclusion on Johnson as a literary critic loses nothing of its humour for being comparatively just: 'It is hardly an exaggeration to say that Johnson's criticisms are such as might have been made by a foreigner of great ability and immense experience who was acquainted with Shakespeare solely in a prose translation.'

Another of his best articles was 'John Milton', an appreciation written in December 1908 to mark the three hundredth anniversary of Milton's birth. Though he responded to Milton's lofty and grandiose vision, the vast sublimity, the superhuman splendour of his poetry, and though he greatly admired Milton's unceasing struggle for artistic perfection in the grand style, yet Lytton was never swayed into overlooking his faults, in particular his withering lack of humour. Nor was he misled, as many critics have been, by the exterior frigidity of Milton's stern self-discipline, into supposing that he was a cold and passionless

---

[1] Massingham later admitted that discharging MacCarthy had been one of his few mistakes as editor. See *Humanities* by Sir Desmond MacCarthy (1953), p. 16n.

man. On the contrary, he maintained that, despite this formidable carapace, Milton was especially susceptible to the charms of attractive women, and afraid of their terrible, illogical power over him. By means of several pertinent quotations, contrasting passages that vibrate almost unwillingly to the agitations of his heart with others emphasizing a narrow, austere, even cruel Puritan dogma, he shows us a Milton torn between his sensibility and his egotism. It is an interpretation at once percipient and convincing, by a critic who always felt that his own unprepossessing outward image of controlled, ironic detachment belied the inner strength and turmoil of his emotions.

But on the whole, as is to be expected, the quality of these reviews does not match those assembled in his collected volumes. Without the attractions of their delicately fashioned aesthetic unity, their studied brightness of phrase, or the absorbing cut and thrust of their narrative, the actual thought that these *Spectator* pieces contain is often revealed as rather commonplace. We learn, for example, that genius is not invariably popular; that great writing is frequently not recognized at once for its true worth; that to see performed on the stage some play of which we have only a literary knowledge is interesting; that Shakespeare is the greatest of poets, and so on. The metaphors, most of which are culinary or architectural, are used unsparingly and, though decorative, seldom carry that original explorative quality which can catch and communicate the uniqueness of a particular book. His images are pleasing, but a little too vague and easy, so that (as words and similitudes become increasingly cheapened and abused) they have in many cases grown too quickly outworn, his recommendations at their worst seeming to resemble advertisement copy instead of valid and positive criticism. Similarly, the analogies which he liked to draw between literature and music or painting – tragedy is a symphony, light comedy is a water-colour sketch, etc. – are facile rather than really illuminating. For to gain certain effects, Lytton tended to separate artificially the intrinsic literary elements of a great work, such as humour and tragedy, which are so essentially part of each other, and did not examine the peculiar composition in which they have been put together.

At other times, at first glance more surprisingly, Lytton is apt to sound a little pompous, as when, for instance, he explains that although literary digressions may be entertaining, they can never be instructive; or that the question of marriage is too complex and serious a business to be treated in a light manner as Shaw does in *Getting Married*. By the same token he almost always qualifies the word 'gaiety' with the epithet 'irresponsible'. But most of this pomposity may fairly be attributed to 'Spectatorial policy', and the dominating influence of St

Loe. Every Tuesday morning Lytton called on St Loe at the *Spectator* offices where they discussed his next article. And very often St Loe would lay down the general lines he would like it to follow.

On the other hand Lytton does not, as in some of his other compositions, sacrifice what he believes to be true for what is overemphatic – perhaps, in part, a consequence of writing anonymously. As a result, many of his own personal opinions and feelings can be read more obviously from these *Spectator* reviews. For him, it appears, the past was not an illustration of the present, but a refuge from it, attracting him by virtue of its associations curiously remote from himself. So eager was he to dispel the shades of sombre and doleful Edwardian England, the ever-watching, ever-disapproving eyes of Mrs Grundy, that even the perusal of some old Elizabethan manuscripts in the illustrative appendix to one of the books he was given to review quickly evaporated the repressive gloom of his immediate surroundings. 'As one reads these dry and faded extracts, these preserved remnants of a vanished age,' he commented, 'the world of which they were a part seems to take shape and substance before the eye of the mind. An air of mysterious antiquity arises from them like the fumes from an alchemist's alembic; the reality of the present disappears; its place is taken by the phantasma of the past.'

One of Lytton's favourite concepts – that of the overwhelming value of original aesthetic unity, of 'significant form' – is almost parodied in a criticism he wrote on an exhibition of pictures at the New Gallery.[1] Noticing a painting that had inadvertently been hung the wrong way round, he describes the effect, with only partial irony, as follows: 'Two dancers seem to be flying upwards in impossible attitudes towards an impossible piece of scenery in mid-air. If the picture were turned round, the dancers would be brought back to earth and the scenery would take up its natural position at the side of the stage. But perhaps after all the change would be a mistake, for as the picture now hangs the lack of verisimilitude is almost compensated for by the curiosity of design.' This same aesthetic emphasis – where pattern is partly divorced from content and given priority over it – is reiterated through much of this literary criticism, where he often likens literature to the art of painting, as when, for example, he writes of the pastoral tradition of the Elizabethans: 'To borrow an analogy from painting, Jonson's introduction of realism has destroyed the harmony of his tones.'

[1] On the one or two occasions when Henry Strachey was ill, Lytton was jockeyed into doing an article on art criticism. These should not be taken too seriously as expressions of his own taste, for he usually went to the exhibitions with Duncan Grant and absorbed his views.

In addition to his rather unsystematic but wide and immensely attentive reading, Lytton possessed a more negative virtue – the amazing lack in a young writer ranging over such a varied field of literature of what E. M. Forster has called 'pseudo-scholarship'. It was this honest and industrious quality, combined with good sense and a really deep love of French and English literature, that elevated his *Spectator* contributions well above the standard of other reviewers. To a large extent he reserves the full measure of his common sense for contemporary writers, indulging his auricular appreciation of fine writing more freely the further back the scene is set in the past. He is admirably sane, for example, when disavowing Professor John Churton Collins's contention that the merit of good poetry is to be weighed by its moral effects, and that the only real justification of poetry lies in its educative influence. After ridiculing the notion that one must, or could, compare the benefits of poetry with those of the birch-rod, and pointing out that, judged by such pragmatic standards, no great poetry ought to be pessimistic, he then gives expression to his own personal response to poetry: 'For it is not by its uses that poetry is to be justified or condemned. Its beauty and its goodness, like the beauty or the goodness of a human being, have a value of their own, a value which does not depend on their effects. We love poems, as we love fields and the rivers of England, and as we love our friends, not for the pleasure which they may bring us, nor even the good they may do us, but for themselves.'

This literary credo, which could hardly be improved on as a concise statement of Lytton's critical beliefs, is crucial to the understanding of all his writing, and goes some way to explaining why it is that these and his other literary essays have tended to be undervalued in comparison with his purely biographical work. Unlike his biographies, his criticism is not, on the whole, polemical, but impressionistic; and although it is sometimes more imaginative, it is also apt to be rather diluted of intellectual matter. In some of these essays there is not enough solid meat: they represent the hors d'œuvre, as he would say, not the main dish.

A humanist by temperament, Lytton was very far from being a 'practical critic'. If asked what use great literature could be – and forced to reply – he might have given Coleridge's answer that it increases our range of understanding of ourselves, of other people, of our world; that it has the power of humanizing human beings, that it can revitalize the mind away from narrow prejudice, and magnify our sympathetic awareness. Literature and the arts offered Lytton a surcease from pain, protecting his senses from the atrophy of a vibrant, restless tedium, and opening up a more abundant avenue of imaginative existence which might lead away from his half-life of agonized self-scrutiny. In short, the arts were 'life-enhancing', not in the sense that they promoted good citizenship, but because they increased 'the pleasure which there is in life itself'. Such are, or can be, the benefits conferred on us by other people's books. But for the genuine creative writer – in whatever field of literature – the *effects* of writing are of secondary interest. It is not what one gets out of any art that is important, but what one puts into it. In this, the truest sense, literature is a culmination of life, concentrating and releasing our past experience, and divining that current of poetry which flows beneath all the whirlpools and waterfalls of our immediate joy, perplexity, sorrow. The purpose of literature, in so far as the word is applicable, is therefore to discover the truth. Not merely the objective, 'scientific' truth, but that residuum of happiness barely noticeable in the stress and discord of living, that aspect of reality which emerges from the relationship between the writer and his material – be it his own or other men's lives or work – an inner truth, refined and made subject to the laws of reason; something personal which rises to a universal yet still individual significance. All reasonable beings love truth; but it is not primarily a functional commodity. Rather it stands like a rock amid all the swirling eddies and passing torrents of our conflicting egotisms, and, being constant itself, promises something that does not pass away.

In order to account for the relative neglect shown to Lytton's critical essays in general, one must set against them those aesthetic standards and values which he upheld, the critical precepts that have emerged ever higher in the ascendant since his death. It is a popular misconception to believe that impressionistic criticism can only flourish in an atmosphere of ethical indifference. According to Desmond MacCarthy, Lytton was often moved in his writing by moral passion, but this was always controlled so as not to disrupt the artistic unity of his compositions. 'The public thought he was a frivolous and detached ironist,' MacCarthy wrote, 'but he was much more of a moralist. Only in writing he avoided carefully, for aesthetic reasons, the portentous frown of the earnest writer.' And Clive Bell, too, observed: 'Like all moralists he had his standards, unlike most he kept his temper and was never self-righteous.' Lytton had too much humour to be accepted as a moralist in the traditional sense, for he never made any book the platform from which to pontificate on all manner of biologico-social activities. But he was, of course, a moralist in the sense that we all are: he held strong, sincerely felt and reasoned opinions on fundamental and controversial topics, and he believed passionately in certain qualities in human nature. In our critical jargon and classification none

George Mallory, 1910

carried away. I think your book has not only wrecked & shattered all writers on Ethics from Aristotle & Christ to Herbert Spencer & Mr Bradley, it has not only laid the 〈for〉 true foundation of Ethics, it has not only left all modern Philosophy bafouée – these seem to me small achievements compared to the establishment of that method which shines like a sword between the lines. It is the scientific method deliberately applied, for the first time, to Reasoning. Do

that time? You perhaps shake your head, but henceforward who will be able to tell lies one thousandth time as easily as before? The truth, there can be no doubt, is really now upon the march. I date from Oct. 1903 the beginning of the Age of Reason.

The last two chapters interested me most, as they were nearer to me than the rest. Your grand conclusion made me gasp – it was so violently definite. Lord! I can't get altogether

agree – I think with some horror of a Universe deprived for ever of real slaughters & tortures & lusts. Isn't it possible that the real Ideal may be an organic unity so large & of such a nature that it is, precisely, the Universe itself? In which case Dr Pangloss was right after all.

I long to talk to you about a great many things. I come up probably on Tuesday, & and as I don't know where you are

69, LANCASTER GATE. W.

I send this there. Dear Moore, I hope & pray that you realise how much you mean to us. It was very pleasant to be able to feel that one came into the Dedication. But expression is so difficult, so very difficult, & there are so many cold material obstructions, that the best of life seems to be an act of faith.

This is a confession of faith, from your brother

Lytton Strachey.

Facsimile of part of a letter from Lytton Strachey to G. E. Moore, 11 October 1903 of this signifies very much. What matters, and what is beyond dispute, is that he was not an *Arnoldian* moralistic critic. And in this obvious fact lies much of the cause for his neglect in this branch of writing.

Lytton died in 1932, the same year as *Scrutiny*, that organ of the new criticism, was founded.[1] Since that time the task of formulating modern critical principles has been increasingly taken over by dons and teachers of the English language, who have developed and sophisticated the kind of dogma propounded as early as 1906 by Professor John Churton Collins.[2] These men have felt strongly that in this age of unprecedented scientific progress, literature was in danger of becoming regarded as a thing of the past, a quaint relic of some defunct and antique civilization, without any place in the modern world. This danger was, for the professional and academic literary disseminator, a very real one: it threatened to affect his job, his prestige and his position in society. To avoid the risk of useless and humiliating redundancy – in inverse

[1] In a review of *Characters and Commentaries* which appeared in *Scrutiny*, Vol. II, No. 3 (December 1933), T. R. Barnes dismissed Lytton Strachey's literary criticism as nothing more than a string of epithets, and described his prose style as a tasty pastiche, a skilfully sentimental compact of snobbery and querulous inferiority feelings. '[Lytton Strachey's] success among the "middlebrow" public was, I think, based on the fact that Strachey competently and directly, with judicious subtlety, and appropriately Freudian and free-thinking reasoning, appealed to that desire for fantasy satisfaction through "characters" or substitute lives, which is the basis of commercial fiction. His attitude flattered post-war up-to-date mechanized amoralism. . . . His formula was the familiar Metro-Goldwyn-Mayer heart-throb and mirthquake one. . . . Always the patina, not the form excites him. . . . But more surprisingly, he has a following. Though Sitwellism is no longer *chic*, Strachey is an influence in life as well as in letters; he set a tone which still dominates certain areas of the highbrow world – e.g. that part of Bloomsbury which has a well-known annex in Cambridge. The deterioration and collapse represented by Mrs Woolf's latest phase (*Orlando, Common Reader 2nd Series, Flush*) is one of the most pernicious effects of this environment.'

[2] John Churton Collins (1848–1908), who had been at Balliol College, was bitterly disappointed at having failed to secure the Merton Professorship of English at Oxford. A teacher of Greek and English literature at W. P. Scoones's coaching establishment, he soon made himself into a much-feared literary reviewer, the scourge of the late Victorians. He was also a keen amateur student of criminology, and incorporated some astringent police methods into his criticism. One of his favourite targets was Sir Edmund Gosse, then Clerk Professor of English literature at Cambridge. 'What has embittered Mr Collins against me, I cannot imagine,' complained another of his victims, John Addington Symonds. '. . . Do you observe how a creature like Churton Collins omits in his review all real discussion of the material in books, confining himself to the one object of carping, sneering and personal insult?' Collins always strenuously denied being a spiteful or malicious critic. His literary censure, he claimed, implied no personal animosity, but was a means of upholding true scholarship and accuracy. Lytton, it appears, was generally sympathetic to Collins. After reading his *Ephemera Critica*, he wrote to Lady Strachey (2 May 1901): 'It is vigorous enough and also amusing, and I really hardly think exaggerated or unnecessarily enraged.' In 1904, Collins was appointed Professor of English at the University of Birmingham. Four years later he was drowned at Oulton Broad, near Lowestoft.

proportion to the expanding authority of his scientific colleagues – he had to advertise literature as a craft with a future, with new frontiers to cross. Much dead wood from the past had to be eliminated; the study of English had to be brought up to date, given a new look – a practical function in a practical world. The benefits of literature as thought of by Coleridge and Strachey were at best too vague and insubstantial to recapture the interest of a materially minded population. Other less romantic slogans had to be adopted and drilled into the students. With this object in mind they cultivated and improved on the original precepts of Matthew Arnold – himself, of course, a schools inspector and son of a headmaster – gearing it up to keep abreast with scientific advancement.

By these means they attempted, and still attempt, to foist literature on the community as a National Moral Health Service, essential to the proper evolution of society. Science may provide its power, but only with modern, new-look literacy can one settle the direction in which it should travel. Only thus, it was felt, could the literary educationalist command the respect of the scientist. In fact, however, the dictatorial, poker-faced, rigidly exclusive dogmas which have been propounded especially under the dynamic management of Dr F. R. Leavis,[1] amounted at worst – and increasingly as time went on – to a vote of no confidence in the real afflatus of literature. Dressed up on the shelf as a revolutionary wonder-drug, providing new knowledge and stimulating new disciplines, it is bound eventually to lose out to the scientific range of products. And why, after all, should the so-called two cultures be combined either in collaboration or in rivalry? – you cannot harness a steam-roller and a gazelle together and look for a multiplication of horsepower. The one attempt leads only to the most flatulent banalities; and under the futile influence of the other in the form of cut-throat literary criticism, the springs of modern literature have, if anything, been weakened, its imaginative purpose degenerated and funnelled down from 'life-enhancement' into a single, monotonous paean of paranoiac self-importance.

[1] In the 70th Foundation Oration at University College, London (March 1966), Lord Annan compared the influence of the Bloomsbury Group on the generation which followed the 1914–18 war with that of Dr F. R. Leavis after the 1939–45 war. The Bloomsbury Group took Voltaire and Hume as their models and never lost an adolescent delight in shocking people. They thought the artist laboured under only one obligation, the duty to express himself. Their first commandment was a respect for the integrity and happiness of other people. While they came from the upper-middle class, Dr Leavis was the son of a small Cambridge businessman, a vigorous rationalist and a republican. Most of his followers, the detractors of Bloomsbury, came from the same background as himself, but 'he [Leavis] has an eagle eye for anyone who wants to join the bandwagon and even the devout are snubbed'.

In all this muddled modernizing, Lytton's contribution to literary criticism has played no part at all, since it is not a branch of school-mastering, but of the old-fashioned humanities. He is, in fact, more of a critical essayist than a critic pure and simple. Consider, for example, his views on Shakespeare. 'Shakespeare', he wrote in one of his *Spectator* pieces, 'is a standing dish at the literary board; and to this one can take no objection.' From his 'Shakespeare's Final Period' to 'Othello', an unfinished paper on which he was working at the time of his death, he produced a far greater volume of criticism on Shakespeare than on anyone else. But he was, in fact, a sounder critic of Shakespearian commentators than of Shakespeare himself, whose poetry liberated in him emotions too vast and universal to be coaxed into words and reduced to a neatly contrived essay. He is, on the other hand, adroit in using other critics' commentaries as a foil to sharpen up his own sensible opinions about Shakespeare, before launching into his some-times rather watery impressionistic appreciation. He argues well, for instance, against Sir Sidney Lee's assertion that the sonnets, far from being the outcome of any intense emotion, were mere literary exercises addressed formally to his patron, the Earl of Southampton. After quoting some instances of the emotional tone which dominates this entire series of sonnets, Lytton then proceeds to offer his own reasons for preferring William Herbert, Earl of Pembroke, as the person to whom they were written. He could feel the thrill of literary detective work, and the emotions of those who set out at length to establish the true identity of Mr W.H., yet his common sense was not to be over-persuaded, and he reminds us that the 'enjoyment of Shakespeare's sonnets need not – fortunately enough! – wait on our unravelment of the mystery of "W.H."'.

Mystery, however, always added a certain spice to his literary com-positions. From the dozen articles which he wrote on Shakespeare for the *Spectator*, it is evident that, quite aside from the pure and miraculous melodies of Shakespeare's poetry, Lytton was attracted partly by the lack of firm biographical data surrounding the subject (which conferred upon it that touch of magic and of curiosity that made absolute the divorce of art from day-to-day living), and partly by the immense complexity and passionate force of Shakespeare's genius, which shone through his poetry and brought with it a sweet eclipse to Lytton's own unhappy and debilitated self-consciousness.

Most writers tend to be unreliable judges of the work of their con-temporaries, which they relate too intimately with their own. Yet since even the wildest aberrations of the creative man – Tolstoy on Shake-speare, for example – are often of more interest than the reasoned and better proportioned views of less exceptional men, what Lytton had to say on the poets and playwrights of his day would in any case be worth recording. Because his love of literature was fastidiously partitioned off from the present, he was apt to evaluate the work of contemporary poets by rather settled and unadventurous standards. Rudyard Kipling was the only modern writer of verse whose genius he considered to be indisputable. All the other celebrated poets, Austin Dobson, Edmund Gosse, Herbert Trench, lacked inspiration. He was excessively bored, too, on one occasion at Arnold Bennett's house, where he was mercilessly subjected to a recitation by Edith Sitwell of some passages from her versifying, which he dismissed as 'absurd stuff'. He also found the long, over-ambitious fiction of Thomas Hardy terribly tedious, and much preferred the condensation of his poetry, with its undecorated, unromantic sobriety, its bitter speculation and appealing undertow of regretful recollection. As for A. E. Housman, he was delightful of course, but he had narrowed his territory and 'was content to reign over a tiny kingdom'. Of J. C. Squire he thought nothing, and of Robert Nichols only a little more. About the earlier poems of T. S. Eliot his feelings were more mixed: he seems to have recognized a genuine poetic quality in them, but to have felt that they were still not to his taste. W. B. Yeats's poems he defined as 'romance in process of decomposition'. Despite some Celtic charm and an obvious felicity of expression, the cumulative effect of Yeats's poetry was faint and rather innocuous. Lytton's final conclusion has about it something of the annihilating logic of Dr Johnson: 'The poem is not only completely divorced from the common facts of life, but its structure is essentially unreasonable, because it depends on no causal law, and thus the effect which it produces is singularly fragmentary and vague. It is full of beauties, but they are all unrelated, and slip out of one's grasp like unstrung pearls.' Much later Lytton was to meet Yeats as a fellow guest of Lady Ottoline Morrell. A photograph of them, taken in about 1923, shows them seated next to each other in garden chairs. Yeats, looking somewhat stout and business-like, appears absorbed in his own monologue, while Lytton, all beard and spectacles, is twisted round in his chair towards the poet, and wears an expression which conveys not so much an air of genuine rapt attention, but the strain of trying to indicate such attention. Yet perhaps the impression of the camera is misleading, and they are discussing with animation the Wildean theory, which they both seem to have shared, that life does not create form, but form life; that so long as the writer possesses a style he has something significant to say. One would like, also, to imagine them debating, with equal enthusiasm, the bizarre and highly strung individuality of Donne, whose hatred of the commonplace, whose love poems so ingeniously worked out with dialectical quibbling, and whose devotional verses full of rhetorical eccentricity, appealed enormously to them both.

Apart from his unsigned book reviews, Lytton also contributed to the *Spectator* over a dozen theatrical reviews above the pseudonym 'Ignotus'. This appointment as dramatic critic was a high tribute to his skill and trustworthiness as a Spectatorial writer. 'The *Spectator*, in all its long history, had never printed an article on the theatre,' James Strachey records.[1] 'But now, on 30 November 1907, the revolutionary step was taken. Very special measures had, of course, to be provided for blanketing the shock to vicarage nerves. The articles were to be signed *"Ignotus"*, to insulate them from editorial responsibility.' At the termination of the first of these articles, St Loe Strachey appended an explanatory note which reads as follows: 'We hope to publish from time to time papers by "Ignotus" dealing with the theatre, but we desire to take the opportunity of pointing out that the critic in question expresses his personal views, and that we are not to be held editorially responsible for his judgements. As long as the opinions given make "les honnêtes gens"[2] laugh or think, and are honest opinions honestly expressed, as unquestionably they will be, we shall be content to leave our readers to determine for themselves whether "Ignotus" distributes his praise or blame successfully.' In the somewhat pompous and long-winded tone of this exposition, one can understand clearly the essential difference between the sort of freedom permitted Lytton on the *Spectator* as opposed to that, say, of the *New Quarterly*. The type of periodical which needed to broadcast the exceptional circumstances of a contributor's written opinions coinciding with his actual thoughts irrespective of editorial policy was obviously far less congenial to his individualistic temperament.

These theatrical reviews are marked by the same qualities of reason and insistence upon an 'attachment with the common facts of life'

---

[1] The *Spectator* was not quite so bereft of theatrical notices as James Strachey suggested. Although Lytton was the paper's first dramatic critic, he was not the first contributor to appraise the contemporary theatre. In a letter to *The Times Literary Supplement* (31 December 1964), Robert H. Tener from the University of Alberta, Calgary, points out that 'during Richard Holt Hutton's editorship of the literary pages (1861–97) a number of non-professional critics reviewed current performances, for, right or wrong, the *Spectator* believed, according to a sub-leader of 22 June 1867, that "every cultivated man, with a love for dramatic literature, and no fettering relations with the theatres and leading performers, will give a better conception of the merits or demerits of any actor, or actress, or any piece", than would a professional critic'. Among these amateur critics of the stage were F. W. Myers, Oliver Elton, Frederick Wedmore, Wilfrid Ward, Meredith Townsend and Hutton himself.

[2] This referred to a quotation from Molière in the article.

which characterize his criticisms of contemporary poets. His case, for example, against the establishment of a National Theatre – that an element of officialdom might well stifle all independent effort, and that State control could so easily lead on to a dull uniformity – is very cogently argued. But his literary appreciation, on the whole, is less acute, so that his censure is usually of more value than his praise. He admired Harley Granville-Barker both as an actor and producer, but had little that was original to write about him. His strictures on Beerbohm Tree and J. M. Barrie, on the other hand, are revealing. Of the imaginative delicacy and pathos which Tree sometimes displayed in the delineation of straight romantic parts, and which so greatly impressed dramatic critics such as Max Beerbohm, Desmond MacCarthy and Bernard Shaw, Lytton has nothing to say. He missed, too, those moments of subtle, imaginative sympathy when Tree's metamorphic genius, in the words of his biographer Hesketh Pearson, 'transcended the art of acting and lifted the spectator out of the world of make-believe'. But almost certainly he was unlucky on the few occasions he saw him act, for Tree was a notoriously erratic and unpredictable performer. In any event, he dealt only with Tree's characteristic habit of clowning, accusing him, with some justice, of preferring what was stagy to the image of life it-self, and describing him as a man obsessed with his audience – 'a great dumb-show actor, a master of pantomime', whose performances held one while they lasted, but left one with 'a feeling of flatness and barren-ness, a feeling almost of dejection', once the curtain had come down.[1]

Lytton diagnosed Tree's failure to produce a convincing, compre-hensive impression as being due to his predilection for a succession of isolated, momentary effects, uncoordinated and contributing nothing to the inner consistency of the play: and he detected a similar failing in

[1] Strong and convincing support for Lytton's denigration of Beerbohm Tree comes from James Strachey who, with what seems incredible fortitude, saw all his Shakespeare productions and a great many others. 'I'm astonished that you should have anything to say in favour of Tree. He was *appalling* in every respect. You should have *seen* his production of *Antony and Cleopatra*. Not thinking it fair that Cleopatra should mono-polize such a large bit at the end of the play, he rearranged it so that both of them died in the same scene. But good heavens! his way of reciting Shakespeare! How on earth can you quote that remark by Hesketh Pearson! And Christ! you should have seen the final scene in the *Tempest*, with Caliban (Sir Herbert Tree) sitting by himself on a rock in gloomy despair – the hero of the play. The only thing he was any good at was pure melodrama – *A Man's Shadow* [adapted by Robert Buchanan from the French play *Roger la Honte*, and first produced in 1889 at the Haymarket Theatre] doubling the parts of the hero and the villain – most enjoyable.' In fairness to Tree, however, it must be pointed out that neither Lytton nor James Strachey have anything to say of his best parts – as Fagin, or Svengali, or Thackeray's Colonel Newcome, as Paragot in *The Beloved Vagabond*, or even as Beethoven in a dreadful play by René Fauchois. It was in parts such as these that he impressed his critics and fellow actors.

J. M. Barrie, upon whose grossly inflated dramatic reputation he poured a much-needed cold douche. In a review of *What Every Woman Knows*, he described the progress of the event-plot as a 'succession of disconnected notes leaving an effect of emptiness'. He was not so taken in by the machine-made neatness of the play as to imagine that the presentment of character was anything but indistinct. Nor was his mood sweetened by Barrie's excessive sentimentality, and he came to the conclusion that 'Mr Barrie is in reality a master in the art of theatrical bluffing'.

Most authors, according to Raymond Mortimer, will prefer reading to the labour of literary composition, and almost anything to weekly reviewing. Lytton was no exception; but despite the very evident dislike he felt for working at articles the compass of which inevitably excluded so much that he was often able to attempt little more than a brief exposition of what was best worth picking out in a writer, yet his period of employment with the *Spectator* was of much practical benefit to him. He was obliged to study many new biographies, and crystallized during this time his own views as to how, artistically, to reconstruct a person's life. He also gained in self-confidence, and was able to condense and refine his prose style. At the end of 1905 he had, for example, written: 'The splendours of triumphant art are often so dazzling as to blind us as to the actual detail of its qualities; and it is only when we have coolly examined a bad imitation that we come to comprehend the hidden values of the original.' Three years later this same idea had been compressed in the columns of the *Spectator* to: 'It is only after a study of an imitation that we begin to understand the real qualities of an original.'

There are many other illustrations of such simplification and improvement. At Cambridge, one of his aphorisms had run: 'It is the highest proof of the genius of Byron that he convinced the world that he was a poet.' More just and hardly less epigrammatic is an ordinary sentence which crops up in 'Andrew Marvell': 'In English, the most notorious example of a poet without style is Byron.' Throughout his *Spectator* reviews are scattered many similarly compact sentences which, if they do not always reveal any unsuspected profundity that he did not exhibit already at Trinity, do indicate a natural tightening up of his style:

'The surest test of the eminence of a poet is the number and variety of literary dogmas which he sets at nought.'

'Nothing can be vainer than promiscuous praise.'

'It is difficult to decide which is the most remarkable thing about Napoleon – his generalship or his lack of humour.'

'The fun of a parody often lies simply in its likeness to the original.'

'A beautiful country is like a beautiful woman – none the worse for a veil.'

(Of Voltaire): 'The most consummate of artists, dancing in a vacuum on the tightrope of his own wit.'

'Laughter is the expression of a simple emotion; but a smile (no less than a tear) is an intellectual thing.'

'The basis of all true comedy is ethical.'

(Of Coleridge as a philosopher): 'He speculated too much and thought too little.'

(Of Chaucer): 'A page or two of his writings will no more contain the true significance of his work than a bucket of sea-water the strength and glory of the sea.'

Although surprisingly few of Lytton's sentences, as George Carver has observed, 'are detachable as aphorisms or quotations of a wider implication', his writing, as it matured, gives increasingly the impression of an uninterrupted flow of intimacy, wit and effortless imagery. In the leisurely atmosphere of Cambridge he had been too preoccupied with the morbid abstractions and intricacies of stylization, with the result that his prose sometimes becomes too languid and self-conscious. But now, when turning out hebdomadal reviews for the *Spectator*, he found that he no longer had time or space for over-elaborate convolutions. The pace and immediacy which were injected into his pieces did much to liberate him from a self-imposed enslavement to extended similitude and metaphor. For the most part his images, such as the one about Chaucer, gained in effect by their greater directness. And by 1910, when he was preparing to start work on his first book, *Landmarks in French Literature*, he had learnt to manipulate his prose with such enviable skill that, with the minimum amount of effort, the reader could receive at once the exact nuance of meaning that he wished to convey.

3

END AS A JOURNEYMAN

'It is many years since he wrote for us,' the *Spectator* said of Lytton on his death in 1932, 'but we remember with some pride his early literary criticisms, particularly of French literature, that appeared in the *Spectator*.' As with most obituary appreciations of the newly dead, the retrospective impression given here of Lytton's special relationship with the *Spectator* is misleading. For although St Loe Strachey was highly delighted with his cousin's contributions, their relationship was curious and uneasy, while Lytton's own feelings as a member of the paper's staff became increasingly unsatisfactory.

With the exception of 'A Russian Humorist', a paper on Dostoievsky which was the last of his criticisms to appear in the *Spectator*, and which was later included by James Strachey in the posthumously assembled *Characters and Commentaries* and *Literary Essays*, none of these *Spectator* pieces were reproduced in his volumes of collected essays. 'I've got a huge box full of *Spectator* reviews – 2 columns I wrote every week for a year and a half,' Lytton wrote to Lady Ottoline Morrell on 18 March 1912. 'I've sometimes had thoughts of collecting the least offensive and trying to have them published in a volume. But I'm afraid it would mean touching them up again, which would be a great bore. I wish I had some faithful acolyte who'd do it for me.' Though it was sometimes suggested to him after the publication of *Eminent Victorians* that he ought to make such a collection, he always put it off.[1] The reasons for this disinclination were various, some of them practical, others more personal. For a start, he felt, there was not much pleasure to be derived from recollecting the circumstances under which these reviews had first appeared. Drafted at speed and with little enough sense of enjoyment, they would have to be passed through a fine comb of textual emendation. For he was well aware that a number of these essays contained, almost word for word, repetitions of metaphor and idea, hardly detectable in the continuing stream of periodical writing, but heavily accentuated, of course, when bound together in a single volume. Besides which, he sometimes used these unsigned and pseudonymous reviews as germs for longer, more elaborately constructed essays. His 'French Poetry' (December 1907), for example, acted as the starting point for his celebrated essay 'Racine' in the *New Quarterly* six months later. Many of his other contributions dealing with French literature were to reappear at least in substance and with many delightful variations and additions in *Landmarks in French Literature*; while the gist of several others again – on the Elizabethans, on Carlyle, Macaulay, Pope and Shakespeare – can be found elsewhere. There was, to Lytton's mind, little additional prestige to be gained from reissuing in a more durable form what sometimes amounted to hardly more than an echo of his other writings. By the time he was famous enough to make this selection of essay-reviews an

---

[1] In the autumn of 1964, James Strachey brought out *Spectatorial Essays*, a volume containing thirty-five of Lytton's contributions to the *Spectator*. Deliberately, this selection was not just a compilation of the best of Lytton's essay-reviews, but the most representative.

attractive publishing venture, he was no longer in urgent need of money, the lack of which had provided the original occasion for their composition. As for the dramatic criticisms of 'Ignotus', they would perhaps never be worth resurrecting, since, as he himself wrote of A. B. Walkley's *Drama and Life*, 'there is no form of literature more apt to be ephemeral than the review of a theatrical performance written for the daily press'.

Then there were other considerations, too, which weighed in his mind. He need never, it was true, look back on his early published work with that acute nausea of embarrassment that afflicts so many authors on re-reading their juvenilia. Even 'Two Frenchmen', the very first of his essay-reviews to be printed, had been remarkable mature. But the reviews he penned each weary week for the *Spectator* re-called to him not simply the drudge of repetitive literary hack work, but a whole period of his career that seemed to hold more misery than happiness and almost no prospects of personal advancement. These Spectatorial essays symbolized his failure to create a com-pletely independent way of life, and reflected back his prolonged reliance on his family, from whom, he knew, he must break free if he were to enjoy life fully and develop his literary talent to anything like its real potential. Frustration mounted within him to an almost un-bearable tension as he laboured week after week at articles that were promptly dispatched and circulated among those hundreds of eager country clergymen. The incongruity between himself and his readers was too preposterous, hardly to be endured. If only the circulation figures had *dropped* while he was taken on the reviewing staff, that at least would have been something. But no, they actually increased! What was happening to him? Possibly, though, it was fortunate that he so seldom had the opportunity for doing more than 'bringing out' an author, of realizing his strong points and enabling him to display himself at his very best. It was an arduous enough task, but one that never approached the final criticism which must discriminate accurately and comprehensively between an author's grain and chaff. After so much time spent picking out only the grain, it was not surprising that after he broke free from the *Spectator*, he should eventually write a book, *Eminent Victorians*, which laid such refreshing emphasis on the chaff in human nature.

As editor of the *Spectator*, St Loe Strachey did not actively interfere with his cousin's compositions to any significant extent, yet it was tacitly assumed by him, as by most subscribers, that the literary section of the paper should consist of a co-ordinated series of articles planned to reinforce, wherever practicable, the political opinions which were expressed in the main body of the paper. St Loe's son, the late John Strachey, told the present author that 'my father always said he [Lytton] was the one reviewer he ever had in whose work he never altered a word'. But James Strachey remembered having seen a few small editorial alterations on Lytton's typescripts. If such interventions were seldom called for, it was largely due to the form of pre-censorship that Lytton himself adopted. The situation with which he had to contend has been described by James Strachey, who for six years worked as St Loe's private secretary. 'Numbers of contributors called on him [St Loe] in the early part of each week: leader-writers (Harold Cox, the economist, John Buchan, the unknown journalist), Eric Parker, who wrote the nature article, the clergyman who wrote the weekly sermon, and, later in the week, the various reviewers. To all of these, indifferently, the same treatment was applied. St Loe was a tremendously fluent talker, producing floods of remarkable ideas and amusing anecdotes – many of which would have startled the vicarages. These he poured over the heads of his visitors at top speed, interlaced with detailed instructions about what was to be written in the leader, the sermon or the review concerned. The visitors had hardly a moment for breathing before they were whirled out of the room. But this was not all. On Thursday afternoons, silent, perhaps, for the first time in the week, St Loe sat back comfortably in a chintz-covered armchair with a pencil in his hand, and read through the galley proofs of the whole of the forthcoming issue. He altered a word here and there, he scribbled a fresh sentence in the margin, he struck out a whole paragraph and replaced it by one of his own.'

These most drastic intrusions were never necessary with Lytton's reviews, yet some of St Loe's unmistakable editorial first person plurals do occasionally crop up, and his unseen influence and guiding hand is discernible in a few of these pieces – 'William Barnes', for example; and 'America in Profile', in which Lytton launches on an uncharacteristic and unconvincing eulogy of the United States; and again in 'Bacon as a Man of Letters'; and 'The Grandiloquence of Wordsworth', a typically Spectatorial title. The most blatant example of St Loe Strachey's own opinions obtruding into an article retrospectively attributed to Lytton is 'The Prose Style of Men of Action', a subleader which they may in fact have written in collaboration. After a chronological description of the enthralling and stately sentences of Elizabeth and of Essex, the 'stupendous power' of Cromwell, the 'charm and force' of Lincoln, and, of course, 'the splendid trenchancy' of Clive, together with the 'swelling and romantic utterance' of Warren Hastings, the piece concludes that men of action make better writers than men of letters. No mere scribbler, working from hearsay, could ever hope to compress into the printed page the spirit of such turbulent and splendid epochs. This lowly concept of the vocational writer in the hierarchy of worldly values was one of which St Loe was always firmly convinced. But Lytton, though he sometimes felt his own miserable inferiority to men of action – in something of the same romantic and frustrated fashion as Walter Scott – nevertheless had begun to rebel against it, and later, in 'The End of General Gordon' and elsewhere, attempted to turn the tables on them. This major change in his attitude was only completed after what he termed his 'Spiritual Revolution' in about 1911, before which, though he had no sympathy with St Loe's opinions on morals, religion or intellectual politics, he did share something of his un-dismayed, sentimental adulation of the Strachey family. This adulation, which again began to assert itself in his last years, was particularly potent in any matter with which his father had been personally con-nected, and perhaps its most direct expression is contained in a review of Colonel Sir G. J. Younghusband's *The Story of the Guides*, which shows that he was still under the spell of the history of British India – a history with which his own ancestors on both sides had played such a prominent part. For this reason, it is easy to exaggerate St Loe's influence over him as his 'secret collaborator'. In fact Lytton was never prevailed upon to write anything in which he did not believe. The pre-censorship he practised was not a perversion but a dilution of the truth; the mixture was less Lytton-and-St Loe than Lytton-and-water. And this restraint and careful inhibition actually assisted his development as a mature writer, giving his hand an added cunning and sense of irony.

In the long run, however, the temperaments of Lytton and St Loe Strachey were bound to clash. St Loe was some twenty years older than Lytton, and his childhood at Sutton Court had been spent in what he called 'a *Spectator* atmosphere', regaled by anecdotes of Clive – 'the Patron saint of the family' – by stories of the American Civil War, and by the recapitulated exploits of countless Stracheys who had been on intimate terms with the famous. After he had come down from Balliol College, Oxford, his father, who was a frequent contributor to the *Spectator*, introduced him to the paper's two editors, R. H. Hutton and Meredith Townsend, and so successful did he turn out as a writer of political and literary articles that he soon gave up his original intention of studying at the Bar and submitted himself to the careful journalistic tuition of these two men. With the years, his influence on editorial policy increased, until, in 1898, at the age of thirty-eight, he became the sole editor and proprietor. From this time onwards the *Spectator* was to be the central pivot of his life.

In the last quarter of the nineteenth century there had been a close tie between the Strachey family and the *Spectator*; and during St Loe's editorship this connexion had been drawn even closer, so that no less than ten Stracheys were numbered among its contributors. This was a result of the particular pride which St Loe took in his heritage. He saw his paper as 'the watch dog of the nation', a means by which to maintain and strengthen the British Empire, that very bulwark of all that was finest in modern civilization. And he was equally determined that the Strachey family, which could boast of such magnificent historical associations in the past, should continue to take its place in the shaping of British political policy and cultural environment. Consequently his own strong and easily recognizable opinions were transparently reflected in each issue of the paper. Being a man of great energy, he never allowed, we are told, 'the slightest news item to find its way into the *Spectator* without first dominating it with his own mind and fixing upon it the special impress of his own character. As many have said, he *was* the *Spectator* for more than twenty five-years.'

This, then, was the peculiar atmosphere that St Loe had established by the time he took Lytton on to his reviewing staff, an atmosphere which united so much that Lytton, in his bid for liberty, had hoped to leave behind him. There were, however, no arguments, no outward show of irritation or hostility between the two cousins while they were working together, and perhaps the best indication of the marked if latent incompatibility between them is to be found in that final essay of *Eminent Victorians*, that account of 'The End of General Gordon', with its distinctive portrait of Sir Evelyn Baring.

Sir Evelyn Baring, or Lord Cromer as he became, had been a colleague of Lytton's father and of his uncle, Sir John Strachey, on the India Council. But by far his most intimate friend among the Stracheys was St Loe. 'I had a regard for him,' confessed St Loe, 'and for his wise, stimulating mind which touches the point of veneration.' And it is no surprise to find that in his autobiography, *The Adventure of Living*, Cromer is placed first in a chapter entitled 'Five Great Men' – all of whom, of course, were soldiers or statesmen. The extent of St Loe's veneration may be measured by the fact that, while his elder son was christened Thomas Clive, his second was named Evelyn John St Loe after Sir Evelyn Baring, who was also his godfather.[1]

For Lytton – during his 'Spiritual Revolution' or period of inverted

---

[1] Evelyn John St Loe Strachey (1901–64), who preferred to be known as John Strachey. He was Minister of Food and Secretary of State for War in the Labour Cabinet of 1945–51. A political economist, he was the author of several brilliant books on the theory and practice of socialism, including *The Coming Struggle for Power*.

admiration – the name of Evelyn Baring came to represent that part of his inheritance which he was most determined to shed. Baring was a reviewer for the *Spectator* at about the same time as himself, and, ironically, they were bracketed together by St Loe as the two most brilliant critics in his employment. Baring, we are told, took immense trouble to understand the *Spectator* point of view, and to submit to St Loe nothing that might prove distasteful. But, since his outlook, unlike Lytton's, was already remarkably similar to his editor's, there was really little enough need for such trouble.[1] 'We wanted the same good causes to win, and we wanted to frustrate the same evil projects,' wrote St Loe. 'In public affairs we agreed not only to what was injurious and to what was sound, but, which is far more important, we agreed to what was *possible*.' When Lord Cromer died in 1917, the year before *Eminent Victorians* was published, St Loe composed a long obituary notice of him, which opened with a characteristically generous and provocative challenge: 'The British people may be stupid, but they know a man when they see him. That is why for the last thirty years they have honoured Lord Cromer.'

St Loe was not to know that while he was penning this tribute to the man whose attitude was so similar to his own, his cousin was already taking up his challenge and drawing a pen-portrait of Lord Cromer that must surely rank among the coldest and most hostile in the whole gallery of his work. This portrait appeared in print the following spring, and a summary of it, fairly recording the part which Sir Evelyn Baring is given to play in 'The End of General Gordon', will, by direct implication, reveal some of those deep temperamental differences that Lytton and St Loe had for so long concealed under a dissembling, politely non-committal front:

'When he [Sir Evelyn Baring] spoke, he felt no temptation to express everything that was in his mind. In all he did, he was cautious, measured, unimpeachably correct. It would be difficult to think of a man more completely the antithesis of Gordon. His temperament, all in monochrome, touched in with cold blues and indecisive greys, was eminently unromantic. He had a steely colourlessness, and a steely pliability, and a steely strength. . . . His life's work had in it an element of paradox. It was passed entirely in the East; and the East meant very little to him; he took no interest in it. It was something to be looked

---

[1] It should be noted that, although in political opinions Cromer and St Loe Strachey were practically identical, their personalities were totally dissimilar. Cromer was a cautious, reserved, methodical man; St Loe a frantically wild character, whose chimerical schemes – the hundred-pound cottage, the National Reserve, the Referendum Bill – were proverbial. Cromer could never have fabricated such schemes, all of which, from the very start, were doomed to failure.

after. It was also a convenient field for the talents of Sir Evelyn Baring. Yet it must not be supposed that he was cynical; perhaps he was not quite great enough for that. He looked forward to a pleasant retirement – a country place – some literary recreations. . . . His ambition can be stated in a single phrase; it was, to become an institution; and he achieved it. No doubt, too, he deserved it.'

The passage is interesting for more than literary-aesthetic reasons. Set in its true biographical context, it may be taken as an affirmation of the precarious new freedom that, in the war years, Lytton had finally managed to secure for himself, an independence, financial and emotional, from the dead trappings of his family. His attitude towards his family had for long been very ambivalent, and was to remain so, with several lurches one way or the other, till the end of his life. St Loe he always regarded as belonging to the other side of the family – the Sutton Court Stracheys, who, to his mind, never had the true Strachey character at all. So far as religion was concerned, he frankly despised their ways and the ways of the *Spectator* – as, for example, his 'Colloquies of Senrab' shows. His political and social opinions, however, were only now shaping themselves, and turning against the Spectatorial St Loe. Like much in *Eminent Victorians*, the caricature of Evelyn Baring as a totally orthodox, passionless and insensate being, was intended to provoke, to sting into anger those intolerant, militaristic bigots whom he associated with the Spectatorial régime. At the same time he was still fond of St Loe, who had always been kind to him, and who had a quite special affection for his mother. Nevertheless, St Loe's public personality was Spectatorial, and Lytton must have written on Baring with the editor of the *Spectator* very much in mind. Thus, there was a complete and quite unrealistic division in his feelings. He did not wish to hurt or offend his cousin personally; yet unless he retaliated, Lytton knew that his onslaught had not been really effective. If he had written really well, St Loe could not ignore it.

And so it turned out. After some weeks of stunned and bewildered silence, St Loe was moved to inform Lady Strachey that the *Spectator* felt a moral duty to attack her son's clever but unfair book. Lytton was at once relieved and concerned. 'As you say,' he wrote to his mother (5 June 1918), 'it's really surprising that there have been no attacks to speak of. I was beginning to feel rather uneasy, but I am reassured by your news of the *Spectator*. This is certainly quite as it should be. I only hope that St Loe was not personally annoyed by my remarks on Lord Cromer.'

It is, however, well nigh impossible to be annoyed *impersonally*. St Loe was closely identified with Lord Cromer, and his annoyance

provided a sure test of the strength and point of Lytton's writing. The
first notice taken of this hostile study by the *Spectator* was mild enough.
A letter appeared in the correspondence columns, in which Maurice
Baring stated that he wished 'to correct one or two errors of fact in this
delicate impressionistic portrait'. He then went on to state that he had
known Lord Cromer personally, that Lord Cromer *had* taken an interest
in the East, that his retirement consisted of incessant work in London,
and that he had looked forward only to what he could look back on,
'tireless devotion in the service of his country'.

But this, as it happened, was no more than an overture to the main
offensive. The following week St Loe himself charged in with a letter
of his own, in which his efforts to be as bland and courteous as Maurice
Baring are almost totally expunged by the pressure of his outraged
sensibilities. Lytton Strachey, he maintained, had launched a thoroughly
ridiculous and ill-informed attack upon Lord Cromer. To say that he
took no interest in the East was 'the most absurd and unpardonable
blunder'. And he drove home his protest in language that verges on a
spluttering incoherence: 'But it is impossible to follow Mr Lytton
Strachey in his farrago of conventional unconventional misapprehen-
sions of Lord Cromer and his attitude. Instead of Lord Cromer being a
kind of embalmed Bureaucrat, he possessed one of the most alert and
least hidebound and least limited intelligences that I have ever encountered.'

More was to follow, for still, even after this outburst, St Loe could
not leave the matter alone. Further letters of disagreement were
printed, and then, nearly two months after the actual publication date
of *Eminent Victorians*, the *Spectator* gave the book a leading review –
described by St Loe as 'trenchant' – which again picked up the question
of 'misstatements about Lord Cromer', of whose invaluable and public-
spirited work Lytton Strachey had given no suggestion. After allowing
that the four essays contained in the book all exhibited a quota of
literary skill, the anonymous Spectatorial reviewer went on to point
out other errors, if not of fact at least of interpretation of fact, and
ended up by stating that the author was 'lacking a sense of responsibility
for the truth of his historical portraits'.

To all this censure Lytton himself replied nothing, and indeed never
contributed another word to the *Spectator* during the remainder of his
life. It was, of course, a favourite literary technique of his to make use
of a subsidiary character as a foil to the principal figure in his books and
essays, and in this role, as the absolute antithesis of General Gordon,
he had cast Sir Evelyn Baring. But in the particular selection of Baring
to fulfil this part, and in the zeal which went towards dressing him up for

it, Lytton may be said to have been flaunting his freshly won independence. Certainly St Loe appears to have taken the whole affair in a highly personal way. Only a grievous and acutely felt injury could have driven him to criticize so adversely and in public a fellow Strachey. Even four years later, in 1922 when his autobiography came out, he had not forgotten the matter, and he is obviously – though now only by implication – slighting his cousin when, in the course of summarizing Lord Cromer's attributes as a writer, he comments: 'He [Lord Cromer] gave "lively characters" of the men described, without being unduly literary or rhetorical. What fascinated me about these portraits, however, was that they were like the best literature, you felt that Cromer had never let himself be betrayed into an epigram, a telling stroke, or a melodramatic shadow in order to heighten the literary effect. The document was a real State Paper, and not a piece of imitation Tacitus or Saint-Simon.'

The interest of this episode is that it shows Lytton's break with his past, Spectatorial self to have been, for all its vigour and intensity, incomplete. In *Eminent Victorians* and elsewhere he did not openly attack his own family, but his family's friends and associates. Baring became the embodiment of the *Spectator*'s public policy, while St Loe he liked to think of as being in many ways far from Spectatorial. Had it not been for the war, perhaps there would have been no attack at all. For though, in peacetime, he had felt stifled by the monstrous regiment of relatives who, like himself, were connected with the paper, he had always taken what opportunities there were for sounding an individual note. But at the outbreak of war, sanity and forbearance were thrown out of the window, and Lytton's political views and those of Lord Cromer and St Loe Strachey, which the *Spectator* lost no chance of advocating each week, were in such total opposition that it became almost impossible for either side to consider the other's point of view with detachment. The *Spectator* proclaimed that there was a fundamental debility in the German mind, and a natural supremacy in the British. It refused to apologize for or feel ashamed of the hostilities between the two countries. Rather it rejoiced in the holocaust. Though entirely of Germany's making, the fight soon took on the aspect of a 'righteous war', in which Britain was undertaking to save the civilized world by replacing German militarism with benefits indistinguishable from those bestowed upon the colonies of the British Empire.

Lytton, of course, was a conscientious objector, as was his brother James, whose position as St Loe's private secretary became increasingly awkward. Eventually, early in December 1915, James was dismissed. 'Apparently he was not altogether surprised at what happened,'

Lytton wrote to Dorothy Bussy (7 December 1915), 'as St Loe has been for months past saying in the Spec. that it was the duty of all employers to dismiss young men in their employment unless they joined the army. He at last told James that he could not continue to employ him consistently with these views. He was very polite and nervous, and they parted in quite a friendly way. It seems to have been inevitable, as St Loe is a conscriptionist, and James's opinion on that subject as on all others, are diametrically the opposite of his.'

Four days later, in a letter to Lady Strachey – 'Aunt Janie' – St Loe expressed something of the same sadness and inevitability. 'In the first place let me assure you that I have no sort of doubt about James's personal courage and good heart. He behaved throughout the whole transaction as I felt sure he would, like a Strachey and a gentleman. His first thought was not to embarrass me or to make me feel that I was doing anything brutal. He told me he recognized that the position had become impossible and unbearable and that I had no other course to take. I was very sorry to part with him for I like him very much, and I feel most awfully sorry for him in the position into which he has got himself, owing I fear, alas, to his sophisticated, socialistic point of view. I am afraid he is very unhappy, and it is dreadful to see that in a person one likes and not to be able to help them[sic]. I suppose I am a monster, but to me the notion that it is so dreadful to take human life, or indeed any life, seems so amazingly foolish that I get quite rabid and unjust about it. It is a commonplace to say so, but I feel sure James will grow out of it . . . I do hope in the first place that he will keep quiet and not go and affiche his follies. I have good hopes that he may keep quiet, because, oddly enough, when he is as it were on the other side he begins to see all their stupidities and finds he cannot go with them. Now the rock-bed of his trouble is a sort of indecision and a sort of intellectual fastidiousness which makes him unable to take any course, and also, as you know, to admire anything.'

Lytton shared exactly James's 'sophisticated, socialistic point of view', his intellectual fastidiousness, his pacifism and pessimism over the war. He, too, did not wish to embarrass St Loe unnecessarily, and seems to have felt no personal antipathy for him despite the wide divergence of their opinions. But for all the diffidence, the nervous good manners, the clannish regret, the dissension between them ran deep. Lytton did not keep quiet, but threw off his indecisiveness and chose to ventilate his 'follies' in his work, the clash between St Loe and James and himself helping to act as a catalyst in the production of 'The End of General Gordon'. Yet even at this moment of utmost, wartime rebellion, at heart Lytton himself still remained a 'Strachey and a gentleman'.

CHAPTER IX

Bloomsbury:
The Legend and the Myth

'For those too young to have known it, the Bloomsbury world is like the memory of a legendary great-aunt; a clever, witty, rather scandalous great-aunt, who was a brilliant pianist, scholar and needlewoman, who could read six languages and make sauces, who collected epigrams and china and daringly turned her back on charity and good works. The influence of Bloomsbury can still be found in the adulation of France; in the mixture of delicious food with civilized values, and in "saying what you mean". Religion was covered by a belief in the importance of human relationships, and the belief seems reasonable enough, though one gets the impression that the milk of human kindness was kept in the larder and that the tea was usually served with lemon. But Bloomsbury, at least in its own eyes, stood for something more important; it stood for tolerance and intelligence, for seriousness about art and scepticism about the pretensions of the self-important, and it carried on a crusade about the conscious philistinism of the English upper classes. Lytton Strachey displayed all these aspects better than any other writer connected with Bloomsbury, and its faults and virtues reflect and explain his own.'

Times Literary Supplement (17 July 1949)

I

THE VISIGOTHS

As we have seen, the five years immediately succeeding Lytton's time at Cambridge form the most unsettled and indeterminate period of his adult life. Everything was speculative, uncertain, fluctuating. He had plenty of plans, but they were all vague and impractical, so that he pursued them only with faint heart. After quitting the one society of which he had managed to become an integral part, he had been pitch-forked back to London, to his family, to nothing. His environment was still largely that of his childhood days, which he had partly outgrown and from which he alternately longed and feared to cut free. At the same time he felt his most urgent need was to merge with – perhaps to create – another congenial society where he could lay the foundations of a successful career; a society that would help to assuage his longing, and comfort his sense of fear. 'Oh dear me!' he had written to Maynard Keynes six months after coming down from Trinity, 'when will my Heaven be realized? – My Castle in Spain? Rooms, you know, for you, Duncan and Swithin, as fixtures – Woolf of course, too, if we could lure him from Ceylon; and several suites for guests. Can you conceive anything more supreme! I should write tragedies; you would revolu-tionize political economy, Swithin would compose French poetry, Duncan would paint our portraits in every conceivable combination and permutation, and Woolf would criticize us and our works without remorse.'

Such was the dream; and reality approximated to it only haphazardly. Three years later a substitute community for Cambridge, something along the lines which Lytton envisaged, had already taken shape in the purlieus of unfashionable Bloomsbury. It was not, of course, the ideal, Castilian concourse of Lytton's quixotic yearnings, nor did he succeed in planting within it the seeds of his own propitious future. In a sense it held him back from realizing his ambitions sooner, for Bloomsbury took the edge off his discontent, making discomfort and obscurity almost endurable. It mitigated, too, a little the claustrophobia of family life. In a letter to his sister, Dorothy Bussy (25 February 1909), he wished desperately that he had achieved something spectacular, but 'I seem to be as far off from even starting as he confesses that ever. My condition is not encouraging. With this damned *Spectator* every week I see no hope of ever doing anything. It's pretty sicken-ing. On Monday I shall be in my 30th year, and if I happened to die there'd be precious little to show for them all – perhaps one or two poems of highly doubtful taste, et voilà tout. It's sickening and occasionally I'm absolutely in despair. If I had decent health I should go into a garret and starve until I'd done something, but that's im-possible. The only consolation is that as it is I lead a very tolerable life.

'At the present moment, as usual, I take more interest in Duncan than in anyone else. He's a genius and charming, but I think he's still rather younger than his age, so that what he does seems to me immature. But I suppose there's no harm in that. Otherwise the people I see and like most are two women – viz. Vanessa and Virginia, with neither of whom I'm in love (and vice versa).'

As Duncan Grant gradually faded from the forefront of Lytton's life, these two custodians and hostesses of the so-called Bloomsbury Group began to figure more prominently. While at Cambridge he had some-times been invited by Thoby to 22 Hyde Park Gate, where the two girls lived and cared for their invalid father. Deaf, suffering from internal cancer, almost completely helpless, Sir Leslie Stephen was wholly dependent upon his daughters. On 22 February 1904 he died, and the four children, Vanessa and Virginia, Thoby and Adrian, left their old home to set up house together at 46 Gordon Square.

Lytton's visits to the Stephens had now grown more frequent. 'On Sunday I called at the Gothic mansion,' he wrote to Leonard Woolf (21 December 1904) not long after they had moved into their new home, 'and had tea with Vanessa and Virginia. The latter is rather wonderful, quite witty, full of things to say, and absolutely out of rapport with reality. The poor Vanessa has to keep her three mad brothers and sister in control. She looks wan and sad.'

At this time, however, the two sisters existed in Lytton's mind as little more than spectral adjuncts to the magnificent Goth, and he used to refer to them collectively as the 'Visigoths'. After Thoby's tragic death, they had not vanished from his life, but slowly asserted them-selves as separate individuals, full of their own interest and fascination. When Clive Bell married Vanessa, Virginia and Adrian moved to a near-by house previously occupied by Bernard Shaw, 29 Fitzroy Square, so as to allow the newly married couple to live alone in Gordon Square. Their circle of friends, of which Thoby's Cambridge contem-poraries formed the nucleus, was not broken up by this move, but enlarged. 'If ever such an entity as Bloomsbury existed,' wrote Clive Bell, 'these sisters with their houses in Gordon and Fitzroy Squares, were the heart of it. But did such an entity exist?' To offer anything like a coherent answer to this vexed and deceptively simple question, it is necessary to disentangle the origins of Bloomsbury from its retro-spective and legendary reputation.

As has already been explained, the group of friends surrounding Lytton, Leonard Woolf and Thoby Stephen were in a sense the original source of Bloomsbury. To most of them, any girl (who was not also a sister) might, for all they knew, have been a species of creature belong-ing to some other planet; and when Thoby had first introduced them to Vanessa and Virginia – shy and alarming in their long white Victorian dresses with lace collars and cuffs, and their large hats, delicately balancing parasols and looking as if they had stepped out of some romantic painting by Watts or Burne-Jones – this double apparition took away their breath. They were speechless and nonplussed. Leonard Woolf recalls that 'it was almost impossible for a man not to fall in love with them, and I think I did so at once. It must, however, be admitted that at the time they seemed to be so formidably aloof and reserved that it was rather like falling in love with Rembrandt's picture of his wife, or Velasquez's picture of an infanta, or the lovely temple of Segesta.'

After Thoby's death, Lytton had got to know the two sisters more intimately, to see some way behind the aloofness and to discriminate more perceptively between their individual characters. In his opinion, and probably in the opinion of most other people, Vanessa was the more beautiful. Her figure was tall and imposing, her face perfectly oval with gray-blue eyes, hooded lids and a full sensitive mouth. In these days she radiated a sense of mature physical splendour, moving with an attractive, undulating walk that later earned for her the nick-name of 'the Dolphin'. Though often severe in the judgements she fixed upon people, her manner was usually gay and spontaneous. At the same time there was also something magisterial about her presence, a quality of quietude and tranquillity that befitted the eldest child of Leslie Stephen's second marriage. This element increased with the years and is vividly conveyed by Duncan Grant's portrait of her[1] – a sensitive yet uncompromising figure seated imperiously upon a high-backed Victorian chair. Despite being the member of a new, deter-minedly enlightened set of artists and writers, she still liked to segregate the human race into two elementary classes – those who basked within the charmed circle of her youthful friends, and those who, possibly through no fault of their own, had been born into a less privileged stratum of society. To one side of this division, she erected a third tiny kingdom within which none of her progressive and emancipated principles were allowed to operate – her children. Over them she watched with a jealous and possessive eye. When Julian, her son, was killed during the Spanish Civil War, she broke off for life her friendship with the painter Wogan Philipps (Lord Milford), who had travelled with him to Spain. And when her daughter Angelica wanted to marry David Garnett, she opposed the match violently, even though Garnett was a personal friend and member of Blooms-bury.

Though his relationship with her was made a little uneasy and con-fused by her far more intimate association with Duncan Grant, Lytton

[1] This portrait, which is reproduced in the Penguin volume *Duncan Grant* by Raymond Mortimer, now hangs in the Tate Gallery.

did experience some mild flutter of physical attraction towards Vanessa. Her collapsed and dreamy attitudes, however, and her wild inconsequence often exasperated him. Her nature was entirely feminine, and though she enjoyed entering into men's discussions and even making bawdy jokes, she had no interest in current affairs. An artist of considerable talent, she scanned only the illustrations in the newspapers, seldom bothering to read through the dull grey columns of print; and on one notable occasion, seated next to a man whose features were intolerably familiar to her, she innocently asked Asquith, then the prime minister, whether, unlike herself, he was interested in politics.

In spite of a natural, unselfconscious humour and gaiety, Vanessa's thoughts were largely disconnected from everyday affairs. She often seemed in the dark over the most ordinary and commonplace matters, and in casual conversation her metaphors were delightfully mixed. Her best and most original remarks, David Garnett observed, were vaguely experimental. 'When she coined an epigram it was often because she had forgotten a cliché.

'"In that house you meet a dark horse in every cupboard," she exclaimed with some indignation. And of Maynard: "It runs off his back like duck's water." But of all her sayings the most withering was: "Ah, that will be canker to his worm."'

The same spirit of haphazard vagueness seems to have informed her painting, much of which is strangely diluted. Though at one time or another she was influenced by Post-Impressionism – in particular Cézanne – and by the Fauvists, she retained an overall detachment from the stylistic movements of her day. Possibly her finest painting was to be a self-portrait done in 1958. Here there is no dilution, no dreamy uncertainty: the face under its almost comically wide-brimmed hat is steeped in wistful sadness and resignation, the once sensuous mouth now tired and tremulous, the eyes from behind the large spectacles focused beyond the limits of the surrounding world.[1]

Early photographs of Virginia Stephen show her as less robust and comely than Vanessa, rather anaemic and ethereal. From out of a thin anxious face, her enormous green eyes gaze out fearfully at the cold, slow terrors of the universe. There was always something unsubstantial and impalpable about her. She appeared to glide below the turbulent seas of life as in a dream that would pitch without warning into the terrifying troughs of nightmare. The mystic aura that during her life enveloped her fragile being like a cocoon has caused many of her friends' retrospective memories to take on the illusion of reverie. For

[1] This painting is now in the collection of Sir Kenneth Clark.

though she could be as animated as her sister, when her haunted, melancholy expression would suddenly light up with a smile, making her face look oddly different, yet her nature was perpetually clogged with morbid self-obsession, the intensity of which would recurrently build up and explode, leaving her in a shattered state of sick, mental collapse. Even in lighter moments, her compulsive fits of vitality seemed to come not from her physical resources, but through a painful, electric system of nerves.

Tall and slender, with a noble forehead and narrow, aquiline features, she radiated an ascetic, sexless charm which contrasted strangely with her zestful, restless enthusiasm when excited by the curiosity of some discussion. Leaning forward in her chair, a cigarette held limply in her long fingers, her head cocked to one side like an intelligent dog, she would talk in her throaty, deepish voice with a keen sensibility, wit and an inquiring passion that was altogether dissimilar to Vanessa's balanced, judicial tone. Her mental animation mounted rapidly as she spoke, but if someone dared stupidly to interrupt her in full flight she would all at once grow fierce, flashing back some sharp and scathing repartee and then reverting to her sullen posture of unapproachable and frigid aloofness.

At her most sympathetic, most relaxed, Virginia displayed a warmth and power of direct friendship that hinted at the deep burden of loneliness from which she was always endeavouring to escape. In convivial surroundings, among trusted friends, she gave the impression of brittle high spirits that might at any second '"leave the ground" and give some fantastic, entrancing, amusing, dreamlike, almost lyrical description of an event, a place, or a person', or alternatively snap and in a trice capsize her frail being into unexpected, imponderable gloom. The peculiar remoteness of personality which manifested itself amusingly in Vanessa's social gaffs and off-beat colloquialisms was present in a far more intensive and terrifying form in Virginia. And whereas Vanessa's feminine intellectual vagueness exasperated Lytton, Virginia's asexual, twilight elusiveness he found psychologically curious. The one, a result of muddled absent-mindedness, jarred upon his matronly sense of order and proportion; the other, the consequence of a strange and original emphasis of concentration, chimed in with his own mystical apprehensions, running to some extent parallel with that ever-present desire of his to find release from the prison of his physical self. He admired her; but her novels were not to his taste. Virginia's strong, masculine intelligence and heightened feminine sensibility seemed almost to cancel each other out, producing a sort of eddying, cross-current of nihility, a bleak no-man's-island that is reproduced in the aseptic, vestal texture of her fiction – a literary quality that dismayed Lytton. Bi-sexuality would have fascinated him; but he abhorred a vacuum.

Despite Virginia's militant feminism and Lytton's radical passivism, neither of them were well-suited to the sort of conscious Fabian worrying that was then forming so great a part of intellectual discussion. But whereas Lytton's pensive silences were rather stylized, Virginia's were more distracted and impenetrable. She seemed oddly isolated from it all, at once half-eager and half-frightened of breaking free from the coiling meshes of her absorbed and tortured self-preoccupation. This spirit of sharply alternating animation and reserve had been conditioned by her father. Leslie Stephen was an enlightened man, but sexually repressed and maladjusted, so that although his children had benefited from his literary tolerance and sagacity, they had also suffered grievously under the meanness and dogmatic puritanism of his household. Perhaps the pathos of such a man's life could only be appreciated by his friends, most of whom thought him very lovable. The contrast between Vernon Whitford in Meredith's *The Egoist* and Mr Ramsay in Virginia Woolf's *To the Lighthouse* underlines Leslie Stephen's opposing roles as friend and father. Virginia herself was directly affected by this duality. In her obituary notice of him in *The Times* she pays tribute to his vigour of mind, his honesty, and endearing eccentricities. But her fictional portrait of him depicts a man essentially unimaginative, joyless, tyrannical. However she might respect his various gifts and achievements objectively, she still felt in an organic sense that his dominating presence had squeezed the very lifeblood from her veins. Somehow he had taken away from her the ability to nourish her ravenous unappeased appetite for life. As she helped to nurse him through his long, last appalling illness she must already have known that her hopes of liberation, of spiritual release, centred upon his death. The consciousness of this had filled her with a dreadful sense of guilt, and in 1903, a few months before her father's death, she suffered a mental breakdown. Both of them could no longer continue that half-life in such close proximity. She recovered and he died. From him she had inherited a strong egoism together with a neurotic and demanding conscience; from her mother, a fine, artistic delicacy and sensitivity. These diverse elements were not to be resolved, but waged within her a tangled and exhausting conflict. Her increasing obsession with death indicated a growing awareness that a part of her father still lived on in her. While she breathed, his alien spirit continued to enshroud her. She could not wash it off. So death became for her the ultimate release, the resurrection through patricide by *felo de se*.

Though she had been well cared for as a child, the comfort of her early years had been punctuated by a series of traumatic shocks – madness, senility and death itself. Before she was ten years old, her first cousin, the handsome and talented J. K. Stephen, had begun to show alarming symptoms of a worsening mental instability. His eccentricities were so unpredictable and extreme that he was soon expelled from his club, and later, after making violent advances to Virginia's half-sister, Stella Duckworth, he was committed to an asylum where in 1892 he died. His father – Virginia's uncle Fitzjames – was inconsolable. He retired; his health rapidly deteriorated; he became within a few short months an old man, and died not long afterwards. The following year had brought the greatest disaster of all, when Julia Stephen, Virginia's mother, died. The shock of this had led to a complete breakdown, and she tried to commit suicide by throwing herself out of a window. It was from this time, too, that her father's health had steadily worsened, and when in 1898, within a year of her marriage, Stella Duckworth died, the old man came to rely entirely on his two daughters. Although Virginia's life was never inactive, the environment at Hyde Park Gate, especially when her brothers were away at school or university, had grown dull and overcast. She longed for the sunlit holidays by the sea; and the sea became for her a symbol of life and freedom. Her poetic genius needed stimulus from the outside world, yet she felt an even stronger need for protection against the ruthless, unheeding cruelty of which the world was so full. Her wraith-like spirit seemed never completely drawn into her body, never entirely possessed by it. In consequence, the probing, innocent curiosity she felt about all human activity, though often passionate, remained peculiarly bloodless and trivial. In place of direct personal involvement, she continued with unanswerable child-like persistence to pose strings of improbable questions that could become tedious and embarrassing. What must it feel like to be a king? A newly-married bride? A bus conductor? Craving to be set free from her egomania by something or someone stronger and altogether dissimilar to herself, she speculated endlessly upon the unknown: and for her the unknown was frequently the commonplace. Thoby might have rescued her, but he, too, had died. And there was no one else.

What temporary respite from introspection she did find, came not through the composition of her books – as was the case with Lytton – which were merely intricately charted extensions of this process of self-examination, but in appraising a sequence of vicarious sensations, and in screwing her concentration round upon diverse but coincidentally simultaneous happenings which, by their very lack of all personal connexion, seemed to diminish the status of the individual and his subjective agonies. In such piecemeal fashion did she hope to reconcile her yearning for poetic experience without personal immolation. Like a bat, relying on sound waves alone to tell it the geography of its surroundings, she put together a vision of the world full of wisps and fragments – a shadow, a silhouette, a twig in the wind, the mark on a wall. If Lytton was like some theatrical director and producer rolled into one, passionately excited not only by the professional décor and costume, but also by the positioning of the *dramatis personae* upon the stage and the synchronization of their rehearsed speeches, Virginia was the special freelance correspondent who, unconcerned by the event-plot, lies concealed in the dark recesses behind the stage and spies on the actors as they retouch or take off their make-up between the acts. Her novels, which involved much anguished self-observation, are delvings into the sick, neurasthenic depths of her nature, which, like that of Coleridge, was subterranean. As an ordinary, open-air land-animal she was inexplicable. 'Virginia is I believe a more simple character than appears on the surface,' Lytton wrote many years later to Ralph Partridge (1 September 1920). 'Her cleverness is so great that one doesn't at first see a kind of ingenuousness of feeling underneath.' He saw her, and rightly, as some deep sea-creature, whose habits and moods could not be properly understood on the hard matter-of-fact surface of things. There are many exquisite vignettes scattered through her work that convey her unique sensibility with a lyrical, muted radiance, which seems to tremble from the refracted rays of a sunlight playing far below the green waves to the soundless bed of the ocean. She breathed in the oxygen of life and gave out in her novels only carbon dioxide. Her view of the universe was somnabulistic; she felt remote from waking reality, and indulged in few of the ordinary adult appetites, eating only a bare minimum and shying hysterically away from sexual intercourse. Though she saw humanity through a glass lucidly, she seemed paralysed from translating her interests into active participations, so that she remained a connoisseur of feeling rather than a lover of life. Her observation of human relationships is always subtle and accurate, but comes little nearer to the wonder and ecstasy of real love than, as William Gerhardie has said, a medical analysis of the menstrual cycle.

Although she resented his superior education, mistrusted his cynical tendency to gossip, and later, for a time, rather envied his meteoric rise to fame, Virginia always felt a peculiarly warm affection for the sickly, hypochondriac Lytton. She was often at her most enchanting, most self-forgetful with those who were ill. Invalids, with their impaired vitality and excessive self-preoccupation, she welcomed as fellow creatures in her dimly-lit underworld. In company with Thoby's other Cambridge friends, several of whom had found asylum in Bloomsbury, she was as relaxed, as whimsically amusing as her difficult temperament permitted. But her moods were unpredictable, and behind her brilliance there was always some hint of pain and stress. Deep beneath her sensitive geniality were sown the seeds of suspicion and envy. In self-protection she assumed an air of wariness, treating everyone as a potential rival. Touchy and mistrustful, she held herself for the most part in check. But when someone happened casually to mention that Vanessa must find it very tiring to stand long hours at her easel, she was at once outraged, and promptly stalked off to buy herself a tall desk at which, for the rest of her life, she made a point of standing while writing her novels. It was characteristic of her deep-seated neurosis that she should read into some harmless remark a non-existent slight, and then set about punishing herself because of it.

Her nervous sensibility could be easily inflamed into a burning sense of persecution. If one congratulated her on looking well she interpreted one's remark as meaning she appeared red and coarse. Should one praise her latest novel, she might read into it a dislike of her last but one. When the Germans bombed London, she calculated the serious damage in terms of decreased book-sales. Tense and shy in company, she could turn bitter and malicious behind her friends' backs in order to repay imaginary aspersions and grievances. She was jealous, too, of their achievements, at one time expressing a wish that Duncan Grant had followed his father into the army, and at another announcing that Lytton should have been an Anglo-Indian Civil Servant. T. S. Eliot, also, she once observed, had he stayed in banking, might well have ended up as a branch manager! She can be, and has been, put down as a textbook example of a leptosome whose neurosis was schizophrenic though, most probably, her condition was that of a manic depressive. Yet (curiously, since Leonard Woolf was an early enthusiast of Freud's) she was never psycho-analysed, merely treated by doctors, as each medical crisis arose.

The atmosphere within the two Bloomsbury salons at Vanessa and Virginia's houses was in several respects quite different, and reflected to some degree their differing personalities. The Bells 'are a wild sprightly couple', Lytton wrote to Duncan Grant soon after they had married and set up house together (2 June 1907). 'The drawing-room has no carpet or wall-paper, curtains some blue and some white, a Louis XV bed (in which they lie side by side), two basket chairs, a pianola, and an Early Victorian mahogany table!' Number 46 was a spacious house set in the centre of the east side of Gordon Square. Clive Bell's hospitality was warm and jovial, reminding his guests of the hunting and shooting milieu in which he had been brought up, and contrasting oddly with the pictures of Picasso and Vlaminck which hung on the walls. His exuberance and the extrovert heartiness which overlaid a morbid fear of illness and pain, lent muscle to the bleak and fastidious gatherings of his intellectual companions, and went some way to prevent the Bloomsbury Group from turning into another Clapham Sect. 'When the door was opened,' wrote David Garnett, who was to join this circle of friends at the beginning of the war, 'a warm stream of Clive's hospitality and love of the good things of life poured out, as ravishing as the smell of roasting coffee on a cold morning.'

Some affinities there still were, however, with the Claphamites. Bloomsbury, like Clapham, was a coterie, Noël Annan points out in his *Leslie Stephen*: 'It was exclusive and clannish. It regarded outsiders as unconverted and was contemptuous of good form opinions. Remarks which did not show that grace had descended upon the utterer were met with killing silence. Like the Claphamites they criticized each other unsparingly but with affection. Like Clapham, Bloomsbury had discovered a new creed: the same exhilaration filled the air, the same conviction that a new truth had been disclosed, a new Kingdom conquered. . . .

'. . . the fourth generation of the Clapham Sect naturally repudiated the moral code of their forefathers. The doctrine of original sin was replaced by the eighteenth-century belief in man's fundamental reasonableness, sanity and decency. They violently rejected Evangelical notions of sex, tossed overboard any form of supernatural belief as so much hocus-pocus, and set their sails in the purer breezes of neo-Platonic contemplation. And yet one can still see the old Evangelical ferment at work, a strong suspicion of the worldly-wise, an unalterable emphasis on personal salvation and a penchant for meditation and communion among intimate friends.'

For Lytton, at least, the Bloomsbury atmosphere represented primarily an invitation to congenial friendship. Though he found sympathetic companions hard to come by, he was never an outcast in Bloomsbury. For there the tables were turned, and it was the ordinary proletariat, the 'unconverted', who found themselves out of place, who were encouraged to feel ill-at-ease and rather inadequate. Outsiders were apt to be particularly disconcerted at Virginia and Adrian's house in the south-west corner of Fitzroy Square. The large drawing-room on the ground floor was decorated in a quite different style from the interior of Gordon Square. There were no cubist paintings, only a

Dutch portrait of a lady and Watts's portrait of Sir Leslie Stephen. Soon after the two of them had settled down there, Lady Strachey came to have tea with Virginia and look over the house where Lytton was to spend so much of his time. During the early part of the meal Hans, the Stephens' dog, made a large, conspicuous mess on the carpet directly between the two women; but such was the impeccable self-control laid upon them by the pressure of late-Victorian etiquette that the ceremony of afternoon tea proceeded on its unhurried way without either of them alluding to the disaster.

Guests would encounter a more Spartan and dismaying welcome here than at Clive Bell's home. Virginia, especially, reacted with the *gaucherie* of an awkward child; but it was a *gaucherie* stylized and tempered into what was later to be recognized as the perfect Bloomsbury manner. None of them, for instance, would smile as they shook hands, a habit which proved extremely effective in unsettling strangers. Adrian, then studying Law, was moreover a confirmed and celebrated practical joker. Led on by his accomplice Horace de Vere Cole, a kindly but clownish retainer to Augustus John, he helped to perpetrate a number of daring, widely publicized hoaxes – digging up Piccadilly as a navvy, and at another time arranging a party for all the citizens of Birmingham whose names – beginning with 'Row', 'Ram', 'Side', 'Higgin' or 'Winter' – ended with 'bottom', and who, finding their unknown host had failed to arrive, were obliged to introduce themselves to one another. Probably the most notorious of all these practical jokes took place on board H.M.S. *Dreadnought*, one of whose officers was persuaded that the Emperor of Abyssinia together with his retinue desired to be officially shown round the ship. Cunningly disguised with thick make-up and extravagant theatrical costumes, and countering all questions with the same mumbled phrase, 'Bonga-Bonga', Duncan Grant, Virginia and Adrian Stephen, Horace Cole and two friends were welcomed aboard the Admiral's flagship with magnificent pomp and formality. There, despite a number of narrow escapes, the masquerade was brought off with the dexterity and finesse of a professional ballet performance: the band struck up with the anthem of Zanzibar, the mariners were paraded and inspected, innumerable salutes were exchanged, several decorations proffered. Only later, to the great scandal of the Press and embarrassment of the authorities, was the true identity of the visitors revealed. Questions were asked in Parliament: the joke was complete.

Besides the live-wire hoaxes of Adrian and Horace Cole, who was at any moment liable to put salt in the cocoa or to spit in the whisky, an unwary guest might also have to contend with the inner ferocity of

Virginia's character, concealed under a delusive, diffident manner, at once subversive and inexorable. 'Upon an unforeseen introduction, for instance,' wrote Duncan Grant, 'there was an expression of blazing defiance, a few carefully chosen banalities and a feeling of awkwardness.' Those whose wish to proceed further had not been successfully eliminated by this welcome would then be shown into Adrian's or Virginia's study. Adrian's was on the ground floor, well ordered, neat and handsomely lined with books. Virginia's workroom was directly above, untidy, books littered all over the floor and furniture, her tall desk – at which she stood writing for two hours each day – positioned near the window.

It was in Adrian's ground-floor study that their friends assembled on Thursday evenings – 'a continuation', Duncan Grant explains, 'of those evenings which began in Gordon Square before Thoby died and Vanessa married. It was there that what has been called "Bloomsbury" for good or ill came into being.

'About ten o'clock in the evening people used to appear and continue to come at intervals till twelve o'clock at night, and it was seldom that the last guest left before two or three in the morning. Whisky, buns and cocoa were the diet, and people talked to each other. If someone had lit a pipe he would sometimes hold out the lighted match to Hans the dog, who would snap at it and put it out. Conversation; that was all. Yet many people made a habit of coming, and few who did so will forget those evenings.

'Among those who consistently came in early days were Charles Sanger, Theodore Llewelyn Davies, Desmond MacCarthy, Charles Tennyson, Hilton Young (later Lord Kennet), Lytton Strachey.'

The mood and atmosphere of these Thursday-night congregations were an extension to those of the Cambridge Conversazione Society, and Lytton soon found in Fitzroy Square a tolerable substitute for the delights of Trinity and King's. This was better than he had expected. Less than four years ago he had crept away from the divine amenities of Cambridge into 'the limbo of unintimacy', prepared for a silent and wretched exile. But Bloomsbury had taken him in, soothed and warmed him a little. There was a strong affinity between the scheme of things in Gordon and Fitzroy Squares, and the courts of Trinity and King's. The rooms were different, but the same tobacco-smoke stole up the windows against the night sky, the same talk of Greeks and Romans – mostly Greeks – sped on around him. 'Talking, talking, talking,' sighed Virginia Woolf in recollection of those days, '– as if everything could be talked – the soul itself slipped through the lips in thin silver discs which dissolve in young men's minds like silver, like moonlight.

Oh, far away they'd remember it, and deep in dullness gaze back on it, and come to refresh themselves again.'

Though the routine of his life, divided between his family and friends, Hampstead and Bloomsbury, was less well arranged and homogeneous than before, though perhaps he was less contented inwardly than as an undergraduate, Lytton did not appear to languish in greater gloom and despair. No longer, surrounded by kindred spirits, did his long, emaciated form crouch in odd and angular shapes on sofas, tables, basket-chairs, wrapped for hours in deep imponderable silence. For now that he and his friends were less absurdly young, their methods of communal conviviality, if still idiosyncratic, had grown more relaxed and mature. The infiltration of feminine society into the circle also did something to lighten the intensity of austere scholasticism that had so resolutely typified their Cambridge dialectics. The Cambridge garrison of Bloomsbury, a civilized fortress, as they saw themselves, isolated amid the hostile, native population of London, was inevitably less immune than the university itself from the vulgar assaults of ignorant masses. Life was necessarily composed of less subdued and even tones, less prim and exclusive conduct, less absolute free thinking, less rigid informality, now that they were no longer sequestered from everyday, human activity in the dingy, antiquarian charm of a few literary backwaters. 'In exchange for the peace of Cambridge,' J. K. Johnstone acutely comments, 'the traffic of London clattered by on the pavements just outside. The world was closer, and there was certain to be a new awareness of it.'

What passing references there are in Lytton's essays to the boom and bombast of twentieth-century living show his deeply ingrained dislike, and even horror of it. 'He was quite definitely,' wrote Max Beerbohm in his Rede Lecture, 'and quite impenitently, what in current jargon is called an escapist.' Bloomsbury society was for him a quiet but active oasis in this desert of loud, claustrophobic loneliness. Yet he was always conscious of those vast, unplanned areas of city life which began only a few steps away and sprawled in all directions for so many hideous miles. He dreamed of an ordered, reasonable, unrespectable, tidy, refreshingly simple world, where happiness, beauty and companionship were not stigmatized as immoral – the very antithesis of sophisticated London. The seven consecutive years he spent there after coming down from Trinity served to widen that fissure in his nature which he was later to dramatize so successfully.

This peculiar dualism was at the same time echoed in his strange, carefully modulated speech. He used two strikingly different types of voice. One, high-pitched and tinny, was employed deliberately to deflate pomposity; to express astonished disagreement with some opinion (when it was often accompanied by a raising of the eyebrow); to introduce either an element of clowning or baiting into the conversation; or to tease someone he liked. 'Sometimes in this mood,' recalled E. B. C. Lucas,[1] 'his splendid, architectural nose would appear larger than usual, presumably owing to an angle of the head. The high voice, then, was an affectation. Lytton would not have denied this. The comment on a friend's narrative: "*Too* ghastly, my dear," was an affectation so transparent that it constituted a sort of musical phrasing, part of a style. Like all "Bloomsberries", he disliked pretension and silliness – the former much more than the latter, which after all could be a trait in youth, and so, forgivable; and in order to show up pretension, he would assume the high voice and the high brows, and so prick the bubble.' Occasionally, to parody or ridicule some attitude, he would chant whole sentences in a feeble, monotonous falsetto. At other times – in moments of intimacy or when reading out loud – he would employ a rather deep, bass voice, which with a strange inversion of stress might all at once rise to a reedy crescendo in emphatic termination of his sentence. As shown by his letters, he was much affected by the weather, and in rain and cold was apt to fall silent for long stretches. He did not often laugh. But an expression which was not exactly a smile would slip over his face, his eyes gleaming and fixed on whoever was speaking, and the mental climate grew warm and sunny. His two celebrated voices were, then, not entirely natural, but a contrived over-emphasis of a natural idiosyncrasy. In 1909, this dual voice was still something of a novelty, adopted to help establish for himself the *persona* which he wished others to accept and remember. But later in his life these voices, together with other distinctive appendages to his new Bloomsbury image – the beetroot-brown beard, the attenuated fingers, and a variety of runcible hats and cloaks – worked themselves into the recognized fabric of his highly stylized personality. They were no longer put on, but came as it were spontaneously to him, just as lines do to a good actor. In the opinion of Ralph Partridge, who knew Lytton only during the last twelve years of his life, 'these two voices of his were not an affectation but a natural gamut of expression – and the top notes were an echo of Voltaire's "high cackle" from the eighteenth century'.

In spite of his involuntary contact with a wider, more cosmopolitan

[1] E. B. C. Jones, the novelist, and first wife of F. L. Lucas of King's College, Cambridge. Known to her friends as 'Topsy', she had a rather arch way of referring to herself, in a deep voice, as 'Monkey' – 'Monkey doesn't read Shakespeare', etc. Living in Cambridge, she exerted a considerable influence on some of the most gifted undergraduates there.

world than Cambridge, Lytton's demeanour could still be as rigidly uncompromising as ever. When Clive Bell invited some French friends of his to Gordon Square, the francophil Lytton responded in a manner highly reminiscent of his grandfather, Edward Strachey. Resenting the intrusion of strangers, and uncomprehending foreigners at that, he stubbornly pretended to be incapable of speaking or understanding a word of the French language, and retreated into one of his grim spells of non-communication. Like Virginia Stephen he tended to distrust people whom he did not know well, and was supremely anxious not to fail in any attempt to impress them. But then again, if they were not handsome, or quick-witted, what, in any case, could possibly be the point in impressing them? They hardly existed. All the same he detested obscurity, and dreamt of being welcomed on his own terms by a society that he scorned. This feeling was shared by several of his friends, and it was on a superfine mixture of arrogance and diffidence, of ambitious talent and crippling shyness, that the Bloomsbury Group was largely founded. Such were some of its biographical and psychological origins; the various and conflicting myths which were erected round the group during later years were vaguer and vaster. But since the sociological and literary legends of Bloomsbury have, as the phrase is, 'caught the public imagination', and gained a wide acceptance despite only random approximation to the truth, they can no longer be corrected and set aside by a simple, qualified alternative statement, but call for some rather more detailed re-examination.

2

HOME THOUGHTS ON HUMAN GROUPS

About 1910 or 1911, Molly MacCarthy, the wife of Desmond Mac-Carthy, in the course of a letter to Frank Swinnerton, described the Stephen family and their associates as 'Bloomsberries'. The word caught on, and it was not long before Arnold Bennett and other writers outside this tiny oligarchy were referring to Virginia Woolf, as she had then become, as 'the Queen of Bloomsbury'. The phrase, used mostly in a derogatory sense, was intended to convey a meaning similar to 'highbrow', the leader of a semi-precious, achromatic, brittle form of mock-Hellenic culture, encased in a Gallic frame. But, as Vanessa Bell pointed out in a paper entitled 'Old Bloomsbury', the original circle, which had started to meet in 1904 and broke up at the beginning of the war, had really ceased to exist several years before the term became fashionable, and other people inherited its name and reputation.[1]

In the years that followed, two divergent fables of Bloomsbury arose and were given wide controversial publicity. Though opposite in many respects, both fostered one common and fundamental fallacy – that the Bloomsbury Group was a strategically planned and predetermined literary movement, starting in about 1905 and continuing on with various alterations in membership and in emphasis of sacred doctrine until the early 1930s. In much authoritative French, German and Russian criticism of early twentieth-century literature in England, the Bloomsbury myths were, and still are, strongest, perhaps because the individuals involved are less well known. Yet even in England numerous essays and theses have been produced which imply or state categorically that the work of Clive and Vanessa Bell, David Garnett, Duncan Grant, Maynard Keynes, Leonard and Virginia Woolf, E. M. Forster, Lytton Strachey and several others, shares an identical system of aesthetics, the same philosophy and values, all of which stem from *Principia Ethica* and that unsuspecting innocent, G. E. Moore.

Despite their superficial contradictions, the twin concepts of Bloomsbury were closely related to each other, and seem to have taken root from a variety of human motives. Those contemporary writers who were not admitted to the select band thought they saw in it a dangerous organic unity which it did not really possess. Others disliked these eminent late-Victorians for their socially secure antecedents and inherited financial independence. And for still others again, Bloomsbury represented a new exclusive movement, an *avant-garde* fashion of superior, voluntary ostracism from life – 'life' so often meaning a mixture of politics and cricket. At the same time, the more obscure rank and file of nonentities on the fringe of the set lent currency to this damaging mystique so as to attract unto themselves a reflected glory from the luminaries of W.C.1. Then more recently, studious literary

[1] Vanessa Bell lists the original members of Bloomsbury as herself, her sister Virginia, Thoby and Adrian Stephen, Clive Bell and Leonard Woolf, Maynard Keynes, Duncan Grant and Roger Fry, Desmond and Molly MacCarthy, Lytton, Oliver, Marjorie and James Strachey, Saxon Sydney-Turner, Harry Norton, E. M. Forster and Gerald Shove. In the opinion of Leonard Woolf, Bloomsbury 'came into existence in the three years 1912 to 1914', after he himself had returned from Ceylon. Thoby, therefore, who died in 1906, was not, in his version, a member. There were, he states, thirteen of them in all. He excludes from the above roll-call Gerald Shove, Harry Norton and Lytton's brothers and sister. Of the ten men in this group, MacCarthy, Lytton, Saxon Sydney-Turner, Forster, Keynes and himself had been 'permanently inoculated with Moore and Moorism'. The basis of this assembly, however, was simply friendship. James Strachey, who denied belonging to Bloomsbury, also disagreed with Leonard Woolf, believing that the group came into existence precisely during his absence in Ceylon, that is in about 1907.

critics, who appear to comprehend next to nothing of the isolated way in which a work of art is evolved, have prolonged the legend to a point where it threatens to become established tradition. With the result that now, what had initially been useful as a quick, rough-and-ready term of classification to the journalist, has been built up into a very real obstacle in the labours of the literary historian and biographer.

The two imaginary Bloomsburies are in amusing disaccord. For many years the Press notices which this largely fictitious coterie drew were unfavourable. An over-serious, self-important Bohemia, Bloomsbury was said to be composed of highly pretentious, ill-mannered dilettanti, who derived a masochistic excitement from casting themselves in the role of supersensitive martyrs to the coarse insensitivity of the barbarian world of twentieth-century London. Arrogant, squeamish pedagogues, their desire to take in people whom they affected to consider their antipodean inferiors in every way belied their assumption of conceit. It was all a sham. Their pseudo-Greek culture, their overriding contempt for the less well educated, at whose head they placed D. H. Lawrence, their insularity and the uncertain grimaces, mock-frivolity and infantile practical hanky-panky which passed among them for humour, were in fact outlets of a rigid and reactionary class system such as, perhaps, only England could boast of. Under their wincing, spinsterish mannerisms these world-shunners were immensely, ruthlessly ambitious. They possessed, however, little potent or vivacious imagination and to attain their aims they formulated a set of restricting artistic rules which had the effect of substituting phoney aestheticism for genuine creative talent. Exclusive not by virtue of any extraordinary ability, but mainly through a supercilious, studiously cultivated priggism, they were too clever by half to perform ordinary services on behalf of the community, yet too 'arty' and unreliable to find places in the universities where they might otherwise have been usefully employed.

Strange rites, sinister rituals and unmentionable initiation ceremonies were soon attributed to those who tended the dark flower of Bloomsbury. Beside this exotic growth, the green carnation was a very tame and pallid cosmetic. According to the would-be tough extrovert poet Roy Campbell, the Bloomsbury equivalent to shaking hands was a pinch on the bottom accompanied by a mouse-like squeak – a salutation that does not appear to have varied with the sexes. Yet in spite of many such emphatically sub-normal and heterologous characteristics, no one seemed able to agree as to who precisely made up this queer tribal faction. Everyone, of course, knew the chieftains – Lytton Strachey, Virginia Woolf, Clive Bell and so on – but after them, as Osbert

Sitwell put it, there 'followed a sub-rout of high-mathematicians and low-psychologists, a tangle of lesser painters and writers'. Taking a census of these lesser breeds was no easy matter since, as another wit explained, 'all the couples were triangles and lived in squares'. Free speech, of course, abounded. They held forth in the mixed company of their late-night cocoa parties with the greatest freedom about sexual generalities, but, in the words of E. M. Forster, 'would have shrunk from the empirical freedom which results from a little beer'. According to Frank Swinnerton, Lytton's level of free speech was somewhat in advance of that of the others, and he dangled before them 'the charms of lasciviousness, the filth of Petronius, the romance of the Arabian Nights'. Love, too, so the rumour went, was uninhibitedly free; and yet there seemed little enough ebullience and gaiety:

> *'Here verse and thought and love are free;*
> *Great God! Give me captivity.'*

despairingly cried E. W. Fordham in the *New Statesman*. Second to no one in the violence and invective of his hostility towards Bloomsbury was Percy Wyndham Lewis, who depicted it as a select and snobbish club comprising a disarray of catty, envious and shabby potentates, collectively bent upon getting the better of himself. Making a cultural stronghold of the Victorian hinterland where they resided, these freakish monsters of his imagination had managed to set up a *societification* of art, substituting money for talent as the qualification for membership. Private means, he explained, was the almost invariable rule. 'In their discouragement of too much unconservative originality they are very strong. The tone of "society" (of a spurious donnish social elegance) prevails among them. . . . All are "geniuses" before whose creations the other members of the Club, in an invariable ritual, must swoon with appreciation.' There was another rather curious way in which they differed – namely in their dress. 'For whereas the new Bohemian is generally as "mondain" and smart, if a little fantastic, as he or she can be, this little phalanstery of *apes of god* went the length of actually dressing the part of the penniless "genius". They presented, Lewis affirmed, a curious spectacle of a group of financially secure men and women, 'drifting and moping about in the untidiest fashion'.

And then, of course, there was the Bloomsbury voice, an appendage of the Strachey clan – 'bringing to one's mind', Wyndham Lewis commented, 'the sounds associated with spasms of a rough Channel passage' – which further cut off this abominable company of citizen-intellectuals from the commonplaces of burgess life. Modelled on the infectious Strachey falsetto – in whom it was doubtless the result of some unfortunate internal malformation – this rare and peculiar dialect was taken up and soon spread from Cambridge to Bloomsbury and thence to the outlying regions of Firle and Garsington. 'The tones would convey with supreme efficiency the requisite degree of paradoxical interest, surprise, incredulity,' observed Osbert Sitwell, 'in actual sound, analysed, they were unemphatic, save when emphasis was not to be expected; then there would be a sudden sticky stress, high where you would have presumed low, and the whole spoken sentence would run, as it were, at different speeds and on different gears, and contain a deal of expert but apparently meaningless syncopation.' By this manner of communication, Osbert Sitwell continues, were the true adherents to the cult of Bloomsbury to be recognized. 'The adoption by an individual of the correct tones was equivalent, I apprehend, to an outward sign of conversion, a public declaration of faith, like giving the Hitler salute or wearing a green turban.'

The great exemplars of Bloomsbury remained for a long time un-recognized by the general public, who are always indifferent to such cliques and juntas unless they are represented as having other than artistic significance. But in the First World War, the Bloomsbury Group was advertised as a left-wing pressure organization which aimed at taking over the Labour Party and establishing an intellectual dictatorship that had little or nothing in common with the ordinary working man. It was hinted darkly that they had built up a sinister hold over the Press, though no one, it seems, thought of asking why, with such a powerful underground network of public relations, they were not depicted by journalists in a rather more attractive light. In the latter part of the war, when most of Bloomsbury came out as agricul-tural pacifists and rustic conscientious objectors, hostility towards them greatly intensified, and ardent-eyed patriots, who had hitherto dismissed the group as a bunch of harmless prigs, now pointed with alarm to the explosive danger, in the very centre of London, of an obviously militant pro-German force. During the twenties, this hysterical enmity abated: some critics, feeling themselves prematurely outdated, still poured out derision, but many more expressed admiration qualified only by envy. *Queen Victoria*, for example, was greeted with almost universal approbation, and from America Hugh Walpole reported that Lytton Strachey was worshipped, 'the God of the moment everywhere'.

Probably the chief cause for aversion still felt by some outsiders was the blatant overblown approbation which members of the *élite* ex-changed among themselves in books, and reviews – the most notorious example being Clive Bell's *Te Deum* sung in joint praise of Duncan Grant and Vanessa Bell, which was especially interesting in the light of these artists' very close relationship. But for the most part this reciprocal, closed-shop admiration was greatly exaggerated by outsiders. For in England, where the creative artist is regarded as an anti-social delinquent or lunatic, writers and painters inevitably turn to one another for the warmth and reassurance with which to lighten their unenviable task, and dispel the cold foggy climate of alien indifference that envelops them. This sympathy – often rather hypocritical and amply compensated for by the adverse criticism expressed to third parties – which members of Bloomsbury extended to each other was interpreted by the less favoured as a peculiarly unhealthy, almost incestuous outbreak of mutual patronage and self-admiration – a view which was neatly summed up in Roy Campbell's narcissistic epigram, 'Home Thoughts on Bloomsbury':

> *Of all the clever people round me here*
> *I most delight in me –*
> *Mine is the only voice I hear,*
> *And mine the only face I see.*

The other popular and complementary version of Bloomsbury may be briefly defined as a counter-interpretation of the same abstract assumptions. The group is said to have comprised an alert and original band of men and women whose splendidly unfashionable and undemocratic enlightenment proved too strong for our universities and too subtle and idiosyncratic for our uncultured, unimaginative society. The much derided Bloomsbury voice, believed to symbolize in some mysterious way all that the movement stood for, came naturally to Lytton Strachey in whom it was so delightful and captivating that it charmed everyone and soon spread equally naturally to his friends. Occasionally it might be put on a little to tease – for there was perpetual gaiety in Bloomsbury – and sometimes, by the sly cadence of a single word – '*Really?*' or 'Extra*ord*inary!' – an outsider's truism was horribly crushed – for Bloomsbury could never gladly suffer fools. But there was more to it than this. By certain bold and original inflexions of emphasis, they could induce rather hidebound conventional people, who would have resented direct opposition, to question and revalue their long-cherished principles.

During the war, the Bloomsberries were said to have displayed marked moral courage by resisting the attractions of armed combat, and by persisting in their rational aversion to senseless avoidable slaughter. In a time of crass barbarism they alone retained their sanity. When an

angry old pullover-knitting lady asked an elegant young man-about-
Bloomsbury whether he wasn't ashamed to be seen out of uniform
while other young men were fighting for civilization, the reply was
confident and characteristic: 'Madam, *I* am the civilization they are
fighting for.' That their united pacifism was practical and common-sense,
not cowardly, was proved in the Second World War – a very different
affair involving different points of Moorish ethics – when many of them
came out as staunch and active patriots. In the opinion of many,
including Roy Harrod and Rosamond Lehmann, Lytton also might
have come out strongly in favour of war in 1939 had he been alive.
David Garnett is more assured and surprising in his suppositions.
'Lytton was maturing and developing,' he wrote. 'The rise of Hitler,
the abominations carried out in Germany before the war and in almost
all countries of Europe and Asia during it, the legacy of evil that the
Germans have left behind them in France, would have been to him
what the Calas affair was to Voltaire.

'Lytton, if he had lived, would have spoken for mankind on
Auschwitz, Hiroshima, the nuclear bomb and torture in France with a
clarity and force with which the political leaders of the world would
have had to reckon. He could not have been neglected as Russell and
Forster are.'

In between these wars we are to picture Lytton and other brave
Bloomsbury spirits with their copies of *Principia Ethica* debating how
best to translate its message into the various realms of art, economics,
literature (subdivided into fiction and non-fiction), painting and
politics. All members chose or were allocated particular fields in which
to work, and spent the remainder of their careers running this specialized
school for higher philosophical propaganda.

Such, in essence, is the view of Bloomsbury projected recently, in
particular by J. K. Johnstone in his closely reasoned study, *The
Bloomsbury Group* (1954).[1] Treating the individual differences between
the novels of Virginia Woolf and E. M. Forster, the biographies and
essays of Lytton Strachey, and the aesthetic criticism of Roger Fry
as being merely superficial variations on a generic pattern, he set out to
discover some basic agreement between their work and the ethical
pronouncements of G. E. Moore. And in the Conclusion at the end of
his book, the author recapitulates his findings. 'There is', he declared, 'a
common respect for things of the spirit; a belief that the inner life of the

---

[1] *The Bloomsbury Group*, written as a thesis at the University of Leeds by J. K. Johnstone, was undertaken at the suggestion of Professor Bonamy Dobrée, and read in
typescript by Noël Annan. It was published in 1954 by Secker and Warburg, under the
supervision of one of the firm's directors, Roger Senhouse, himself on the fringe of
Bloomsbury during the 1920s and 1930s.

soul is much more important than the outer life of action or the outer world of material things; an admiration for the individual and for the virtues of courage, tolerance and honesty; a desire that man shall be whole and express himself emotionally as well as intellectually; a love of truth and of beauty. And the integrity and careful composition of their books demonstrate a profound respect for art, and a conviction that form is as important to a work of art as content; that, indeed, the two are inseparable since the artist cannot express emotions and ideas adequately except in significant form.'

But are these really the qualities by which we recognize the characteristic output of Bloomsbury? Surely in so far as they apply to each and every member of the group they may be said to apply equally to nearly *all* artists – a fact which perhaps explains why so many dissimilar writers working in the first part of the twentieth century, and ranging haphazardly at one time or another from William Gerhardie to F. R. Leavis (who hold nothing in common except their complete independence from the clan) have quite erroneously been classified in print by various ill-informed critics as 'typical Bloomsbury'. Besides which, not all Bloomsbury did hold these values. A number of them, being devout atheists, cherished little respect for the inner, immortal life of the soul.[1] And if this inner life was counted so very much more important than the life of action, why was it that Lytton chose two queens, a general and a dynamic woman of action as subjects for his biographies? The all-embracing importance which he himself certainly attached to significant form was by no means shared by all the others – Desmond MacCarthy, for example, whom Johnstone mentions as another member of the sect.

Some attempt to interweave these two fables of Bloomsbury into a convincing, comprehensive pattern has been made by the poet Stephen Spender. In setting about this he has been obliged to treat as indivisible 'Old Bloomsbury' and the new-look Bloomsbury of the 1920s. The plausibility of his version springs from the literary skill with which it is presented and from his wisdom in not regarding Bloomsbury as a proselytizing body, but simply as a tendency. In this diluted form the myth is given a certain flexibility and plain dealing. To qualify for membership, Spender explains, one had to be agnostic, responsive to French impressionist and post-impressionist painting, and in politics a liberal with slight leanings towards socialism. The group represented

[1] I have presumed from the wording that he employs that J. K. Johnstone used the word 'soul' as meaning the immaterial part of man 'regarded', in the words of the *Oxford Dictionary*, 'as immortal or as subject to salvation and damnation or as animating the body or as existing independently of it or as the true self . . .' It is possible, however, that he used it simply in its subsidiary meaning as the organ of emotion, thought and will.

'the last kick of an enlightened aristocratic tradition'. Setting their standard at five hundred pounds a year and a room of one's own (in Virginia Woolf's words), they sought to entrench themselves within an impenetrable, class-conscious ring against the social revolution advancing on all sides. Their tolerant, scrupulous, cerebral flirtation with left-wing politics was an indication of the guilt which they felt at their own inborn and untouchable snobbery. In short, Stephen Spender's Bloomsbury is chiefly sociological – the symbol of a cultured, intelligent, politically naïve era, as seen by a representative of the 1930s – a less aesthetic but more serious and politically responsible decade.

In the sinking of unique differences beneath a general classification, critics have incorrectly assumed that, in matters of taste and judgement, the writers and artists whose names are linked with Bloomsbury were in accord with one another, and that they presented to the world a united if not easily definable front. The danger of seeking common trends within any set of people is that one is obliged to misrepresent, now slightly, now more drastically, the actual individual truth in order to preserve an even façade. In the case of Bloomsbury this has been particularly noticeable, for often the opinions and inclinations of its members were very far from being uniform. Leonard Woolf was always passionately interested in politics; Lytton, though he inclined to become more leftish under his brother James's persuasion during the war, was largely indifferent to political questions of the hour. Clive Bell enthused over the most abstract art; Roger Fry held aloof;[1] while Lytton himself was even more conservative and dismissed Clive Bell's *Art*, in a letter to James Strachey, as 'utter balls' (22 February 1914). Though he had learnt at Cambridge to enjoy a literary appreciation of the visual arts, Lytton considered that both Clive Bell and Roger Fry were downright silly in their highflown admiration of Matisse and the early Picasso, and he made some attempt through Vanessa Bell to discourage Duncan Grant from the post-impressionist and cubist influences under which he was falling. As for Maynard Keynes, Lytton maintained that he possessed no aesthetic sense whatever; and Clive Bell held a similar opinion of Harry Norton. Despite his tenuous friendship with E. M. Forster, who was certainly no atheist or even agnostic, Lytton found his novels

[1] Clive Bell has generally been put down as a popularizer of Roger Fry's aesthetic theories; and while there is much truth in this, it is not wholly true. After the failure of the Omega Workshops in 1919, Fry grew much less concerned with contemporary art. He had, in any case, from the first felt doubts about Clive Bell's theory of 'significant form', and wondered whether 'it might be possible', Professor Quentin Bell writes, 'that some paintings were "operatic" in the sense of being a perfect fusion of two different kinds of art. It was towards a solution of this nature that he was looking in his last years.' When, in 1925, I. A. Richards published his *Principles of Literary Criticism*, a work which strongly attacked Fry's standpoint, Lytton welcomed this new attitude.

quite unreadable – a view similar to that which Virginia Woolf affected to hold of his own biographies – while his aesthetic differences with Roger Fry,[1] who injected a mood of earnest Quakerism into the group, effectively stifling the movement towards sybaritic pleasure, were, according to Gerald Brenan, enlivened by personal antipathy. Nor had Lytton much in common with Arthur Waley whose scholarship he respected – though it does not seem to have inspired him as did the work of the non-Bloomsbury Professor Giles – but whose egocentricity bored and exasperated him. Several of the so-called group he hardly knew at all! Sir Charles Tennyson, whom Duncan Grant names as one of the original intimate circle which met at Fitzroy Square, wrote to the present author: 'I was fairly often in the same room with him [Lytton], but never really knew him. He was a good many years younger than me and in a more highbrow set, so that I really have nothing beyond a quite superficial and useless impression.' Another critical mistake has been to assume that all Bloomsbury was nourished on Moore's ethics. The two Stephen sisters seldom if ever discussed questions of academic moral philosophy, while some later recruits to the group, Raymond Mortimer, Ralph Partridge and Roger Senhouse who were all at Oxford, and Gerald Brenan, who did not go to Cambridge, never burnt the midnight oil over the complicated pages of *Principia Ethica*. Roger Fry, whose aesthetic principles J. K. Johnstone claims were closely integrated with Moore's work, and in a sense completed it, actually dismissed *Principia Ethica* as 'sheer nonsense'.

According to the Freudian definition, 'two or more people constitute a psychological group if they have set up the same model-object (leader) or ideals in their super-ego, or both, and consequently have identified with each other'.[2] If one accepts this conception, then clearly Bloomsbury was not strictly a group at all. But it did comprise something – an atmosphere, a mood, a culture which today can be detected in those who have inherited its tradition, Noël Annan, Quentin Bell, Kenneth Clark, Cyril Connolly and others. Although it accepted part of the Apostolic severity – a then idiosyncratic belief in good moral values, true personal relationships, free and more or less reasonable thinking and speech – it was permeated with other qualities that made it very unlike the original Cambridge Conversazione Society. Maynard Keynes and Harry Norton, two Apostles of the highest-grade intellect who belonged to Bloomsbury, were rather despised by most of the

[1] Of another of the Bloomsbury literary critics, Fry seems to have held a distinctly mediocre opinion. 'I don't mind a weather-cock,' he once remarked of him, 'but a weather-cock that crows is too much.'

[2] This definition is given by S. Scheidlinger in *Group Dynamics* (1954), p. 56, edited by D. Cartwright and A. Zander.

others. For Bloomsbury was deficient in purely intellectual interests, being strongly dominated by the visual arts and literature. Science was unheard of, and even music was almost absent.

Today the name of Bloomsbury is respectable – perhaps too respectable – while at the same time remaining unfashionable. Its collective reputation had declined with that of Lytton's individual status, for its present comparatively low quotation is felt by many to be due to its characteristic Stracheyesque shortcomings – in particular a fondness for exaggeration leading to distortion of truth and a fake aestheticism which was already beginning to bring the author of *Elizabeth and Essex* into some disfavour by 1930 and which has helped to prolong the usual widespread denigration after death – a recognition, David Garnett believes, of the influence he would have exerted had he lived. Of his two Cambridge idols, Lowes Dickinson had devoted his life to the task of interpreting, for the benefit of his compatriots, Plato and the Greek ideals of civilization; while G. E. Moore, in the words of Maynard Keynes, was even 'better than Plato'. The Apostles who immediately succeeded Moore, and who were led by Keynes and Lytton, modified these ideals, which were later transferred to Bloomsbury, making them more worldly and sophisticated. There these ideals were translated into a neo-Greek cult of friendship, donnish rather than Hellenic. In his book *Civilization: An Essay*, Clive Bell echoed a recurrent theme of Bloomsbury writers: that to be completely civilized a human being must be liberated from material cares and vexations. Indisputably the best example of such a scheme in practice was given by Plato. The Greeks, he pointed out, because they had slaves who freed the citizens from everyday chores so that they might concentrate on other, worthier affairs of the mind, had attained a standard of civilization that came nearer the heart's desire than was conceived possible by any other people in history. And so it should be with Bloomsbury, which took its inspiration from the Greek example. Virginia Woolf's celebrated 'five hundred a year each of us and rooms of our own' is anticipated by Lytton in a letter to Duncan Grant (23 August 1909): 'Good God! to have a room of one's own with a real fire and books and tea and company, and no dinner-bells and distractions, and a little time for doing something! – It's a wonderful vision, and surely worth some risks!'

Independence founded on the Hellenic model – that was what so many of them aspired after. Lytton had no very scholarly knowledge of the Greek language, but he saw in the *élite* at Cambridge the centre of a new and expanding civilization, sweetened by the free, venturesome flavour of ancient Greece and the sentiment of Athens. Having shed the dry Victorian ectoderm, the world seemed solid and fruitful, and he and his friends all felt convinced that fresh progress would now start up, and that they would contribute something of value to this advancement. It was this undefined, hopeful, reforming spirit of 'neo-Platonism' which spread from Trinity and King's to the literary salons of London that later became recognized as the distinctive religion of Bloomsbury. 'A strange thing – when you come to think of it – this love of Greek,' Virginia Woolf reflected in her novel, *Jacob's Room*, 'flourishing in such obscurity, distorted, discouraged, yet leaping out, all of a sudden, especially on leaving crowded rooms, or after a surfeit of print, or when the moon floats among the waves of the hills, or in hollow, sallow, fruitless London days, like a specific; a clean blade; always a miracle.'

The inevitable reaction to this 'civilization' came, ironically, from Cambridge itself, starting with I. A. Richards, whose *Principles of Literary Criticism* (1925) aimed at exploding the aesthetic approach to literature, and declared the concepts of 'beauty' and 'pure aesthetic value' to be myths. From then on literary criticism was to be led by precept rather than example, and under the new dictatorial authority, impressionistic writing lost favour. The disciples of this new 'scientific' criticism were irritated by the extreme aestheticism of Bloomsbury, which, they proclaimed, accentuated strangeness and fascination at the expense of heart and conscience, and which had tended to evolve a flippant society where, to use the words of Lord David Cecil, 'it is more important to be clever than good, and more important to be beautiful than to be either!'

This new wave of criticism subsequently gained in strength and reached its full impetus under the redoubtable leadership of Dr F. R. Leavis, whose dislike of Lytton – the Mephistopheles of the Bloomsbury World – rested on his antipathy to what he saw as an immature valuation of life masquerading under an air of detached irony, a ruthless sacrifice of truth for literary purpose, and a puny, irresponsible assertion of personal prejudice over serious sociological scrutiny. That divine confluence of Cambridge amenities, hymned by E. M. Forster in his Life of Goldsworthy Lowes Dickinson, was denounced by Leavis as: 'Articulateness and unreality cultivated together; callowness disguised from itself in articulateness; conceit casing itself safely in a confirmed sense of sophistication; the uncertainty as to whether it is serious or not taking itself for ironic poise; who has not at some time observed the process?'

The narrowly blinkered Leavis could observe little else. To him the charmed circle of Bloomsbury and Lytton's lucid interval of prestige both of which dominated temporarily the metropolitan centres of taste and fashion, was an unforgivable departure from the great tradition of powerful representative Cambridge men of their time – Sidgwick and Leslie Stephen, Maitland and Dr Leavis. 'Can we', he asked with rather Stracheyesque rhetoric, 'imagine Sidgwick or Leslie Stephen or Maitland being influenced by, or interested in the equivalent of Lytton Strachey?' Can we imagine Dr Leavis being so interested? And this same derisory question is, by implication, repeated again and again and again throughout his writings. For as the conviction of personal persecution thickened round his critical faculties and choked his already turgid prose style, so he laid greater and greater emphasis on the inessential trappings of literature, its civic importance and tutorial status.

Despite these frantic objections from Downing College, many of the King's and Trinity members of Bloomsbury were undoubtedly perfect representatives of the Cambridge culture of their generation. They were passionately attached to the beauty and emotional flavour of the place, and in London looked for what most resembled it. If the Bloomsbury Group has to be treated as a homogeneous entity, then it can in no manner be dissociated from Cambridge, and all Cambridge stood for. The best features in their environment of privileged culture – the play of mind with mind on literary and other topics, and a sane and humane morality – Lytton with his sensitive intelligence and irregular deviations was well qualified to absorb and enjoy. Nor was Bloomsbury the wholly desiccated intellectual unit it is so often depicted as being, but was bound together by intense and enduring personal relationships, which for all their complexity were managed in a very civilized and sensible way. For a number of years, however, after going down from Cambridge – years of self-discontent and aimlessness – Lytton also exemplified the limitations of the over-cultivated. By a perversion of language, good taste came to mean not the taste of persons with healthy appetites, but of persons with weak digestions. The collective literary voice – described by F. L. Lucas in a letter to Irma Rantavaara as 'shepherd's piping in Arcadia' – is distinctive in its thinness and its clarity. Moreover, the superhuman detachment and remoteness on which they sometimes prided themselves did sever them from the deeper sources which stem out of a vital, raw and vulnerable contact with reality. Romantic academics and quietists, deeply allergic to the humdrum, many of them were, to use the words of E. M. Forster, full of the wine of life without having tasted the cup – the teacup – of experience.

The myths which have billowed up round the name of Bloomsbury are like voluminous clouds arising from a small central flame. For although these friends who met on Thursday evenings before the war shared no fixed and common values germinating from an original gospel, they may be said to have been permeated with similar intuitions. The keystone to these intuitions was a desire for partial independence from the parochial and pretentious fog of Victorianism. They were alike in their determined opposition to the religious and moral standards of Victorian orthodoxy; and in their work they represented more truly than anything else the culmination and ultimate refinement of the aesthetic movement. Essentially they were reformers rather than revolutionaries. Virginia Woolf's concept of a proper financial and domestic standard, no less than Lytton's Preface to *Eminent Victorians*, was a declaration of this spirit of partial independence, a wish to cut herself off from the immediate past by escaping from the family sitting-room to another, unopened wing of the same house – not to a new house or town or country.

And if they looked back to the example of ancient Greece, in the modern world they turned their eyes towards the Continent. Under the delusion that things were ordered differently in France, they made an attempt to establish on French lines a society fit for the discerning minority. 'A time had come,' wrote Virginia Woolf in her biography of Roger Fry, 'when a real society was possible. It was to be a society of people of moderate means, a society based on the old Cambridge ideal of truth and free speaking, but alive, as Cambridge had never been, to the importance of the arts. It was possible in France; why not in England? No art could flourish without such a background. The young English artist tended to become illiterate, narrow-minded and self-centred with disastrous effects upon his work, failing any society where, among the amenities of civilization, ideas were discussed in common and he was accepted as an equal.'

But Bloomsbury did not transform the naturally isolated and painful process of artistic creation. Once 'Old Bloomsbury' had lost its bloom and become moribund, the new Bloomsbury Group flowered into a gayer, more pleasure-loving and intellectually fashionable clique, tripping in quicker, high-stepping time to the light fantastic twenties. But, like all rather self-conscious 'modern' movements, this phase was destined, as surely as the coming of death itself, to dwindle and wither into an extinct relic in the history of artistic taste. For all their elegant and ingenious tinkerings, most of the Bloomsbury writers and artists were unable finally to sever the umbilical cord joining them to the inherited traditions of the past. Theirs was a tenuous transitory mood, largely barren and inbred, a suspension bridge which now forms our authentic link back to the solid cultural traditions of the nineteenth century. They modified, romanticized, avoided those traditions with varying degrees of success. But rather than being the real founders of a new and originally conceived civilization as Virginia Woolf supposed, they were, in the words of Roger Fry himself, 'the last of the Victorians'.

CHAPTER X

The Wrong Turning

All, all of a piece throughout:
Thy chase had a beast in view:
Thy Wars brought nothing about;
Thy Lovers were all untrue.
'Tis well an old Age is out,
And time to begin a New.
Dryden – *The Secular Masque*

I

A PROPOSAL OF MARRIAGE

By far the most arid and oppressive moments of family life for Lytton were public holidays and anniversaries. Whenever practicable he would arrange to be elsewhere, anywhere, with his friends or even alone. For the Christmas festivities of 1908 and the New Year celebrations he fled down once again to the Mermaid Inn at Rye. 'This is a scene of complete desolation,' he wrote to James (31 December 1908), '– rain, snow, fog, dimness unimaginable.' Nevertheless there was absolute rest, which was something, and he was able to read his Merimée, his Voltaire and his Saint-Simon unimpeded. He even had dreams of writing poetry.

For the first week, he appears to have had the place entirely to himself. At least there was no one else who *counted*; no one he could talk to or even look at for long. He sat on there alone 'in a semi-stupor among mists and golfers', he told Virginia Stephen. '. . . Their conversation is quite amazing, and when I consider that there *must* be numbers of persons more stupid still, I begin to see the human race *en noir*. Oh God! Oh God! The slowness of them, the pomp, and the fatuity.' But early in the New Year the Mermaid Inn received two visitors of note – R. Vere Laurence, his old enemy from Trinity who had rejected his Fellowship dissertation, and his old literary hero, Henry James. Both arrivals were amusingly observed and reported by letter to his brother James (4 January 1909): 'The other day as I was snoozing after lunch I had a surprise, looked up and there was Laurence, in furs and beard complete; fortunately only passing through. My final reflection was that if I were to grow a beard we should be indistinguishable.

'I've also seen Henry James – twice. Both times exceedingly remarkable, but almost impossible to describe. He came in here to show the antique fireplace to a young French poet and you never saw such a scene – the poor man absolutely *bouche béante*, and all the golfers and bishops sitting round quite stolidly munching buttered buns. He has a colossal physiognomy, and it's almost impossible to believe that such an appearance could have produced the Sacred Fount. I long to know him.'

Even more impressive was the second vision of Henry James – at a window of Lamb House. He had just appeared there as Lytton passed by, to examine more minutely some momentous manuscript, a silent but masterly performance – the polite irony of it! He looked immensely serious, and quite extraordinarily slow. 'So conscientious and worried and important,' Lytton described the scene to Virginia Stephen, '– he was like an admirable tradesman trying his best to give satisfaction, infinitely solemn and polite. Is there any truth in this? It has since occurred to me that his novels are really remarkable for their lack of humour. But I think it's very odd that he should have written precisely them and look precisely so. Perhaps if one talked to him one would understand.'

These were the only highlights of Lytton's visit to Rye, and he returned to London two days later. Virginia had invited him to dine at Fitzroy Square on the evening of 7 January. He was to meet her cousin, H. A. L. Fisher, the historian and Oxford don whose father had married into the Stephen family. 'Summoned from the writing of history,' as one of his pupils at New College described his subsequent elevation to the post of president of the Board of Education, 'to a share in muddling it,' his paroxysms of awe and homage before the men who had converted him into a subject for future historical research, in combination with the book learning he was anxious to put at their disposal, gratified those politicians who might otherwise have regarded a history don with distaste. But in achieving this modest eminence and popularity, he had succeeded only in transferring the burden of hostility from his political to his literary associates. 'You are going to meet the Fishers on Thursday,' Virginia had written to Lytton (4 June 1909). 'You and Herbert must talk about Voltaire, and I shall say how I have been seeing his waxwork at Madame Tussaud's. I can't help thinking he is rather a fraud (H.F. I mean). He is impossibly enlightened and humane. She is a bright woman.'

'I shall be able to speak of nothing but cleeks and greens,' Lytton wrote back from the Mermaid, 'though no doubt Herbert would be very well able to cope with that. Besides the golfers there are some of the higher clergy – bishops and wardens – and two lawyers at the chancery bar. Of course these are all golfers as well, so it all comes to very much the same thing.'

H. A. L. Fisher turned out to be less interested in golf than riding, and after some false starts, the conversation switched to the subject of French literature, about which everyone professed to know something. Lytton, as was customary in front of strangers – especially Oxford dons – was silent and mainly unresponsive. But luckily Fisher, not unaware that his father had been a distinguished general, refused to be unimpressed. 'I well remember my first interview with Strachey,' he recollected over twenty years later, 'a sensitive ungainly youth; awkward in his bearing, and presenting an appearance of great physical debility, as if he had recently risen from the bed of an invalid. His voice was faint and squeaky. His pale face was at that time closely shaven. The long red beard of Lamb's portrait which has made him so familiar, was a thing of the future. He was very silent, but uncannily quick and comprehending.'

The impression which Lytton made that evening on Fisher was favourable and long-lasting. And although no one present realized it at the time, this meeting was in due course to lead to a crucial development in Lytton's career.

Meanwhile his routine continued on much as before – labouring over endless *Spectator* reviews; lunching whenever possible at Simpson's; dining at Fitzroy and Gordon Squares; and the sporadic week-end foray to Cambridge where, released from polite family inhibitions, he could enter into the social life around him and feel free to speak his mind more plainly. 'On Sunday at breakfast,' Maynard Keynes reported to Duncan Grant (19 January 1909), 'Sheppard delivered an indictment on poor Rupert [Brooke] for admiring Mr Wells and thinking truth beauty, beauty truth. Norton and Lytton took up the attack and even James and Gerald [Shove] (who was there) stabbed him in the back. Finally Lytton, enraged at Rupert's defences, thoroughly lost his temper and delivered a violent personal attack.'

Lytton's letters over these weeks are full of dismal complaints – about the bad weather, about the 'ghastly solitude' of Belsize Park Gardens, and the feverish colds which seemed persistently to assail him. Some of his days were spent up in his bed, dosed with Sanatogen and quinine; and others, huddled in front of the fire, reading amongst other things the notebooks of Samuel Butler and an eighteenth-century life of

Madame de Maintenon. One thing alone he looked forward to; and that was a journey he was planning later in the year to Italy. There, in the warm and friendly climate, he felt confident of shaking off his depression. In the meantime, he must live as economically as possible, save every penny. He even had to refuse Moore's invitation to the Lizard for that year's Easter reading-party: 'If I had a little more money it would be different,' he explained (5 February 1909), 'but I'm poor, and I've got to choose one thing or the other.'

Between colds, he emerged into the outside world like a mole from below ground, and suffered himself to be taken to the random concert or picture gallery. At such moments, London, for all its incursive horrors, would hold him enthralled. There were so many amenities, opportunities, people of interest and attraction. Accidentally he would forget his own ailments and become absorbed by all the curious and entertaining sights around him – in particular by glimpses of the aristocratic world of high fashion and artistic culture.

'I looked in for an hour at the New Gallery,' he wrote in one letter to Duncan Grant (21 February 1909), '. . . and was carried away with excitement. It's packed with the most interesting things of the most varied kinds. . . . There are Whistlers and Reynoldses, and a divine Gainsborough, and Wattses that even I found charming, and amazing Monticellis, and a superb Manet, and a John à faire mourir de peur. The Simon [Bussy] I found rather a difficult affair to take in at the first go off, but I seemed to be making progress as time went on. The excitement was increased for me by the immense distinction of the audience. – Among others, Mrs Carl Meyer was present, in ermine, the Duchess of Portland and Lady Ottoline Morrell, the Marquis de Soveral, accompanied by Señor Villaviciosa, Lord Musk and Master Musk. Mrs George Batten was talking to Lady Strachey, while Mr Lytton Strachey, who was wearing some handsome Siberian furs, was the centre of an animated group. Mr E. Marsh came in later with the President of the Board of Trade[1] – to say nothing of Mr Edmund Gosse and Mr Sidney Colvin. – The Rothenstein woman, even more painted than usual, flowed in your praises to her Ladyship.'

This world of eminent personages and splendid upper-class names held him spellbound. Intellectually he repudiated it and, as his deliberate caricature style indicates, mocked his own feeling of fascination. Nevertheless it seemed to defy all reason and satire, and persisted in its

[1] The President of the Board of Trade at this time was Winston Churchill. Edmund Gosse had worked as a translator in the Board of Trade with Austin Dobson, the poet. Sidney Colvin, who had been Slade Professor of Fine Art at Cambridge and Director of the Fitzwilliam Museum, was now keeper in the Department of Prints and Drawings at the British Museum.

romantic hold over his imagination. He was like a child enraptured by some fabulous Arthurian legend. But part of the allure lay in his pre-occupation with prestige and with personal success, its trappings and rigmarole; and part again in his devouring curiosity over the more exaggerated aspects of human nature.

Another indication of this potent and childlike spell is provided by *Lord Pettigrew*, a novel which Lytton had begun to work on that winter. Written after the style of Anatole France's *M. Bergeret à Paris*, it is ostensibly a satire directed against the snobbery and the intrigue of fashionable society and reactionary politics.[1] Altogether he completed four chapters, that is between eight and nine thousand words, before giving it up. In this surviving fragment there are some good observations, and the narrative runs along smoothly enough. But because Lytton could not conceive of the aristocracy as being composed of real people like himself, his characters remain mere mouthpieces and never really come to life. For a time, though, he felt excited about the book's possibilities. He would lie in bed in the morning imagining its various dramatic incidents, and each day they would grow more extraordinary. 'You have never heard such conversations or imagined such scenes!' he wrote to Virginia Stephen, who had urged him to continue with it. 'But they're most of them a little too scabreux, and they're none of them written. What's so remarkable is the way in which I penetrate into every sphere of life. My footmen are amazing, and so are my prostitutes. There's a Prime Minister à faire mourir de rire. But it's impossible to get any of it together.'

Lord Pettigrew, so far as it went, was a fantasy which his mind fertilized with ideas as far removed as possible from customary experience, and it may be regarded as a symptom of his desire to escape from the familiar drudgery and ennui of family life in London. There were several other such symptoms, since his need for independence was now more urgent than ever before. His letters from the country have a

[1] In 1909, the House of Lords rashly rejected the Liberal reforms implemented by the budget. Asquith then dissolved Parliament and, in January 1910, won the election. Soon afterwards he introduced proposals for altering the powers of the House of Lords, but at that moment Edward VII died, and in the new reign a constitutional conference was held between the parties. This broke down in the autumn and Asquith dissolved Parliament a second time and held a second election in December 1910. Having won this too, he introduced the Parliament Bill, at the same time threatening to abolish the Lords' veto by advising the Monarch to create, if necessary, some five hundred new peers sympathetic to his measures. Rather than be flooded out in this manner, the Upper House gave way. Lytton bought the *Times* booklet reporting in full the historic debate in the House of Lords on the second reading of the Finance Bill of 1909, and marked a number of the more extreme effusions to assist him with the dialogue of his novel. This whole constitutional affair was perhaps the start of Lytton's serious political interest. He became strongly anti upper class – an attitude that was the obverse of his pseudo-snobbery.

natural melancholy about them; but those he wrote from Belsize Park Gardens are steeped in adolescent romanticism, a day-dream sentimentality released by the surrounding pressure of prosaic realism. 'If I could have my way,' he wrote after returning from Rye, 'I should go out to dinner every night, and then to a party or an opera, and then I should have a champagne supper, and then I should go to bed in some wonderful person's arms.'

Another aspect of Lytton's longing for liberty, leading to a most improbable moment of crisis, is shown in his letters to Virginia Stephen, of which there were an increasing number over this period. The relationship between these two gifted writers is interesting. Their correspondence, especially in these early years, has a self-consciousness, a stiltedness, which was entirely typical of neither, and which, in the opinion of both Leonard Woolf and James Strachey, was due to their mutual respect and admiration. But it was probably more than ordinary respect that accounted for this awkwardness. It was, at least partly, a lively apprehension of each other's power, of criticism. Virginia Stephen distrusted Lytton's Cambridge education, with its overtones of ethical and intellectual superiority. Easily discouraged, she feared his quick irony – so reminiscent of her father's – his ridicule that could instantly disintegrate the vague shadows and shapes which she was trying to crystallize into something palpable. To some extent, also, she envied and resented his apparent self-assurance which tended to make her follow where he led; and she was always distressingly susceptible to his 'hints and subtleties and catlike malice' which could pierce the web of delicate, protective speculation, and leave her numbed and solitary.

As for Lytton, his apprehension of her was more indirect. His assumed self-confidence came from creating a fictitious image of himself which he dramatized with an elegant sureness of touch. Virginia Stephen's greater doubts suggested a more disturbing introspective honesty. Though she might follow the tune that he played, he was always looking back over his shoulder, aware that she could see through the paraphernalia of his acting. And although, too, she may have envied his earlier and more popular success as a writer, she considered his reputation rather exaggerated. To Lytton himself she was highly, almost implausibly, flattering; but to others she could criticize his work rather spitefully. He was the hare in the race for fame and she the tortoise who, with greater patience and imaginative endeavour, would eventually catch up and overtake him at the winning-post. Meanwhile, like eternal correctives, each brought out a latent feeling of inferiority in the other, raising doubts as to his or her intrinsic capabilities and achievements. Was she deluding herself with worthless, twittering phantoms, peopling her novels with airy ghosts? Was he exploiting a verbal felicity in facile and frivolous story-telling, scattering his biographies with shallow caricatures? Such uncertainties helped to confuse and unsettle their relationship.

They shared, however, much in common. Both were brought up in large Victorian households, and being considered too delicate to attend the type of school to which an upper-middle-class child was usually sent, had become dominated by a stultifying family system. To a large extent literature now held a similar appeal for them. They welcomed with relief the lush, unrestrained articulation of the Elizabethans, and on the whole preferred to contemplate writers who had themselves lived in comfortable, independent circumstances – Horace Walpole, Gibbon, Henry James. Through the eyes of such men, the past might be convincingly transformed into an attractive sanctuary from the present. In addition to these special preferences, they shared several literary attributes – a vein of refined feminine malice, a sharp eye for salient facts and an intense curiosity about human nature. But the comparison between them can be extended little farther than this. For all their sensitivity and unstable passion they were both somewhat removed from the quickening flow of humanity; but whereas Virginia, attracted like a moth to the light, was always trying to warm herself dangerously close to the fire of life, Lytton, like a man who has been scalded once too often, draws back, affecting to find warmth in the cold. She was absorbed by the spectacle of London; he was largely appalled by it. Her sense of character, if less vivid and clear-cut, is more genuinely subtle, and the transforming process of the past was less complete with her than with him. Her novels were the fluttering butterfly wings with which she set out on an impossible journey over the ocean to some far-off shore. His biographies were the gorgeous sweetmeats with which he consoled himself for never having attempted the journey. Writing, which fatally concentrated her self-absorption, dispersed his; and though her work is neither so perfect nor so readable as Lytton's, yet it retains the fragile, uneven pulse of original genius, while, by comparison, his is the successful achievement of a man of high talent and refinement.

The spirit of half-amused, diffident rivalry which existed between Virginia and Lytton was created as much by their similarities as by their differences in character, and below it ran a smoother undercurrent of real affection. 'Love apart, whom would you most like to see coming up the drive?' Lytton asked Clive Bell one rainy afternoon in the depths of the country. Clive Bell hesitated a moment and Lytton replied to his own question: 'Virginia, of course.'

Admiration and great affection, not love, were then what Lytton felt
for her. Physically she did not appeal to him, and as a confidante she
could not be trusted. His relationship with her was unique. He saw in
her the presiding chatelaine of Bloomsbury, and in 29 Fitzroy Square a
possible alternative to his mother and Hampstead. What else was there –
loves apart? Now that Duncan and Maynard, the two emotional and
intellectual props of his life, had collapsed, his platonic friendship with
Virginia had been promoted to a new and unexpected importance. He
knew, of course, that they were far from being ideally suited to each
other, yet her extraordinary percipience and sensibility might prove
vastly preferable to the communal incomprehension, the loving lack-
of-understanding of his female relatives. This thought germinated
inside him until on 17 February, despite a heavy cold, he boldly made
his way across London to Fitzroy Square and, on the spur of the
moment, proposed to Virginia – who, to his immediate horror and
consternation, accepted him. The vague, escapist day-dream was instantly hardened into impossible reality, and it was only her quickness
and sensitivity – these qualities which had originally made her seem so
eligible as a wife – that enabled Lytton hurriedly to extricate himself.
Writing the following month to James, he gave an account of the
episode: 'Im my efforts to escape, I had a decided reverse the other day.
I haven't mentioned the incident before for various reasons. On
Feb 19th[1] I proposed to Virginia, and was accepted. It was an awkward
moment, as you may imagine, especially as I realized, the very minute
it was happening, that the whole thing was repulsive to me. Her sense
was amazing, and luckily it turned out that she's not in love. The result
was that I was able to manage a fairly honourable retreat. The whole
story is really rather amusing and singular, but its effect has been to
drive me on to these shoals more furiously than ever. I need hardly
mention the immense secrecy of the affair. . . .'

This incident is made doubly ludicrous by the fact that Virginia found
Lytton so physically unattractive that the prospect of their marriage
was almost as repulsive to her as to him. For both of them it represented
part of a psychological escape, a way out from something worse. He
had proposed in an endeavour to cut free from Belsize Park Gardens;[2]

---

[1] February 19 was a mistake for February 17.

[2] An additional explanation for Lytton's impulsive proposal of marriage to Virginia
Stephen has recently been advanced by Professor Gabriel Merle – that it was occasioned
by a wish to escape not only from his family at Lancaster Gate, but also from his most
persistent visitors there, namely Duncan Grant and Maynard Keynes. Although the
crisis between the three of them had exploded almost eight months back, it was still not
properly resolved. Lytton, fluctuating between a wide variety of moods and attitudes –
anger and resignation, curtness and magnanimity, sexual jealousy and philanthropic

and she had at once accepted him as a means of dragging herself out from under the imaginary shadow of her dead father. At the same time she was not searching for a husband; rather the reverse. Marriage was a condition of life which held only limited appeal for her. Walter Lamb, who was supposed to be courting her at one time, received scant encouragement; and when Hilton Young proposed to her in a punt on the Cam, he was told that she could only marry one person – Lytton Strachey, and this though she did not love him. But what she did value above all other men was his understanding, his diplomacy, his kindness. These were the only sort of qualities that had any relevance to her. Nevertheless both she and Lytton must have realized almost simultaneously that so far from solving their separate problems, such a union could only add new mutual ones. Each was inadequate for the other's peculiar purpose.

At this time Virginia Stephen was already working at her first novel, *The Voyage Out*, which was eventually published in 1915, and which contains a portrait of Lytton under the name of St John Hirst. Naturally cautious, irretrievably intellectual, a devoted admirer of Gibbon and a confirmed misogynist, Hirst cherishes his memories of Cambridge but finds the company of his own family intolerable: 'They want me to be a peer and a privy councillor.' His appearance and mannerisms are closely observed. When he leans against a window-frame his figure looks like 'some singular gargoyle' – a shrewd use of one of Lytton's own favourite adjectives. When, in sprawling relaxation, he subsides into a chair, he seems 'to consist entirely of legs'. Overhearing a group of ordinary people in ordinary conversation, he feels nauseated by their stupidity. But though he tries to isolate himself from these stupid and ignorant persons, telling another character that 'there will never be more than five people in the world worth talking to', yet he is prevented from sealing himself off completely by his thwarted ambition, and is forced to confess at one point: 'I hate everyone. I can't endure people who do things better than I do – perfectly absurd things too.' At another stage in the narrative, when he stings Rachel Vinrace, the heroine based on Virginia Stephen herself, with some sharp and sober criticism to

---

tolerance – presented a formidable antipathetic face to Keynes who, that February, broke down and cried in front of James. This mounting tension immensely deepened for Lytton the instability and unhappiness of this 'black period' of his life. His sudden proposal to Virginia, therefore, which arose from an uprush of despair rather than from enthusiasm or calculation, was partially an effort to break this circle of intrigue, and amounted, Professor Merle argues, to a renunciation, hurriedly withdrawn, of his homosexual ties and of homosexuality itself – that intermittent revulsion, sometimes comically expressed, which may infrequently be read into his letters.

which she can find no quick, articulate repartee, she reflects to herself that he is 'ugly in body, repulsive in mind'.

For the most part, St John Hirst presents an unflattering likeness to Lytton, and Virginia was probably reflecting on the inaptitude of a marriage between them in a passage which describes some party at which they attempted to dance together.

'"We must follow suit," said Hirst to Rachel, and he took her resolutely by the elbow. Rachel, without being expert, danced well, because of a good ear for rhythm, but Hirst had no taste for music, and a few dancing lessons at Cambridge had only put him in possession of the anatomy of a waltz, without imparting any of its spirit. A single turn proved to them that their methods were incompatible; instead of fitting into each other their bones seemed to jut out at angles making smooth turning an impossibility, and cutting, moreover, into the circular progress of the dancers.

'"Shall we stop?" said Hirst. Rachel gathered from his expression that he was annoyed.'

Despite his uncomplementary nature and the physical aversion she felt for him, Virginia liked Lytton; she pitied him for the unmelting, cold kernel of loneliness he carried within, and for his outward show of phoney romantics; and she admired at the same time his 'mind like a torpedo'. She sums up her compound impressions of him near the end of *The Voyage Out*, in a passage which brings together his morbid sensitivity and isolation, his envy and contempt, arrogance and self-absorption, his unhappiness and the restless fretting of his ambition: 'But St John thought that they were saying things which they did not want him to hear, and was led to think of his own isolation. These people were happy, and in some ways he despised them for being made happy so simply, and in other ways he envied them. He was much more remarkable than they were, but he was not happy. People never liked him. . . . To be simple, to be able to say simply what one felt, without the terrific self-consciousness which possessed him, and showed him his own face and words perpetually in a mirror, that would be worth any other gift, for it made one happy. Happiness, happiness, what was happiness? He was never happy. . . . But it was true that half the sharp things he said about them were said because he was unhappy or hurt himself. But he admitted that he had very seldom told anyone that he cared for them, and when he had been demonstrative, he had generally regretted it afterwards.'

The danger of identifying actual people in the creations of novelists is that, through a too literal transposition of the event-plot, the critic will misread not so much the character as the situations in which that

character is involved. *The Voyage Out*, and that later and more subjective novel, *The Waves*, give some testimony of what Virginia really
felt and thought of Lytton, and the manner in which her feelings for
him developed.

'The characters in *The Waves*', Leonard Woolf cautiously tells us,
'are not drawn from life, but there is something of Lytton in Neville.
There is no doubt that Percival in that book contains something of
Thoby Stephen, Virginia's brother.' J. K. Johnstone, with more
temerity, also affirms that 'there is much of Lytton Strachey in Neville',
and he goes on, 'though Neville's intellect is so splendid and brave, he
is too timid in some respects. He is very like St John Hirst of *The
Voyage Out*. His body is ugly, and, he fears, disgusting. He wonders
whether he is "doomed always to cause repulsion in those [he] loves".
He loves Percival, who is intensely his opposite, with an "absurd and
violent passion" which he is afraid to expose . . . for he is one of those
who love men more than women. At moments his emotions inspire
him to write poetry, but then his intellect draws him up short, and ends
his inspiration.' St John Hirst's uncommunicative misogamy has
flowered in the fifteen years which separate *The Voyage Out* from *The
Waves* into the fruitless, romantic homosexuality of Neville. And the
lyrical yearning relationship depicted in this later novel accurately
reproduces Lytton's physical and emotional susceptibility to the whole
class of person whom Percival represents – in his own life Thoby
Stephen, George Mallory, and, to a large extent, Ralph Partridge – 'the
normal English Public School type', as David Daiches describes
Percival, 'neither intellectual nor particularly perceptive, but well
adjusted and at ease in life'.

Although the character of Neville was never intended to be taken as
a photographic representation of Lytton, it does provide an interesting
fictional portrait, incomplete but nevertheless containing several
intimate aspects of Lytton's personality as Virginia Woolf was shrewdly
to interpret them – as opposed to the more shallow flattery or denigration of her letters and reported conversations.[1] The bleak, dehumanized
arrogance revealed in *The Voyage Out* has softened and is now more
sympathetically presented, and his contempt for the facile and complacent mediocrity of others is seen as a stimulant to his own superior,
yet precarious, sense of individuality. Precise and neat as a cat, he seeks
to oppose the chaos and hubbub of the world with his love of order and

[1] The portraits of Lytton in Virginia Woolf's novels undoubtedly give an accurate
reflection of what she felt about him. However, James Strachey notes that 'so far as my
observation goes she never had any real notion of what other people were like. She had
some very crooked ideas.'

exactitude. But he is never at home in this world, never at ease as Percival is, in the random company of others, feeling their presence 'like a separating wall'. Whenever he attempts to transmute his emotions of love into poetry, he automatically heightens the effect, becoming artificial and insincere, so that, as he confesses in one of the recitative lyrical monologues of which the book is made up, 'I shall be a clinger to the outside of words all my life.' Though successful, his wide literary reputation has, in itself, brought him no real happiness, and only applies a balm to soothe the pangs of his envy. 'Yet we scarcely breathe, spent as we are,' sighs Neville near the end of *The Waves* when, tired by his continual opposition to the natural forces of life, he expresses something of Virginia Woolf's own sickness of living. 'We are in that passive and exhausted frame of mind when we only wish to join the body of our mother from whom we have been severed. All else is distasteful, forced and fatiguing.'

Their affection for one another persisted and even perhaps deepened after Lytton's proposal of marriage to Virginia. The letters which they exchanged became, too, a little less stilted and protectively self-conscious. Writing over fifteen years later to Victoria Sackville-West, Virginia Woolf described Lytton as 'infinitely charming, and we fitted like gloves'. But they were both gloves for the same hand, differently styled yet a duplication rather than a complement of each other. They could never have made a pair.

After his proposal, Lytton hurried back again across London to Hampstead, from where, that same evening, he dashed off a note to Virginia: 'I'm still rather agitated and exhausted . . . I do hope you're cheerful! As for me, I'm still of a heap, and the future seems blank to me. But whatever happens, as you said, the important thing is that we should like each other: and we can neither of us have any doubt that we do.'

But by now, Lytton could see no practical alternative to the dingy mode of existence that he had been carrying on for nearly four years. Even his day-dreams were, one by one, being extinguished. He had tried everything, and nothing had come of it all. 'This world', he confessed in a mood of hopeless dejection, 'is so difficult to manage.'

2

ON GRAY AND PURPLE SEAS

'I'm more exhausted than it's easy to imagine,' Lytton wrote to Duncan Grant a few hours after the disastrous proposal of marriage to Virginia Stephen. 'I've been having an agitated day, but it can't be explained yet, and don't mention it, only I do sometimes wish that I was hundreds of leagues away from everything, and everybody, floating alone on purple seas.'

Pending Italy, the nearest approximation to this dream of romantic escape was to purchase a large bottle of medicine and take himself off for a week-end to the gray, wintry seas of Brighton. He spent much of his time there writing poetry, which was a pleasant and therapeutic occupation – even though he dared not show it to anyone. Far removed from the sort of idyll he had in mind, this brief week-end none the less helped repair his shattered nerves and on the last day of his visit (Sunday, 21 February 1909), he was able to report back to Duncan that 'my health so far is flourishing. I suppose the combination of Brighton and Sanatogen has done the trick!'

In the third week of March, Lytton heard that Maynard Keynes had been awarded a Fellowship at King's, and wrote off at once to offer his congratulations. He had been looking for an excuse to correspond with Keynes for some weeks. Eight months had passed since he had learnt of his friend's relationship with Duncan Grant, and almost all the old bitterness and envy had by now evaporated. His reversal with Virginia Stephen – a full realization of the practical limits to *that* association – had produced two immediate effects: first, that of re-emphasizing the value of his old friendships; and second, that of reviving temporarily his passion for Duncan Grant. He appreciated, of course, that Duncan was impossibly vague and childish – but who could deny that he was also wonderfully good-looking? And besides, who else was there? Perhaps, even now, he might salvage something from the shipwreck of that divine friendship. Duncan and Maynard were still on the very best of terms, so it would be impossible to re-establish his intimacy with Duncan without regenerating his amiable feelings for Maynard, and attributing the estrangement that had grown up between them to trivial, involuntary causes for which he himself was largely to blame. Probably nothing would come of it, but he was in no frame of mind to ignore even the faintest chance of happiness. His letter to Maynard was a difficult one to write, and 'I think it's hardly necessary – only to say that you must always think of me as your friend. I shall think of you in the same way. But I've been rather afraid that lately you may have felt things had become different. I don't think it's the case. The only thing is that I'm sometimes uneasy and awkward perhaps, partly I suppose because of my nervous organization which isn't particularly good – but I don't see how it can be helped. I can only beg that you'll attend to it as little as you can, and believe me to be a sensible decent person who remembers and knows.'

Lytton's nervous organization during these weeks had in fact been surprisingly, even embarrassingly, steady. For no reason whatever he felt wonderfully well, and, more incredible still, quite cheerful – ominously so. It must, he believed, all be due to the astonishing quantities of Sanatogen he was consuming. But it was all very extraordinary. 'By every rule,' he explained to Duncan Grant (4 March 1909), 'I ought to be shivering on the edge of moral and physical annihilation, and I find I'm a healthy, energetic, efficient and resourceful member of society. How dreadful it sounds! I expect before the week's out I shall have joined the territorial army, and become a tariff reformer. However in the meantime I pass the time of day pleasantly enough.'

The most important outcome from this inexplicable bonus of vitality was another vigorous drive to embark on an independent way of life. The old domestic solitude-without-privacy was no longer to be endured. This time he must be more severely practical and down-to-earth, for if he failed yet again, he might never escape at all. He had three concurrent plans in mind. The first, most positive and long-term, was a scheme to set up house with his brother James somewhere in London – possibly Bloomsbury. The obstacles and perplexities of putting this move into operation seemed to him enormous, but he was firmly determined that somehow they must be overcome. 'I've practically decided to leave the house,' he wrote to James (9 April 1909), who had gone off to join Moore's reading-party at the Lizard. 'My last few days have been terrible – from every point of view. I hardly know where I am or what I'm doing; and it's quite uncertain whether I shall be any better anywhere else. But it seems clear that the time has come for trying. As far as I can see my fate is mere touch and go. The probabilities are I suppose against me. Oh heavens! What infernal horrors one has to face!

'Why shouldn't you come back on Tuesday? Is there any point in staying longer? The solitude here is accablant, and if you come it would be amusing to do a little house-hunting . . .

'. . . The grave or the lunatic asylum – which will it be? I daresay both. How unfortunate it is that the only woman who behaves with decency and propriety in this house is Pippa, and that she's never in it.'

To discover and then occupy a suitable house with James would, of course, take several weeks, perhaps even months. Meanwhile, Lytton put into effect his second interim plan, which was to follow the example of his sister Pippa, and spend as much time as conveniently possible away from 67 Belsize Park Gardens. With this idea in mind, he decided to join the Savile Club, then in Piccadilly.[1] Naturally, this institution in no respect measured up to the ideal home from home for which he was always searching, but as a temporary oasis it should, he felt, prove extremely useful, since he could spend much of his free time there in reasonable comfort, tolerably segregated from his ever-present, over-attentive mother and sisters. He therefore joined the Savile at the beginning of April. But his first appearance there was a fiasco, the pre-posterous details of which he amusingly recounted to James (6 April 1909): 'My adventures on Friday, when I arrived here for the first time, were extremely painful. After having been certified as a member by a purple-bottle-nosed servitor in a guichet in the hall, I didn't in the least know what to do. There was a door, a staircase, and a notice-board; I was in my hat and coat, carrying an umbrella; the servitor merely stared from his guichet. In a moment of weakness I began to read the notices on the notice-board, and while I was doing so the servitor became involved in an endless conversation with an imbecile Major. I was therefore lost. I couldn't ask him where I was to put my hat, coat and umbrella, I had read every notice six times, and there seemed no hope. At last I made a wild plunge at the door – opened it, entered, and found myself in the dining-room, nose to nose with a somewhat surprised and indignant waiter. I then fled upstairs, and so managed to get here* safely. But there are further mysteries still to be explained – the second floor? – dare I penetrate there? . . .

'*The Smoking room, overlooking Green Park.'

A more serious proposition was his third plan – a new bid to liberate himself from the clutches of the *Spectator*. 'Perhaps Duncan has told you of my probable abandonment of the *Spectator*,' he wrote to Maynard Keynes (29 March 1909). 'At present it had better not be mentioned. I think it's the only thing to do, though it terrifies me out of

---

[1] In the Savile Candidates Book No. 3, it is recorded that Lytton was proposed by J. E. McTaggart on 13 February 1908 and elected on 31 March. His referees were H. L. Stephen, W. H. C. Shaw (who had married Frances, younger sister of St Loe Strachey), H. G. Dakyns, Hilton Young, John Pollock, A. Chichele Plowden (Lytton's cousin), J. B. Atkins (a friend of St Loe Strachey's and his second in command as assistant editor of the *Spectator*), and (the Rev.) H. F. Stewart, author of *A Century of Anglo-Catholicism* (1929), a Trinity don, friendly with Lytton and with Pernel who was then a Newnham don in the same modern languages department.

my wits.' Keynes, as usual, agreed. 'I think you're much to be congratulated on getting rid of the *Spectator*,' he replied (4 April 1909),
'– if you're prepared to risk poverty and pawn your coat.' It was, he
implied, easy to overestimate the importance of money. Nevertheless,
Lytton's apprehensions were very understandable. It was a brave
decision, and one that James had predicted he could never have the will
to make. From the *Spectator* he received almost all his independent
means of livelihood. Yet while he continued to expend so much of his
time and precious store of energy working away for it, there could be
little or no chance of composing the literary masterpieces on which he
had set his sights. Most men spent all their time amassing money, but *he*
wanted money in order to buy him more free time – and it had not
worked out like that. Still, it was not too late. He was now twenty-
nine years of age – surely not too moribund to emerge from his
anonymous, journalistic obscurity and start a new career in literature.
Molière, for instance, had not written his first play until he was twenty-
nine, and he was as ancient as thirty-five before he began to be eminent.
Lytton felt fortified by this example. The *Spectator* was like a millstone
round his neck; but to cut free was tantamount to loosing anchor
and setting one's sails irretrievably towards some limitless, uncharted
ocean. 'I fancy myself alone before eternity,' he exclaimed. And he saw
visions of himself as a perennial wanderer in mid-seas, never able to
complete his voyage. Moore was an alarming embodiment of such aimlessness. On the other hand, the pleasure to be derived from drifting
across the high seas might be enormous – and the profit, too, if he had
any luck!

The last of his regular pieces for the *Spectator* – a rather indifferent
article on Carlyle's letters – appeared on 10 April; though in the course
of the next five years he did contribute five more long essay-reviews to
the paper, which were specially commissioned by James – then working as St Loe Strachey's private secretary. The decision to terminate his
employment with the *Spectator* was hastened by a sudden crisis in
health. For a week he lay in bed feeling wretched. 'My health', he wrote
to James (12 April 1909), 'has collapsed rather more seriously than
usual. I've been attacked by some unpleasant diseases, among which is
vertigo! The man Roland has been called in, and has ordered a complete cessation of work, and absolute mental rest. – How am I to get
that, I wonder? It would be a great thing to have someone to talk to.
I'm not even allowed out, for fear of falling down in the middle of
Piccadilly, and I sit all day trying to read, and not succeeding very
well.'

And so, once more, his plan for establishing himself on some permanent basis apart from his family had been undermined by illness, and would have yet again to be postponed. As soon as he was allowed out of doors, he left Belsize Park Gardens and went to stay for two weeks at King's. Here he encountered many of his old friends – Keynes, Harry Norton, Sheppard and several others – and was whirled into the throbbing vortex of undergraduate romance. The colleges seemed thick with amorous crises and stupendous rumours, and Lytton rolled from one to the other in fits of laughter and floods of sentimental tears. Cambridge had infected him with a fresh and delightful sense of vitality. But eclipsing all else was his first meeting with the mythical George Mallory, a figure cut authentically in the heroic mould. Next to the shadow of George Mallory's muscular strength, Lytton seemed to shrink back into child-size. As with Thoby Stephen, everything about him appeared larger than life – the manly shoulders, the magnificent torso, the wide open smile, white teeth and blue eyes – so large he felt he could curl up within its shadow, and sleep. He had heard of Mallory earlier from James, who was said to treat him rather severely, and from Duncan Grant, who placed him 'easily first' of all the handsome young men there. But their stories, Lytton decided, had conspicuously failed to do him justice. From the start, he was swept off his feet by the sight of this splendid, godlike phenomenon. Mallory was not so much a person with whom one slipped into an intimate, lasting friendship as someone whom one worshipped humbly from afar, someone whose very existence seemed to justify all the pain and perplexity of this world – the perfect human specimen. Something of the peculiar quality of his feelings towards Mallory – which, like those for Thoby Stephen, were more idealistic than sensual – are explained by, and can be further deduced from, a very articulate letter which he wrote to Clive and Vanessa Bell (21 May 1909):

'Mon dieu! – George Mallory! – When that's been written, what more need be said? My hand trembles, my heart palpitates, my whole being swoons away at the words – oh heavens! heavens! I found of course that he'd been absurdly maligned – he's six foot high, with the body of an athlete by Praxiteles, and a face – oh incredible – the mystery of Botticelli, the refinement and delicacy of a Chinese print, the youth and piquancy of an unimaginable English boy. I rave, but when you see him, as you must, you will admit all – all! The amazing thing, though, was that besides his beauty, other things were visible, more enchanting still. His passion for James was known, but it so happened that during my visit he declared it – and was rejected. . . . Poor George! I met him for the first time immediately after this occurrence, and saw in my first glance to the very bottom of his astounding soul. I was écrasé. What followed was remarkable – though infinitely pure. Yes! Virginia alone will sympathize with me now – I'm a convert to the divinity of virginity, and spend hours every day lost in a trance of adoration, innocence, and bliss. It was a complete revelation, as you may conceive. By God! The sheer beauty of it all is what transports me. . . . To have sat with him in the firelight through the evening, to have wandered with him in the Kings Garden among violets and cherry blossom, to have – no, no! for desire was lost in wonder, and there was profanation even in a kiss. . . . For the rest, he's going to be a schoolmaster, and his intelligence is not remarkable. What's the need?'

Early in May Lytton left Cambridge and moved to Burley Hill, which Thena Clough had lent him for the month and where he was soon joined by Pippa. He still felt rather enfeebled after his sickness and excitement, but there was no more vertigo or gastric capitulation. In his weakened condition, the comfort and the fine spring weather were very wonderful at first. 'I've grown used to annihilation,' he admitted to James, 'and have at last learnt the art of not expecting very much.' Calm was not life's crown, but calm was best. In this mood of tranquil renunciation, he felt happy simply to sit out in the sun, flowers carpeting the ground, birds packed tight upon the trees, and *The Faerie Queene* (unopened) within reach. If only his physique had been more robust, everything would have been perfect, for then he could have explored the depths of the New Forest, and composed perhaps a century of sonnets enhaloing the resplendent beauty of George Mallory, every line of which would breathe the purest spirit of idealistic and exotic love – wafted over seas of amaranth, plunged up to the eyes in all the spices of Arabia, and lulled in the bosom of eternal spring. As it was, he had to content himself writing letters, to George Mallory of course and to his other friends. 'I can never have been in the country before at this time of year – it's all most amazing, and I'm beginning to understand the sentimentality of poets on the spring,' he told Duncan Grant (7 May 1909), delineating his placid and ethereal convalescence. 'Their preposterous descriptions are here, actually existing, under my very nose. Beds of violets, choirs of birds, blossoms and butterflies and balmy breezes and scents and everything else.'

And so the days slipped by in charming vagueness and contentment. Why should it not always be so? He had declared a truce on his passions, and from this sanctuary the world of the emotions appeared farcical. Besides which, he had to think carefully about his future. He possessed, he felt sure, the two essential qualities that in the long run ought to give him success – a decent competency and the capacity and desire for doing work of importance. Love might be the very devil in disrupting one's plans, but it *was* Time's fool; and once it had flown out of the window, one was always astonished to find just how well one could get along without it.

Soon enough, however, Lytton's mood began to change, his reflections to veer off on to a new course. After a fortnight of uninterrupted composure, his improving health started again to disturb him. He felt bored, smothered by the rich, tropical profusion of the spring, wearied by the simple happenings of the country – and he wrote off eagerly for news of the latest affairs at Cambridge. 'I live in complete silence, infinite dimness, and absolute monotony,' he complained to James (16 May 1909). 'The weather, too, has turned icy, so that I now spend my days over a sea-coal fire, reading Joan of Arc. My nights I pass in incredible virginity among the folds of a highly tantalizing double-bed. In the intervals, I dream and wonder, but to no avail. My heart, my mind, and my honteuses parties – all are in Cambridge, though nobody seems to mark them.'

To relieve the monotony, he invited Duncan Grant to stay, but Duncan could not make it. So much for that day-dream. A few days later he was even further dismayed by an unwelcome visit from Mrs Humphry Ward. 'I looked at that shapeless mass of meaningless flesh,' he wrote savagely to James (26 May 1909), '– all old and sordid and insignificant – and could hardly believe that humanity could contain that and – you know what.' Mrs Humphry Ward represented for Lytton all that was ugly and distasteful. His dislike of her persisted strongly over a number of years, and was, indirectly, to act as an effective catalyst in the third essay of *Eminent Victorians*.

By the end of May, Lytton's tenancy of Burley Hill was up and he had to leave. The prospect of London was wormwood to him, but it was extremely difficult to find any *pied-à-terre* elsewhere. He retreated to Hampstead for a few uneasy days, and then – he could not resist it – ran off to Cambridge for a further week. Later in June he was forced to go back to Belsize Park Gardens again. 'I was just beginning to feel mildly happy,' he told James, 'when my internal economy gave way and now I have the worst fears – it's quite sickening. The power of digestion seems to have abandoned me altogether, and I think I shall never be able to eat again. Damn! Damn! And my temper too is deteriorating.'

Lytton's hopes of escaping to the sunshine of Italy had by this time been altogether relinquished. But his mother, worried over his inexplicable bouts of sickness, felt strongly that he needed some sort of restorative holiday. It was therefore decided that he should spend a few weeks in Sweden, a clean, enlightened country, notorious for its up-to-date clinics, where he might at last find some explanation and remedy for

his perpetual invalidism. Lytton did not greatly look forward to this
trip which was something of an anti-climax after his Roman dreams, but
he felt obliged to go through with it. At least he would be out of
Hampstead. And if the Swedish doctors could work some miraculous
cure, perhaps he might then build up the vigour and vitality to make a
successful bid for liberty, for happiness and a new career.

In any event, it was worth a shot.

3

THE SWEDISH EXPERIMENT

Lytton started out on his quest for health in mid-July, spending one
day and a night in Copenhagen before arriving in Sweden. With him
went two female attendants – Daisy McNeil, an eccentric aunt of
Duncan Grant's who ran a private nursing home in Eastbourne for the
superannuated and infirm members of well-to-do families; and one of
her elderly, affluent patients, a woman by the name of Elwes, 'a poor
dried-up good-natured old stick with an odd tinge of excitability, alias
madness I suppose, but always absolutely insipid'. These two ladies
were not perhaps ideal travelling companions, but they both turned out
to be very obliging, constantly offering to mend Lytton's socks,
presenting him at all times of the day with cups of weak tea, and insisting that he read the out-of-date newspapers before themselves. In
return for this hospitality, he could only repay them by cracking polite
jokes and elaborately admiring, for their benefit, the scenery. But this
rendering seemed more than sufficient to delight them both. 'Even La
Elwes's conversation has its charms', he reported back to Duncan Grant
(1 August 1909). 'At first I was terrified by her hatchet nose and slate-
pencil voice – and I still am occasionally – but on the whole I now view
her with composure. Never have I met a more absolutely sterile mind –
and yet how wonderfully cultivated! It's like a piece of flannel with
watercress growing on it.'

On their arrival in Stockholm, Daisy McNeil, who spoke Swedish,
arranged for Lytton to have some medical tests performed by a Dr
Johanson. These turned out to be rather fearful encounters, chiefly
because they had to be carried on in broken French. 'Pas de laxatifs,
monsieur!' were the doctor's first and last words; and he sent Lytton
down with his retinue of old ladies to Badanstalten, a health sanatorium
for 'physical therapeutics' at Saltsjöbaden, by the sea, not far from
Stockholm. This sanatorium specialized in the treatment of heart
conditions, nervous illnesses, stomach, intestine and digestive com-

plaints and was presided over by a charming, 'cello-playing Dr Zander, himself a heart-and-nerve specialist, who attended personally to Lytton.

About Saltsjöbaden itself there seemed very little to fire anyone. Everything appeared indefinite and infinitely negative. The water was undoubtedly the best feature of the place, and if he had only owned a small sailing boat, life might have been perfect. As it was he saw a great many boats going about, but unfortunately they were all private, and it seemed out of the question to hire one. The rest of the surroundings struck Lytton as rather second-rate, though he courteously refrained from saying so. They were very much built over, and to his eye quite shapeless. The woods were scrubby, the inhabitants more middle-class than could easily be imagined, the whole atmosphere distinctly hydro-pathetic – and far too much of the hydro and too little of the pathetic for his taste. However, he did feel really extraordinarily contented. By dint of never thinking, he managed to pass through the invariable daily life there pretty comfortably. It proved, no doubt, how appallingly degraded his character had become – to be able to spend week after week after week without a murmur of discontent in the company of two inconceivably dull old maids. The flatness of their trio conversations was inexpressible, and on all sides boredom reigned supreme.

'I believe I'm the only person of our acquaintance who could do what I'm doing,' he wrote to James. 'The dullness is so infinite that the brain reels to think of it, and yet I might almost be called happy. The whole place is too unimaginably bourgeois. I had quite a shock when I entered the dining-room for the first time and saw the crowd of middle-aged and middle-class invalids munching their Swedish cookery. For complete second-rateness this country surpasses the wildest dreams of man. I sometimes fear that it may be the result of democracy, but I imagine really that it's inborn, and brought to its height by lack of cash. All the decent Scandinavians, no doubt, left the place a thousand years ago, and only the dregs remain. Yet they're amazingly good-looking; and the sailors in Stockholm, with their décolleté necks, fairly send one into a flutter. The bath-attendants, however, so far, have not agitated me, and this in spite of the singular intimacies of their operations. Even the lift boys leave me cold. My health seems to be progressing rather well, but my experiences have been more ghastly than can be conceived, medical experiences, I mean – oh heavens!'

It was the sustained and startling improvement in his health that made the overall tedium supportable, even unimportant. The subject of health absorbed and dominated existence, and so long as it continued on the upgrade Lytton believed that he could put up with anything. He had started off the first week with nothing more strenuous than some insignificant baths ('Finsenbad'), but almost immediately he began to gain in weight, his digestion improved – also his temper – and other departments. 'Conceive me if you can a healthy and pure young man,' he wrote to Maynard Keynes (13 August 1909). 'My only terror is that none of it'll last.' But this apprehension appeared quite groundless. After the first successful week he graduated from the bathroom to the gym. 'I hope when I get on to the mechanical gymnastics, etc., that I shall swell out of my clothes,' he told Duncan Grant. And so it actually came about! His appetite increased still further, and the female attendants were asked to let out his waistcoats.

Lytton's régime at Saltsjöbaden, though not complicated, was certainly formidable, and his various cures occupied him on and off for almost the whole day. At eight o'clock each morning he was called by Sister Fanny who brought him a glass of 'Carlsbad water' – a mild tonic. Half an hour later he breakfasted off a locally concocted simulacrum of porridge and sour cream. At nine-thirty he paraded at the gym for a thirty-minute period of mechanical exercises. These operations took place in a large hall decked out with gadgets and appliances of the most gruesome and mediaeval appearance, which were worked partly by electricity, partly by the patient. In spite of his quota of electricity, Lytton found them sufficiently exhausting. All the collaborative, semi-mechanized apparatuses on which he and the other invalids performed were made up, so Lytton explained to his mother (3 August 1909), of 'most singular arrangements, by means of which the various muscles are worked without being tired. The hall where one does them [the exercises] looks exactly like a torture chamber – terrific instruments of every kind line the walls, and elderly gentlemen attached upon them go through their evolutions with the utmost gravity.'

After these exertions were over, Lytton was allowed nearly two hours of freedom and relaxation. When the sun shone, the air would glow miraculously light and clear, and he was able to sit out on his special deck-chair among the pines, and the fat and perspiring Swedish patients, wonderfully comatose, idly dreaming and idly doing nothing whatever, all with the greatest satisfaction. To his tired mind everything might seem dubious, anaemic and uncertain; but at the back of every dream and every expectation was the heroic figure of George Mallory. To everyone he poured out a constant stream of letters which amusingly describe the rigours and incongruities of this 'Swedish experiment'. And when he had wearied of writing, he would read Tolstoy, Saint-Simon, Voltaire and Swinburne. 'I only regret that I forgot to bring a copy of the Holy Bible,' he wrote to his mother. But to make up for this deficiency he eagerly devoured the *Daily Mail* – two days late –

and the *Gloucester and Wilts Advertiser*, in many ways more interesting than the *Daily Mail*, and he began to get quite heated over far-off local affairs. Swedish politics also claimed his attention when, early in August, a general strike was called. However, the alarmist reports in the newspapers seemed purely fictional. There was, at any rate, no symptom of any strike or even the mildest ripple of a disrupting influence in those placid, medicinal halls at Saltsjöbaden.

It was during these morning periods of dreaming, reading and writing letters, that Lytton conceived a plan for compiling an anthology of English heroic verse. 'I think it might be very interesting, and that one might get a great many good extracts which people don't know of,' he wrote to his mother (21 August 1909). 'The interest would be to trace the development up to Pope, etc., and then the throw back with Keats and Shelley. I think Pope made more advance on Dryden – in the mere technique of the line – than is usually recognized. Dryden's line, though of course it's magnificent, lacks the weight of Pope's. I once analysed some passages in the Dunciad, and found that the number of stressed syllables in each line was remarkable – sometimes as many as seven or eight. It's difficult to believe that this is the same metre as Epipsychidion which rushes along with three stresses to a line at most. I've written to Sidgwick[1] proposing to do this. I hope he'll accept.' Unfortunately nothing came of this plan, though fifteen years later Lytton incorporated some of these reflections on the heroic couplet into his Leslie Stephen lecture on Pope.

Shortly before midday, the treatment was resumed with a vigorous session of massage which in turn was followed up with a warm undoctored bath, superintended by various Scandinavian stewards and officials. Lunch was at one o'clock, and two hours afterwards, once the patient had properly digested his food, he was plunged into a medicinal bath. These were rather strict, inaudacious affairs, even more meticulously supervised by attendants, but never very varied and always too cold for pleasure. After tea at four, Lytton was again allowed two hours' rest until dinner, which, much to his disgust, was served at the unbelievably *bourgeois* time of six o'clock. Communal walks were generally taken after dinner, under the pallid sky and among the mangy conifers of the so-called 'English Park'. It was a shocking experience to be encompassed by all the other inhabitants on these slow, pedestrian expeditions. There were *millions* of them – all either Swedes

---

[1] Frank Sidgwick, the publisher, best remembered perhaps for his collaboration with Eddie Marsh on Marsh's *Memoir* of Rupert Brooke, and selections from Brooke's poetry. He was also responsible for bringing out Brooke's first book, *Poems*, which the house of Sidgwick and Jackson published on 4 December 1911.

or Finns – and, despite their regrettably middle-class habits, secretly believed by Lytton to be counts and countesses incognito. Wherever he went they surrounded him in hordes – fat, old, ugly and imbecile – dotted across the shapeless nondescript countryside, or bobbing about in boats, or streaming endlessly through the corridors to their various meals and cures, or chattering over their symptoms in the 'Salong'. There was no escaping them.

In the later evening, after promenading about in the park, Lytton usually played a few games of billiards with the ever-faithful and kind Daisy. Soon, much to his amazement, he discovered that he had somehow gained an immense reputation as a billiards expert among the other inmates of the clinic. 'Directly we begin to play,' he informed his mother (21 August 1909), 'crowds enter the room, and take seats to watch the Englishman playing "cannon-ball" as they call it. As the table is very small and the pockets are very large I occasionally manage to make a break of 15 or 20 which strikes astonishment in the beholders. Apparently the Swedish game consists entirely of potting the red ball with great violence, so that cannons and losing hazards brought off with delicacy appear to these poor furriners wonderful and beautiful in the extreme.'

At half-past nine play was interrupted while Lytton was brought a large evening bowl of pseudo-porridge. And an hour later he retired upstairs to his bedroom, drew down his special blinds and went off into a long and dreamless sleep.

He had originally intended to leave Sweden at the end of August, but though he was anxious not to miss all the English summer, his health was going up to such an extent in the spick-and-span, disinfected atmosphere of Saltsjöbaden that he felt obliged to extend his stay there for another fortnight. He had, in fact, become attuned to this ingeniously monotonous existence, and could, so he said, hardly believe in any other mode of living which did not comprise dinner-at-six, mechanical gymnastics, porridge and sour cream, hot and cold baths, and communal perambulations with dubious Scandinavian countesses. It was not the unremitting hell it sounded, but rather a purgatory where he had absolved himself through suffering.

Early in September Daisy McNeil and 'La Elwes' gave up the struggle and fled to England; but James bravely came out to stay with Lytton for the remaining days of his treatment. 'It was very fortunate,' Lytton explained to Maynard Keynes (17 September 1909), 'as otherwise I should have been alone and moribund in this ghastly region.' But then, at about the same time, he was quite suddenly and inexplicably struck down by illness, losing much of the weight which he had spent the previous seven weeks so carefully amassing. By the third week of September he had recovered, but decided to remain on for a further ten days to re-establish 'my now normal condition of corpulence' and to swell out again into his enlarged clothes, which for a time hung round him in folds.

Eventually, Lytton and James left Saltsjöbaden on 23 September, arriving back in London two days later. After a week at Belsize Park Gardens, suffering acutely from piles and carrying with him everywhere an air cushion which he had hired for the fee of one-and-six a week, Lytton travelled down with his mother and Harry Norton to Brighton, where, at the Queen's Hotel and subsequently at the Belvedere Mansion Hotel, he set about trying 'to recover from the effects of Sweden'.

4

FOR TRAVEL'S SAKE

No sooner was Lytton safely installed back in London than he evolved a new scheme to ensure his future independence. This entailed going to live at Grantchester as a neighbour of Rupert Brooke's, in 'my moated grange' as he called it in happy anticipation of his tenancy. From Saltsjöbaden he had already written to Brooke inquiring after the Old Vicarage, next to The Orchard where Brooke was then living. This house, which Brooke himself later occupied and made famous with his Grantchester poem, was owned by a Mr and Mrs Neeve, who were at that time anxious to find lodgers. 'So far they have been singularly unsatisfied,' Brooke reported in an epistolary style that bears many similarities to Lytton's own. 'Mr Neeve is a refined creature, with an accent above his class, who sits out near the beehives with a handkerchief over his head and reads advanced newspapers. He knows a lot about botany. They keep babies and chickens; and I rather think I have seen both classes entering the house. But you could be firm. The garden is the great glory. There is a soft lawn with a sundial and tangled, antique flowers abundantly; and a sham ruin, quite in a corner; built fifty years ago by Mr Shuckbrugh,[1] historian and rector of

---

[1] In his biography of Rupert Brooke, Christopher Hassall noted that this actually referred to Samuel Widnall, 'author and printer of several topographical books, and pioneer in photography; he was never ordained but affected the appearance of a clergyman, and in 1853 erected a Folly at the bottom of his garden, the ruinated fragment of what might be a medieval nunnery.

And spectral dance, before the dawn,
A hundred Vicars down the lawn . . .'

Grantchester; and *most* attractive. . . . There are trees rather too closely all round; and a mist. It's right on the river.'

James was sceptical about this plan. 'I gather Lytton's corresponding with you about a house in Grantchester,' he wrote. 'Would you hate anyone being near you? though I suppose you both dislike one another too much to meet often.' But Brooke was quite unaware of disliking Lytton; and Lytton himself felt enthusiastic about the venture. 'If I can, I shall stay there for ever,' he told Virginia Stephen (13 October 1909), 'but I suppose I can't. My health still seems to be something of a Mahomet's coffin. However, *vogue la galère!*'

All this, however, was before he had gone down to reconnoitre the place. In order to do this in comfort, he spent one night as Brooke's guest at The Orchard where he was observed 'to have a habit of sitting with his back against the book-shelves, reaching a hand over his shoulder, and bringing forward without looking the first book he touched, reading a snatch of it, putting it back, and grabbing another, all without turning round'. On first inspection, the Old Vicarage seemed fairly tolerable and even in some respects charming, so he decided that he would definitely try this experiment, at least for a short while – one of the advantages being that it was very cheap. If it failed, then he would have no alternative but to go back and live in Hampstead. Everything seemed fixed for a new phase in his life, but, as with so many of his previous projects, it all fell through at the last moment when Brooke casually explained to him the reason for the inexpensive rental – that the house was easily and frequently flooded in all seasons, and impossibly frigid in the winter. Perhaps James's intuition had been right in the first place. In any case, with his Mahomet's coffin, the Old Vicarage was obviously no place for Lytton; and so yet another scheme had hastily to be abandoned.

He had almost resigned himself to a further arid stretch of family life, when George Mallory came miraculously to the rescue, telling him that he was going to stay with Arthur Benson [1] and that his old rooms in Cambridge were consequently empty. Lytton hurried round there at once, and after some agitating negotiations secured the place for a

---

[1] Arthur Christopher Benson (1862–1925), possibly the least talented of the three gifted Benson brothers, sons of E. W. Benson, Archbishop of Canterbury. A. C. Benson was the Master of Magdalene and a copious and indifferent author of sugar-and-water verse and prose. At the suggestion of Edward VII, he wrote the words for the air in Elgar's Pomp and Circumstance March No. 1: 'Land of Hope and Glory'. After the death of Henry James in 1916, he went to live in Lamb House at Rye, replacing Percy Lubbock, who had lived there in the intervening half-dozen years, but who was then 'cast out to seek for rest in dry places – his own mind, for instance'. (A. C. Benson to George Rylands, 26 December 1922.) The unsuspecting Lubbock later edited Benson's Diaries for publication (1926).

relatively cheap sum. He settled down there at once, writing to explain the summary change of plan to his mother (18 October 1909). 'I have now found some other rooms on the outskirts of Cambridge (much nearer than Grantchester) which I have taken for the term at 35/– a week for board and lodging. I think they will do very well, but I can only have them for this term. It's rather a piece of luck my getting them – the real tenant is ill, and cannot use them, so that they are perfectly civilized in the way of furniture. The people who keep them I know to be trustworthy. I hope now to be able to do some writing. My health appears to be quite satisfactory. . . .

'I forgot to mention the charming name of my new abode – Pythagoras House.'

Pythagoras House became Lytton's headquarters for the next ten weeks – almost to the end of the year. 'I'm wonderfully comfortable and healthy here – also at present shockingly lazy,' he wrote to Duncan Grant (1 November 1909). 'I occasionally wish that I could glide on here for ever, but no doubt in a week or two I shall be horribly sick of the whole place.'

But for once his doleful prognostications were not to be fulfilled. Every day Cambridge grew more gay and debonair. How delightful it was to linger among such memories! He wished that he might go on living there for longer than a single term; but by December, of course, Hampstead *would* be inevitable. Perhaps, though, by that time he might not be so sorry. At any rate, for the moment he remained remarkably well and happy. Such leisure! Such repose! And then, too, the weather was still warm enough for the occasional morning in the garden. 'I find the beauty of the trees and the country quite divine', he wrote to Clive Bell (21 October 1909). 'The view from the King's bridge this morning – you should have seen it! Certainly this is the most beautiful time of the year for Cambridge. Won't you come up for a week-end?'

Clive and Vanessa Bell did come and visit him the following month, and so did Virginia Stephen. Lytton also attended several meetings of the Apostles, and saw much of Rupert Brooke, Harry Norton, Sheppard, Gerald Shove, Saxon Sydney-Turner and the non-Apostolic Walter Lamb. Most notable among his new and younger Cambridge associates was Francis Birrell:[1] 'I have made the acquaintance of Mr Birrell's small son, who is at King's,' he informed his mother. 'He is very gay, and has apparently never heard of Ireland.'[2]

[1] Francis Birrell (1889–1935), journalist and dramatic critic, who after the war started a bookshop with David Garnett.

[2] Francis Birrell's father, Augustine Birrell, the politician and man of letters, was Chief Secretary for Ireland in Asquith's Cabinet. He resigned after the Easter Week Rebellion in Dublin in 1916.

During this stay at Pythagoras House, Lytton composed a blank verse tragedy for a Stratford on Avon Prize Play Competition. From the sixteenth century onwards nearly every would-be poet has attempted to write at least one blank verse drama, and the unlikely chorus of praise accorded such playwrights as Stephen Phillips and Christopher Fry has only shown up the dearth of really effective blank verse theatre in the last hundred years. *Essex: A Tragedy*, as Lytton's production was entitled, embodies several of the characteristic short-comings one would expect to discover in modern blank verse. It is competently, even ingeniously constructed, but rather lifeless. Where the verse needs to be strong and concentrated, it is often merely windy and rhetorical; where it should communicate the more subtle shades of emotion, it reveals instead the naked machinery of the plot or merely etches in by conversational reference and allusion the historical background. Perhaps the most interesting lines are those given to Queen Elizabeth as she reflects on the difference between her own advanced age and that of the youthful Essex. There is a pathos and tenderness in her monologue which conveys something of Lytton's own worship of splendid masculine youth, and the sense of premature middle-age which sometimes overcame him in his blacker moods.

> *For I was old*
> *Ere he was young, and years before he breathed*
> *These locks had worn the coronet of a queen.*
> *Rather it was that in my age I knew him,*
> *And to my setting skies he came to lend*
> *The freshness of a star. Am I a dotard*
> *Dreaming on fantasies? Or is it true*
> *That frozen years can snatch from fiery youth*
> *Some palpable warmth and the reflected radiance*
> *Of life's meridian splendour? No, 'tis no dream;*
> *For often in the midst of my dull days,*
> *My councils, and my creeping policies,*
> *I have known a look from Essex light the clouds,*
> *And make earth glory.*

Such soliloquies were to play a large part in *Elizabeth and Essex*, which Lytton subtitled 'A Tragic History'; and the chief interest that *Essex: A Tragedy* now holds lies in its relationship to that later work. The action of the play is spread only over some four chapters – XIII to XVI – of the book, and it opens very dramatically with Essex's unannounced and forbidden return from Ireland on 28 September 1599. The last passage of Chapter XII in *Elizabeth and Essex* is in fact an exact description of the opening scene, and reads in places like the stage and costume directions for it:

'A quarter of an hour later – it was ten o'clock – the Earl was at the gate. He hurried forward, without a second's hesitation; he ran up the stairs, and so – oh! he knew the way well enough – into the presence chamber, and thence into the privy chamber; the Queen's bedroom lay beyond. He was muddy and disordered from his long journey, in rough clothes and riding boots; but he was utterly unaware of any of that, as he burst open the door in front of him. And there, quite close to him, was Elizabeth among her ladies, in a dressing-gown, unpainted, without her wig, her grey hair hanging in wisps about her face, and her eyes starting from her head.'

The prior composition of *Essex: A Tragedy* shows that Lytton believed that the enigma of the Queen's relationship with her famous courtier was ideally suited to a theatrical treatment, and helps to explain why *Elizabeth and Essex* was aesthetically conceived in a dramatic form, unlike all his other books – even *Queen Victoria* and *Landmarks in French Literature* – which, though visually dramatic, are in construction successions of cleverly interrelated essays. The play is yet another pointer, also, to the fact that, unknown to his later critics, Lytton had a long-standing interest and thorough knowledge of the Elizabethan age; and it reveals that his opinion and attitude towards Essex and Elizabeth herself, notwithstanding the added Freudian interpretations incorporated into the biography, remained pretty well consistent throughout his adult life.

During the autumn evenings at Pythagoras House, Lytton would read out scenes from his competitive tragedy to several friends. Shortly before Christmas the play was completed and sent off to Stratford in the vain hope that it would be performed there during the Festival Week. 'When it's acted,' he optimistically wrote to Moore, 'I'll send you a box.' But the occasion never arose.

Life at Pythagoras House had been wonderfully luxurious, and in his last week or two it grew if anything more so, full of charm and sweetness and that warm humanity which was for Lytton the essence of Cambridge – 'I suppose the result of the end of term,' he told James. 'People seem to draw closer.' One constant pleasure was the proximity of George Mallory, living near by with Arthur Benson. But, as he had dreaded from the first, Mallory's good looks were beginning to deteriorate. The hand of Time had already started to work its havoc. He was growing fat, and his complexionless face was becoming rather washy and bulbous, its contours too lunar – like a cheese. Lytton turned away in despair. He still thought him exquisite as an ideal human concept, but it was now easier to picture him as such if he forgot, or at least blurred over, certain physiognomical and corpulent developments. Sometimes, of course, this was not possible, and he would feel heart-broken and oppressed by the agony of human relationships, by those awful shadows of mortality – the inevitable melancholy end of all that is beautiful, all that is lovely on earth. His pessimism, shot through with iridescent irony and laughter, was deepened by the news that Mallory was planning to go off on one of his dangerous Alpine expeditions. 'It's not only the love affairs that are bound to fail!' he wrote to James in explanation of the low spirits which recurrently sucked him down. 'And now I shall never see him again, or if I do, it'll be an unrecogniz-able middle-aged mediocrity, fluttering between wind and water, probably wearing glasses and a timber toe.'

As with A. E. Housman, Lytton's reactions to intense emotionalism or despair were invariably gastric. At the end of December he returned to Hampstead where, almost immediately, he caught gastric influenza, and had to be fed on pap for a fortnight. For his convalescence it was arranged that he should go to spend a few days by the sea, and in the last week of January he set off for Daisy McNeil's private nursing home at 12 Devonshire Place in Eastbourne, just two hundred yards from the front. He had expected to find Daisy alone, and was horrified on dis-covering that the house was full of muttering old invalid hags, among whom he felt like Orpheus surrounded by the Scythian women, about to tear him to pieces. 'The place is rather bizarre,' he wrote to James (26 January 1910). 'I arrived at teatime – entered a room almost pitch dark, and apparently full of females – one of them I gathered a hospital nurse – the others being presumably morphine maniacs. I don't at all know whether I'm a guest or a patient.' Lytton had rarely been so gloomy as in these demure surroundings; but even here there were slight compensations – good food and an attractive German waiter to serve it.

He returned to Hampstead at the beginning of February, but suc-ceeded almost at once in escaping again, for 'a dream of a week' to Clive and Vanessa Bell in Gordon Square. 'Dignity, repose, and medical consolations,' he wrote to them after leaving (15 February 1910), '– I feel that I shall never find the divine conjunction again.' Apart from the occasional poem, he wrote nothing. James had by this time started full-time work as St Loe Strachey's private secretary, and most of his friends – Clive and Vanessa Bell, Ralph Hawtrey, Bertrand Russell, C. P. Sanger, Gerald Shove, R. C. Trevelyan, and Virginia Stephen (who was suffering from a nervous breakdown) – had gone down to Cornwall, so that instead of spending his afternoons and evenings in

Bloomsbury, he would wander dispiritedly off to the Savile Club to sit among the intolerable old gentlemen there and gaze forlornly at the footmen. In an endeavour to revive his cheerfulness, he took himself off for a solitary few days to the Old George House, a private hotel in Salisbury. But it was no use. 'My health has become quite filthy, and the future seems very black,' he wrote to Duncan Grant (4 April 1910). 'I think I shall *have* to give up living here – which points to Cambridge – oh dear! it's very melancholy. I've been almost perpetually ill here since I came back in December – and there seems now no possible reason, except the place and entourage, for this happening. If I was well, I should like London far better than Cambridge; but it's too much never to be able to work for more than a fortnight at a time. I've been too feeble to do a stroke. . . .'

To infuse into his decrepit frame some semblance of vitality before embarking on the arduous business of finding new lodgings in Cambridge, Lytton decided that he must go off to some seaside town for a week's 'change of air'. The prospect of staying anywhere alone appalled him and he wrote off diffidently to Rupert Brooke to ask if he might consider accompanying him (31 March 1910): 'Is there any chance of your being able to go with me, only, for a week or so? James thinks there may be, and says that you know of a cottage on Dartmoor. . . . My health seems to be giving way, and I want to go off somewhere; but I fear its hardly possible that you're still free. If you were I could go as soon as you liked, with songs of Thanksgiving.'

Rupert Brooke at once agreed to go, but as the Dartmoor cottage, Becky House, was not vacant, he made arrangements for them to spend the second week in April at the Cove Hotel, at West Lulworth in Dorset. No sooner was this irrevocably fixed than Lytton received an invitation from George Mallory urging him to come to Paris. Since he was now obliged to spend all his available money on his 'change of air', this new and infinitely preferable holiday had to be put out of mind. Far from sounding off songs of Thanksgiving, therefore, he felt particularly embittered, cursing himself for having written off to Brooke in the first place simply because no one else seemed free. The expectation of West Lulworth now singularly failed to thrill him, but on his arrival there all this bitterness and disappointment quickly melted away. Rupert was a charming and decorative companion, and the hotel was warm and cosy. 'Rupert read me some of his latest poems on a shelf by the sea,' he wrote to James, 'but I found them very difficult to make out, owing to his manner of reading. I could only return the compliment by giving him the first act of Essex to read – he didn't seem quite so bitter about it as you; but that may have been his politeness. I found him, of course, an extraordinarily cheerful companion. I only hope though, that he won't think me (as he does George Trevy) "an old dear". I thought I saw some signs of it.'

The two of them had never been on friendlier terms, and Lytton was always to remain grateful to Brooke for helping to pull him out of the troughs of his melancholia. Health was the order of the day at the Cove Hotel, frequent jumpings in and out of cold baths, and a pulley for developing the biceps which both poet and dramatist worked at very vigorously.

After their week together Brooke hurried off to join a reading-party assembled at the Lizard, while Lytton dragged himself back to London and then to Cambridge where he set about searching for new lodgings. It was almost a month before he succeeded in engaging suitable rooms at 14 St John Street for two pounds a week. This was rather more than he had wanted to pay but turned out to be well worth it since, though his financial position was worrying, he felt better here than at any time since the beginning of the year. On 15 June he went back again to Hampstead where he was soon engulfed in the Suffrage Movement – 'demonstrations and petitions in every direction', as he described it to Maynard Keynes (7 July 1910). 'I hope to get a seat in the House for Tuesday, and if I do, of course, I shall have to shriek and be torn to pieces. An uncomfortable, but no doubt noble death.'

Predictable as ever, his health had once again deteriorated during these weeks at Belsize Park Gardens. 'Such is my low ebb,' he admitted to Saxon Sydney-Turner, 'that I'm reduced to reading the life of Cardinal Manning!' Lady Strachey had run out of new ideas to contend with his illnesses, and the only possible remedy that anyone could think of was another sojourn in the Saltsjöbaden sanatorium. Lytton's previous course of treatment there, though ultimately disastrous, had almost been successful. But for that freak set-back at the end, he had looked like benefiting enormously and might have been able to avoid what had turned out one of his worst years of sickness. This time, with reasonable luck, the venture ought to pay off, making up to his body for the horrors it would certainly inflict on his mind. At any rate he could only hope so. Accordingly he set off in the second week of July for another ten weeks' spell in Sweden. This time the female cortège consisted of his sister Pernel and Jane Harrison, the fifty-nine-year-old classical anthropologist, who was using this pharmaceutical holiday 'to get new heart' for the writing of *Themis*, her celebrated study on the social origins of Greek religion.

On disembarking at Gothenburg, Lytton promptly missed his train, spent the night there, and travelled up the next day to Stockholm. As the journey progressed his spirits sank rapidly. What a very plain, featureless, unappealing country Sweden was! Nearly everyone was good-looking, but there was a monotonous chastity about the type that was mortifying. Even the Swedish sailors, with their pretty *décolleté* necks, now failed to agitate him. And when he arrived back at the Saltsjöbaden clinic, there, to welcome him, was that same veteran brigade of patients going through the same hectic and idiotic pro-gramme of porridge and baths. Nothing had changed, and Lytton him-self quickly settled down again to the old routine. 'I already feel as if I'd been here for twenty years,' he began a letter to James written on his first day (18 July 1910), 'and should be quite put out if dinner was later than six or the porridge was made of porridge.'

His régime was almost identical to that of the previous year. Instead of the *Daily Mail* he took *The Times*, studying with great interest the Minority Report on the Poor Law; and he also read Dumas's *Memoirs* and Lecky's *Eighteenth Century*. While Jane Harrison took advantage of her stay to learn Swedish principally from the writings of Selma Lagerlöf, Lytton, rather perversely, concentrated on mastering Italian – for his dreams had revived of going south to the more sympathetic climate of Italy. He still, of course, went through the same pantomime of billiards, gymnastics and massage, but this time the medical treat-ment was if anything rather more stringent. He was placed under the care of the unmusical Dr Olof Sandberg, the specialist in digestive complaints, who favoured a liberal use of the stomach pump. At the same time he insisted that Lytton should eat a great deal – 'as much as possible and sometimes a little more'. This drastic dietary and emetic treatment, however, appeared to pay dividends, and by the middle of August he could report to Pippa: 'My cure has been going very well.'

For Jane Harrison, suffering under a similar course of treatment, there were no such redeeming features. Unlike Lytton she could not attune herself to the colourless oddity of the place; and Pernel fared little better. 'They both find the place very singular,' Lytton explained to his mother (5 August 1910), 'and I should think the place returns the compliment so far as Jane is concerned – she makes a strange figure among the formal Scandinavians, floating through the corridors in green shawls and purple tea-gowns, and reciting the Swedish grammar at meals.'

Suddenly, in the third week of August, the weather became piercingly cold, unlike anything he had experienced on his previous stay there, 'so I fear that the summer is now over', he lamented to Pippa (17 August 1910). 'As the Salong is the only hot room, I spend most of my days in it, among a shrieking crowd of foreigners, who discuss their symptoms in every language from Chinese to Peruvian. At the present moment I'm *accablé* by three fat women talking Esperanto.' Despite an occasional day of heavy sunshine, the cold persisted and proved too much for Lytton's two companions who soon hastened back to England. 'This is the last anyone will hear of my health,' remarked Jane Harrison ruefully.

Lytton's invalidism, however, was made of sterner stuff, and for him the rigorous cure continued on unchecked. He felt as if he had become lodged in Saltsjöbaden for the next century. 'One leads such a sheltered life!' he reminded James. 'Nothing but meals, torpor, and senselessness.' His apathy was relieved for a time by the arrival of Pippa, but even she could only endure a fortnight of the sanatorium before retreating to England. Yet still Lytton stayed on. His health, meanwhile, had improved, though not so noticeably as on his first visit. Then, just as before, he suffered a sudden relapse, the cause of which none of the specialists could diagnose. Once again all his suffering and patience had been to little or no purpose. 'I've stayed on here week after week,' he complained to Maynard Keynes (26 September 1910), 'lured by the hope of attaining eternal health: on Friday I shall drag myself away. . . . I feel that this has been a wasted summer for me.'

To wile away the long hours at the clinic Lytton had been working spasmodically at a rather heavy *facétie* on the Suffrage Movement. 'I fear, even if it's finished, that it will never see the light of day,' he confessed to Pippa. 'The scene is the infernal regions, and the principal character so far Queen Victoria.' More serious was the work he had now resumed on his Warren Hastings dissertation. If he was to get anywhere in the literary world, he felt that he must produce a book. And he was still sure that *Warren Hastings* would be his first *magnum opus*. After all, what else was there? But now, in these last days at Saltsjöbaden, his literary horizon was suddenly transformed when, out of the blue, he received a letter from H. A. L. Fisher asking him to write a brief panoramic study of French literature for a series that he and Gilbert Murray were editing. Lytton at once accepted, though he felt sure the project would prove difficult chiefly owing to its restricted length – not exceeding fifty thousand words. 'Herbert Fisher and Gilbert Murray have asked me to write a history of French lit for upperclass citizens,' was how he announced the news to James on a postcard (21 September 1910), 'and I shall accept. It will amuse me, and perhaps pay better than reviews. "If", Herb says, "75,000 are sold you will get £290." Isn't it a bright prospect? But at any rate I gather I'll get £50.'

Lytton returned to England at the beginning of October and quickly succeeded in arranging his autumn and winter programme to such effect that hardly more than a week of it was to be passed in Hampstead. His continuous peregrinations about the countryside at this time have about them an air of desperation. He whisked and shuttled from one place to another, visiting old friends and his old rural haunts, and always avoiding London. Waiting for him on his arrival back from Sweden was an invitation from Maynard Keynes to spend a couple of days at the Little House at Burford (Oxon.) which Keynes had hired the previous year as a haven where he might concentrate undisturbed on his *Treatise on Probability*. Desmond MacCarthy, too, had invited him for a week's visit, but on arriving from Burford, Lytton found that his host had absent-mindedly left for Paris. However, he passed a very agreeable and comfortable time with Molly MacCarthy in the Cloisters at Eton waiting for Desmond's unannounced return. 'After a few happy quiet days in the Cloisters London fills me with terror and disgust,' he confided to James. It was not in London, however, that he next turned up, but at Charterhouse, where George Mallory had taken up a temporary post as schoolmaster. From here he went for a further week to the Homere sisters at Kingham 'in a state bordering on collapse – mental and physical', he told Duncan Grant (19 October 1910), adding all the same that 'in spite of the hounds, the piano, and the intellectual annihilation, I'm now beginning to pull round'. In the fourth week of October he shuffled decrepitly off from Kingham, but still managed to skirt Belsize Park Gardens, veering off instead, for a very pleasant but exhausting fortnight, to Cambridge.

During these itinerant weeks he squeezed in an afternoon's discussion of his projected history of French literature with Herbert Fisher, 'who struck me as an Academic Fraud', he informed Keynes (9 October 1910), echoing Virginia Stephen's earlier view. Fortunately, Fisher's opinion of Lytton was unrepentantly high. When, earlier that summer, the editors of the Home University Library, casting round to find the right person to compose a short one-volume survey of the literature of France, asked him for his nomination, he had at once recalled his conversation in Fitzroy Square eighteen months previously. The favourite candidate for the authorship of this book was Edmund Gosse, then an established oracle on the subject. But Fisher submitted Lytton's name, recommending him as the writer of 'Two Frenchmen', his first contribution to the *Independent Review*. In urging Lytton's particular merits and qualifications, he pointed, with justification, to the superior versions of the original French which, in the course of his long review, Lytton had offered in order to bring out various fine and subtle shades of meaning in the work of La Bruyère and Vauvenargues which Elizabeth Lee, a conscientious though clumsy and inexact translator, had

altogether missed. Fisher also drew the attention of the editors to
Lytton's own prose style, and the aesthetic cohesion of his essay-review,
reminding them that the avowed policy of the Home University Library
was to select authors not for academic distinction alone, but also for
their literary skill in combining learning with artistic lucidity. The
editors were suitably impressed by Fisher's advocacy, and soon agreed
to his candidate.

It was at this autumn meeting that Fisher explained the details of their
proposition to Lytton. He was to receive from Williams and Norgate,
the publishers, the sum of fifty pounds down for the copyright, and a
royalty of one penny per copy sold. 'I told him that I wanted him to
write a sketch of French Literature in fifty thousand words,' Fisher
later recorded, 'and showed him J. W. Mackail's *Latin Literature*, with
which he was not then acquainted, as a model which he might be content
to follow. He assented to my proposal with rare economy of speech,
and with none of the usual expressions of diffidence, which an editor is
accustomed to hear from an untried author to whom he has offered a
task of exceptional difficulty.'

The result of this interview was that Lytton finally committed himself to the writing of *Landmarks in French Literature*, once and for all
abandoning his *Warren Hastings*. His plans now took on a fresh
practical immediacy and resolution. During the autumn he would in-
tensively read and re-read a large number of French classics; while for
the winter he decided to go off and live with Simon and Dorothy Bussy
down at Roquebrune, where he believed that he stood the best chance
of escaping the psycho-somatic illnesses of the preceding year, and
where, from past experience, – having written part of his Fellowship
dissertation and several of his more elaborate essays at La Souco – he
knew he could work in comparative tranquillity and concentration.
With the commission of this first book, his years of obscurity and
pessimism had reached their end, and to coincide with the new emer-
gent phase, his social and emotional life were also about to undergo
some dramatically involved variations of pattern. The composition of
Landmarks in French Literature injected into him a rejuvenated,
long-sought-after burst of self-confidence which, like an expanding
spring, released him from the lugubrious routine of the past, its
frustrations and lethargic aimlessness, and led on to what he himself described as his 'Spiritual Revolution'.

So that now, in the autumn of 1910, he stood on the perimeter of a
new and ultimately happier world.

Index

461

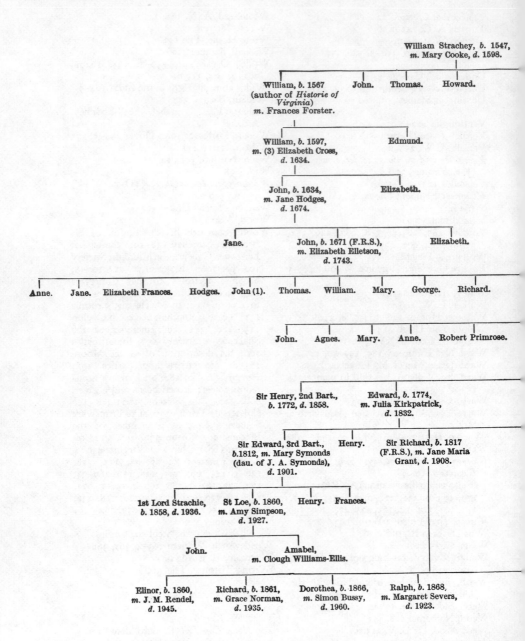

William Strachey, *b.* 1547,
m. Mary Cooke, *d.* 1598.

William, *b.* 1567
(author of *Historie of
Virginia*)
m. Frances Forster.

John. Thomas. Howard.

William, *b.* 1597,
m. (3) Elizabeth Cross,
d. 1634.

Edmund.

John, *b.* 1634,
m. Jane Hodges,
d. 1674.

Elizabeth.

Jane.

John, *b.* 1671 (F.R.S.),
m. Elizabeth Elletson,
d. 1743.

Elizabeth.

Anne. Jane. Elizabeth Frances. Hodges. John (1). Thomas. William. Mary. George. Richard.

John. Agnes. Mary. Anne. Robert Primrose.

Sir Henry, 2nd Bart.,
b. 1772, *d.* 1858.

Edward, *b.* 1774,
m. Julia Kirkpatrick,
d. 1832.

Sir Edward, 3rd Bart.,
*b.*1812, *m.* Mary Symonds
(dau. of J. A. Symonds),
d. 1901.

Henry.

Sir Richard, *b.* 1817
(F.R.S.), *m.* Jane Maria
Grant, *d.* 1908.

1st Lord Strachie,
b. 1858, *d.* 1936.

St Loe, *b.* 1860,
m. Amy Simpson,
d. 1927.

Henry. Frances.

John.

Amabel,
m. Clough Williams-Ellis.

Elinor, *b.* 1860,
m. J. M. Rendel,
d. 1945.

Richard, *b.* 1861,
m. Grace Norman,
d. 1935.

Dorothea, *b.* 1866,
m. Simon Bussy,
d. 1960.

Ralph, *b.* 1868,
m. Margaret Severs,
d. 1923.

Frances.   Maria.   Anna.

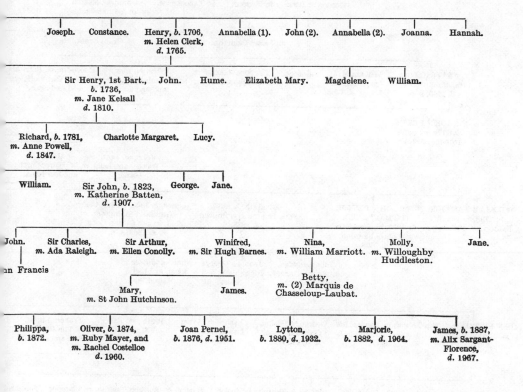

Joseph.   Constance.   Henry, *b.* 1706,   Annabella (1).   John (2).   Annabella (2).   Joanna.   Hannah.
m. Helen Clerk,
d. 1765.

Sir Henry, 1st Bart.,   John.   Hume.   Elizabeth Mary.   Magdelene.   William.
b. 1736,
m. Jane Kelsall
d. 1810.

Richard, *b.* 1781,   Charlotte Margaret.   Lucy.
m. Anne Powell,
d. 1847.

William.   Sir John, *b.* 1823,   George.   Jane.
m. Katherine Batten,
d. 1907.

John.   Sir Charles,   Sir Arthur,   Winifred,   Nina,   Molly,   Jane.
an Francis   *m.* Ada Raleigh.   *m.* Ellen Conolly.   *m.* Sir Hugh Barnes.   *m.* William Marriott.   *m.* Willoughby
Huddleston.

Mary,   James.   Betty,
m. St John Hutchinson.   *m.* (2) Marquis de
Chasseloup-Laubat.

Philippa,   Oliver, *b.* 1874,   Joan Pernel,   Lytton,   Marjorie,   James, *b.* 1887,
b. 1872.   *m.* Ruby Mayer, and   *b.* 1876, *d.* 1951.   *b.* 1880, *d.* 1932.   *b.* 1882, *d.* 1964.   *m.* Alix Sargant-
m. Rachel Costelloe   Florence,
d. 1960.   *d.* 1967.

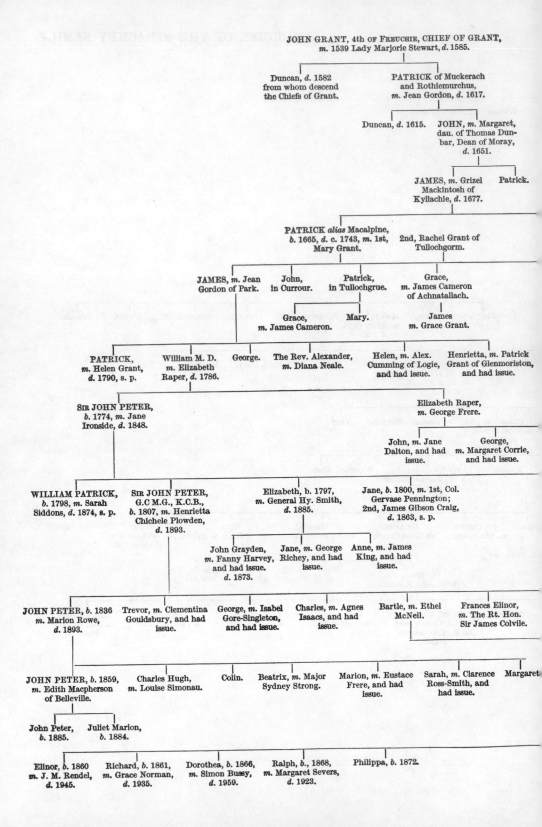

JOHN GRANT, 4th of FREUCHIE, CHIEF OF GRANT,
m. 1539 Lady Marjorie Stewart, *d.* 1585.

Duncan, *d.* 1582
from whom descend
the Chiefs of Grant.

PATRICK of Muckerach
and Rothiemurchus,
m. Jean Gordon, *d.* 1617.

Duncan, *d.* 1615.

JOHN, *m.* Margaret,
dau. of Thomas Dunbar, Dean of Moray,
d. 1651.

JAMES, *m.* Grizel
Mackintosh of
Kyllachie, *d.* 1677.

Patrick.

PATRICK *alias* Macalpine,
b. 1665, *d.* c. 1743, *m.* 1st,
Mary Grant.

2nd, Rachel Grant of
Tullochgorm.

JAMES, *m.* Jean
Gordon of Park.

John,
in Currour.

Patrick,
in Tullochgrue.

Grace,
m. James Cameron
of Achnatallach.

Grace,
m. James Cameron.

Mary.

James
m. Grace Grant.

PATRICK,
m. Helen Grant,
d. 1790, s. p.

William M. D.
m. Elizabeth
Raper, *d.* 1786.

George.

The Rev. Alexander,
m. Diana Neale.

Helen, *m.* Alex.
Cumming of Logie,
and had issue.

Henrietta, *m.* Patrick
Grant of Glenmoriston,
and had issue.

SIR JOHN PETER,
b. 1774, *m.* Jane
Ironside, *d.* 1848.

Elizabeth Raper,
m. George Frere.

John, *m.* Jane
Dalton, and had
issue.

George,
m. Margaret Corrie,
and had issue.

WILLIAM PATRICK,
b. 1798, *m.* Sarah
Siddons, *d.* 1874, s. p.

SIR JOHN PETER,
G.C M.G., K.C.B.,
b. 1807, *m.* Henrietta
Chichele Plowden,
d. 1893.

Elizabeth, b. 1797,
m. General Hy. Smith,
d. 1885.

Jane, *b.* 1800, *m.* 1st, Col.
Gervase Pennington;
2nd, James Gibson Craig,
d. 1863, s. p.

John Grayden,
m. Fanny Harvey,
and had issue.
d. 1873.

Jane, *m.* George
Richey, and had
issue.

Anne, *m.* James
King, and had
issue.

JOHN PETER, b. 1836
m. Marion Rowe,
d. 1893.

Trevor, *m.* Clementina
Gouldsbury, and had
issue.

George, *m.* Isabel
Gore-Singleton,
and had issue.

Charles, *m.* Agnes
Isaacs, and had
issue.

Bartle, *m.* Ethel
McNeil.

Frances Elinor,
m. The Rt. Hon.
Sir James Colvile.

JOHN PETER, *b.* 1859,
m. Edith Macpherson
of Belleville.

Charles Hugh,
m. Louise Simonau.

Colin.

Beatrix, *m.* Major
Sydney Strong.

Marion, *m.* Eustace
Frere, and had
issue.

Sarah, *m.* Clarence
Ross-Smith, and
had issue.

Margaret

John Peter,
b. 1885.

Juliet Marion,
b. 1884.

Elinor, *b.* 1860
m. J. M. Rendel,
d. 1945.

Richard, *b.* 1861,
m. Grace Norman,
d. 1935.

Dorothea, *b.* 1866,
m. Simon Bussy,
d. 1959.

Ralph, *b.,* 1868,
m. Margaret Severs,
d. 1923.

Philippa, *b.* 1872.

PEDIGREE OF THE GRANTS OF ROTHIEMURCHUS

Showing the Strachey connexion

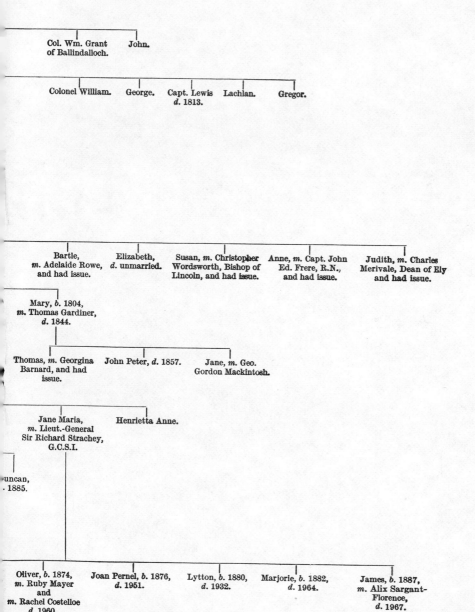

Col. Wm. Grant of Ballindalloch.   John.

Colonel William.   George.   Capt. Lewis d. 1813.   Lachlan.   Gregor.

Bartle, m. Adelaide Rowe, and had issue.   Elizabeth, d. unmarried.   Susan, m. Christopher Wordsworth, Bishop of Lincoln, and had issue.   Anne, m. Capt. John Ed. Frere, R.N., and had issue.   Judith, m. Charles Merivale, Dean of Ely and had issue.

Mary, b. 1804, m. Thomas Gardiner, d. 1844.

Thomas, m. Georgina Barnard, and had issue.   John Peter, d. 1857.   Jane, m. Geo. Gordon Mackintosh.

Jane Maria, m. Lieut.-General Sir Richard Strachey, G.C.S.I.   Henrietta Anne.

uncan, . 1885.

Oliver, b. 1874, m. Ruby Mayer and m. Rachel Costelloe d. 1960.   Joan Pernel, b. 1876, d. 1951.   Lytton, b. 1880, d. 1932.   Marjorie, b. 1882, d. 1964.   James, b. 1887, m. Alix Sargant-Florence, d. 1967.